I0120818

De Gruyter Handbook of Citizens' Assemblies

Citizens' Assemblies and Mini-Publics

Series Editor
Stephen Elstub

Volume 1

De Gruyter Handbook of Citizens' Assemblies

—

Edited by
Min Reuchamps, Julien Vrydagh, and Yanina Welp

DE GRUYTER

This publication is based upon work from COST Action COST Action 'Constitution-making and deliberative democracy' (CA17135), supported by COST (European Cooperation in Science and Technology).

COST (European Cooperation in Science and Technology) is a funding agency for research and innovation networks. Our Actions help connect research initiatives across Europe and enable scientists to grow their ideas by sharing them with their peers. This boosts their research, career and innovation.

www.cost.eu

cost
EUROPEAN COOPERATION
IN SCIENCE & TECHNOLOGY

Funded by
the European Union

ISBN 978-3-11-163243-8
e-ISBN (PDF) 978-3-11-075826-9
e-ISBN (EPUB) 978-3-11-075834-4
ISSN 2751-3505
e-ISSN 2751-3513
DOI https://doi.org/10.1515/9783110758269

(cc) BY-NC-ND

This work is licensed under the Creative Commons Attribution-NonCommercial-NoDerivatives 4.0 International License. For details go to https://creativecommons.org/licenses/by-nc-nd/4.0/.

Library of Congress Control Number: 2023931046

Bibliographic information published by the Deutsche Nationalbibliothek
The Deutsche Nationalbibliothek lists this publication in the Deutsche Nationalbibliografie; detailed bibliographic data are available on the Internet at http://dnb.dnb.de.

© 2024 the author(s), editing © 2024 Min Reuchamps, Julien Vrydagh, Yanina Welp,
published by Walter de Gruyter GmbH, Berlin/Boston
This volume is text- and page-identical with the hardback published in 2023.
The book is published open access at www.degruyter.com.

Cover image: DA4554/iStock/Getty Images Plus

www.degruyter.com

Acknowledgments

The open access publication of this *Handbook* has been made possible thanks to the generous support of the COST Action 'Constitution-making and deliberative democracy' (CA17135). The COST Action ConstDelib, as it is known by its members, is funded by the COST Association that is also funded by European research framework programmes. For four years, it has been one of the largest COST Actions, that is a network of members from over 40 countries all across Europe and beyond. In fact, the purpose of such an Action is not to undertake one single research project but rather to form a network of many people with different and possibly diverging approaches. Despite their different and diverging views, together, these researchers, practitioners, public servants, civil society actors have reflected upon and have written reports and papers on constitution-making and deliberative democracy that are available on the Action's online portal: www.constdelib.com.

This *Handbook* is not only a by-product of the COST Action 'Constitution-making and deliberative democracy', but also and above all the product of the hard work of many dedicated people. First and foremost, no fewer than 43 contributors, from all over the world, have brought in their expertise in order to shape this comprehensive overview of citizens' assemblies. Their contributions form the building blocks of the inaugural volume for the series 'Citizens' Assemblies and Mini-Publics' edited by Stephen Elstub for De Gruyter, an independent academic publisher. At De Gruyter, the book was initiated by Faye Leerink, managed by Maximilian Gessl and produced by Anett Rehner. Last but not least, Axel Humbert-Labeaumaz carefully followed the proof-reading and index-making process, putting the last touches to this *Handbook of Citizens' Assemblies.*

∂ Open Access. © 2023 the author(s), published by De Gruyter. (cc) BY-NC-ND This work is licensed under the Creative Commons Attribution-NonCommercial-NoDerivatives 4.0 International License. https://doi.org/10.1515/9783110758269-001

Contents

Part 3: **Assessment**

List of contributors

John Boswell is an Associate Professor in Politics at the University of Southampton. His research interests span deliberative democratic theory, public policy and administration, and interpretive research methods. He has written four books and over 30 articles on these themes, including in recent times *Mending Democracy: Democratic Repair in Disconnected Times* (Oxford University Press, 2020) with Carolyn M. Hendriks and Selen A. Ercan.

Jehan Bottin is a PhD candidate and teaching assistant in Political Science at the Université catholique de Louvain (UCLouvain), Belgium. His research interests are democratic innovations, deliberative democracy, and participatory governance. More specifically, his PhD analyses the effects of the institutionalization of deliberative processes on the public servant's job in Belgium.

Sonia Bussu is associate professor of Public Policy at the Institute of Local Government Studies (INLOGOV), University of Birmingham. Her main research interests are democratic innovations, participatory governance, and participatory action research. Over the years, she has led research and published on democratic innovations, community engagement, and coproduction of public services. Following her PhD in Government at the LSE, she spent a few years working for the third sector, where she designed and evaluated innovative participatory processes and community development programmes.

Didier Caluwaerts is Associate Professor of Political Science at the Vrije Universiteit Brussel. His research and teaching deal with Belgian and comparative politics, democratic governance in deeply divided societies, and democratic innovation. His work has been published in among others *European Political Science Review*, *West European Politics*, *Parliamentary Affairs*, the *Journal of Legislative Studies*, and *Acta Politica*. With Min Reuchamps, he published *The Legitimacy of Citizen-led Deliberative Democracy. The G1000 in Belgium* (Routledge, 2018), and co-edited *Belgian Exceptionalism: Belgian Politics between Realism and Surrealism* (Routledge, 2022).

Armando Chaguaceda is Researcher in Government and Political Analysis A.C. Degree in Education and History, Master in Political Science, and PhD in History and Regional Studies. He has been a professor at the University of Havana, El Colegio de Veracruz, Universidad Veracruzana, Universidad Iberoamericana and Universidad de Guanajuato. He was Visiting Professor at the Polytechnic University of Nicaragua, the Central University of Venezuela, the University of Girona, and the Sorbonne University. He is a Member of the National System of Researchers (SNI) of the National Council of Science and Technology (Mexico), and a Country Expert (Cuba and Venezuela) of the V-Dem project (University of Gothenburg). He has specialized in studying the processes of democratization and autocratization in Latin America and Russia. He is the compiler and co-author of six books and author of about 30 academic articles on the subjects mentioned above (see https://ongbrotar.academia.edu/ArmandoChaguaceda).

Nicole Curato is a Professor of Political Sociology at the Centre for Deliberative Democracy and Global Governance. She is the author of *Democracy in a Time of Misery: From Spectacular Tragedy to Deliberative Action* (Oxford University Press, 2019) and one of the leads of a multi-authored book *Deliberative Mini-Publics: Core Design Features* (Polity Press, 2021).

Stephen Elstub is a Reader in British Politics, Newcastle University. He is a member of the Tyndall Centre and a Fellow of the Centre of Deliberative Democracy and Global Governance. He has research interests in participatory and deliberative democracy and the role democratic innovations can play in environmental politics. He is the editor of the book series 'Citizens' Assemblies and Deliberative Mini-Publics' (De

𝝏 Open Access. © 2023 the author(s), published by De Gruyter. (CC) BY-NC-ND This work is licensed under the Creative Commons Attribution-NonCommercial-NoDerivatives 4.0 International License. https://doi.org/10.1515/9783110758269-002

Gruyter), and co-editor of *Representation: Journal of Representative Democracy* and the *Handbook of Democratic Innovation and Governance* (Edward Elgar, 2019).

Selen A. Ercan is a Professor of Political Science at the Centre for Deliberative Democracy and Global Governance, University of Canberra. Her work sits at the intersection of normative democratic theory and empirical political research, and examines a wide range of topics on public deliberation, social movements, democratic governance, and interpretive methods. Her recent publications include *Mending Democracy: Democratic Repair in Disconnected Times* (Oxford University Press, 2020, with Carolyn M. Hendriks and John Boswell) and *Research Methods in Deliberative Democracy* (Oxford University Press, 2022, with Hans Asenbaum, Nicole Curato, and Ricardo F. Mendonça).

David Farrell (MRIA) is Professor at the School of Politics and International Relations, University College Dublin. His current work is focused primarily on deliberative mini-publics. To date he has advised and/or researched six government-led deliberative mini-public processes in Ireland, the UK, and Belgium; and most recently he also provided support for one of the citizen panels of the Conference on the Future of Europe. His most recent books include: *The Oxford Handbook of Irish Politics* (co-edited, Oxford University Press, 2021), and *Deliberative Mini-Publics: Core Design Features* (co-authored, Bristol University Press, 2021). In 2021 Professor Farrell was elected the Chair of the European Consortium for Political Research (ECPR).

Andrea Felicetti (PhD, Australian National University) is Assistant Professor at the Faculty of Political and Social Sciences, Scuola Normale Superiore. He is the author of *Deliberative Democracy and Social Movements* (Rowman & Littlefield International, 2016) and co-author of *Discursive Turns and Critical Junctures* (Oxford University Press, 2020). Andrea has published in international academic journals including *Science, Journal of Politics, European Journal of Political Research, Social Movement Studies*, and *Journal of Business Ethics*. Andrea works on governance, social movements, and theories of democracy.

Irena Fiket is a Senior Research Fellow and academic coordinator of the laboratory for Active Citizenship at the Institute for Philosophy and Social Theory, University of Belgrade. Her current research interests lie in deliberative democracy, citizens' participation, democratic innovation and social movements and Western Balkans. On those topics she published in journals such as *Southeast European and Black Sea Studies, Italian Political Science Review, Javnost—The Public, European Union Politics*, and others. She has been involved in numerous international projects and is currently serving as academic coordinator of Jean Monnet Network 'Active Citizenship: Promoting and Advancing Innovative Democratic Practices in The Western Balkans' and principal investigator of the Serbian team for a Horizon 2020 project, EnTrust.

Dannica Fleuß is a postdoctoral researcher in School of Communication at Dublin City University (Ireland). Her research focuses on theories of democratic legitimacy, the theoretical and empirical inquiry of deliberative democracy, and approaches to decolonizing democratic theory. Her book *Radical Proceduralism: Democracy from Philosophical Principles to Political Institutions* (Emerald, 2021) proposes a theory of political legitimacy, advocates for "democratizing democratic theory" and explores the role of political theorists in democratic societies.

Brigitte Geissel is Professor at Goethe University Frankfurt for Political Science and Political Sociology, and Head of Research Unit 'Democratic Innovations'. Her research interests include democratic innovations, new forms of governance, political actors (new social movements, associations, civil society, parties, political elites, citizens). Her research has received a number of awards, including a Democracy Fellowship from Harvard University's Ash Center for Democratic Governance and Innovation, a Senior Fellowship from the Alfried Krupp Foundation, and a Marie-Curie-Fellowship from the European Commission. Her most recent publication is *The Future of Self-Governing, Thriving Democracies: Democratic Innovations By, With and For the People* (Routledge, 2022).

Saskia Goldberg is a postdoctoral researcher at KU Leuven. Her research focuses on legitimacy perceptions, process preferences, and deliberative democratic innovations. She has recently published with *British Journal of Political Science* ('Catching the 'deliberative wave'? How (disaffected) citizens assess deliberative citizen forums'), *Journal of Deliberative Democracy* ('Towards a more robust, but limited and contingent defence of the political uses of deliberative minipublics'), and *Political Studies* ('Deliberating or thinking (twice) about democratic preferences: What German citizens want from democracy').

Clodagh Harris (PhD) is a Senior Lecturer in the Department of Government and Politics, University College Cork and an affiliate of the Environmental Research Institute (ERI) and the Research Centre for Energy, Climate and Marine research and innovation (MaREI). Her research focuses on deliberative and participatory democracy, democratic innovations, and deliberative democracy and climate governance. She is currently serving on the expert advisory group of Ireland's Citizen Assembly on biodiversity loss and is part of a wider consortium funded by the Department of Housing, Local Government and Heritage to design and implement a young person and children's assembly on biodiversity loss. She was co-PI of the EPA funded Imagining 2050 project and EU Horizon 2020 funded ENTRUST project each of which employed deliberative forums as a participatory research method in the co-development of community visions and pathways to climate resilience.

Baogang He is Alfred Deakin Professor, Chair in International Relations, School of Humanities and Social Sciences, Faculty of Arts & Education, Deakin University, and the Fellow of the Academy of Social Sciences in Australia. Graduated with PhD in Political Science from Australian National University in 1994, Professor He has become widely known for his work in Chinese politics, in particular the deliberative politics in China as well as in Asian politics covering regionalism, international relations, federalism, and multiculturalism in Asia. Professor He has published 6 single-authored books, one co-authored book, 7 co-edited books, 88 international refereed journal articles, and 66 book chapters. His publications are found in top journals including *Science*, *British Journal of Political Science*, *Journal of Peace Research*, *Political Theory*, *Political Studies*, and *Perspectives on Politics*. In addition, he published 3 books, 18 book chapters and 82 journal papers in Chinese.

Carolyn M. Hendriks is a Professor at the Crawford School of Public Policy at the Australian National University. She undertakes engaged interpretive social research that brings democratic practice into dialogue with political theory. Carolyn has published widely on democratic aspects of contemporary governance, including participation, deliberation, inclusion, listening, and representation. Carolyn's current research is exploring how citizens themselves are leading collective problem-solving efforts to address governance voids or to repair dysfunctional institutions. Carolyn is the author of three books, including *Mending Democracy: Democratic Repair in Disconnected Times* (Oxford University Press, 2020, with Selen A. Ercan and John Boswell), *The Politics of Public Deliberation* (Palgrave, 2011), *Environmental Decision Making: Exploring Complexity and Context* (Federation Press, 2009, with Ronnie Harding and Mehreen Faruqi).

Kristof Jacobs is an Associate Professor at the Department of Political Science (IMR, Radboud University). His research focuses on contemporary challenges to democracy, the responses to them, and whether these responses work as proposed (or perhaps rather backfire). One of these challenges to democracy is populism, one of the responses to populism is to implement democratic innovations. Whether or not these innovations work as proposed, is his current research focus. Other topics he studies are electoral systems change, social media and democracy, and electoral behaviour. He was the director of the Dutch 2016 and 2018 national referendum study and the co-director of the 2021 Dutch national election study. He published in such journals as *European Journal of Political Research*, *West European Politics*, and the *British Journal of Political Science*.

Vincent Jacquet is a F.R.S.-FNRS research associate at the University of Namur. He studies transformation of contemporary democratic regimes by focusing on the development of participatory and deliberative procedures, the evolution of local politics, and different forms of political engagement.

Louise Knops is post-doctoral researcher at the Université catholique de Louvain (UCLouvain) and the Vrije Universiteit Brussel (VUB). She completed her doctoral thesis on the concept of indignation and her research interests include social movements, representation, climate change, and emotions. She was previously a researcher for the Centre for European Policy Studies, and has published in leading international journals such as *Mobilization*, *Representation*, and the *International Journal of Communication*. She is involved in several working groups of the European Consortium for European Research (ECPR) and civil society organizations on the topics of democracy, social movements, and climate change.

Zohreh Khoban is a postdoctoral researcher in Political Science at the Institute for Housing and Urban Research at Uppsala University. Her research focuses on inclusion and equality in citizen deliberation and issues of representation in randomly selected citizens' assemblies.

Antonin Lacelle-Webster is a PhD candidate in political theory at the University of British Columbia. He is broadly interested in issues related to contemporary democratic theory, democratic innovations, and the politics of hope.

Cristina Lafont is Harold H. and Virginia Anderson Professor of Philosophy at Northwestern University where she is Chair of the philosophy department and Director of the Program in Critical Theory. Her current research focuses on issues in contemporary political philosophy such as deliberative democracy and citizen participation, human rights and global governance, religion and politics. She is the author of *Democracy without Shortcuts. A Participatory Conception of Deliberative Democracy* (Oxford University Press, 2020), *Global Governance and Human Rights* (Spinoza Lecture Series, van Gorcum, 2012), *Heidegger, Language, and World-Disclosure* (Cambridge University Press, 2000), *The Linguistic Turn in Hermeneutic Philosophy* (MIT Press, 1999). Some of her recent articles include 'Deliberative minipublics and the populist conception of representation as embodiment' in *Contested Representation: Challenges, Shortcomings, and Reforms* (Cambridge University Press, forthcoming, edited by Claudia Landwehr, Thomas Saalfeld and Armin Schäfer); 'Citizen juries/minipublics', in *The Cambridge Handbook of Constitutional Theory* (Cambridge University Press, forthcoming, edited by Richard Bellamy and Jeff King).

Marina Lindell is an Academy Research Fellow at the Social Science Research Institute at Åbo Akademi University. Dr Lindell received her PhD in 2015. She holds the title of Docent in political science. Her research interests encompass participatory and deliberative democracy – primarily citizen deliberation, polarization, and the impact of social-psychological processes on opinions and behaviour. Her current research focuses on the impact of framing on opinions, and whether deliberation can mitigate these effects. She analyses attitudinal change in different experimental settings – depending on the framing of issues and group composition, communicative dynamics (speaking/acting/listening) and personality traits. She is the head of the Barometern online citizens' panel and leads several projects in conjunction to this. She has vast experience on conducting survey-based panel research and experimental research. She is an Assistant Editor of the *Journal of Deliberative Democracy* and the Convenor of the ECPR SG on Democratic Innovations.

Michael K. MacKenzie is an Associate Professor in the Department of Political Science at the University of Pittsburgh. His research interests include democratic theory, democratic institutions and innovations, intergenerational relations, political representation, and deliberative democracy. He is the author of *Future Publics: Democracy, Deliberation, and Future-Regarding Collective Action* (Oxford University Press, 2021). He is also the lead editor (with Maija Setälä and Simo Kyllönen) of *Democracy and the Future: Future-Regarding Governance in Democratic Systems* (Edinburgh University Press, forthcoming).

Rousiley C. M. Maia is Professor of Political Communication at the Federal University of Minas Gerais, Brazil. She is a researcher from The National Council for Scientific and Technological Development (CNPq) and member of the National Institute for Democracy and Democratization of Communication (INCT), and leader of the Research Group in Media and the Public Sphere (EME/UFMG). She is the author of *Deliberation across Deeply Divided Societies* (Cambridge University Press, 2017, with Jürg Steiner, Maria Clara Jaramillo, and Simona Mameli), *Recognition and the Media* (Palgrave McMillan, 2014), *Deliberation, the Media and Political Talk* (Hampton Press, 2012), *Mídia e Deliberação* (FGV, 2009), *Comunicação e Democracia* (Paulus, 2008, with Wilson Gomes). Her work has been published in journals such as *European Political Science Review, Political Studies, Policy Science, Journal of Democratic Deliberation, Human Communication Research, Journal of Computer-Mediated Communication, International Press Politics, Representation, Journal of Political Power.* She is currently associate editor of *Journal of Communication* and *Journal of Information, Communication & Society.*

Alice Mazeaud is lecturer in political science in La Rochelle University (LIENSS UMR 7266). Her research mainly concerns local public action in line with participatory democracy and climate issues. Among her recent publications is 'From the participatory turn of administrations to the bureaucratisation of participatory democracy: Study based on the French case' (*International Review of Administrative Sciences*, 2021, with Guillaume Gourgues and Magali Nonjon).

Elisa Minsart is a F.R.S.-FNRS PhD candidate in political science at the Transitions Institute of the University of Namur. Her research interests focus on democratic innovations such as participatory and deliberative mechanisms, as well as their articulation with the traditional model of governance. Her doctoral thesis addresses the influence of citizens' climate assemblies on the decision-making process.

Rasmus Øjvind Nielsen is Post-doc at Department of Social Sciences and Business at Roskilde University. He has practical experience with employing citizen assemblies as a tool in policy development and knowledge production from seven years as project manager at the Danish Board of Technology. His research interests circulates around the role of public institutions in innovation and sustainability, and the practices and governance of multi-stakeholder partnerships, transdisciplinary policy support, co-creation processes, and citizens' participation. Among his publications are 'Options for improving e-participation at the EU level', in *European E-democracy in Practice* (Springer Verlag, 2020, edited by Leonhard Hennen et al.) and 'Institutional Turnaround in Public Value Organizations: The Case of the Danish Board of Technology', PhD Dissertation, Roskilde University.

Christoph Niessen is post-doctoral researcher in political science at Université catholique de Louvain and the European University Institute. His research deals with deliberative citizen participation and multi-level governance. More specifically, he has researched how deliberative democratic innovations are received by traditional decision-making actors and studied the determinants of evolving sub-state autonomy demands and statutes in Western Europe.

Kei Nishiyama is an Assistant Professor of Policy Studies at Doshisha University (Japan) and will move to Kaichi International University (Japan) in 2023. He is also an associate of the Centre for Deliberative Democracy and Global Governance at the University of Canberra (Australia). Kei studies deliberative theory and applies it to childhood studies, democratic education studies, and social movement studies to examine children's democratic agency from both normative and empirical points of view. Kei's recent work has appeared in various journals, including *Journal of Youth Studies, International Journal of Social Research*

Methodology, Theory and Research in Education, Journal of Human Rights, Journal of Public Deliberation, Education, Citizenship and Social Justice, Childhood and Philosophy, among others.

Raudiel Francisco Peña Barrios is Jurist (2013) and Master in Constitutional and Administrative Law (2018) from the Faculty of Law of the University of Havana, Cuba. He is a student of the Masters Degree in Political Science at El Colegio de México (COLMEX) and of the Doctorate in Legal Sciences at the University of Havana. He worked as a professor of constitutional law at the University of Havana between 2016 and 2018. His areas of interest are linked to political systems, political regimes, party systems, transparency, political participation, mechanisms of direct democracy, among others. He has published articles on these and other topics in magazines and books from Argentina, Brazil, Cuba, Spain, the United States, Mexico, the United Kingdom, among other countries.

Jean-Benoit Pilet is Professor of Political Science at Université libre de Bruxelles (ULB), Belgium. He coordinates the project POLITICIZE on public attitudes towards non-elected politics, including support for citizens' assemblies. He has recently published a comparative study on the topic in the *European Journal of Political Research* (2022, with Damien Bol, Davide Vittori and Emilien Paulis). He has also published books and articles on elections, electoral systems, political parties, and the personalization of politics.

Min Reuchamps is Professor of Political Science at the Université catholique de Louvain (UCLouvain), Belgium. His teaching and research interests include federalism and multi-level governance, democracy and its transformations and innovations, participatory and deliberative methods, as well as relations between language(s) and politics and in particular the role of metaphors in political discourse. He has published over twenty books and edited volumes on these topics. In the wake of these works, he initiated the COST Action 'Constitution-making and deliberative democracy'. He is regularly invited to observe and assess democratic processes as well as to appear in the media and in the public debate. In Belgium, he actively contributed to the design of the Permanent Citizens' Dialogue of the Parliament of the German-speaking Community and of the mixed parliamentary committees for the Parliament of the Region of Brussels, the French-speaking Parliament in Brussels and the Walloon Parliament, as well as the federal online platform for the future of the country.

John Rountree is an Assistant Professor of Communication Studies and Assistant Director of the Center for Public Deliberation at the University of Houston-Downtown. His research investigates the intersection of rhetoric and democratic deliberation and has appeared in *Rhetoric & Public Affairs, Western Journal of Communication, and Journal of the Scholarship of Teaching and Learning.*

Eva Sørensen is Professor in Public Administration and Democracy at the department of Social Sciences and Business at Roskilde University. Her main research interests are democratic and administrative implications of emerging forms of interactive governance, and transformations in the role that politicians, public administrators, and citizens play in governing modern representative democracies, and prospects for strengthening democratic governance through the search for innovative forms of dialogue between political and administrative elites and the public. She has published several books and articles reflecting on theoretical and empirical aspects of these issues. Resent books are *Interactive Political Leadership: The Role of Politicians in Interactive Governance* (Oxford University Press, 2020) and *Political Innovations: Creative Transformations in Polity, Politics and Policy* (Routledge, 2021).

Nenad Stojanović is a Swiss National Science Foundation Professor of Political Science at the University of Geneva. His main research topic is democracy, with a focus on political institutions for multicultural societies. In recent years he has conducted numerous "deliberative mini-publics" (i. e. citizens' assemblies selected via lot) in several Swiss cantons and cities (www.demoscan.ch), and has collaborated in similar projects in Bosnia and Herzegovina. He is the author of *Dialogue sur les quotas: Penser la représentation* *dans une démocratie multiculturelle* (Presses de Sciences Po, 2013; Il Mulino, 2014) and *Multilingual Democracy: Switzerland and Beyond* (ECPR Press, 2021).

Jane Suiter is Professor at the School of Communications at Dublin City University and is the Director of the university's Institute for Future Media Democracy and Society. She has worked on or advised every Irish deliberative mini-public from We the Citizens to the citizens' assemblies from 2012–2014, 2016–2018, 2020, and 2022. She also worked on and advised processes in Scotland and France and is an observer on the Conference on the Future of Europe. She has published widely including in the *International Political Science Review*, *Science*, and the *Journal of European Communication* as well as a number of books.

David Talukder is a post-doctoral researcher at the Université libre de Bruxelles (ULB) and a post-doctoral fellow of the Wiener-Anspach Foundation at the University of Cambridge. He wrote a dissertation about underrepresented citizens' evaluation of the political system and his main research interests are democratic attitudes, political (under)representation, and participatory reforms of representative democracy. He recently co-authored an article regarding disadvantaged groups' support for deliberative democracy in *Innovation: The European Journal of Social Science Research* and an article on MPs' discourse regarding deliberative democracy in *Acta Politica.*

Pierre-Étienne Vandamme is a F.R.S.-FNRS Postdoctoral Researcher at Université libre de Bruxelles (Cevipol). His current research deals with democratic theory, democratic innovations, representation, and legitimacy. He has published articles on citizens' assemblies and other uses of sortition in *Politics & Society*, *Journal of Deliberative Democracy*, *Contemporary Political Theory*, and the *Swiss Political Science Review*. He is also the author of a book in French entitled *Démocratie et justice sociale* (Vrin, 2021).

Julien Vrydagh is a postdoctoral researcher at the University of Stuttgart, where he works on the ERC funded project "Designing Democracy on Mars and Earth". He holds a joint PhD from the at the Vrije Universiteit Brussel (VUB) and the Université catholique de Louvain (UCLouvain), Belgium. He is also a research associate at the Centre for Deliberative Democracy and Global Governance at the University of Canberra. His PhD thesis investigated the influences of mini-publics on public decisions in Belgium. His broader research interests include citizen participation, democratic theory, systems thinking, deliberative democracy, collaborative governance, and public policy. He has already published articles in European Political Science Review, Policy Studies, *Representation*, the *Journal of Legislative Studies*, the *Journal of Deliberative Democracy*, among others.

Mark E. Warren is Professor Emeritus of Political Science at the University of British Columbia, where he held the Harold and Dorrie Merilees Chair for the Study of Democracy. Warren's research focuses on contemporary democratic theory and democratic innovations.

Yanina Welp is a Research Fellow at the Albert Hirschman Centre on Democracy, Graduate Institute in Geneva (Switzerland), and co-founder of the Red de Politólogas. She is currently the Chair of COST Action 'Constitution-making and deliberative democracy'. Between 2008 and 2018 she was a principal researcher at the Centre for Democracy Studies and co-director of the Zurich Latin American Centre (2016–2019), both at the University of Zurich. She finished her Habilitation in 2015 at the University of St Gallen. She holds a PhD in Political and Social Sciences from the Pompeu Fabra University (Spain) and two Bachelor degrees in Social Communication and Political Science from the University of Buenos Aires (Argentina). Recent representative publications include the edited books *The Politics of Recall Elections* (Palgrave, 2020) and *El diablo está en los detalles. Referéndum y poder político en América Latina* (*The Devil is in the Details. Referendum and Political Power in Latin America*, PUCP, 2020).

Julien Vrydagh

1 Citizens' assemblies: An introduction

Abstract: Citizens' assemblies are advanced as one promising institutional solution to tackle some of the challenges facing representative democracies. The introduction to the *Handbook* offers a definition of citizens' assembly, which is understood as a participatory institution that brings together an inclusive group of lay citizens who engage in a deliberation on a public issue so as to exert a public influence. Such understanding differs from the western-centric and stricter approach to deliberative mini-publics, allowing a broader and more inclusive examination of the global practice of citizens' assemblies. The three core principles that underpin citizens' assemblies – deliberation, inclusion and public influence – and the ways in which each principle is embodied by the design features is then presented. The introductory chapter concludes with an overview of the structure of the *Handbook* and a brief description of each contribution.

Keywords: Citizens' assemblies, mini-publics, deliberative democracy, participatory democracy, deliberation, inclusion, public influence, sortition, citizens, public participation

1.1 The crisis of democracy and the rise of citizens' assemblies

Representative democracies are facing a series of serious challenges. Citizens feel increasingly more disconnected from their elected representatives, resulting in a broad distrust of public institutions, political parties and politicians (Dalton 2004, 2013). The foundations of representative democracies are undermined by a decline in electoral turnout and membership in traditional mobilization organizations such as political parties and unions (Mair 2013; Papadopoulos 2013). The augmentation of polarization further makes it increasingly difficult to adopt policies that receive public support beyond partisan lines. The idea of democracy itself is being challenged by illiberal and authoritarian threats, such as the rise of illiberal democracies (e.g., Hungary, Poland or Turkey) and leaders (e.g., Donald Trump, Narendra Modi or Jair Bolsonaro), and the direct attacks from authoritarian regimes (e.g., Russia or China) that seek to discredit democracy in order to legitimize its own rule. The concept of democracy has room for various interpretations (Held 2006), therewith implying that the realization of democracy is a never-ending project that is constantly in crisis (Ercan and Gagnon 2014; Rosanvallon 2000) and subjected to the criticisms of theorists (for an overview, see Merkel 2014). In this turbulent time, many people seek to address these democratic challenges with various solutions. Chief among them is greater citizen involvement in

Julien Vrydagh: University of Stuttgart, Germany.

∂ Open Access. © 2023 the author(s), published by De Gruyter. (cc) BY-NC-ND This work is licensed under the Creative Commons Attribution-NonCommercial-NoDerivatives 4.0 International License. https://doi.org/10.1515/9783110758269-003

political decision-making. Increasing the participation of citizens through democratic innovations and other participatory governance schemes is expected to generate multiple benefits that can help improve democracy and offer a response to the aforementioned issues (Elstub and Escobar 2019; Smith 2009).

Among various participatory processes, so-called *citizens' assemblies* (CAs) have been set up in many places across the world. CAs have become a popular institutional solution to address a series of symptoms of the democratic crisis. Their implementation in the past decade has mushroomed (Paulis et al. 2021) to the point that the Organization for Economic Co-operation and Development (OECD) describes their proliferation as a "deliberative wave" (OECD 2020). The French Climate Convention epitomizes their increasing political presence: the head of a major international power, President Emmanuel Macron, convened a CA to elaborate the national climate plan. Supranational institutions are relying on CAs as well: the European Commission recently implemented a large-scale CA to discuss the future of the European Union, while 100 citizens worldwide took part in a Global Assembly to deliberate on climate and the ecological crisis ahead of the 2021 United Nations Climate Change Conference. Likewise, scholars have devoted increasingly more attention to CAs, as illustrated by the proliferation of scientific publications (Jacquet and van der Does 2021b).

The increasing popularity and political implementation of CAs calls for a holistic reflection and evaluation of origins, current uses, and future directions. Most of the academic literature on CAs stems from the subfields of democratic innovations and deliberative democracy. In the literature on democratic innovations, CAs are described as one of the most sophisticated institutions to involve citizens thanks to the provision of balanced information before and during the process, the structured process of deliberation which allows all participants to express themselves, and the specific attention to the inclusion of a diverse group of lay citizens. As a result, CAs are expected in theory to draw a unique picture of what the whole citizenry thinks about a public issue were it to have the time to deliberate on the matter. In the literature on deliberative democracy, CAs were initially seen as the way to realize deliberative democracy in the sense that researchers used them as a social experiment to assess whether citizens were able to deliberate and to identify the conditions enabling them to do so. The assumptions from both subfields are however being challenged internally and in other social science fields. Empirical examples of CA show its shortcomings in generating large-scale political changes and addressing other societal issues such as populism, climate change, or post-truth thinking. Increasing implementation and visibility put a public spotlight on CAs, but many questions remain unanswered or less accessible to a non-academic readership. This *Handbook* seeks to address the profusion of questions that emerge from the scientific and societal debate about the potential and limits of CAs with a target audience that extends beyond scholars of deliberative democracy and democratic innovations. In the following section, I define the concept of CAs, presenting their core principles and how their design features aim to realize them in practice, before presenting an overview of the 28 chapters that compose this *Handbook*.

1.2 Definition

We understand *citizens' assembly* as a generic term for all participatory institutions which brings together an inclusive group of lay citizens who deliberate together on a public issue so as to exert a public influence. CA may seem to be an odd terminology for many scholars, as the scientific literature commonly uses the term *deliberative mini-publics* (Curato et al., 2021; Grönlund, Bächtiger and Setälä 2014; Smith 2009). There are several reasons behind this editorial choice. First, we want to depart from the term "deliberative mini-public" because it is academic jargon and has not (yet?) reached the broader public. We speculate with confidence that most researchers use an alternative terminology to describe their work on mini-publics to people external to their scientific community. Accordingly, all large surveys polling the public about deliberative mini-publics use a different term, such as a citizens' meeting (Bedock and Pilet 2020), citizens' forum (Goldberg and Bächtiger 2022), citizens' panels and even "a legislative chamber composed of randomly selected citizens" (Jacquet, Niessen and Reuchamps 2022).

One issue with this parlance is that it projects the image of a mini-public as both a new institutional invention and a Western phenomenon. This projection is problematic for at least two reasons. It first suggests that the Western mini-publics, created by Ned Crosby and Pieter Dienel, were the pioneering participatory institutions that successfully brought together a diverse group of citizens to deliberate on a public issue. This belief boils down to reinventing the wheel: while Dienel and Crosby may indeed be the first to implement mini-publics in the West, this perspective overleaps their older theoretical and practical origins. It is sometimes assumed that CAs come from the ancient democratic city of Athens due to the conflation with civic sortition (Van Reybrouck 2016; for a discussion of the different understandings of democracy behind civic sortition and CAs, see Sintomer 2018). John Keane (2009: 107–123) however challenges this theory as he argues that prototypes existed in the cities of Syria-Mesopotamia, long before this participatory invention was imported to Greece by the Phoenicians. Similarly, Parthasarathy and Rao (2018: 808–809) highlight the resemblance of CAs to Mohandas Gandhi's (1963) concept of a *panchayat raj*, wherein participants engaged in a cooperative discussion among equal citizens (Mantena 2012), and provides the example of the Indian state of Uttar Pradesh which instituted a deliberative assembly in 1947, the *gaon sabha* (Parthasarathy and Rao 2018: 809). We hence opt for the term Citizens' Assembly because it not only has greater resonance among a nonacademic readership but also because it opens the discussion to include new, non-western perspectives and studies on CAs.

This editorial choice compels us to clarify our generic definition of CAs regarding the scientific literature, which understands CA as a specific type of deliberative mini-public that involves a lengthy process (over a series of weekends) gathering at least a hundred randomly selected citizens and producing detailed policy recommendations (Elstub 2014; Setälä and Smith 2018). Scholars distinguish the CA-model from others because it involves a larger number of citizens who receive more time to delve into a topic. Such CAs are therefore commonly implemented to deal with salient and important public issues, such as the constitution (Farrell and Suiter 2019; Reuchamps and Suiter 2016), electoral reform (Smith 2009; Warren and Pearse 2008), or climate change (Courant 2020; Elstub et al. 2021). This *Handbook* deviates from a model-based approach to deliberative mini-publics that often seek to differentiate them into typologies. Each model of deliberative mini-public indeed tends to be associated with the inventor of a specific design, such as the Deliberative Poll with James Fishkin, the Planning Cell with Pieter Dienel, the Citizens' Jury with Ned Crosby and the Consensus Conference with the Danish Board of Technology (Elstub 2014; Setälä and Smith 2018). The corollary of these canonical approaches is that the theoretical design characteristics of the models often overlap, while their implementation in practice often diverges from the initial theoretical model (see for instance Vrydagh et al. 2020). And when one seeks to categorize the actual diversity of designs into a typology, they end up with a dozen different models (OECD 2020: 33–60). Opting for a CA terminology hence enables us to not only reach a broader public but also to go beyond a more orthodox definitional approach and understanding of deliberative mini-publics.

1.3 The three core principles of citizens' assemblies

A CA is a participatory institution which brings together an *inclusive group of lay citizens* to *engage in deliberation* on a public issue so as *to exert a public influence.* CAs hence rely on three core principles: deliberation, inclusion and public influence. We briefly describe the substance of each, before presenting how the design features of CAs seek to realize them in practice, allowing us to set the conceptual contours of the definition of CA used in this *Handbook.*

1.3.1 Deliberation

The participants of a CA engage in a deliberation on a public issue. Deliberation can be minimally understood as "mutual communication that involves weighing and reflecting on preferences, values and interests regarding matters of common concern" (Bächtiger et al. 2018: 2). This form of communication differs from others, like debating, negotiating, or conversing, because it involves mutual reason-giving and reciprocity. The former refers to the exchange of reasons, which seeks to change judgements, preferences, and views of participants through persuasions instead of coercion, manipulation, or deception (Bächtiger and Parkinson 2019: 2; Dryzek 2002: 1). Reciprocity – i.e., mutual respect – means that participants must respect the views and the right of others to deliberate and be open-minded when considering the merits in the others' views (Bächtiger and Parkinson 2019: 22; Gutmann and Thompson 1998; Mansbridge et al. 2010). It hence implies that participants adopt a *deliberative stance*, that is "a relation to others as equals engaged in the mutual exchange of reasons oriented as if to reaching a shared practical judgement" (Owen and Smith 2015: 228).

This communicative action lies at the roots of the broader theoretical paradigm of deliberative democracy. According to Floridia (2017), the theory of deliberative democracy is the result of a dialogue among various approaches to philosophy (Cohen 1989; Manin 1987), laws and constitutions (Bessette 1980; Habermas 2015; Sunstein 1985), social theory (Elster 1986) and political theory and science (Dryzek 1994; Fishkin 1991; Mansbridge 1983). We can summarize the main distinctive contribution of deliberative democracy using Simone Chambers' definition (2003: 308), for whom deliberative democracy is a "talk-centric" approach to democracy that replaces the traditional and widespread "vote-centric" perspective: "Voting-centric views see democracy as the arena in which fixed preferences and interests compete via fair mechanisms of aggregation. In contrast, deliberative democracy focuses on the communicative processes of opinion and will-formation that precede voting". In other words, the purpose of deliberation is to form a collective will, considering the various solutions and weighing the pros and cons of each, before making a decision about one of them (Manin 1987: 345).

Deliberating prior to deciding confers many benefits. It can for example improve the epistemic credentials of decisions: through the exchange of arguments, participants can broaden their perspectives, understand the rationale of others, and identify potential flaws or particular interests (Bächtiger and Parkinson 2019: 2; Manin 1987: 351–355). Most notably, deliberation holds the potential to increase the legitimacy of public decisions. For deliberative democrats, a law is legitimate to the extent that it is the result of democratic deliberation, which implies that all citizens and points of view affected by that law can participate in the deliberation and receive an equal consideration and are freely compared (Floridia 2017: 108; Habermas 2015; Manin 1987). The theory of deliberative democracy is essential to understand the more recent creation, development, and functions of CAs. These were for a time commonly conceived as a micro strategy for testing and realizing deliberative democracy (Elstub, Ercan and Mendonça 2016; Hendriks 2006; see also Nielsen and Sorensen, in this *Handbook*), although it has now changed. Following the systemic turn to deliberation (Dryzek 2010; Mansbridge et al. 2012), scholars now tend to highlight CAs' contributions to the broader deliberative system (see the contributions by Lacelle-Webster and Warren; Roundtree and Curato; Goldberg in this *Handbook*).

CAs possess a series of design features to ensure their deliberative character. First, deliberation must be inclusive, that is making sure that everyone participating has the effective opportunity of expressing her opinions, values, and preferences. This not only requires that deliberation must engage a diverse group of citizens (see below), but that everyone at the table has an equal opportunity to participate. As Curato, Hammond and Min point out, "getting a seat at the table is vastly different from having a voice at the table" (2019: 68). Research has shown that some citizen groups are less likely to participate in a deliberation – for instance, women, people with lower income or lower formal education, ethnic minorities – while other groups tend to dominate the discussion – for instance, male, people with higher income and formal education (Carpini, Cook and Jacobs 2004; Karpowitz, Mendelberg and Shaker 2012; Lupia and Norton 2017). An essential design feature of CA is the facilitation, which ensures that everyone receives an equal opportunity to express themselves, and that each voice is equally respected. Facilitation is a delicate task, as it must spot the subtle and implicit ways through which inequalities occur and distort genuine deliberation (Curato et al. 2021: 62–63; Landwehr 2014). Inclusion also involves allowing a wide range of expression styles, so that everyone feels it is legitimate to participate (Curato et al. 2021), thereby broadening the scope of deliberation beyond the Habermasian ideal of rational discourse (Bächtiger et al. 2010; Young 2000). Another important design characteristic is the provision of information: participants in a CA should receive information so as to inform their deliberation, stimulate the production of informed judgement and considered reflection, and to compensate for some internal qualities among participants (Curato et al. 2021: 71–72; Drury et al. 2021). Information provision can take different forms, from information booklets distributed before a CA, to hearings of experts, stakeholders, and advocates.

1.3.2 Inclusion

CAs seek to create the ideal conditions for a deliberative democracy, which implies that the diversity of its participants mirrors the heterogeneity of the broader population. As Dryzek (2009: 1382) famously argued: "without inclusiveness, there may be deliberation but not deliberative democracy". Ideally, all citizens affected by a public decision should have the equal opportunity of providing input to collective decision-making to ensure that the public decision is seen as legitimate (Dryzek 2010; Goodin 2007; Manin 1987). Inclusion is however constrained by the impossibility of realizing simultaneously the three principles of political equality, deliberation, and mass participation (Fishkin 2018, 2020). Typically, institutions that combine political equality with mass participation fail to be deliberative, for example elections. Alternatively, deliberation and mass participation are likely to result in an unequal involvement of citizens in deliberation. The final configuration with political equality and deliberation, incarnated by CAs, fails to realize mass participation because deliberation requires small groups in order to be effective (for an institutional proposal to solve this issue, see Ackerman and Fishkin 2004). Inclusion is moreover difficult to realize in practice because power is unequally distributed among citizens. Political participation is indeed determined by income, wealth, and education and other attributes (Gallego 2015; Verba, Nie and Kim 1978). These factors correlate with who participates not only in elections but also in other ad hoc participatory processes that rely on self-selection, such as participatory budgeting, referenda, or public hearings. As Smith (2009: 15; see also 163–169) points out, "the widely held concern among democratic theorists is that extending opportunities for citizen participation in the political process will simply reinforce and amplify the existing differentials of power and influence within society". CAs are attractive because they ensure a certain degree of political equality in the deliberation, an achievement that no other participatory institutions have yet equalled. By gathering a group of diverse citizens, CAs help to artificially repair the unequal distribution of power and voices in representative democracy (Curato, Hammond and Min 2019; see also the chapter by Vandamme in this Handbook). The design of CAs seeks to realize inclusion by addressing the inequality of power through different design features, both through the aforementioned structured deliberation and its selection procedure.

Ryan and Smith's (2014) definitional work on CAs provides a great typology to present the three main approaches to selection procedures and how these aim to realize inclusion. A stricter and more orthodox approach implies that CA participants must precisely mirror the demographics of the broader population. Stemming from the work of James Fishkin on his deliberative polls (2011), CAs are supposed to create "deliberative microcosms", which are legitimate to the extent that they are statistically representative of the broader public. He conceives his deliberative polls as a survey that reveals "what the public would think, had it better opportunity to consider the question at issue (Fishkin 1997: 162). Such a CA model must thus achieve the same standards as a survey or a poll, because the legitimacy of its results depends on the inferences we can draw from the broader population. It therefore implies that their democratic credentials rely on a "pure" sortition, without the use of quotas or targeted recruitment (see below) of a group of lay citizens large enough to be statistically representative of the relevant population. Pure random sampling is essential because it enacts the principle of equality that "gives the same probability of being included in the sample" (Curato et al. 2021: 39). This more restrictive approach to selection has however been criticized because it dismisses the added value of quasi-random sampling techniques, and it repudiates any CAs that are not large enough to uphold the criteria of statistical representativeness. Nevertheless, if CAs were supposed to meet the standards of statistical validity, they should contain at least 1,000 participants. The large number of participants in practice (between 100 and 500) puts a strain on the quality of deliberation, which is difficult to organize in practice for so many participants (Curato et al. 2021: 39) and results in costly short deliberation meetings (Elstub 2014).

Scholars have therefore advocated for an alternative approach to select a diverse group of lay citizens. Goodin and Dryzek (2006: 220) famously argued that CAs are "groups small enough to be genuinely deliberative, and representative enough to be genuinely democratic (though rarely will they meet standards of statistical representativeness, and they are never representative in the electoral sense)". This definition adjusts the principle of representativeness so that it needs not only to be realized in a statistical sense but instead representative of the *diversity* of the broader population. As Ryan and Smith (2014: 20) summarize: "the primary aim is clearly to engage an inclusive subgroup of participants from the affected population, from which no social group or perspective, particularly those who are traditional politically marginalized, is excluded". CAs can thus convene smaller groups of lay citizens, as long as all perspectives from the affected population are included. Departing from the demanding statistical representativeness, CAs can rely on stratified random sampling and targeted mobilization strategies to make sure that all groups are represented. The former implies that CA designers use various socio-demographic, geographic, and political criteria (Curato et al. 2021: 39–41; Dryzek and Niemeyer 2008). The sortition thus commonly follows a two-stage process (OECD 2020; for a detailed description of the procedure, see Curato et al. 2021: 41–46): the CA organizers first send a bulk of invitations to randomly selected citizens. They next use a stratified random sampling to select the participants from the citizens who accepted the invitations. In addition, since some groups remain difficult to reach through the communication channels commonly used (letters, telephone, door-to-door), organizers sometimes employ targeted mobilization strategies, like the British Columbia Citizens' Assembly which recruited two representatives from aboriginal communities (Smith 2009: 81).

CAs can finally rely on an open self-selection to convene a diverse group of citizens. In theory, allowing entry to all is likely to reproduce the inequality of political participation but CA designers can actively seek to advertise and recruit among the more politically marginalized groups. Including open selection for CAs departs from most definitions in the literature, which conceive near-random selection as a distinctive feature of CAs (Ryan and Smith 2014; Setälä and Smith 2018). In line with Curato et al. (2021: 3–4), we do not wish to be prescriptive, so that we allow CAs that "may need a little tweaking in design to suit local contexts". Loosening this criterion allows us to consider more unconventional cases of CAs that do not use civic sortition but still feature a group of lay citizens representing different viewpoints that deliberate together on a public issue. In so doing, we want to go beyond a Western-centric approach to CAs and to open the research agenda to include cases with inventive designs, such as the National Public Policy Conferences in Brazil (Pogrebinschi and Ryan 2018) or the world's largest deliberative assembly ever seen, the Gram Sabha in India (Parthasarathy and Rao 2018; Singh 2002); or in peculiar contexts, like in authoritarian regimes (see the chapters respectively by He and by Chaguaceda and Peña Barrios, in this *Handbook*). We should finally mention that the selection procedure is not the only way of ensuring the principle of inclusion. Besides inclusion within deliberation, various mechanisms have been implemented to increase the response rate from groups that are more difficult to reach. For instance, CA organizers commonly cover the travel and accommodation expenses of participants and offer supporting infrastructures, such as childcare. We also increasingly witness the use of various financial incentives, which are intended to attract individuals with lower incomes.

1.3.3 Public influence

CAs must be consequential in the sense that deliberation should result in some public influence. Public influence can refer to any effects a CA has on the public. So far, the theory has mainly focused on contributions to policymaking, mainly regarding how CA recommendations help policymakers adopt more informed and responsive decisions (Grönlund, Bächtiger and Setälä 2014; Setälä 2017). The rationale behind influencing policymaking consists of the need for a CA to see some of its deliberative outcome translated into public decisions. Like any participatory processes, citizen participation should result in some effects on decision-making (Rowe and Frewer 2000; Smith 2009: 22–23); otherwise it dissolves into tokenism and leads to the frustration of its participants (Fernández-Martínez, García-Espín and Jiménez-Sánchez 2020; Pateman 2012). It is moreover a basic question of respecting the engagement of the participating citizens who have devoted time and energy to deliberation during evenings and weekends. Empirical studies indeed show that citizens deem it to be important for CAs to impact public decisions if they want to participate or perceive the process as legitimate (Germann, Marien and Muradova 2021; Gundelach, Buser and Kübler 2017; Jacquet 2017). Their inconsequentiality also questions their *raison d'être:* CAs are in principle used to enhance "the democratic legitimacy of the political decision-making process" (Setälä and Smith 2018: 306), a contribution that can only be realized if the outcome of deliberation is to some extent integrated in public decisions.

Given little or no impact of many CAs in practice, some scholars have formulated theoretical proposals to give decision-making authority to CAs (Courant 2022; Gastil and Wright 2019; Landemore 2020). Nevertheless, over the past decade many theoretical essays have advocated for examining and assessing broader public contributions, mainly as a result of the systematic turn to deliberation (Dryzek 2010; Mansbridge et al. 2012) and Cristina Lafont's argument against the use of CAs as a shortcut to public deliberation (2015 2019). Deliberative democrats argue that CAs should primarily aim to improve public deliberation, distil reasoned and informed arguments among the citizenry, build the deliberative capacity of the system and foster a macro-deliberative culture (Böker 2017; Dryzek 2017; Niemeyer 2014; Rountree and Curato, in this *Handbook*). Other scholars have also highlighted the long-term effects of CAs on the institutional culture of public institutions or have considered the extent to which recommendations made in CAs are taken up in political debates (Jacquet and van der Does 2021a; Minsart and Jacquet, in this *Handbook*). We can also mention the more subtle political influences, such as when a CA weakens or strengthens the political positions of actors involved in policymaking, thereby shaping indirectly the final public decision (Michels and Binnema 2019: 753–754; Vrydagh 2022: 82). All of these views either seek to replace the conception of CAs as consultative processes for policymaking with a deliberative purpose, or to encourage a broader understanding of the effects of CAs on policymaking and politics. Yet, all in all, we should not lose sight of two facts. First, most CAs in practice are still implemented as a consultative institution for policymaking (OECD 2020; Paulis et al. 2021) and only several instances target the broader citizenry or the public debate (Gastil, Richards & Knobloch 2014; Stojanović, in this Handbook). Second, these kinds of public influences should ultimately result in some impact on public decisions and policies as well. For instance, when a CA is implemented to spread reasoned arguments among the citizenry, it is with the hope that the more informed public deliberation influences, in turn, public decisions considering that a deliberative system ought to be consequential (Curato, Hammond and Min 2019: 5; Dryzek 2009; Mansbridge et al. 2012).

CAs are mainly designed in a way that allows for deliberation to produce some tangible results for the public. The deliberative process is thus result-oriented, meaning that after allowing all participants to share their views, the group must seek to formulate a collective judgement on a question (Curato et al. 2021; Landwehr 2014). The provision of information also enables participants to make recommendations that take into account the various legal and substantive factors that constrain decision-makers. The outcome of deliberation aims to form an informed collective will, which was initially often intended to be based on consensus. Yet, more recent theoretical and empirical accounts of deliberation and decision-making procedures point out the risk for consensus-seeking deliberation to end up in anodyne outcomes that favour the status quo (Curato et al. 2021: 93–94). CA procedures for collective decision-making therefore often consist of voting procedures allowing participants to support or oppose the recommendations and ideas resulting from deliberation. Minority views are also integrated in the description of the collective will. The outcome can thus take various forms in practice. Many end up with a series of recommendations on public policy, which entail abstract or concrete proposals for policymaking, as well as a description of the reasoning that led to such recommendations. CAs can also feature the results of a survey of its participants: they commonly measure the epistemic transformation, showing how participants have changed their opinions on the question thanks to the deliberative experience. A collective judgement is then compiled in an official public report, which is circulated among the broader public and policymakers. That report is the main channel through which CAs pursue public influence (see Minsart and Jacquet, in this *Handbook*), although media coverage (see Maia, in this *Handbook*) and the involvement of elected representatives (see Harris, Farrell and Suiter, in this *Handbook*) can also allow a CA to exert public influence.

1.4 Structure of the *Handbook*

The *Handbook* compiles a series of contributions that present a comprehensive and state-of-the-art overview of the ongoing scientific debate on CAs. In addition to reviewing the latest empirical findings and theoretical developments, it also features innovative and original pieces that tap into the insights from alternative scientific fields and explore innovative thinking about these deliberative processes. We hope that this *Handbook* can serve as a resource to fuel, initiate, and shape an informed discussion about a participatory institution whose presence is growing worldwide. It is structured around four parts: (1) theoretical perspectives, (2) the uses of citizens' assemblies, (3) assessment, and (4) different perceptions of citizens' assemblies.

The first part presents various theoretical perspectives on CAs. It starts with MacKenzie's discussion of how the concept of representation is articulated within CAs and how the representative mandates of its participants differ from the representation of other political actors in democratic systems. He argues that CAs should be evaluated with distinct standards. Vandamme's contribution complements this discussion as he reflects on the accountability of CAs and suggests different ways to maintain accountability to the broader public. In the third chapter, Cristina Lafont tackles the question of whether CAs have the authority to make binding decisions, adding to her previous theoretical work on the topic (Lafont 2019) by proposing two implementation options for CAs that do not undermine the legitimacy of the democratic system. Brigitte Geissel next addresses the gap in the literature about the connections between CAs and decision-making. Based on a literature review, she categorizes different types of realist and visionary connections. The following two chapters discuss the connections between CAs and the broader public sphere. John Rountree and Nicole Curato argue that CAs should primarily seek to influence public deliberation. Reviewing the empirical literature, they outline three ways through which CAs can foster deliberation in the public sphere: contribute to public deliberation, inviting it, or triggering meta-deliberation. In a similar vein, John Boswell, Carolyn Hendriks, and Selen Ercan propose implementing CAs so that they can help 'mend' the fabric of democracy by improving the democratic connections between people and the empowered spheres. The section concludes with two pieces that interrogate the strengths and weaknesses of CAs with different approaches. Antonin Lacelle-Webster and Mark Warren opt for a problem-based approach to democracy to theorize the contributions of CAs in democratic systems and the authors analyse several sites where CAs could interact with other spaces, institutions, and democratic practices. Finally, Stephen Elstub and Zohreh Khoban present six prominent criticisms against CAs to which they answer by considering the configurations under which CAs can address these criticisms to produce democratic values.

The following part consists of eight chapters that deal with the various uses and practices of CAs. Rasmus Ø. Nielsen and Eva Sørensen commence with a chronological literature review that discusses how CAs and other deliberative participatory processes are used and depicted in the light of the broader debate about the crisis of representative democracy. The next duo with Sonia Bussu and Dannica Fleuß elaborate a theoretical framework that distinguishes top-down from bottom-up CAs based on the initiating actors, the process design, and normative values and the core aims. They next conduct a comparative analysis of ten cases before concluding with a broader reflection advocating for a combination of both top-down and bottom-up CAs. The following two chapters delve into the internal dimension of CAs. First, Clodagh Harris, David Farrell, and Jane Suiter offer the first scientific contribution on the use of mixed deliberative forums, which include both randomly selected lay citizens and elected representatives. After defining this uncommon practice, they empirically analyse six cases that took place in Ireland, the United Kingdom, Belgium, and Finland, before discussing the risks of political domination by elected representatives. Next is Kei Nishiyama's piece on the lack of inclusion of children in CAs, which stems from the use of voter lists to select participants and the implicit assumptions that children are incapable of deliberation. He opens the discussion about how children could still be included via four alternative routes: representation by adults, representation by children, consultative participation, and systemic inclusion.

The second part goes on with chapters that discuss the use of CA in specific contexts, and it starts with Nenad Stojanović, whose contribution seeks to reconcile deliberative and direct democracy by elaborating a conceptual roadmap to connect CAs and the various processes of direct democracy by empirically examining how the so-called "Oregon" or "Demoscan model" of CAs influence voters. Irena Fiket next dissects how various actors at the European and Global levels rely on CAs to address their lack of legitimacy and bridge the gap with citizens. After describing the multiple initiators behind these supranational CAs, she analyses different empirical cases to assess their capacity to actually fulfil the intended democratic outcomes. We then find Louise Knops and Julien Vrydagh's piece, which discusses the potential of CAs to deal with climate change. Adopting a problem-based approach to climate change, distinguishing its different problematic political dimensions, they discuss which contributions we can and cannot expect from climate assemblies. Finally, Armando Chaguaceda and Raudiel Peña Barrios focus on an often-overlooked topic of the use of CAs in authoritarian regimes. They conduct a comparative analysis of the legal framework, institutions and processes of three cases of CAs at the local level in Cuba, Nicaragua, and Venezuela. They conclude with a discussion of the logic of authoritarian participationism, and whether these deliberative processes lead to more democracy or authoritarianism.

The assessment of CAs is the theme of the third part that comprises five chapters. Didier Caluwaerts and Min Reuchamps open it with a piece that designs a Citizen Assembly Evaluation Survey (CAES), a practical methodological instrument to evaluate the process design integrity, the deliberative experience, the policy impact, and the transformative effects on the broader public. The following chapter, written by Marina Lindell, anatomizes the internal effects of CAs, reviewing the literature to disentangle how various elements of a CA, such as the deliberation, the diversity of the group, or the expert evidence, affect the participating citizens. Whereas the literature has been prolific to look into the impact inside the process, little is known about how CAs influence people who have not participated in the deliberation. Saskia Goldberg builds upon the few existing theoretical and empirical studies to offer an overview and develop an integrative framework to assess the effect of CAs on the population. On a similar question, Elisa Minsart and Vincent Jacquet look at the impact of CAs on policymaking. They conceptualize three sorts of impacts – the congruence between a CA recommendation and the public decision, consideration in the policymaking process, and structural changes – and propose different methods to measure each. Part 3 finishes with He's chapter, wherein he investigates the degree of empowerment of CAs in the context of the authoritarian regimes of China, Cuba, and Libya. He enquires into three conditions (leadership, ideology, and market development) that enable or constrain the empowerment of CAs in these autocracies.

The final part of the *Handbook* focuses on how CAs are perceived by different actors and in different literature. David Talukder and Jean-Benoit Pilet begin with a chapter that analyses public support for the use of CAs. Relying on comparative survey data from 15 European countries, they examine overall support in the population as well as the factors that account for (lack of) support. Their findings reveal that the citizenry on the whole does not want CAs to replace traditional elected assemblies. Levels of support depend however on a series of factors, such as political dissatisfaction, political engagement, trust in politicians and fellow citizens, and the way a CA is institutionalized. In the next chapter, Christoph Niessen looks into support from elected officials as he builds an innovative conceptual framework that explains whether and under which conditions elected officials perceive CAs negatively or positively. His insightful matrix furthermore distinguishes between types of CAs, and whether they aim to complement representative democracy or to disrupt it. He finishes with a review of the existing quantitative and qualitative studies to test the empirical validity of his framework. We then find Jehan Bottin and Alice Mazeaud's contribution in which they investigate the support of public servants for CAs. Commonly skimmed over in the literature on deliberative democracy and CAs, they define their profiles, roles, and attitudes towards CAs and, in doing so, demonstrate the key importance of these actors for the organization, institutionalization, and follow-up of CAs.

The three remaining chapters in this part offer new insights into the research on CAs, as they discuss them from the perspective of external fields. Kristof Jacobs starts with a contribution to the literature on populism in which he analyses how populist parties and citizens with populist attitudes perceive CAs. Examining the French Climate Convention and three cases of participatory budgeting in the Netherlands, he reveals that populist parties support CAs when outcomes coincide with their political agenda, whereas populist citizens are less "outcome-driven" and show the same support for CAs as their non-populist counterparts. The next piece, written by Rousiley C. M. Maia, approaches CAs from the angle of communication studies and advocates for an integrative research agenda through which the role of citizens in deliberative politics is not only analysed within CAs but also in the broader sets of formal and informal political discussions. Andrea Felicetti offers the final contribution of the fourth part with a discussion on the increasing interactions between CAs and social movements. Reviewing the literature, he argues that these can develop a mutually beneficial relationship that can generate democratic values, provided that they succeed in reconciling different logics.

Yanina Welp concludes the *Handbook* with a discussion of the main outcomes and trends. She seeks to strike a balance between utopian and dystopian approaches to CAs as she reviews seven primary dimensions emerging from the 27 contributions: (1) the global spread of CAs; (2) their authorization, accountability, and legitimacy; (3) their outcomes and evaluation; (4) their scalability and best design; (5) their public support; (6) their capacity to solve global challenges, and (7) their connection to regime type. While she does not settle on either a utopian or dystopian perspective on CAs, Yanina Welp wraps up the *Handbook* with a nuanced discussion of what we can reasonably expect from CAs in the lights of the latest theoretical and empirical research.

References

Ackerman, B. A., & Fishkin, J. S. (2004). *Deliberation Day.* New Haven, CT: Yale University Press.

Bächtiger, A., Dryzek, J. S., Mansbridge, J., & Warren, M. (2018). Deliberative democracy. In A. Bächtiger, J. S. Dryzek, J. Mansbridge, & M. Warren (eds), *The Oxford Handbook of Deliberative Democracy*, 1–32. Oxford: Oxford University Press.

Bächtiger, A., Niemeyer, S., Neblo, M., Steenbergen, M., & Steiner, J. (2010). Disentangling diversity in deliberative democracy: Competing theories, their blind spots and complementarities. *Journal of Political Philosophy* 18 (1), 32–63.

Bächtiger, A., & Parkinson, J. (2019). *Mapping and Measuring Deliberation: Towards a New Deliberative Quality.* Oxford: Oxford University Press.

Bedock, C., & Pilet, J.-B. (2020). Enraged, engaged, or both? A study of the determinants of support for consultative vs. binding mini-publics. *Representation*, 1–21.

Bessette, J. M. (1980). Deliberative democracy: The majority principle in republican government. In R. A. Goldwin & W. A. Schambra (eds), *How Democratic Is the Constitution?*, 102–116. Washington D.C.: American Enterprise Institute for Public Policy Research

Böker, M. (2017). Justification, critique and deliberative legitimacy: The limits of mini-publics. *Contemporary Political Theory* 16 (1), 19–40.

Carpini, M. X. D., Cook, F. L., & Jacobs, L. R. (2004). Public deliberation, discursive participation, and citizen engagement: A review of the empirical literature. *Annual Review of Political Science* 7, 315–344.

Chambers, S. (2003). Deliberative democratic theory. *Annual Review of Political Science* 6 (1), 307–326.

Cohen, J. (1989). Deliberation and democratic legitimacy. In A. Hamlin & P. Pettit (eds), *The Good Polity. Normative Analysis of the State*, 67–92. Oxford: Basil Blackwell.

Courant, D. (2020). Des mini-publics délibératifs pour sauver le climat? Analyses empiriques de l'Assemblée citoyenne irlandaise et de la Convention citoyenne française. *Archives de philosophie du droit* 62 (1), 485–507.

Courant, D. (2022). Institutionalizing deliberative mini-publics? Issues of legitimacy and power for randomly selected assemblies in political systems. *Critical Policy Studies* 16 (2), 162–180.

Curato, N., Farrell, D., Geissel, B., Grönlund, K., Mockler, P., Pilet, J.-B., Renwick, A., Rose, J., Setälä, M., & Suiter, J. (2021). *Deliberative Mini-Publics: Core Design Features.* Bristol: Policy Press.

Curato, N., Hammond, M., & Min, J. B. (2019). *Power in Deliberative Democracy.* Cham: Palgrave Macmillan.

Dalton, R. J. (2004). *Democratic Challenges, Democratic Choices.* Oxford: Oxford Univ Press.

Dalton, R. J. (2013). *Citizen Politics: Public Opinion and Political Parties in Advanced Industrial Democracies.* Washington D.C.: Cq Press.

Drury, S. A., Elstub, S., Escobar, O., & Roberts, J. (2021). Deliberative quality and expertise: Uses of evidence in citizens' juries on wind farms. *Journal of Public Deliberation* 17 (2).

Dryzek, J. S. (1994). *Discursive Democracy: Politics, Policy, and Political Science.* Cambridge: Cambridge University Press.

Dryzek, J. S. (2002). *Deliberative Democracy and Beyond: Liberals, Critics, Contestations.* Oxford: Oxford University Press.

Dryzek, J. S. (2009). Democratization as deliberative capacity building. *Comparative Political Studies* 42 (11), 1379–1402.

Dryzek, J. S. (2010). *Foundations and Frontiers of Deliberative Governance.* Oxford: Oxford University Press.

Dryzek, J. S. (2017). The forum, the system, and the polity: Three varieties of democratic theory. *Political Theory* 45 (5), 610–636.

Dryzek, J. S., & Niemeyer, S. (2008). Discursive representation. *American Political Science Review* 102 (4), 481–493.

Elster, J. (1986). The market and the forum: Three varieties of democratic theory. In J. Elster & A. Hylland (eds), *Foundations of Social Choice Theory*, 104–132. Cambridge: Cambridge University Press.

Elstub, S. (2014). Mini-publics: Issues and cases. In S. Elstub & P. McLaverty (eds), *Deliberative Democracy: Issues and Cases*, 166–188. Edinburgh: Edinburgh University Press.

Elstub, S., Ercan, S., & Mendonça, R. F. (2016). Editorial introduction: The fourth generation of deliberative democracy. *Critical Policy Studies* 10 (2), 139–151.

Elstub, S., & Escobar, O. (2019). *Handbook of Democratic Innovation and Governance.* Cheltenham: Edward Elgar Publishing.

Elstub, S., Farrell, D. M., Carrick, J., & Mockler, P. (2021). *Evaluation of Climate Assembly UK.* Newcastle: Newcastle University Press.

Ercan, S. A., & Gagnon, J.-P. (2014). The crisis of democracy: Which crisis? Which democracy? *Democratic Theory* 1 (2), 1–10.

Farrell, D. M., & Suiter, J. (2019). *Reimagining Democracy: Lessons in Deliberative Democracy from the Irish Front Line.* Ithaca, NY: Cornell University Press.

Fernández-Martínez, J. L., García-Espín, P., & Jiménez-Sánchez, M. (2020). Participatory frustration: The unintended cultural effect of local democratic innovations. *Administration & Society* 52 (5), 718–748.

Fishkin, J. S. (1991). *Democracy and Deliberation: New Directions for Democratic Reform.* New Haven, CT: Yale University Press.

Fishkin, J. S. (1997). *The Voice of the People: Public Opinion and Democracy.* New Haven, CT: Yale University Press.

Fishkin, J. S. (2011). *When the People Speak: Deliberative Democracy and Public Consultation.* Oxford: Oxford University Press.

Fishkin, J. S. (2018). *Democracy When the People are Thinking: Revitalizing Our Politics Through Public Deliberation.* Oxford: Oxford University Press.

Fishkin, J. (2020). Cristina Lafont's challenge to deliberative mini-publics. *Journal of Deliberative Democracy* 16 (2), 56–62.

Floridia, A. (2017). *From Participation to Deliberation: A Critical Genealogy of Deliberative Democracy.* Colchester: ECPR Press.

Gallego, A. (2015). *Unequal Political Participation Worldwide.* Cambridge: Cambridge University Press.

Gandhi, M. K. (1963). *Village Swaraj.* Ahmedabad: Narajivan Publishing House.

Gastil, J., Richards, R. C., & Knobloch, K. (2014). Vicarious deliberation: How the Oregon Citizens' Initiative Review influenced deliberation in mass elections. *International Journal of Communication* 8 (1), 62–89.

Gastil, J., & Wright, E. O. (2019). *Legislature by Lot: Transformative Designs for Deliberative Governance.* London: Verso Books.

Germann, M., Marien, S., & Muradova, L. (2021). Scaling up? Unpacking the effect of deliberative mini-publics on legitimacy perceptions. https://dx.doi.org/10.2139/ssrn.3954035

Goldberg, S., & Bächtiger, A. (2022). Catching the 'deliberative wave'? How (disaffected) citizens assess deliberative citizen forums. *British Journal of Political Science*, 1–9.

Goodin, R. E. (2007). Enfranchising all affected interests, and its alternatives. *Philosophy & Public Affairs* 35 (1), 40–68.

Goodin, R. E., & Dryzek, J. S. (2006). Deliberative impacts: The macro-political uptake of mini-publics. *Politics & Society* 34 (2), 219–244.

Grönlund, K., Bächtiger, A., & Setälä, M. (2014). *Deliberative Mini-Publics: Involving Citizens in the Democratic Process.* Colchester: ECPR Press.

Gundelach, B., Buser, P., & Kübler, D. (2017). Deliberative democracy in local governance: The impact of institutional design on legitimacy. *Local Government Studies* 43 (2), 218–244.

Gutmann, A., & Thompson, D. F. (1998). *Democracy and Disagreement.* Cambridge, MA: Harvard University Press.

Habermas, J. (2015). *Between Facts and Norms: Contributions to a Discourse Theory of Law and Democracy.* Cambridge, MA: MIT Press.

Held, D. (2006). *Models of Democracy.* Redwood City, CA: Stanford University Press.

Hendriks, C. M. (2006). Integrated deliberation: Reconciling civil society's dual role in deliberative democracy. *Political Studies* 54 (3), 486–508.

Jacquet, V. (2017). Explaining non-participation in deliberative mini-publics. *European Journal of Political Research* 56 (3), 640–659.

Jacquet, V., Niessen, C., & Reuchamps, M. (2022). Sortition, its advocates and its critics: An empirical analysis of citizens' and MPs' support for random selection as a democratic reform proposal. *International Political Science Review* 43 (2), 295–316.

Jacquet, V., & van der Does, R. (2021a). Deliberation and policy-making: Three ways to think about minipublics' consequences. *Administration & Society* 53 (3), 468–487

Jacquet, V., & van der Does, R. (2021b). The consequences of deliberative minipublics: systematic overview, conceptual gaps, and new directions. *Representation* 57 (1), 131–141..

Karpowitz, C. F., Mendelberg, T., & Shaker, L. (2012). Gender inequality in deliberative participation. *American Political Science Review* 106 (3), 533–547.

Keane, J. (2009). *The Life and Death of Democracy.* London: Simon and Schuster.

Lafont, C. (2015). Deliberation, participation, and democratic legitimacy: Should deliberative mini-publics shape public policy? Deliberation, participation & democratic legitimacy. *Journal of Political Philosophy* 23 (1), 40–63.

Lafont, C. (2019). *Democracy Without Shortcuts: A Participatory Conception of Deliberative Democracy.* Oxford: Oxford University Press.

Landemore, H. (2020). *Open Democracy: Reinventing Popular Rule for the Twenty-First Century.* Princeton, NJ: Princeton University Press.

Landwehr, C. (2014). Facilitating deliberation: The role of impartial intermediaries in deliberative mini-publics. in K. Grönlund, A. Bächtiger and M. Setälä (eds),*Deliberative Mini-Publics: Involving Citizens in the Democratic Process*, 77–92. Colchester: ECPR Press.

Lupia, A., & Norton, A. (2017). Inequality is always in the room: Language & power in deliberative democracy. *Daedalus* 146 (3), 64–76.

Mair, P. (2013). *Ruling the Void: The Hollowing of Western Democracy.* London and New York: Verso.

Manin, B. (1987). On legitimacy and political deliberation. *Political Theory* 15 (3), 338–368.

Manin, B. (1997). *The Principles of Representative Government.* Cambridge: Cambridge University Press.

Mansbridge, J. J. (1983). *Beyond Adversary Democracy.* Chicago: University of Chicago Press.

Mansbridge, J., Bohman, J., Chambers, S., Christiano, T., Fung, A., Parkinson, J., Thompson, D. F., & Warren, M. E. (2012). A systemic approach to deliberative democracy. In J. Parkinson and J. Mansbridge (eds), *Deliberative Systems: Deliberative Democracy at the Large Scale*, 1–26. Cambridge: Cambridge University Press.

Mansbridge, J., Bohman, J., Chambers, S., Estlund, D., Føllesdal, A., Fung, A., Lafont, C., Manin, B., & Martí, J. L. (2010). The place of self-interest and the role of power in deliberative democracy. *Journal of Political Philosophy* 18 (1), 64–100.

Mantena, K. (2012). On Gandhi's critique of the state: Sources, contexts, conjunctures. *Modern Intellectual History* 9 (3), 535–563.

Merkel, W. (2014). Is there a crisis of democracy? *Democratic Theory* 1 (2), 11–25.

Michels, A., & Binnema, H. (2019). Assessing the impact of deliberative democratic initiatives at the local level: A framework for analysis. *Administration & Society* 51 (5), 749–769.

Niemeyer, S. (2014). Scaling up deliberation to mass publics: Harnessing mini-publics in a deliberative system. In K. Grönlund, A. Bächtiger, & M Setälä (eds), *Deliberative Mini-Publics: Involving Citizens in the Democratic Process*, 177–202. Colchester: ECPR Press.

OECD. (2020). *Innovative Citizen Participation and New Democratic Institutions: Catching the Deliberative Wave.* Paris: OECD Publishing.

Owen, D., & Smith, G. (2015). Survey article: Deliberation, democracy, and the systemic turn. *Journal of Political Philosophy* 23 (2), 213–234.

Papadopoulos, Y. (2013). *Democracy in Crisis? Politics, Governance and Policy.* Houndmills, Basingstoke: Macmillan.

Parthasarathy, R., & Rao, V. (2018). Deliberative democracy in India. In A. Bächtiger, J. S. Dryzek, J. Mansbridge, & M. Warren (eds), *The Oxford Handbook of Deliberative Democracy*, 805–818. Oxford: Oxford University Press.

Pateman, C. (2012). Participatory democracy revisited. *Perspectives on Politics*, 10 (1), 7–19.

Paulis, E., Pilet, J.-B., Panel, S., Vittori, D., & Close, C. (2021). The POLITICIZE dataset: An inventory of deliberative mini-publics (DMPs) in Europe. *European Political Science* 20 (3), 521–542.

Pogrebinschi, T., & Ryan, M. (2018). Moving beyond input legitimacy: When do democratic innovations affect policy making? *European Journal of Political Research* 57 (1), 135–152.

Reuchamps, M., & Suiter, J. (2016). *Constitutional Deliberative Democracy in Europe.* Colchester: ECPR Press.

Rosanvallon, P. (2000). *La démocratie inachevée: Histoire de la souveraineté du peuple en France.* Paris: Éditions Gallimard.

Rowe, G., & Frewer, L. J. (2000). Public participation methods: A framework for evaluation. *Science, Technology, & Human Values* 25 (1), 3–29.

Ryan, M., & Smith, G. (2014). Defining mini-publics. In K. Grönlund, A. Bächtiger, & M. Setälä (eds), *Deliberative Mini-Publics: Involving Citizens in the Democratic Process*, 9–26. Colchester: ECPR Press.

Setälä, M. (2017). Connecting deliberative mini-publics to representative decision making. *European Journal of Political Research* 56 (4), 846–863.

Setälä, M., & Smith, G. (2018). Mini-publics and deliberative democracy. In A. Bächtiger, J. S. Dryzek, J. Mansbridge, & M. Warren (eds), *The Oxford Handbook of Deliberative Democracy*, 300–314. Oxford: Oxford University Press.

Singh, Y. (2002). Decentralised governance in Madhya Pradesh: Experiences of the gram sabha in scheduled areas. *Economic and Political Weekly* 37 (40), 4100–4104.

Sintomer, Y. (2018). From deliberative to radical democracy? Sortition and politics in the twenty-first century. *Politics & Society* 46 (3), 337–357.

Smith, G. (2009). *Democratic Innovations: Designing Institutions for Citizen Participation.* Cambridge: Cambridge University Press.

Sunstein, C. R. (1985). Interest groups in American public law. *Stanford Law Review*, 38, 2987.

Van Reybrouck, D. (2016). *Against Elections: The Case for Democracy.* London: The Bodley Head.

Verba, S., Nie, N. H., & Kim, J. (1978). *Participation and Political Equality: A Seven-Nation Comparison.* Cambridge: Cambridge University Press.

Vrydagh, J. (2022). Measuring the impact of consultative citizen participation: Reviewing the congruency approaches for assessing the uptake of citizen ideas. *Policy Sciences* 55 (1), 65–88.

Vrydagh, J., Devillers, S., Talukder, D., Jacquet, V., & Bottin, J. (2020). Les mini-publics en Belgique (2001–2018): Expériences de panels citoyens délibératifs. *Courrier Hebdomadaire Du CRISP* 32, 5–72.

Warren, M. E., & Pearse, H. (2008). *Designing Deliberative Democracy: The British Columbia Citizens' Assembly.* Cambridge: Cambridge University Press.

Young, I. M. (2000). *Inclusion and Democracy.* Oxford: Oxford University Press.

Part 1: **Theoretical perspectives**

Michael K. MacKenzie

2 Representation and citizens' assemblies

Abstract: Citizens' Assemblies (CAs) are commonly seen as institutions that provide descriptive representation, but this is only one type of representation that CAs can provide. In this chapter, I address several concerns that have been raised about CAs as representative institutions. I then discuss four types of representation that they provide: 1) descriptive; 2) discursive; 3); surrogate; and 4) gyroscopic. These forms of representation, as realized in the CAs, do not provide, or require direct links of accountability between the representatives and the represented. Indeed, the latter three forms of representation are made possible only because the representatives who serve on CAs are not constrained by the demands of specific constituencies. I argue that this is a strength, rather than a weakness of the CA model, and it does not undermine the democratic character of these institutions. The CAs are democratically legitimate, just in different ways than elected assemblies.

Keywords: random selection, sortition, descriptive representation, discursive representation, surrogate representation, gyroscopic representation, democratic innovations, deliberative systems, deliberative democracy, discursive accountability

2.1 Introduction

Citizens' Assemblies (CAs) are commonly seen – and justified – as institutions that provide descriptive representation in political systems (e.g., Brown 2018; Fournier et al. 2011; Warren 2008). In many cases, the members of a CA are randomly selected from a larger public to create a "mini-public" that is (ideally) a smaller version of the larger one in all its relevant diversity.[1] But the descriptive features of CAs are only *one* component of the representation that they provide. In this chapter, I examine CAs as institutions of descriptive representation, but I also explore some of the other representational functions that CAs can perform in democratic systems.

There are questions about whether the members of CAs can be considered legitimate representatives. Are they authorized to act on behalf of others? Are they accountable to those they represent? Authorization and accountability are hallmarks of dem-

---

Michael K. MacKenzie: University of Pittsburgh, USA.

1 For the purposes of this chapter, I will assume that CAs are randomly selected. They might be different sizes, ranging from a dozen participants at their smallest to more than 1000 at their largest (see, e.g., Setälä and Smith 2018). They may be temporary assemblies designed to deal with specific issues, or they may be permanent advisory or legislative bodies with representatives who serve short terms and are regularly replaced by others (e.g., Abizadeh 2021; Gastil and Wright 2018; MacKenzie 2016b, 2021; Van Reybrouk 2019).

∂ Open Access. © 2023 the author(s), published by De Gruyter. [CC] [BY-NC-ND] This work is licensed under the Creative Commons Attribution-NonCommercial-NoDerivatives 4.0 International License. https://doi.org/10.1515/9783110758269-004

ocratic representation, and randomly selected representatives are not authorized or accountable in the same ways as elected representatives. Random processes ensure that *no one* has authorized *specific* individuals to serve as representatives, and unelected representatives cannot be voted out if they make decisions that their publics disagree with. Randomly selected representatives are not accountable to voters directly, but they are *discursively* accountable to other empowered actors. CAs cannot act without providing justifications for their actions that others, such as elected officials, might plausibly accept, and this helps ensure that they are (in this sense, at least) accountable for whatever actions they take or recommendations they make.

CAs do not provide *the same sort* of representation as elected legislatures, and randomly selected representatives do not face the same incentives as elected ones. But that is precisely the point. The Citizens' Assemblies on Electoral Reform, which were held in Canada in 2004 and 2006, were useful *precisely because* they were populated with randomly selected and thus *un*elected representatives. Elected officials have a vested interest in preserving the electoral systems that were used to elect them. The designers of the Canadian CAs believed that it was therefore necessary to have unelected – but nevertheless representative – assemblies if critical assessments of the electoral systems were to be made (Gibson 2002). In more general terms, CAs will be useful and valuable only if they *add* something to our democratic systems, as opposed to merely reproducing more of what we already have.

In this chapter, I argue that CAs should not be judged according to the standards and expectations used to judge elected representatives. Standards for assessing representation in elected assemblies tend to focus on the qualities and characteristics of individual representatives. They focus on whether *individual* representatives are competent, authorized, or accountable to constituencies or groups. Instead of viewing the CAs as institutions in which individual representatives act as agents for other individuals or groups, an alternative approach is to view each CA as a single, collective representative. This way of thinking shifts the unit of analysis from the individual representative to the institution itself. This shift helps focus our attention on the representational roles that CAs might play *as institutions* that are situated in ecologies of other democratic institutions that *are* authorized by, and directly accountable to, the publics they serve. Those who apply the standards of electoral democracy to their assessments of CAs, often fail to recognize the potential benefits that unelected but nevertheless democratically legitimate representatives can provide in democratic systems.

In what follows, I address several concerns that have been raised about CAs as representative institutions. I then discuss four types of representation that CAs can provide: 1) descriptive; 2) discursive; 3); surrogate; and 4) gyroscopic. These forms of representation, as realized in the CAs, do not provide, or require direct links of accountability between the representatives and the represented. Indeed, the latter three forms of representation – at least in the ways provided by CAs – are made possible because the representatives who serve on CAs are free to act without being constrained by the demands of specific constituencies. CAs are well positioned to play these roles precisely because the representatives who serve on them are not directly accountable to individuals or constituencies with specific demands or interests (Mansbridge 2004; Warren 2008).

2.2 Critiques of citizens' assemblies as representative institutions

Mini-publics, such as CAs, are often called participatory institutions because they empower "ordinary" people in political processes. But as Mark Warren (2008) has argued, this way of thinking about CAs neglects the fact that very few individuals – a vanishingly small percentage of any public – will be members of any particular CA. This fact has led some observers to critique CAs on the grounds that they do not help make our democratic systems, overall, more deliberative (e.g., Lafont 2015, 2020; Owen and Smith 2015). Viewing CAs as representative, rather than participatory institutions may help mitigate these concerns, at least to some extent. The number of representatives in any situation or institution is, by definition, always smaller than the number of represented, and the work of enhancing deliberation in the public sphere can be continued alongside whatever efforts are made to create representative mini-publics.

As mentioned above, it has also been argued that CAs – and other mini-publics – are not democratically legitimate because the members are not authorized by, or accountable to the people they are meant to represent (e.g., Lafont 2015: 52; Parkinson 2006: 33). This critique, which is situated in discussions about the role of mini-publics in deliberative systems more generally (see, e.g., Erman 2016), raises legitimate concerns, but it is important to acknowledge the many forms of representation that exist in our democratic systems that are not directly legitimated through electoral processes. Some forms of representation are formal and institutionalized, others are less formal and exist *despite* the constraints imposed by formal institutional structures. Those who speak in deliberations represent those who do not speak. Those who attend protests represent those who do not. Those who start or participate in advocacy groups represent those who do not. The fact that some forms of representation do not – or cannot – be authorized in advance or sanctioned in retrospect through elections does not necessarily make them democratically illegitimate (see, e.g., Mansbridge 2003; Montanaro 2018). As Setälä and Smith (2018) have argued, it "is striking that the fetish for electoral modes of authorization and accountability is so deeply engrained in deliberative democratic theory" (p. 310). The focus on electoral accountability persists even though elections, partisan commitments, and demands from constituencies or special interests with wealth and influence can work to undermine the conditions needed for good deliberations – and representation – to take place. In what follows, I argue that the absence of electoral forms of authorization and accountability between representative CAs and the people they are meant to serve does not necessarily undermine their democratic legitimacy, and it can, instead, have some positive benefits, such as making supplementary forms of representation possible.

CAs may be considered legitimate when they are situated in, or integrated with, other institutions that are authorized and accountable to the publics they serve. A randomly selected second chamber – a sort of permanent CA with a continually rotating membership – would not be directly accountable, in electoral terms, to the people it serves, but it would nevertheless (at least in most proposals) have its decisions scrutinized and sanctioned or rejected by an elected chamber (see, e. g., Abizadeh 2021; Gastil and Wright 2018; MacKenzie 2016b, 2021; cf Bouricius 2018).

There are other representatives who derive their legitimacy from the fact that they have been authorized by elected governments. Appointed judges, members of cabinet in presidential systems, central bankers, public commissioners, citizen jurors, and public servants, more generally, are examples. Some of these representatives are more independent than others, but it is the independence of indirectly authorized representatives that allows them to do the work they need to do. CAs derive their legitimacy in the same way: they are not bodies of appointed experts, but they are representative assemblies appointed by duly elected officials to perform functions within a larger political or policymaking system. As Warren (2008) explains, the British Columbia Citizens' Assembly on Electoral Reform "was a body legislated into existence by an elected government. Authorization was explicit, coming in the form of enabling legislation that specified the manner in which CA members would be chosen, the task, and the timetable for completion" (p. 57). It would be a mistake to hold the CAs to a higher (or different) standard of authorization and accountability simply because they are *more* representative, in various ways, than most other appointed institutions in our democratic systems.

2.3 Types of representation

In this section, I discuss four types of representation that CAs can provide: 1) descriptive; 2) discursive; 3) surrogate; and 4) gyroscopic. These four types of representation do not require strong links of authorization and accountability between the represented and the representatives. Indeed, the latter three types are only possible where links of accountability between individual representatives and specific constituencies are weak or non-existent. These forms of representation – as provided by CAs – can be considered legitimate *even when the represented are unaware that they are being represented*, as is the case when mini-publics are used to inform and democratize policymaking processes *within* bureaucracies or other governance structures (Warren 2009). The CAs may be considered democratically legitimate because they provide forms of representation that are not normally provided elsewhere, while at the same time operating under the purview of other institutions that are subject to democratic control.

2.3.1 Descriptive representation

CAs are commonly understood and justified as institutions that provide descriptive forms of political representation (Brown 2018; Fournier et al. 2011; Warren 2008). Members are carefully selected to ensure that each assembly adequately reflects the diversity of the larger public from which its members are drawn. Elected assemblies are representative in different ways. The members of an elected assembly are authorized to act on behalf of others by the individuals and constituencies who vote for them. Elected assemblies could, in principle, adequately reflect the diversity of the publics from which their members are drawn, but this not normally the case. Instead, elections tend to select for only certain types of people. It is for this reason that Bernard Manin (1997) calls elections aristocratic: they tend to select for people who are wealthy, well connected, well organized, and well educated. In most democratic systems, elected assemblies have been dominated by men and members of majority groups, as well as those who are gregarious.

In many cases, random selection is used to ensure that the CAs are, in fact, descriptively representative. In principle, random processes will not be biased in favour or against certain types of people. All different types of people will be included in approximate proportion to their numbers in the population if a randomly selected assembly is large enough and everyone is equally willing (or required) to serve. In practice, randomly selected assemblies are not *perfectly* representative because they are not large enough to include all different types of people (and different combinations of types of people), and individuals are not normally equally willing to serve (Jacquet 2017).

In order to address these concerns, stratified random selection can be used to ensure that certain types of people (such as people of different ages, genders, and members of minority groups) are adequately represented. Stratified processes involve putting people from an initial sample into groups and then randomly selecting individuals from among those groups. If the objective is to ensure that an assembly includes people of all ages, for example, candidates would be placed in separate age groups and an appropriate number of representatives would be randomly selected from each age group.

Random processes have their own force of legitimacy. They are used in political contexts because they are a means of making choices in unbiased ways. Random processes take decisions about *who* should be a representative out of the hands of humans who have biases, preferences, and selfish (or insufficiently public) motives (e.g., Manin 1997). Random processes also support a certain version of democratic equality: in principle every person will have an equal chance of being selected to serve as a representative, which is decidedly not the case in electoral processes. Random processes substantiate the Aristotelian notion of democracy as a system in which we are, all, ruled by others and rulers in turn.

One of the problems with using stratified random processes is that stratification brings human judgement and biases back into the selection process, thus potentially undermining the legitimizing force of using random selection in the first place. This is a legitimate concern, but it is one that must be balanced against the benefits of stratification. Random selection is used to take human judgements out of selection processes, and to give everyone an (ideally) equal chance of being selected, but stratification is used to ensure that each iteration of an assembly includes categories of people whose adequate or proportional presence is thought to be essential for the legitimacy of the assembly as a whole. In striking this balance, the objective, then, is to use stratification to ensure that the CAs are descriptively representative *in the right ways* but to use it as little as possible. As the number of representatives increases more categories of stratification might be used but they also become less necessary because a larger randomly selected assembly will be more likely to include all relevant types of people.

Stratified random processes do not help solve the problem of self-selection. In most cases, individuals are randomly selected from a larger population of people, such as taxpayers, citizens, voters, or residents of a particular area, and *invited* to participate in a CA process. Typically, a large majority of those who are invited *do not* accept the invitation (e. g., Fournier et al. 2011; Jacquet 2017; Warren and Pearse 2008). If those who are willing to serve are systematically different from those who do not accept the invitation, a CA will not be truly descriptively representative even if it is large and stratification is used to ensure that the group selected *is* representative on a small number of demographic or political dimensions (e. g., Elstub 2014). At the extreme, the CAs may then be viewed as no better than elected assemblies in terms of descriptive representation: both types of assemblies will over-represent those who are politically eager, savvy, and motivated to participate for public or selfish reasons. For example, "joiners" (i. e., people who were already active in other political or voluntary organizations) were over-represented in the British Columbia CA (Warren and Pearse 2008).

Some scholars, such as Leib (2004), have argued that individuals should be compelled to serve on randomly selected assemblies, in much the way that jurors are compelled to report for jury duty when their names have been selected. This approach *could* help make CAs more descriptively representative, but most scholars believe that it is normatively problematic, potentially counter-productive, and unnecessary (e. g., Gastil and Wright 2018). It would be normatively problematic because both reflective participation *and* reflective (or thoughtful) non-participation can produce democratic benefits. For example, individuals who have been invited to participate in a CA might decline the invitation if they believe that they are not sufficiently affected by the issues being dealt with or that others who are more – or more directly affected – should have more influence in making those decisions (MacKenzie and Moore 2020). In systems with mandatory voting, citizens are required to show up to vote, but they are not required to cast a valid ballot. Mandatory participation in CAs would be more demanding than mandatory voting but it would also provide people with fewer (or no) options for reflective non-participation. Relatedly, mandatory service in a CA may be counter-productive because those who are uninterested and unwilling to participate, but nevertheless required to do so, may be less likely to participate productively. Lastly, mandatory service may be unnecessary because voluntary CAs that use stratified random processes to select members are normally representative of the publics from which they are drawn, even if they are not perfectly accurate reflections of those publics.

As a practical matter, we cannot, and should not, demand perfection in any of our political institutions. Elections are supposed to provide each person with equal influence (i.e., "one person, one equal vote"). This ideal is a source of legitimacy, but it is not ever fully realized; in part, because we also care about other principles, such as fair representation for communities of interest, which might justify some deviation from the ideal of equal votes. Randomly selected CAs will not *perfectly* reflect the publics from which they are drawn, but they are *more* descriptively representative than other democratic institutions.

It is also worth noting that self-selection does not undermine the principle of equality at work in random processes. Random selection ideally provides individuals with equal *opportunities* to participate, but as Abizadeh (2021) point outs, "no one's opportunity for holding office is diminished by her own power of declining" (p. 799). Furthermore, people should be free to decide whether they will participate, or not, in democratic processes – and some forms of non-participation can be beneficial rather than detrimental (see, e.g., MacKenzie and Moore 2020). Lastly, although self-selection will, inevitably produce some deviations from "pure" descriptive representation, it can also be advantageous. Warren (2008) argues that "self-selection into the pool of potential CA members biased the [British Columbia Citizens'] Assembly toward public-spirited individuals" (p. 65). In addition, those who volunteer for public service, when given the opportunity to do so, may be more committed, eager, and willing than those who would be forced to serve if service were mandatory (Gastil and Wright 2018). As evidence of this advantage, the Canadian Citizens' Assemblies on Electoral Reform experienced almost no attrition of participants even though the assemblies each sat for several months (Fournier et al. 2011).

The fact that CAs broadly reflect the diversity of the publics from which their members are drawn, says nothing about *how* those members should *act* as representatives (Pitkin 1967). But descriptive representation provides a foundation for better – more just or legitimate – substantive representation (Fournier et al. 2011). Collective decisions made by unrepresentative groups may be unfair or even unjust to those who are excluded because the interests of the excluded can be (and often are) ignored, undervalued, or summarily dismissed by those who are included (Young 2000). Descriptive representation may be especially important when representatives are navigating emerging or unfamiliar issues that will affect different types of people in ways that are not fully understood or anticipated. In these circumstances, as Mansbridge (1999) has argued, most of us probably want to be represented by people who are "like us" in various relevant ways because those people are more likely to think about emerging or unfamiliar issues in ways that reflect our interests (even if we do not know what our interests or concerns are in relation to those issues).

Random processes can ensure that many (but not all) types of people are present in a representative assembly. In a large enough assembly, random processes should, in principle, include not only different types of people but also different combinations of both observable and latent characteristics and beliefs. Random processes mean that CAs may be descriptively representative even in ways that we do not anticipate or fully realize.

2.3.2 Discursive representation

John Dryzek (2010) argues that the quality of representation in a democratic system should not be judged solely on whether individuals, groups, or constituencies are well represented. The legitimacy of a democratic system should also be judged according to whether "collective outcomes are responsive to the balance of competing discourses in the public sphere" (p. 24). According to Dryzek a discourse can be defined as:

> a set of concepts, categories, and ideas that will always feature particular assumptions, judgments, contentions, dispositions, intentions, and capabilities ... Accordingly, any discourse will have at its center a story line, which may involve opinions about both facts and values. Discourses involve practices, not just words, as social actions are generally accompanied by words that indicate the meaning of action (Dryzek 2010: 31).

The relevant discourses that need to be represented at any moment will depend on which issues are being addressed. As Dryzek (2010) explains, examples of economic discourses might include, "market liberalism, antiglobalization, social democracy, and sustainable development" (p. 32). Examples of environmental discourses might include "wildlife management, conservation, preservation, reform environmentalism, deep ecology, environmental justice, and ecofeminism, along with an antienvironmental discourse of 'manifest destiny'" (p. 55).

Dryzek (2010) argues that descriptive representation does not ensure that all relevant discourses will be represented. As he explains: "There is no guarantee or even strong likelihood that people with different social characteristics will in fact represent different discourses; or that a reasonably full range of social characteristics will guarantee a reasonably full range of discourses present in a forum" (p. 52). Relying on demographic, or socio-economic, characteristics as proxies for the representation of discourses will be insufficient because discourses do not map cleanly onto specific demographic characteristics. If, for example, age is used as a proxy for environmentalism, on the assumption that young people are more likely to support environmentally sustainable policies, a political forum could end up with a group of young people who all adhere to only a small subset of environmental discourses (such as those associated with conservation and preservation), and no one representing more radical discourses or anti-environmental ones (such as deep ecology or manifest destiny).

With this in mind, Dryzek (2010) argues that small deliberative forums, such as CAs, could be designed to represent discourses instead of individual persons or constituencies. The members of a CA would not be mandated to represent "their" discourses regardless of what other representatives might argue. Instead, they would deliberate with each other to clarify the points of tension or conflict between them, find positions or options for action that minimize those disagreements, or identify options that most of them support – even if they support them for different reasons (p. 58). To remain discursively accountable to the publics they serve, such representatives would be expected to explain or justify any changes of position "in terms set by the discourse(s) they represent" (p. 61).

To perform these functions, however, the representatives would need to be selected in ways that do not create direct links of authorization and accountability to specific individuals or constituencies – precisely because those linkages would also create obligations to represent and reconcile the (normally conflicting) preferences or interests of individuals within those constituencies rather than the various discourses that may be relevant to particular issues. Discourses that divide rather than mollify, for example, may be avoided by elected representatives who must seek to maintain positions that as many people as possible will support within their constituencies.

How can representatives be selected to ensure that all (or most) relevant discourses are adequately represented in deliberative forums such as CAs? Dryzek (2010) recommends using the tools of social science, such as Q-sorting, opinion surveys, in-depth interviews, or focus groups, to identify individuals who may be either strongly or moderately aligned with one or more relevant discourses. Such methods might also identify relevant discourses that the organizers of a deliberative forum were not previously aware of.

One problem with this approach is that it would give social scientists a decisive role in selecting which people – and thus which discourses – are *or are not* represented in a deliberative forum. This may be a relatively minor concern when a CA is meant to play an advisory role in policymaking processes. It will be a more significant concern when CAs are given more substantive powers in those processes. One way to address this concern is to combine the social science methods used to identify individual representatives of discourses with random selection. Q-sort methodologies, or other survey instruments, could be used to identify individuals who are aligned with specific discourses, and then random processes could be used to select specific representatives of those discourses. This would be analogous to using stratified random selection to ensure that those from diverse backgrounds are included in a CA. The difference is that instead of randomly selecting from among demographic or socio-economic categories, people would be grouped according to how they *think* about the relevant issues (i.e., according to which discourses they adhere to).

2.3.3 Surrogate representation

Jane Mansbridge (2003) argues that surrogate representation is a common practice in electoral politics. It occurs when a politician actively represents individuals who do not live, and thus do not vote, in that politician's electoral district. Mansbridge gives the example of Barney Frank, a long-serving and openly gay representative from Massachusetts, who actively represented gay rights activists across the country. Links of authorization and accountability between representatives and their surrogate constituencies may be anchored in financial donations or other contributions to the representatives' campaigns. These resources may be withheld if the represented feel as if they are not being adequately represented by their surrogate. But, as Mansbridge (2003) explains: "In the kind of surrogate representation that is not anchored in money or other contributions ('pure' surrogate representation), there is no relation of accountability between the representative and the surrogate constituent" (p. 523).

Surrogate representation helps fill gaps in the representative system: it provides groups or individuals (such as Republicans in heavily Democratic urban areas or LGBTQ people in rural areas, for example) with representation for their interests that they are unlikely to obtain through their elected representatives. As Mansbridge explains, the normative criteria for judging surrogate representation do not have to do with whether there are links of authorization and accountability forged between individuals and their representatives. Instead, this form of representation should be judged at the systems-level. The relevant question "is whether, in the aggregate, each conflicting interest has proportional adversarial representation in a legislative body" (p. 524).

Thinking about CAs as surrogates shifts the unit of analysis from the individual representative to the institution. CAs can be understood as surrogates to the extent that they can – or are well positioned to – represent interests that are not otherwise represented in our existing democratic systems. CAs are surrogates because they "stand in" for other representatives that should (or could) exist but do not. As surrogates CAs are well positioned to represent many different latent or unorganized interests, such as non-voters, immigrants or migrants (whether documented or undocumented), and, as Brown (2018) points out, "people in other countries, children, future generations, and nonhumans" (p. 172). The CAs can also act as representatives of a broadly conceived public interest (Warren 2008). CAs can play a role as surrogates precisely, and *only*, because the individuals who serve as representatives on them are not incentivized to represent only – or primarily – the demands of existing and organized interests and constituencies.

There is, of course, no guarantee that CAs will represent relevant interests that are unorganized (or unorganizable, such as future generations). The point is that they will not be *disincentivized* from doing so like elected politicians who face strong incentives to respond to organized and articulate interests over unorganized and inarticulate or latent ones.

CAs can also be designed to represent unorganized interests as surrogates. I have argued elsewhere, that randomly selected legislatures could be given an explicit mandate to represent the potential interests of future others in our collective decision-making processes (MacKenzie 2021: chapter 7). There is evidence that people will seek to play the roles they are asked to play in institutional settings (e. g., Goodin 1986: 89). If we ask people who serve on CAs to represent future others or other latent or unorganized interests, many of them will try to do so. In a deliberative forum – like a CA – the very fact that some representatives might come to see themselves as surrogates of latent or inarticulate interests may be enough to make the assembly attentive to those otherwise under-represented (and hard-to-represent) interests and concerns.

2.3.4 Gyroscopic representation

Mansbridge (2003) identifies another form of representation that is relevant in the current context: gyroscopic representation. As she explains:

> In this model of representation, voters select representatives who can be expected to act in ways the voter approves *without* external incentives. The representatives act like gyroscopes, rotating on their own axes, maintaining a certain direction, pursuing certain built-in (although not fully immutable) goals (Mansbridge 2003: 520).

Gyroscopic representatives look *within* to their own beliefs, commitments, or interests as guidance for how they should act when representing others. This form of representation is especially desirable when the represented are not sure how their interests are likely to be affected by policy options or choices. In these cases, the represented can rely on gyroscopic representatives to think and act as they would because they share certain interests, aims, or principled commitments with those representatives.

When Mansbridge writes about gyroscopic representatives, she is thinking about individuals acting as gyroscopes, but the concept can be usefully applied to institutions as well. CAs will not act as gyroscopic representatives of particular individuals or constituencies, but they may be viewed as institutions that are capable of gyroscopically representing the public as a whole – or something like a public interest – on different political issues and concerns.

There are several reasons why CAs are particularly well positioned to play the role of a gyroscopic representative of the public interest. First, randomly selected CAs are, as explained above, broadly representative of the publics from which they are drawn. Second, they can be designed to adequately represent not only different types of people and groups but also different relevant discourses (Dryzek 2010). Third, the members of CAs are given the time and resources needed to understand the political, technical, cultural, or sociological complexities of the issues they are dealing with. Fourth, the members are not selected as partisan actors or as representatives of particular communities or constituencies. The members will have their own perspectives, preferences, and beliefs – as they should – but they will be *encouraged* through deliberation with others to consider how their personal perspectives are related to the beliefs and interests of others and the public interest more generally. Fifth, the members of a CA must deliberate the issues with one another to formulate a common will or collective position on those issues. In some cases, a CA may be able to transform conflicting interests and beliefs into articulations of shared commitments or acceptable compromises. In other cases, CAs might issue public statements or clarifications of unresolved (or unresolvable) disagreements or conflicts. In either case, the collective outputs of a sufficiently inclusive, informed, and deliberative CA may be viewed as articulations of a public interest. Given the structure of the CAs – with their always rotating memberships of randomly selected individuals – we can have a certain amount of confidence that they will act as gyroscopes of a public interest more generally, even as the diverse publics they serve change over time, and as new or unfamiliar issues emerge, or old ones come to be understood in new ways. The CAs will rotate on their axes and maintain a focus on representing the public as a whole, even when a common interest or collective will can only be articulated as a clarification of divergent interests or concerns.

2.4 Conclusion

There are many different types of representatives in democratic systems. Some are directly elected and accountable to the people they serve. Many officials, such as commissioners, (most) judges, and jurors, are appointed by others to play representational roles. Others, such as members of advocacy groups, are self-appointed representatives: they take it upon themselves to speak and act on behalf of others (e.g., Montanaro 2018). CAs have a unique place in democratic systems. They are representative assemblies like elected legislatures, but they are populated by unelected representatives.

The similarities between CAs and elected legislatures may help account for the fact that CAs are often judged according to the same standards and expectations as elected legislatures, while many other representative bodies, such as judicial panels and juries, are not. The members of CAs, like judges and jurors, are not directly accountable to the people they serve, but CAs, like these other institutions, are legitimated by their positions within a large ecology of political institutions.

I have argued that CAs can perform their representative functions well because their members are unelected. The members of CAs can deliberate with each other without being constrained by the demands of specific constituencies or groups. They can seriously consider and represent popular, unpopular, or unfamiliar discourses in their deliberations without fear of being silenced by the people they serve. They are not disincentivized from representing unorganized or latent interests or groups, such as noncitizens, future generations, or nonhumans, and they can represent the public interest, as they understand it, without having to also justify public interest claims in particularistic or partisan terms. The fact that randomly selected CAs are (typically) more descriptively representative than elected legislatures means that they are well positioned to make plausible and legitimate claims about what is, or might be, in the public interest. In short, CAs have a unique and useful, but nevertheless legitimate, place within our democratic systems precisely *because* their members are not elected officials.

References

Abizadeh, A. (2021). Representation, bicameralism, political equality, and sortition: Reconstituting the second chamber as a randomly elected assembly. *Perspectives on Politics* 19, 791–806.

Bouricius, T. (2018). Why hybrid bicameralism is not right for sortition. *Politics & Society* 46, 435–451.

Brown, M. (2018). Deliberation and representation.' In J. Dryzek, A. Bachtiger, J. Mansbridge, & M. E. Warren (eds), *The Oxford Handbook of Deliberative Democracy*, 171–186. Oxford: Oxford University Press.

Dryzek, J. S. (2010). *Foundations and Frontiers of Deliberative Governance*. Oxford: Oxford University Press.

Elstub, S. (2014). Minipublics: Issues and cases. In S. Elstub & P. McLaverty (eds), *Deliberative Democracy: Issues and Cases*, 166–188. Edinburgh: Edinburgh University Press.

Erman, E. (2016). Representation, equality, and inclusion in deliberative systems: Desiderata for a good account. *Critical Review of International Social and Political Philosophy* 19, 263–282.

Fournier, P., van der Kolk, H., Carty, K. R., Blais, A., & Rose, J. (2011). *When Citizens Decide: Lessons from Citizen Assemblies on Electoral Reform*. Oxford: Oxford University Press.

Gastil, J., & E. O. Wright. (2018). Legislature by lot: Envisioning sortition within a bicameral system. *Politics & Society* 46, 303–330.

Gibson, G. (2002). *Report on the Constitution of the Citizens' Assembly on Electoral Reform*. Victoria, BC: Attorney General of British Columbia.

Goodin, R. E. (1986). Laundering preferences. In J. Elster & A. Hylland (eds), *Foundations of Social Choice Theory*, 75–101. Cambridge: Cambridge University Press.

Jacquet, V. (2017). Explaining non-participation in deliberative mini-publics. *European Journal of Political Research* 56, 640–659.

Lafont, C. (2015). Deliberation, participation, and democratic legitimacy: Should deliberative mini-publics shape public policy? *The Journal of Political Philosophy* 23, 40–63.

Lafont, C. (2020). *Democracy without Shortcuts: A Participatory Conception of Deliberative Democracy*. Oxford: Oxford University Press

Leib, E. J. (2004). *Deliberative Democracy in America: A Proposal for a Popular Branch of Government*. University Park, PA: Pennsylvania State University Press.

MacKenzie, M. K. (2016a). Institutional design and sources of short-termism. In I. Gonzalez-Ricoy & A. Gosseries (eds), *Institutions for Future Generations*, 24–48. Oxford: Oxford University Press.

MacKenzie, M. K. (2016b). A general-purpose, randomly selected chamber. In I. Gonzalez-Ricoy & A. Gosseries (eds), *Institutions for Future Generations*, 282–298. Oxford: Oxford University Press.

MacKenzie, M. K. (2021). *Future Publics: Democracy, Deliberation, and Future-Regarding Collective Action*. New York: Oxford University Press.

MacKenzie, M. K., & Moore, A. (2020). Democratic non-participation. *Polity* 52 (3), 430–459.

Manin, B. (1997). *The Principles of Representative Government*. Cambridge; New York: Cambridge University Press.

Mansbridge, J. (1999). Should Blacks represent Blacks and women represent women? A contingent 'Yes'. *The Journal of Politics* 61, 628–657.

Mansbridge, J. (2003). Rethinking representation. *The American Political Science Review* 97, 515–528.

Mansbridge, J. (2004). Representation revisited: Introduction to the case against electoral accountability. *Democracy and Society* 2.

Montanaro, L. (2018). *Who Elected Oxfam?: A Democratic Defense of Self-Appointed Representatives*. Cambridge: Cambridge University Press.

Owen, D., & Smith, G. (2015). Survey article: Deliberation, democracy and the systemic turn. *Journal of Political Philosophy* 23 (2), 213–234.

Parkinson, J. (2006). *Deliberating in the Real World: Problems of Legitimacy in Deliberative Democracy*. New York; Oxford: Oxford University Press.

Pitkin, H. F. (1967). *The Concept of Representation*. Berkeley: University of California Press.

Setälä, M., & Smith, G. (2018). Mini-publics and deliberative democracy. In J. Dryzek, A. Bachtiger, J. Mansbridge & M. E. Warren (eds), *The Oxford Handbook of Deliberative Democracy*, 300–314. Oxford: Oxford University Press.

Van Reybrouck, D. (2019). Belgium's democratic experiment: Europe's smallest federal entity is setting a big precedent. *Politico EU*, 04/25/2019.

Warren, M. (2008). Citizen representatives. In M. Warren & H. Pearse (eds), *Designing deliberative democracy: The British Colombia Citizens' Assembly*, 50–69. Cambridge: Cambridge University Press.

Warren, M. (2009). Governance-driven democratization. *Critical Policy Studies* 3, 3–13.

Warren, M., and Pearce, H. (2008). *Designing Deliberative Democracy: The British Columbia Citizens' Assembly*. Cambridge, UK; New York: Cambridge University Press.

Young, I. M. (2000). *Inclusion and Democracy*. New York; Oxford: Oxford University Press.

Pierre-Étienne Vandamme

3 Citizens' assemblies and accountability

Abstract: The main theoretical objection pressed against empowered citizens' assemblies is that randomly selected representatives would not be accountable. In contrast, accountability is often held to be one of the key benefits offered by elections. To allow readers to assess the validity of this objection, this chapter starts by distinguishing different understandings of accountability. It then explains why citizen representatives would not be accountable in the same way as elected representatives are, while qualifying the accountability of the latter. It explores the notion of deliberative or discursive accountability, which can apply to CAs, and different forms of non-electoral sanctions that may strengthen the accountability of citizen representatives. Finally, considering that it is often the organizers of CAs that make the representative claim as well as key design choices, the chapter explores different ways in which organizers can be made accountable.

Keywords: sortition, citizens' assemblies, accountability, legitimacy, control, representation

3.1 Introduction

Citizens' assemblies (CAs) composed through random selection (or stratified sampling) are increasingly seen as offering a new form of democratic representation, complementing or competing with electoral representation (Warren 2008; Farrell and Stone 2020; Landemore 2020; MacKenzie in this *Handbook*). The main objection pressed against this new form of representation is that randomly selected representatives (hereafter "citizen representatives") would not be accountable (Parkinson 2006; Lafont 2015; Pourtois 2016; Abizadeh 2021; Landa and Pevnick 2021). In contrast, accountability is often held to be one of the key benefits offered by elections, along with authorization (Pitkin 1967: 55–59; Young 2000: 128–132). As CAs become more and more empowered and achieve genuine influence on policymaking or even constitution-writing in some contexts (see Reuchamps and Suiter 2016), this question of accountability matters increasingly. The very democratic legitimacy of CAs is at stake, as it is often considered that an unaccountable political power is undemocratic.[1]

Pierre-Étienne Vandamme: Université libre de Bruxelles, Belgium.

[1] Another interesting debate about the legitimacy of CAs is whether it can be claimed to derive from a form of popular authorization. The process of authorization of CAs certainly does not work in the same way as in elections, but elections are not the only possible vehicle of authorization. In the case of CAs, authorization can be indirect, either by an electoral mandate received by those who set up the CA, or a

∂ Open Access. © 2023 the author(s), published by De Gruyter. [CC] [BY-NC-ND] This work is licensed under the Creative Commons Attribution-NonCommercial-NoDerivatives 4.0 International License. https://doi.org/10.1515/9783110758269-005

Arguably, the lack of direct popular accountability is a less salient problem when CAs are embedded in a broader democratic system (see Parkinson and Mansbridge 2012) where key decision-makers are accountable, and when the output of CAs is submitted for approval either to elected representatives or to the general population through a referendum. Nevertheless, as many roles can be imagined for CAs, including strongly empowered ones, the question is worth investigating.

To allow readers to assess the validity of the claim that citizen representatives would not be sufficiently accountable, this chapter starts by distinguishing different understandings of accountability. It then explains why citizen representatives would not be accountable in the same way as elected representatives are, while qualifying the accountability of the latter. The next section explores the notion of deliberative or discursive accountability, which can apply to CAs. I argue that citizen representatives can be made accountable without sanction, but that this form of accountability may seem insufficient to non-participating citizens, especially if the CA is empowered. Therefore, I explore different forms of non-electoral sanctions that may strengthen the accountability of citizen representatives. Then, considering the fact that it is often the organizers that make the representative claim – not citizen representatives themselves – as well as key design choices, I mention different ways in which organizers can be made accountable.

One aspect of the relation between CAs and accountability that is not discussed in this chapter is the way CAs can be used to hold elected actors accountable (see Goodin 2008: 33–34; Setälä 2021). It is discussed in another chapter of this volume (MacKenzie in this *Handbook*).

3.2 A polysemic notion

The validity of the accountability objection to representation by lot largely hinges on the definition of accountability that is used. As Robert Goodin (2008: 156) puts it, accountability "is a concept that takes a three-part predicate: the accountability is *of* some agent *to* some other agent *for* some state of affairs". Within electoral representation, it is 1) elected officials who are accountable 2) to their constituents (at least) 3) for their (in)actions in office. Within representation by lot, it would be 1) citizen representatives (individually or collectively) who would have to be accountable 2) to the whole citizenry (at least) 3) for their (in)actions in office.

Now, what does it mean for representatives – be they elected or randomly selected – to be accountable? In the most general contemporary sense of the word, it means that they can be asked to give an account of their decisions, to justify themselves for what they do or fail to do in their function of representatives. See Goodin again:

referendum legitimizing (at regular intervals) the use of CAs for predefined purposes (see Landemore 2020: 108).

"For public officials, accountability requirements are characteristically satisfied when they show that the action was within the scope of their official powers, and that some reason (within the scope of legitimate reasons) was given for the action" (Goodin 2008: 164).

In political science and political philosophy, accountability is often associated with sanctions. In their important book on electoral representation, Przeworski, Stokes and Manin (1999: 10) thus affirm that governments are accountable "if citizens can discern representative from unrepresentative government and can sanction them appropriately, retaining in office those incumbents who perform well and ousting from office those who do not" (conditions, they argue, often fail to be met[2]). The reason for this association of accountability with sanction is probably that it is harder to imagine what could force representatives to justify themselves if they did not face the prospect of popular sanction (in the form of deselection). And if they are not forced, if they can escape the duty to give accounts, are they really accountable in a meaningful sense?

Nevertheless, sanctions are not necessary for accountability to occur. Initially, accountability did not have this restrictive meaning that became dominant in political science (see Bovens, Goodin and Schillemans 2014). It meant "having to describe, explain, and justify one's actions to those to whom one is responsible" (Mansbridge 2019: 194). People can feel accountable and can decide to justify themselves even when they are not sanctionable. As Jane Mansbridge (2014) has argued, there are at least two different forms of accountability: sanction-based and trust-based. The former is relevant in contexts where agents cannot be trusted by principals to behave appropriately; the latter in contexts where there are enough agents with an intrinsic motivation to behave as expected by principals. To give examples, when a lot of power is at stake and when we know that the agent (a minister, typically) will face a risk of corruption, the threat of sanction seems appropriate. In contrast, when we can expect an agent to do her job properly because we can count on her innate motivation (a researcher, for example?), trust and discursive accountability (like a frequent report on activities) may be more appropriate than sanctions (like the threat of dismissal).

Accountability always incorporates a discursive element – the demand and supply of reasons or justifications – which can (but need not) be completed with an element of sanction. In contexts of trust, it can take a purely discursive form, without an institutionalized mechanism of sanction. People – including citizen representatives – can internalize an expectation to provide justifications and do it spontaneously. Or they can be asked – by citizens, journalists, or associations, for example – to justify things in the absence of a sanction mechanism. In such cases, one can speak of "discursive" (Dryzek and Niemeyer 2008: 490; Goodin 2008: 155–185; Warren 2008: 61) or "deliberative" (Mansbridge 2019: 197–199) accountability.

---

2 To mention just a few problems: citizens often lack relevant information, partisans may not want to sanction their misbehaving leaders, and as a result many politicians stay in power even when there is evidence of misconduct. Furthermore, several politicians do not run again for office anyway. Qualifications to elections' capacity to deliver accountability are introduced below.

One advantage of this form of accountability is that it extends the scope of account-ability beyond the constituents. In a world where decisions made locally have huge im-pacts elsewhere, where only a slight portion of affected interests are enfranchised, this is desirable. It means that people can be asked to justify their actions by affected par-ties (or in the name of affected parties) that do not have the power to sanction them electorally. As Goodin (2008: 148) puts it a bit emphatically, with discursive accountabil-ity "the problem of political boundaries disappears." Hence, it can be a "powerful sup-plement to electoral accountability" (p. 149).

Note however that sanctions are not entirely absent from such deliberative forms of accountability. When expectations are attached to actions, there is always a social form of sanction faced by people who act against these expectations. Thus, even if some public officials or representatives cannot be dismissed or deselected, they can suffer from the sanction associated with public disapproval, or even shaming. Imagine for example a CA neglecting completely the interests of foreigners or future genera-tions. It could be blamed and shamed by spokespersons of these affected interests, which would be a form of social sanction. As we shall see, sanctions can take very dif-ferent forms. At this stage, the key point is that accountability does not necessarily en-tail an *institutionalized sanction mechanism*, nor does it entail sanctions as costly as losing one's job.

3.3 Accountability beyond electoral sanction

The exploration of the different possible meanings of accountability shows that ac-countability is conceivable independently of electoral sanction. So, the accountability-based objection to CAs is not valid if the claim is that citizen representatives *cannot* be made accountable. It is valid, however, if the claim is that citizen representatives would not be accountable in the same way as elected representatives are. They would not be because they would not face the same incentives. As they do not have the possibility to run for reelection, they are dispensed from the electoral obligation to defend their performance at the end of their mandate. And as most of them are not member of political parties, they do not have to care about the party's reputation either. Whether the public is satisfied or not with their performance in office matters only for their reputation and self-esteem – which is not negligible – but not for their career as such.

Admittedly, electoral accountability is deficient in many respects (see Przeworski, Stokes and Manin 1999; Guerrero 2014; Achen and Bartels 2017). In most democracies, voters have been found largely ignorant about the work (or even identity) of their rep-resentatives (Brennan 2016; Achen and Bartels 2017). Most of them also face profound difficulties "in connecting specific policy proposals to their own values and interests" (Bartels 2008: 27). Therefore, they are often not properly equipped to judge their repre-sentatives' policy choices. What is more, according to some scholars, they usually "have great difficulty making sensible attributions of responsibility for hard times" (Achen and Bartels 2017: 304) or even to assess whether times have been good or bad during a term in office. As a result, when voters do vote retrospectively, they may reward or sanction representatives for things they are not responsible for, such as droughts, floods, or a suddenly changing economic dynamic in the months preceding an election (whatever the economic results of the whole term in office). Finally, it seems that things are getting worse with time, as contemporary democracies are witnessing a decline of accountability as a result of a shift of decision-making power from the frontstage to the backstage of politics, with an increasing amount of power in the hands of actors that are not electorally accountable (see Papadopoulos 2013).

Hence, the degree to which existing democracies honour the value of accountability should not be overestimated. Yet it does not invalidate the accountability objection. It is not because electoral accountability is deficient that it is useless. As Achen and Bartels (2017: 318) themselves recognize, reelection-seeking politicians will at least "strive to avoid being caught violating consensual ethical norms in their society". And parties still clearly face incentives to monitor their representatives in power and to encourage them to honour most of their electoral promises. From this viewpoint, if accountability is already fragile within electoral representation, there would be a high danger of reducing it further in alternative forms of representation.

What can advocates of representation by lot respond to this challenge? Either they can downplay the importance of accountability for democracy, or they can put forward ways other than elections to promote accountability within a CA. The first strategy is for example used by Hélène Landemore (2020: 88, 103–104), who argues that accountability is a concern of secondary importance. It is not essential for a regime to count as democratic, but it is a matter of good governance. Hence, democrats should first identify institutions that respect core democratic values such as inclusiveness and equality, and then see how to promote accountability within the most inclusive and equal political system. In a slightly different perspective, Alexander Guerrero (2021) argues that responsiveness matters more than accountability as such, and that citizen representatives can be expected to be responsive to the demands of the general public without being accountable in the way elected representatives are.

Let us now focus on the second strategy: promoting accountability without electoral sanctions. The deliberative form of accountability presented above can be promoted in several ways. First, if participants deliberate before reaching collective decisions, they will feel accountable to one another. Some attitudes or ideas will be challenged, and it can be expected that the social norm condemning purely self-interested behaviour in public missions will play its civilizing role (see Elster 2000). Yet what the accountability objection points out is not a lack of *mutual* accountability within a CA, it is a lack of accountability to the general public, to non-selected citizens. Such outward accountability can be promoted by demanding public reports on the assembly's activities and deliberations. One could imagine that citizen representatives have at least a collective obligation to motivate their decisions. This, however, could be considered insufficient if the public has no power to challenge these official justifications or to demand more. Hence, one could imagine allowing the press to interview citizen representatives (or their spokesperson).

The important thing to see is that there is a trade-off between accountability and independence, and one between accountability and participation or inclusion (see Vandamme and Verret-Hamelin 2017). The more the deliberations and decisions of a CA are open to public scrutiny (for the sake of accountability), the more their independence will be weakened. If citizen representatives are public figures rather than anonymous citizens, they become more exposed to undue influence and risks of capture (Guerrero 2014). This is why Gastil and Wright (2019: 28) recommend the use of secret ballots in their legislature by lot. They want the whole assembly to give accounts of its collective decisions, but they do not want individual citizen representatives to be exposed to public pressure and lobbying.

One additional reason to limit individual accountability to the public within a CA is that it could discourage participation. As Mansbridge (2019: 200) notes, 40 per cent of US citizens "say they fear speaking in public in front of an audience". This number is likely to be much higher for disadvantaged groups. Hence, if we want to avoid very low rates of participation by randomly selected citizens – and if we want to include members of disadvantaged groups in particular – we should pay attention not to put too much pressure on participants' shoulders. An obligation to defend their positions in public would certainly increase accountability yet be dissuasive for many. This is the second trade-off, between accountability and inclusion.

To sum up, a deliberative form of accountability can be fostered not only within a CA, but also in its relation to the wider public (on which, see also Rountree and Curato in this *Handbook*). However, this accountability is likely to be somewhat limited in order to preserve the independence of citizen representatives and to keep the mission attractive to a wide diversity of social profiles. And it will also be limited by the fact that citizen representatives would not face the same incentives to stay aligned with public opinion as elected politicians and parties.

Because deliberative accountability will be limited, one could consider it insufficient. As argued by Elizabeth Anderson (2006), there is a discursive dimension in electoral accountability as well, but recurring elections also have the added value of incentivizing representatives to take people's discursive feedback more seriously. So, without any threat of sanction other than public blaming or shaming, one might consider that discursive or deliberative accountability alone is not enough.

3.4 Sanctions within representation by lot

There is a diversity of sanctions that can be imagined in order to promote adequate behaviour in CAs. Participants could be asked to take an oath or sign a chart of conduct, deviations from which could be sanctioned by the steering committee, by their peers, or a combination of both. Taking some inspiration from ancient practices of accountability in Athens – which were particularly harsh (see Elster 1999) – one might also imagine popular juries (also randomly selected) tasked with assessing the appropriate behavior of citizen representatives (Landemore 2020: 100 – 101).

To allow non-selected citizens to sanction misbehaviour, one could also imagine a right of popular recall.[3] Several countries allow citizens to recall elected representatives through the gathering of a required threshold of signatures followed by a popular vote (see Welp and Whitehead 2020). In the absence of elections, one might see the recall as the ideal way to empower non-selected citizens and to hold citizen representatives accountable. However, leaving aside the broader discussion about the benefits and limits of the recall in general, one might see a public revocation as excessively harsh for citizen representatives who have not asked to be there and who are just kind enough to accept a time-consuming public mission (see Vandamme 2020: 9). Moreover, there is once again an important trade-off between accountability and participation/inclusion. Allowing for the recall of citizen representatives might make the mission unattractive to many, and in particular to those who are not full of self-esteem – at the cost of inclusion and descriptive representation. Finally, even if the recall of individual representatives were desirable, it might be illusory to think that the public will be sufficiently informed about the actions and opinions of individuals within the CA to exercize such form of control. It is likely that part of the deliberations (and maybe even final decisions) will occur behind closed doors. And even if votes and deliberations were public, the process is likely to be less readable for citizens than the opposition of a few coherent political visions offered by parties (see Rummens 2016).

On all these accounts, a right of *collective* recall might sound more appealing, certainly if terms in office are relatively long. The idea, here, would be to allow non-selected citizens to demand the dissolution of the CA in cases where its decisions deviate too much from public opinion in a way that citizen representatives cannot convincingly justify. This is unlikely to be necessary with low-empowered CAs, but it might be a way to hold powerful CAs accountable in a meaningful way. This right of collective recall (for elected assemblies, though) is currently practiced in Latvia, Slovakia, and in six Swiss Cantons (Magni-Berton and Egger 2019: 81– 82). It might be better suited to a CA than the individual recall. Furthermore, recall initiatives, whether successful or not, might have the benefit of politicizing the work of the CA for the wider public, thus attracting the latter's attention and giving the CA's work more visibility.

Nevertheless, it is worth pointing again to the classical trade-off between accountability and independence. It is often the independence of CAs from electoral promises and public pressure that is invoked to justify their epistemic added value. Yet, if they cannot deviate from public opinion without sanction, these epistemic benefits (including the possibility to leave room for the interests of foreigners and future generations)

---

3 In the *popular* recall, the idea is to allow non-participants to sanction participants. An *internal* recall mechanism can also be used to strengthen mutual accountability among participants. In the mixed "deliberative committees" of the Brussels Parliament, the rapporteurs, who are randomly selected among the participants, can be recalled by the rest of the group (subject to 90 % of approval). I thank Min Reuchamps for attracting my attention to this rule.

might be jeopardized. This, however, will depend on the degree of demandingness of the recall procedure. One could imagine a demanding threshold of signatures, and possibly a demanding quorum of participation in the recall referendum that would make of the recall more a last resort option for serious deviations from public opinion than the norm. It could also play a symbolic role: reassuring non-selected citizens about their empowerment (Vandamme 2020: 4–5), thereby partly countering the objection that CAs making final decisions harm the agency of the non-selected (see Abizadeh 2021) and require them to defer blindly to their unchosen representatives (Lafont 2020).

3.5 The accountability of the organizers

There are at least four reasons why a CA might deviate importantly from public opinion, and two of them raise important accountability concerns:
– The information acquired through hearings of experts and stakeholders improves their understanding of the issue at stake and corrects for mistakes that are widespread among the general population.
– Deliberations within the CA can lead to a revision of the dominant view on an issue through the consideration of a legitimate minority perspective.
– Citizen representatives may pursue private interests at the expense of the general public.
– Distortions of judgement may occur through bad or voluntarily biased organizational choices: the framing of the question dealt with by the CA, the governance committee, the sample of participants, and the panel of auditioned experts might all be biased; besides, deliberations might be dominated by charismatic or skilled participants.

If the panel of experts is not biased and if deliberative domination is weak, the first two reasons to deviate from the dominant public opinion seem legitimate. In such cases, the independence of the CA from popular accountability mechanisms can even be desirable. The third calls for forms of control as the ones put forward in the previous section. The fourth set of reasons falls within the responsibility of the organizers of the CA and calls for additional accountability considerations.

It is important not to neglect the power of influence in the hands of organizers. They are usually the actors making the representative claim (Gül 2019) – claiming that the CA they designed reasonably reflects the diversity of relevant social categories among the population, will deliberate in appropriate conditions, hear a balanced set of experts[4] and stakeholders, and hence can be trusted to represent the whole population

---

[4] Experts themselves are usually subject to a deliberative form of accountability through peer networks relying on mutual monitoring and reputational sanctioning (Goodin 2008: 162).

in an appropriate way. Hence, they should be accountable – and possibly more so than participants themselves.[5]And this accountability should concern the whole process. Design choices should be transparent and justified publicly *before* the CA starts, to allow for contestation and revisions. Choices made *during* the meetings of the CA should also be justified – to participants in particular, but also to the general public. And finally, organizers should be held accountable for the follow-up of the CA's recommendations and their possible implementation.

This question of the accountability of organizers, however, cannot be dealt with appropriately in abstraction from the institutional context in which the CA is embedded. If it is elected actors (be it the executive or the parliament) who initiate the CA, like the recent French citizen convention for climate, they can be made accountable through the traditional electoral way. Most likely, initiating political actors will appoint an organizing or supervising committee, that will be accountable to them, while they remain accountable to their electors.

If it is a grass-root initiative, the question will be different (see Bussu and Fleuß in this *Handbook*). We would then face "self-selected representatives" (see Montanaro 2012) who claim that the CA they set up is representative, without clear accountability mechanisms. This might not be too much of a problem, however, given that CAs initiated by civil society actors in isolation from public authorities usually do not have much power and do not produce major impacts on policymaking. The demand for accountability grows with the political power of CAs.

In a political system where a CA would be permanently integrated, as is the case in East Belgium (Ostbelgien) for example (Niessen and Reuchamps 2022), there would be a need for a clear chain of accountability. One would have to hold accountable the actors in charge of the selection of participants, of experts and stakeholders, and of moderators. This could be achieved, for example, by the inclusion in a steering committee of people accountable to the parliament, or even members of the different parties. Yet even if there is a specific institution – like the Citizen Council in East Belgium, also composed of lay citizens – designed to supervise CAs and make sure that the initial aims and requirements are met, these processes cannot be entirely self-regulated

In the more utopian scenario where elections would have been entirely replaced by CAs (or would still exist, but where a CA would be the main locus of power), the problem would be more salient.[6] One possibility would be to have clearly identifiable decision-makers (elected, or randomly selected and revocable) in charge of all these choices and directly accountable to the whole population. Another one would be to count on a form of self-regulation by citizen representatives. The method of random selection would have been decided once and for all, and the remaining decision (whom to invite for hearings, how to moderate deliberations, etc.) would be taken

---

5 One might also think that organizers should be accountable to participants themselves, at least in a deliberative way: they should be able to justify their organizational choices to the first affected and willing to consider the latter's alternative suggestions.

6 Along with other problems discussed in Gastil and Wright 2019; Lafont 2020; Abizadeh 2021.

by citizen representatives themselves in the assembly. Alternatively, a specific CA could be designed to oversee the correct application of rules previously set (and open to revisions) by yet another citizen body, as is the case in Terrill Bouricius' (2013) multi-body sortition model. In all these cases, it could seem wise to allow for a right of collective recall of the different bodies by non-selected citizens in cases of abuses of power.

3.6 Conclusion

One of the most powerful objections to representation by lot is that citizen representatives would not be accountable enough, as they could not be sanctioned through elections and would not face the same incentives as elected actors. In this chapter, I argued against the view that citizen representatives would not be accountable at all. There are different ways of being accountable, and different possible strategies for promoting accountability besides the electoral sanction. It remains true, however, that citizen representatives would not be accountable in the same way as elected representatives. Whether that is a reason to reject representation by lot altogether, to oppose democratic systems that would rely exclusively on sortition, to object to the transfer of important political power to CAs, or whether that brings more democratic benefits than losses are normative questions on which this contribution does not wish to take a stance. My hope is that it helps the reader see more clearly through this debate and to make an informed judgement about the validity and strength of the accountability objection and about possible ways of making CAs more accountable when it is judged desirable.

References

Abizadeh, A. (2021). Representation, bicameralism, political equality, and sortition: Reconstituting the second chamber as a randomly selected assembly. *Perspectives on Politics* 19 (3), 791–806.

Achen, C., & Bartels, L. (2017). *Democracy for Realists*. Princeton, NJ: Princeton University Press.

Anderson, E. (2006). The epistemology of democracy. *Episteme* 3 (1–2), 8–22.

Bartels, L. (2008). *Unequal Democracy: The Political Economy of the New Gilded Age*. Princeton: Princeton University Press.

Bouricius, T. G. (2020). Democracy through multi-body sortition: Athenian lessons for the modern day. *Journal of Deliberative Democracy* 9 (1).

Bovens, M., Goodin, R. E., & Schillemans, T. (eds). (2014). *The Oxford Handbook of Public Accountability*. Oxford: Oxford University Press.

Brennan, J. (2016). *Against Democracy*. Princeton, NJ: Princeton University Press.

Bussu, S. & Fleuß , D. (2023). Citizen's assemblies: Top-down or bottom-up? - both, please! In M. Reuchamps, J. Vrydagh & Y. Welp (eds). De Gruyter Handbook of Citizens' Assemblies. Berlin: De Gruyter.Dryzek, J. S., & Niemeyer, S. (2008). Discursive representation. *American Political Science Review* 102 (4), 481–493.

Elster, J. (1999). Accountability in Athenian politics. In A. Przeworski, S. C. S. Stokes, & B. Manin (eds), *Democracy, Accountability, and Representation*, 253–278. Cambridge: Cambridge University Press.

Elster, J. (2000). Arguing and bargaining in two constituent assemblies. *University of Pennsylvannia Journal of Constitutional Law* 2, 345–421.

Farrell, D., & Stone, P. (2020). Sortition and mini-publics: A different kind of representation. In R. Rohrschneider & J. Thomassen (eds), *The Oxford Handbook of Political Representation in Liberal Democracies*, 228–246. Oxford: Oxford University Press.

Gastil, J., & Wright, E. O. (2019). *Legislature by Lot: Transformative Designs for Deliberative Governance*. London: Verso Books.

Goodin, R. E. (2008). *Innovating Democracy: Democratic Theory and Practice After the Deliberative Turn*. Oxford: Oxford University Press.

Guerrero, A. A. (2014). Against elections: The lottocratic alternative. *Philosophy & Public Affairs* 42 (2), 135–178.

Guerrero, A. (2021). The morality of democracy (has nothing to do with elections). Presentation at the MANCEPT workshop "Rethinking Elections".

Gül, V. (2019). Representation in minipublics. *Representation* 55 (1), 31–45.

Lafont, C. (2015). Deliberation, participation, and democratic legitimacy: Should deliberative mini-publics shape public policy? *Journal of Political Philosophy* 23 (1), 40–63.

Lafont, C. (2020). *Democracy Without Shortcuts: A Participatory Conception of Deliberative Democracy*. Oxford: Oxford University Press.

Landa, D., & Pevnick, R. (2021). Is random selection a cure for the ills of electoral representation? *Journal of Political Philosophy* 29 (1), 46–72.

Landemore, H. (2020). *Open Democracy: Reinventing Popular Rule for the 21st Century*. Princeton, NJ: Princeton University Press.

MacKenzie , M. K. (2023). Representation and citizens' assemblies. In M. Reuchamps, J. Vrydagh & Y. Welp (eds). De Gruyter Handbook of Citizens' Assemblies. Berlin: De Gruyter.

Magni-Berton, R., & Egger, C. (2019). *Le référendum d'initiative citoyenne expliqué à tous: Au coeur de la démocratie directe*. FYP éditions.

Mansbridge, J. (2014). A contingency theory of accountability. In M. Bovens, R. Goodin, & T. Schillemans (eds), *The Oxford Handbook of Public Accountability*, 55–68. Oxford: Oxford University Press.

Mansbridge, J. (2019). Accountability in the constituent-representative relationship. In J. Gastil and E. O. Wright (eds.), *Legislature by Lot: Transformative Designs for Deliberative Governance*, 189–204. London: Verso.

Montanaro, L. (2012). The democratic legitimacy of self-appointed representatives. *The Journal of Politics* 74 (4), 1094–1107.

Niessen, C., & Reuchamps, M. (2022). Institutionalising citizen deliberation in parliament: The permanent citizens' dialogue in the German-speaking community of Belgium. *Parliamentary Affairs* 75 (1), 135–153.

Papadopoulos, Y. (2013). *Democracy in Crisis? Politics, Governance and Policy*. Houndmills, Basingstoke: Palgrave Macmillan.

Parkinson, J. (2006). *Deliberating in the Real World: Problems of Legitimacy in Deliberative Democracy*. Oxford: Oxford University Press.

Parkinson, J. & Mansbridge, J. (eds). 2012. *Deliberative Systems: Deliberative Democracy at the Large Scale*. Cambridge: Cambridge University Press

Pitkin, H. F. 1967. *The Concept of Representation*. Berkeley: University of California Press.

Pourtois, H. (2016). Les élections sont-elles essentielles à la démocratie?. *Philosophiques* 43 (2), 411–439.

Przeworski, A., Stokes, S. C. S., & Manin, B. (eds). (1999). *Democracy, Accountability, and Representation*. Cambridge: Cambridge University Press.

Reuchamps, M., & Suiter, J. (2016). *Constitutional Deliberative Democracy in Europe*. Colchester: ECPR Press.

Rountree, J. & Curato, N. (2023). Citizens' assemblies and the public sphere. In M. Reuchamps, J. Vrydagh & Y. Welp (eds). De Gruyter Handbook of Citizens' Assemblies. Berlin: De Gruyter.

Rummens, S. (2016). Legitimacy without visibility? On the role of mini-publics in the democratic system. In M. Reuchamps & J. Suiter (eds), *Constitutional Deliberative Democracy in Europe*, 129–146. Colchester: ECPR Press.

Setälä, M. (2021). Advisory, collaborative and scrutinizing roles of deliberative mini-publics. *Frontiers in Political Science* 2, 19.

Vandamme, P. E. (2020). Can the recall improve electoral representation? *Frontiers in Political Science* 2, 6.

Vandamme, P. E., & Verret-Hamelin, A. (2017). A randomly selected chamber: Promises and challenges. *Journal of Public Deliberation* 13 (1).

Warren, M. E. (2008). Citizen representatives. In M. E. Warren & H. Pearse (eds), *Designing Deliberative Democracy: The British Columbia Citizens' Assembly*, 50–69. Cambridge: Cambridge University Press.

Welp, Y., & Whitehead, L. (eds.). (2020). *The Politics of Recall Elections.* Cham: Springer Nature.

Young, I. M. (2000). *Inclusion and Democracy.* Oxford: Oxford University Press.

Cristina Lafont

4 Which decision-making authority for citizens' assemblies

Abstract: The increased interest in citizens' assemblies has generated a heated debate about precisely which decision-making authorities they should be able to exercise. A key question in this debate is whether it is democratically legitimate to confer decision-making authority upon citizens' assemblies. To help answer this question, I distinguish between two ways in which citizens' assemblies can be institutionalized: a vertical or "top-down" approach versus a horizontal or "bottom-up" approach. Whereas the first approach seeks to empower citizens' assemblies to do the deliberating and deciding for the rest of the citizenry, the second approach seeks to institutionalize citizens' assemblies with the aim of empowering the entire citizenry to influence policy-making, set the political agenda, and have the final say on certain political decisions. After analysing various proposals, I conclude that conferring decision-making authority upon citizens assemblies can be democratically legitimate only insofar as it empowers the entire citizenry.

Keywords: citizens' assemblies, decision-making authority, citizen empowerment, deliberation, legitimacy, participation.

4.1 Introduction

Citizens' assemblies (CAs) are groups of 40 to 200 or more citizens tasked with learning, deliberating, and then advising or deciding upon a law or policy. Such bodies are typically sponsored by a political authority and organized by an independent agency that facilitates group deliberation among a near-random or stratified sample of citizens which is descriptively representative of the constituency that will be subject to the law or policy in question. CAs provide a space for high quality, face-to-face deliberation. Randomly selected participants who would otherwise not interact receive balanced, expert information on an issue. They are exposed to a variety of relevant social perspectives and, via facilitated group discussions, have the opportunity to weigh the reasons and arguments both "for and against" specific laws or policies before reaching a considered judgement or making a recommendation. This information can be made available to policymakers, voters, or the general public.

In the 2000s CAs were launched in British Colombia (2004), Ontario (2006), and the Netherlands (2006) to discuss proposals for electoral reform. They offered a model for subsequent assemblies that have been established with broader mandates such as the recent Irish Citizens' Assembly (2016–2018) that issued reports on several topics (some

Cristina Lafont: Northwestern University, USA.

∂ Open Access. © 2023 the author(s), published by De Gruyter. (cc) BY-NC-ND This work is licensed under the Creative Commons Attribution-NonCommercial-NoDerivatives 4.0 International License. https://doi.org/10.1515/9783110758269-006

constitutional in nature) or the Citizens Convention for Climate (2019 and 2020) that discussed reducing France's carbon emissions by 40 per cent. Institutions that include *both* randomly selected citizens and other political actors are a more recent development. The best-known examples are the Convention on the Constitution in Ireland (2013–2014) or the G1000 Citizens' Summits in Belgium (2011) and in the Netherlands (2014). But, due to their "mixed" composition, these institutions fall outside the standard meaning of the term "citizens' assemblies."

As these examples show, CAs can be used to address a wide variety of topics and their decision-making authority can also vary. Given the increased interest in CA and their recent proliferation, there has been a lot of debate about precisely *which* decision-making authority they should be able to exercise. Proposals abound and are continuously added to the discussion. The various options can be helpfully thought of on a spectrum (see examples in the table below).

4.2 Different types of decision-making authority

On the weakest side of the spectrum, CAs can be convened merely for consultative purposes about policy issues that have already been determined. Such assemblies do not have any agenda-setting capacity or decision-making authority conferred upon them. This minimal political role reflects the bulk of current practice. In most cases, CAs are convened to discuss a pre-selected menu of policy issues; they are non-mandatory, one-off processes that only have the power to influence political actors such as legislatures or administrative agencies via consultation or advisement. Moreover, since CAs are not permanent institutions and most citizens are unfamiliar with them, any policy recommendations they make can be easily ignored without fearing any public pressure. With few exceptions, the political impact of citizens' assemblies has been rather modest (Pogrebinschi and Ryan 2018; Font et al. 2018; Farrell, Suiter and Harris 2019). Frustration with this lack of uptake fuels demands for strengthening the decision-making authority of CAs (Fuji-Johnson 2015; Setälä 2011). Stronger proposals would require legislatures or administrative agencies to directly act upon the policy recommendations of CAs or to make it mandatory that their recommendations are submitted to a referendum within a specified period of time so that action cannot be deferred indefinitely.

On the strongest side of the spectrum, we find proposals that would give CAs *binding* decision-making authority. These proposals would confer various powers and authorities upon assemblies such as the power of *legislative review* (e.g. by establishing assemblies of randomly selected citizens which would complement or partially replace existing legislative assemblies of elected representatives, see Abizadeh 2020; Gastil and Wright 2018), the power of *constitutional review* (e.g. by replacing or complementing Constitutional Courts with citizens' juries, see Ghosh 2010, 2018; Spector 2009; Zurn 2011), or the power of *constitutional amendment* (e.g. by replacing or complementing constitutional assemblies of elected representatives with CAs, see Landemore 2020).

Among these proposals, there is an important division between those who favour *supplementing* current electoral institutions, e.g. by instituting a sortition chamber alongside an elected chamber (Abizadeh 2020; Fishkin 2018; Gastil and Wright 2018; Leib 2004; O'Leary 2006; Vandamme and Verret-Hamelin 2017; Zakaras 2010), and those who advocate for *replacing* electoral institutions altogether, e.g. by instituting a form of lottocratic democracy without elections in which CAs of randomly selected citizens replace legislative assemblies of elected representatives (Guerrero 2014; Landemore 2020; Van Reybrouck 2016). In the latter case, CAs would not only have decision-making authority over an antecedently specified menu of issues. Rather, as fully functional legislatures, they would have some of the broadest agenda-setting and decision-making powers possible.

4.3 Decision-making authority and legitimacy

Recent debates have focused on the question of whether it would be democratically legitimate to confer decision-making authority upon CAs and similar mini-publics (Lafont 2015, 2020; Parkinson 2006). This issue is contested. While some scholars advocate strong policymaking powers for CAs (Gastil and Wright 2019; Hennig 2017; Van Reybrouck 2016), many others would hesitate to go so far as to hand over actual political power (e.g., of legislation or constitutional interpretation) to CAs (Pettit 2013; Mansbridge 2019; Niemeyer 2014). In fact, recent empirical studies suggest that ordinary citizens are generally opposed to giving CAs the power to make binding decisions (Goldberg 2021; Rojon, Rijken and Klandermans 2019), though opposition is slightly less strong among politically dissatisfied yet engaged citizens (Bedock and Pilet 2020).

Those who advocate conferring decision-making authority upon CAs often base their proposals on the claim that, in using stratified random sampling to compose the group of ordinary citizens who participate, assemblies effectively create an accurate "mirror" of the citizenry; consequently, their views, interests, values, and attitudes reflect those of the people at large. Since participants are *like us*, it is plausible to assume that their judgements after the deliberative experience reflect *what the people would think if they were informed and had the opportunity to deliberate about the matter.* They represent "the considered judgments of the people." (Fishkin 2009: 28)

There are several claims involved in this argument. Participants in CAs are certainly *like us* in that they are ordinary citizens. Thus, in contrast to politicians, lobbyists, and other specialized political actors they are unlikely to have hidden agendas or conflicts of interest that may cloud their deliberations about the public interest. We can trust them as our representatives in that we don't need to monitor them or threaten them with sanctions since they are independently motivated to figure out what's best for the polity. But they are supposed to be *like us* in a *stronger* sense as well: they supposedly share our interests, values, policy objectives, and so on. This is why we can assume that their recommendations coincide with what we would have thought if we had participated. But *this* claim is quite implausible. Since there is so much ethical and political disagreement among citizens in pluralistic societies this assumption can hardly be true of any genuinely representative sample of the population. The more that diverse evaluative perspectives (concerning need interpretations, value orientations, comprehensive views, etc.) are included in the sample, the less sense it makes for non-participant citizens to assume that their own particular interests, values, and political objectives will invariably coincide with those of *the majority of the sample* regardless of the issue. Non-participants cannot assume that the recommendations of the majority of the participants in the CA reflect what *they would have thought if they had participated.* For, in principle, the opposite is equally possible. After all, the participants who endorse a minority view have reviewed the exact same information and deliberated just as much as other participants. They have just reached the opposite conclusion. Even if citizens can trust that all participants were conscientious and genuinely interested in figuring out what is best for the polity, they nevertheless know that, in pluralistic democracies, there is contestation over a variety of social, moral, ethical, religious, and economic views and values, and that this significantly influences political questions and policy objectives. Far from constituting a homogeneous body, in pluralist societies that are committed to the maintenance of free institutions citizens have ongoing political disagreements with each other. Consequently, without first knowing whether *the majority took the side in the political spectrum that they would have taken if they had participated,* citizens cannot simply "trust" that the decisions of the majority of the sample will invariably coincide with what they themselves would have concluded with respect to a contested political issue.

In fact, if the materials and deliberations of the assembly were made public, then many citizens would find out that the majority of the sample was actually *not like them,* since they oppose their own professed views, values, and policy objectives on the issue in question. At this point, the claim that non-participants should just trust the recommendations of CAs *because* their participants are *like them* becomes dubious. The fact that the random sample is a microcosm of *the people taken collectively* means that, especially on hotly contested issues, there will be a majority defending one view and a sizeable minority defending the opposite view. This means that it cannot be strictly true of *all the people considered individually* that the majority of the sample is *like them.* But if this is so, then in what sense can we say that sample participants are *their representatives?* If the majority of the sample is neither like them nor accountable to them, then on what basis can we reasonably expect non-participant citizens to blindly trust *this majority?* Since citizens have not selected their own representatives to participate in the CA, they have no particular reason to assume that the recommendations of either the majority or the minority would coincide with what they would have thought if they had been informed and deeply thought about the issue on their own. The legitimacy of conferring decision-making authority upon CAs is called into question by the fact that relations of authorization and accountability don't exist between participants in CAs and the rest of the citizenry.

However, worries about legitimacy do not merely impact proposals that would empower CAs to make binding political decisions. Legitimacy concerns also crop up with respect to the more-widely endorsed proposals to institutionalize CAs for the purposes of mere public consultation. Indeed, within debates on whether and how the political uses of CAs can be democratically legitimate the central question is not simply about *how much power* their participants ought to exercise but rather, and above all, *the specific capacity* in which they are supposed to exercise that power. The concern is that, in contrast to other political actors, CAs can easily be taken to be "proxies" for the citizenry as a whole.

In comparison to other political institutions, CAs, as mini-publics, are special in that they are composed of ordinary citizens who are supposed to exclusively act in that capacity, i.e. as members of the citizenry. The mini-publics' composition is supposed to reflect or descriptively represent the composition of the entire citizenry. Yet, at the same time, members have neither been selected by the citizenry nor are they required to act as political representatives of individuals or groups that they represent in a descriptive sense. There is no sense in which female participants are supposed to defend the views of women or Californians the views of other Californians. They are and remain members of the citizenry who, as such, only represent themselves. They participate as individual citizens with total freedom to express whichever views and opinions they happen to have and to change them in whichever way they see fit. But, for that very same reason, they are in no way accountable to citizens outside of the assembly. This is problematic in light of potential differences of opinion between participants and non-participants. The purpose of having a process of public consultation is for officials to be able to find out the opinion and will of the citizenry regarding certain policy decisions. But if participants in CAs and non-participating citizens disagree about the decisions at hand, then who is supposed to speak in the name of the citizenry? Whose views ought to count as the views of "the public" that officials are supposed to consult?

John Parkinson's pioneering research on the relationship between deliberative mini-publics and the broader public illustrates this problem through a case study of a citizens' jury that was convened to consider hospital restructuring in Leicester, England. In that case, decision-makers were confronted with the results of a deliberation by a citizens' jury that recommended one course of action, and a petition of 150,000 signatories demanding another (Parkinson 2006: 33). The citizenry neither elected the mini-publics' participants nor had any way of holding them accountable. In such a situation of conflict it is normatively unclear whether and why officials should just follow the judgement of a CA over the judgement of the citizenry at large. Of course, this problem is not unique to CAs. It can also arise with other forms of public consultation (e.g., town hall meetings, focus groups, and so on). Thus, it is possible that, in some cases, the recommendations of a CA might be better aligned with the views of the relevant constituency than the recommendations defended by participants in other fora or activist movements and organizations which may be less representative, more polarized, or "captured" by particular interests (see e.g. Beauvais & Warren, 2019). However, just because this *can* be the case doesn't mean that it will *always* be the case. Indeed, given the extensive empirical evidence about drastic changes of opinion among participants in CAs on contested political issues (see e.g., Fishkin 2009), the legitimacy concerns remain for all cases in which there is a conflict between the recommendations of CAs and the opinions of the relevant constituency. Expecting public officials to simply follow the policy recommendation of a CA against the opinion and will of the bulk of the citizens who will be subject to the policy in question would hardly be a democratically legitimate option (Chambers 2009; Lafont 2020; Parkinson 2006).

The presence of such a conflict indicates that the issue is not yet "settled" within the political community in question. In such cases, a proper public debate is needed in which the information and reasons that led the recommendations of the citizens are made readily available to the citizenry so that they can determine for themselves whether they can, upon reflection, come to the same conclusion. The institutionalization of CAs would enhance the democratic legitimacy of political decision-making *only* if the desirable qualities of deliberation within CAs could positively impact and improve the quality of the deliberative process of opinion- and will-formation in which the citizenry participates. One of the biggest challenges that the design and institutionalization of CAs faces is how to "scale up" deliberation from CAs to the wider public (Niemeyer 2014; Curato and Rountree, in this *Handbook*).

4.4 Two approaches to institutionalization

A larger issue lurks behind the questions about whether and when it is legitimate to confer *binding* decision-making authority upon CAs: namely, what are the various political uses and functions that these institutions can fulfil? Proposals vary alongside several dimensions, perspectives, and aims (Courant 2022). It would be nearly impossible to provide an exhaustive list of the proposals that are currently under discussion. However, as an organizing principle, it is helpful to distinguish between two fundamentally different ways of thinking about how to institutionalize CAs: a vertical or "top-down" approach versus a horizontal or "bottom-up" approach (see table below). The first approach would aim to integrate CAs into the political system as either advisory bodies or to supplement (or replace) some of the functions and the decision-making authority of existing political institutions (Setälä 2021). They would be directly coupled with formal political institutions with varying degrees of decision-making authority. In contrast, the second approach would institutionalize CAs as mediating bodies between formal political institutions and the wider public to strengthen the agenda-setting capacity of the citizenry and their ability to make political institutions more responsive to their interests, values, and policy objectives. The ultimate goal of each of these approaches is fundamentally different. Whereas the first approach seeks to *empower the (relatively few) participants in citizens' assemblies* to do the thinking, deliberating, and deciding on political issues for the rest of the citizenry, the second approach seeks to *empower the whole citizenry* to initiate public debate, influence policymaking, set the political agenda, and/or have final say on certain political decisions.

So far, most actual CAs have followed the top-down approach in so far as they have been organized by policymakers or administrators with the aim of delivering some "input" that was of interest to the sponsors (Setälä 2017: 851). But this approach is also followed by proposals that seek to enhance the power of CAs to make binding political decisions by either supplementing or replacing existing representative institutions. An actual example that falls on the stronger side of the spectrum of empowerment are several CAs that have been organized in the city of Gdansk, Poland. While the issues under discussion are not selected by the assemblies, the mayor agreed to treat their recommendations as binding if they achieved the support of at least 80 per cent of participants. In fact, several recommendations have already been implemented (Gerwin 2018).

There are also actual examples of CAs that can be characterized as following a bottom-up approach while pursuing different levels of citizens' empowerment. On the weakest end of the spectrum, there are CAs that are organized independently of formal institutions and with the exclusive aim of activating public debate on contested issues. Fishkin's deliberative polls such as "America in One Room" (A1R) would fit in this category. AIR gathered 500 American voters for a nonpartisan discussion of the major issues in the 2020 presidential election. Although it was organized in the run-up of a presidential election, it was not institutionally connected to a formal decision-making process. Its potential to induce broader debate entirely depends on uptake by the media (social media included). Another actual example of CAs that tends toward the stronger end of the citizen's empowerment spectrum is the Citizens' Initiative Review (CIR) in Oregon. After having the opportunity to become informed and deliberate about an active ballot measure, participants in the citizens' jury are asked to produce a statement that contains key facts, the best reasons to vote for the measure, and the best reasons to vote against the measure. This statement is then sent to every registered voter in the state as part of the official Voters' Pamphlet.

But many proposals that follow a bottom-up approach expect CAs to serve as tools for stronger forms of citizen empowerment. Let me mention just two proposals that exemplify different degrees of empowerment. On the strongest side of the spectrum is a proposal that would enable deliberative agenda-setting for ballot propositions. Fishkin has articulated this proposal based on his experience with a deliberative poll that he organized in California in 2011 (*What's Next California*). This proposal would give citizens both the power of agenda-setting and of ratification (Fishkin et al. 2015; 2019). The idea is to periodically convene CAs to assess proposals for various initiatives submitted by civic groups that satisfy some low threshold of signatures, and to then determine which should go on the ballot. Participants would receive relevant, balanced information about the proposed initiatives. After deliberating about the "pros and cons" they would then have the power to select the best initiatives to be included on the ballot and to even amend those initiatives based on their deliberations. This proposal would give some decision-making authority to CAs (e. g., selecting among initiatives and amending them) but the citizenry would retain the power to both propose initiatives and ratify them. Moreover, as Fishkin indicates, if the entire electorate is provided with not only the initiatives but also the best arguments both for and against them, then this use of CAs "would add a truly deliberative element to mass direct democracy and fulfill many of the initial aspirations of the initiative to empower the people to engage in thoughtful self–government" (Fishkin 2019: 101).

Another proposal that exemplifies a similar bottom-up approach is the citizen-initiated citizens' assemblies recently discussed by the Flemish parliament in Belgium. According to a bill proposed by the Green Party, after gathering 80,000 signatures, citizens could then demand a CA on any topic belonging to the competencies of Flanders. The CA would scrutinize the proposal in question and have the power to amend it accordingly. Although the bill was defeated in parliament, it offers an ambitious model for how CAs could be institutionalized with strong participatory aims in mind (Van Crombrugge 2020). Whereas Fishkin's proposal to use CAs and other mini-publics for agenda setting in ballot propositions would give citizens the power to make binding decisions on certain laws or policies, the proposal to institutionalize citizen-initiated CAs would only give citizens the power to petition parliament to consider certain policies. This would certainly enhance citizens' ability to set the political agenda, but it would not give them the final say. To that extent, this proposal falls on the weaker side of the citizen empowerment spectrum (see table below).

Table 4.1: An overview of the political uses of CAs

Type of Power/ Form of Integration	Weak (e.g., advisory)	Intermediate (e.g., restricted agenda setting)	Strong (e.g., unrestricted agenda setting & ratification)
Top-down approach			
(empowering citizens' assemblies)	Citizens Convention for Climate (2019 and 2020)	Citizen's Assembly on Electoral Reform (British Columbia, 2004; Ontario, 2006; Netherlands, 2006)	Citizens' Assemblies in Gdansk, Poland
			Legislature by Lot (Gastil & Wright)
		Irish Citizens' Assembly (2016 – 18)	Sortition Chamber (Abizadeh)
			Open Democracy (Landemore)
Bottom-up approach			
(empowering the citizenry)	America in One Room (2019)	Citizens' Initiative Review (Oregon)	Deliberative agenda setting for ballot propositions (Fishkin)
		Citizen-initiated citizens' assemblies	

4.5 Conclusions

CAs are fascinating institutional innovations that offer promising venues for democratization. However, whether they have a positive democratic impact will very much depend on how they are institutionalized. If the aim of institutionalizing CAs is to empower a few participants to do the thinking, deliberating, and deciding for the rest of the citizenry, then it is hard to see how these innovative institutions can have a positive *democratic* impact. Giving decision-making authority to the few who are well-informed and who have access to good-quality deliberation while simply expecting the rest of the citizenry to blindly defer to their decisions would predictably increase the disconnect between citizens' actual beliefs or attitudes and the political decisions to which they are subject. Far from having a positive democratic impact, it could make the problem which CAs are meant to solve even worse; citizen's alienation from the political process would grow rather than shrink. By contrast, if CAs are institutionalized with the aim of empowering the citizenry to catalyse public debate, set the political agenda, and have final say on important political decisions then such institutions could clearly contribute to democratization. In the end, the answer to the question of which decision-making authority CAs ought to have essentially depends on whether providing such authority serves the democratic aim of empowering the citizenry.

References

Abizadeh, A. (2020). Representation, bicameralism, political equality, and sortition: Reconstituting the second chamber as a randomly selected assembly. *American Political Science Association* 19 (3), 791807.

Beauvais, E., & Warren, M. E. (2019). What can deliberative mini-publics contribute to democratic systems? *European Journal of Political Research* 58 (3), 893–914.

Bedock, C., & Pilet, J. (2020). Enraged, engaged, or both? A study of the determinants of support for consultative vs. binding mini-publics. *Representation*, doi: 10.1080/00344893.2020.1778511.

Chambers, S. (2009). Rhetoric and the public sphere: Has deliberative democracy abandoned mass democracy? *Political Theory* 37 (3), 323–350.

Courant, D. (2022). Institutionalizing deliberative mini-publics? Issues of legitimacy and power for randomly selected assemblies in political systems. *Critical Policy Studies* 16 (2), 162–180.

Farrell, D. M., Suiter, J., & Harris, C. (2019). 'Systematizing' constitutional deliberation: the 2016–18 citizens' assembly in Ireland. *Irish Political Studies* 34 (1), 113–123.

Fishkin, J. (2009). *When the People Speak: Deliberative Democracy and Public Consultation.* Oxford: Oxford University Press.

Fishkin, J. (2018). *Democracy When the People are Thinking: Revitalizing Our Politics Through Public Deliberation.* Oxford: Oxford University Press.

Fishkin, J. (2019). Random assemblies for lawmaking: Prospects and limits. In J. Gastil and E. O. Wright (eds), *Legislature by Lot: Transformative Designs for Deliberative Governance*, 79–103. London: Verso,

Fishkin, J., Kousser, T., Luskin, R. C., & Siu, A. (2015). Deliberative agenda setting: Piloting reform of direct democracy in California. *Perspectives on Politics* 13 (4), 1030–1042.

Font, J., Smith, G., Galais, C., & Alarcon, P. A. U. (2018). Cherry-picking participation: Explaining the fate of proposals from participatory processes. *European Journal of Political Research* 57 (3), 615–636.

Fournier, P., van der Kolk, H. & Carty, R. K. (2011). *When Citizens Decide: Lessons from Citizen Assemblies on Electoral Reform*, Oxford: Oxford University Press.

Fuji-Johnson, G. (2015). *Democratic Illusion: Deliberative Democracy in Canadian Public Policy.* Toronto: University of Toronto Press.

Gastil, J., & Wright, E. O. (2018). Legislature by Lot: Envisioning Sortition within a Bicameral System. *Politics & Society* 46 (3), 303–330.

Gastil, J., & Wright, E. O. (2019). *Legislature by Lot: Transformative Designs for Deliberative Governance*, London: Verso.

Gerwin, M. (2018). *Citizens' Assemblies. Guide to Democracy that Works.* Krakow: Otwarty Plan.

Ghosh, E. (2010). Deliberative democracy and the countermajoritarian difficulty: Considering constitutional juries. *Oxford Journal of Legal Studies* 30, 327–59.

Ghosh, E. (2018). Deliberative constitutionalism: An empirical dimension. In R. Levy, H. Kong, J. King & G. Orr (eds), *The Cambridge Handbook of Deliberative Constitutionalism*, 220–232. Cambridge: Cambridge University Press.

Goldberg, S. (2021). Just advisory and maximally representative: A conjoint experiment on non-participants' legitimacy perceptions of deliberative forums. *Regular Issue* 17 (1), Article 1. https://doi.org/10.16997/jdd.973

Grönlund, K., Bächtiger, A., & Setälä, M. (eds). (2014). *Deliberative Mini-Publics: Practices and Prospects*, Colchester: ECPR Press.

Guerrero, A. A. (2014). Against elections: The lottocratic alternative. *Philosophy & Public Affairs* 42 (2), 135–178.

Hennig, B. (2017), *The End of Politicians*, London: Unbound.

Lafont, C. (2015). Deliberation, participation and democratic legitimacy: Should deliberative minipublics shape public policy? *The Journal of Political Philosophy* 23 (1), 40–63.

Lafont, C. (2020). *Democracy without Shortcuts. A Participatory Conception of Deliberative Democracy*, Oxford University Press.

Landemore, H. (2020). *Open Democracy: Reinventing Popular Rule for the Twenty-First Century*, Princeton, NJ: Princeton University Press.

Leib, E. J. (2004). *Deliberative Democracy in America: A Proposal for a Popular Branch of Government*, University Park: Pennsylvania State University Press.

Mansbridge, J. (2019). Accountability in the constituent-representative relationship. In J. Gastil and E. O. Wright (eds). *Legislature by Lot. Transformative Designs for Deliberative Governance*, 185–197. London: Verso.

Niemeyer, S. (2014). Scaling up deliberation to mass publics: Harnessing mini-publics in a deliberative system. In K. Grönlund, A. Bächtiger, & M. Setälä (eds), *Deliberative Mini-Publics: Involving Citizens in the Democratic Process*, 177–201. Colchester: ECPR Press.

O'Leary, K. (2006). *Saving Democracy: A Plan for Real Representation in America.* Stanford, CA: Stanford University Press.

Parkinson, J. (2006). *Deliberating in the Real World: Problems of Legitimacy in Deliberative Democracy.* Oxford: Oxford University Press.

Pettit, P. (2013), *On the People's Terms: A Republican Theory and Model of Democracy*, Cambridge: Cambridge University Press.

Pogrebinschi, T., & Ryan, M. (2018). Moving beyond input legitimacy: When do democratic innovations affect policy making? *European Journal of Political Research* 57 (1), 135–152

Rojon, S., Rijken,A., & Klandermans, B., (2019). A survey experiment on citizens' preferences for 'vote–centric' vs. 'talk–centric' democratic innovations with advisory vs. binding outcomes. *Politics and Governance* 7 (2), 213–226.

Setälä, M. (2011). The role of deliberative mini-publics in representative democracy: Lessons from the experience of referendums. *Representation* 47 (2), 201–213.

Setälä, M. (2017). Connecting deliberative mini-publics to representative decision making. *European Journal of Political Research* 56 (4), 846–863.

Setälä, M. (2021). Advisory, collaborative and scrutinizing roles of deliberative minipublics. *Frontiers in Political Science.* DOI: 10.3389/fpos.2020.591844

Spector, H. (2009). The right to a constitutional jury. *Legisprudence* 3 (1), 111–123.

Van Crombrugge, R., (2020). The derailed promise of a participatory minipublic: The Citizens' Assembly Bill in Flanders. *Journal of Deliberative Democracy* 16 (2), 63–72.

Vandamme, P.-E., & Verret-Hamelin, A. (2017). A randomly selected chamber: Promises and challenges. *Journal of Public Deliberation* 13 (1). doi: https://doi.org/10.16997/jdd.271

Van Reybrouck, D. (2016). *Against Elections: The Case for Democracy.* London: Random House.

Zakaras, A. (2010). Lot and democratic representation: A modest proposal. *Constellations* 17 (3), 455–471.

Zurn, C. (2011). Judicial review, constitutional juries and civic constitutional fora: Rights, democracy and law. *Theoria* 58 (2), 63–94.

Recommended reading

Fishkin, J. (2018). *Democracy When the People are Thinking: Revitalizing Our Politics Through Public Deliberation.* Oxford: Oxford University Press.

Gastil, J., & Wright, E. O. (2019). *Legislature by Lot: Transformative Designs for Deliberative Governance.* London: Verso.

Ghosh, E. (2010). Deliberative democracy and the countermajoritarian difficulty: Considering constitutional juries. *Oxford Journal of Legal Studies* 30, 327–359.

Goodin, R. E., & Dryzek, J. S. (2006). Deliberative impacts: The macro-political uptake of mini-publics. *Politics & Society* 34 (2), 219–244.

Lafont, C. (2020). *Democracy Without Shortcuts. A Participatory Conception of Deliberative Democracy.* Oxford: Oxford University Press.

Landemore, H. (2020). *Open Democracy: Reinventing Popular Rule for the Twenty-First Century.* Princeton, NJ: Princeton University Press.

Leib, E. J. (2004). *Deliberative Democracy in America: A Proposal for a Popular Branch of Government.* University Park: Pennsylvania State University Press.

MacKenzie, M. K., & Warren, M. E. (2012). Two trust-based uses of minipublics in democratic systems. In J. Parkinson & J. Mansbridge (eds), *Deliberative Systems: Deliberative Democracy at the Large Scale,* 95–124. New York: Cambridge University Press.

Mansbridge, J. (2019) Accountability in the constituent-representative relationship. In J. Gastil and E. O. Wright (eds). *Legislature by Lot. Transformative Designs for Deliberative Governance,* 185–197. London: Verso.

Niemeyer, S. (2014). Scaling up deliberation to mass publics: Harnessing mini-publics in a deliberative system. In K. Grönlund, A. Bächtiger, & M. Setälä (eds). *Deliberative Mini-Publics: Involving Citizens in the Democratic Process,* 177–201. Colchester: ECPR Press.

Parkinson, J. (2006). *Deliberating in the Real World: Problems of Legitimacy in Deliberative Democracy.* Oxford: Oxford University Press.

Smith, G., & Setälä, M. (2019). Mini-publics and deliberative democracy. In A. Bächtiger, J. S. Dryzek, J. Mansbridge, & M. Warren (eds), *The Oxford Handbook of Deliberative Democracy,* 299–314. Oxford: Oxford University Press.

Van Reybrouck, D. (2016). *Against Elections: The Case for Democracy.* London: Random House.

Warren, M. E., & Pearse, H. (eds), (2008). *Designing Deliberative Democracy: The British Columbia Citizen's Assembly.* Cambridge: Cambridge University Press.

Brigitte Geissel

5 Linking citizens' assemblies to policymaking: Real-life and visionary connections

Abstract: We currently witness the mushrooming implementation of CAs. But CAs do not necessarily guarantee that citizens' refined preferences feed into political decision-making. How can we ensure that recommendations made by CAs do not disappear unnoticed in pigeonholes? How can we guarantee that CAs are not misused? Academia has neglected the connections between CAs and decision-making for too long. However, we have to think about (new ways of) connecting CAs to decision-making. This chapter first provides theoretical arguments for respective connections. It proceeds with a state of the art and then presents a categorization for sorting existing examples of connections. The main and visionary part of the chapter is dedicated to developing novel models for connecting collective, inclusive will-formation to decision-making.

Keywords: participatory governance, participatory constitution-building, political decision-making, mini-publics, multi-issue referendum, multi-options referendum, deliberation day, randomly selected parliament

5.1 Introduction: Connecting citizens' assemblies to policymaking

This edition proves vividly the mushrooming implementation of CAs. But CAs do not necessarily guarantee that citizens' refined preferences feed into political decision-making. A legion of examples shows severe flaws (see also Minsart and Jacquet in this *Handbook*). Officially, policymakers claim to implement CAs in order to receive informed judgment and refined public opinion. But too often CAs serve as symbolic or "simulative" participation (Blühdorn 2011), as "particitainment" – which means participation as entertainment without influence – or as distracting participation. Curato et al. (2021: 22), who have evaluated many CAs, ask accordingly: "What use are intelligent recommendations from CAs if these recommendations are silenced by politicians?" Furthermore, CAs are misused for political cherry-picking – politicians choose recommendations they like and neglect those they dislike (Font, Amo and Smith 2016). We also find "token" CAs implemented to pacify and "to silence critical voices" (Setälä 2017: 846) as well as CAs set up for co-optation (Lafont 2015) or for manipulation (Bua and Bussu 2020). CAs turned out to run the risk of elite capture (Neblo 2015; Beauvais and Warren 2019) leading to skewed decisions in the interests of the well-off.

Brigitte Geissel: Goethe-Universität Frankfurt, Germany.

Open Access. © 2023 the author(s), published by De Gruyter. (CC) BY-NC-ND This work is licensed under the Creative Commons Attribution-NonCommercial-NoDerivatives 4.0 International License. https://doi.org/10.1515/9783110758269-007

How can we ensure that recommendations made by CAs do not disappear unnoticed in pigeonholes? How can we guarantee that CAs are not misused? Academia has neglected the connections between CAs and policymaking for too long (see also Lafont in this *Handbook*). *But we have to think about (new ways of) connecting CAs to policymaking.*

This chapter first provides theoretical arguments for respective connections. It proceeds to the state of the art and then presents a categorization for sorting existing examples of connections. The main and visionary part of the chapter is dedicated to developing novel models for connecting collective, inclusive will-formation to decision-making. The conclusion summarizes the main points.

5.2 Theoretical approach: Why connect citizens' assemblies to decision-making?

Democracy means rule of the people as self-government. But what does that mean exactly? Many citizens as well as scholars link – or even reduce – democracy to elections and competition. Some consider these features as the main characteristics of democracy. They judge a political system as a democracy, when free and fair elections are held, in which citizens have the choice between two or more parties (see Geissel, Kneuer and Lauth 2016). But these practices turned out to be increasingly dysfunctional. They can no longer guarantee that citizens' preferences and political decisions are connected.

A novel approach has recently been provided by Mark Warren (2017), who reminded us that democracy cannot be defined in terms of practices such as elections, but rather in terms of the problems the democratic system needs to solve. To be considered democratic, a political system must realize empowered inclusion, collective will-formation and decision-making (see Lacelle-Webster and Warren in this *Handbook*).

I find great value in Warren's explanation of democracy, but I am convinced we have to advance his approach. Democracy is about *connecting* citizen will-formation and decision-making systematically. A political system may be successful in hosting well-designed CAs – as practices for refining citizen will-formation. But this is not enough if it fails to feed the outputs of these CAs into decision-making. Democratic systems require such connections. Intuitively, most scholars seem to support the focus on connections. Some of the most famous CAs are those that are designed to feed into processes of decision-making. Among the best-known examples are the British Columbia Citizens' Assembly in Canada (Warren and Pearse 2008), or the Constitutional Assemblies in Ireland. In these cases, CAs were systematically connected to decision-making, both via referendum.

In this sense, I also advance the debate on *deliberative systems* towards *participatory systems*. While the deliberative system approach advocates multiple sites of deliberation (Mansbridge et al. 2012), the participatory system approach advocates the systematic and systemic connection of collective will-formation with decision-making (Deligiaouri and Suiter 2019; Geissel 2019: 414 ff.). This approach transcends the dichotomies that have long defined democratic theory, such as representation versus participation and deliberation versus aggregation of "raw" opinions in electoral or direct democracy. Participatory systems entail intelligent linkages of representative, deliberative and participatory elements in order to ensure connections between citizen will-formation and decision-making.

5.3 State of the art on connecting citizens' assemblies to decision-making

Although scholars increasingly advocate more connections between citizen will-formation and decision-making, the literature is divided in fragmented (sub-)disciplines working on, for example, elections and representation or deliberative practices.

Traditional studies focus on elections as the supposed warrantor for connecting citizens' wills to decision-making, with intermediaries like parties and interest groups as additional "transmission belts". They describe and prescribe connections between citizens' preferences and political decisions with focus on representatives. Concepts like responsiveness (Geißel 2004), congruence, and accountability put representatives into the centre, who supposedly ensure such connections. This research community starts to realize the dysfunctions of these supposed warrantors and admits that responsiveness, congruence, and accountability do not function as described in the handbooks of representative democracy. Yet, it just starts to include developments with novel procedures of citizen will-formation such as CAs and seems to hope that connections could be restored via better representation.

In contrast, scholars of deliberative democracy published very actively on respective procedures (see e.g. Geissel and Newton 2012; Elstub and Escobar 2019). This epistemic community, however, showed and partly still shows two shortcomings. First, it mainly worked on practices of citizen will-formation but overlooked the decision-making side of the equation for a long time (Pateman 2012). Recently, it began to ponder on connections to political decision-making. And here the second shortcoming comes into play. It provides normative political philosophy, e.g. the "deliberative systems" approach recommending "nodes" and "multiple forms of communication" (Mansbridge et al. 2012), Christina Lafont's (2019) advocacy for a "democracy without shortcuts" with a "long, participatory road", Hélène Landemore's (2020) promotion of an "Open Democracy", or Michael Saward's (2021) encouragement for novel democratic design thinking. However, it remains unclear, how respective "nods", "roads", and "systems" would look like and how they connect citizen will-formation and decision-making concretely.

Empirical studies in the field mostly focus on single or a few, mostly famous procedures, e.g. the Citizen Initiative Review in Oregon (Knobloch, Gastil and Reitman 2019) connecting referendums and CAs, the Brazil's National Public Policy Conferences (Pogrebinschi and Samuels 2014), which links CAs to administrative agenda-setting and policy-drafting; and the Citizen Council in the East Belgian parliament (Niessen and Reuchamps 2019), which connects CAs to decision-making in parliament. Different terms were applied to describe such connections, for example transmission (Boswell, Hendriks and Ercan 2016), coupling (Hendriks 2016), or sequencing (Goodin 2008). But all in all, the literature on this topic is still theoretically and empirically underdeveloped and underspecified. In the reminder of this chapter, I will take up the threads presented in the literature and advance them.

5.4 Existing examples and experiments

As might become apparent throughout this *Handbook*, a variety of examples and experiments exist, which aim at connecting CAs to political decision-making. Up to now, these variations of connections look rather "messy". A categorization sorting the variations does not yet exist but would be useful. I have developed a preliminary categorization, which includes a) connections of CAs to either decision-making by representatives or by citizens and b) connections of CAs to decision-making bodies either as one-time events or institutionalized. In detail:

First, I differentiate, whether the output of CAs is connected to decision-making by representatives, e.g. parliaments, or by referendums. Today, recommendations provided by CAs are mostly decided by the former and only seldom by the latter. The designed connections can look very different. Representatives might announce vaguely that they will take CAs' recommendations into account and justify the decisions accordingly. One example for such a promise of justification is the French CA on Climate (*Convention Citoyenne pour le Climat*), where the French president promised to answer to the recommendations. Connections can be, yet, more prescriptive. The design of a CA can stipulate for example that its recommendations are put on a referendum for decision, which puts of course more value and importance on the CA.

The table below differentiates, first, between the connections of CAs to decision-making by representatives and citizens.[1]

The second differentiation refers to the level of institutionalization. Is the connection a one-time event or is it formalized as a permanent endeavour? Most participatory procedures are designed as one-time events, for example the 2019 Citizens' Dialogue in The Hague conducted by the European Commission. Few procedures are formalized and designed to take place routinely, e.g., the National Public Policy Conferences, Brazil, the Observatory of the City in Madrid, the East Belgian Citizen Council, or the Brus-

---

1 Parsimony is the reason why very few special connections are not included. For example, in Poland, some mayors had committed to implementing the recommendation agreed by CAs in broad consensus, which means that CAs can under certain circumstances be empowered to decide themselves (Gerwin 2018: 14–15). However, such practice are very seldom used and would blow up the categorization below unnecessarily.

sels deliberative committees (Vrydagh et al. 2021). Table 5.1 illustrates my categorization.

Table 5.1: Categorization of connections between CAs and decision-making

	CA + decision-making by *representatives*	CA + decision-making by *citizens*
One-time event	French Citizens' Convention on Climate Citizens' Dialogue in The Hague conducted by the European Commission	Irish Constitutional CAs British Columbia CA on Electoral Reform
Formalized	Citizen Council in East Belgian parliament Brazil's National Public Policy Conferences Observatory of the City in Madrid Standing CA in Paris	Swiss/New England Town Hall Meetings Participatory Budgeting, Porto Alegre, Brazil Citizens' Initiative Review, Oregon

Most of these examples have been discussed in this *Handbook* on CAs at length-and there is no need to describe them again in this chapter.

5.5 The future of democracy – how to connect citizens' assemblies to decision-making

In order to deepen and to strengthen the connection of CAs with decision-making, novel visions of democracy can serve as lighthouses showing the way. Therefore, this chapter is devoted to developing such visionary models. I start with the description of novel practices and then procedure to suggesting how they can be connected.

Up to now, I have applied the loose definition of CAs provided in the introduction of this *Handbook*. In the following visionary part, CAs are always defined as randomly selected – in the sense of mini-publics (see Curato et al. 2021).

5.5.1 Visionary practices (modules)

The following lines describe five novel practices, which are applied in the visionary models developed below:
– CAs with different tasks
– Multi-level CAs
– Multi-Issue Referendum
– Randomly selected parliament
– Deliberation Day

Citizens' assemblies with different tasks

Real-life experiments have already demonstrated that CAs can be commissioned with a variety of assignments (see Figure 5.1). CAs have drafted legislative bills, e.g. in British Columbia. They have identified important issues and put them on the political agenda, e.g. in Ireland. Or, they provide considered recommendations for parliaments, e.g. in East Belgian and Paris. CAs are applied at several phases of policy processes, from agenda-setting to monitoring and evaluating, and can be placed at various places within political systems. In future models, we could make more use of these variations and link such various CAs.

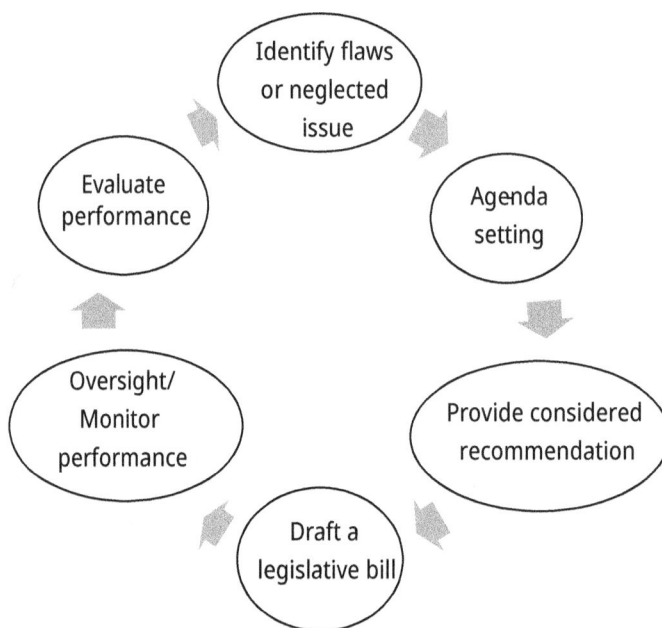

Figure 5.1: Example of CAs with different tasks

Multi-level citizens' assemblies

Inspired by the Policy Conferences in Brazil and CAs taking place at the EU level (see Fiket, this *Handbook*), multi-level CAs might be implemented. They start at the local level, where randomly selected citizens discuss political issues. Each of these local CAs selects one or two delegate/s who represents the outputs in the "Assembly of Delegates". This assembly bundles the recommendations and summarizes proposals. Competing proposals are possible, if agreement cannot be reached.

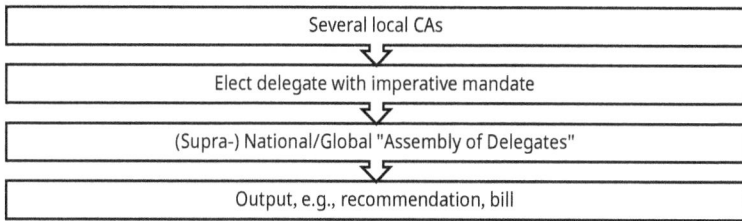

Several local CAs
⇩⇧
Elect delegate with imperative mandate
⇩⇧
(Supra-) National/Global "Assembly of Delegates"
⇩⇧
Output, e.g., recommendation, bill

Figure 5.2: Linking CAs in multi-level democracy (vertically)

Multi-Issue Referendum

Decision-making via referendum is available in some democracies. However, referendums are up to now mostly limited to "yes-no" options on single issues. These are rather crude devices to identify citizens' preferences. More sophisticated practices of citizens' decision-making would be helpful, which allow citizens to express their preferences in a more nuanced way. Such a novel and enhanced direct democratic practice was recently developed by Jonathan Rinne (2020) at the Research Unit 'Democratic Innovations', Goethe University Frankfurt. The Multi-Issues Referendum allows citizens to articulate their interests and priorities more accurately, comprehensively, and precisely than in elections. They can express their preferences on a large number of topics, which they can also prioritize. Thus, they are not limited to elect a party programme with only some policies they like and other policies they dislike.

CAs can play a crucial role for putting issues and options on the *ballot sheet*. For example, CA 1 might suggest minimum wage of 9 €/h, CA 2 might suggest "no minimum wage", CA 3 might opt for 15 €/h, and another CA for 20 €/h.

Voters get a certain number of votes, e.g., 30, and can allocate their votes. If they favour one topic more than another, they can give the respective one e.g., up to three votes ("cumulative-voting"). They can choose issues across lists. They can, for example, give three votes for "Minimum wage: 9 €/h per hour" suggested by CA 1, endorse Issue 2 of CA 2 and Issue 3 of the CA 3 proposal. Thus, voters can compile their own "programme".

A ballot sheet might look like the following one (Table 5.1).

Table 5.1: Ballot sheet of Multi-Issues Referendum (Rinne 2020, adapted)

○	Proposal CA 1 CA 1	○	Proposal CA 2	○	Proposal CA 3	○	Proposal CA 4
○ ○ ○	Minimum wage: 9 €/h	○ ○ ○	No minimum wage	○ ○ ○	Minimum wage: 15 €/h	○ ○ ○	Minimum wage: 20 €/h
○ ○ ○	Issue 2	○ ○ ○	Issue 2	○ ○ ○	Issue 2	○ ○ ○	Issue 2
○ ○ ○	Issue 3	○ ○ ○	Issue 3	○ ○ ○	Issue 3	○ ○ ○	Issue 3

Table 5.1: Ballot sheet of Multi-Issues Referendum (Rinne 2020, adapted) *(Continued)*

○ **Proposal CA 1** CA 1	○ **Proposal** CA 2	○ **Proposal CA 3**	○ **Proposal CA 4**
○ ○ ○ Issue 4	○ ○ ○ Issue 4	○ ○ ○ Issue 4	○ ○ ○ Issue 4

Similar to elections, Multi-Issue Referendums might be set up at all political levels (local, state, national, and supranational) covering respective topics. For example, the local ballot sheet might cover issues like local public transport, the local library, or local energy production. Ballot sheets on national topics might relate, for example, to international treaties, membership of the country in international organizations, and military missions abroad. And like elections, it might be a good idea to hold Multi-Issue Referendums recurring periodically, for example once per year. When they take place at periodic intervals, referendum campaign can act within a clear time frame. And citizens know the date in advance.

Randomly selected parliament

The idea of a randomly selected parliament is rather novel for us. Selecting decision-makers by lot sounds strange to most people today. But the inhabitants of the Athenian Polis, the origin of today's democracy more than two millennia ago, preferred sortition as the most democratic choice – and considered elections as a bad way of selecting people for political office (e.g., Sintomer 2019). Today, the idea of a randomly selected parliament increasingly inspires scholars as well as politicians. In my description of the randomly selected parliamentarian chamber, I start with the potential advantages and proceed to critical voices (Van Reybrouck 2016; Vandamme and Verret-Hamelin 2017; Gastil and Wright 2019).

What are the advantages of a randomly selected chamber of parliament? First, such a chamber, if recruited properly, will *mirror the composition of society* (descriptive representation). Most parliaments today are heavily skewed towards well-off men. Random selection is expected to mend such inequalities. Members of this chamber will come from different contexts and backgrounds and thus be familiar with the needs and interests of all citizens (see also MacKenzie, in this *Handbook*). A second potential benefit is the option for *deliberation beyond party lines.* Whereas members in current parliaments are often bound by party and caucus discipline, randomly selected members can discuss and decide without these restrictions (Sintomer 2018). They can decide based on arguments.

Third, *elected politicians execute a lot of political activities to secure their political career.* Based on my own experiences, I can say that, in order to be reelected, for example they have to please the media, satisfy their party, and establish a favourable public image. This is not necessary for randomly selected members. They do not want to be reelected. They also will most likely not seek a career within a party and do not need to build up a respective reputation. Thus, they are free to follow their own conscience. A final potential positive aspect might be the *diminished access of lobby groups.* Lobby groups cannot rely on party discipline, and they might have more difficulties "bribing" randomly selected members with attractive jobs in the private economy.

But there are also critical voices. One critique is the *presumable lack of accountability and legitimacy,* because members of the selected chamber are not elected. However, the concepts of accountability and legitimacy sound reasonable in the theoretical model of representative democracy but do not work as expected in reality. This is not the place for discussing these complex concepts and the empirical problems (Geissel 2023). It might suffice that some authors argue that randomly selected chambers could be more legitimate than elected ones, because citizens would have more trust ("perceived legitimacy"). They might feel better represented by people, who are "like them" (see Gastil and Wright 2019; Sintomer 2019).

Another critical voice addresses the challenge that the members of the selected chambers – as ordinary citizens – *lack competencies necessary for parliamentarians.* They would not be able to deliberate meaningfully on complex subjects, have no experience with politics and political strategies, do not know how to interact with the media, and so on. They miss the long phase of "apprenticeship" professional politicians pass before they enter parliament. Accordingly, they have to complete a steep learning curve within a relatively short time period. Comprehensive training and professional assistance are necessary to enforce such a learning curve. And finally, whereas elected parliamentarians have access to a whole party backing their work, the randomly selected citizens lack such a helping environment. Again, professional assistance might balance this shortcoming (see Gastil and Wright 2019).

Deliberation Day

Two political scientists, Bruce Ackerman and James Fishkin (2005), came up with the idea of a *Deliberative Day* a couple of decades ago. The main rationale of a Deliberation Day is to foster broad and in-depth deliberation within a community on a prominent topic. This includes balanced a priori information in all channels. At the Deliberation Day, schools, universities, churches, sports clubs, unions, kindergartens, and work-places discuss the respective topic. Especially politically marginalized groups and citizens are invited, and mobilizing strategies are applied to incentivize their involvement.

Within a Deliberation Day also *Democracy Games* might be employed. Democracy Games cover a variety of topics, for example creating a constitution for a fictional state or discussing rules for referendums. They allow for learning about many aspects of democracy and are available for all educational levels, from kindergarten to adult education. They also have the potential to inspire politically less interested people. They learn in a playful way what democracy entails and they may start to reflect what democracy means to them.

Up to now, there are few examples of such Deliberative Days. The Estonian People's Assembly Deliberation Day is one of them. In 2013, all Estonians were invited to propose ideas on certain topics, for example funding of political parties, on an online website. This also included the consultation of scholars and practitioners as well as an offline workshop. Yet, the topics were rather limited and the connection to decision-making remained vague. Another, yet imperfect example is Macron's Grand Débat National, which was also only vaguely connected to decision-making.[2]

5.5.2 Visionary combinations

Applying the visionary practices described above, I propose innovative models of connecting CAs and decision-making. The following models systematically connect representative and direct democratic elements with various forms of CAs and other practices of citizen will-formation. They are set up as multi-level, multi-actor, and multi-modular. They not only integrate the multi-level system at federal, state, and municipal levels. They also integrate various actors from politicians, administration, the general public and organized groups, as well as individual citizens (multi-actors). They use a variety of practices of will-formation and decision-making (multi-modular)

The sequencing of such practices might look different for different kinds of political decisions. Will-formation and decision-making on simple laws require less sophisticated procedures than will-formation and decision-making on novel constitutions and constitutional revisions. The following two processes provide suggestions for how such connections could look like in future democracies (Figures 5.3 and 5.4).

Plain law: Collective will-formation and decision-making

Legislature on plain laws should be linked to citizens' refined preferences and run through a procedure of collective, inclusive will-formation. It might start with a CA that identifies an issue crucial for the community but neglected by parliament. The legislative process might then proceed with public deliberation. Based on the different suggestions and claims put forward, a CA might draft a recommendation. (The chambers of) Parliament draft a second bill, which inspires a second public deliberation. A second CA drafts a third bill based on the discussions, which is then decided by parliament (Figure 5.3).

Novel constitution and constitutional amendments: collective will-formation and decision-making

---

2 https://www.democracy-international.org/2019-grand-debat-national-france-participatory-experiment-limited-legitimacy.

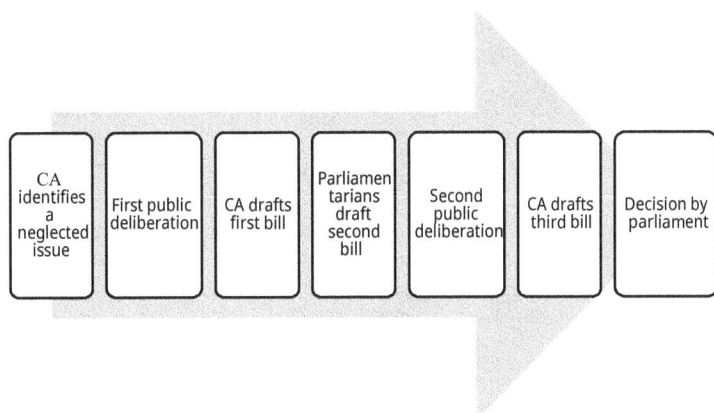

Figure 5.3: Procedure for connecting CAs and decision-making on simple laws (exemplarily)

The following visionary model describes a complex, deliberative, participatory constitutional revision procedure. In this model, various tools and practices are linked in a clearly structured sequence guaranteeing comprehensive will-formation connected to decision-making.

Let's start with the first step, the initiation of a constitutional revision. In the visionary model, the initiative is started by a petition, i.e. a certain number of supporters for a constitutional revision automatically starts the procedure. Once the procedure has been initiated, a Constitutional Assembly is set up, which consists of a CA and experts. This Assembly drafts first proposals that are discussed in the general public with face-to-face and online hearings, (social) media debates, open conferences, and so on. As part of this public deliberation, interest groups, parties, and movements are invited to get involved and make their suggestions. Experts are available to provide information about experiences in other countries, empirical findings, and scientific controversies. A multi-level CA is then implemented to bundle and to summarize the discussions and provide second proposals. These proposals are discussed in parliament, which might consist of an elected as well as a selected chamber. The parliament suggests third (counter-)proposals. These proposals are discussed in the second public deliberation. Based on these debates, parliament drafts the fourth round of proposals. Finally, a Deliberation Day takes place, where citizens debate on these proposals extensively in schools, universities, civil society, and at workplaces. A second multi-level CA drafts the fifth and final proposals and puts them on the ballot sheet of the Multi-Issue Referendum. Citizens decide on the proposal via the Multi-Issue Referendum (see Figure 5.4).

Figure boxes in flow:

```
Petition asks for          Constitutional          First public
constitutional             Assembly                deliberation
revision                   (CA and experts)        including interest
                           draft first proposals   groups, parties,
                                                    movements, experts

Second public              Parliament (elected     Multi-level CA
deliberation               and selected            suggests second
                           chambers) suggests      proposals
                           third (counter-)
                           proposals

Parliament (elected        Deliberation Day        Multi-level CA
and selected                                       develops fifth and
chambers) suggest                                  final proposals
fourth proposals

                                                   Decision-making
                                                   via
                                                   Multi-Issue
                                                   Referendum
```

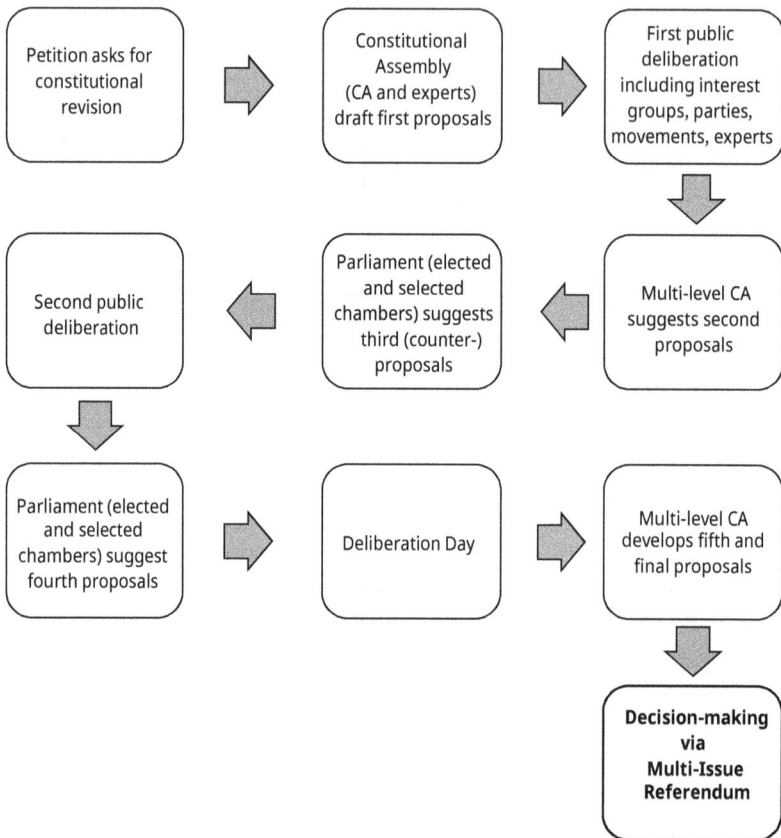

Figure 5.4: Procedure for connecting CAs and decision-making on novel constitution (exemplarily)

5.6 Conclusion

This chapter argues that democracies should connect citizens' inclusive will-formation more systematically to political decision-making. It portrays CAs as crucial jigsaw piece for inclusive will-formation and describes how existing CAs are connected to decision-making. But it goes beyond the state of the art by providing novel ideas of how respective connections might look. Thus, I advance the theory of participatory systems with visionary suggestions for practices and procedures.

The main part of the chapter is dedicated to visionary models of how CAs and other practices of will-formation could be integrated into comprehensive procedures of decision-making. Research on respective connections is just starting and real-world examples of CAs indicate rather limited linkages. Going beyond these experiments, I develop novel modular models, which combine CAs and other deliberative practices with direct democratic and representative elements. These models are multi-level – covering all political levels–multi-actor – including citizens, representatives, civil society, interest groups etc. – and multi-module – providing suggestions for systems with modular design.

Which problems can be solved with these models? The novel models will most likely connect inclusive, collective will-formation and decision-making significantly better than current procedures. The suggested models guarantee *inclusiveness* with the mixture of randomly selected CAs and broad public deliberation. The use of different practices ensures that all preferences can be expressed as well as refined and all perspectives are "on the table". The outputs and recommendations of the different *CAs feed systematically into the decision-making process.* Such complex models would achieve exactly what democracy means: connecting collective will-formation and decision-making in order to provide a democracy "of, by and for the people" (Lincoln, 1994).

References

Ackerman, B., & Fishkin, J. (2005). *Deliberation Day.* New Haven & London: Yale University Press.

Beauvais, E., & Warren, M. E. (2019). What can deliberative mini-publics contribute to democratic systems? *European Journal of Political Research* 58 (3), 893–914.

Blühdorn, I. (2011). *Simulative Demokratie.* 1st edn. Berlin: Suhrkamp (edition suhrkamp). Available at: http://www.worldcat.org/oclc/706072443.

Boswell, J., Hendriks, C. M., & Ercan, S. A. (2016). Message received? Examining transmission in deliberative systems. *Critical Policy Studies* 10 (3), 263–283.

Bua, A., & Bussu, S. (2020). Between governance-driven democratisation and democracy-driven governance: Explaining changes in participatory governance in the case of Barcelona. *European Journal of Political Research* 60 (3), 716–737.

Curato, N., Farrell, D. M., Geißel, B., Grönlund, K., Mockler, P., Pilet, J.-B., Renwick, A., Rose, J., Setälä, M. & Suiter, J. (2021). *Deliberative Mini-Publics: Core Design Features.* Bristol: Bristol University Press.

Deligiaouri, A., & Suiter, J. (2019). Assessing democracy in vitro, in vivo, and in actu and the role of democratic theory today. *Democratic Theory* 6 (2), 70–84.

Elstub, S., & Escobar, O. (eds). (2019) *Handbook of Democratic Innovations and Governance.* Cheltenham & Northampton: Edward Elgar Publisher.

Fishkin, J. S. (2011). *When the People Speak: Deliberative Democracy and Public Consultation.* Oxford: Oxford University Press.

Font, J., Amo, S. P. del, & Smith, G. (2016). Tracing the impact of proposals from participatory processes: Methodological challenges and substantive lessons. *Journal of Public Deliberation,* 12 (1). https://doi.org/10.16997/jdd.243

Gastil, J., & Wright, E. O. (2019). *Legislature by Lot: Transformative Designs for Deliberative Governance.* Cambridge: Verso Books.

Geißel, B. (2004) Responsivität und Responsivitätswahrnehmung – Thesen zu einem undurchsichtigen Verhältnis. *Zeitschrift für Politikwissenschaft* 14 (4), 1235–1255.

Geissel, B. (2023) *The Future of Self-governing, Thriving Democracies – Democratic Innovations by, with and for the People.* New York: Routledge

Geissel, B. (2019). Democratic innovations in Europe. In S. Elstub & O. Escobar (eds), *Handbook of Democratic Innovation and Governance,* 404–420. Cheltenham: Edward Elgar,.

Geissel, B., Kneuer, M., & Lauth, H.-J. (2016). Measuring the quality of democracy: Introduction. *International Political Science Review* 37 (5), 571–579.

Geissel, B., & Newton, K. (eds). (2012). *Evaluating Democratic Innovations. Curing the Democratic Malaise?* New York: Routledge.

Gerwin, M. (2018). *Citizens' Assemblies: Guide to Democracy That Works.* Krakow: Otwarty Plan.

Goodin, R. E. (2008.) *Innovating Democracy: Democratic Theory and Practice after the Deliberative Turn.* Oxford: Oxford University Press.

Hendriks, C. M. (2016). Coupling citizens and elites in deliberative systems: The role of institutional design. *European Journal of Political Research* 55 (1), 43–60.

Knobloch, K. R., Gastil, J., & Reitman, T. (2019). Connecting micro-deliberation to electoral decision making: Institutionalizing the Oregon Citizens' Initiative Review. *Participations* 1, 93–121.

Lafont, C. (2015). Deliberation, participation, and democratic legitimacy: Should deliberative mini-publics shape public policy? *Journal of Political Philosophy* 23 (1), 40–63.

Lafont, C. (2019). *Democracy without Shortcuts: A Participatory Conception of Deliberative Democracy.* Oxford: Oxford University Press.

Landemore, H. (2020). *Open Democracy: Reinventing Popular Rule for the Twenty-First Century.* Princeton, NJ: Princeton University Press.

Lincoln, A. (1994). *Gettysburg Address, 1863.* Chicago: Lakeside Press.

Mansbridge, J., Bohman, B., Chambers, S., Christiano, T., Fung, A., Parkinson, J., Thompson, D. F., & Warren, M. E. (2012). A systemic approach to deliberative democracy. In J. Parkinson & J. Mansbridge (eds), *Deliberative Systems*, 1–26. Cambridge: Cambridge University Press.

Neblo, M. A. (2015). *Deliberative Democracy between Theory and Practice.* Cambridge: Cambridge University Press.

Niessen, C., & Reuchamps, M. (2019). *Designing a Permanent Deliberative Citizens' Assembly: The Ostbelgien Modell in Belgium.* Centre for Deliberative Democracy and Global Governance Working Paper Series 6, University of Canberra.

Pateman, C. (2012). Participatory democracy revisited. *Perspectives on Politics* 10 (1), 7–19.

Pogrebinschi, T., & Samuels, D. (2014). The impact of participatory democracy: Evidence from Brazil's national public policy conferences. *Comparative Politics* 46 (3), 313–332.

Rinne, J. (2020). *Reforming Democratic Systems: Improving the Realization of the Normative Standards of Democracy with Enhanced Policy Voting (EPV).* Frankfurt: Goethe University.

Saward, M. (2021). *Democratic Design.* Oxford: Oxford University Press.

Setälä, M. (2017). Connecting deliberative mini-publics to representative decision making. *European Journal of Political Research* 56 (4), 846–863.

Sintomer, Y. (2018). From deliberative to radical democracy? Sortition and politics in the twenty-first century. *Politics and Society* 46 (3), 337–357.

Sintomer, Y. (2019). From deliberative to radical democracy? Sortition and politics in the twenty-first century. *Participations* 23 (1), 33–59.

Van Reybrouck, D. (2016). *Against Elections: The Case for Democracy.* London: Random House.

Vandamme, P.-E., & Verret-Hamelin, A. (2017). A randomly selected chamber: Promises and challenges. *Journal of Public Deliberation*, 13 (1). https://doi.org/10.16997/jdd.271

Vrydagh, J., Devillers, S., Jacquet, V., Talukder, D., & Bottin, J. (2021). Thriving in an unfriendly territory. In D. Caluwaerts & M. Reuchamps (eds), *Belgian Exceptionalism*, 59–76. London: Routledge.

Warren, M. E. (2017). A problem-based approach to democratic theory. *The American Political Science Review* 111 (1), 39–53.

Warren, M. & Pearse, H. (eds). (2008). *Designing Deliberative Democracy: The British Columbia Citizens' Assembly.* Cambridge, UK; New York: Cambridge University Press.

John Rountree and Nicole Curato

6 Citizens' assemblies and the public sphere

Abstract: This chapter investigates the relationship between CAs and discourse in the public sphere. Rather than consider CAs as authoritative forums, it argues that CAs should be viewed as conduits of public deliberation that are influenced by public discourse and have the potential to reshape public sphere deliberations in turn. This chapter first establishes the normative basis for linking CAs to the public sphere by focusing on their external quality. Then, it uses the empirical literature on CAs to outline three ways they can be linked to public sphere deliberations in practice: by contributing to public deliberation, by inviting public deliberation, or by triggering meta-deliberation.

Keywords: CAs, public sphere, deliberative mini-publics, public discourse, legitimacy, meta-deliberation, capacity building, media, deliberative system

6.1 Introduction

Citizens' assemblies (CAs) have been the subject of high praise and intense criticisms. Advocates portray these forums as a "defibrillator" that can jolt democracies back to life (Wilson and Mellier 2021). They are a "transformative experience" that demonstrate the power of ordinary citizens coming together to collectively discuss their differences of opinion in a respectful and open-minded manner (*The Financial Times* 2019). Many, however, are not persuaded. What gives a randomly selected group of ordinary people the power to make recommendations to policymakers on complex political issues? Why should the public place trust or even give attention to citizens who have no authority to deliberate on their behalf (see Lafont 2015)?

In this chapter, we argue that the praises and criticisms against CAs can be bridged by emphasizing the connection between deliberations taking place in these assemblies to deliberations taking place in the public sphere. We characterize CAs' relationship with the wider public as an iterative one, such that the perspectives and prejudices participants bring in these forums are shaped by on-going conversations in the public sphere, while the reasons, considerations, and recommendations that emerge from these assemblies can, in turn, reshape wider public conversations. Viewed this way, CAs can be characterized as conduits of public deliberation instead of authoritative forums that "shortcut" democratic decision-making (Lafont 2015).

We begin this chapter by revisiting the normative basis for situating the legitimacy of CAs in the wider deliberative system. We argue that these forums' legitimacy rests on

John Rountree: University of Houston-Downtown, USA; **Nicole Curato:** University of Canberra, Australia. The first draft of this chapter appeared at the Centre for Deliberative Democracy and Global Governance's Working Paper Series. Parts of this book chapter are based on the research conducted for an Australian Research Council Discovery Project (DP DP180103014) on the Metastudy of Democratic Deliberation.

∂ Open Access. © 2023 the author(s), published by De Gruyter. [CC] [BY-NC-ND] This work is licensed under the Creative Commons Attribution-NonCommercial-NoDerivatives 4.0 International License. https://doi.org/10.1515/9783110758269-008

their connection to the public sphere. Based on a review of literature, we find that CAs can be linked to the wider citizenry by (1) contributing to public deliberation; (2) inviting public deliberation; and (3) triggering a meta-deliberation on the value of these assemblies in public life. We conclude the chapter by identifying open questions for scholars, advocates, and critics of CAs, and how the field of deliberative democracy can address these gaps.

6.2 Connecting citizens' assemblies to the deliberative system

CAs, by design or circumstance, are not one-off events of citizen engagement that are disconnected from the broader discussions taking place in the public sphere. Indeed, many CAs are organized in response to the deficits of representative democracy, such as political parties that are unresponsive to the demands of ordinary citizens or the hyper-partisanship of commercial media that further polarizes public opinion. From this perspective, the legitimacy of mini-publics should not only be judged based on its "internal quality", or the extent to which the process upholds norms of inclusive and reasonable deliberation. The legitimacy of mini-publics should also be judged based on its "external quality", or how they enhance deliberations in the wider deliberative system (Curato and Böker 2016: 174).

What then are the functions of mini-publics in the deliberative system? There are many answers to this question, which can be summarized to three functions, as described by Curato and Böker (2016). These functions are deliberation-making, legitimacy-seeking, and capacity building.

1. Deliberation-making refers to the role of mini-publics as knowledge brokers to the wider public (see Niemeyer 2014). The outcomes of mini-publics, as well as the reasons that support these outcomes, should be communicated to those who were not part of the forum as another input to on-going public deliberations. Boswell, Hendriks and Ercan (2016) refer to this as the "transmission" role of mini-publics or their function as a connector of claims and ideas between the public sphere and empowered sites of decision-making. In theory, mini-publics can provide a distilled and nuanced position on a complex issue as a result of the learning, deliberation, and reflection that unfolded in the forum. This, however, is not to say that outcomes of mini-publics are necessarily more superior than the discourses already articulated in the public sphere. This is why we emphasize deliberation-making as a core feature of external validity, for we think that mini-publics should extend and deepen ongoing public deliberations, instead of asserting epistemic superiority and democratic authority which could undermine other views.

2. Legitimacy-seeking underscores the imperative for mini-publics to seek "public authorisation and accountability" (Olsen and Trenz 2014: 118). Regardless of the popularity of mini-publics, their legitimacy is not predetermined but constituted by (1)

demonstrating that the reasons circulating in the public sphere have been serious-ly considered in their deliberations and (2) justifying the outcomes of deliberation to people who did not take part in the mini-public. This, for Curato and Böker, ad-dresses the criticism that mini-publics are a form of "participatory elitism" (Cham-bers 2009). Inviting scrutiny to the process and outcomes of mini-publics build their legitimacy through deliberative accountability.

3. Capacity-building stresses the purpose of mini-publics beyond the forum, which is to build the deliberative system's capacity to facilitate inclusive, authentic, and con-sequential deliberations (Stevenson and Dryzek 2014). One could argue that as mini-publics become institutionalized, more people get to experience what it means to engage in careful deliberation (see Suiter 2021). This, in turn, builds citi-zens' capacities to model deliberative behaviour even outside the forum. This vi-sion, however, still warrants empirical evidence. The scholarship on deliberative democracy has yet to understand the long-lasting effects of deliberative mini-pub-lics to its participants because the evidence base is still small (van der Does and Jacquet 2021; but also see Boulianne, Chen and Kahane 2020). Another possibility is for mini-publics to serve as "circuit breakers" in highly-charged issues (Sondha 2019). The Irish CAs on abortion and same sex marriage are often used as the para-digmatic examples of this claim, although again, the systemic effects of iconic mini-publics warrants further investigation.

Focusing on mini-publics' external quality allows us to characterize mini-publics as conduits to public deliberation, instead of narrowly focusing on their potential to be authoritative forums where political decisions are made. As conduits, deliberative mini-publics can serve to deepen existing conversations through their deliberation-making function, facilitate and distil the flow of discourses through their legitimacy-seeking function, and strengthen the deliberative system through their capacity-build-ing function. We argue that portraying mini-publics as conduits to public deliberation is a more normatively defensible position for it recognizes the many ways in which de-liberative democracy can be enriched beyond structured forums.

Now that we have discussed the normative basis for linking mini-publics to delib-erative systems, the next question now is how exactly can they be linked, especially to the public sphere? The next sections present three examples of how CAs have been linked to wider public conversations.

6.3 Contributing to public deliberation

CAs contribute to public deliberation by helping initiate and frame the discussion over specific policies. This appears to be the model that most CAs rely on. An engaged public hears about the assembly and its recommendations. As a result, the assembly starts a public debate about a specific policy, or it reframes an existing public debate.

Hypothetically, the policies favoured by an assembly would have some recommending force for non-participating citizens. In one model of influence, a public audience would trust the judgement of a representative group of fellow citizens who went through an extensive deliberative process. Ferejohn (2008) endorses this division of labour where onlooking citizens do not have to deliberate on the policy proposal directly but instead weigh the competence and representativeness of assembly members. For example, the public can evaluate the expertise of assembly members through observations of their proceedings. In the case of the British Columbia Citizens' Assembly, Ferejohn concludes that public deliberation following the assembly was indeed indirect. He found that "rather than direct deliberation on the merits of the alternative proposals, the CA process itself acquired a trustworthy reputation that gave voters a reason to support its recommendation" (Ferejohn 2008: 202). This act of deference and trust need not be limited to the public.

As McNamara (2019) argues, the Irish government used the 2018 Irish Citizens' Assembly to sidestep revising its controversial abortion law directly and instead defer to the will of the assembly. While the Irish example may present an "abdication of responsibility" by the government, it points to a broader capacity for assemblies to help elected officials navigate highly polarized issues by conferring legitimacy on a citizen deliberation process (Setälä 2017).

Following our normative discussion in the earlier section, this model of influence could be critiqued as anti-democratic. It promotes what Lafont (2020) calls "blind deference" to an assembly and does not empower the public to directly engage in deliberation on important policy issues (see also Lafont 2015). The recommendation of an assembly could alternatively require serious consideration rather than deference, and public debate would centre on the merits of policy proposals rather than the recommending power of the assembly. This route, we argue, is more appealing, as it could empower citizens for further deliberation in the public sphere. In other words, an assembly could provide the public with the raw materials for public debate, including a solid information base, key values at stake, an array of policy options, and the benefits and drawbacks of each approach (Gastil and Black 2007). Especially when connected to mechanisms of direct democracy, such as a referendum, CAs have the ability to improve the deliberative qualities of existing democratic processes (Gastil and Richards 2013).

What remains unclear is the avenue by which the public would become aware of the CA in the first place. Three different routes can be considered: (1) members of the public may watch the deliberations unfold live or through recordings of the proceedings, (2) learn about the deliberations through the media, or (3) review the final report from the assembly.

The first option would position members of the public as direct consumers of CA deliberations who then respond to the proceedings, for example through discussions on social media platforms or current affairs talk shows. However, it is unrealistic to expect a large segment of a population to follow along with an assembly's proceedings. Assembly proceedings are long and demand a lot from audiences. Besides, the purpose of deliberative mini-publics is to create a functional division of labour that lays some of the cognitive and temporal demands of deliberation on participants (Warren and Gastil 2015). If the public was willing and able to spend hours each week following the proceedings closely, then there would be less need for such a division of labour. It is therefore unsurprising that the views on YouTube videos for CAs seem to be generally low (e. g., Cahillane 2020).

The second option is for the public to learn second-hand about an assembly through the media. This is a much more likely outcome. If the media covered an assembly, the recommendations from the process, and the reasoning of an assembly, then the coverage could spark a public conversation and develop political will to move a policy forward. The BBC and ARTE France, for example, produced documentaries on the CAs on climate in the UK and France, respectively. The public may also develop interest in the process from media coverage and seek to learn more (Goodin and Dryzek 2006). Hartz-Karp and Carson (2013) conclude that media coverage is essential to the success of mini-publics, reflecting that mini-publics "may not be capable of achieving transformational change without extensive and impartial media coverage, together with new forms of collaborative governance" (Hartz-Karp and Carson 2013: 32).

Unfortunately, research on the media uptake of CAs is still scarce, so it is difficult to reach general conclusions about how often CAs receive extensive coverage in actual cases or what type of coverage they receive. While one could reasonably anticipate that the novelty of a CA process would attract some media attention, scholarship in this area has shown that the mere existence of an assembly does not by itself lead to much media coverage and subsequent impact on public debate. In fact, in most cases where researchers have studied the media uptake of CAs, they have shown a considerable lack of media visibility and public awareness of an assembly's policy recommendations (LeDuc 2011; Rinke et al. 2013; Warren and Pearse 2008; for an exception, see McNamara 2019). Fournier et al. (2011) have suggested that CAs lack core elements that attract media attention: conflict, polarization, and a clear spokesperson vying for attention. Thus, even if assemblies receive media coverage, Parkinson (2006a) warns that media organizations will pick and choose which parts of deliberative processes are most newsworthy to appeal to mass audiences. In the case of a Deliberative Poll, Parkinson (2006a) shows that coverage highlighted conflict and "significant personalities" rather than the deliberation done in small group discussions.

The Australian Citizens' Parliament, for example, involved a process that engaged in lengthy online and offline deliberations to generate policy recommendations to the national government. The Citizens' Parliament received some positive media coverage on the value of the event for democratic engagement, but the vast majority of this coverage happened *prior* to the deliberations actually taking place. Coverage of the final recommendations of the Citizens' Parliament were scant, thus the event may have stimulated interest in deliberation but did not raise awareness of its outcomes (Rinke et al. 2013).

Scholarship on CAs suggests that some conditions of the assembly design would likely increase its media visibility. A few scholars have suggested that assemblies need to allocate significant resources for a media and public information strategy to improve the visibility of their findings (LeDuc 2011; Ratner 2008). Additionally, compared with CAs that are formed from civil society, assemblies that are commissioned by a government seem to be more likely to gain attention from the media for their perceived policy impact and for the involvement of political figures. As we will discuss in the third section of this chapter, this visibility can be a double-edged sword: the involvement of a prominent political leader in the advocacy for or planning of an assembly can make the assembly appear to be a partisan tactic rather than a true attempt at collaborative governance (Boswell, Niemeyer and Hendriks 2013; Carson 2013; McNamara 2019).

The third option is for the public to read an assembly report. CA reports could be condensed to a page or two and disseminated to every residence. Indeed, some CA processes have distributed copies of their findings to residents, but there is not currently research on the reception or use of these recommendation reports.

Research on the Oregon Citizens' Initiative Review (CIR) may offer some hope for positive impacts from disseminated reports. While not a CA, it shares many of its features. Some assemblies are tied to a referendum process, and the CIR is attached to a ballot initiative process. The CIR relies on a citizens' jury model of deliberation with a stratified randomly selected group of 20–24 participants. After four to five full days of hearing from experts and advocates on a ballot initiative, the CIR writes a one-page report outlining key findings, arguments in favour, and arguments against a particular measure. The subsequent "Citizens' Statement" is mailed to every voting household prior to the election to help inform voters' choices. While the CIR has not significantly filtered into public debate in the media, awareness of the process and the CIR findings are relatively high and may influence informal channels of political conversation (Gastil, Richards and Knobloch 2014; Gastil and Knobloch,2020).

6.4 Inviting public deliberation

While not ubiquitous, some CAs have included a public consultation phase as part of the deliberative process. This shows that participants in CAs do not only hear from experts but also from lay citizens or the wider public. Assemblies are capable of inviting or staging public deliberation through public hearings and soliciting written public input. This can create incentives for the public to participate in debate because that input can feed directly into assembly deliberations, and it does not require the public to stay tuned in throughout the assembly proceedings. Furthermore, engagement between the public and assembly members could draw focus away from conflict-driven public discourse. Grant (2014), for example, argues that assembly members meeting with other citizens have the potential to supplant "the plebiscitary rhetoric of argument winning" with "the deliberative rhetoric of reason giving" (Grant 2014: 544).

One key difference between an assembly organizing public debate rather than merely influencing public debate is that the assembly can use public input to create a feedback mechanism between the public and assembly members. This, as we discussed earlier, forms a critical part of the mini-public's legitimacy-seeking function. The potential to offer feedback can create a virtuous cycle where participants are more motivated to engage productively because an assembly has responded to their ideas and concerns. The consultation could also increase public perceptions of an assembly's legitimacy if interested groups who are not randomly selected can still have influence over the process.

Some CAs have combined public meetings and written submissions in a broad and robust public consultation phase. The British Columbia Citizens' Assembly had 50 public hearings with 1600 written submissions, the Ontario Citizens' Assembly ran 41 public hearings with 1000 written submissions, and the Netherlands' Electoral System Civic Forum (Burgerforum) held 18 hearings with 1400 written submissions (Fournier et al. 2011: 6). In addition, the Australian Citizens' Parliament created an ad hoc online deliberation for participants to jointly create proposals for the Parliament to consider (Sullivan and Hartz-Karp 2013), and the Irish Citizens' Assembly included only a written submission process (Devaney et al. 2020). While the public meetings seem to be the most obvious case of public discourse, Ward (2008) observes that online submitters in the British Columbia case would reply to each other, creating a type of public dialogue across submissions. A mixture of online input and public meetings also was used in the Grand Débat National in France where citizens made contributions to be considered in a series of regional deliberative mini-publics (Courant 2019).

Much more research should be done on the intersection of public input and CAs. Notably, the British Columbia Citizens' Assembly's consultation process has received some scholarly attention. Ratner characterizes the public hearings as attracting useful public engagement to inform the Assembly: "Rooms were crowded at times, but that added to an aura of intense involvement [...] the mood at the hearings was one of genuine engagement" (Ratner 2005: 25–26). According to Ratner, the public consultations revealed that the Assembly and public sentiment were aligned in their distaste for the first-past-the-post electoral system; however, they were not aligned in the system they preferred to replace the current electoral system.

In a case where an assembly's recommendations do not align with public input, that does not necessarily signal a problem. Deliberation is a transformative process, and assembly members after going through deliberation would not be expected to mirror public opinion. As mentioned previously, CAs have an obligation to seek legitimacy by showing that public input is being seriously considered and by giving justifications to those outside of the assembly. In addition, CAs should not be disconnected from more traditional mechanisms of electoral accountability and authorization (Parkinson 2006b: 34).

There is potential for a positive feedback loop between an assembly and the public, but we should be cautious about concluding public consultations influence a CA in practice. In the case of the Grand Débat National, the volume of public contributions was too much for the regional mini-publics to process (Courant 2022). Even if there is time to fully consider public input, it is possible that assembly members will pay lip service to the importance of public consultations or cherry-pick elements of the consultations to reinforce their own decisions. At the three assemblies on electoral reform, assembly members rated the public hearings as "helpful", "informative", and "interesting", and reported that the consultations reinforced assembly members' confidence in their own efficacy and legitimacy (Fournier et al. 2011: 42, 108). However, scholars also observed that "the consultations did influence the members but did not substantially affect the final outcomes" (Fournier et al. 2011: 107).

It could be that public consultation did not appear to influence the final outcome because the public input favoured the direction the Assembly was already going. At least in the British Columbia Assembly, this is not the case. The vast majority of participants at the public meetings advocated for a Mixed Member Proportional (MMP) voting system, whereas the Assembly ultimately recommended a Single-Transferable Vote (STV) system. It could also be that the public input was useful, but the Assembly still exercised its own independent judgement in advocating for STV. Yet, this does not seem likely either, as only 10 of the 364 registered presentations delivered at the public meetings were brought to the attention of the full assembly. Ward (2008) explains that many of the presentations at the public meetings were off-topic or provided misinformation, while other public meetings were subjected to professional lobbying campaigns, leaving some assembly members dissatisfied.

There is also a risk in this process that, rightly or wrongly, assembly members will perceive public input as less legitimate than the Assembly's own deliberations and thus not give it careful consideration. When compared with an assembly, the members of the public who show up to these consultations are less representative of the population and likely less knowledgeable about the issue at hand (Fournier et al. 2011: 41).

The problem may partially reside with the format these public consultation forums have taken. It is ironic that participants in a CA would rely on traditional public consultation formats, such as inviting a series of presentations or speeches rather than facilitating interactive group discussion. Such formats invite monologic, professional lobbying or an airing of grievances rather than dialogic weighing of relevant issues. More innovative consultation designs, in line with the spirit of a CA, could result in more helpful public discussion that informs the assembly deliberations.

6.5 Trigger meta-deliberation

As multiple scholars have shown, CAs themselves often become the subject of public debate. Rather than debate the policies under consideration at the assembly, commentators may debate the assembly model as a process for public engagement. Rinke et al (2013) term this outcome "mediated meta-deliberation" when media outlets foster public deliberation *about* deliberation. It is unsurprising that when CAs receive media coverage, much of the coverage focuses on the uniqueness of the form. Most of the public will not be familiar with a CA or how it operates, so the "news" in a CA is simultaneously the findings of the assembly and the process itself.

Deliberative scholars have argued that meta-deliberation can have positive impacts on public discourse. Rinke et al. (2013) identify four important functions that it may serve. First, it can raise awareness about the outcomes from a deliberative event, such as a list of recommendations or an advisory report. Second, it can foster interest in issues that were under deliberation. Third, it can persuade people that deliberation is a valuable political process. Finally, it can put forward public deliberation as a standard against which other public engagement processes are evaluated.

On the other hand, the case study literature on CAs reveals that meta-deliberation does not necessarily work in favour of a CA. Scholars have shown how focused criticism of the CA can threaten its perceived legitimacy and even derail CAs from ever forming. One prominent example is the failed 2010 proposal for an Australian citizens' assembly on climate change. During the 2010 election campaign, Julia Gillard proposed a CA to form recommendations on climate change, but the proposal received harsh criticism from media commentators and political opposition. Some perceived it as a delaying tactic on climate change, while others speculated that assembly members would be manipulated towards specific policy recommendations. Eventually, the proposal was discarded in favour of an expert panel (Boswell, Niemeyer and Hendriks 2013; Carson 2013). LeDuc observes similar media criticism of the Ontario Citizens' Assembly, where the Assembly process was characterized as "populist pandering" while "papers in Ontario saw Assembly members as largely invisible or often maligned them, sometimes referring to them as government appointees or political pawns" (LeDuc 2009: 34–36).

The negative reactions to CAs in these cases may arise from genuine scepticism of the legitimacy of CAs as a form. Nevertheless, there is the danger that politicians or lobbying groups, distrustful that an assembly will serve their interests or dissatisfied with the assembly's recommendations, will attempt to de-legitimize the process (Setälä 2017; Dryzek 2015). It will not always be clear whether genuine concern or strategic interest leads groups to criticize assembly processes, but practitioners should be concerned that attacking the assembly process rather than its recommendations is a common rhetorical tactic for dissatisfied interest groups. For example, when the Irish Citizens' Assembly deliberated over abortion, some pro-life groups attacked the legitimacy of the assembly process itself, claiming that it had a predetermined outcome and was comprised of biased members (McNamara 2019).

In another case described by Magnusson (2020), a local CA in Vancouver motivated the creation of an oppositional organization. The Grandview-Woodland Citizens' Assembly was formed in 2014 by the Vancouver city government in response to public uproar at their initial community plan for the city. Considering the city had already gone through a public consultation process, the CA was met with extreme scepticism by members of the community. The group Our Community, Our Plan (OCOP) formed in opposition to the assembly, claiming that the assembly was exclusionary. They repeatedly attempted to delegitimize the assembly online and in the media.

While public criticisms of the CA could derail its implementation or threaten its legitimacy, it can also lead assembly organizers and participants to be more reflexive about their own process. This, after all, is the value of meta-deliberation – to examine the way we deliberate on our shared concerns (Holdo 2020). In the Grandview-Woodland Citizens' Assembly case, the opposition from OCOP goaded participants to be reflexive and even self-critical about who was represented within the assembly and more diligent about soliciting public input (Magnusson 2020). Even harsh criticism can be a useful feedback mechanism for deliberative processes. It contributes to both the legitimacy-seeking function of mini-publics and builds the deliberative system's overall capacity to critically examine the democratic quality of democratic innovations.

Each of the cases described here involve the short-term meta-deliberation resulting from CAs. The longer-term impact of CA meta-deliberation on the deliberative system remains to be seen. As noted with the Grandview-Woodland Citizens' Assembly, even harsh criticism can promote critical reflexivity to make an assembly more dynamic and responsive. In practical terms, it could offer lessons to organizers that improve the design of future assemblies, but such criticism could also detract support for future deliberative initiatives. More research should be done to examine the long-term impacts of meta-deliberation on CAs.

6.6 Conclusions

This chapter provided an overview of the normative justifications for connecting deliberative mini-publics, particularly CAs, to the public sphere. We discussed three ways in which these forums can be linked to the system and provided a measured empirical narration of how these connections unfolded in some of the most popular CAs. Spotlighting some of the criticisms of these assemblies was driven by our hope that future assemblies can build on both successes and shortcomings of those that come before them. We were also careful to not to over-assert our claims, for one key takeaway from this chapter is there still much we do not know about CAs – from understanding their long-term impact to participants and the public to learning about ethical and practical ways in which they can be connected to the deliberative system. May these open questions serve as an invitation for scholars and practitioners, advocates and critics of CAs to continue experimenting, observing, and scrutinizing the role of these democratic innovations in shaping public deliberation.

References

Boswell, J., Hendriks, C. M., & Ercan, S. A. (2016). Message received? Examining transmission in deliberative systems. *Critical Policy Studies* 10 (3), 263–283.

Boswell, J., Niemeyer, S., & Hendriks, C. M. (2013). Julia Gillard's citizens' assembly proposal for Australia: A deliberative democratic analysis. *Australian Journal of Political Science* 48 (2), 164–178.

Boulianne S., Chen K., & Kahane, D. (2020). Mobilizing mini-publics: The causal impact of deliberation on civic engagement using panel data. *Politics* 40 (4), 460–476.

Cahillane, L. (2020). Ireland as a learning experience for the Scottish Citizens' Assembly. *The Edinburgh Law Review* 24, 95–103.

Carson, L. (2013). How not to introduce deliberative democracy: The 2010 Citizens' Assembly on Climate Change proposal. In L. Carson, J. Gastil, J. Hartz-Karp, & R. Lubensky (eds.), *The Australian Citizens' Parliament and the Future of Deliberative Democracy*, 274–288. University Park, PA: The Pennsylvania State University Press.

Chambers, S. (2009). Rhetoric and the public sphere: Has deliberative democracy abandoned mass democracy? *Political Theory* 37 (3), 323–350.

Courant, D. (2019). Petit bilan du Grand Débat National. *AOC Media*, 1–7. https://aoc.media/analyse/2019/04/09/petit-bilan-grand-debat-national/

Courant, D. (2022). Institutionalizing deliberative mini-publics? Issues of legitimacy and power for randomly selected assemblies in political systems. *Critical Policy Studies* 16 (2), 162–180.

Curato, N. & Böker, M. (2016). Linking mini-publics to deliberative systems: A research agenda. *Policy Sciences* 49 (2), 173–190.

Devaney, L., Brereton, P., Torney, D., Coleman, M., Boussalis, C., & Coan, T. G. (2020). Environmental literacy and deliberative democracy: A content analysis of written submissions to the Irish Citizens' Assembly on climate change. *Climatic Change* 162, 1965–1984.

Dryzek, J. S. (2015). Deliberative engagement: The forum in the system. *Journal of Environmental Studies and Sciences* 5, 750–754.

Ferejohn, J. (2008). Conclusion: The citizens' assembly model. In M. E. Warren & H. Pearse (eds.), *Designing Deliberative Democracy: The British Columbia Citizens' Assembly*, 192–213. Cambridge: Cambridge University Press.

Financial Times Editorial Board (2019). Deliberative democracy is just what politics needs. *The Financial Times.* 11 August. Available at: https://www.ft.com/content/6bc199c8-b836–11e9–96bd-8e884d3ea203 [Last accessed: 9 September 2021]

Fournier, P., van der Kolk, H., Carty, R. K., Blais, A., & Rose, J. (2011). *When Citizens Decide: Lessons from Citizen Assemblies on Electoral Reform.* Oxford: Oxford University Press.

Gastil, J. & Black, L. (2007). Public deliberation as the organizing principle of political communication research. *Journal of Public Deliberation* 4 (1), article 3. DOI: 10.16997/jdd.59

Gastil, J. & Knobloch, K. (2020). *Hope for Democracy: How Citizens Can Bring Reason Back into Politics.* Oxford: Oxford University Press.

Gastil, J. & Richards, R. (2013). Making direct democracy deliberative through random assemblies. *Politics & Society* 41 (2), 253–281.

Gastil, J., Richards, R., & Knobloch, K. (2014). Vicarious deliberation: How the Oregon Citizens' Initiative Review influenced deliberation in mass elections. *International Journal of Communication* 8, 62–89.

Goodin, R. E. & Dryzek, J. S. (2006). Deliberative impacts: The macro-political uptake of mini-publics. *Politics & Society* 34 (2), 219–244.

Grant, J. (2014). Canada's republican invention? On the political theory and practice of CAs. *Political Studies* 62, 539–555.

Hartz-Karp, J. & Carson, L. (2013). Putting citizens in charge: Comparing the Australian Citizens' Parliament and the Australia 2020 Summit. In L. Carson, J. Gastil, J. Hartz-Karp, & R. Lubensky (eds.), *The Australian Citizens' Parliament and the Future of Deliberative Democracy*, 21–34. University Park, PA: The Pennsylvania State University Press.

Holdo, M. (2020). Meta-deliberation: everyday acts of critical reflection in deliberative systems. *Politics* 40 (1), 106–119.

Lafont, C. (2015). Deliberation, participation, and democratic legitimacy: Should deliberative mini-publics shape public policy? *The Journal of Political Philosophy* 23 (1), 40–63.

Lafont, C. (2020). Against anti-democratic shortcuts: A few replies to critics. *Journal of Deliberative Democracy* 16 (2), 96–109.

LeDuc, L. (2009). The failure of electoral reform proposals in Canada. *Political Science* 61 (2), 21–40.

LeDuc, L. (2011). Electoral reform and direct democracy in Canada: When citizens become involved. *West European Politics* 34 (3), 551–567.

Magnusson, R. (2020). Unsettled democracy: The case of the Grandview-Woodland Citizens' Assembly. In L. Levac & S. M. Wiebe (eds.), *Creating Spaces of Engagement: Policy Justice & the Practical Craft of Deliberative Democracy*, 117–138. Toronto: University of Toronto Press.

McNamara, P. (2019). *Vox Populi* or abdication of responsibility?: The influence of the Irish Citizens' Assembly on the public discourse regarding abortion, 2016–2019. *The Copernicus Journal of Political Studies* 2, 131–156.

Niemeyer, S. (2014). Scaling up deliberation to mass publics: Harnessing mini-publics in a deliberative system. In K. Grönlund, A. Bächtiger, & M. Setälä (eds.), *Deliberative Mini-Publics: Involving Citizens in the Democratic Process*, 177–202. Colchester: ECPR Press.

Olsen, E. D. & Trenz, H. J. (2014). From citizens' deliberation to popular will formation? Generating democratic legitimacy in transnational deliberative polling. *Political Studies* 62 (S1), 117–133.

Parkinson, J. (2006a). Rickety bridges: using the media in deliberative democracy. *British Journal of Political Science* 36 (1), 175–183

Parkinson, J. (2006b). *Deliberating in the Real World: Problems of Legitimacy in Deliberative Democracy*. Oxford: Oxford University Press.

Ratner, R. S. (2005). The BC Citizens' Assembly: The public hearings and deliberations stage. *Canadian Parliamentary Review* 28 (1), 24–33.

Ratner, R. S. (2008). Communicative rationality in the citizens' assembly and referendum process. In M. E. Warren & H. Pearse (eds.), *Designing Deliberative Democracy: The British Columbia Citizens' Assembly*, 145–165. Cambridge: Cambridge University Press.

Rinke, E. M., Knobloch, K. R., Gastil, J., & Carson, L. (2013). Mediated meta-deliberation: Making sense of the Australian Citizens' Parliament. In L. Carson, J. Gastil, J. Hartz-Karp, & R. Lubensky (eds.), *The Australian Citizens' Parliament and the Future of Deliberative Democracy*, 260–273. University Park, PA: The Pennsylvania State University Press.

Setälä, M. (2017). Connecting deliberative mini-publics to representative decision making. *European Journal of Political Research* 56 (4), 846–863.

Sondha, S. (2019) A citizens' assembly can sort Brexit mess. *The Guardian*. 3 March. Available at: https://www.theguardian.com/politics/2019/mar/03/brexit-citizensassembly-compromise [Last accessed 9 September 2021]

Stevenson, H. and Dryzek, J. (2014*). Democratizing Global Climate Governance*. Cambridge: Cambridge University Press.

Suiter, J. (2021) A modest proposal: Building a deliberative system in Northern Ireland. *Irish Studies in International Affairs* 32 (2), 247–270.

Sullivan, B. & Hartz-Karp, J. (2013). Grafting an online parliament onto a face-to-face process. In L. Carson, J. Gastil, J. Hartz-Karp, & R. Lubensky (eds.), *The Australian Citizens' Parliament and the Future of Deliberative Democracy*, 49–62). University Park, PA: The Pennsylvania State University Press.

van der Does, R. & Jacquet, V. (2021). Small-scale deliberation and mass democracy: A systematic review of the spillover effects of deliberative minipublics. *Political Studies*. DOI: 10.1177/00323217211007278

Ward, I. (2008). An experiment in political communication: The British Columbia Citizens' Assembly on Electoral Reform. *Australian Journal of Political Science* 43 (2), 301–315. DOI: 10.1080/10361140802035796

Warren, M. & Pearse, H. (eds.) (2008). *Designing Deliberative Democracy: The British Columbia Citizens' Assembly*. Cambridge: Cambridge University Press.

Warren, M. E. & Gastil, J. (2015). Can deliberative minipublics address the cognitive challenges of democratic citizenship? *The Journal of Politics* 77 (2), 562–574.

Wilson, R. and Mellier, C. (2021) Defibrillating democracy. *New Internationalist*. 4 March. Available at: https://newint.org/features/2021/02/08/defibrillating-democracy [Last accessed: 9 September 2021]

John Boswell, Carolyn M. Hendriks, and Selen A. Ercan

7 Beyond citizens' assemblies: Expanding the repertoire of democratic reform

Abstract: There is broad support for democratizing the policy process by better connecting mass publics and governing elites. In policy terms, these efforts have become closely associated with deliberative mini-publics, especially CAs (CA). The wisdom accumulated on these novel practices is impressive, but also highlights important limitations. Drawing on recent developments in deliberative theory and our own empirical work on other democratic practices, we suggest expanding the repertoire of democratic reform beyond the current focus of "designing" one-off novel deliberative forums to thinking more systemically about ways to "mend" the fabric of democracy. Democratic mending involves strengthening and sustaining democratic connections between people and the processes and institutions that govern them. We argue that mending is a vital component both of better integrating forums like CAs into their political and administrative context, and, more radically, for expanding the repertoire of practices for democratic reform in contemporary governance.

Keywords: democratic mending, design thinking, deliberative systems, deliberative mini-publics, CAs, representative government, public sphere, public policy, innovative governance, pragmatic experimentalism

7.1 Introduction

The rapid rise of the citizens' assembly (CA) into everyday policymaking parlance in many parts of the world is, in broad terms, a welcome development for those interested in deepening democracy in governance. CAs are celebrated for breaking policy deadlocks even on the most contentious policy issues and for offering an open and direct democratic experience to ordinary citizens (see Landemore 2020; OECD 2020). They are proposed as solutions to democracy's many pressing problems such as rebuilding national unity and repairing the trust deficit between citizens and politicians (Brown 2019). According to their advocates, CAs can even solve the "echo chamber" problem of democracy "by making people talk to others who don't share their opinions" (Benedictus 2019).

While most CA efforts are founded in good intentions on the part of key advocates and champions, they are not without their drawbacks and risks. The existing literature emphasizes these risks eloquently (see, for example, Lee 2015; Fuji-Johnson 2015; van Dijk and Lefevere 2022). What is less problematized is that CAs are mostly rooted in

John Boswell: University of Southampton, UK; **Carolyn M. Hendriks:** Australian National University, Australia; **Selen A. Ercan:** University of Canberra, Australia.

Open Access. © 2023 the author(s), published by De Gruyter. [CC] BY-NC-ND This work is licensed under the Creative Commons Attribution-NonCommercial-NoDerivatives 4.0 International License. https://doi.org/10.1515/9783110758269-009

what we call "big-D Design" thinking in democratic governance – an abstract and technocratic exercise in developing and implementing institutional interventions to democratize the policy process. Big-D design thinking is the opposite of "small-d" design thinking – or, as we ultimately prefer to call it, "mending" – which problematizes reaching for "off-the-shelf" solutions like CAs, at least without adopting and adapting them significantly for local conditions and contexts. When underpinned by big-D design thinking, CAs can easily become vulnerable to *realpolitik* and can struggle to realize much impact in practice because the political context is hostile or unfamiliar (see e.g., Flinders et al. 2016).

In this chapter, we consider alternatives to the big-D Design approach to democratic reform as manifested in deliberative mini-publics such as CAs. Our contribution expands the focus from "designing" to "mending" democracy where the broader goal centres on strengthening connections among the citizens themselves and between the citizens and governing elites. Democratic mending refers to "the intentional, creative, everyday practices that seek to repair and renew connections in the fabric of democratic life" (Hendriks, Ercan and Boswell 2020: 2). It draws our attention to often overlooked agents and agency in creating and sustaining these democratic connections. While the primary purpose of the mending approach is to expand the existing repertoires of democratic reform beyond designed forums, it also has important implications for how we think about CAs and their underlying design logic (big-D vs small-d). Taking a mending approach, we can show why and how CAs need careful integration into existing institutions and policymaking practices if they are to realize the benefits their advocates in academia and practice hope they will. More fundamentally still, taking a mending approach allows us to appreciate a wide repertoire of democratic repair alternatives beyond "off-the-shelf" interventions such as CAs.

The chapter proceeds in three sections. The first section sets out in greater detail the limitations of "the forum" in the context both of what we know empirically about contemporary governance trends and what leading theorists argue normatively about ideal democratic practices. The next section outlines our idea of "democratic mending". We show here both how an emphasis on mending can inform contemporary research and practice on CAs, and also how it can encourage scholars and practitioners of democratic reform to look beyond these sorts of forums and recognize/make use of a wider repertoire of repair. The conclusion then draws together key lessons for further research and experimentation, advocating in particular a grounded, pragmatic emphasis on policy learning through trial and error rather than seeking to replicate the rigid "social laboratory" approach associated with a big-D Design approach.

7.2 Citizens' assemblies and their limits

The public policy and public administration literatures (and cognate fields such as health, environmental, and innovation governance) now abound with systematic efforts to define and map out democratic innovation (see e.g., Abelson et al. 2003; Knobloch, Gastil and Reitman 2015; Smith 2009). The practice of democratic innovation has become an important field of consulting and expertise, as specialists hone a toolkit of techniques, and the skills to execute them, across sectors and settings (see Hendriks and Carson 2008; Cooper and Smith 2012; Lee 2015; Escobar 2018). The touchstone, in both research and practice, has been on participatory forums – the CA perhaps chief among them—that seek to institutionalize many of the ideals of deliberative democracy.

On the one hand this focus on "the forum" is entirely understandable, especially given emphasis in policy theory and practice on using public engagement processes to democratize governance (see Fung 2006; Nabatchi et al. 2012). Below we briefly run through what makes "the forum" so appealing for democratic reform in the policy process to illustrate how successful it has been on some dimensions, and also to foreshadow its limits and alternatives.

(a) *Forum as a shortcut to democracy/democratic representation:* This point is well articulated by Christina Lafont (2019), in her recent book, *Democracy without Shortcuts.* What Lafont rightly criticizes is that the forum is often seen as a shortcut to democratic practice. It is seen as a remedy to many systemic problems, most notably to the broken system of democratic representation in modern governance. In a context of deepening disaffection with representative democracy and a growing chasm between elites and everyday citizens, the forum appeals as an ideal augmentation which can reinject inclusivity into the making of key policy decisions. Archon Fung (2006), for example, argues that elected institutions provide only a minimally representative process, and that acute pathologies afflict contemporary governance as a consequence, providing evidence that "institutional remedies" (imagined as the forum) can address the democratic shortcomings of contemporary governance. These forums can be both designed as part of existing institutions (Neblo, Esterling and Lazer 2018), or outside of them.

(b) *Forum as a remedy to distorted public sphere and uninformed public opinion:* The forum promises to cut through the "noise" of an increasingly distorted public sphere. The perceived problem here is that the conduits of public opinion outside of electoral representation – the traditional media and increasingly social media especially – are seen to reinforce and generate a lot of heat and little light, such that we cannot be sure what policy preferences an informed and rational debate among citizens would lead to. There is sound evidence that the forum provides an alternative, controlled conduit which can enable better and more legitimate decision-making (see especially Fishkin 2009; Niemeyer 2011). The forum offers a platform for testing policy ideas and proposals. It provides policymakers with an answer as to whether a policy can be "sold" to the public (Goodin and Dryzek 2006: 228). It offers politicians the possibility of finding out "what the public *would* think about an issue if it were to experience better conditions for thinking about it" (Fishkin 2009: 13).

(c) *Forum as a solution to complex policy issues:* The forum also promises to generate and protect capacity for lay citizens to engage with the complexities, risks, and uncertainties of contemporary policy issues. It seeks to address the perceived growing disconnect between democracy and bureaucracy, where non-majoritarian institutions and a raft of powerful private actors shape policymaking "on the ground" through Byzantine processes in the messy, "real world" of policymaking (see Flinders 2008). The forum appeals as a means to bridge this disconnect. It allows lay citizens and stakeholders to become better informed about the complexities of policymaking, and to use that knowledge to deliberate on otherwise hidden or opaque decisions about policies and services – with a considerable literature suggesting that citizens are capable of coming to grips with governing complexities in the right circumstances (see, for example, Abelson et al. 2003; Gronlund, Bächtiger and Setälä 2014). Another additional layer here is that our knowledge and understanding of many contemporary public policy issues is often incomplete and highly contested. Ideally the forum offers a 'clearing house' where citizens can learn about and question the unknowns, risks, and uncertainties of knowledge, and develop 'common sense' judgements. In some policy areas, such as climate change, the forum has found particular appeal because citizens are encouraged to look beyond the short-term and consider the interests of future generations (Devaney et al 2020; Smith 2021).

There is also a practical utility to the forum. In countries like Ireland and the UK, the CA has become a salient tool for tricky political problems (Farrell and Suiter 2019). For example, comparisons of the botched handling of Brexit in the UK with the widely acclaimed Irish abortion referendum in Ireland are thought to provide clear evidence of the potential of CAs (Brown 2019). It is easy to imagine, and plan, a forum as an intervention in the policy process – indeed it is an ideal input in the policy stages or cycle heuristic which continues to predominate. It is a convenient "social laboratory" to study and assess the effects of deliberation in empirical research. It is an off-the-shelf solution for the challenges of governing complex issues in practice. It is, in other words, a tried and tested product of "big-D Design".

But, as this might suggest, the forum model also has important limitations. According to some scholars of democracy, it is deeply problematic to equate democratic reform of the policy process with "the forum" (see e.g. Hammond 2019; Hendriks, Ercan and Boswell 2020; Lafont 2015; 2019; Pateman 2012). These concerns can be traced back to the compelling logics underpinning the appeal in the first place.

a) *The legitimacy and accountability of designed forums:* Current practices of designed forums such as CAs operate according to certain principles (such as random selection) that seem to violate or bypass established canons of existing representative democracy (Parkinson 2003, 2006). They provide little scope for the sort of scrutiny or accountability typical to established democratic institutions. And, certainly, there are prominent examples of forums or planned forums which have generated considerable antipathy in the broader public sphere – none more so than the proposed CA on climate change in Australia that was written off and ridiculed across the political spectrum (Boswell, Niemeyer and Hendriks 2013).

b) *Top-down nature of designed forums:* There is also concern about the potential for top-down democratic innovations like CAs to crowd out or marginalize organic, bottom-up participation in civil society (see e.g. Mansbridge et al. 2012). Others worry that deliberative forums are too discrete and isolated, and thus have limited engagement or capacity to address democratic disfunctions in conventional institutions (Pateman 2012). There is also a growing critique that the refined and routinized practices of professional forum-making can function as a tool by which governing elites seek to tame difficult issues, shutting out or quietening the "noise" from the public sphere (see Lee 2015; Fuji-Johnson 2015).

c) *Unclear/uncertain role of designed forums:* The forum does not necessarily produce immediate policy clarity or certainty – mostly it forms part of, and becomes absorbed within, the complex, recursive, sporadic practices of policy work (e.g. see Wells, Howarth and Brand-Correa 2021). In other words, the forum can be lost in and swamped by the vast array of other discussions and sources of policy input surrounding any given issue (see Hendriks 2011), and can struggle to produce tangible reforms (see Michels 2011). Certainly, for instance, the messy and incomplete integration of the recent spate of climate assemblies in Europe speaks to a complexity that forum-designers seldom bear in mind (see Torney 2021; Wells, Howarth and Brand-Correa 2021). The particular concern is that forums might end up offering little more than the veneer of democratic inclusion within a context of continuing elite domination (Fuji-Johnson 2015).

These concerns about "the forum" share affinities with more recent scholarship on democratic and policy design – a small-d approach to "design thinking'. This more nuanced approach to design recognizes the importance of context in shaping and constraining interventions (see in political theory Saward 2021; in policy studies Lewis, McGann and Blomkamp 2020). Small-d design thinking emphasizes the need for locally meaningful, contextual solutions to policy problems. In what follows, we elaborate our mending approach which has important affinities with this kind of small-d design thinking, and which opens up the possibilities for democratic reform beyond designed forums.

7.3 From "designing" to "mending" democracy: "Stitching in" citizens' assemblies

The approach we advance in this chapter shares some affinities with this shift towards small-d design thinking in democratic governance, although as our point of departure we draw on "systemic" thinking in democratic democracy. Here deliberative democrats have expanded their view of public deliberation beyond something that occurs in a singular ideal forum, towards thinking of it as something that occurs across a more complex system made up of many communicative activities and spaces, ranging from highly structured assemblies (such as legislatures), to loose informal social gatherings and public interactions (Hendriks 2006; Parkinson and Mansbridge 2012; Elstub, Ercan and Mendonça 2016).

While the existing literature tends to draw on idea of deliberative systems as a way of thinking big and scaling up the democratic effects of deliberative mini-publics, in our view, a deliberative systems approach also offers a way of reconceptualizing democratic reform beyond the forum. Inherent in the idea of a legitimate deliberative system is the notion of connectivity. Connections not only help link different actors, practices, and institutions across a deliberative system, but they are crucial for ensuring undistorted communication between citizens and decision-makers (including elected representatives, and those making and implementing public policy). Despite the centrality of connectivity in deliberative systems thinking, it is curiously under-developed concept in theories of deliberative democracy.

We can flesh out the idea of connectivity by turning to democratic practice. Our empirical work on contemporary democratic practices show that connectivity is enacted in democratic systems in multiple ways as diverse actors, activities, settings, and practices relate to and influence one another (Hendriks, Ercan and Boswell 2020). In studying these diverse connective practices we uncovered the important – yet largely hidden – small-scale efforts of citizens, elected officials, civil society activists, and public administrators to connect citizens with each other as well as with the governing elites. These are not high-profile democratic wonders but everyday actors doing incremental connective work often in and around conventional or unassuming institutions, such as local cafés and libraries, election campaigns, and administrative committees.

We label this intentional, creative, and everyday work to repair and renew connections in the fabric of democratic life as *mending democracy* (Hendriks, Ercan and Boswell 2020: 2). Practices of democratic mending entail the gradual, small-scale, incremental, mundane work of people working inside the system, rather than imposing something on the system. They occur in and around political and policymaking institutions that already exist, and involve reimagining and remaking this institutional architecture as more deliberative and democratic. They emerge through mostly bottom-up efforts of citizens, activists, and civil society groups, as well as professionals, public managers and officials. Often these practices are not products of conscious big-D design or high-minded initiatives to enhance deliberative democracy. More commonly they emerge out of collective problem-solving efforts, whether to address a policy issue or to resolve a political or administrative challenge (such as a broken electoral relationship, a divisive public sphere, an opaque and confusing institutional make-up) (see Hendriks and Dzur 2022). Finally, practices of democratic mending are not usually off-the-shelf or codified. They are instead contingent on the complex constellation of factors that have fostered and channelled their emergence.

The idea of democratic mending we propose in this chapter has important implications for the way we think about and design interventions like CAs. At first blush, our emphasis on democratic mending might imply that we are critical of designed forums. But we still believe forums can be valuable – indeed, a key principle is that actors should "mend and make do" with the resources at their disposal, and the opportunities that come along. The proliferation of assemblies in the recent "deliberative wave" (OECD 2020) is one such opportunity to grasp. CAs have developed a mainstream cache that opens up exciting possibilities for meaningful democratic repair.

A mending approach emphasizes the importance of integrating forums into the existing political system and policy process and shifts our attention to the actors involved in doing the integration work. To extend the metaphor, a CA represents a "patch" that might help repair the connection between citizens and democratic policymaking. But patches do not work on their own. They need to be carefully "stitched in". That work has important parallels with the work of democratic mending; it is time-intensive, relational, and context-specific.

"Stitching in" requires more than linking CAs to formal decision-making processes, which seems to be the priority of most of the existing efforts. It also requires ensuring that CAs are not isolated spaces of deliberation and instead well integrated into the wider public sphere (Curato and Böker 2016). Only when they are part of the broader public sphere can they contribute to not only to "decision-making" but also "deliberation-making" (Niemeyer 2014).

We can look to a nascent literature on the integration of forums like CAs for promising signs on how such "stitching in" might occur. To date, much of focus has been on establishing elite champions for the cause. One approach is to engage elite actors directly. Notably, for instance, politicians were intimately involved in the deliberations of the Irish Citizens' Assembly, which made them much more receptive to the ideas emanating from the forum (Farrell, Suiter and Harris 2019). But that success was not just a question of big-D Design – it took ongoing relational work on the part of committed activists (Enright, McNeilly and De Londras 2020) and other civil society actors to build and sustain that sort of elite buy-in, as reflected by relative failures to emulate the Irish model elsewhere (see Flinders et al. 2016). Another approach entails "institutional coupling", whereby empowered institutions (often legislative committees) sponsor and support a designed forum (Hendriks 2016). Early experiments in this regard have proven somewhat successful, although again they stress the importance of everyday, relational work to sustain the link. The recent experience of the Climate Assembly UK on this front is instructive – the CAUK lost much of its impetus following significant turnover across the Parliamentary select committees that had co-sponsored the process. The new committee chairs were much less enthusiastic to endorse and follow through on an innovation they had played no part in establishing (Elstub et al. 2021).

But "stitching in" could also mean connecting CAs (whether instigated by state or non-state actors) to wider public discourse – to embed and sustain better links with the media, community initiatives, and the broader public. We see signs of this sort of wider "stitching in" in recent climate assemblies in France and Germany, for instance (Boswell, Dean and Smith 2022). Indeed, the newly formed Knowledge Network On Climate Assemblies (KNOCA) in Europe offers a promising model for exploring these modes of integrative innovation. This is an active network of practitioners, advocates, and experts developed to share experiences from the recent wave of national climate assemblies in Europe, learn from successes and failures from mini-public intervention in practice, and develop strategies for better enhancing profile and impact for the long term.

7.4 Beyond citizens' assemblies: A much wider repertoire of democratic repair

While CAs can, with a mending orientation, go some way to helping democratize policy work, it is important to retain perspective. In the task of democratizing the policy process, they remain minor and niche in the grand scheme of things. They command a lot of media attention, and attract considerable academic attention and analysis because of their novelty. They are increasingly recognized in policy practitioner circles, too – but the bulk of this audience would still consider them relatively peripheral to the everyday work of governing (e.g., Sasse, Allan and Rutter 2021).

There is instead a lot more activity already happening in the more mundane spaces of policy work that can and does have much greater impact on the real lived experience of democratic governance. In our own empirical work on democratic mending we identified the careful, creative, intensive work done by actors on the ground to make democracy work better for them (Hendriks, Ercan and Boswell 2020). For example, we observed a group of alienated voters reclaim the electoral process from the inside out, and in the process reimagine representative democracy outside of the traditional strictures of party politics. We observed a collection of concerned citizens working creatively to change the terms of a polarized environmental debate and seeking to mend a fractured public sphere in Australia. We observed civil society activists and officials seize on newly re-made institutional arrangements to pry open the complex and opaque health system in the UK, ensuring greater public inclusion and scrutiny over policymaking and implementation. In the space available we cannot do justice to these rich cases – all are recorded in more detail in our book-length treatment (see Hendriks, Ercan and Boswell 2020) – but they speak to the importance of placing equal analytical attention on the ordinary, mundane, low-profile spaces of democratic governance as has been granted to novel deliberative forums.

Pleasingly, our observations and insights also gel with insights beginning to emerge elsewhere in the field. Escobar's (2022) recent account of Scottish participatory engagement practitioners on the "frontlines" of public encounters describes them as being engaged in the careful, skilful, and resourceful work of democratic mending; in the face of bureaucratic obstacles and political dynamics, they adapt and reimagine established tools and practices of participatory engagement to keep the show on the road. Wood's (2022) study of the European Medicine's Authority showcases democratic mending in public hearings, demonstrating how seemingly mundane and dry committee work can link affected publics to this technocratic supranational body. Beyond work that expressly adapts and builds on our ideas, we see affinities elsewhere, too. For instance, something very close to democratic mending appears in the creative and forceful work of Scottish health activists who resist tightly scripted, top-down engagement activities while at the same time forging opportunities for more expansive "fugitive co-production" to ensure greater inclusion and accountability on healthcare priorities (Stewart 2021). Likewise, we see something like democratic mending emerging in various trust-restoring and community-building efforts, for example, locally-led housing and economic development initiatives in England (Healey 2015), or parents engaged in after school programmes in Chicago (Barnes 2020).

In other words, there are hopeful stories emerging for everyday practices of mending that can democratize the policy process from the ground up. We need to know much more about what different practices of democratic mending are out there, how they emerge in practice, if (and how) they interrelate, and how well (or badly) they can be sustained against a wider background of disconnection in the representative relationship, in the public sphere, and in the policy process. CAs – as occasional but potentially useful integrated "patches" – can only ever be a small part of a much broader systemic approach to democratic repair work.

7.5 Conclusion

CAs are "just one piece of the puzzle when it comes to creating a more deliberative democracy" (Dryzek 2015: 753). Much more is needed for advancing both deliberation and democratic reform in contemporary societies. In this chapter, we have provided a glimpse of what a mending approach to democratic reform entails, but much more experimentation is needed. We use the term experimentation with particular purpose – in the pragmatist tradition, with the soft sense of encouraging trial-and-error through experience, rather than the hard sense of imagining complex contemporary policy settings as controlled environments into which it is possible to input innovative democratic "treatments". None of the examples we draw on above, either of our own work or of others, lend themselves to neat replication across context. The work of "stitching in" CAs and other deliberative forums will by necessity be contingent on local context. The practices within the broader repertoire of mending beyond the forum are not off-the-shelf products or services. There may be ways to seed or promote similar practices elsewhere, but such efforts will always take on their own local hue. And, in any case, there may be more value in promoting and protecting local practices which emerge organically.

We conclude, then, that the pursuit of democratic repair needs to move away from a "social laboratory" mode and towards an approach associated with "reflexive governance" (see Hendriks and Grin 2007) and "policy learning" (see Dunlop and Radaelli 2013). That will entail looking for, seeding, and supporting organic opportunities to "stitch in" forums or, more often, draw on a much wider range of democratic mending practices. In other words, pursuing democratic reform now requires a form of experimentation based on experiential knowledge, historical understanding, a nuanced appreciation of local practice, and a thoughtful, flexible and piecemeal approach to learning by doing.

References

Abelson, J., Forest, P. G., Eyles, J., Smith, P., Martin, E., & Gauvin, F. P. (2003). Deliberations about deliberative methods: issues in the design and evaluation of public participation processes. *Social Science & Medicine* 57 (2), 239–251.

Barnes, C. (2020). *State of Empowerment: Low Income Families and the New Welfare State.* Ann Arbor: University of Michigan Press.

Benedictus, L. (2019). Power to the people – could a citizens' assembly solve the Brexit crisis. *The Guardian*, 17 January.

Boswell, J., Niemeyer, S., & Hendriks, C. M. (2013). Julia Gillard's citizens' assembly proposal for Australia: A deliberative democratic analysis. *Australian Journal of Political Science* 48 (2), 164–178.

Boswell, J., Dean, R., & Smith, G. (2022, Early View). Integrating citizen deliberation into climate governance: Lessons on robust design from six climate assemblies. *Public Administration.* https://doi.org/10.1111/padm.12883

Brown, G. (2019). A citizens' assembly is now the only way to break the Brexit deadlock. *The Guardian*, 21 January.

Cooper E., & Smith, G. (2012). Organizing deliberation: The perspectives of professional participation practitioners in Britain and Germany. *Journal of Public Deliberation* 8 (1). doi: https://doi.org/10.16997/jdd.125

Curato, N., & Böker, M. (2016). Linking mini-publics to deliberative systems: A research agenda. *Policy Sciences* 49 (2), 173–190.

Devaney, L., Torney, D., Brereton, P., & Coleman, M. (2020). Ireland's Citizens' Assembly on Climate Change: Lessons for deliberative public engagement and communication. *Environmental Communication* 14 (2), 141–146.

Dryzek, J. S. (2015). Deliberative engagement: the forum in the system. *Journal of Environmental Studies and Sciences* 5 (4), 750–754.

Dunlop, C. A., & Radaelli, C. M. (2013). Systematising policy learning: From monolith to dimensions. *Political Studies* 61 (3), 599–619.

Elstub, S., Ercan, S., & Mendonça, R. F. (2016). Editorial introduction: The fourth generation of deliberative democracy. *Critical Policy Studies* 10 (2), 139–151.

Elstub, S., Carrick, J., Farrell, D. M., & Mockler, P. (2021). The scope of climate assemblies: Lessons from the Climate Assembly UK. *Sustainability* 13 (20), 11272.

Enright, M., McNeilly, K., & De Londras, F. (2020). Abortion activism, legal change, and taking feminist law work seriously. *Northern Ireland Legal Quarterly* 71 (3). 359–385.

Escobar, O. (2015). Scripting deliberative policy-making: Dramaturgic policy analysis and engagement know-how. *Journal of Comparative Policy Analysis: Research and Practice* 17 (3), 269–285.

Escobar, O. (2022). Between radical aspirations and pragmatic challenges: Institutionalising participatory governance in Scotland. *Critical Policy Studies* 16 (2), 146–161.

Farrell, D. M., Suiter, J., & Harris, C. (2019). 'Systematizing' constitutional deliberation: The 2016–18 Citizens' Assembly in Ireland. *Irish Political Studies* 34 (1), 113–123.

Farrell, D. M., & Suiter, J. (2019). *Reimagining Democracy.* Ithaca, NY: Cornell University Press.

Fishkin, J. (2009). *When the People Speak: Deliberative Democracy and Public Consultation.* Oxford: Oxford University Press.

Flinders, M. (2008). *Delegated Governance and the British State: Walking Without Order.* Oxford: Oxford University Press.

Flinders, M., Ghose, K., Jennings, W., Molloy, E., Prosser, B., Renwick, A., ... & Spada, P. (2016). *Democracy Matters: Lessons from the 2015 CAs on English Devolution.*

Fuji-Johnson, G. (2015). *Democratic Illusion: Deliberative Democracy in Canadian Public Policy.* Toronto: University of Toronto Press.

Fung, A. (2006). Democratizing the policy process. In M. Moran, M. Rein & R. E. Goodin (eds), *The Oxford Handbook of Public Policy*, 669–685. Oxford: Oxford University Press

Goodin, R. E., & Dryzek, J. (2006). Deliberative impacts: The macro-political uptake of mini-publics. *Politics and Society* 34 (2), 219–244.

Grönlund, K., Bächtiger, A., & Setälä, M. (eds.) (2014) *Deliberative Mini-Publics: Involving Citizens in the Democratic Process.* Colchester: ECPR Press.

Hammond, M. (2019). Deliberative democracy as a critical theory. *Critical Review of International Social and Political Philosophy* 22 (7), 787–808.

Healey, P. (2015). Civil society enterprise and local development. *Planning Theory & Practice* 16 (1), 11–27.

Hendriks, C. M. (2006). Integrated deliberation: Reconciling civil society's dual role in deliberative democracy. *Political Studies* 54, 486–508.

Hendriks, C. M. (2011). *The Politics of Public Deliberation. Citizen Engagement and Interest Advocacy.* Basingstoke: Palgrave Macmillan.

Hendriks, C. M. (2016). Coupling citizens and elites in deliberative systems: The role of institutional design. *European Journal of Political Research* 55 (1), 43–60.

Hendriks, C. M., & Grin, J. (2007). Contextualizing reflexive governance: the politics of Dutch transitions to sustainability. *Journal of Environmental Policy & Planning* 9 (3–4), 333–350.

Hendriks, C. M., & Carson, L. (2008). Can the market help the forum? Negotiating the commercialisation of deliberative democracy. *Policy Sciences* 41 (4), 293–313.

Hendriks, C. M., & Dzur, A. W. (2022). Citizens' governance spaces: Democratic action through disruptive collective problem-solving. *Political Studies* 70 (3), 680–700.

Hendriks, C. M., Ercan, S. A., & Boswell, J. (2020). *Mending Democracy: Democratic Repair in Disconnected Times.* New York: Oxford University Press.

Knobloch, K. R., Gastil, J., & Reitman, T. (2015). Connecting micro-deliberation to electoral decision making: Institutionalizing the Oregon Citizens' Initiative Review. In A. Przybylska, S. Coleman & Y. Sintomer (eds.) *Deliberation: Values, Process, Institutions*, 21–40. Frankfurt: Peter Lang Publishing.

Lafont, C. (2015). Deliberation, participation, and democratic legitimacy: Should deliberative mini-publics shape public policy? *Journal of Political Philosophy* 23 (1), 40–63.

Lafont, C. (2019). *Democracy Without Shortcuts.* Oxford: Oxford University Press.

Landemore, H. (2020). *Open Democracy. Reinventing Popular Rule for the Twenty-First Century.* Princeton: Princeton University Press.

Lee, C. W. (2015). *Do-It-Yourself Democracy. The Rise of the Public Engagement Industry.* Oxford: Oxford University Press.

Lewis, J. M., McGann, M., & Blomkamp, E. (2020). When design meets power: Design thinking, public sector innovation and the politics of policymaking. *Policy & Politics* 48 (1), 111–130.

Mansbridge, J., Bohman, J., Chambers, S., Christiano, T., Fung, A., Parkinson, J., Thompson, D. F., et al. (2012). A systemic approach to deliberative democracy. In J. Parkinson & J. Mansbridge (eds.), *Deliberative Systems: Deliberative Democracy at the Large Scale*, 1–26. Cambridge: Cambridge University Press.

Michels, A. (2011). Innovations in democratic governance: how does citizen participation contribute to a better democracy? *International Review of Administrative Sciences* 77 (2), 275–293.

Nabatchi, Tina, John Gastil, Michael G. Weiksner, & Matt Leighninger (eds). (2012). *Democracy in Motion: Evaluating the Practice and Impact of Deliberative Civic Engagement.* New York: Oxford University Press.

Neblo, M. A., Esterling, K. M., & Lazer, D. M. (2018). *Politics with the People: Building a Directly Representative Democracy.* Cambridge: Cambridge University Press.

Niemeyer, S. (2011). The emancipatory effect of deliberation: empirical lessons from mini-publics. *Politics & Society* 39 (1), 103 – 140.

Niemeyer, S. (2014). Scaling up deliberation to mass publics: Harnessing mini-publics in a deliberative system. In K. Grönlund, A. Bächtiger, & M. Setälä (eds.), *Deliberative Mini-Publics: Involving Citizens in the Democratic Process*, 177 – 202. Colchester: ECPR Press.

OECD (2020). *Innovative Citizen Participation and New Democratic Institutions: Catching the Deliberative Wave.* Paris: OECD Publishing.

Parkinson, J. (2003). Legitimacy problems in deliberative democracy. *Political Studies* 51 (1), 180 – 196.

Parkinson, J. (2006). *Deliberating in the Real World. Problems of Legitimacy in Deliberative Democracy.* New York: Oxford University Press.

Parkinson, J., & Mansbridge, J. (eds). (2012). *Deliberative Systems: Deliberative Democracy at the Large Scale.* Cambridge: Cambridge University Press.

Pateman, C. (2012). Participatory democracy revisited. *Perspectives on Politics* 10 (1), 7 – 19.

Sasse, T., Allan, S., & Rutter, J. (2021). Public engagement and net zero. *IfG Insight.* London: Institute for Government.

Saward, M. (2021). *Democratic Design.* Oxford: Oxford University Press.

Smith, G. (2009). *Democratic Innovations: Designing Institutions for Citizen Participation.* Cambridge: Cambridge University Press.

Smith, G. (2021). *Can Democracy Safeguard the Future?* Cambridge: Polity Press.

Stewart, E. (2021). Fugitive coproduction: Conceptualising informal community practices in Scotland's hospitals. *Social Policy & Administration* 55 (7), 1310 – 1324.

Torney, D. (2021). Deliberative mini-publics and the European Green Deal in turbulent times: The Irish and French Climate Assemblies. *Politics and Governance* 9 (3), 380 – 390.

Van Dijk, L., & Lefevere, J. (2022). Can the use of minipublics backfire? Examining how policy adoption shapes the effect of minipublics on political support among the general public. *European Journal of Political Research.* DOI 10.1111/1475 – 6765.12523

Wells, R., Howarth, C., & Brand-Correa, L. I. (2021). Are citizen juries and assemblies on climate change driving democratic climate policymaking? An exploration of two case studies in the UK. *Climatic Change* 168 (1), 1 – 22.

Wood, M. (2022). Can independent regulatory agencies mend Europe's democracy? The case of the European Medicines Agency's public hearing on Valproate. *The British Journal of Politics and International Relations* 24 (4), 607 – 630.

Antonin Lacelle-Webster and Mark E. Warren

8 A problem-based approach to citizens' assemblies

Abstract: Growing concerns with legitimacy deficits in democracies are motiving interest in CAs. These processes can address some of these deficits quite well, especially, citizen representation and considered deliberation of issues by non-elites. However, CAs are not the solution to every problem of democratic legitimacy. How should we understand their strengths and weaknesses within democratic systems? We address these questions by drawing on a problem-based approach to democracy. To count as a democratic, a political system must empower inclusions, form popular collective wills and agendas, and make decisions that provide collective goods, such that a people is acting on its own behalf. This framework allows us to theorize the contributions of CAs within the context of democratic systems. We examine seven sites of potential contributions: elections, ballot measures, legislatures, executive agencies, public spheres, political parties, and constitutional processes. This approach specifies and calibrates our expectations for CAs.

Keywords: democracy, problem-based approach, political institutions, political practices, deliberative democracy, democratic innovations, democratic systems, CAs

8.1 Introduction

Most democratic polities today are struggling with legitimacy deficits that manifest as political polarization, political disaffection, distrust of government, and sometimes as popular organization that can wield significant veto-powers over policies and governments. In the long-standing democracies, it is not likely that key democratic mechanisms such as elected representation will fail, not least because in these countries democratic values remain strong, despite the surprising strength of right-wing authoritarianism in some places such as the US (Norris 2011). But over time, legitimacy deficits can erode their capacities – on display, for example, in the many democracies that have struggled to manage the COVID-19 pandemic.

Can citizens be brought back on board through institutional supplements that deepen democracy? An increasingly popular approach is to initiate citizens' assemblies (CAs) (e. g., Setälä and Smith 2018). However, this popularity comes with risks: CAs are not solutions to every problem of democratic legitimacy. By design, they have strengths in representing citizens who are often marginalized in electoral democracy, and strengths in capturing the perspectives and wisdom of ordinary citizens, deliberating

Antonin Lacelle-Webster: University of British Columbia, Canada; **Mark E. Warren:** University of British Columbia, Canada.

🔓 Open Access. © 2023 the author(s), published by De Gruyter. (CC) BY-NC-ND This work is licensed under the Creative Commons Attribution-NonCommercial-NoDerivatives 4.0 International License. https://doi.org/10.1515/9783110758269-010

difficult issues, and finding win-win solutions. They appear to garner trust from citizens in ways that other political institutions do not (Warren and Gastil 2015). But, they also have limitations built into their design. They are often organized by political elites; they do not provide broad opportunities for political participation as they are closed processes so to be demographically representative; and they have limited capacities for broad, programmatic agenda-setting. Thus, what we expect of CAs, democratically speaking, should be appropriate to their design, as well as specific to their locations and roles within political systems (Jacquet 2019). We need to understand how and why CAs should be integrated into democratic systems, in ways that capitalize on their strengths, while avoiding uses that are likely to disappoint and undermine their legitimacy and the legitimacy of democratic systems (Curato and Böker 2016; Lafont 2019).

In this chapter, we ask: How should we understand the role of CAs in democratic systems, and in what ways can they strengthen democracy? We rely on a problem-based approach of democracy to help conceptualize how CAs might supplement the more familiar institutions of democratic political systems, and in what ways they might deepen democracies in doing so (Warren 2017). We first introduce the problem-based approach by focusing on its motivating question: What kinds of normative problems does a political system need to solve in order to count as "democratic"? To count as "democratic" a system needs to (a) empower inclusions of those affected by collective decisions, (b) form preferences and interests into collective agendas and wills, and then (c) convert these into collective decisions, such people rule over themselves. Second, we discuss seven sites within democratic systems through which CAs might serve one or more of these normative functions: elections, ballot measures, legislatures, executive agencies, public spheres, political parties, and constitutional processes. The democratic possibilities will vary by site, the structure and design of CAs, and their integration into political systems. We conclude that we should advocate for CAs in places where they can strengthen the deliberative and representative dimension of democratic polities, while looking to other kinds of institutions and practices for other democratic goods, such as broad citizen participation.

8.2 A problem-based approach to democratic theory

Problem-based approaches to democratic theory and practice have emerged over the last few years with the aim of moving beyond models of democracy that emphasize one kind of practice or norm, such as deliberative, participatory, electoral, republican, agonistic, or other of the many kinds of "democracy with adjectives" (Warren 2017; Bächtiger and Parkinson 2019). The model-based thinking that has dominated democratic theory over the last few decades has been useful in identifying and justifying specific democratic norms and practices (Held 2006). However, it has also made it difficult to think about democratic political systems, within which differing institutions and practices have distinct and often complementary, normative strengths. As Warren (2017: 41) puts it,

> [W]e might think that models are different answers to the same problem – usually the democratic legitimacy of political order. But what we actually get … is something more like the same answers (e.g., deliberation or elections) to different problems of democratic political organization (in particular, empowered inclusion, collective agenda and will formation, and collective decision making). Rather than modeling democracy after a mechanism, practice, or norm, we should build democratic theory as a set of responses to the question: What kinds of problems does a political system need to solve to function democratically?

Warren identifies three broad classes of functional problems, each with democratic normative justifications. First, political systems should empower the inclusion of those affected or potentially affected by collective decisions (Warren 2017: 44). Second, political systems should provide ways in which affected individuals can communicatively transform their interests, values, perspectives, and preferences into collective agendas and wills. Individuals should understand how their preferences relate to collective judgements and have the space and opportunities to justify their views, positions, and decisions to one another (Warren 2017: 44). Finally, political systems should empower the collective capacity to make and impose binding decisions to provide collective goods, thus empowering people as collective agents (Warren 2017: 45).

Political systems can achieve these normative functions through a range of practices associated with democracy such as deliberation, voting in competitive elections, recognizing others, representing, resisting and protesting, joining and exiting (Warren 2017: 45–51). Each kind of practice, either singly or combined into institutions, can be assessed according to their contributions to one or more of the three (normative) problems. Thus, for example, distributing equal rights to vote in competitive elections is a good way of empowering inclusion, but less good at communicating, as a vote is a signal rather than an argument. Deliberation is a good way of forming collective wills and agendas, but less good as a means of distributing empowerments. *Institutions* are typically combinations of these practices, and so can be assessed by the ways their constitutive practices address one or more of the problems a democratic system must address (e.g., Beauvais and Warren 2019; Jäske and Setälä 2020). A problem-based approach holds that no single practice or institution can address all three functions that make a political system "democratic." Rather, democratic systems rely on a complex ecosystem of political practices and institutions, each with strengths and weaknesses relative to these functions.

8.3 What problems of democracy can citizens' assemblies address?

This problem-based approach allows us to specify and calibrate our expectations of CAs. From a problem-based perspective, CAs combine two core democratic practices – representing and deliberating – in ways that can strengthen empowered inclusion and collective will-formation and may, sometimes, strengthen collective decision-making capacities. But they do so in very specific ways, inherent in their design. (1) They are composed of a (near) random sample of citizens selected to be representative of a relevant public. (2) They are typically tasked with a bounded issue, about which they learn, deliberate, and issue recommendations (Curato et al. 2021; Setälä and Smith 2018). These design features come with strengths and weaknesses relative to the three problems political systems must solve to count as "democratic."

With respect to empowered inclusion, CAs should be viewed as a representative institution rather than (say) a participatory one (Warren 2013; cf. Lafont 2019). By design, participation in CAs is limited to a very small sample of a population. They are closed to broader participation in order to (a) provide demographic representation of a relevant public, and (b) comprise a body small enough to engage in high-quality deliberation. What is gained is a form of representation that elected (e. g., legislatures) and self-selected (e. g., town hall meetings) institutions do not provide – namely, representation of those who are often marginalized along the cleavages of education, class, race, ethnicity, and/or sex (e. g., Fung 2007; Setälä and Smith 2018). And because CAs typically reflect issue constituencies, they can often represent publics that are not defined by existing territorial jurisdictions (Warren 2009). These contributions to empowered inclusion, however, come with trade-off among democratic goods. Issues must be defined and organized by the institutions that sponsor and organize CAs. With the exception of CAs attached to ballot measures, they have agendas set for them by political elites, and they are convened only when other institutions have the political will and capacity to do so (see Bussu and Fleuß in this *Handbook*). Likewise, their representative qualities depend upon institutions with the authority and capacity to select, invite, and convene. So, owing to their organizational and representative requirements, they are usually elite-driven, and provide only limited opportunities for political participation.

The deliberative qualities of CAs strongly support the capacities of political systems to form collective wills (Curato et al. 2021; Jäske and Setälä 2020). CAs are designed for high-quality deliberation, as they typically involve members learning about issues from experts and advocates, followed by facilitated deliberation aimed at producing recommendations. The selection process is also important for these collective will-formation functions. In contrast, say, to legislatures, because members of CAs have no strategic interests in election or re-election, deliberative processes are generally sheltered from strategic communications with constituents or strategic posturing in the media (Lacelle-Webster and Warren 2021). And because participants are near-randomly selected, those with intense interests and motivated reasoners are not over-represented, probably producing bodies that are better able to consider alternative viewpoints (Warren and Gastil 2015). This way of constituting a body is likely to bring a greater diversity of viewpoints, perspectives, and experiences – and the epistemic gains that follow – than bodies that are elected or self-selected (Mercier and Landemore 2012). Research does indeed show impressive epistemic results: members typically show a high capacity to learn about complex issues and reach considered judgements (e. g., Knobloch, Barthel and Gastil 2020; Lindell in this *Handbook*). They often do so without reverting to partisan cleavages, and they are often take long-term perspectives (Bächtiger and Goldberg 2020). There is some evidence that citizens within broader publics are more likely to trust CAs and their recommendations than they are to trust other kinds of political bodies or political elites (MacKenzie and Warren 2012; Warren and Gastil 2015).

Can CAs contribute to the third problem political systems need to solve to count as "democratic" – that is, the capacity to make decisions, such that a people can be said to govern itself? To date, CAs have not done so directly, as they are typically advisory rather than empowered bodies, although there is a lively debate as to whether such unelected bodies would be democratically legitimate (Lafont 2019; Gastil and Wright 2019; Landemore 2020; Courant 2021). But if CAs generate advice that citizens view as legitimate owing to other features – likely their demographic representativeness and their credible investments in learning and deliberation – then empowered bodies, particularly legislatures and bureaucracies, might borrow legitimacy and find their decision-making capacities increased. These effects might be greater if and when processes are formally coupled with representative institutions and processes, or with bureaucratic decision-making processes (Hendriks 2016; Mansbridge et al. 2012). Influences on collective decision-making capacities might also be greater when issues are tough, divisive, or deadlocked, as the Irish CAs on abortion and gay marriage demonstrated (Farrell and Suiter 2019) and was likely the case with a CA focused on a divisive urban planning process in Vancouver, Canada (Beauvais and Warren 2019). This said, we still know too little about how broader publics view CAs, despite some promising evidence (cf. Bächtiger and Goldberg 2020; Már and Gastil 2021; Warren and Gastil 2015; Goldberg in this *Handbook*).

8.4 Citizens' assemblies as democratic supplements to institutions

Beyond their core deliberative and representative features, CAs' designs, mandates, and locations in the political system remain contingent on a particular set of political circumstances, norms, and structures (Curato et al. 2021). CAs operate within ecosystems in which institutions and processes (e. g., elections, political parties, parliaments, social movements) may play distinct and complementary roles in deepening democracy. This kind of contingency provides a theoretical opportunity: we can analyse CAs not just as discrete institutions, but also through their potential democratic functions as parts of democratic systems.

In this section, we look at seven kinds of institutions within political systems, and discuss whether and how CAs might supplement them in ways that deepen democracy: elections, ballot measures, legislatures, executive agencies, public spheres, political parties, and constitutional processes (Table 8.1). While our approach is primarily theoretical, we are interested in developing middle-level theory that is sufficiently fine-grained to relate more focused, often case-study research to the broader contexts of democratic systems. We draw on recent examples to illustrate the ways in which CAs might address the problems a political system needs to solve to count as "democratic."

Table 8.1: Potentials for citizens' assemblies to strengthen democracy in political systems

Sites	Empower inclusion	Collective agenda and will formation	Collective decision- making
Elections	Representing typically excluded voices	Improving campaign-focused public deliberation, reducing partisan polarization	–
Ballot measures	Representing unorganized voters	Connecting learning and deliberation to voting	Connecting policy decisions to learning and deliberation
Legislatures	Expanding representation beyond organized interest groups	Providing legislatures with considered public opinion beyond organized interest groups	Providing legislatures with political cover for hard choices, enabling legislative leadership
Executive agencies	Expanding representation beyond organized interest groups	Defining constituency views and preferences	Increasing democratic legitimacy for agency policies and decisions
Public spheres	Expanding voice representation beyond organized interest and advocacy groups	Setting public agendas outside party platforms and negotiated coalitions; pushing back against epistemic bubbles, polarization	–
Political parties	–	Creating new narratives against elite intransigence or gridlock; transforming social movement issues into political agendas	–
Constitutional processes	Enabling a people to own constitutional processes	Enabling a people to connect democratic values to political processes	Providing constituent power for a people

8.4.1 Elections

Voting is a relatively strong way of empowering inclusions, and so we should see the supplementary value of CAs as primarily in connecting voting to considered public opinion. Public debate and deliberation during campaigns are often low information, highly polarized processes – indeed, so much so that much of the voting public will avoid or dismiss campaigns altogether, leaving public debate to highly intense partisans (Neblo et al. 2010). CAs could be proposed to deliberate campaign issues in advance of elections, with the aim of deepening collective agenda-setting. Their representative and deliberative qualities make it less likely that they will be colonized by polarizing partisans, and less likely to be coopted by the targeted framing practices of professional campaigners (Calvert and Warren 2014). This kind of supplementary use will depend, of course, on CAs themselves becoming sites of publicity, much like the staged debates in US presidential elections. The idea here is not to put aside conflicts, but rather to find ways to introduce more reflexivity into debates during moments of high political intensity, as well as introducing a more diverse set of voices and perspectives into election-focused public deliberation. This kind of possibility is not entirely fanciful: another kind of deliberative mini-publics, a Deliberative Poll called "America in One Room," was organized in the run-up to the 2020 US presidential election (America in One Room 2019). The process showed that Americans can, in fact, deliberate with one another, even within highly polarized contexts. The process gained some publicity, although not enough to penetrate the attention of most voters. Nonetheless, "America in One Room" showed that CA type processes could improve both the representativeness and quality of election-focused public deliberation.

8.4.2 Ballot measures

Like voting for representatives, ballot measures are strong ways of empowering inclusions. By their very nature, ballot measures have strong decision-making capacities – indeed, they are one of the only ways citizens can directly decide public policies in mass democracies As is well-known, however, their key weakness is that, when citizens vote, they often lack the knowledge and considered judgement to make good choices, particularly when the issues are complex (like the Brexit referendum), or important but not widely understood (as, say, with popular mandatory minimum sentences initiatives in the US). Low information voters are relatively easily swayed by well-funded advocacy campaigns, which tends to undermine the empowering potentials of ballot measures. A demonstration *ex-post* CA on Brexit showed that, if citizens had learned and deliberated about the proposal, a decisive number would have changed their votes (Renwick et al. 2018). Indeed, an increasingly common use of deliberative mini-publics is to convene them in advance of ballot initiatives and referendums. A CA can, potentially, raise the profile of an issue, induce citizens to learn more about the issue, or sometimes serve as a trusted information proxy (Warren and Pearse 2008; Gastil and Knobloch 2020). There are a few cases – notably in Ireland – in which CAs have been used to propose agendas that are then put to a referendum. Or, in less open-ended cases, CAs in British Columbia and Ontario, were tasked with setting electoral reform agendas in the form of a referendum question. As with voting for representatives, then, the most important contribution of CAs would be to strengthen collective will-formation. Again, there is some evidence that highly publicized CAs or similar deliberative mini-publics can improve citizen attentiveness and information in ways that deepen democracy by connecting their voting powers to collective will-formation (Warren and Gastil 2015).

8.4.3 Legislatures

Legislative bodies are, of course, the apex decision-making bodies in democratic political systems. Their weaknesses, however, include hard or stalemated issues, or issues where there are well-organized minorities that effectively hold veto power over broadly popular agenda items. These weaknesses are exacerbated by separated power systems that effectively require supermajorities for legislation, and by single member plurality electoral systems, which can often magnify political polarization. Moreover, legislative bodies are often subject to "democratic myopia" generated by electoral incentives that can prioritize short-term over long-term decision-making (MacKenzie 2021; Smith 2021). For example, the ways legislatures are addressing the climate crisis suggest weakness in their capacities to address long-term issue, indicative of more general failures to represent (non-voting) future generations. As advisory to legislatures, CAs can contribute by increasing collective decision-making capacities and providing citizen-based leadership against political deadlock, thus giving legislatures cover for taking on difficult issues, even against well-organized interest groups and veto players.

These kinds of capacities depend upon the new forms of representation that CAs provide as well as their visibility in forming and deliberating collective wills. The examples are not common, but they do exist. In the early 1980s, the Oregon state legislature pushed a Medicaid reform proposal into a set of public processes (Kitzhaber 1993). While not a CA process in the sense defined here, the case was important because it was the first time (we believe) that a legislature pushed a hard issue into a citizen-based deliberative process. More recently, the Irish parliament established CAs on the hard cases of abortion and gay marriage. They likely provided the political cover necessary for the legislature to establish referendums on the issues – both of which were overwhelmingly successful (Farrell et al. 2020). Similarly, "climate assemblies" are gaining traction with legislative bodies. In proposing ambitious solutions to the climate crisis, CAs can provide political cover and legitimacy for legislative actions. However, there is also a risk that without a clear understanding of their functions in democratic systems and implications, CAs might also serve as political cover for legislative inaction, (Willis, Curato, and Smith 2022), a hazard that is likely lessened when they are paired with civil society advocacy and public sphere publicity.

There are some cases in which CAs are used more formally to set legislative agendas. For instance, in Paris and Ostbelgien, the German-speaking Community of Belgium, there are now standing CAs tasked with agenda-setting (OECD 2021). The Ostbelgien case is the first example of a permanent CA directly linked to the parliamentary system (see Niessen and Reuchamps 2022; OECD 2021, 12–14). This process is designed around a Citizens' Council composed of 24 randomly selected members, tasked with initiating, and organizing up to three CAs every year, and following up on their recommendations. These CAs issue policy recommendations and take part in three joint sessions with elected representatives to discuss the recommendations (Niessen and Reuchamps 2022, 149), in this way connecting CAs with legislative processes. The Council of Paris also recently instituted a permanent CA linked directly to its legislative functions (OECD 2021, 14–17). This body is composed of 100 members selected by lot and can, importantly, organize a citizen's jury on a particular topic and submit its recommendation as a local bill to the Council of Paris. In addition, it can submit current affairs questions to the Council, initiate an evaluation process of a public policy once every year, submit non-binding "wishes" during the council sessions, and decide the themes for participatory budgeting processes. What distinguishes these two examples are the careful ways in which standing CAs are integrated into legislative processes.

8.4.4 Executive agencies

By far the most common uses of CAs to date have been in policy-defined governance spaces, organized primarily by executive agencies and ministries. Their most important democratizing function is to increase collective decision capacities by generating democratic legitimacy for governance domains defined by agency mandates. The reasons are not difficult to find. In the post-WWII era, governments grew in their mandates and size, enabling legislation directed agencies and ministries to consult with "stakeholders," "communities," or other such terms meant to indicate that agencies have constituencies that are more intensively interested or affected by the issues within an agency's domain or mandate. Moreover, whatever legitimacy is generated by elections often fails to feed through to the agencies that actually carry out government and governance (Warren 2009). Increasingly, agencies seek to generate democratic legitimacy with citizens assembly-like processes (OECD 2020). Sometimes, CAs function as democratic push-back against well-organized pressure and interest groups, driven by professionals who recognize that they serve poorly organized or marginalized constituencies (e. g., Beauvais and Warren 2019). In other cases, agencies may seek proactively public guidance on issues that have little public profile, but might generate public backlash should they go sideways, as (for example) genomic research-driven biobanking proposals have the potential to do, should they come to be viewed as a reservoir of personal information to be exploited by for-profit pharmaceutical companies (MacKenzie and Warren 2012). For these kinds of issues, CAs can proactively probe where public interest might develop, particularly in response to executive agency policymaking. CAs can help agencies avoid missteps and false starts in sensitive areas of policy (Lafont 2019: 158–59). Although the key democratic contributions of CAs here involve building out collective decision capacities, these contributions build on empowering inclusions of those poorly represented through other processes, as well as forming collective wills. Collective agendas, in these cases, are elite-driven, indirectly by legislatures, and directly by agencies and ministries.

8.4.5 Public spheres

Free and open public spheres are essential to democracy, particularly in forming collective agendas and wills. Many different kinds of actors comprise publics, including the media, social movements, and advocacy and interest groups. While it is possible to do a fine-grained analysis of these highly pluralistic domains (Cohen and Arato 1992; Habermas 1996), public spheres have in common a dynamic of self-selection: individuals join, exit (follow or ignore) groups and media, in such a way that public spheres often lack the deliberative qualities that strongly democratic public spheres should have. Nowhere is this more evident today than in social media, which reinforces and intensifies epistemic bubbles, low information, polarization, and other features of public spheres that undermine collective agenda and will formation (McKay and Tenove 2021). But similar kinds of weaknesses are evident across the landscape of self-selected associations, groups, and organizations. We know that the representative qualities of these kinds of groups often exclude interests that are unorganized or marginal. Social movements and public interest advocacy groups are, typically, more sensitive – but also require high levels of organizational skills, pursued over long periods of time, groups (Warren 2001). Other kinds of interest groups seek to set agendas in non-public ways, especially through lobbying, and sometimes, in the cases of industry groups, through threats of disinvestment. In all such cases, CAs have two democratic advantages: their demographically representative qualities help to provide voice for those who are less organized or otherwise marginalized, and they can do so without the enormous resources required for effective social movement, advocacy, or political organization. CAs can push back against epistemic bubbles, polarization, and low information, just because they do not self-select for motivated reasoners (America in One Room 2019). They are thus likely to supplement existing vectors of public agenda-setting with empowered inclusions and collective agenda-setting.

This said, there are currently only few cases of this kind of use of CAs. Interest groups and advocacy groups may have fraught relationships with deliberative minipublics (Hendriks 2006; Vrydagh, Devillers and Reuchamps 2020). For instance, Gastil and Knobloch (2020: 161) discuss a case in which an interest group – the Washington State's teachers' union – ran against a Washington ballot initiative to establish a Citizens' Initiative Review process (which attaches citizen juries to ballot initiatives), probably because the union was unwilling to dilute their own public influence with the uncertainties of a representative and deliberative process. But there are also a few cases of social movements asking for CAs on issues that are gridlocked at elite levels, and where movements judge that the public is on their side (e. g., Extinction Rebellion, Fair Vote Canada). CAs can help democratize collective agenda and will formation, while contributing to empowered inclusion by providing a voice for those who may be poorly represented by social movements, and advocacy and interest groups.

8.4.6 Political parties

Political parties translate public agendas into actionable legislative agendas, and they gain the powers to do so by putting together coalitions that can win elections. On average, we should not expect political parties to be friendly to CAs. Because they operate within competitive electoral systems, parties are and must be strategic actors. They do, of course, contribute to public deliberation as strategic participants. They seek to convert public positions into votes, and votes into legislative power. Of course, there are important differences in political parties owing largely to differing electoral and constitutional systems. But because in all democracies parties operate in competitive environments, we should expect their partisan natures to exclude public interests and win-win solutions for which there is no electoral advantage, and often to increase polarization around non-negotiable identity issues. Parties often do not reflect or represent marginalized citizens and "moderate" citizens who are interested in public interest platforms, negotiated solutions, but who "hate politics" (Neblo et al. 2010). This said, especially in contexts within which big tent brokerage parties (e. g., Canada's Liberal Party or Germany's Christian Democrats) find themselves losing vote shares, parties may become more open to representative deliberative processes such as CAs (e. g., Gherghina and Jacquet 2022). Were this to happen, CAs could strengthen collective agenda and will formation through political parties (Kuyper and Wolkenstein 2019). However, we have yet to see such developments, and we probably should not expect to see them until parties find strategic advantages in using these kinds of processes.

8.4.7 Constitutional processes

Finally, CAs can be used to recommend constitutional processes. The broad democratic argument is that establishing or reforming constitutions is something that should be owned by the people, at least in the form of a representative process, and that the task is complex enough to require a long-form deliberative process (Fishkin 2018; Reuchamps and Suiter 2016). Used within constitutional processes, CAs could, in principle, contribute to all three democratic functions: empowering inclusion through demographic representation, strengthening collective agenda and will formation, and underwriting decision capacities. We have seen examples of CAs for limited constitutional reform – specifically, electoral system reform – in British Columbia and Ontario, Canada, in both cases combined with referendums (Fournier et al. 2011; Warren and Pearse

2008). Similarly, Ireland's CAs on abortion and gay marriage were both constitutional reform issues (Farrell, Suiter, and Harris 2019). Iceland convened a much more extensive process that included CA processes in the aftermath of the 2008 financial crisis that undermined public confidence in political elites, although the process was, in effect, set aside by political elites after it was concluded (Landemore 2015; 2020). The fate of Iceland's process raises the question as to what kind of constituencies such constitutional processes would need to be successful – a question that probably does not have generalizable theoretical answers. And there is some new thinking about the roles that representative deliberative processes might play in post-conflict contexts within which political elites have little or no broad popular credibility (Levy, O'Flynn, and Kong 2021)

8.5 Conclusion: What cizizens' assemblies can and cannot do

CAs can, potentially, supplement political systems in ways that make them more democratic, particularly in those sites and venues that could benefit from better representation, and higher quality collective agenda and will-formation. Approaching this question from the standpoint of a problem-based approach to democratic theory helps to identify the site-specific ways in which CAs might deepen democracy by supplementing the more familiar and traditional institutions of democratic political systems. However, there are many kinds of democratic functions that CAs cannot address or address only weakly owing to their design. Their limitations include the following:

a) CAs are usually elite-driven in their definition, organization, and scope, and so usually have limited collective agenda-setting powers.

b) As closed processes, they are not highly participatory, meaning that vectors of empowered inclusion work only through representative relationships.

c) Because they are comprised of non-professionals, they will have limited technical expertise, in contrast to (say) agencies and even legislative committees.

d) Because they are not partisan, their motivational attractions may remain weaker than parties and advocacy groups, although much research remains to understand the incentives of publics, partisans, and governments to support them.

e) We still need to understand the relationship between CAs, and the (democratic) hazards that accompany their integration into political systems, such as capture by special interests, their degrees of autonomy or connection, and the dangers that they may be convened primarily for elites to claim them for political show ("democracy washing").

This said, when we calibrate our expectations to fit with the design of CAs and their potentials to supplement institutions within democratic systems, they count as one of the most important innovations we currently have to revitalize and deepen democratic political systems.

References

America in One Room. 2019. Stanford Center for Deliberative Democracy. https://cdd.stanford.edu/2019/america-in-one-room/.

Bächtiger, A., & Goldberg, S. (2020). Towards a more robust, but limited and contingent defense of the political uses of deliberative minipublics. *Journal of Deliberative Democracy* 16, 33–42.

Bächtiger, A., & Parkinson, J. (2019). *Mapping and measuring deliberation: Towards a New Deliberative Quality.* Oxford: Oxford University Press.

Beauvais, E., & Warren , M. E. (2019). What can deliberative mini-publics contribute to democratic systems? *European Journal of Political Research* 58 (3), 893–914.

Calvert, A., & Warren, M. E. (2014). Deliberative democracy and framing effects: Why frames are a problem and how deliberative mini-publics might overcome them. In K. Grönlund, A. Bächtiger, & M. Setälä (eds), *Deliberative Mini-Publics: Involving Citizens in the Democratic Process*, 203–246. Colchester: ECPR Press.

Cohen, J., & Arato, A. (1992). *Civil Society and Political Theory.* Cambridge. MA: MIT Press.

Courant, D. (2021). Institutionalizing deliberative mini-publics? Issues of legitimacy and power for randomly selected assemblies in political systems. *Critical Policy Studies* 16 (2), 162–180.

Curato, N., & Böker, M. (2016). Linking mini-publics to the deliberative system: A research agenda. *Policy Sciences* 49 (2), 173–190.

Curato, N., Farrell, D. M., Geissel, B., Grönlund, K., Mockler, P., Pilet, J.-B., Renwick, A., Rose, J., Setälä, M., & Suiter, J. (2021). *Deliberative Mini-Publics: Core Design Features.* Bristol: Bristol University Press.

Farrell, D. M., & Suiter, J. (2019). *Reimagining Democracy: Lessons in Deliberative Democracy from the Irish Front Line.* Ithaca, NY: Cornell University Press.

Farrell, D. M., Suiter, J., Cunningham, K., & Harris, C. (2020). When mini-publics and maxi-publics coincide: Ireland's national debate on abortion. *Representation* https://doi.org/10.1080/00344893.2020.1804441

Farrell, D. M., Suiter, J., & Harris, C. (2019). 'Systematizing' constitutional deliberation: The 2016–18 Citizens' Assembly in Ireland. *Irish Political Studies* 34 (1), 113–123.

Fishkin, J. S. (2018). *Democracy When The People Are Thinking: Revitalizing Our Politics Through Public Deliberation.* Oxford: Oxford University Press.

Fournier, P., van der Kolk, H., Carty, R. K., Blais, A., & Rose, J. (2011). *When Citizens Decide: Lessons from Citizen Assemblies on Electoral Reform.* New York: Oxford University Press.

Fung, A. 2007. Democratic theory and political science: A pragmatic method of constructive engagement. *American Political Science Review* 101 (3), 443–458.

Gastil, J., & Knobloch, K. R. (2020). *Hope for Democracy: How Citizens can Bring Reason Back into Politics.* Oxford: Oxford University Press.

Gastil, J., & Wright, E. O. (2019). *Legislature by Lot: Transformative Designs for Deliberative Governance.* London: Verso.

Gherghina, S., & Jacquet, V. (2022). Why political parties use deliberation: A framework for analysis. *Acta Politica*, February.

Habermas, J. (1996). *Between Facts and Norms: Contributions to Discourse Theory of Law and Democracy.* Cambridge, MA: The MIT Press.

Held, D. (2006). *Models of Democracy.* Third edition. Redwood City, CA: Stanford University Press.

Hendriks, C. M. (2006). Integrated deliberation: Reconciling civil society's dual role in deliberative democracy. *Political Studies* 54 (3), 486–508.

Hendriks, C. M. (2016). Coupling citizens and elites in deliberative systems: The role of institutional design. *European Journal of Political Research* 55 (1), 43–60.

Jacquet, V. (2019). The role and the future of deliberative mini-publics: A citizen perspective. *Political Studies* 67 (3), 639–657.

Jäske, M., & Setälä, M. (2020). A functionalist approach to democratic innovations. *Representation* 56 (4), 467–483.

Kitzhaber, J. A. (1993). Prioritising health services in an era of limits: The Oregon experience. *British Medical Journal* 307, 373–377.

Knobloch, K. R., Barthel, M. L., & Gastil, J. (2020). Emanating effects: The impact of the Oregon Citizens' Initiative Review on voters' political efficacy. *Political Studies* 68 (2), 426–445.

Kuyper, J. W., & Wolkenstein, F. (2019). Complementing and correcting representative institutions: When and how to use mini-publics. *European Journal of Political Research* 58 (2) 656–675.

Lacelle-Webster, A., & Warren, M. E. (2021). CAs and democracy. *Oxford Research Encyclopedia of Politics.* https://doi.org/10.1093/acrefore/9780190228637.013.1975.

Lafont, C. (2019). *Democracy Without Shortcuts: A Participatory Conception of Deliberative Democracy.* Oxford: Oxford University Press.

Landemore, H. (2015). Inclusive constitution-making: The Icelandic experiment: Inclusive constitution making. *Journal of Political Philosophy* 23 (2), 166–191.

Landemore, H. (2020). *Open Democracy: Reinventing Popular Rule for the Twenty-First Century.* Princeton, NJ: Princeton University Press.

Levy, R., O'Flynn, I., & Kong, H. L. (2021). *Deliberative Peace Referendums.* Oxford: Oxford University Press.

MacKenzie, M. K. (2021). *Future Publics: Democracy, Deliberation, and Future-Regarding Collective Action.* Oxford: Oxford University Press.

MacKenzie, M. K., & Warren, M. E. (2012). Two trust-based uses of minipublics in democratic systems. In J. Parkinson & J. Mansbridge (eds), *Deliberative Systems: Deliberative Democracy at the Large Scale*, 95–124. Cambridge: Cambridge University Press.

Mansbridge, J., Bohman, J., Chambers, S., Christiano, T., Fung, A., Parkinson, J., Thompson, D. F., & Warren, M. E. (2012). A systemic approach to deliberative democracy. In J. Parkinson & J. Mansbridge (eds), *Deliberative Systems: Deliberative Democracy at the Large Scale*, 1–26. Cambridge: Cambridge University Press.

Már, K., & Gastil, J. (2021). Do voters trust deliberative minipublics? Examining the origins and impact of legitimacy perceptions for the Citizens' Initiative Review. *Political Behavior.* https://doi.org/10.1007/s11109-021-09742-6.

McKay, S., & Tenove, C. (2021). Disinformation as a threat to deliberative democracy. *Political Research Quarterly* 74 (3), 703–17.

Mercier, H., & Landemore, H. (2012). Reasoning is for arguing: Understanding the successes and failures of deliberation. *Political Psychology* 33 (2), 243–258.

Neblo, M. A., Esterling, K. M., Kennedy, R. P., Lazer, D. M. J., & Sokhey, A. E. (2010). Who wants to deliberate—and why? *American Political Science Review* 104 (3), 566–583.

Niessen, C., and Reuchamps, M. (2022). Institutionalising citizen deliberation in parliament: The permanent citizens' dialogue in the German-speaking Community of Belgium. *Parliamentary Affairs* 75 (1), 135–153.

Norris, P. (2011). *Democratic Deficit: Critical Citizens Revisited.* New York: Cambridge University Press.

OECD. (2020). *Innovative Citizen Participation and New Democratic Institutions: Catching the Deliberative Wave.* Paris: OECD Publishing.

OECD. (2021). *Eight Ways to Institutionalise Deliberative Democracy.* OECD Public Governance Policy Papers. Paris.

Renwick, A., Allan, S., Jennings, W., McKee, R., Russell, M., & Smith, G. (2018). What kind of Brexit do voters want? Lessons from the Citizens' Assembly on Brexit. *The Political Quarterly* 89 (4), 649–658.

Reuchamps, M., & Suiter, J. (eds). (2016). *Constitutional Deliberative Democracy in Europe.* Colchester: ECPR Press.

Setälä, M., & Smith, G. (2018). Mini-publics and deliberative democracy. In A. Bächtiger, J. S. Dryzek, J. Mansbridge, & M. E. Warren (eds), *The Oxford Handbook of Deliberative Democracy*, 300–314. Oxford: Oxford University Press.

Smith, G. (2021). *Can Democracy Safeguard the Future?* Cambridge: Polity.

Vrydagh, J., Devillers, S., & Reuchamps, M. (2020). The integration of deliberative mini-publics in collaborative governance through the perspectives of citizens and stakeholders: The case of the education reform in French-speaking Belgium. *Representation*, December, 1–22. https://doi.org/10.1080/00344893.2020.1853599.

Warren, M. E. (2001). *Democracy and Association.* Princeton, NJ: Princeton University Press.

Warren, M. E. (2009). Governance-driven democratization. *Critical Policy Studies* 3 (1), 3–13.

Warren, M. E. (2013). Citizen representatives. In J. Nagel & R.Smith (eds), *Representation: Elections and Beyond*, 269–294. College Station: Pennsylvania State University Press.

Warren, M. E. (2017). A problem-based approach to democratic theory. *American Political Science Review* 111 (1), 39–53.

Warren, M. E., & Gastil, J. (2015). Can deliberative minipublics address the cognitive challenges of democratic citizenship? *The Journal of Politics* 77 (2), 562–574.

Warren, M. E., & Pearse, H. (eds). 2008. *Designing Deliberative Democracy: The British Columbia Citizens' Assembly.* Cambridge: Cambridge University Press.

Willis, R., Curato, N., & Smith, G. (2022). Deliberative democracy and the climate crisis. *WIREs Climate Change*, no. September 2021, 1–14.

Stephen Elstub and Zohreh Khoban

9 Citizens' assemblies: A critical perspective

Abstract: There are a number of significant concerns about the democratic legitimacy of CAs. In this chapter we identify six of the most prominent critiques. Firstly, that members of the public do not have the capacity to engage in meaningful deliberation and decision-making. Secondly, that CAs do not contest power relationships in society. Thirdly, that they are excessively manipulated spaces, with participants having little control over their own agendas. Fourthly, that they are easily co-opted by public authorities and have little policymaking impact. Fifthly, they only include small numbers of participants, and therefore exclude most of the public from deliberation and decision-making. Sixthly, because they are representative, they do not do enough to promote the voice and interests of minorities and marginalized groups. While these problems are significant, we conclude by arguing that CAs can provide democratic value in the right circumstances.

Keywords: Deliberative democracy, deliberative systems, CAs, mini-publics, political participation, representation, power, agenda-setting, co-option, inequality

9.1 Introduction

Citizens' assemblies (CAs) have been lauded as one of the best ways to institutionalise deliberative democracy (Curato et al. 2021; Landemore 2020). Recently we have seen a significant increase in the number of CAs being used to enable representative samples of the public engage in informed deliberation on topical issues and make policy recommendations on how to address these issues (OECD 2020; Paulis et al. 2020). The extent that this trend is a good thing for democracy is disputed. There are a number of significant concerns about the democratic legitimacy of CAs. In this chapter we identify, and consider, six of the most prominent critiques. Firstly, that members of the public do not have the capacity to engage in meaningful deliberation and decision-making. Secondly, that CAs do not contest power relationships in society that is the essence of democracy. Thirdly, that they are excessively manipulated spaces, with participants having little control over their own agendas, evidence, and programme of activities. Fourthly, that they are easily co-opted by public authorities and have little policymaking impact, and are consequently often symbolic exercises. Fifthly, they only include small numbers of participants, and therefore exclude most of the public from deliberation and decision-making, representing an unacceptable short-cut to the institutionalization of deliberative democracy. Sixthly, because they are representative, they do not do enough to promote the voice and interests of minorities and marginalized groups who are most

Stephen Elstub: Newcastle University, UK; Zohreh Khoban: Uppsala University, Sweden.

Open Access. © 2023 the author(s), published by De Gruyter. (CC) BY-NC-ND This work is licensed under the Creative Commons Attribution-NonCommercial-NoDerivatives 4.0 International License. https://doi.org/10.1515/9783110758269-011

adversely affected by the policy issues. In this sense they exacerbate inequalities rather than alleviate them. While these problems are significant, we do not think they are terminal for the democratic legitimacy of CAs. Rather, we argue they can be mitigated if we take a deliberative systems approach and CAs are democratized, appropriately linked with other democratic institutions, and legally embedded in political systems. We deal with each critique in turn, before proving our defence.

9.2 Critique 1: Public incapacity

The first critique dates back to, at least, ancient Athens and Plato (2007). The argument is that the public do not have the capacity to meaningfully deliberate and make decisions on the complex issues that society faces. CAs are therefore dangerous for the effective functioning of the political system. Schumpeter (1952) concluded that there was no will of the people, as the public are incapable of forming one. He distinguished between the market and the forum to explain why. People are capable of rational choices when purchasing as they will be affected directly by the decision. However, most public policies only affect certain groups in society directly so there is little incentive for the unaffected to become informed about these issues. Consequently, their views are irrational, impulsive, prejudicial, and easily swayed by advertising, rhetoric, and propaganda. Similarly, Converse (1964) argues that the public have "non-attitudes" on public issues, which are inconsistent and fluctuate greatly, due to low levels of knowledge. For Zaller (1992), this means public opinion can be "induced" by political elites. Each concludes that democracy can, at best, be competition between political elites, facilitated by elections. The only involvement of the public in democratic decision-making is to vote periodically to select who will make decisions on their behalf. Downs (1957) argues, as a result, that public ignorance, and political apathy, are actually rational choices, as each individual has such a small chance of affecting public policy decisions in an election. These arguments were presented before the proliferation of CAs, and Böker and Elstub (2015) argue that empirical evidence from mini-publics challenges these arguments as it has demonstrated that, in the right circumstances, where participants engage with a range of information and views in a facilitated, supportive, and inclusive environment, people can deliberate complex issues and develop informed and coherent views. Furthermore, they argue that, theoretically, if mini-publics afford their participants meaningful opportunities to influence policy through credible institutional links with legislatures, governments, and referendums, they can mitigate the "rational" incentives not to engage. Nevertheless, "public incapacity" arguments have been resurrected and aimed specifically at deliberative democracy; labelled as "an idealistic version of liberalism" (Achen and Bartels 2016: 217) or a "fantasy" (Brennan 2016: 60) due to being based on naive perceptions of the public's capacity to reason and become informed. Whilst they do acknowledge that mini-publics are "creative" (Achen and Bartels 2016: 2) and provide "evidence that this kind of moderated deliberation can work" (Brennan 2016: 66), they have concerns about their scalability to political systems as a whole. Achen and Bartles (2016) refer to the lack of influence the British Co-lombia CAon electoral reform had on the broader public,[1] whilst Brennan (2016) is con-cerned they will become overly politicized if given decision-making authority and as a result pressurized by partisan political bodies such as parties and interest groups.

9.3 Critique 2: A neglect of power

CAs can be criticized from radical views of democracy that see any political order as the expression of particular power relations. This critique is rooted in an understand-ing of democracy as disruptions of the established order. It is usually either anti-institu-tional or opposes the deliberative democratic ideal of free and unconstrained public deliberation.

Rancière exemplifies the anti-institutional strand of radical democracy. He argues that the administrative and distributive arrangements that normally goes by the name of politics, and which he calls "the police", inevitably rest on norms that decide who is included and excluded and who is entitled to govern others and who is not (Rancière 1999). In other words, the police order determines hierarchical relationships between human beings. For Rancière, politics proper implies a disruption of the police order. It occurs when a group that is excluded from the political community asserts its equality by undoing the naturalness of the police order. From this perspective, inclusive and democratic politics cannot be institutionalized – not even through CAs, which aim to select a diverse body of citizens. Politics, which for Rancière always means democratic politics, is rare, sporadic and temporary, and comes as a surplus to the established po-litical order (Rancière 1999, 2001).

Wolin also offers an anti- and extra-institutional account of democracy. He charac-terizes democracy as a "rebellious moment" that is "doomed to succeed only tempora-rily" (Wolin 1996: 43). Thus, democracy, for Wolin, is not a form of government or social life – it is a spontaneous moment of rupture carried along by uprisings and revolu-tions. Consequently, Wolin conceives democracy as only existing outside of established institutions. He asserts that the institutionalization of politics "marks the attenuation of democracy: leaders begin to appear; hierarchies develop; experts of one kind or an-other cluster around the centres of decision; order, procedure, and precedent displace a more spontaneous politics" (Wolin 1996: 39). From such a perspective, CAs are funda-mentally anti-democratic because, like other formal political institutions, they are in-evitably governed by rules, procedures, and norms of practice. This remains the case even if the CA is convened by a civil society organization or social movement as it will still be operating in a rigged and biased system. Hammond (2020) argues that de-liberative processes can be systems disruptors but to do so the established norms of the

---

1 See Jacquet and Minsart's chapter in this *Handbook* on 'The impact of citizens' assemblies on policy-making', for a further discussion of this case.

CA format (e.g. participant recruitment, evidence provision, discussion facilitation) need to be relaxed, with the focus on the number, rather than the design of social spaces for deliberation, and aiming to generate societal debate rather than to influence policy.

In addition to the anti-institutional critique, radical democrats have criticized the deliberative democratic ideal of free and unconstrained, rational, argumentation. Most notably, Mouffe (1999) argues that the deliberative democratic idea to ground legitimacy on pure rationality fails to recognize the link between legitimacy and power. For Mouffe, rules and processes that are believed to be rational or natural are in fact always constrained by, and supportive of, particular power relations (Mouffe 1999, 2005). Hence the main task of democracy cannot be to eliminate power – but to acknowledge and transform power relations by enabling diversity and conflict (Mouffe 1999). According to this view, the deliberative democratic quest for public reasoning and mutual understanding, which is usually adopted by CAs, forecloses possibilities for democratic politics.

The deliberative idea of rational argumentation has also been criticized by so-called "difference democrats". While these scholars usually do not reject the whole project of deliberative democracy, they argue that there are good reasons to believe that marginalized groups' arguments and modes of expression will be perceived as unreasonable in deliberation, especially if they threaten the position of advantaged groups (e.g., Williams 2000; Young 1996). In short, these theorists claim that the norms of deliberation often operate as forms of power, and risk excluding and constraining certain voices and kinds of people. To resist such exclusions, they encourage deliberative democrats to tolerate group-based struggles, and to allow for other forms of reason-giving than rational argumentation (Williams 2000; Young 1996). This certainly poses a challenge to CAs as they are usually conducted.

9.4 Critique 3: Manipulated spaces

CAs are often commissioned by parliaments and governments (OECD 2020). Although they are sometimes called for by civil society organizations and social movements, public authorities are often in charge of their design. This has given rise to strong criticism. Scholars have argued that institutional engineering from the centre of political power has inherent control mechanisms that tames radical energy and gives government authorities control over political processes and discourses (Blaug 2002; Böker 2017).

CAs, as with all mini-publics, are certainly highly artificial and controlled spaces. However, not all control mechanisms are destructive. Some of them are meant to be positive for the institutionalization of deliberative democracy. For example, there is control over who can participate to ensure diversity, and the discussions are facilitated to promote deliberative norms (Elstub 2014). Nevertheless, other common characteristics risk being manipulative and having less positive consequences for deliberative democracy. These include elite control of the assembly agenda and the information and evidence fed into the assembly. We deal with each in turn.

Firstly, the remits of CAs are usually pre-determined by the commissioning authorities and are therefore "elite-driven" (Warren 2009: 6). This can be done instrumentally and strategically to advance the interests of political elites (Dryzek and Tucker 2008). Agenda-setting is the stage of the CA process where the "mobilisation of bias is at its highest" (Smith 2001: 84) as the assembly remit generates a path-dependency that determines most aspects of the design of the process (Goodin 2005; Elstub et al. 2021a). For Richardson (2010: 184), this means that CAs "will tell us little of value about the popular will" as the pre-determined agenda means we do not know what the public's policy priorities are, just what they think about the issue they have been asked to reflect on.

Secondly, in CAs, the information, and the experts and advocates that provide it, are selected by the assembly organizers. These choices frame the debate on the issue and can heavily influence the outcome of the assembly (Fournier et al. 2011; Elstub et al. 2021a). Smith and Wales' (2000: 58) point about citizens' juries seems to apply equally to CAs that "there is a danger that even before citizens are directly involved, issues, information and witnesses might be mobilised out of the process" (see also Roberts et al. 2020 and Curato et al. 2021). To mitigate this danger balanced advisory boards usually select relevant experts and advocates to speak to the assembly members and guide them on, and review, the specific information to provide, and the manner in which they provide it (Elstub 2014). Whilst this type of oversight is essential, it is not sufficient to prevent manipulation as it "recreates existing power relationships" (Roberts et al. 2020: 7). Indeed, CAs have been criticized for excluding interest groups and thereby promoting co-opted processes rather than an open, and inclusive dialogue (Elstub 2014; Böker and Elstub 2015). This is important as research indicates that it is the information provided that has the greatest influence on the opinions of mini-public participants (Goodin and Niemeyer 2003; Setälä, Grönlund and Herne 2010; Thompson et al. 2021). This is also the case in CAs specifically, especially early on in the assembly when the participants learn the most (Elstub et al. 2021a).

Because Böker and Elstub (2015: 5) see deliberative democracy as a critical theory that opposes illegitimate hierarchies and elitist governance structures, they see the manipulation of the agenda and information in a CA as significantly compromising the contribution they can make to institutionalizing deliberative democracy. This is a more acute problem for CAs than smaller mini-publics, with fewer participants, as they allow less citizen control over the process than citizens' juries and consensus conferences, for example (Elstub 2014).

9.5 Critique 4: Symbolic engagement

The impact of mini-publics on policy is unclear and difficult to assess despite extensive research in this area (Jacquet and van der Does 2021). As a result, one of the most persistent critiques of mini-publics is that they are benign and easily co-opted by public authorities who organize them for symbolic reasons, to provide a veil of legitimacy to elitist policymaking and to make it look as though they are enabling the public to have a say, when the decisions have already been made (Dryzek and Goodin 2006; Böker and Elstub 2015; Curato et al. 2021). Indeed, even when it appears that a mini-publics' recommendations have been implemented by a public authority, this could be the result of "cherry-picking" and "retro-fitting", whereby authorities select recommendations they already planned to implement and ignore the others that they do not support (Smith and Wales 2000; Andrews et al. 2022). Consequently, mini-publics have been criticized as potentially "becom[ing] useful legitimating devices for an already decided policy" (Pateman 2012: 9). If the recommendations do not align with the public authority's initial priorities then they are unlikely to be adopted (Vrydagh 2022). The danger is then that they are a "tokenistic consultative exercise convened to legitimize predetermined policy outcomes" (Curato et al. 2021: 107). Other stakeholders, opposed to the recommendations, may critique the mini-public in order to prevent their uptake (Dryzek 2010: 27).

However, CAs are often linked with other democratic institutions in order to overcome this critique. They have preceded referendums (Farrell et al. 2020), and been linked with governments (OECD 2020) and parliaments (Beswick and Elstub 2019; Elstub at al. 2021a; Elstub et al. 2021b) in order to give them some leverage in the political system. The outputs of a CA are usually detailed policy recommendations which make it easier to see if they have been implemented and thereby hold the relevant policymakers to account. According to some studies these institutional features are seeing the recommendations emerging from CAs being increasingly adopted into policy (OECD 2020; Paulis et al. 2020).[2] As a result the emancipatory potential of CAs is greater than other types of mini-public (Böker and Elstub 2015).

Nevertheless, CAs remain susceptible to the symbolic engagement critique. In Gdansk, the Mayor has committed to implementing any CA recommendations that receive over 80 per cent support (Carson and Gerwin 2018). But this is still ultimately influence at the discretion of the elected representatives. Even with CAs where there is a prior commitment to implement recommendations, implementation does not necessarily happen as was the case with Convention Citoyenne pour le Climat (Courant 2020). In other cases, policy impact is reduced due to the absence of clear plans to deal with the recommendations (Elstub et al. 2021a). Even in Ireland, which has some of the most celebrated CAs producing recommendations on abortion and marriage equality which were adopted into legislation via referendums and parliament, most of the other recommendations have not been picked up (Harris 2019). Cherry-picking is rife then even with the CA model.

---

2 Although see Vrydagh (2022) for a critique of the approach adopted by these studies to assessing the policy impact of mini-publics.

9.6 Critique 5: A short-cut to deliberative democracy

In order to facilitate both genuine deliberation, and a diversity of experiences and perspectives, CAs usually consist of around 100 participants. One of the loudest criticisms against these institutions has been that the small numbers of participants generate a problematic or illegitimate short-cut to deliberative democracy. According to Chambers (2009), a full theory of deliberative democracy needs to include the mass public. She warns that abandoning the mass public in favour of institutionally bounded deliberation risks sending deliberative democracy on a path toward participatory elitism. Making a distinction between "deliberative democracy" and "democratic deliberation", Chambers argues that mini-publics are exercises in the latter and thus only internally democratic. She considers them to be fully democratic to the extent that they can convince the general public that they have made policy choices worth pursuing. Chambers therefore emphasizes the importance of deliberation in the mass public sphere and the deliberativeness of the political system as a whole.

Lafont (2015) offers a similar, albeit more pessimistic, account of mini-publics. She asserts that a deliberative assembly of randomly selected participants does not provide any mechanisms of direct authorization and accountability to the wider citizen body (see also Parkinson 2006). At the same time, participants in that assembly might change opinions as a result of their internal discussions, and end up in a position that is not representative of the broader public. Granting these participants decision-making powers is, according to Lafont, in line with elite models of democracy, which ask citizens to blindly defer to the deliberations of a few. While the participants might very well end up being more knowledgeable than those who have not deliberated, a blind deference to their deliberation would imply that a vast majority of the people are dominated by a few selected citizens. Thus, Lafont concludes that it is democratically illegitimate for CAs, and other mini-publics, to directly feed into a decision-making process. As she discusses in more detail in her later work (2017, 2019),[3] they can serve democratic goals and improve the quality of deliberation in the public sphere when they contest the majority opinion, play a vigilant role, or anticipate issues.

Finally, the critique that CAs constitute a problematic short-cut to deliberative democracy has been expressed from a critical democratic perspective. According to Böker (2017), deliberative democratic theory should conceptualize ways of opening up social and political space for critical scrutiny of authorities, and enable emancipation from structural forms of domination. While Böker acknowledges that mini-publics can enable emancipatory critique, she argues that this possibility hinges on a political culture characterized by genuinely critical attitudes. According to her, participants in a deliberation would not assume a position to critique in an emancipatory sense as a result of

---

3 See also Lafont, in this *Handbook.*

a facilitator's instructions. Rather, "emancipation requires a self-empowering potential within citizens themselves" (Böker 2017: 31), and has to do with their own norms and expectations. Thus, in Böker's view, deliberative democracy cannot be artificially engineered through a set of institutional specificities. It can only self-evolve gradually and bottom-up, through a long-time process of cultural change. Like Chambers and Lafont, Böker's account of deliberative democracy, and critique of mini-publics, emphasizes the role of the informal public sphere in deliberative democratic theory.

9.7 Critique 6: Exacerbating inequality

The small numbers of participants in CAs have also given rise to discussions about their representativeness. While, pure random sampling, and the equal probability to be selected, has been considered to guard the democratic legitimacy of unelected deliberative bodies (Fishkin 2009; Khoban 2021), CAs usually use stratified random sampling based on demographic criteria to try to ensure a diversity of social perspectives, and to counteract self-selection biases (Escobar and Elstub 2017). Nevertheless, since there is no compulsion to participate, a degree of self-selection is unavoidable, and risks exacerbating inequalities in political influence between resourceful and marginalized groups.

Another problem with random sampling to CAs is that small minorities risk not being represented. A proposal that can, to some extent, solve this problem is to maximize the number of different social perspectives, rather than to try to achieve demographic proportionality (Brown 2006). According to this view, the injustice of oversampling minority groups is outweighed by a more socially diverse deliberative body, which may improve the quality of the deliberation and increase feelings of being represented among non-participants. While some have pointed to the impracticality of oversampling minorities (Landemore 2013), others have argued that it addresses social inequities that skew sampling frames, and counterbalances social injustices that are prevalent in other arenas of society (Steel et al. 2020).

In addition to injustices that affect the composition of CAs, it is likely that CAs reproduce inequalities in voice among those who participate. Studies on small group deliberations show different results. While some have found that inequalities in skills and social status do not translate into inequalities in speaking time and influence (Siu 2017), others have observed that women and working-class participants tend to make fewer contributions to the discussions (Gerber 2015; Setälä, Grönlund and Herne 2010). A recent study on Ireland's Convention on the Constitution finds that men tended to speak more frequently than women in the plenary debates, while women participated more than men in the roundtable sessions (Harris et al. 2021). However, privilege might not necessarily express itself in more contributions. An analysis of Deliberative Polls in the United States shows that white, highly educated, and older participants did not provide as many reasons for their arguments as non-white, less-educated, and younger participants, suggesting that privileged individuals might believe their statements carry more weight because of their social position (Siu 2017).

As a case of a formal institution for citizen participation, CAs are also subject to criticism that highlights participatory and consultative processes' embeddedness in social structures that reproduce oppression and racism. According to Almeida (2019), who has studied diversity and political participation in the City of Toronto, consultation with ethnic minority and immigrant groups converges with the racial norms of diversity discourse to reproduce and occlude colonial and racial thinking. Almeida shows that labour market and economic disparities identified by racialized minorities during a consultation process on how to address racism and discrimination was met with suggestions by the city to implement mentoring programmes to assist immigrant workers. Thus, residents' input was contextualized under the city's broader diversity narrative, which emphasized racial *lack* rather than racial *exclusion*.

Almeida's finding on the reproduction of racial practices in participatory processes further underlines the risk of CAs being overlooked and co-opted (see critique 4). It demonstrates that co-option can take place at a structural, rather than agential, level, and has particularly negative consequences for marginalized social groups. In addition, her observation of a diversity discourse that emphasizes racial lack gives reason to be vigilant against certain types of arguments about the desirability of CAs. While CAs have different goals, scholars often emphasize that they can improve participants' civic skills and knowledge of issues (Bächtiger et al. 2018; Fishkin, Luskin and Jowell 2000). Knowledge acquisition is indeed an important aspect of CAs. However, an overemphasis on the educative function of CAs may risk overshadowing their empowering and emancipatory capacity (cf. Böker and Elstub 2015). Such a tendency is most likely to disarm and inhibit participants who are considered to have relatively little knowledge and skills, i.e. those who are assumed to have a lot to learn.

9.8 In defence of citizens' assemblies

We have highlighted six important critiques of CAs. However, some of them do contradict each other. For example, it would be inconsistent to conclude that the public are incapable of meaningful participation in CAs (critique 1) and maintain that assembly members should have more control over the assembly process than they are usually afforded (critique 3). Indeed we reject critique 1 outright with respect to its limited normative vision of what democracy entails and the conclusions it draws from the empirical evidence about public participation. We believe the evidence from mini-publics, and many other avenues for political participation and deliberation, clearly demonstrate the capacity of the public to make meaningful contributions to policy debate and formation. Elsewhere, there are clear synergies between critiques, 2, 3, 4, 5 and 6 that ultimately all call for a more radical approach to democracy than the use of CAs can deliver. We therefore agree with Curato et al. (2020) that we should take an ecumenical approach to CAs. They should not be seen as necessarily positive contributions to democracy.

Nevertheless, we still maintain that CAs can provide democratic value in the right circumstances. The opportunities they afford for a diverse group of people to deliberate important political issues together, in a rather supportive and inclusive environment, are rare elsewhere in the political system. Consequently, we take a deliberative systems approach (Elstub, Ercan and Mendonça 2016). Accordingly, CAs should not be seen in isolation and should not be expected to promote all of the norms of deliberative democracy themselves: "conceptualizing mini-publics not as full instances but as incomplete parts of a wider system of deliberative democracy allows for acknowledgement of their inevitably limited nature, contributing certain specific components to the overarching system but failing at providing others" (Böker and Elstub 2015: 17).

This would help CAs democratize, not just by giving participants more say over the remit and information they receive (critique 3), but enabling non-participants to have input on these issues too (critiques 5 and 6). There needs to be concrete and established links between CAs and other parts of the political system including civil society, parliaments, government, and the media to enhance their impact on policy debate and opinion in the informal and formal public spheres (critiques 4, 5 and 6). To help achieve this there needs to be laws on when CAs are held, how they are organized, and on what should happen to the resulting recommendations, to reduce elite control over the process (critiques 3 and 4). We need an array of democratic innovations, not just CAs, to provide opportunities for the public to engage in meaningful participation and deliberation. As each "family" of democratic innovation contribute different types of democratic norms, and include different types of publics, they need to be combined in varying ways in different contexts (critiques 5 and 6) (Elstub and Escobar 2019). Furthermore, the democratic qualities of claimed participatory spaces, such as occupied public squares, should not be underestimated (critique 2).

The good news is that we are starting to see CAs become embedded in democratic systems and connected with established democratic institutions and democratic innovations in a variety of ways (OECD 2020, 2022; Paulis et al. 2020). We need to learn from these cases, but also push the experimentation further. We can do so without assuming that CAs will ever be fully inclusive, and while being responsive to groups that claim to be excluded and oppressed by the political system (critique 2). There will always be barriers. The critiques of CAs are real and significant. However, they apply to other parts of the democratic system too. If we learn how these parts can be most effectively combined, we can move towards deliberative systems, and CAs can play an important role in this.

References

Achen, C. H., & Bartels, L. M. (2016). *Democracy for Realists: Why Elections do not Produce Responsive Government.* Princeton, NJ: Princeton University Press.

Almeida, S. (2019). Mythical encounters: challenging racism in the diverse city. *International Journal of Sociology and Social Policy* 39 (11/12), 937–949.

Andrews, N., Elstub, S., McVean, S., & Sandie, G. (2022). *Scotland's Climate Assembly Research Report – Process, Impact and Assembly Member Experience*, Edinburgh: Scottish Government Research (Available at: https://www.gov.scot/isbn/9781804353073)

Bächtiger, A., Dryzek, J. S., Mansbridge, J., & Warren, M. E. (2018). Deliberative democracy: An introduction. In A. Bächtiger, J. S. Dryzek, J. Mansbridge & M. E. Warren (eds), *The Oxford Handbook of Deliberative Democracy*, 1–31. Oxford: Oxford University Press.

Beswick, D., & Elstub, S. (2019). Between diversity, representation and 'best evidence': Rethinking select committee evidence-gathering practices. *Parliamentary Affairs* 72 (4), 945–964.

Blaug, R. (2002). Engineering democracy. *Political Studies* 50 (1), 102–116.

Brennan, J. (2016). *Against Democracy.* Princeton, NJ: Princeton University Press.

Brown, M. B. (2006). Survey article: Citizen panels and the concept of representation. *Journal of Political Philosophy* 14 (2), 203–225.

Böker, M. (2017). Justification, critique and deliberative legitimacy: The limits of mini-publics. *Contemporary Political Theory* 16 (1), 19–40.

Böker, M., & Elstub, S. (2015). The possibility of critical mini-publics: Realpolitik and normative cycles in democratic theory. *Representation* 51 (1), 125–144.

Carson, L. & Gerwin, M. (2018). Embedding deliberative democracy in Poland, *New Democracy. Research and Development Note* (Available at: https://newdemocracy.com.au/wp-content/uploads/2018/05/docs_researchnotes_2018_May_nDF_R-N_20180508_EmbeddingDeliberativeDemocracyInPoland.pdf)

Chambers, S. (2009). Rhetoric and the public sphere: Has deliberative democracy abandoned mass democracy? *Political Theory* 37 (3), 323–350.

Converse, P. E. (1964). The nature of belief systems in mass publics. In D. E. Apter (ed.), *Ideology and Discontent*, 206–261. Glencoe: Free Press.

Courant, D. (2020). La Convention citoyenne pour le climat: Une représentation délibérative. *Revue Projet* 378, 60–64.

Curato, N., Vrydagh, J., & Bächtiger, A. (2020). Democracy without shortcuts: Introduction to the Special Issue, *Journal of Deliberative Democracy* 16 (2), 1–9.

Curato, N., Farrell, D. M., Geißel, B., Grönlund, K., Mockler, P., Pilet, J.-B., Renwick, A., Rose, J., Setälä, M., & Suiter, J. (2021). *Deliberative Mini-Publics: Core Design Features.* Bristol: Bristol University Press.

Downs, A. (1957). *An Economic Theory of Democracy.* New York: Harper & Row.

Dryzek, J. S. (2010). *Foundations and Frontiers of Deliberative Governance*, Oxford: Oxford University Press.

Dryzek, J. & Goodin, R. (2006). Deliberative impacts: The macro-political uptake of mini-publics. *Politics and Society* 34 (2), 219–244.

Dryzek, J. S. & Tucker, A. (2008). Deliberative innovation to different effect: Consensus conferences in Denmark, France, and the United States. *Public Administration Review* 68 (5), 864–876.

Elstub, S. (2014). Mini-publics: Issues and cases. In S. Elstub & P. McLaverty (eds), *Deliberative Democracy: Issues and Cases*, 166–188. Edinburgh: Edinburgh University Press.

Elstub, S., Carrick, J., Farrell, D. M., & Mockler, P. (2021a). The scope of climate assemblies: Lessons from the Climate Assembly UK. *Sustainability* 13 (20), 11272.

Elstub, S., Carrick, J., and Khoban, Z. (2021b). Democratic innovation in the Scottish Parliament: An evaluation of committee mini-publics. *Scottish Affairs* 30 (4), 493–521.

Elstub, S., Ercan, S., & Mendonça, R. (2016). The fourth generation of deliberative democracy. *Critical Policy Studies* 10 (2), 139–151.

Elstub, S., & Escobar, O. (2019). Defining and typologising democratic innovations. In S. Elstub & O. Escobar (eds), *The Handbook of Democratic Innovation and Governance*, 11–31. Cheltenham: Edward Elgar.

Escobar, O., & Elstub, S. (2017). Forms of mini-publics: An introduction to deliberative innovations in democratic practice. *New Democracy. Research and Development Note, 4.* (available at: https://www.newdemocracy.com.au/2017/05/08/forms-of-mini-publics/).

Farrell, D. M., Suiter, J., Cunningham, K., & Harris, C. (2020). When mini-publics and maxi-publics coincide: Ireland's national debate on abortion. *Representation.* DOI: 10.1080/00344893.2020.1804441

Fishkin, J. S. (2009). *When the People Speak: Deliberative Democracy and Public Consultation.* Oxford: Oxford University Press.

Fishkin, J. S., Luskin, R. C., & Jowell, R. (2000). Deliberative polling and public consultation. *Parliamentary Affairs* 53 (4), 657–666.

Fournier, P., van der Kolk, H., Carty, K., Blais, A., & Rose, J. (2011). *When Citizens Decide: Lessons from Citizen Assemblies on Electoral Reform.* Oxford: Oxford University Press.

Gerber, M. (2015). Equal partners in dialogue? Participation equality in a transnational deliberative poll (Europolis). *Political Studies* 63, 110–130.

Goodin, R. E. (2005). Sequencing deliberative moments. *Acta Politica* 40, 182–196.

Goodin, R. E. & Niemeyer, S. (2003) When does deliberation begin? Internal reflection versus discussion in deliberative democracy. *Political Studies* 51 (4), 627–649.

Hammond, M. (2020). Democratic deliberation for sustainability transformations: Between constructiveness and disruption. *Sustainability: Science, Practice and Policy* 16 (1), 220–230.

Harris, C. (2019). Deliberative mini-publics: Design choices and legitimacy. In S. Elstub & and O. Escobar (eds), *The Handbook of Democratic Innovation and Governance*, 45–59. Cheltenham UK and Northampton, MA: Edward Elgar.

Harris, C., Farrell, D. M., Suiter, J., & Brennan, M. (2021). Women's voices in a deliberative assembly: An analysis of gender rates of participation in Ireland's Convention on the Constitution 2012–2014. *The British Journal of Politics and International Relations* 23 (1), 175–193.

Jacquet, V., & van der Does, R. (2021). The consequences of deliberative minipublics: Systematic overview, conceptual gaps, and new directions. *Representation* 57 (1), 131–141.

Khoban, Z. (2021). Interpretative interactions: An argument for descriptive representation in deliberative mini-publics. *Representation* 57 (4), 497–514.

Lafont, C. (2015). Deliberation, participation, and democratic legitimacy: Should deliberative mini-publics shape public policy? *Journal of Political Philosophy* 23 (1), 40–63.

Lafont, C. (2017). Can democracy be deliberative & participatory? The democratic case for political uses of mini-publics. *Daedalus* 146 (3), 85–105.

Lafont, C. (2019). *Democracy Without Shortcuts: A Participatory Conception of Deliberative Democracy.* Oxford: Oxford University Press.

Landemore, H. (2013). Deliberation, cognitive diversity, and democratic inclusiveness: an epistemic argument for the random selection of representatives. *Synthese* 190 (7), 1209–1231.

Landemore, H. (2020). *Open Democracy: Reinventing Popular Rule for the Twenty-First Century.* Princeton, NJ: Princeton University Press.

Mouffe, C. (1999). Deliberative democracy or agonistic pluralism? *Social Research* 66 (3), 745–758.

Mouffe, C. (2005). *The Return of the Political.* London: Verso.

OECD (2020). *Innovative Citizen Participation and New Democratic Institutions: Catching the Deliberative Wave.* Paris: OECD Publishing.

OECD (2022). *Eight Ways to Institutionalise Deliberative Democracy.* Paris: OECD Publishing.

Pateman, C. (2012). Participatory democracy revisited. *Perspectives on Politics* 10 (1), 7–19.

Parkinson, J. (2006). *Deliberating in the Real World: Problems of Legitimacy in Deliberative Democracy.* Oxford: Oxford University Press.

Paulis, E., Pilet, J.-B., Panel, S., Vittori, D., & Close, C. (2020). The POLITICIZE dataset: An inventory of deliberative mini-publics (DMPs) in Europe. *European Political Science* 20, 521–542.

Plato (2007). *The Republic.* London: Penguin Classics.

Rancière, J. (1999). *Disagreement: Politics and Philosophy.* Minneapolis, MN: University of Minnesota Press.

Rancière, J. (2001). Ten theses on politics. *Theory and Event* 5 (3).

Richardson, H. S. (2010). Public opinion and popular will. In D. Kahane, D. Weinstock, D. Leydet & M. Williams (eds), *Deliberative Democracy in Practice*, 177–193. Vancouver: University of British Columbia Press.

Roberts, J., Lightbody, R., Low, R., & Elstub, S. (2020) Experts and evidence in deliberation: scrutinising the role of witnesses and evidence in mini-publics, a case study. *Policy Sciences* 53, 3–32.

Schumpeter, J. (1952.) *Capitalism, Socialism and Democracy.* London: Allen & Unwin.

Setälä, M., Grönlund, K., & Herne, K. (2010) Citizen deliberation on nuclear power: A comparison of two decision-making methods. *Political Studies* 58 (4), 688–714.

Siu, A. (2017). Deliberation & the challenge of inequality. *Daedalus* 146 (3), 119–128.

Smith, G. (2001). Taking deliberation seriously: institutional design and green politics. *Environmental Politics* 10 (3), 72–93.

Smith, G., & Wales, C. (2000). Citizens' juries and deliberative democracy. *Political Studies* 48 (1), 51–65.

Steel, D., Bolduc, N., Jenei, K., & Burgess, M. (2020). Rethinking representation and diversity in deliberative minipublics. *Journal of Deliberative Democracy* 16 (1), 46–57.

Thompson, A. G. H., Escobar, O., Roberts, J. J., Elstub, S., & Pamphilis, N. M. (2021) The importance of context and the effect of information and deliberation on opinion change regarding environmental issues in citizens' juries. *Sustainability* 13 (17), 9852.

Vrydagh, J. (2022). Measuring the impact of consultative citizen participation: reviewing the congruency approaches for assessing the uptake of citizen ideas. *Policy Sciences* 55, 65–88.

Warren, M. E. (2009). Governance-driven democratization. *Critical Policy Studies* 3 (1), 3–13.

Williams, M. (2000). The uneasy alliance of group representation and deliberative democracy. In W. Norman & W. Kymlicka (eds), *Citizenship in Diverse Societies*, 124–154 Oxford: Oxford University Press.

Wolin, S. S. (1996). Fugitive democracy. In Seyla Benhabib (ed.), *Democracy and Difference*, 31–45. Princeton, NJ: Princeton University Press.

Young, I. M. (1996). Communication and the other: Beyond deliberative democracy. In Seyla Benhabib (ed.), *Democracy and Difference*, 120–135. Princeton, NJ: Princeton University Press.

Part 2: **The uses of citizens' assemblies**

Rasmus Ø. Nielsen and Eva Sørensen

10 Citizens' assemblies and the crisis of democracy

Abstract: For decades, citizens' assemblies (CAs) have served as one of the remedies that scholars have advocated and decision-makers have employed in their efforts to overcome the crisis of representative democracy. In the back-and-forth between CA promoters and critical evaluators, the recent discourse around CAs follows a familiar pattern recurring since the 1970s. The chapter argues that a systemic approach is necessary to fully understand the potential and limitations of CAs for remedying the crisis of democracy. The chapter makes this case in relation to four sets of mini-public methods and draws the conclusion that the degree to which arenas for citizen deliberations contribute to overcoming the democratic crisis hinges on how they are integrated in the larger democratic process. Institutionalizing such arenas as competitors to formal representative assemblies will tend to weaken representative democracy further, whereas building productive synergies between them will enhance the effectiveness and legitimacy of representative democracy.

Keywords: citizens' participation, crisis of democracy, citizens' assemblies, systemic turn, democratic innovations

10.1 Introduction

In one form or another, representative democracy has been in a state of crisis ever since the rise of the new social movements in the late 1960s (Ercan and Gagnon 2014; Sørensen 2020) While the content of this crisis has changed, the establishment of citizens' assemblies (CAs) (used in this *Handbook* interchangeably with Robert Dahl's "mini-publics" (Dahl 1970, 1989)) has continued to be one of the remedies for which scholars have advocated and which decision-makers have employed in their efforts to counteract the crisis (Ryan and Smith 2014). Current proponents argue that CAs hold the potential for overcoming the current rise in political polarization and the surge in authoritarian values (Warren 2013; Dryzek et al. 2019; Daly 2020). The expectations are that involving a diverse group of citizens in joint policymaking and deliberation will not only stimulate mutual understanding between citizens but also between citizens and politicians. However, critical assessments of the actual impact of CAs document that they are no panacea (see e. g., Goodin and Dryzek 2006; Edelenbos, van Meerkerk and Koppenjan 2017; Caluwaerts and Reuchamps 2016).

In the back-and-forth between CA promoters and critical evaluators, the recent discourse around CAs follows a familiar pattern recurring since the 1970s: every decade or

Rasmus Ø. Nielsen: Roskilde University, Denmark; **Eva Sørensen:** Roskilde University, Denmark.

∂ Open Access. © 2023 the author(s), published by De Gruyter. (cc) BY-NC-ND This work is licensed under the Creative Commons Attribution-NonCommercial-NoDerivatives 4.0 International License. https://doi.org/10.1515/9783110758269-012

so, a new deliberative mini-public variant has been promoted as a tool for policymakers to counteract the crisis of representative democracy, such as this crisis was understood at the time. In response, critics have then found some way of discounting the potential of mini-publics, either due to a lack of solid evidence for specifically measurable effects or by pointing to negative unintended consequences for democracy (Stadelmann-Steffen and Dermont 2016; Gerber, Schaub and Mueller 2019). The question, of course, is whether achieving precisely these effects was ever the real ambition of those who have experimented with and promoted mini-public formats (Warren 2009; Setälä 2011), and whether continuing this ping-pong between promoters and critics is productive for democracy.

This chapter argues that a systemic approach is necessary to fully understand the potential and limitations of CAs for remedying the crisis of democracy. The chapter makes this case in relation to four sets of mini-public methods, namely: i) the Citizens' Jury and the Planning Cell (German: *Planungszelle*), ii) Open Space Technology, Future Search, and World Café, iii) the Consensus Conference and the Deliberative Poll, and, finally, iv) the Citizens' Assembly method pioneered in British Columbia. For each set of methods, we describe the developments and crisis tendencies in democracy that motivated the invention of new mini-public formats and list the claims made by promoters about the democratizing potentials of these methods. We show the results of evaluations of the experiments and then shift the perspective to what decision-makers (could have) gained from the full-scale deployment of these innovations as a routine part of democratic decision-making. We conclude our tour with a discussion of how the evaluation of the current CA wave can best underpin the realization of its democratizing potential.

10.2 A systems-theoretical perspective on citizens' assemblies and the crisis of democracy

For our analysis, we draw inspiration from the "systemic turn" literature in participatory research, which was initiated by contributions from Mansbridge et al. (2012) and Dryzek (2012) and which others have since developed further (see also Lacelle-Webster & Warren, in this *Handbook*). This turn was proposed as a way of achieving a more productive dialogue between the practitioners working to develop, refine, and institutionalize mini-public innovations and the academics who critically scrutinize their contributions to democracy. The basic idea is to shift or expand the scope of how mini-public formats are evaluated: from the direct and measurable effects of individual experiments to the broader functional effects that putting different mini-public formats in the toolbox of decision-makers and institutions has on the democratic system (Setälä 2017). This shift in perspective lends itself to an evaluative approach that is more complex than the binary empowerment-or-not narrative traditionally associated with citizens' participation (Arnstein 1969). When conducting evaluations from a systems perspective, researchers can broaden their questions from the (in)ability of citizens to affect the decisions of political leaders and system; they may also evaluate what the CA does (or fails to do) to help elected political leaders lead (Sørensen 2020). At the same time, the systemic perspective opens the door to a productive form of evaluation that is less concerned with proving or disproving the immediate effects of mini-public innovations (Curato et al. 2017) and more concerned with *how* and *under what conditions* new mini-public formats can best provide the functional enhancements to the democratic system that they promise (Mansbridge et al. 2012). In short, the conceptual framework of the systemic turn is useful for understanding the potential of CAs to counteract current crisis tendencies in representative democracy.

10.3 Countering crises of democracy through democratic innovations: A movement in four parts

The story of the evolving relationship between the crisis of democracy and mini-public formats akin to CAs can roughly be divided into four parts (see also Elstub, Ercan and Mendonça 2016; Curato, Vrydagh and Bächtiger 2020). First, the 1960–1970s, when CAs were motivated by a perceived democratic deficit originating from state centralization and resulting in alienation; second, the 1980s, when CA inventions were motivated by societal conflicts over structural change; third, the 1990s, when CA formats were invented to address the inability of public organizations to handle complex challenges; and fourth, the 2000–2010s, during which time CAs were motivated by the inability of democratic institutions to govern efficiently and legitimately. The four parts are schematically represented in the Table 10.1.

Table 10.1: Schematic overview of democratic crises and corresponding CA interventions

Decade	New methods invented	Crisis tendencies motivating innovation	Benefits claimed by promoters	Critical points of external evaluation	Possibilities from a systems perspective	Institutionalization strategy
1970s	*Citizens' Jury Planning Cell*	Anti-authoritarian movements protest centralized policymaking.	Changes the role of the citizen in democracy.	Lacks representativeness Only little policy effect.	Empower policymakers vis-à-vis interest groups	Outside-in, bottom-up
1980s	*Consensus Conf. Deliberative Poll*	Citizens reject structural adjustment, demand partici-	Enhances governability of potential conflicts	Co-opts citizens into government policy.	Give citizens a voice in 24-hr news cycle	Outside-in, top-down

Table 10.1: Schematic overview of democratic crises and corresponding CA interventions *(Continued)*

Decade	New methods invented	Crisis tendencies motivating innovation	Benefits claimed by promoters	Critical points of external evaluation	Possibilities from a systems perspective	Institutionalization strategy
		pation in planning.				
1990s	*Open Space Tech.* *Future Search* *World Café*	Political decision-makers lack information and knowledge for complex problem-solving	Enables innovation through collective intelligence	Decoupled from formal democratic processes.	Democratize decision-making inside the hierarchical systems	Inside-out, bottom-up
2000–2010s	*Citizens' Assembly*	Democratic institutions need citizens' resources to address societal challenges.	Engage citizens to make possible needed reforms	Powerful actors shape deliberations	Empower political leadership	Inside-out, top-down

10.4 1960–1970s: Citizens' Juries and Planning Cell

Citizens' Juries and Planning Cells are two very similar mini-public methods developed in the 1970s by Ned Crosby in the US and Peter Dienel in West Germany respectively, each initially unaware of the other's work (Crosby 2007). Their work has played a foundational role in the development of CA methods in contemporary Western democracies.

The two "inventors" shared a similar dissatisfaction with the state of democracy in the late 1960s and early 1970s. At the time, the crisis of democracy manifested itself in the form of anti-authoritarian movements protesting centralized policymaking on a range of issues, including civil rights, environmental policy, gender policy, and foreign policy. In response to this crisis, Dienel (1978) explicitly posits the methods as "an alternative to establishment democracy" (title page). In the US, Crosby and his colleagues were similarly motivated by a feeling among citizens that "participation through normal institutional channels has little impact on the substance of government policies" (Friedland and Alford 1975, quoted in Crosby, Kelly and Schaefer 1986). This dissatisfaction was not limited to traditional forms of democratic representation and bureaucratic decision-making (e.g., elections, plebiscites, local councils); it also extended to new forms of citizen participation emergent during the 1960s and early 1970s, including the organization of protest through social movements.

Dienel (1978) argued that neither the new social movements, heralded by many of his contemporaries as a reinvigoration of democratic participation, nor the advocacy planning experiments, which were closer to his own enterprise, would be able to create the opportunities needed for meaningful citizen participation. In his view, the new social movements were too reactive in their motivations and too unconnected to administrative planning to serve as a stable platform for participation and rational discourse. On the contrary, these movements could ultimately lead to increased dissatisfaction with the system among citizens, while the need to attract attention to one's cause could create increasingly emotional and chaotic forms of manifestation (Dienel 1978: 52–58). Crosby and colleagues took an equally critical view of the results of the first two decades of the citizen participation movement, citing flaws such as a lack of representativeness, a lack of policy impact, and a lack of ambition regarding the required expertise levels and the scope of the decision-making processes addressed by citizens participation (Crosby, Kelly and Schaefer 1986). From this dual motivation – dissatisfaction with both the overall state of democracy and with current reform practices – came two remarkably similar solutions.

The central hypotheses forwarded by Dienel (and implicitly supported by Crosby and colleagues) was that a system-wide adoption of the Planning Cell or Citizens' Jury would substantially change the role of citizens in society. Rather than being divided between those who apathetically freeride on the benefits of democracy and those who, for various self-interested reasons, make a paid or voluntary career out of making themselves heard, a fully institutionalized participation format based on random selection would mean that every citizen would at some point participate in a deliberative process and, more importantly, would expect at some point to play the part of "citizen advisor". This expectation would in turn shape the image of what it means to be a citizen in general and, as such, would help change the parameters of the democratic crisis.

Dienel's hypothesis is well-aligned with the systems perspective and evaluating its merits would demand focusing not only on individual cases and methodology but also on the outcomes of the *democratic change project* of institutionalizing mini-publics. Along these lines, Peter Dienel's son, Hans-Liudger Dienel, and an international group of co-authors argue in a 2014 contribution that the spread of the Planning Cell countries across the world (even to non-democratic countries like China) has created an empirical basis for broader system-level evaluation (Dienel et al. 2014). The authors, however, seem to operate with a theory of change that moves via increasing professionalization and standardization (meaning shared standards for diverse practices, not homogenization) to institutionalization; that is, a bottom-up approach to the project of changing the role of the citizen in the democratic system. As such, their contribution ultimately becomes dominated by internal questions of quality assurance, which – while certainly pertinent – still leaves us with the questions: What would a system-level approach to institutionalizing mini-publics look like? And what kind of strategy could bring it about? The three remaining parts of our story account for some of the attempts made at such an institutionalization of mini-publics.

10.5 1980s: The Consensus Conference and the Deliberative Poll

In the 1980s, the crisis of democracy manifested itself in the popular rejection of neo-liberal and technology-centric economic policies (OECD 1988; Glynos and Howarth 2007). What citizens demanded instead, inspired in part by the bottom-up mini-public experiments of the previous decade, was the right to participate in the decision-making by which economic and technological policies were designed and adopted.

In response, attempts at institutionalizing system-level CAs began to emerge in the late-1980s. CAs were perceived as potentially serving as valuable, consensus-building platforms supplementing the expert advisory functions already serving public deci-sion-makers. Bringing citizens together with experts would produce new ideas and in-sights that could qualify policymaking. Two notable examples of this strategy were the Participatory Consensus Conference (hereafter: Consensus Conference) developed by the Danish Board of Technology (DBT) and the Deliberative Poll developed by Jeremy Fishkin at the Stanford Center for Deliberative Democracy. Both of these formats were formulated against the backdrop of rising opposition to government decision-making and sought to empower decision-makers to proactively avoid making decisions that would generate government-citizen conflict (Fishkin 1995; Vig and Paschen 2000).

From a systemic perspective, deliberative methods deployed as means for demo-cratic governments to avoid conflict and navigate toward a national consensus on dif-ficult issues such as technological change and structural transformation have been en-duringly criticized for serving to co-opt citizens into supporting government policy (Joss and Durant 1995). But while such intentions on the part of officials making use of these methods cannot be disproven, the argument seems in a certain way to miss the entire point of the exercise: these methods, which bring ordinary citizens into tra-ditional forms of government advice, could instead be seen as mechanisms for circum-venting the interest group politics in which co-optation becomes a necessary part of the game. Precisely because participants are not there as representatives of the rest of the citizenry, mini-publics that advise public decision-makers provide a way for non-organ-ized citizens to be heard amidst the growing noise of interest group politics (Goodin and Dryzek 2006).

10.6 1990s: Open Space Technology, Future Search, and the World Café

In the 1990s, newly recognized systemic challenges (e.g., global warming, biodiversity) shifted the perspective on the crisis of democracy. What came to the fore was the inability of policymakers to solve complex global problems, largely due to a lack of information and knowledge about the multitude of ongoing actions and interactions in society. In response, a new answer began to emerge to the question how (and why) system-level mini-publics could be institutionalized. Like Dienel (cited above), the inventors of Open Space Technology, Future Search, and the World Café sought to create "an alternative to establishment democracy" , i.e., another process for enabling collective community action. But whereas Dienel rejected the democracy of the affected in favour of randomly selected citizens' groups, the inventors of these methods leaned into the idea of mobilizing affected and concerned citizens and stakeholders and sought to provide methods for dialogue and deliberation that would avoid the chaos of competition between special interests. Inspired by theories of self-organizing systems (Wheatley 1992) and convinced that the alienation and lack of responsiveness produced by centralization begins at the heart of the hierarchically structured and silo-based decision-making process of democratic government (i.e., in the practical way meetings are organized and decisions are made), several groups of academics and practitioners set out to revolutionize the basic unit of rational planning and decision-making – the meeting – to better facilitate change processes (Saam 2004).

The methods discussed here are community-centric and therefore agnostic about whether they are deployed in connection to representative democratic institutions, grassroots organizing, or private corporations. For this reason, a debate can be had whether these methods strictly meet the definitional criteria for deliberative mini-publics or CAs. We have chosen to include them here, nevertheless, because the development and proliferation of these methods have played an important role in expanding the ways that practitioners and academics imagine what "democratizing democracy" can look like – especially when we look beyond the confines of advanced Western democracies (de Sousa Santos 2005).

Open Space Technology (OST) was invented (or "rediscovered," as the inventors would say) in the preparation for the *3rd Annual International Symposium on Organizational Transformation* in Monterey in 1985. Their basic insight was that much more knowledge exchange and creativity took place in the coffee breaks of the symposium than in the planned activities. To make space for this creativity, the arrangers sought to make space for the self-organizing group intelligence of the participants by abandoning pre-planned schedules; instead, participants would show up and organize the three-day event themselves.

The Future Search Conference and World Café formats represent variations on the same theme and approach, the former emphasizing the "whole system" approach even more strongly, while the latter takes a more open approach to participant selection. In the Future Search Conference, the objective is for a community of people united by having a stake in a complex and conflictual situation to find common ground and agree to proceed toward a shared vision of the future. Here, getting the "whole system" in the room is of particular importance because it is necessary to avoid scapegoating and to create a sense of mutual empowerment (Weisbord 1992). The World Café, on the other hand, has a more open-ended approach to participation in that the method does not assume the ability to identify clearly who the relevant stakeholders may be, especially regarding issues in the public sphere. Instead, the World Café would seem conceived to function as a space in which those choosing to participate in a workshop on a given theme are already representatives of the social networks existing around that theme. Facilitating the creation of novel ideas and plans for future actions to set change in motion among these participants is therefore already a way of setting those ideas in motion in much wider networks (Brown and Isaacs 2005).

The literature concerned with these methods tends to focus on their ability to instigate change through mutual learning and collective intelligence. In this respect, the methods are evaluated on the merits of serving as change engines for communities in a mode that cuts across public/private, professional/amateur, and top/bottom divisions. As such, they are obvious tools for collaborative governance *by* and *with* public institutions.

10.7 2000s – The Citizens' Assembly (and the Constitutional Convention)

This brings us to the Citizens' Assembly method, so named when it was first launched in British Columbia in 2003. Like the experimental methods of the 1990s, the invention of the Citizens' Assembly format was motivated by the belief that maladies internal to the democratic system were to be blamed for (some of) the ills of society (Warren and Pearse 2008). But whereas the former wave of mini-public experiments had focused on overcoming the informal organizational practices and institutional silo effects that stood in the way of creative solutions to complex problems, the Citizens' Assembly format focused on overcoming the lack of decision-making capacity that arose from the formal strictures of representative democracy. Commenting on CAs in British Columbia, Warren and Pearse (2008: 2) thus identify the motivation for this innovation as being a perceived "misalignment between citizen capacities and demands, and the capacities of political institutions to aggregate citizen demands and integrate them into legitimate and effective governance". To overcome longstanding gridlocked policy issues and address societal challenges, democratic institutions would need to mobilize citizen resources.

In designing the method, the importance of achieving a legitimate connection to the representative democratic system was a key concern (entirely contrary to the utopic revolutionism of the methods from the 1990s). The Citizens Assembly method as developed in British Columbia is thus mandated by the legislature to produce recommendations for legislative change within certain scope conditions, such as remaining within the Westminster system and the Canadian constitution. This emphasis on the compatibility of the CA with the core values of the existing representative democratic system – e.g., representativeness, pluralism, evidence-based decision-making, and transparency – is clearly apparent in the design choices made. To ensure representativeness in a geographical and sociological sense, participating citizens are selected through stratified random selection and from the full list of registered voters. During the learning phase, participants engage with all sides of an issue, and stakeholders and citizens are able to give testimony regarding their preferences through an open hearing invitation in the "listening" phase. Any lack of clarity in the transmission of recommendations from the CA to the representative system (a drawback of many other mini-public designs; see Hendriks 2016) is eliminated by the demand that the CA produces recommendations for the adoption of a solution that can be decided on a straight "Yes" or "No" vote, and – in the British Columbia and certain other high-profile cases – that the decision is made by a popular referendum (see also the *Introduction* to this *Handbook*).

This latter feature is obviously also the one characteristic that raises the stakes for the entire process to a new level compared to earlier mini-public formats. On the one hand, a follow-up referendum puts the results of the deliberative process under a magnifying glass within the public sphere. The referendum thus provides a highly dramatized possibility that the perceived crisis of democracy embodied in the particularly gridlocked issue, which the CA is mandated to address, could be "solved" in one fell swoop. In the British Columbia case: if the first-past-the-post system seems to produce somehow "rigged" or unfair results, setting in motion a participatory process that ultimately involves the entire voting-age population in changing the rules of the game would provide a swift, specific response to the perceived injustice and thereby a breath of life to the meaningfulness of democracy. On the other hand, the sharpness of the will-they-or-won't-they moment can also potentially exacerbate the disappointment and subsequent backlash from participating citizens if change is rejected. We know from other participatory formats that such backlash can further sour citizens' views on democracy (Lindner and Aichholzer 2020).

For this reason and others, evaluations of the effects of mixed-membership versions of CAs are of particular interest (see also Harris, Farrell and Suiter in this *Handbook*). In the Irish Constitutional Convention of 2012–2014, a novel model was implemented in which 66 randomly selected citizens participated in the convention along with 33 self-selected parliamentary politicians. The purpose of this novel setup was to ensure two mutually reinforcing effects: firstly, to create a greater degree of realism in relation to what political parties would be able or willing to adopt as policy and, secondly, to thereby unlock the force of political parties being motivated to drive voters to the subsequent referendum. This innovation thus seeks to soften the sharpness of the encounter between the deliberative process and the party-political system as compared to the Canadian CA format.

From a systems point of view, the Irish mixed-membership variant of the CA format instantiates a "directly representative democracy" (Neblo, Esterling and Lazer 2018). This interactive form of democracy seems to some observers not only to hold the potential to overcome the "gladiatorial contests between parties and among highly organized interest groups" (Neblo, Esterling and Lazer 2018: 11) by allowing for productive citizen–politician dialogue; contrary to a zero-sum understanding of power and participation, it may also thereby strengthen the ability of elected politicians to exert political leadership (Sørensen 2020). How? By giving elected leaders a rational and considered mandate to act decisively; a mandate that comes without strings attached in terms of parliamentary *quid pro quos* or backroom deals with civil society supporters.

10.8 Conclusion and reflections

In response to the persistent crisis of representative democracy, the particular Citizens' Assembly format developed in British Columbia and later refined in Ireland and elsewhere is the latest stem on a growing branch of democratic innovations, the family name of which is the deliberative mini-public. Over the last 50 years, the mini-public format has assumed many different guises sharing certain common features and motivations, although they also differ in important ways. The many academics and practitioners who have contributed to this development share the assumption that involving citizens in policymaking can reduce the political tensions in society, and they hold the view that institutionalizing deliberative arenas holds the potential to strengthen democracy. Over the years, empirical studies have documented how CAs are not always able to fulfil this potential. A systemic approach is helpful in pointing out how the degree to which arenas for citizen deliberations contribute to overcoming the democratic crisis hinges on how they are integrated in the larger democratic process. Institutionalizing such arenas as competitors to formal representative assemblies will tend to weaken representative democracy further, whereas building productive synergies between them will enhance the effectiveness and legitimacy of representative democracy.

References

Arnstein, S. R. (1969). A ladder of citizen participation. *Journal of the American Institute of Planners* 35 (4), 216–224.

Brown, J., & Isaacs, D. (2005). *The World Café: Shaping our Futures through Conversations that Matter.* Oakland: Berrett-Koehler.

Caluwaerts, D., & Reuchamps, M. (2016). Generating democratic legitimacy through deliberative innovations: The role of embeddedness and disruptiveness. *Representation* 52 (1), 13–27.

Crosby, N. (2007). Peter C. Dienel: Eulogy for a deliberative democracy pioneer. *Journal of Deliberative Democracy* 3 (1).

Crosby, N., Kelly, J. M., & Schaefer, P. (1986). Citizens panels: A new approach to citizen participation. *Public Administration Review* 46 (2), 170–178.

Curato, N., Dryzek, J. S., Ercan, S. A., Hendriks, C. M., & Niemeyer, S. (2017). Twelve key findings in deliberative democracy research. *Daedalus* 146 (3), 28–38.

Curato, N., Vrydagh, J., & Bächtiger, A. (2020). Democracy without shortcuts: Introduction to the Special Issue. *Journal of Deliberative Democracy*, 16 (2), 1–9.

Dahl, R. (1970). *After the Revolution.* New Haven: Yale University Press.

Dahl, R. (1989). *Democracy and its Critics.* New Haven: Yale University Press.

Daly, T. G. (2020). Designing the democracy-defending citizen. *Constitutional Studies* 6, 189–193.

Dienel, H. L., Franzl, K., Fuhrmann, R. D., Lietzmann, H. J., & Vergne, A. (2014). Die Qualität von Bürgerbeteiligungsverfahren. *Evaluation und Sicherung von Standards am Beispiel von Planungszellen und Bürgergutachten.* München: Oekom Verlag

Dienel, P. C. (1978). *Die Planungszelle: der Bürger plant seine Umwelt. Eine Alternative zur Establishment-Demokratie.* Opladen: Westdeutscher Verlag.

Dryzek, J. S. (2012). *Foundations and Frontiers of Deliberative Governance.* Oxford: Oxford University Press.

Dryzek, J. S., Bächtiger, A., Chambers, S., Cohen, J., Druckman, J. N., Felicetti, A., … & Warren, M. E. (2019). The crisis of democracy and the science of deliberation. *Science* 363 (6432), 1144–1146.

Edelenbos, J., van Meerkerk, I., & Koppenjan, J. (2017). The challenge of innovating politics in community self-organization: The case of Broekpolder. *Public Management Review* 19 (1), 55–73.

Elstub, S., Ercan, S., & Mendonça, R. F. (2016). Editorial introduction: The fourth generation of deliberative democracy. *Critical Policy Studies* 10 (2), 139–151.

Ercan, S. A., & Gagnon, J.-P. (2014). The crisis of democracy: Which crisis? Which democracy? *Democratic Theory* 1 (2), 1–10.

Fishkin, J. S. (1995). *The Voice of the People.* New Haven: Yale University Press.

Gerber, M., Schaub, H. P., & Mueller, S. (2019). O sister, where art thou? Theory and evidence on female participation at citizen assemblies. *European Journal of Politics and Gender* 2 (2), 173–195.

Glynos, J., & Howarth, D. (2007). *Logics of Critical Explanation in Social and Political Theory.* London: Routledge.

Goodin, R. E., & Dryzek, J. S. (2006). Deliberative impacts: The macro-political uptake of mini-publics. *Politics & Society* 34 (2), 219–244.

Hendriks, C. M. (2016) Coupling citizens and elites in deliberative systems: The role of institutional design. *European Journal of Political Research* 55, 43–60

Joss, S., & Durant, J. (eds). (1995). *Public Participation in Science: The Role of Consensus Conferences in Europe.* London: NMSI Trading Ltd.

Lindner, R., & Aichholzer, G. (2020). E-democracy: Conceptual foundations and recent trends. In L. Hennen, I. Korthagen, I. van Keulen, G. Aichholzer, R. Lindner, & R. Ø. Nielsen (eds), *European E-democracy in Practice*, 11–45. Cham: Springer.

Mansbridge, J., Bohman, J., Chambers, S., Christiano, T., Fung, A., Parkinson, J., … & Warren, M. E. (2012). A systemic approach to deliberative democracy. In J. Parkinson & J. Mansbridge (eds), *Deliberative Systems: Deliberative Democracy at the Large Scale*, 1–26. Cambridge: Cambridge University Press.

Neblo, M. A., Esterling, K. M., & Lazer, D. M. (2018). *Politics with the People: Building a Directly Representative Democracy.* Cambridge: Cambridge University Press.

OECD (1988). Technology for growth and employment: Science Policy in the 21st Century 1. *OECD Observer, 1988: 1.* OECD iLibrary

Ryan, M., & Smith, G. (2014). Defining mini-publics. In K. Grönlund, A. Bächtiger & M. Setälä (eds), *Deliberative Mini-Publics: Involving Citizens in the Democratic Process*, 9–26. Colchester: ECPR Press

Saam, N. J. (2004). Towards a rational foundation of open space technology. *Organization Development Journal* 22 (1), 76–92.

de Sousa Santos, B. (ed.). (2005). *Democratizing Democracy: Beyond the Liberal Democratic Canon.* London: Verso.

Setälä, M. (2011). The role of deliberative mini-publics in representative democracy: Lessons from the experience of referendums. *Representation* 47 (2), 201–213.

Setälä, M. (2017). Connecting deliberative mini-publics to representative decision making. *European Journal of Political Research* 56 (4), 846–863.

Stadelmann-Steffen, I., & Dermont, C. (2016). How exclusive is assembly democracy? Citizens' assembly and ballot participation compared. *Swiss Political Science Review* 22 (1), 95–122.

Sørensen, E. (2020). *Interactive Political Leadership*. Oxford: Oxford University Press.

Vig, N. J., & Paschen, H. (2000). *Parliaments and Technology: The Development of Technology Assessment in Europe*. Albany, NY: SUNY Press.

Warren, M. E. (2009). Citizen participation and democratic deficits: Considerations from the perspective of democratic theory. In J. DeBardeleben & J. H. Pammett (eds), *Activating the Citizen*, 17–40. London: Palgrave Macmillan.

Warren, M. E. (2013). Citizen representatives. In J. H. Nagel & R. M. Smith (eds), *Representation: Elections and Beyond*, 269–294. University Park: University of Pennsylvania Press.

Warren, M. E., & Pearse, H. (2008). Introduction: Democratic renewal and deliberative democracy. In M. E. Warren & H. Pearse (eds), *Designing Deliberative Democracy: The British Columbia Citizens' Assembly*, 1–19. New York: Cambridge University Press.

Weisbord, M. R. (1992). *Discovering Common Ground*. Oakland: Berrett-Koehler.

Wheatley, M. (1992). *Leadership and the New Sciences. Learning about Organisation from an Orderly Universe*. San Francisco: Berrett-Koehler Publications Inc.

Sonia Bussu and Dannica Fleuß

11 Citizens' assemblies: Top-down or bottom-up? – both, please!

Abstract: This chapter provides a critical reflection on conceptualizations of top-down and bottom-up citizens' assemblies (CAs). Through a review of the literature and analysis of paradigmatic examples we identify main characteristics of each ideal type. Ideal-type top-down assemblies are opened by state institutions to address a predefined policy issue and strengthen the legitimacy of the commissioning body. Ideal-type bottom-up assemblies are led by civil society, provide space for citizen agenda-setting and might have ambitions for more radical reform projects but struggle to have tangible impact because of looser or no links with centres of power. However, the practice of CAs is less clear-cut: bottom-up approaches are not always better at ensuring more inclusive processes, and top-down CAs do not seem to have such a good record in terms of impact just because they work closely with state institutions. Our assessment of four different dimensions of the top-down/bottom-up heuristic allows for a more differentiated assessment of types of CAs that may also flexibly combine bottom-up and top-down elements.

Keywords: deliberative democracy, participatory democracy, citizens' assembly, institutional design, civil society, social movements, democratic legitimacy, constitutional reform, governance-driven democratization, democracy-driven governance

11.1 Introduction

The debate over top-down (Fishkin 2009) versus bottom-up approaches (Papadopoulos 1998) is a heated one, not only with regard to citizens' assemblies (CAs) but participatory governance more broadly (Richardson, Durose and Perry 2019). The top-down/bottom-up dichotomy is frequently understood in terms of the actors initiating the process and determining core design features. This heuristic has been used to distinguish between different scales of government, whereby top-down refers to central government and bottom-up to the local level, closer to the citizens (Willett and Giovannini 2013). More commonly within the literature on democratic innovations, a top-down process is understood as opened by state actors, irrespective of the tier, and a bottom-up process will be one led by civil society. Based on this definition, the CA on Electoral Reform in British Columbia (Warren and Pearse 2008) is an oft celebrated example of top-down processes. By contrast, cases such as the Belgian G1000 project (Caluwaerts

Sonia Bussu: University of Birmingham; **Dannica Fleuß:** Dublin City University, Ireland (dannica.fleuss@dcu.ie).

∂ Open Access. © 2023 the author(s), published by De Gruyter. (cc) BY-NC-ND This work is licensed under the Creative Commons Attribution-NonCommercial-NoDerivatives 4.0 International License. https://doi.org/10.1515/9783110758269-013

and Reuchamps 2015), led by civil society, social movements or grassroots groups, are defined as bottom-up.

Scholars and practitioners frequently emphasize the need to strengthen the links between an assembly and "empowered' political and institutional actors to increase impact on binding decisions. A CA initiated by state actors or public agencies would therefore appear to guarantee greater influence on decision-making institutions, as well as stronger legitimacy, as it is sanctioned by elected representatives or accountable public agencies. However, to date amongst the many examples of CAs commissioned and endorsed by public actors, only a small number could be said to have led directly to policy or constitutional change, generally when coupled with mechanisms of direct democracy, such as referendums (Jacquet and Minsart, in this *Handbook*; Gastil and Richards 2013; Farrell et al. 2019). Civil society-led processes, although mostly failing to connect citizens' recommendations to the political agenda, are perceived to be better able to mobilize civic participation (Cornwall 2004) and generate stronger links to the wider public sphere (Perry and May 2010; Wagenaar and Wood 2018). For this reason, participatory and deliberative democrats frequently "fetishize" bottom-up processes (for a critique of this literature see Richardson, Durose and Perry 2019).

In this chapter, we move away from black and white distinctions and recognize that top-down and bottom-up approaches might in fact exist in a dynamic relationship (Bua and Bussu 2021). We note how the rise in "hybrid processes" on the ground is stimulating new thinking towards more systemic approaches to participatory governance (Bussu 2019). Different components, top-down and bottom-up, might in fact be sequenced and/or interact with each other (see Elstub, Ercan and Mendonça 2016; Parkinson and Mansbridge 2012), as a variety of participatory spaces, including but not only CAs, can create channels for different publics to participate at different points in the policy process.

The chapter first reviews the literature on CAs to describe salient traits of both top-down and bottom-up ideal types. We flesh out core characteristics in each case and identify four different dimensions that characterize top-down/bottom-up CAs based on: (1) initiating actors, (2) process design, (3) normative values, and (4) core aims guiding the process. The following sections present examples of CAs that are described as top-down, such as the recent Climate Assembly UK (Elstub et al. 2021) or bottom-up, such as the German Citizens' Assembly on the Future of Democracy (e. g., Della Porta and Felicetti 2022; Fleuß 2021; Landemore 2020). By applying the four dimensions to the analysis of these and other cases, we show that top-down and bottom-up tend to operate on a *continuum* or *spectrum* (combining the four dimensions in different ways) and display varying degrees of top-down/bottom-up orientation. We elaborate a new gradual categorization of top-down and bottom-up CAs, reflecting on ways in which characteristics of each type could help us develop more effective and legitimate processes.

11.2 Top down or bottom up? Beyond black and white distinctions

The literature on mini-publics has historically focused on top-down (i.e., state-led) deliberative initiatives (e.g., Bächtiger and Parkinson 2019; Elstub and McLaverty 2014). These processes have a long history which predates the deliberative turn in the field (Floridia 2017); they are often presented as "democratic innovations" (Smith 2009; Elstub and Escobar 2019) that can help public officials deal with complex policy issues that "traditional" forms of governing fail to deliver (Warren 2009). Mark Warren's (2014) work on governance-driven democratization offers the best description of *elite-led* forms of democratic innovations, where the aim is both to address the legitimacy crisis of representative institutions and experts and to improve policymaking, by involving new voices and interests. Due to close ties with established political elites and institutions (often reflected in government funding), top-down CAs in principle are more closely linked to the political agenda of the day and pursue less "disruptive" goals (Caluwaerts and Reuchamps 2016). Accordingly, their results appear to be, at least in rhetoric, more likely to be endorsed and implemented.

Bottom-up (i.e., civil society-led) approaches to CAs are on the rise, as civil society actors and social movements become more familiar with and reclaim and reinvent the deliberative toolbox (Della Porta and Felicetti 2022; Bua and Bussu 2021). These processes may be crowdfunded and/or funded by charitable organizations. A bottom-up approach is generally understood to be less concerned with specific designs and instead provide opportunities for participants to influence both the content and direction of the process. Thus, it might open the space to pursue more radical and even disruptive aims to challenge established power relations (Caluwaerts and Reuchamps 2015). However, bottom-up processes raise practical challenges. As they might lack clear connections to existing institutions and policymaking processes, they might risk producing less specific and actionable recommendations, reducing opportunities for concrete outcomes, and they might lack legitimacy without the endorsement of elected bodies (Lafont 2015; 2020).

Whilst this brief outline of bottom-up and top-down processes suggests that CAs' categorization strongly relies on the agents who initiate and steer these processes, a closer look reveals that the matter is more complex. Irrespective of which *actors* (i.e. state v. non-state) initiate the CA, the *process* itself can also be described as either top-down or bottom-up. Top-down assemblies tend to be tightly organized around a clearly defined problem, with a top-down approach to process design, which is pre-determined, and with expert evidence, structure, and voting options agreed in advance by the commissioning or organizing body. Citizens are expected to engage in a deliberation around predefined policy options, with limited opportunities to reframe the issue and expand the scope of the evidence around it. The recommendations citizens are able to put forward are therefore shaped by the way the process is designed. In a top-down process, assembly members' function is to provide the views of citizens to inform decisions, but they are not expected to engage with the wider political context (Cherry et al. 2021).

A bottom-up approach, by contrast, is characterized by a more open structure that allows participants to set the agenda, with greater emphasis on citizen-driven questions. Whilst public agencies will often prefer a top-down process that is easier to control and manage, and civil society actors might favour a bottom-up approach, this distinction does not always stand. There are increasing examples of bottom-up processes opened by state actors which involve the public directly in agenda setting in an attempt to tackle distrust and grapple with wicked problems, from increased polarization to societal impacts of new technology or climate change. *Le Grand Débat* launched in France by President Macron in January 2019 could be seen as a recent example of this more hybrid approach.

A third distinction concerns *normative values* informing the preference for top-down versus bottom-up, which also underpin different conceptions of democracy and reasons for expanding the scope and reach of democracy. The idea of "bottom-up legitimacy" remains at the heart of the participatory and deliberative project, whereby legislation and the "rules of the democratic game" must ultimately be rooted in affected citizens' perspectives, needs and preferences (Fleuß 2021). In this respect, a bottom-up approach might appear to be more attuned to the normative ambitions of participatory democracy as it responds better to more radical participatory aspirations for inclusion and social justice (Bua and Bussu 2021). Participatory democrats such as Pateman (2012) have critiqued the top-down nature of most CAs and other mini-publics; they have accused deliberative democrats of having renounced the aspirations of broad participation. Deliberative democrats such as Fishkin (2009) are less concerned with mass participation and would perceive social movements as inferior, or even harmful, compared to the "enlightened opinion" of a randomly selected panel.

The last dimension describes the *core aims*. The rationale behind a top-down approach is generally *functionalistic*; the agenda is shaped from above based on the technocratic needs of the public agency(ies) that "invite" citizen participation (Cornwall 2004). Within this context, CAs can help generate new information to strengthen effective governance but might also be designed to increase popular support for specific policy outcomes, in order to pre-empt social opposition (Papadopoulos 2012). Within a bottom-up approach, the concern might be more explicitly on disruptive change to political, social, and economic structures that would ensure meaningful opportunities for citizens to participate. The new wave of bottom up CAs led by social movements and grassroots group can be interpreted as a promising synthesis between these two normative positions, as it reclaims the deliberative toolbox to foster epistemic value but also more radical participation that challenges the socio-economic and political status quo (Bua and Bussu 2021).

Table 11.1 summarizes these ideal-typical characteristics of top-down and bottom-up CAs and categorizes them under the four dimensions described above: 1) the actor(s) leading the process (state v. non state); 2) the approach to the process itself (open v.

close); 3) the normative values (epistemic v. democratic); and 4) their core aims to either strengthen or challenge existing institutions.

Table 11.1: Ideal types: Top-down/Bottom-up CAs

Dimensions	Top-down CA	Bottom-up CA
1.(Initiating) Actors	Public agencies/state institutions	Social movements, civil society, grassroot initiatives
– *Funding*	Commissioning organization	Crowdfunding, charity
– *Implementation*	Potentially stronger links to policymakers and focus on policy on the agenda might increase impact	Looser links to policymaking and political agenda
2. Process design	Process design predetermined based on predefined goals	Process design (at least partly) a result of co-production
– *Agenda-setting*	Agenda, goals and core questions/issues predefined	Agenda-setting as part of the CA-process
3. Normative values informing CAs	*Primarily epistemic:* Informing public decision-making based on "enlightened" citizen deliberation	*Primarily democratic inclusion:* bottom-up legitimacy of collectively binding laws/policies
4. Core aims – *Relationship to institutions*	Preferences on predefined policy issues; legitimation of (potentially controversial) policies	Broader/more comprehensive and potentially radical reform projects
	Functionalistic; improving/strengthening existing institutions	Disrupting the status quo

We must emphasize that the top-down/bottom-up dichotomy is not always clear-cut. Real world processes can rarely be subsumed under one "top-down" or "bottom-up" ideal type and rather operate on a continuum, combining the elements summarized in Table 11.1 in different ways, for example by involving a mix of state, civil society and grassroots actors, or by having a state-led but open process or *vice versa.*

11.3 Top-down citizens' assemblies: Towards systemic designs

Since the turn of the century, top down, state-led CAs have grown in scope and numbers across polities from the local to the EU level, as an attempt to address the crisis of legitimacy of representative institutions and as part of efforts to tackle so-called wicked policy problems, such as climate change. We are witnessing increasing experimentation to couple top-down CAs with parliamentary committees as in Australia (Hendriks 2016) or with processes of direct democracy, such as referendums, as seen in Canada (Warren and Pearse 2008) and Oregon (Gastil and Richards 2013), over a range of policy areas. There are also increasing examples of mixed-deliberation involving both citizens and elected officials or bureaucrats, as in the case of the Irish Constitutional Convention (ICC) (Farrell et al. 2019).

The Climate Assembly UK (CAUK) is a recent example that helps analyse the limitations and opportunities of an approach that we define as top-down in terms of 1) the actors leading the process, 2) the process itself, 3) the normative values underpinning it, and 4) the core aims. Whilst following the same broad format as many of the exemplary cases often covered in the literature, such as the BCCA, CAUK presents some characteristics that make it a paradigmatic case of the new wave of state-led CAs on climate change; it provides an indication of what state-led digital-analogue CAs might look like and what challenges they raise. The CAUK was commissioned in 2020 by the UK parliament (*state-led*) to agree measures that would help the UK meet its target of net zero greenhouse gas emissions by 2050 (*epistemic value*) (Elstub et al. 2021). The CA was structured based on a classic format, with 108 randomly selected assembly members engaging in deliberation with guidance from facilitators. External experts and advocates providing evidence were chosen by the organizers, through what can be described as a *close process*, with the core aim to *strengthen and legitimize* decision-making on climate policies. Similarly to other recent processes such as the French Climate Convention (FCC), and differently from a traditional format, CAUK assembly members were split into different topic groups for part of the process, to optimize the limited time available to cover a range of topics. This meant that members did not always have access to the same information and were not able to make decisions on all issues. This might have compromised the ability of the assembly to co-ordinate recommendations across all topics. As was the case for other CAs happening during the pandemic, and possibly indicative of future trends in a pragmatic effort to reduce costs and increase reach, part of the deliberation process moved online to meet social distancing regulations. The overall experience was quite positive for participants, and this hybrid (digital/analogue) approach might help address some of the criticisms levelled against top-down CAs that they have limited reach, are expensive and difficult to scale up.

Although CAUK was commissioned by the UK Parliament, the connection with representative structures, as is often the case with CAs and democratic innovations more broadly, had many shortcomings. The high turnover in committee membership following snap general elections in 2019, shortly after the CA had been commissioned, affected political engagement with the process. Furthermore, CAUK never gained full support from government; a lack of planning and guidance on follow up on recommendations also limited its impact (Elstub et al. 2021). These are persistent barriers that continue to plague even processes with strong political backing. The claim that a top-down/state-led approach increases opportunities for impact is often challenged by the reality that these processes are still vulnerable to changes in the political cycle, resistance to citizen influence among public servants, and the complexities of policymaking. The CAUK was more effective than previous deliberative initiatives in the UK at gaining media coverage. However, public awareness of the process remained low, particularly in a context where public attention was grabbed by the pandemic and Brexit.

Whereas the benefits of CAs in terms of learning outcomes for participants and the quality of policy ideas and recommendations emerging though facilitated deliberation are well documented, the *ad hoc*, top-down process design has several limitations when it comes to tangible policy and democratic impact. As a reaction, more innovative designs are increasingly taking a systemic lens. The recent Ostbelgien Model, in the German-speaking region of Belgium, has become a trailblazer of this systemic approach to CAs. Niessen and Reuchamps (2019) identify several aspects in which this process differentiates itself from previous initiatives. It responds to the limited policy impact that plagues most CAs, firstly by creating a quasi-institutional connection to parliament and secondly by making this connection permanent. Further, Ostbelgien attempts to broaden the scope of a top-down process design, by giving substantive autonomy to the new permanent Citizen Council, which can set the agenda and institute three CAs each year to deliberate and propose recommendations over the issues identified by the Council itself. In so doing, Ostbelgien, which based on the actor dimension can be described as top-down (*state-led*) is incorporating bottom-up elements when it comes to process, as the latter is open to citizen agenda-setting. By embedding these CAs within the yearly policy and political cycle, with opportunities for oversight and follow up, Ostbelgien realizes the aspiration of ongoing, back-and-forth dialogue between citizens and policy-makers. In this way, normative values and core aims respond both to the top-down functionalistic orientation to strengthen epistemic utility and produce better policies, and bottom-up democratic aspirations, with potentially disruptive effects on the working of traditional institutions.

11.4 Bottom-up citizens' assemblies: Reclaiming the deliberative toolbox to meet bottom-up demands

Typically, when CAs are launched and funded independently from state actors or public agencies (i.e. civil society/grassroots-led), they are ascribed more disruptive potential and often presented as better equipped for bringing marginalized voices to the fore (see Table 11.1). Whilst random selection in state-led processes is also presented as a way of including voices that are often at the margins of political and public life, as it claims to provide every citizen with an equal chance of being invited (although this is debatable), it does little to remove many of the barriers to participation that stand in the way of lower socioeconomic cohorts and other marginalized segments of the population (Harris 2021). There may be a host of factors that alienate these groups (e.g., a sense of self-inefficacy, distrust, cynicism, as well as material and time poverty). Embeddedness within communities is essential to foster inclusive participation. In this respect, civil society can play a crucial role in anchoring participation in the community and reaching out to disempowered groups (Bussu et al. 2022). However, as civil society-led processes can be more or less open in terms of focus and process, they can also be vulnerable to capture by the most resource-rich citizens.

Based on the dimensions examined above (actors, process, normative values, and core aims), we can distinguish two sub-types in the vast array of bottom-up initiatives that took place in the past decade. Assemblies such as the Irish Initiative *We the Citizens* (2011; henceforth: WtC) and the more recent *Citizens' Assembly on Brexit* (2017; henceforth: CAB) have focused on a particularly salient and heavily disputed political issue which political elites and routinized democratic procedures could not adequately deal with (also see Renwick et al. 2018: 656). Both WtC and the CAB were launched by teams of researchers (e. g., Renwick et al. 2018: 650). Whilst these assemblies were initiated by civil society actors, they largely used a top-down approach to process design and dealt with a comparatively narrow range of topics and questions on abortion policies in Ireland, and trade and migration policies in post-Brexit UK. In terms of normative values, the focus was on citizens' epistemic advantage, "to demonstrate the value of citizen-oriented, deliberative approaches to achieving large-scale political reform" (Farrell, O'Malley and Suiter 2013: 100). Yet, in practical terms core rationales of both initiatives were to "feed deliberately and publicly into the political reform agenda" and to contribute to a more inclusive and constructive dialogue in the broader public sphere and society (Farrell, O'Malley and Suiter 2013: 100).

More radical approaches have aimed at challenging and reconceptualizing the very "rules of the democratic game". The *Icelandic Initiative for Constitutional Reform* (2010 – 2013; henceforth: ICR) and the German *Citizens' Assembly on the Future of Democracy* (2019; henceforth: CAD) were explicitly framed and designed as "disruptive" initiatives, i. e., they "challenge[d] the political status quo, by targeting the perceived gap between elites and citizens" (Caluwaerts and Reuchamps 2016: 16). They differ from "more piecemeal" efforts aiming at changing particular laws or policies and explicitly explore options for innovating and/or complementing the existing institutional infrastructure of democratic politics (Landemore 2020: 152–153; Fleuß 2021: 147). In the ICR's case, Iceland's political and financial crisis in 2008 triggered a protest movement which called for more and more immediate citizen involvement in political decision-making that culminated in drafting a novel constitutional document (Della Porta 2020: 36–38). Whilst the German CAD's initiative did not evolve out of a particular protest or social movement, it was nevertheless a response to German citizens' increasing disinterest and distrust in representative politics.

In all these initiatives, policy options were co-created by experts and citizens, through an open process. This involved a multi-staged approach, integrating citizens in (online) initiatives for crowdsourcing ideas and agenda-setting (Della Porta 2020: 36–38; Fleuß 2021: 159; Landemore 2020: 157–182). The funding approach and limited ties, if any, to established political elites were instrumental in "keeping the agenda open" (Caluwaerts and Reuchamps 2015: 157). Whilst ICR explicitly adopted crowdfunding and crowdsourcing approaches, the German CAD's process was funded and designed by a charitable civil society organization, *Mehr Demokratie*, to strengthen lay citizens' impact on collectively binding decision-making (Mehr Demokratie 2021). CAD was the first German CA that involved citizens systematically in "co-developing" German democracy and thinking about institutional reforms at the federal level. Participants proposed to combine deliberative forums with referendums; they advocated for "citizens' councils with randomly selected citizens at the federal level", "nationwide referendums" and "an independent staff unit for citizen participation and direct democracy" (Fleuß 2021: 148; also see Bürgergutachten 2019).

Mehr Demokratie combined a public relations campaign with targeted interactions and partnerships with established political elites such as Wolfgang Schäuble, the then president of the German parliament. A core aim here was to "change hearts and minds" of citizens and public officials, rather than implementing *ad hoc* institutional reforms. These strategies certainly contributed to raising awareness for alternative ways of "doing democracy", but their long-term impact on Germany's constitutional and institutional infrastructure might be harder to achieve. The ICR which emerged out of combinations of disruptive protests and government elite interventions was confronted with similar problems: the constitutional reform was at the end of the day blocked by conservatives in the Icelandic parliament (Della Porta 2020: 37–43). Problems concerning the implementation of bottom-up CAs' decisions are also rooted in the ways in which liberal or representative democracies conceptualize and generate "legitimate" collectively binding decisions: in this respect, the legitimacy of bottom-up CAs, as they bypass institutionalized, constitutionally embedded channels for decision-making, is often questioned.

CAs such as CAD or the ICR can be described as bottom-up across the four dimensions we have identified (Table 11.1): they were led by civil society actors (1), and they were based on an open process that enabled citizens' agenda-setting, creating new space for citizen-led democratic innovation (2). Their normative aspirations were to widen the scope of democracy, bridging the gap between citizens and representatives (3), with the core aims of disrupting the status quo and building new support for a participatory society (4). Whilst in both cases there were important efforts at working with political elites, these processes also illustrate the complexity of working with state institutions when the latter are not the commissioners with stakes in the process: "collaboration with the state is not simply a resource to secure even the highest type of impact (i.e., constitutional change). The state actually exposes democratic experiments to legal, political and administrative dynamics that might halt the process of change" (Della Porta and Felicetti 2022: 78). Cooperation and ties to government elites can significantly limit CAs' disruptive potential, independence, and credibility, yet substantive political change requires civil society actors to navigate existing power structures.

Table 11.2 summarizes the cases described based on the four dimensions of actor, process, normative values, and core aims.

Table 11.2: Top-down and bottom-up CA across four dimensions

Cases	Actor	Process	Normative Goals	Core aims
BCCA	State-led	Close	Epistemic	Functionalistic
CAUK	State-led	Close	Epistemic	Functionalistic
FCC	State-led	Open	Epistemic and Democratic	Functionalistic
OSTBELGIEN	State-led	Hybrid	Epistemic and Democratic	Functionalistic
CAB	Civil society-led	Close	Epistemic and Democratic	Functionalistic
ICC	State-led	Open	Epistemic and Democratic	Functionalistic
WtC	Civil society-led	Close	Epistemic and Democratic	Functionalistic
CAD	Civil society-led	Open	Democratic	Disruptive
ICR	Civil society-led	Open	Democratic	Disruptive
G1000	Civil society-led	Open	Democratic	Disruptive

11.5 Top-down and bottom-up: A dynamic relationship

The top-down vs. bottom-up heuristic has underpinned many analyses of democratic innovations. The focus has often been on actors opening the process: bottom-up as in civil society-led governance is generally presented as better able to mobilize wider participation (Cornwall 2004) and produce radical transformation (Bua and Bussu 2021); top-down, as in state-led participation, is depicted as more effective at producing impact through links to the political and policy agenda. "Expert citizens" attending these "invited" forums, however, might be disconnected from the wider public and at risk of co-optation (Bang 2005). A closer look at exemplary top-down and bottom-up initiatives, however, leads to more nuanced conclusions.

Firstly, we argue that the distinction between bottom-up and top-down CAs should not be merely drawn in terms of actors initiating the process. The openness of the process and whether participants are able to set the agenda as well as values and goals underlying, informing, and structuring the CA might have as big an impact on citizen empowerment as the actors initiating it. Along these lines, Richardson et al. (2019) argue that civil society-led initiatives can be equally at risk of capture by sectional interests – and disconnected from the needs and preferences of affected citizens – if the process is not open and aiming at broad inclusion. Depending on the context and the issue, a state-led approach might indeed provide better democratic channels to broker between hotly contested claims.

Secondly, an adequate combination of the characteristics of our ideal types of bottom-up and top-down assemblies can be helpful to achieve different goals in different contexts. Whilst some CAs primarily wish to foster new discourses in the broader society about political alternatives, others aim to have concrete impact on policies or constitutional decisions. The elements that characterize ideal-types of top-down and bottom-up initiatives can thus be used as a "toolbox" that allows for flexible design and combination in democratic processes. A top-down process design with a predefined agenda may be well-suited for a "consultative" use of CAs, to gauge the views of the general public if it had access to balanced and as far as possible unbiased information and had the opportunity to deliberate with peers. Such CAs can perform an ancillary role to increase the effectiveness of representative institutions and strengthen existing governance structures. Yet, processes that exclude citizens from agenda-setting and process design will be ill-suited if the core aim is to challenge and question hegemonical discourses or the very "rules of the democratic game". Here, we need to keep in mind that different *kinds* of initiating actors (state/civil society) *tend* to pursue and prioritize different goals: state-led initiatives are more likely to make consultative use of CAs whilst civil society-led initiatives are prone to challenge established institutions.

Nevertheless, in recent years CAs have grown in complexity and new hybrid experiments have emerged on the ground that synthesize different democratic practices involving a range of actors (Felicetti 2021), and increasingly including a mix of deliberative, representative, and participatory aspects (Felicetti 2021; Caluwaerts and Reuchamps 2015; Gastil et al. 2018). These are often complex arrangements including a series of interacting arenas, whilst "hybridized and inventive" radical experiments have been emerging, which attempt to combine top-down and bottom-up elements (Sintomer 2018). Whilst more technocratic and consultative CA, such as the Citizen Assembly UK, continue to gain popularity amongst politicians, observers are paying greater attention to their limitations, and we are seeing renewed efforts at institutionalizing permanent CAs that influence the cycle of policymaking in a continuous fashion, such as the above mentioned Ostbelgien. New movement parties and political coalitions, such Barcelona en Comú in Spain (Bua and Bussu 2021) or the Agora party in Belgium have embedded sortition and deliberative and participatory tools (which normally characterize top-down processes) within their organizational structures. The Agora case is particularly interesting in this respect, as their CAs are organized by volunteers, but citizen recommendations are then defended in the Brussels Regional Parliament through the elected Agora MP (Junius et al. 2021).

Different top-down and bottom-up CAs can therefore be usefully linked with each other and the democratic system at large. The disappointing record of most CAs, whether top-down or bottom-up, in influencing decisions, as policymakers continue to ignore or cherry pick citizens' recommendations, has informed theory and practice to better link CAs to representative institutions (e.g., Sintomer, Herzberg, and Röcke 2008). But there are also increasing calls and experimentation in linking CAs to the wider society, amid growing concerns, particularly amongst participatory democrats (see Pateman 2012), that CAs may otherwise become apolitical remedial action.

11.6 Conclusion

This chapter has provided an overview and a critical reflection on conceptions of top-down and bottom-up CAs. We have identified four main characteristics of each ideal type, as described in the literature. Ideal-type top-down assemblies are opened by state institutions to address a predefined policy issue and strengthen the legitimacy of the commissioning institution. Ideal-type bottom-up CAs are led by civil society and provide space for citizen agenda-setting and might have ambitions for more radical reform projects, whilst struggling to have tangible impact because of looser or no links with empowered decision-making spaces. However, the practice of CAs is less clear-cut and if bottom-up approaches are not necessarily better than top-down initiatives at bringing in disempowered interests and ensuring more inclusive processes, top-down CAs do not seem to have such a good record in terms of impact just because they work closely with state institutions. Our assessment of four different dimensions of the top-down/bottom-up heuristic facilitates a more differentiated assessment of types of CAs that also may flexibly combine bottom-up and top-down elements. For instance, CAs can be bottom-up because they are led by non-state actors and yet top-down in terms of process, with a predefined policy focus, as in the case of CAB. Away from fetishizing one or the other, different approaches might be better suited to different contexts and different goals. Overall, we are seeing promising developments away from one-off *ad hoc* initiatives and towards processes combining top-down and bottom-up elements in a systemic fashion, potentially strengthening opportunities for more tangible impact and citizen empowerment.

References

Bächtiger, A., & Parkinson, J. (2019). *Mapping and Measuring Deliberation: Towards a New Deliberative Quality.* Oxford: Oxford University Press.

Bang, H. (2005). Among everyday makers and expert citizens. In J. Newman (ed.), *Remaking Governance: Peoples, Politics and the Public Sphere*, 159–179. Bristol: Policy Press

Bua, A., & Bussu, S. (2021). Between governance-driven democratisation and democracy-driven governance: Explaining changes in participatory governance in the case of Barcelona. *European Journal of Political Research* 60 (3), 716–737.

Bussu, S. (2019) Collaborative governance: between invited and invented spaces. In S. Elstub & O. Escobar (eds), *Handbook of Democratic Innovation and Governance*, 60–76. Cheltenham: Edward Elgar Publishing.

Bussu, S., Bua, A., Dean, R. & Smith, G. (2022). Embedding participatory governance, *Critical Policy Studies* 16 (2), 133–145.

Bürgergutachten. (2019). [Citizens' report: recommendations from the German citizen assembly on the future of democracy in Sept. 2019]. Retrieved from:
https://www.mehr-demokratie.de/fileadmin/pdf/Buergerrat/2019–11–07_Bu__rgergutachten_Web.pdf

Caluwaerts, D., & Reuchamps, M. (2015). Strengthening democracy through bottom-up deliberation: An assessment of the internal legitimacy of the G1000 project. *Acta Politica* 50 (2), 151–170.

Caluwaerts, D., & Reuchamps, M. (2016). Generating democratic legitimacy through deliberative innovations: the role of embeddedness and disruptiveness. *Representation* 52 (1), 13–27.

Cherry, C. E., Capstick, S., Demski, C., Mellier, C., Stone, L., & Verfuerth, C. (2021). Citizens' climate assemblies: Understanding public deliberation for climate policy. Cardiff: The Centre for Climate Change and Social Transformations
https://cast.ac.uk/wp-content/uploads/2021/07/CITIZENS-CLIMATE-ASSEMBLIES-CAST-July-2021.pdf

Cornwall, A. (2004). Introduction: New democratic spaces? The politics and dynamics of institutionalised participation. *IDS Bulletin* 35, 1–10.

Della Porta, D. (2020). *How Social Movements Can Save Democracy.* Cambridge: Polity Press.

Della Porta, D., & Felicetti, A. (2022). Innovating democracy against democratic stress in Europe: Social movements and democratic experiments. *Representation* 58 (1), 67–84.

Elstub, S., and Escobar, O. (eds.) (2019). *Handbook of Democratic Innovation and Governance.* Cheltenham: Edward Elgar Publishing.

Elstub, S., and McLaverty, P. (eds.) (2014). *Deliberative Democracy: Issues and Cases.* Edinburgh: Edinburgh University Press

Elstub, S., Ercan, S., & Mendonça, R. F. (2016). Editorial introduction: The fourth generation of deliberative democracy. *Critical Policy Studies* 10 (2), 139–151.

Elstub, S., Farrell, D. M., Carrick, J., & Mockler, P. (2021). *Evaluation of Climate Assembly UK.* Newcastle: Newcastle University https://www.parliament.uk/globalassets/documents/get-involved2/climate-assembly-uk/evaluation-of--climate-assembly-uk.pdf

Farrell, D. M., O'Malley, E., & Suiter, J. (2013). Deliberative democracy in action Irish-style: The 2011 *We the Citizens* pilot citizens' assembly. *Irish Political Studies* 28 (1), 99–113.

Farrell, D. M., Suiter, J., & Harris, C. (2019). 'Systematizing' constitutional deliberation: the 2016–18 citizens' assembly in Ireland. *Irish Political Studies* (34) 1, 113–123.

Felicetti, A. (2021). Learning from democratic practices: New perspectives in institutional design. *The Journal of Politics* 83 (4), 1589–1601.

Fishkin, J. S. (2009). *When the People Speak: Deliberative Democracy and Public Consultation.* Oxford: Oxford University Press.

Fleuß, D. (2021). *Radical Proceduralism: Democracy from Philosophical Principles to Political Institutions.* Bingley: Emerald Publishing.

Floridia, A. (2017). *From Participation to Deliberation. A Critical Genealogy of Deliberative Democracy.* Colchester: ECPR Press.

Gastil, J., & Richards, R. (2013). Making direct democracy deliberative through random assemblies. *Politics & Society* 41 (2), 253–281.

Gastil, J., Knobloch, K. R., Reedy, J., Henkels, M., & Cramer, K. (2018). Assessing the electoral impact of the 2010 Oregon Citizens' Initiative Review. *American Politics Research* 46 (3), 534–563.

Harris, C. (2021). Looking to the future: Including children, young people and future generations in deliberations on climate action. Ireland's Citizens' Assembly 2016–2018. *Innovation: The European Journal of Social Science Research* 34(5), 677–693.

Hendriks, C. M. (2016). Coupling citizens and elites in deliberative systems: The role of institutional design. *European Journal of Political Research* 55, 43–60.

Junius, N., Caluwaerts, D., Matthieu, J., & Erzeel, S. (2021). Hacking the representative system through deliberation? The organization of the Agora party in Brussels. *Acta Politica* 1–19.

Lafont, C. (2015). Deliberation, participation & democratic legitimacy. *Journal of Political Philosophy* 23, 40–63.

Lafont, Cristina (2020). *Democracy without Shortcuts. A participatory conception of deliberative democracy.* Oxford: Oxford University Press.

Landemore, H. (2020). *Open Democracy: Reinventing Popular Rule for the Twenty-First Century.* Princeton, NJ: Princeton University Press.

Mehr Demokratie. (2021). Profil von Mehr Demokratie e.V. [Profile of the organization] Retrieved from: https://www.mehr-demokratie.de/ueber-uns/profil

Niessen, C., & Reuchamps, M. (2019). *Designing a Permanent Deliberative Citizens' Assembly: The Ostbelgien Modell in Belgium.* Working Paper Series of the Centre for Deliberative Democracy and Global Governance.

Papadopoulos, Y. (1998). *Démocratie directe.* Paris: Economica.

Papadopoulos, Y. (2012). On the embeddedness of deliberative systems: Why elitist innovations matter more. In *Deliberative Systems: Deliberative Democracy at the Large Scale*, edited by J. Mansbridge & J. Parkinson, 125–150. Cambridge: Cambridge University Press.

Parkinson, J., & Mansbridge, J. (2012). *Deliberative Systems: Deliberative Democracy at the Large Scale*. Cambridge: Cambridge University Press

Pateman, C. (2012). Participatory democracy revisited. *Perspectives on Politics* 10 (1), 7–19.

Perry, B., & May, T. (2010). Urban knowledge exchange: Devilish dichotomies and active intermediation. *International Journal of Knowledge-Based Development* 1 (1/2), 6–24.

Renwick, A., Allan, S., Jennings, W., McKee, R., Russell, M., & Smith, G. (2018). What kind of Brexit do voters want? Lessons from the Citizens' Assembly on Brexit. *The Political Quarterly* 89 (4), 649–658.

Richardson, L., Durose, C., & Perry, B. (2019). Three tyrannies of participatory governance. *Journal of Chinese Governance* 4 (2), 123–143

Sintomer, Y. (2018). From deliberative to radical democracy? Sortition and politics in the twenty-first century. *Politics & Society* 46 (3), 337–357

Sintomer, Y., Herzberg, C. & Röcke, A. (2008). Participatory budgeting in Europe: Potentials and challenges. *International Journal of Urban and Regional Research* 32, 164–178.

Smith, G. (2009) *Democratic Innovations: Designing Institutions for Citizen Participation*. Cambridge: Cambridge University Press

Wagenaar, H., & Wood, M. (2018). The precarious politics of public innovation. *Politics and Governance* 6 (1), 150–160.

Warren, M. E. (2009). Citizen participation and democratic deficits: Considerations from the perspective of democratic theory. In J. DeBardeleben & J. H. Pammett (eds), *Activating the Citizen*, 17–40. London: Palgrave Macmillan.

Warren, M. (2014). Governance-driven democratization. In S. Griggs, A. J. Norval, & H. Wagenaar (eds), *Practices of Freedom: Decentered Governance, Conflict and Democratic Participation*, 38–60. Cambridge: Cambridge University Press.

Warren, M. E., & Pearse, H. (2008). *Designing Deliberative Democracy: The British Columbia Citizens' Assembly*. Cambridge: Cambridge University Press.

Willett, J., & Giovannini, A. (2014). The uneven path of UK devolution: Top-down vs. bottom-up regionalism in England – Cornwall and the North-East compared. *Political Studies* 62 (2), 343–360.

Clodagh Harris, David M. Farrell, and Jane Suiter

12 Mixed-member deliberative forums: Citizens' assemblies bringing together elected officials and citizens

Abstract: Rarer than standard citizens' assemblies, mixed deliberative forums that include both randomly selected citizens and elected political representatives are having an emerging impact on our understanding of deliberative democracy and how deliberative democratic innovations can contribute to the wider deliberative system. This chapter presents a definition and a concise overview and analysis of these mixed deliberative forums with reference to the cases that have been established to date. Drawing from the literature on "democratic coupling", it explores their possible strengths and shortcomings, finding that the inclusion of politicians can enhance the diversity of opinion, add epistemic value and increase the visibility and impact of the process and its recommendations. However, it also notes, that these benefits risk being undermined by the potential for elite domination of the discussions and decisions. It concludes with a discussion of their possible future use within the wider deliberative system.

Keywords: elected representatives, mixed member forum, citizens' assembly, domination, impact

12.1 Introduction

The onset of the "deliberative wave" (OECD 2020) over the past decade has seen a dramatic rise in the number of deliberative mini-publics (DMPs) across OECD countries (and more widely); it has also seen the emergence of hybrids of the existing types of DMPs, to such an extent that the lines between (what had been seen as) different forms of DMPs have become blurred (Curato et al. 2021). A prominent form of hybridization has involved including politicians (elected officials) as members, sitting side by side with "regular citizens" (non-elected residents and/or citizens). These hybrid forums are used less frequently than the standard citizens' assemblies (CAs) but have led to political and constitutional reform as well as increased understanding of how deliberative democratic innovations can contribute to the wider political system. To date, the best-known example of a mixed-member mini-public was Ireland's Convention on the Constitution (2012–2014). Others have emerged more recently in Belgium

Clodagh Harris: University College Cork, Ireland; **David M. Farrell:** University College Dublin, Ireland; **Jane Suiter:** Dublin City University, Ireland.

∂ Open Access. © 2023 the author(s), published by De Gruyter. (CC) BY-NC-ND This work is licensed under the Creative Commons Attribution-NonCommercial-NoDerivatives 4.0 International License. https://doi.org/10.1515/9783110758269-014

and Finland, and again in Ireland, providing important insights into their deliberative quality, impact, and institutionalism.

This chapter presents a concise overview and analysis of these mixed deliberative forums. Drawing from literature in the field, it offers a definition of what is meant by a mixed-member deliberative forum, and outlines where and how they have been established to date. With reference to the literature on "democratic coupling", it explores the potential strengths and shortcomings of these hybrid CAs, and concludes with a discussion of their possible future use.

12.2 What are mixed-member deliberative forums?

Different terms have been used to describe processes in which randomly selected citizens deliberate directly with elected officials in a particular forum. In their work on the Irish Convention on the Constitution, Arnold et al. (2019) talk of a "hybrid sortition chamber". Others refer to them as "mixed". For instance, Flinders et al. (2016) differentiate between pure and mixed assemblies where pure assemblies consist solely of citizens and mixed assemblies include citizens and politicians. Strandberg et al. (2021a) and Vandamme et al. (2019) speak of "mixed deliberation" and a "mixed chamber" respectively. Yet, these terms are not sufficiently comprehensive. Mixed deliberation could be interpreted broadly to include processes that involve the wider citizenry, elected officials, stakeholders, and others in system wide deliberations as opposed to deliberations between citizens and politicians in a discrete deliberative forum as is the objective of this chapter. In their most recent work on the Irish Convention, Farrell et al. (2020) identify it as a mixed-member deliberative forum (MMDF). This is the term employed here as it captures both the forum's membership and process.

In MMDFs the private citizens are randomly selected to fill key demographic descriptors such as age, gender, educational attainment, employment status and so forth (in some instances the stratification might also include attitudinal quotas). The elected officials usually put themselves forward or are nominated by their political party; party representation in the forum often reflects their strength within the parliament, or municipal council. Citizens tend to outnumber elected officials in these processes.[1]

To date, there is no definitive template for MMDFs. Similarly, research on their design, deliberative quality, and impact is limited though – as we shall see – growing. Their membership may differentiate them from "regular" mini-publics, but they share their deliberative virtues of inclusion, justification, and reflection (Dryzek 2016), as well as operational features such as invited expertise, professional facilitation and decision making.

---

[1] Clearly, elected officials are citizens too, but their membership of the deliberative forum recognizes their particular status as elected (professional) politicians.

12.3 Real-world examples of mixed-member deliberative forums

To date there have only been a handful of real-world examples of MMDFs, some established officially (by a government or municipal authority), others as academic experiments. In this section we review cases from Ireland, Belgium, the UK, and Finland.

12.3.1 Ireland

Ireland's Convention on the Constitution (2012–2014) was the first of its kind worldwide (Arnold et al. 2019). Its membership and agenda were the result of a compromise negotiated between the two governing parties at the time. It comprised 66 citizens, 33 politicians, and an independent chair. The citizen members were selected at random and stratified across gender, age, socio-economic status, and geography. The political parties determined how their parliamentary members were selected and the parties' allocations were proportionate to their representation in parliament.

The Convention was asked to consider eight specific issues: the length of the term of office of the Irish President; whether to reduce the voting age to 17; a review of the Dáil (lower house of parliament) electoral system; whether to give non-resident Irish citizens the right to vote in Presidential elections; whether to legalize marriage equality; a review of an existing clause in the Irish Constitution on the role of women in the home and encouraging greater participation of women in public life; increasing the participation of women in politics; and whether to remove the offence of blasphemy from the Constitution. It was allowed to propose other topics after the original eight reports were completed, thereby giving the Convention some limited agenda setting powers. This was to see the addition of two topics: parliamentary reform, and economic, social, and cultural rights.

The Convention voted by secret ballot and it recommendations required only a majority of the votes cast. Its reports were sent to the Houses of the Oireachtas (Parliament) for further discussion and the government committed to respond within four months. The first three reports were all discussed promptly. This was not the case for those that followed; they were discussed much later. In all, the Convention made 38 recommendations of which it is estimated that 18 would require a referendum. Overtime, the majority of the Constitutional Convention's recommendations have been accepted and/or are due to be implemented. Only eight of them were rejected outright. Many of those accepted are still awaiting referendum, for example lowering the voting age and votes for those resident outside the state in presidential elections (Harris et al. 2021).

Undoubtedly, the Convention on the Constitution's most significant impact, was on 22 May 2015, when Ireland became the first country in the world to support the introduction of marriage equality by popular vote. This was the first time a recommendation from a deliberative mini-public resulted in constitutional change. Ireland's subsequent CAs are also part of its legacy (Farrell et al. 2021), as are the impact its processes have had on CAs and MMDFs internationally.

At the time of writing, the Irish houses of the Oireachtas have just established two new mini-publics whose processes will run in parallel. One is a "pure" CA comprising a stratified random selection of residents in Ireland aged 18 and over to address the issue of biodiversity loss. The other is a MMDF that has been charged with deliberating on the direct election of a Mayor for Dublin and other local governance issues in the city. It has used sortition to recruit city residents aged 18 and over (67 members). The councillor members, of whom there are 12, broadly reflect their parties' representation in the respective local authorities, with a slight bias to smaller parties in order to ensure representation of most groups, and have either been self-selected or chosen by their party. Both deliberative forums commenced their work in April 2022. At the time of writing, both are scheduled to finish their work by the end of that year.

12.3.2 Finland

There have been a number of MMDFs in Finland that have occurred primarily at the municipal level. They have varied in duration, recruitment, and impact. The "Turku debates" citizens' panel which took place in 2020 is arguably the most significant of the Finnish cases (Grönlund et al. 2020; Värttö et al. 2021). The panel included 193 participants, consisting of a mix of randomly selected citizens (171) and local councillors (21). The deliberations involved a combination of citizen only small groups and small groups that mixed citizens and councillors. The city's Mayor tasked it with deliberating on future traffic arrangements in Turku, to feed into the city's new "master plan". Similar to the Irish Convention the citizen members outnumbered the councillors in the mixed groups and party representation reflected their representation in the city council. The COVID-19 pandemic resulted in the deliberations taking place online. The panel received a prompt response to their recommendations, which were discussed in a public webinar, attended by the Mayor, a fortnight after the panel concluded its work and were subsequently presented to the city's urban environment department for consideration.

The Korsholm municipality debated a contentious municipal merger in Finland in 2018. This MMDF was officially recognized as part of the municipality's discussions on this topic, but in a limited way. It met a year in advance of a consultative referendum on the issue. Compared to other MMDFs, the process was short: only three separate two-hour sessions in January and February 2018. The events were open to all who were interested in participating. Sortition was not used to recruit participants. Random selection was, however, used to ensure that a mix of citizens and politicians were included in each set of facilitated small group discussions. The deliberative discussions formed part of the municipality's official public hearings of citizens prior to the merger negotiations (Strandberg et al. 2021a; Strandberg et al. 2021b). This was not, however, the first MMDF to take place in Korsholm.

In November 2016, a different MMDF took place in the municipality: this was primarily an academic exercise with little or no official role. Its task was to consider the building of a new school centre and took place after the municipality had made a decision that favoured closing the small schools and replacing them with a single larger one. Strandberg and Berg (2020) note that this forum used an "experimental design" in which half of the groups had a facilitator to support their deliberations while the other half had no facilitator or "discussion rules". There were 35 participants (21 citizens and 14 politicians) who were recruited through local papers, social media and word of mouth (Strandberg and Berg 2020).

12.3.3 Belgium

Belgium has emerged as a world leader in the institutionalization of deliberative and participatory forums (Niessen and Reuchamps 2019). In 2019, the pioneering Ostbelgien model was created, embedding CAs in political decision making in the country's German-speaking community. More recently, following the increased representation of the Green party in the 2019 general elections in both the Brussels and Walloon regional parliaments, the governing coalitions committed to the establishment of MMDFs in the shape of deliberative committees as part of their policymaking processes.

At the time of writing, the Brussels regional parliament and the French-speaking Parliament in Brussels (Cocof) have each established "deliberative committees" that include both members of Parliament and randomly selected residents aged 16 and over, stratified by gender, age, the region's official languages, geographical distribution, and level of education (Reuchamps 2020). The politician members are those who sit in the relevant parliamentary standing committee. The ratio of citizen to politician members is 3 to 1.

Unlike the Irish and Finnish cases discussed above, which were once off and "ad hoc", the Brussels deliberative committees are institutionalized to the extent that they are embedded in the region's democratic process and occur regularly. It should be noted, however, that they are not enshrined in the Constitution and could be abolished, if desired, by a new administration.

An indirect petition process open to the public can be used to determine the topic for deliberation. It requires that a group of 100 or more residents support a call for the collection of signatures on the Parliament's website: when a call receives the support of 1,000 residents it is forwarded to the Bureau of the Parliament for consideration and possible selection. Allowing for greater public say in the choice of topic enhances the processes input legitimacy, yet, as Reuchamps observes, the relevant parliament "retains the ultimate agenda-setting power" (2020).

In terms of the final decision-making process, the Brussels' MMDFs take a twin track approach with different processes for the citizen and politician members. The citizens vote secretly on each proposal while the politician members vote publicly with an absolute majority requirement (Vrydagh et al. 2021). In addition the politicians may explain each of their votes. This can make the voting session lengthy but does facilitate justification and reason giving. The process is chaired by the chair of the standing committee (politician) and the deliberations are held in the official buildings of the regional parliament and committee rooms.

Those recommendations that are approved by both groups of members are included in a report that is in turn submitted to the Parliamentary standing committee (of which the 15 parliamentarians are members). This committee must respond by issuing a follow up report, responding to the status of the recommendations within six months. This is done in a public session of the standing committee to which the citizens are invited (Vrydagh et al. 2021).

At the time of writing, three mixed member deliberative committees have been convened and are ongoing in terms of decision-making and official responses. The first two involved members from standing committees in the Brussels regional parliament with the third one linked to the Cocof. The first and second deliberative committees took place during summer 2021 and deliberated on 5G and homelessness respectively, the former topic chosen by the parliamentarians and the latter stemming from the indirect public petition process. The deliberation on 5G focused on technical matters over 5G itself. The framing of the deliberations in this way led to widespread criticism as well as concern that the topic had been somewhat cynically used by a political party to endorse its own position. The Cocof deliberative committee that took place in Autumn 2021 deliberated on resilience, a topic that was favoured by the political leadership.[2] Another has yet to be convened owing to legal issues surrounding the sortition process. At the time of writing, it is expected that a new law permitting the use of the national register for the purpose of random selection will be passed in a matter of months.

12.3.4 The UK

In 2015 a group of academics and civil society actors established the UK's Democracy Matters project to explore the potential for a UK constitutional deliberative forum. The project compared two types of deliberative forums: a "pure", citizens only, assembly and a mixed-member deliberative forum. The research team, funded by the UK's Economic Social and Research Council, designed two city-based mini-publics. Described by the team as a "democratic experiment", participants in Sheffield and Southampton were invited to consider devolution and the future of local democracy over the course of two weekends. The CA included 32 randomly selected residents while the mixed-

---

2 The authors are grateful to Julien Vyrdagh for sharing his knowledge of and expertise on the Belgian deliberative committees. All omissions or errors are our own.

member deliberative forum brought together six local politicians to deliberate with 23 randomly selected citizens.

Table 12.1: Types of MMDFs

	Official or Academic	One-off or Institutionalized
Ireland's Convention on the Constitution, 2012–14	Official	One-off
UK Democracy Matters, 2015	Academic	One-off
Korsholm MMDF, 2016	Academic	One-off
Korsholm MMDF, 2018	Official	One-off
Brussels' Deliberative Committees, 2019	Official	Institutionalized
'Turku debates" citizens' panel, 2020	Official	One-off

This brief snapshot of MMDFs that have taken place to date reveals both commonalities and differences. Shared practice has emerged in participant recruitment and deliberative process. Most of the cases have employed forms of random selection for the citizen participants and, the ratio of citizens to elected officials is heavily weighted in favour of the former. Similarly, all share, albeit to varying degrees, a deliberative process that employs expert input, mixed small group discussions and facilitation. Their agenda-setting powers, duration, and impact of their recommendations differ. The same is true for their status and function. We've observed that an MMDF may be institutionalized or once-off, ad-hoc events (status), as summarized in Table 12.1. There are also variations in terms of the commissioning agent: there are those MMDFs that can be categorized as official, initiated by political institutions (parliaments, councils etc.) with a specific official remit; and then there are experimental MMDFs, established by academic and/or civil society teams who have a research and/or advocacy objective. These experimental projects, while not directly impactful on policy, are emerging as an important source of research on deliberation in MMDFs. They have also increased awareness of this type of deliberative forum amongst officials, policymakers, stakeholders, and residents.

12.4 The risks and rewards of mixing politicians with citizens

Mixing politicians in with regular citizens has its positives and its negatives. In order to assess this, we can draw upon the concept of "designed coupling", which is prominent in debates over deliberative systems. The concept refers to how different sites of deliberation are "connected through institutional mechanisms" (Hendriks 2016: 44). Clearly, in our use of this concept, we are also referring to coupling in a different sense, namely relating to the connecting in the one process of two different sets of individuals: professional politicians and regular citizens. For Mansbridge et al. the coupling, if done well, should allow each part to "consider reasons and proposals generated in other parts" (2012: 23). The challenge is achieving a balance that prevents the "coupling" becoming too tight or too loose. Should the "coupling" prove too tight, the MMDF risks elite domination and the loss of the deliberative democratic system's "self-corrective quality" (Mansbridge et al. 2012: 23). It may also lead to co-option (Hendriks 2016; Setälä 2017) and a distortion of outcomes.

Drawing on the chapter by Caluwaerts and Reuchamps in this *Handbook*, we note in Table 12.2 that elite domination can manifest itself at the input, throughput, and output stages of the process and with varying degrees of impact on the process's deliberative quality and outcomes.

Table 12.2: The potential for political domination within in MMDFs

Deliberative quality/ outcome	Scope for political influence
Input	
Representativeness	– Rules relating to the establishment of the forum
Openness of the agenda	– How the topic(s) is/are chosen
Epistemic completeness	– Forum governance (e. g., the procedure determining how experts are chosen and invited) – Forum design (e. g., membership recruitment; the proportion of politicians to citizen members) – Forum financing and administration – Destination of the forum's report
Throughput	
Quality of participation	– Design of the deliberation; resources for professional facilitators
Quality of decision-making	– Decision-making rules
Contextual independence	– Forum governance (e. g., a role for members?)
Output	
Public endorsement	– Official public response to the output
Political uptake	– Policy and/or legislative commitments
Policy implementation	– Whether implemented in full or in part; and how expeditiously

Arguably, the ways in which the politician members can frame and influence the process at the input stage are as applicable to "pure" assemblies as they are to mixed-member forums. But in the case of MMDFs there are significant additional questions over whether there can be parity of esteem between the citizen members and the elected officials given the latter's role, in certain cases, in the initiation, remit, design, and financing of the forum. Furthermore, there are issues over differences in parity between the politician members themselves; those in the governing parties may be in a stronger position to influence the establishment of a process, its topics, and design than those on the opposition benches. Finally, the decision-making processes used can hinder parity of esteem. This is most notable in the case of the Brussels' MMDFs. The different voting processes used by politician and citizen members indicate how tightly that system is coupled in a way that enshrines political partisanship among the elected officials and risks significantly distorting the outcomes and impact of deliberations.

But, the most significant distinction between traditional or "pure" CAs and MMDFs is the potential for elite domination in the forum's deliberations (throughput influence). There is the risk that politicians, as experienced and confident deliberators, may have more voice in the process. They may dominate the discussions, by simply talking more than the citizen members, and as result unduly shape the recommendations albeit in ways that are more easily implemented.[3] Additionally, their professional experience and knowledge of policy processes and policy details potentially lend greater weight to their views in the group discussions (Strandberg et al. 2021b). These asymmetries of power could serve to limit the contestatory role of these forums (see Lafont 2017; 2020).

In our real-world examples, differences have been observed in levels of politician and citizen members deliberative quality. Politicians, in some processes have achieved higher levels of deliberative quality than citizens (Flinders et al. 2016; Strandberg et al. 2021b). Yet, Grönlund et al. (2020) observe no such difference in the Turku panels.[4] Furthermore, when comparing citizen and politicians in the assembly and in parliamentary committee, Suiter et al. (2021) find that members of the citizens' assembly demonstrate a deeper cognitively complex grasp of the subject matter.

In terms of output influence, the recommendations stemming from MMDFs, to date, have been advisory as they do not take direct effect. They are referred to parliament or the relevant parliamentary committee for consideration and response. Some have also been shelved with little or no official response. The fact that the political elite determine the impact of the recommendations gives the elected officials within the MMDF significant influence. Knowing that they have this power can shape citizen members' and fellow politician members' interactions with them and skew perceptions of the weight of their opinions.

There are measures that can be employed to mitigate a number of these issues. These may include: ensuring a greater proportion of citizens to politicians; granting a role for the wider public in setting the agenda; providing access to the media to the proceedings to ensure transparency and scrutiny; professional facilitation; oversight of expert selection; accessible and balanced information briefings; secret voting

---

3 This raises an ancillary question, namely, is it the objective of a deliberative forum to develop recommendations that are ready to implement or to propose broader, more considered and possibly more innovative reflections on a topic? The authors are grateful to Julien Vrydagh for this observation
4 Interestingly, in their study of a "pure" CA, Suiter et al. (2021) observe greater deliberative quality by citizens in the CA than in parliament by politicians.

at the decision-making stage; selection of an independent chair or convenor; and a clear destination for the recommendations with a specific timeline for a response.

Yet how effective are they against perceptions of power that may be indirect and subconscious in their effect? Is there the risk that even when politicians do not overtly dominate the discussions in terms of the frequency and length of their contributions, their contributions may be subconsciously perceived as more significant by other members (citizens and political representatives) by virtue of their professional position?

Findings on elite domination in such forums are mixed. The UK Democracy Matters project revealed that the inclusion of politicians in the deliberative process negatively impacted on the quality of the deliberations, noting "at least in the short term, inclusion of the politicians decreases the quality of deliberation (including the amount of perceived domination)" (Flinders et al. 2016: 42). Similarly, Strandberg et al. (2021b) in their research on a MMDF in a Finnish municipality observe that politicians dominated the deliberations; however, they note that the dominance may not necessarily have been malign, as shown, for example, by the positive role played by politicians in answering citizens' queries. In their research on the "Turku debates" citizens' panels, Grönlund et al. (2020) find that very few participants said that the deliberations had been dominated. Harris et al.'s (2020) research on the frequency of speech acts in the Irish Convention on the Constitution observe politicians' slight over-participation in the roundtable discussions; however, an analysis of member surveys over the course of the Convention's deliberations, reveals that politicians did not dominate the Convention's deliberations generally (Farrell et al. 2020). The authors speculate that the length of the Convention, its scope, and the higher profile of its politician members may explain the differing results in the Irish and UK processes.

Interestingly, the Farrell et al. (2020) study finds evidence of a "modest liberal bias" amongst the politician members of the Convention, which, they argue, could have "a distinct (and potentially detrimental) impact on the process of deliberation" (p. 69). Consequently they recommend that politician members, like the citizen members, should be selected randomly "to avoid the risk of 'entryism' by politicians of a certain ideological hue" (Farrell et al. 2020: 69). Additionally they call for caution in the selection of topics ascribed to MMDF, suggesting those topics in which politicians may have a vested interest (such as electoral or political reform) should be avoided.

In terms of possible benefits, the mixing of politicians with regular citizens can be impactful in four ways. Firstly, the inclusion of elected representatives directly in the deliberations can ensure visibility for the recommendations. Politicians from across the party system may act as champions for the recommendations in parliament and the government (in the case of those who are members of governing parties) and increase the possibility of "uptake" (see Farrell et al. 2021). Secondly, it may increase politicians' and the political establishment's trust and confidence in deliberative processes. By having them on the "inside", any fears or concerns they may have around citizen competence and citizen capacity as well as the possible manipulation of such processes could be assuaged and lead to greater use of deliberative forums or indeed their institutionalization.

Thirdly, including politicians may lend greater epistemic value to the process as they allow for learning by bringing different perspectives and lived experiences to bear on the given topic (see Vandamme et al. 2019). Owen and Smith, argue "a demographically diverse group is epistemically important for collective knowledge" (2019: 293). This is true of "pure" assemblies but also has a bearing on mixed-member processes, as politicians from different political perspectives may bring different ideological positions on a given topic to the fore. They also have greater experience and expertise in the policy arena and may increase the success of a policy by pre-empting concerns, unintended consequences, implementation challenges, and so forth. It is noteworthy, however, that the research to date on the epistemic value of including politicians produces mixed findings. Research on the Irish Convention on the Constitution finds that politicians were an important source of information on technical issues for some of the citizen members (Harris et al. 2021). Interestingly, Grönlund et al. (2020) do not observe differences in knowledge gains between citizen only and mixed-member deliberations. They note that "the presence of politicians had no effect on knowledge" (p. 10). Determining the epistemic impact, if any, of including politicians as members of a deliberative forum vis-à-vis their possible impact as "experts and/or stakeholders" requires further research.

Finally, MMDFs have the potential to increase trust in politics, politicians, political institutions, and the wider policymaking and legislative process (see Vandamme et al. 2019). Research shows that citizen members learn more about the policy under discussion politics and political life (see Strandberg et al. 2021b; Grönlund et al. 2020, Suiter, Farrell and Harris 2016). They can also contribute to citizens' sense of external efficacy (Setälä 2017) as they give them an opportunity to engage directly with policymakers – a point that emerged in research on the Turku debates panel where councillors "felt they were able to hear those citizens who do not usually voice their concerns in local politics" (Grönlund et al. 2020: 13). This was not the case in the UK, however, where no differences in efficacy (internal and external) were observed between the two assembly types.

Research has also shown that citizens' perceptions of politicians' participation in the process grew more positive over time (Farrell et al. 2020; Flinders et al. 2016). Yet what of politicians' perspectives? For Koskimaa and Rapeli (2020), there is a dearth of research on policymakers' views on deliberative processes generally. Examining Finnish policymakers' attitudes to DMPs, they find they are sceptical towards them, a point contradicted by those councillors who participated in the Turku debates panels who were in favour of increased use of DMPs in local politics (Grönlund et al. 2020). For their part, Hendriks and Lees-Marshment's work on political leaders' attitudes to public input and participatory processes in general note that they are valued for "epistemic and instrumental reasons" (2019: 605). Informal interactions with the public are their preferred form of engagement (Hendriks and Lees-Marshment 2019). The authors suggest "creating participatory spaces where decision makers engage informally and productively with citizens would go a long way to addressing the [preference of] contemporary political leaders [for] constructive conversations with citizens, not staged participatory performances" (Hendriks and Lees-Marshment 2019: 611). This is supported by the reactions of Irish politicians to their experience of deliberating with regular citizens in the Convention on the Constitution (Arnold et al. 2019: 119). The chapter by Niessen in this *Handbook* explores this issue in greater depth.

Our discussion of the strengths and weaknesses of MMDFs begs the question what, if anything, can be done to achieve a "designed coupling" that avoids the risk of elite domination, reflecting existing "imbalances of power" (Smith 2009: 172). Based on deliberative democracy's normative principles of inclusive and equal participation and informed, respectful considered judgement, the potential damage caused by elite domination, the distortion of deliberative quality and outcomes may be greater than the possible rewards of implementation and impact. This may well give some pause for thought.

12.5 Conclusion

As a relatively new, and still rather rare, form of deliberative democratic innovation, there is much we have to learn about MMDFs. Research in the field is still emerging, and, the studies currently underway on the Brussels' deliberative committees, in particular, will add significantly to our understanding of these forums in due course.

What is already apparent is that the inclusion of politicians in deliberative processes can enhance the diversity of opinion, potentially add epistemic value and arguably increase the visibility and impact of the process and its recommendations. However, these benefits risk being undermined by the potential for elite domination of the discussions and decisions. The power asymmetries at the heart of MMDFs pose a substantial obstacle to open, inclusive and equal deliberation. It may be difficult to champion them when "pure" CAs are an alternative option. Yet it would be a mistake to dismiss MMDFs and their potential role in the wider deliberative system.

As the use of new deliberative democratic institutions continues to expand, MMDFs may have a role to play at certain stages in the policy cycle. For instance, they could oversee the implementation of the recommendations coming from a CA. Alternatively, they could be instrumental at the agenda setting stage, acting as a bridge between a public petition process and a CA. Such forums would be most effective if institutionalised as opposed to being set up as once off ad-hoc bodies.

References

Arnold, T., Farrell D. M., & Suiter, J. (2019). Lessons from a hybrid sortition chamber: The 2012–14 Irish Constitutional Convention. In J. Gastil & E. O. Wright (eds), *Legislature by Lot: An Alternative Design for Deliberative Governance*, 101–121. London: Verso.

Curato, N., Farrell, D.M., Geißel, B., Grönlund, K., Mockler, P., Pilet, J.-B., Renwick, A., Rose, J., Setälä, M., & Suiter, J. (2021). *Deliberative Mini-Publics: Core Design Features*. Bristol: Bristol University Press.

Dryzek, J. S. (2016). Deliberative policy analysis. In G. Stoker & M. Evans (eds). *Evidence-Based Policy Making in the Social Sciences: Methods That Matter,* 229–242. Bristol: Policy Press.

Farrell, D. M., Suiter, J., Harris, C., & Cunningham, K. (2020). The effects of mixed membership in a deliberative forum: The Irish Constitutional Convention of 2012–2014. *Political Studies* 68 (1), 54–73.

Farrell, D. M., Suiter, J., Harris C., & Cunningham, K. (2021). Ireland's deliberative mini publics. In D. M. Farrell & N. Hardiman (eds), *Oxford Handbook of Irish Politics,* 627–643. Oxford: Oxford University Press.

Flinders, M., Ghose, K., Jennings, W., Molloy, E., Prosser, B., Renwick, A. Smith, G. & Spada, P. (2016). *Democracy Matters: Lessons from the 2015 Citizens' Assemblies on English Devolution.* University of Southampton. https://eprints.soton.ac.uk/391972/

Grönlund, K., Herne, K., Jäske, M. Liimatainen, H., Rapeli, L., & Värttö, M. together with

Schauman, J., Siren, R., & Weckman, A. (2020). *Implementing a Democratic Innovation: Online Deliberation on a Future Transport System.* City of Turku Urban Research Programme: Research Reports 4/2020.

Harris, C., Farrell, D. M., Suiter, J., & Brennan, M. (2021). Women's voices in a deliberative assembly: An analysis of gender rates of participation in Ireland's Convention on the Constitution 2012–2014. *The British Journal of Politics and International Relations* 23 (1), 175–193.

Harris, C., Farrell, D. M., Suiter J., Cahillane, L., & Stone, P. (2020). *Ireland's experience of Constitutional Deliberation:* report for the ConstitDelib COST Action. https://constdelib.com/wp-content/uploads/2021/04/Ireland-report-CA17135.pdf

Hendriks, C. M., & Lees-Marshment, J. (2019). Political leaders and public engagement: The hidden world of informal elite–citizen interaction. *Political Studies* 67 (3), 597–617.

Hendriks, C. M. (2016). Coupling citizens and elites in deliberative systems: The role of institutional design. *European Journal of Political Research* 55, 43–60.

Koskimaa, V., & Rapeli, L. (2020). Fit to govern? Comparing citizen and policymaker perceptions of deliberative democratic innovations. *Policy & Politics* 48 (4), 637–652.

Lafont, C. (2017). Can democracy be deliberative & participatory? The democratic case for political uses of minipublics. *Daedalus* 146 (3), 85–105.

Lafont, C. (2020). *Democracy without Shortcuts.* Oxford: Oxford University Press.

Mansbridge, J., Bohman, J., Chambers, S., Christiano, T., Fung, A., Parkinson, J., Thompson, D. F., & Warren, M. E. (2012). A systemic approach to deliberative democracy. In J. Parkinson & J. Mansbridge (eds), *Deliberative Systems,* 1–26. Cambridge: Cambridge University Press.

Niessen, C., & Reuchamps, M. (2019). *Designing a Permanent Deliberative Citizens' Assembly: The Ostbelgien Modell in Belgium.* (Working Paper Series No. 2019/6. The Centre for Deliberative Democracy & Global Governance).

OECD (2020). *Innovative Citizen Participation and New Democratic Institutions: Catching the Deliberative Wave.* Paris: OECD Publishing, Paris.

Owen, D., & Smith, G. (2019). Sortition, rotation, and mandate: Conditions for political equality and deliberative reasoning. In J. Gastil & E. O. Wright (eds), *Legislature by Lot: An Alternative Design for Deliberative Governance,* 279–300. London: Verso.

Reuchamps, M. (2020). Belgium's experiment in permanent forms of deliberative democracy. *Constitution Net,* 17 January 2020, http://constitutionnet.org/news/belgiumsexperiment-permanent-forms-deliberative-democracy.

Setälä, M. (2017). Connecting mini-publics to representative decision making. *European Journal of Political Research* 56, 846–863.

Smith, G. (2009). *Democratic Innovations: Designing Institutions for Citizen Participation.* Cambridge: Cambridge University Press.

Strandberg, K., & Berg, J. (2020). When reality strikes: Opinion changes among citizens and politicians during a deliberation on school closures. *International Political Science Review* 41 (4), 567–583.

Strandberg, K., Backström, K., Berg, J., & Karv, T. (2021a). Democratically sustainable local development? The outcomes of mixed deliberation on a municipal merger on participants' social trust, political trust, and political efficacy. *Sustainability* 13 (13), 7231.

Strandberg, K., Berg, K., Karv, T., & Backström, K. (2021b). When citizens met politicians –the process and outcomes of mixed deliberation according to participant status and gender. *Innovation: The European Journal of Social Science Research* 34 (5), 638 – 655.

Suiter, J., Farrell, D. M., Harris, C., & Murphy, P. (2021). Measuring epistemic deliberation on polarized issues: The case of abortion provision in Ireland. *Political Studies Review*, https://doi.org/10.1177/14789299211020909.

Suiter, J., Farrell, D. M., & Harris, C. (2016). A constitutional turn for deliberative democracy in Europe? In M. Reuchamps & J. Suiter (eds), *Constitutional Deliberative Democracy in Europe*, 33 – 52. Colchester, Essex: ECPR Press.

Vandamme, P.-E., Jacquet, V. Niessen, C., Pitseys, J., & Reuchamps, M. 2019. Intercameral relations in a bicameral elected and sortition legislature. In J. Gastil & E. O. Wright (eds), *Legislature by Lot: An Alternative Design for Deliberative Governance*, 123 – 144. London: Verso.

Värttö, M., Jäske, M., Herne, K., & Grönlund, K. (2021). Two-way street: Politicians' participation in a deliberative mini-public. *Politiikka* 63 (1), 28 – 53.

Vrydagh, J., Bottin, J., Reuchamps M., Bouchon, F., & Devillers, S. (2021). Les commissions délibératives entre parlementaires et citoyens tirés au sort au sein desassemblées bruxelloises. *Courrier hebdomadaire* n° 2492, 5 – 68.

Kei Nishiyama

13 Deliberation in citizens' assemblies with children

Abstract: Deliberative democracy researchers argue that CAs practice inclusivity, but, in fact, it is not always the case. Many CAs are normally less child-friendly in that those who fall below a certain age are excluded. One clear reason is that random sampling is usually based on voter lists that have no names of children. And another implicit reason may be that children are assumed to be incapable of deliberation. In such ways, children are normally regarded as individuals who are not eligible to be official participants in CAs. This chapter, however, seeks for the second-best routes for including children in a deliberative process by drawing on the existing attempts and the insights gained from children's participation studies. It classifies possible routes into four categories (representation by adults, representation by children, consultative participation, and systemic inclusion) and examines opportunities and limitations of each route.

Keywords: CA, children, democratic inclusion, participation, representation

13.1 Introduction

Citizens' Assemblies (CAs) are, generally speaking, not child-friendly.[1] To ensure a wide range of citizens' views, CAs recruit participants through random sampling. However, this strategy often fails to reflect *all* relevant views of the population in a pure sense because those who fall below a certain age are not selected in the first place. In British Columbia's CA in 2004, persons under the age of 18 were not subject to random sampling. In the Welsh CA in 2019, children under the age of 16 did not receive an invitation

---

Kei Nishiyama: Kaichi International University.

1 Age often comes to mind when we define children and childhood in the context of politics. The age-based distinction of children from adults is widely shared and institutionally justified, most famously described in the United Nations Convention on the Rights of the Child Article 1 (Every human being below the age of eighteen years unless under the law applicable to the child). However, this definition can encapsulate related or similar concepts (e.g., infant, baby, kid, pupil, juvenile, teenager, young people, and so forth), and political inclusion of these different types of "children" require different strategies. With the above definition in mind, when discussing the inclusion of children in citizens' assemblies, the chapter uses the term (a) *children* if the inclusion strategy is applicable to various types of children of various age group, (b) *younger children* if the strategy is particularly helpful for inclusion of younger preschoolers and pupils, and (c) *older children* to those who are generally referred to as teenagers. Of course, as sociology of childhood studies have tellingly argued, different cultures have different concepts of children, and, therefore, age is not the only indicator to define who children are (James and Prout 2015). In this sense, this classification is not universal but a tentative one. Children are a discursively constructed phenomenon in the first place.

ᵈ Open Access. © 2023 the author(s), published by De Gruyter. (cc) BY-NC-ND This work is licensed under the Creative Commons Attribution-NonCommercial-NoDerivatives 4.0 International License. https://doi.org/10.1515/9783110758269-015

letter. To ensure political equality and fair representation, Curato et al. (2021: 4) observe, "it may be necessary to actively recruit or even oversample minority views that are likely to be glossed over by pure random selection". Nonetheless, such an oversampling strategy is rarely applied to children. One clear reason is that random sampling is usually based on voter lists that have no names of children. Another implicit reason may be that children are assumed to be incapable of deliberation. According to this view, exclusion of children can be justified because children are "future" citizens who require education and preparation for future democracy, rather than participation in today's democracy (see Nishiyama 2017).

However, exclusion of children from CAs on the basis of their age and lack of capacity is problematic. For example, such exclusion ignores the fact that children have *already* become a fundamental part of democratic movements. As best exemplified by the worldwide growth of climate activism, many children across the world show how they are capable of acting as agents of democracy (see also, Nishiyama 2017; Bowman 2020; Nishiyama 2020; Hayward 2021). In addition, the exclusion of children from deliberation about issues concerning their future (e.g., climate change, pensions) is morally and epistemically problematic in a sense that it is the present generation's disregard for the interest and welfare of future generations. Furthermore, exclusion of children undermines fundamental principles of CAs, such as equality and diversity.

Conversely, inclusion of children in a process of CAs promises some general democratic advantages. First, inclusion of children is epistemically beneficial for adult citizens to get a deeper understanding of perspectives and interests of future generations. Second, inclusion of children is also beneficial for children themselves as it enables them to act as agents of democracy who communicate various political agents (e.g., lay citizens, experts, elected officials) and influence the policymaking process, which are usually difficult to achieve in other popular simulative practices such as mock elections or mock parliaments. Third, as to be discussed in this chapter, some forms of inclusion of children in CAs are synergistic in many ways with the existing children's political engagement practices (e.g., children's parliament, social movements).

But what does "inclusion of children in Citizens Assemblies" mean? There are two possible pathways for including children in the process of CAs. The first one is to enable direct participation of children by lowering the age limit. This pathway appears to be a simple solution, but in reality, it is not so straightforward, as it may require a change in the legal voting age, or there may be a never-ending debate about "how old should someone be allowed to participate?" (for instance, is my two-year-old daughter eligible to participate in the CA. Another pathway discussed in this chapter is to examine and identify possible approaches through which children's voices can somehow be included in a deliberative process. Drawing on some real-life attempts, coupled with insights gained from children's participation studies, the chapter examines the opportunities and limitations of four approaches to children's inclusion: representation by adults, representation by children, consultative participation, and systemic inclusion.

13.2 What kind of "inclusion" should be avoided?

According to Young (2000), political inclusion has two meanings: external and internal. External inclusion means to give inclusive access to a deliberative process, while internal inclusion requires removing structural, social, and/or cultural barriers preventing people from being recognized and heard within a process of deliberation. With this categorization in mind, I will first introduce two types of inclusion (imaginary representation and symbolic inclusion) that can occur in CAs. Both can achieve external inclusion to some extent and, nevertheless, run the risk of excluding children internally. Therefore, when this chapter uses the term "inclusion of children", these two types of attempts at inclusion are not included.

The first type is *imaginary representation.* Inclusion of this sort is often discussed in the context of inclusion of the unborn. Precisely because present generations must make political decisions in the absence of future generations who cannot speak for themselves, what is considered as the second-best strategy is to better imagine, predict, and then represent the voices of future generations through deliberation (Smith 2021). As MacKenzie notes, "where sufficient deliberative opportunities do not exist, the interests of the future may be badly misrepresented *precisely because the future cannot answer back to us*" (MacKenzie 2018: 262; original emphasis). In Japan, for example, Hara et al. (2019) designed a participatory practice for imaginary future generations, whereby participants (present generations) represent the potential interests of future generations.

Imaginary representation creates one significant pathway through which voices of the unborn child can be included in a deliberative process. However, situating imaginary representation at the heart of policies to include children who are capable of forming their opinion would be problematic. Malala Yousafzai, Greta Thunberg, Emma González, and many other ordinary older and younger children have demonstrated that they are capable of thinking critically and reflectively about common problems of their future (e. g., women's rights to education, climate change, gun control) and expressing their interests in the broader public sphere (Nishiyama 2017; Hayward 2021). Since present generations can listen to the real voice of children, relying solely on imaginary representation may run the risk that adults unilaterally distort the opinions and interests of children.

Another type is *symbolic inclusion*, whereby adults strategically use (mostly younger) children's presence and "purity" to gain further sympathy from the public. Roger Hart developed a famous classification of children's participation, called the "ladder of participation", and defined symbolic inclusion (or what he called "tokenism") as a practice in which "children seem to have a voice but in fact have little or no choice about the subject or the style of commutating it" (Hart 1997: 41). Such symbolic inclusion has long been used as a key tactic in the context of adult-initiated protest movements (Rodgers 2005), and so too in many children's participation practices. In 2006, for example, several younger and older children were invited as guest speakers at the opening session of the United Nations Conventions on the Rights of the Child General Discussion. However, according to Ennew (2006: 73) who observed the meeting, "children and adults were not treated as equal participants" because three adults dominated discussion of the session, and children had to use what little time remained. Thus, symbolic and tokenistic participation is epistemically and morally problematic because it uses children as a means, not as an end.

13.3 A typology of children's inclusion in citizens' assemblies

Beyond imaginary representation and symbolic inclusion, how can we include children in a democratic manner even though they normally do not receive an invitation letter for CAs? Given that children are not allowed to participate in CAs due to the age restriction, a possible second-best option would be to develop multiple routes through which children's voices and interests are heard and taken seriously by adult participants. To this end, I have identified four key elements (representation, participation, adult-centric practice, adult–child collaboration) that relate to inclusion of children in CAs, and then developed a typology. This typology, derived from existing attempts at CAs coupled with insights gained from children's participation studies, offers insights into possible (and realistic) approaches to children's inclusion, and encourages further research and practical application.

Representation is an integral element of deliberative mini-publics in general (Warren 2008; Curato et al. 2021; see also the chapter by MacKenzie in this *Handbook*), but it is also crucial for achieving democratic inclusion of children. If children's voices, interests, and perspectives are properly and democratically represented and shared in a deliberative process, their non-participation is not necessarily very problematic. As Pow et al. (2020) demonstrated, non-participants in deliberative mini-publics can trust such a representative group of citizens if participants can act and speak like other citizens. However, as noted in the previous section, ill-considered representation or irresponsible representation by adults may amount to imaginary representation. The key question, therefore, is the following: who can and should represent and advocate for the best interests of children in a legitimate manner, and how?

Participation is also an important element of CAs. Participation here refers to direct involvement in a deliberation, and participants are required to express *their own* lived experience and perspectives, rather than represent and speak on behalf of others. Importantly, the term "participants" in the context of deliberative mini-publics does not always refer only to randomly selected citizens. Research has demonstrated that deliberative mini-publics include experts, local/national media, and organizers in addition to lay citizens (Gül 2019; Curato et al. 2021; Smith 2021). These "participants" exercise varying degrees of influence over a deliberative process. The key question here is as follows: what role can children play when they "participate" in CAs? It should be made clear that participation and representation are not mutually exclusive. In the case of deliberative mini-publics, they are different sides to the same coin. My point is to focus on the degree to which a specific inclusion approach places more emphasis on participation or representation.

Adult-child collaboration and *adult-centric practice* make different contributions to the inclusiveness of CAs. The former is a democratic design of a deliberative process whereby children are respectfully treated as having equal voices, and adult participants have rich opportunities to hear and learn from children at various stages of a deliberative process. In this practice, children become actively involved in deliberative activities with adult citizens inside and outside of CAs. In contrast, adult-centric practice refers to a deliberative design that enables children to involve themselves in adult spheres (e. g., adult citizens' deliberative activities, a deliberative forum for those over age 18). Children's voices are heard and considered directly or indirectly only at a specific stage of deliberative process. Children do not need to participate on a long-term basis; instead, deliberation of this kind may become more adult-centric, and therefore imaginary representation or symbolic inclusion may take place.

All in all, children's participation and inclusion in CAs can be implemented differently, depending on how we combine the above four elements. Representation and participation are represented on the horizontal axis, and adult–child collaboration and adult-centric practice are represented on the vertical axis. The combination of "presentation" and "adult-centric practice" takes a form of *presentation by adults*, while the combination of "representation" and "adult–child collaboration" leads to *representation by children*. Children can also be included in a *consultative* process if "participation" and "adult-centric practice" operate in tandem, while "participation" and "adult–child collaboration" will crystallize together in the form of *systemic inclusion*. Figure 13.1 is a visual summary of these categorizations. The following sections will provide further and more detailed explanations about how these different forms of inclusion work.

13.4 Representation by adults

Representation by adults may be the simplest way of including children's voices and interests in a deliberative process, through discussions on behalf of children by adult participants who are familiar with children's current socio-political situations. Such adults might include parents. When the main topic of the CA relates to issues of intergenerational conflict and justice, such as climate change, many parents of young children have thus far discussed this topic while thinking about their children's future. Alternatively, they might talk about it at home with their children and then draw on this experience in the process of public deliberation. Some experts who make it their business to listen to children have rich experiences and insights about interests and perspectives of children. For example, some legal scholars and practitioners who have long been working with younger children in cases of child poverty and

Adult-child collaboration

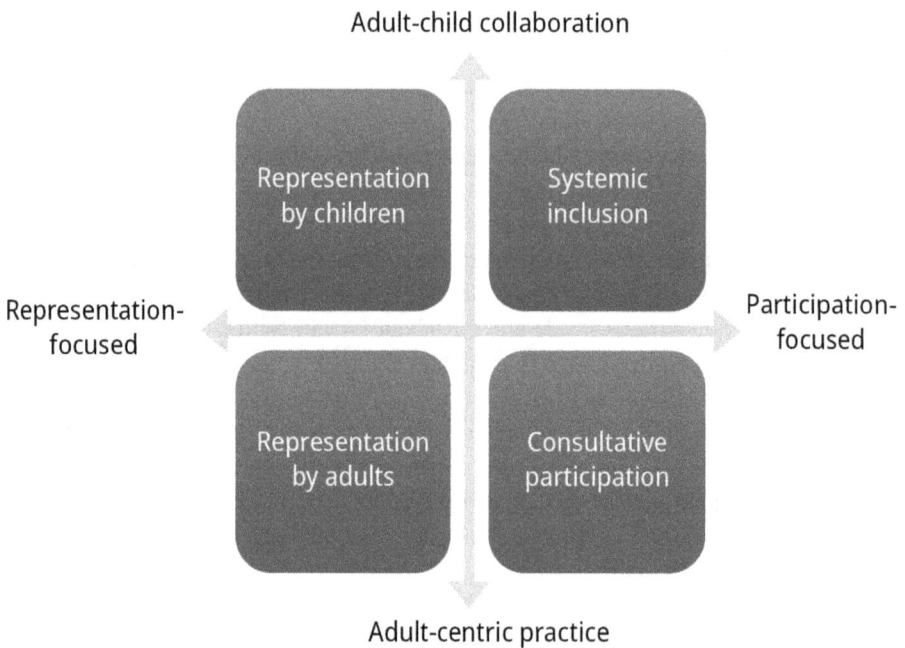

Representation-
focused

Representation
by children

Systemic
inclusion

Participation-
focused

Representation
by adults

Consultative
participation

Adult-centric practice

Figure 13.1: Forms of inclusion of children in a deliberative process

abuse have a greater opportunity to listen to younger children's voices on a regular basis. Despite the lack of reports on how these experts operate in CAs, research has demonstrated that they are fully capable of bringing the expressed interests of younger children into a deliberative process and thereby advocating for their best interests in the public sphere (Henning 2005).

The Norwegian experience of the children's ombudsman (sometimes called "ombudsperson") also provides insights into representation by adults. The children's ombudsman is a public authority advocating for promotion and protection of children's rights, particularly younger children's rights. As Musinguzi and Ellingsen (2017: 148) note, the primary work of a children's ombudsman entails "talking to and seeking advice from children and young people on matters concerning them" and bringing "their perspectives to [the attention of] decision-makers". When a child suffers abuse, neglect, or a range of other physical, mental, or social problems, s/he can consult members of the ombudsman's office about the problem. Through conducting multiple interviews, members listen carefully to the child's views and perspectives and, if needed, set up expert meetings to carry out surveys of the various institutions involved. If these interviews and surveys conclude that the existing system or law should be changed, members of the ombudsman's office and the child work together to make a recommendation and then submit it to decision-makers and decision-making bodies to "bridge the gap between children's perspectives and the actions of decision-maker'" (Musinguzi and Ellingsen 2017: 158).

In some deliberative mini-publics, organizers decide to add special seats for members who would otherwise be excluded from statistics-based random sampling (e.g., indigenous people) (Gül 2019; Curato et al. 2021). By the same token, creating special seats for the above type of adults would allow them to speak on behalf of children, especially younger children, in a democratic manner and thereby contribute to the indirect but meaningful inclusion of children in a deliberative process.

Representation by adults, however, is not without its problems. Even though adult representatives can advocate for the best interests of children, the deliberative process of such representation *per se* proceeds in the absence of children, which can amount to imaginary representation. The alternative is to have only adults take ownership of framing children's perspectives and sharing them with other participants, whereas there is limited scope for children to have substantial influence on how adults speak on behalf of children. In the context of the children's ombudsman in Norway, for example, Musinguzi and Ellingsen (2017: 159–160) report that "there is a risk that important messages may be omitted as the adults decide what to extract in their further proposals", and as a result, children lack a real impact on the quality and content of deliberation. Thus, representation by adults is, for better or worse, an adult-centric approach to children's inclusion.

13.5 Representation by children

Representation by children, a combination of representation with adult–child collaboration, becomes a relatively popular practice in some CAs. It opens pathways through which children work with adult citizens in a collaborative manner and, in parallel, enjoy a greater opportunity and freedom to express their collective views in a way that represents other children. Representation by children values both participation and representation, but it normally places its emphasis more on the latter. Practices based on representation by children are not open to all children, but to those who pass through a selection process. The selected children are expected to deliberate on behalf of opinions and best interests of other children.

Working with external representative organizations, such as children's parliaments, represents one crystallization of representation by children. The core mechanism of such representative organizations is to enable selected or elected children to engage in productive deliberations, participate in surveys, and present their findings and experiences about policies and social issues that affect them in the public sphere. Since the adoption of the United Nations Convention on the Rights of the Child in 1989, this kind of representative body has been established worldwide (Cockburn 2010). In some countries such as Denmark or Portugal, members of parliament actively work with children (Shephard and Patriklos 2013). Incorporating children's experiences and their various outputs (e.g., press releases, policy recommendations, news contributions) into a process of deliberation will offer more opportunities for participants of

CAs to listen to the collective and well-examined voices expressed by the child representatives.

Scotland's Climate Assembly offers an example of how a substantive collaboration and communication between CAs and children's representatives is possible. Since 1996, the Children's Parliament in Scotland has made contributions to various policy processes, including an international Eco-City project and has played a remarkable role in Scotland's Climate Assembly in 2020–2021. Over 100 children aged 7 to 14 from across Scotland participated as official members of the Children's Parliament. The Children's Parliament reflects various social, economic, religious, ethnic, or geographical differences in Scottish society. Before the Climate Assembly, members of the Children's Parliament undertook surveys and interviews to collect data about Scottish children's thoughts, attitudes, and demands with respect to the climate emergency. After collecting diverse perspectives of children on the climate emergency, adult project leaders and children worked together to complete a final report called *It's Up to You, Me, and All of Us* (Children's Parliament 2021) whose content ranged from expressed keywords around climate change (e.g., "animals", "change", "worried", "unsure") to the idea of a fair future defined from children's point of view, and key topics that citizens and the Scottish government were jointly to reflect on (e.g., land and sea use, future lifestyle, travel, work, and learning). The particular significance of this chapter is that this final report was used in the process of deliberation in Scotland's Climate Assembly as an important informational resource for adult participants (Harris 2021). In addition, the report was ultimately incorporated in the final report of Scotland's Climate Assembly as a legitimate document and submitted to decision-makers (Scotland's Climate Assembly 2021: 148–196).

Another progressive example of representation by children is the world's first attempt at a child-and-youth-led CA (the 2022 Youth-Led CA on Climate Change). This CA is planned, designed, and initiated by young staff (aged 10–24) and adult experts in Millennium Kids, a youth organization that has organized various deliberative forums for children and young people in Australia, such as the Western Australian Children's Environmental Conference ('Kids Helping Kids') (Millennium Kids 2020). The assembly was originally planned to be held in 2021, but it had to be postponed to September 2022 due to the worldwide pandemic of COVID-19. Despite this situation, young staff have prepared for the assembly through their regular learning of deliberative theories and practical training on deliberation. According to their plan, and on the basis of the idea of a CA, a representative sample of approximately 100 randomly selected Australian high school students will gather in one room to participate in a learning and deliberative process, and then submit their collective recommendations to decision-makers (Millennium Kids 2020). They will invite local decision-makers either as observers or presenters, so that their deliberation becomes more influential.

13.6 Consultative participation

Even though CAs are normally designed and run only by adults, children can directly participate in their processes if they are invited by guest presenters who share their professional views about the specific issue affecting their current and/or future lives (e. g., education, pensions, climate change, health care). This practice, known as "consultative participation", has occasionally been used in city planning (Grant-Smith and Edwards 2011). Lansdown identifies its core feature as a practice whereby "adults seek children's views in order to build knowledge and understanding of their lives and experience" (Lansdown 2010: 20). Children are not invited to participate in the deliberative forum and cannot, therefore, influence a decision-making process *per se*. Nonetheless, consultative participation allows them to inform adults' decision-making. Importantly, children engaged in consultative participation play different roles from other children with respect to representation by children. While the children in the context of representation by children need to argue for the best interest of other children, children in consultative participation are not requested to argue on behalf of others. Rather, what is required for them is to show how *their own* experience, perspectives, and expert knowledge (e. g., knowledge of childhood, knowledge of their own lives) speak to the issue in question.

Several CAs have already invited older children to serve as guest speakers or even members of the expert panel. Like other invited experts, children (e. g., school children, young activists, street children) are treated with equal respect and have a chance to ask questions of adult participants, make their claims, and offer professional input. The Children's Parliament in Scotland took such a consultative approach at certain stages of Scotland's Climate Assembly, whereby some older children were invited to the deliberative forum, so that the invited children had a chance to share their own views about the climate emergency, answer the questions of adults, and exchange opinions with participants (Harris 2021).

In such a consultative process, Hart (1997: 43) noted that organizers and participants should treat children as more than mere informants; they should also disclose a range of information, including about the purpose and results of the consultation. Indeed, research has shown that some deliberative practices become tokenistic because, while children are formally included, some adults are not so willing to listen to children from the beginning (Nishiyama 2017). In the context of deliberation within the community advisory committee for water planning in Australia, for example, Grant-Smith and Edwards reported that some community representatives underestimated the abilities of invited children and regarded them as "not being mature or knowing how things worked" (Grant-Smith and Edwards 2011: 9). Therefore, consultative participation can be tokenistic and symbolic in its inclusive capacity when children are not fully informed about the degree to which their views are taken seriously and incorporated into a deliberative process, as well as when there is insufficient mutual trust between children and adults.

13.7 Systemic inclusion

While the abovementioned approaches for inclusion are effective for some children, they are not as meaningful for other children. For example, while representation by adults is effective mostly for younger children, older children who are capable of forming their opinions may find it more meaningful to be involved in consultative participation or representation by children. Alternatively, younger children may be less likely to participate in the consultative participation and representation by children where many older children tend to participate. To facilitate *children's* inclusion in CAs, therefore, we need to pay attention to the fourth approach, systemic inclusion. Systemic inclusion is theoretically informed by the deliberative system theory that shifts our focus away from a single deliberative forum toward a functional division of labour involving different aspects of deliberative experiences occurring across society, thereby considering the democratic quality of deliberative governance in terms of how each part constitutes a complex whole (Dryzek 2010; Mansbridge et al. 2012). Viewed in this light, CAs are, ideally, understood as a deliberative forum interconnected with diverse networks of deliberative institutions and deliberative agents. Here inclusion of children in CAs means not only the way in which their voices are, whether directly or indirectly, taken seriously within a deliberative forum, but also a wide range of efforts to maximize opportunities for children to engage in deliberative acts outside the forum, thereby creating new pathways through which their various deliberative experiences contribute to deliberation in a deliberative forum.

Obviously, maximizing the opportunities to enable the above three types of children's inclusion (representation by adults, representation by children, and consultative participation) contributes to making systemic inclusion possible. To this end, some funding for CAs should be distributed to children's out-of-forum deliberative spaces (e.g., the Children's Parliament) and a professional institution where its agents communicate with children on a regular basis (e.g., Children's Ombudsman). In addition, organizers of a CA should encourage children's deliberation and public submissions by making information about a deliberative process and topics widely available to various children who are active in a more child-friendly deliberative space, such as online spaces, protest groups, and/or schools (see Nishiyama 2020). The greater the capacity of CAs to encourage and incorporate representation by adults, representation by children, and consultative participation, the more inclusive and child-friendly they become as a systemic whole.

Another key opportunity for systemic inclusion is to invite children to a meta-deliberative process. Meta-deliberation is a reflective process of deliberation about deliberation, or to put it differently, a self-examination capacity of the deliberative process. Dryzek (2010: 12) defines meta-deliberation as an integral element of a democratic deliberative system, arguing that "a healthy deliberative system therefore needs a capacity for self-examination and self-transformation if need be". Viewed in this light, even though children are not eligible to be official members of CAs due to the age restriction, they can nonetheless contribute to democratization of their deliberative processes by evaluating the epistemic, inclusive, representative, ethical, and democratic quality of deliberation from outside the deliberative forum. If such meta-deliberation concludes that the deliberative process does not mirror children's voices and perspectives or its participants misrepresent children, they can demand improvement.

One possible route for children to participate in the meta-deliberative process is to include some older children (e.g., members of a children's parliament) in the organizational committee of the CA. As Gül (2019) notes, organizers play an essential role in enhancing the representative and democratic quality of deliberation in deliberative mini-publics because they have the power and authority to define what democratic mini-publics look like, determine who and how many people should be invited, and design how deliberation works. Having older children as official organizing committee members allows them to co-design a deliberative process with adult organizers and gives them the right to have a say in the process of selecting experts, as well as regularly control the checks and balances to ensure the representational inclusiveness of the overall process. Sceptics might object to this suggestion, arguing that children, regardless of their developmental stage, are too inexperienced to be able to run a CA as central members. However, as the case of the Youth-Led CA on Climate in Australia has shown, many children, given an adequate opportunity, are fully capable of designing, initiating, and organizing the deliberative forum and process.[2]

Another route is to establish an external body for meta-deliberation. Bouricius (2019: 330) made a similar suggestion in his argument on lottocracy, emphasizing the need for a meta-legislative body whose participants oversaw the efforts of organizers, other participants, and experts to ensure the impartiality of the overall deliberative process. Similarly, a healthy, child-friendly, and inclusive CA might need to own this sort of meta-deliberative body that invites children and adults to serve as its legitimate members; enables their collaboration; encourages them to observe and check adults' deliberation in a deliberative forum; and improves the overall deliberative process from children's point of view.

13.8 Conclusion

The core democratic value of deliberative mini-publics consists of their representative capacity. Exclusion of children as important members of our society because of their age or their maturity greatly undermines this value. If we accept Pow et al.'s (2020) empirical claim that "like-me perception" (i.e., citizen representatives act and speak like non-participants) is key for mini-publics to gain legitimacy, this "me" must include chil-

---

2 Children have demonstrated their capacity for running deliberative mini-publics beyond the case of CAs. For example, children and young people (ages 8–25) played a powerful role as core staff members and participants in Scotland's Youth-led Participatory Budgeting in North Ayrshire (Cook 2021).

dren who can speak for themselves; otherwise, CAs would risk losing their legitimacy. While children are normally not eligible to be official participants in CAs, this chapter makes a case for the second-best routes for including children in a deliberative process, namely, representation by adults, representation by children, consultative participation, and systemic inclusion. This chapter does not contend that we should rely on one of them. Nor should we understand them as mutually exclusive routes. These four routes present not only opportunities but also challenges (e. g., leading to imaginary representation and symbolic inclusion), and it is therefore important to understand the characteristics, benefits, and limitations of these four routes of inclusion and to consider which route fits perfectly into the deliberative process at hand.

References

Bouricius, T. (2019). Why hybrid bicameralism is not right for sortition. In J. Gastil & E. Olin Wright (eds), *Legislature by Lot: Transformative Designs for Deliberative Governance*, 313–332. London: Verso.

Bowman, B. (2020). They don't quite understand the importance of what we're doing today: The young people's climate strikes as subaltern activism. *Sustainable Earth* 3 (16), 1–13.

Children's Parliament. (2021). *It's Up to You, Me and All of Us.* Retrieved from: https://www.childrensparliament.org.uk/wp-content/uploads/Childrens-Parliament_Climate_Assembly_2021.pdf [Last access: 11/Oct/2021].

Cockburn, T. (2010). Children and deliberative democracy in England. In B. Percy-Smith & N. Thomas (eds), *A Handbook of Children and Young People's Participation*, 306–317. London: Routledge.

Cook, A. (2021). Youth-led participatory budgeting in North Ayrshire. *Democratic Society.* Retrieved from: https://www.demsoc.org/blog/youth-led-participatory-budgeting [Last access: 26/Oct/2021]

Curato, N., Farrell, D. M., Geißel, B., Grönlund, K., Mockler, P., Pilet, J.-B., Renwick, A., Rose, J., Setälä, M., & Suiter, J. (2021). *Deliberative Mini-Publics: Core Design Features.* Bristol: Bristol University Press.

Dryzek, J. (2010). *Foundations and Frontiers of Deliberative Governance.* Oxford: Oxford University Press.

Ennew, J. (2006). Children as 'citizens' of the United Nations. In A. Invernizzi & J. Williams (eds.) *Children and Citizenship*, 66–78. London: Sage.

Grant-Smith, D., & Edwards, P. (2011). 'It takes more than good intentions'. Institutional and attitudinal impediments to engaging young people in participatory planning. *Journal of Public Deliberation* 7 (1), Article 11.

Gül, V. (2019). Representation in mini-publics. *Representation* 55 (1), 31–45.

Hara, K., Yoshioka, R., Kuroda, M., Kurimoto, S., & Saijo, T. (2019). Reconciling intergenerational conflicts with imaginary future generations: Evidence from a participatory deliberation practice in a municipality in Japan. *Sustainability Science* 14, 1605–1619.

Harris, C. (2021). Looking for the future? Including children, young people and future generations in deliberations on climate action: Ireland's Citizens Assembly 2016–2018. *Innovation: The European Journal of Social Science Research* 34 (5), 677–693.

Hart, R. (1997). *Children's Participation: The Theory and Practice of Involving Young Citizens in Community Development and Environmental Care.* London and New York: Routledge.

Hayward, B. (2021). *Children, Citizenship and Environment #SchoolStrike Edition.* Abingdon and New York: Routledge.

Henning, K. (2005). It takes a lawyer to raise a child: Allocating responsibilities among parents, children and lawyers in delinquency cases. *Nevada Law Journal* 6, 836–889.

James, A., & Prout, A. (eds). (2015). *Constructing and Reconstructing Childhood: Contemporary Issues in the Sociological Study of Childhood.* London and New York: Routledge.

Lansdown, G. (2010). Challenges of participatory practice with children. In B. Percy-Smith & N. Thomas (eds), *A Handbook of Children and Young People's Participation*, 24–38. London and New York: Routledge.

Mackenzie, M. (2018). Deliberation and long-term decisions: Representing future generations. In A. Bächtiger, J. Dryzek, J. Mansbridge, & M. Warren (eds). *The Oxford Handbook of Deliberative Democracy*, 251–269. Oxford: Oxford University Press.

Mansbridge, J., Bohman, J., Chambers, S., Christiano, T., Fung, A., Parkinson, J., Thompson, D. F., & Warren, M. E. (2012). A systemic approach to deliberative democracy. In J. Parkinson & J. Mansbridge (eds), *Deliberative Systems*, 1–26. Cambridge: Cambridge University Press.

Millennium Kids. (2020). *Youth-led Citizen Assembly on Climate Change.* Retrieved from: https://www.millenniumkids.com.au/wp-content/uploads/2021/04/Youth-Citizen-Assembly-Climate--Change-September.pdf [Last access: 25/Oct/2021]

Musinguzi, P., & Ellingsen, I. (2017). The Norwegian ombudsman for children on child participation: Perceptions, impacts and dilemmas. *Journal of Comparative Social Work* 12 (2), 147–169.

Nishiyama, K. (2017). Deliberators, not future citizens: Children in democracy. *Journal of Public Deliberation* 13 (1), Article 1. https://doi.org/10.16997/jdd.267.

Nishiyama, K. (2020). Between protection and participation: Rethinking children's rights to participate in protests on streets, online spaces, and schools. *Journal of Human Rights* 19 (4), 501–517.

Pow, J., van Dijk, L., & Marien, S. (2020). It's not just the taking part that counts: 'Like me' perceptions connect the wider public to mini-publics. *Journal of Deliberative Democracy* 16 (2), 43–55.

Rodgers, D. (2005). Children as social movement participants. *Sociological Studies of Children and Youth* 11, 239–259.

Shephard, M., & Patriklos, S. (2013). Making democracy work by early formal engagement? A comparative exploration of youth parliament in the EU. *Parliamentary Affairs* 66, 752–771.

Scotland's Climate Assembly. (2021). *Scotland's Climate Assembly: Recommendations for Action.* Retrieved from: https://www.climateassembly.scot/full-report [Last access: 11/Oct/2021]

Smith, G. (2021). *Can Democracy Safeguard the Future?* Cambridge: Polity Press.

Warren, M. (2008). Citizen representatives. In M. Warren & H. Pears (eds), *Designing Deliberative Democracy: The British Columbia CA*, 50–69. Cambridge: Cambridge University Press.

Young, I. (2000). *Inclusion and Democracy.* Oxford: Oxford University Press.

Nenad Stojanović

14 Citizens' assemblies and direct democracy

Abstract: Deliberative and direct democracy should not be seen in opposition: they can support each other and provide a promising way to address the alleged "crisis" of (representative) democracy. The chapter elaborates a conceptual roadmap exploring the linkage between citizens' assemblies and direct democracy and presents an overview of the various points, within the process leading to a popular vote, at which deliberative mini-publics could be meaningfully deployed. It then develops in greater depth one of the possible uses – i.e. the Citizens' Initiative Review (CIR), also called the "Oregon model" or "demoscan" (in the Swiss context) – by presenting selected empirical results from a CIR pilot conducted in Switzerland.

Keywords: direct democracy, referendum, mini-public, deliberation, "demoscan", Switzerland

14.1 Introduction

One of the main objectives of democratic innovations such as randomly selected citizens' assemblies (CAs) is to improve and enhance the role of "ordinary citizens" in political processes. In one way this implies a challenge to the elitist, Schumpeterian conception of democracy that considers citizens as mere providers of legitimacy to elected politicians: their role is to vote for parties and candidates every four to five years and leave the business of politics to elected representatives.

Yet in a number of democracies – and well before CAs started popping up around the globe in recent years – citizens have already had additional channels for genuine and impact-relevant political participation *between* regular elections, for instance in the form of popular votes triggered by referendums and initiatives. Similarly to CAs, the use of such direct democratic instruments challenges the elitist conception of democracy because it gives citizens the possibility both to challenge the decisions taken by government or parliament and/or to propose reforms that ordinary politics was not able or willing to undertake.

Hence, in the context of this *Handbook*, exploring the relationship between CAs and direct democracy (DD) is a logical and necessary step. The main objective of this chapter is to provide a conceptual roadmap that should allow scholars and practitioners alike to assess the links between CAs and DD and to have a – hopefully comprehensive even if not fully exhaustive – overview of various options on how to combine the instruments of DD and CAs so that they become *mutually supportive*. Indeed, the final, normative goal of this endeavour is to avoid CAs and DD being seen as competitors that

Nenad Stojanović: Université de Genève, Switzerland.

∂ Open Access. © 2023 the author(s), published by De Gruyter. (cc) BY-NC-ND This work is licensed under the Creative Commons Attribution-NonCommercial-NoDerivatives 4.0 International License. https://doi.org/10.1515/9783110758269-016

cancel each other out in the attempt to address the current "crisis" of (representative) democracy.

I begin the chapter by presenting key issues, concepts and definitions (Section 14.2) before proceeding with an overview of possible uses of DD in combination with CAs (Section 14.3). That section is mainly theoretical but it is also inspired by real-world examples. I will then (Section 14.4) discuss in greater depth one of the possible uses – i.e. the Citizens' Initiative Review (CIR), also called the "Oregon model" and "demoscan" (in the Swiss context) – by presenting selected empirical results from a CIR pilot that the "demoscan" team conducted in Switzerland in 2019. In the Conclusion I will briefly sum up the discussion and suggest avenues for further research.

14.2 Key issues, concepts and definitions

I start by noting that, generally speaking, deliberative theorists have not been much interested in DD or have dismissed it mainly on the grounds that a popular vote is an aggregation of preferences and, as such, is not really an ideal of deliberation (cf. Elstub 2018). While the instruments of DD have been included among the elements characterizing the "systemic turn" of deliberative theory they are still seen as "necessary evils" due to their presumed lack of deliberative character (for an overview of these critiques, see el-Wakil 2017). Only recently has DD received a more positive appreciation from deliberative theorists. In particular, Parkinson (2020: 486; see also Chambers 2009; Setälä 2011), argues that "referendums can play constructive roles at both the start and the end of a mass deliberative process, connecting political actors with everyday political talk".

Let me now turn to defining the main notions that I will use in this chapter. I consider CAs a synonym of *deliberative mini-publics* whose members are selected via *sortition*. Given that the present *Handbook* is entirely dedicated to CAs, as well as for reasons of space, I will thus mostly focus this section on the definition of DD.

The notion of *direct* democracy is not necessarily the best semantic choice to describe a democratic system in which referendums and citizens' initiatives come into play in order to *complement* the political processes within the institutions of representative democracy. Therefore, some scholars refer to "semi-direct democracy" while others propose to abandon the adjective "direct" altogether and speak of "popular vote processes in democratic systems" (el-Wakil and Cheneval 2018). Nevertheless, the notion of direct democracy is still widely used in the literature and, as long as we know what we are referring to, I suggest that we keep it for the time being.

Direct democracy can take various forms. The two most important criteria to distinguish them is to ask (1) who is legally entitled to initiate the process (government/ parliament or citizens); and (2) whether or not the outcome of the popular vote is binding. Table 14.1 offers a basic overview of the various instruments of direct democracy.

Table 14.1: A basic overview of direct democratic instruments

	Binding	Non-binding
Top-down (decided by parliament/government)	*Obligatory referendum* *Plebiscite*	*Consultative plebiscite*
Bottom-up (it is necessary to collect signatures)	*Facultative referendum* *Citizens' initiative* *Recall*	*Consultative initiative*

Yet the reality is more complex than this overview suggests. For example, some non-binding direct democratic instruments are *de jure* non-binding but, due to a specific context or to political pressures, they are (or they become) *de facto* binding. Think of the role of government-initiated referendums in the United Kingdom (e.g., Brexit) that are legally non-binding – and hence fall into the category of "consultative plebiscites" – but whose results have politically binding effects. On the other side, the result of some *de jure* binding tools, such as popular initiatives in Switzerland, can be put aside if a majority of parliament comes to a conclusion that their implementation would produce major negative drawbacks for the country.[1] The top-down vs. bottom-up distinction can also be questioned because citizens' initiatives are on occasion launched by political parties and/or interest groups and not by citizens' committees or grassroot movements.

Also, notice that the tools of direct democracy typically imply that, at the end of the process, a popular vote should take place. But sometimes the initiators – for example, a citizen's committee that has successfully launched an initiative – can stop the process if some of their demands are met by parliament.[2]

For the sake of parsimony I will develop in further detail the political process that characterizes two direct democratic tools: the facultative referendum (also called "optional referendum"); and the citizens' initiative (also called "popular initiative"). This focus is justified by these being the two most used forms of DD worldwide.[3] It will allow us to see at what points of the process the use of CAs might become interesting as a democratic innovation that improves the use of DD.

---

1 See, for example, the non-implementation of the 2014 popular initiative "against mass immigration" in Switzerland; its implementation would probably have ended the bilateral agreements with the EU that are considered of vital importance for the Swiss economy.

2 Other tools that are often associated with direct democracy – such as European Citizens' Initiative – do not even contemplate the possibility of holding a popular vote and, for this reason, I suggest that we do not take them into account in this analysis.

3 See the online database of the Centre for Research on Direct Democracy (www.c2d.ch). Notice that the dominance of these two instruments "worldwide" is strongly driven by their dominance in Switzerland, where six out of ten popular votes held in the world since the late 18th century, at national level, have taken place (Stojanović 2021: 14). If we include sub-national popular votes, the predominance of the Swiss case would be even stronger.

14.2.1 Facultative referendum

In Switzerland, most bills, acts, and regulations adopted by parliament can be fought via a facultative referendum. "In these cases, a parliamentary decision becomes law unless 50,000 citizens or eight cantons, within 100 days, demand the holding of a popular vote. If a popular vote is held, a simple majority of the voting people decides whether the bill is approved or rejected (…)" (Linder and Mueller 2021: 121). Schematically, the process can be summed up as follows:

> Various inputs suggesting the necessity to adopt a new bill or to reform an existing one → the executive drafts a bill proposal → consultation (pre-parliamentary) procedure in which relevant political actors (parties, interest groups) but also ordinary citizens can provide comments and inputs → the bill is submitted to parliament (parliamentary procedure) → the bill is approved by parliament (post-parliamentary procedure), when the collection of signatures for a referendum can start → if the requested number of valid signatures is collected, the referendum campaign (of both sides) starts → several weeks before the popular vote, all enfranchised citizens receive an official booklet informing them about the topic of the vote → popular vote (the bill is approved or rejected by citizens) → if approved, the implementation of the bill (by the government and public administration) can start.

14.2.2 Citizens' initiative

The second instrument of DD, the citizens' initiative, is triggered from below. In Switzerland, 100,000 citizens can sign, within 18 months, a formal proposal demanding an amendment to the constitution. If the collection of signatures is successful, the initiative is discussed by the executive and parliament. "This can involve drawing up an alternative proposition or, if the popular initiative is couched in general terms, formulating precise propositions. Initiatives and eventual counterproposals are presented simultaneously to the people. As with all constitutional changes, acceptance requires majorities of both individual voters and cantons" (Linder and Mueller 2021: 121). The process can be summed up as follows:

> Various inputs suggesting the necessity to have a political reform that the government and/or parliament are hardly likely to adopt → an initiative committee is set up in order to elaborate a written proposal → the proposal is officially adopted and the collection of signatures can start → if the necessary number of signatures is collected, the government recommends that parliament approve or reject the initiative, or make a counterproposal → the executive and parliament deliberates on the content of the initiative and decide to approve or reject the initiative, or adopt a counterproposal → the initiative committee decides whether or not to withdraw the initiative (in the light of the outcome of parliamentary deliberations and/or the current political context) → if the initiative is not withdrawn, the campaign (of both sides) in view of a popular vote starts → several weeks before the popular vote, all enfranchised citizens receive an official booklet informing them about the topic of the vote → popular vote (the initiative is accepted or rejected by citizens) → if accepted, the procedure concerning its implementation (by the government and parliament) starts

→ decisions on the implementation are carried out by public administration and possibly the courts.

As I will show in the next Section, CAs can be employed in all phases of the process that characterizes a facultative referendum and a citizens' initiative. But, first of all, we should ask what *functions* a CA should be able to accomplish within a political system with DD. The answer will depend mostly on the kind of actors who are the recipients of the CA's outcome, as well as on their expectations. We can broadly distinguish between three kinds of actors: (a) institutional actors (government/parliament/public administration); (b) reform advocates (e.g. a movement that launched the collection of signatures; initiative committee); (c) citizens at large.

For actors of the first (a) category, a CA can be useful to gain an idea of "what the people thinks" on a given issue. Hence a CA may provide an answer to a cognitive demand and perform functions that are similar to opinion surveys – it is not a coincidence that one influential model of CA is called "deliberative polling" (Fishkin 2009). However, it is much more robust than the latter because it does not consist of a mere aggregation of preferences, capturing only "raw opinions", but is based on deliberation and, thus, is able to capture "considered opinion". It is true that, in any political system, institutional actors can see an interest in CAs but, in a system where DD plays a major role, this interest might be further enhanced by a desire to make decisions that can resist the challenge of a popular vote. In Ireland, for example, any modification of the constitution must be approved by a majority of voters and therefore it is *"rational to consult a representative sample of the population before any referendum"* (Courant 2021: 6; my italics).

For (b) the advocates of a reform, a CA can be useful for similar reasons, but from a different perspective. Suppose that we are members of a movement that has set out to reform the fiscal laws in our country because they produce huge social inequalities. Yet before launching a citizens' initiative – a move that will require significant resources in terms of money, time, and personnel – we might wish to know which among the various options is the most promising in terms of being likely to receive the support of a majority of voters.

Finally for (c), citizens at large, a CA can perform the function of "facilitative trust", i.e. it eases their "cognitive expenses of forming opinions" (Warren and Gastil 2015: 566). This is what makes CIRs so interesting: they are held ahead of popular votes and their outcomes are distributed to all enfranchised citizens.

14.3 Overview of possible uses of citizens' assemblies in direct democracy

14.3.1 Pre-parliamentary phase

Option 1a: The government decides to set up a CA during the consultation procedure; that is, before sending the final draft of a new law to parliament. Indeed, the Swiss experience shows that the very goal of this pre-parliamentary phase is to improve the chances that, eventually, the final decision of parliament will be sufficiently "resistant" to possible referendums (*referendumssicher*; Neidhart 1970: 287). Typically, the organizations that participate in the consultation procedures are political parties and interest groups and only rarely groups of citizens. Yet parties and interest groups are anyway actively involved in the parliamentary phase. Hence, an interesting innovation of the already existing consultation procedure would be to organize CAs in that phase, if not permanently then at least on the most disputed topics. This would allow government and parliament to have an idea what a demographically representative sample of citizens thinks of the reform and thus decrease the risk that, at the end of the procedure, the law is defeated in a referendum.

Option 1b: Similarly to (1a), the prospective initiative committees, especially those composed of grassroot citizens' movements with little experience in politics, may have an interest in setting up a deliberative mini-public in order to decide what exactly they want to propose and/or the exact wording of the proposal. Such CAs can be of a relatively small size (about 20 participants, as in CIR processes) and convene during two weekends.[4] The goal is to come up with a proposal – that is, the text of a citizens' initiative – that is most likely to convince a majority of voters. For example, if a movement advocating unconditional basic income wants to launch a citizens' initiative on that topic there are many important details to sort out. One of them is whether or not the text of the initiative should mention the exact amount of that income or remain vague by stipulating that the amount will be decided by parliament but that it must cover the basic needs of every citizen.

14.3.2 Parliamentary phase

Option 2a: In the parliamentary phase CAs can be set up towards the end of the process, in order to check to what extent a new law has the potential to convince a majority

---

4 Notice, however, that grassroot movements might lack the resources to set up a mini-public or may not have access to the official population registers that are typically used to select the members of a CA at random.

of voters in the case that, eventually, a successful referendum is launched against it. But, given the high number of new laws and/or amendments to existing laws that a parliament is called to adopt on a regular basis, organizing CAs on each of them would amount to creating an additional chamber of parliament. While this is certainly an idea worth exploring, for the time being it is more realistic to imagine a mechanism setting up a threshold of MPs – one-third, for example – who can file a request for a CA on certain (presumably the most disputed) topics. The threshold should not be too high in order to allow opposition parties to trigger the mechanism. The distinction with regard to (1a) is that, in the latter case, the decision is taken by the government whereas here it is taken by parliament.

Option 2b: Regarding citizens' initiatives, the parliamentary phase is typically focused on the question of whether or not parliament should elaborate a counterproposal. Indeed, the Swiss experience shows that it is rare for parliament to accept what a citizens' initiative proposes. This refusal has structural grounds: initiatives are typically launched by *minority* groups whose ideas, in the past, have failed to convince a majority of parliament (Vatter 2000). So if a counterproposal emerges in the parliamentary phase, parliament can decide to set up a CA as in (2a). Probably even more interesting would be for the initiative committee to have a mini-public deliberate on the counterproposal as well as on the main proposal, eventually taking into account the conclusions of the CA in order to decide whether or not to withdraw the citizens' initiative if the counterproposal is considered a sufficiently acceptable compromise.

14.3.3 Post-parliamentary phase preceding a popular vote

Option 3a/3b: Once the parliamentary phase is concluded, and supposing that a successful referendum has been launched against the law (3a), or that a popular initiative has not been withdrawn (3b), mini-publics can be put in place in order to provide citizens with the necessary information on the topic of the upcoming popular vote. This is, in a nutshell, the CIR model that has already been experienced in Oregon and other US states and cities, as well as in Finland and in Switzerland. The topic of the deliberations can even be both a citizens' initiative and a law voted by parliament as a counterproposal to the initiative.[5] What makes the CIR model special with regard to the other uses of CAs – in a system with DD but also more generally – is that its conclusions are not simply sent to the government and/or parliament, with these being free to decide what to do with them, but are distributed to all enfranchised citizens of the respective polity.

---

5 This was the case in "demoscan Geneva", held in September 2021 in the canton of Geneva, with regard to a popular initiative and a law (counterproposal) concerning a reform of the pension scheme for members of the cantonal executive (https://demoscan.ch/demoscan-geneve/).

14.3.4 Post-parliamentary phase after the popular vote

Option 4a/4b: Even if a given reform is approved by voters according to the established rules (either a simple majority or qualified majorities), this does not mean that the process has come to an end. Adopted laws (4a) typically require governmental decrees in order to allow public administration (and sometimes also tribunals) to implement them. This could be another point at which a CA could be set up. As for citizens' initiatives (4b), the possible pathways of implementation are even larger, especially if the initiative is an amendment to the constitution that requires parliament to adopt a specific law in order to implement it.

14.3.5 Zooming in: The proposal for a climate council in Switzerland

A particularly inspiring proposal to combine CAs with DD *and* the institutions of representative democracy comes from Switzerland, where in September 2020 the Greens filed a parliamentary initiative demanding the creation of a "climate council"; essentially a CA of 200 members randomly selected for a period of six years from all Swiss residents (Swiss and foreign nationals alike) aged 16 and above.[6] Its task would be "to develop measures to protect the climate and achieve greater climate justice", noting that "these measures must be capable of gaining majority support". Its powers would be analogous to the prerogatives and the legal standing of a committee that has successfully launched a citizens' initiative.

In other words, if the climate council was to make a proposal in the form of a constitutional amendment – requiring in such a case the support of a two-thirds majority within the council – it would be sent to parliament as if it were a citizens' initiative that had succeeded in gathering the necessary number of signatures (i.e. 100,000). Hence, the government and parliament would be obliged to take a stance and decide whether to accept or disapprove the proposal or make a counterproposal. In any event the council would be free to decide to withdraw the proposal, in the light of the conclusions reached by parliament, or to let citizens decide in a popular vote. As in the case of a citizens' initiative, any proposal would need to gather a double majority, of both citizens and cantons, in order to pass. If successful, it would enter the constitution and would thus have a binding character.

Even though in December 2021 the parliamentary initiative of the Greens was eventually rejected by a strong majority[7] of the Swiss National Council, it is worth mentioning in the context of this chapter because it neatly illustrates how a CA could be

---

6 https://www.parlament.ch/en/ratsbetrieb/suche-curia-vista/geschaeft?AffairId=20200467.
7 136 against 33, with 19 abstentions; only Green MPs and a handful of Social Democrat ones supported it.

inserted into a political system that already combines institutions of representative democracy and DD. Contrary to the CAs held in Ireland, British Columbia, and Ontario, which had follow-up referendums (Courant 2021), the decision on whether or not to put the conclusions of a CA to a popular vote ought not to be left to the mercies of the government or parliament but is something that could be enforced by the citizens comprising the mini-public.

14.4 Side-effect: Impact on turnout (the example of "demoscan Sion")

In the previous section I have tried to put forward the possible uses of CAs, within a political system combining DD and representative democracy, from the point of view of its interest for elected politicians, advocacy groups, and ordinary citizens. I have shown that there are many options to use CAs in a meaningful way to enhance articulation between the institutions of DD and representative democracy.

But the interest in holding CAs in such contexts extends far more broadly. When we organized the first[8] randomly selected mini-public in Switzerland ("demoscan Sion"), following the CIR model and as a pilot, there was one aspect that was of upmost importance for the municipal authorities as well as a frequent question among the media: will the citizens' statement – i.e. the formal outcome of the mini-public – improve turnout? The background to this question is the relatively low turnout in Swiss popular votes (46% at national level between 1990 and 2020). The interest in turnout seems to be an exception, however, both in the literature and in real-world experiences; in fact, in other CIRs, in Oregon and in Finland, this issue did not feature at all.[9]

"Demoscan Sion" took place in November 2019, with 20 randomly selected citizens of the town of Sion, the capital of the canton of Valais, and was organized in collaboration with the municipality and in particular with the office of the mayor and the mayor himself. The topic of its deliberations was a federal popular initiative on affordable housing, launched by the main Swiss tenants' association, which is close to the parties of the left. On 9 February 2020 the popular initiative was rejected by 57.1% of Swiss voters. In Valais, the initiative was rejected by 67.1%. In Sion, however, the share of "no" votes was significantly lower than in the rest of the canton (58.7%). It is interesting to note that the result of the vote held within "demoscan Sion" (11 out

---

8 The second "demoscan" took place at cantonal level in Geneva (September 2021) and the third one in the city of Bellinzona (March/April 2023).

9 Gastil et al. (2017) do not even mention the word "turnout" in their assessment of the 2016 CIR held in Oregon. Setälä et al. (2020: 9) mention it only once, simply to inform the reader of the final turnout in the local referendum.

of 19 citizens, that is 57.9%, rejected the initiative) was as close as it could be (given the small N) to the final result both in Sion and at federal level.

The turnout in Sion was 44.0%, which was slightly higher than the turnout in Valais (42.5%) and at federal level (41.7%). Based on comparisons with past popular votes, as well as with turnout rates in Sion compared to those at the level of the district, region, canton, and federation, the citizens' statement distributed to all Sion's voters in early January 2020 might well have had a small positive effect on the turnout. Nevertheless, the increase is almost certainly not as large as one might have hoped for (Geisler and Stojanović 2020).

Table 14.2: Turnout in the popular vote on affordable housing (9 February 2020; %)

	City of Sion	Local district of Sion	Region (Valais central)	Canton (Valais)	Switzerland
Turnout	44.0	45.0	44.3	42.5	41.7
Difference compared to the turnout in Sion	–	+1.0	+0.3	−1.5	−2.3
Average difference compared to turnout rates in Sion between 2016 and 2020	–	+1.7	+2.6	+0.1	−3.2

However, the results of our survey experiment do show a more optimistic picture when we focus on the reported likelihood of voters participating in the popular vote (Geisler and Stojanović 2020).

In fact, in order to determine the impact of the citizens' statement and its support among the wider public, we conducted a survey experiment. A sample of 2500 randomly selected enfranchised citizens of Sion received a letter inviting them to participate in three waves of online surveys. The letter was co-signed by the mayor of Sion and the author of this chapter and bore the municipality's coat of arms. Approximately 1159 respondents (46.4%) responded to the first survey wave.

The survey experiment randomly assigned participants to reading one of four different variations of the citizens' statement; one control group that did not receive a statement; and one modified control group (see Figure 14.1). Once they had completed pre-treatment questions on their awareness of "demoscan Sion" and the topic of the initiative, participants were randomly assigned to either treatment or control conditions. In the four treatment groups, they read one of four otherwise identical statements, including or excluding (1) the result of the vote of "demoscan Sion" on the popular initiative; and (2) the result of the vote on the popular initiative held within the Swiss Federal Assembly. In the two control groups, participants read only a four-paragraph newspaper-style article about the general proceedings of "demoscan Sion", one of them containing a cue (Gastil et al. 2017: 39) that this had voted by a small majority against the initiative.

The mean comparisons in Figure 14.1 show that the citizens' statement significantly enhanced the readiness of respondents to take part in the popular vote. The average intention to participate, measured on a seven-point scale, was up to 8 per cent higher when comparing the control groups and the treatment groups. An exception is the difference between the control group and the group that received the citizens' statement together with the result of the vote of the Federal Assembly. The difference here amounted to just half the size of that with the remaining treatment groups (Geisler and Stojanović 2020).

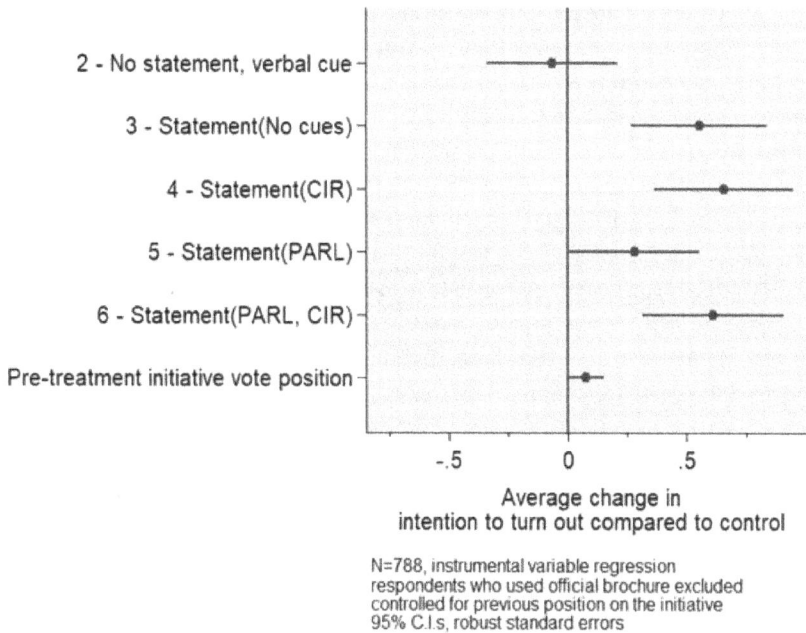

N=788, instrumental variable regression
respondents who used official brochure excluded
controlled for previous position on the initiative
95% C.I.s, robust standard errors

Figure 14.1: Average change per condition in voters' reported intention to take part in the popular vote compared to control groups

To sum up, while is too early to assess the impact of CAs (here: CIR) on turnout, the results of our survey experiment do indicate that an improvement might be an important side-effect if CAs were to be institutionalized and become a permanent component of a political system based on a combination of representative and direct democracy.

14.5 Conclusion

The main goal of this chapter has been to elaborate a conceptual roadmap regarding the linkage between CAs and DD and to present an overview of the various points, within the process leading to a popular vote, at which deliberative mini-publics could be meaningfully deployed. The underlying idea has been that deliberative and direct democracy should not be seen in opposition but that they support each other and ultimately provide a promising way to address the alleged "crisis" in the institutions of representative democracy.

The main difficulty with this approach is that there are simply not too many democracies in which the instruments of DD are employed with a relatively high degree of frequency. In many European countries it is not even legally possible to hold referendums at national level (e.g. Belgium, Germany). In others (e.g. Austria, France) the thresholds for triggering a referendum are so high that the instrument is rarely used. Hence, the discussion on the possible use of mini-publics in DD is *de facto* limited to a handful of polities, mainly to Switzerland, a number of US states and Ireland. Greater variety and frequency, however, can be found at municipal level.

As a consequence, only a few models of mini-publics have so far been used in relation to DD. The most promising are the Irish model (see Courant 2021) and the CIR or Oregon model (Gastil et al. 2017). Since 2019, the Oregon model has found three opportunities for testing in Switzerland, under the label "demoscan", and once in Finland (Setälä et al. 2020). In Section 4 of this chapter, I have thus focused on our main findings from the first "demoscan" pilot, the one held in the city of Sion in November 2019 (Geisler and Stojanović 2020).

I see two main avenues for future research on the use of mini-publics in DD. First, there is a need to provide a comprehensive assessment of the various experiences that have taken place up to now, by comparing the mini-publics held in Ireland, Finland, Oregon (as well as in a couple of other US states), and Switzerland. Second, we need more experiences with mini-publics, ideally one for each of the various stages of the political process, starting with the draft of a law (in the case of referendums) or the draft of a citizens' initiative and ending with the implementation of the decision taken by the citizens in a popular vote.

References

Chambers, S. (2009). Rhetoric and the public sphere: Has deliberative democracy abandoned mass democracy? *Political Theory* 37, 323 – 350.

Courant, D. (2021). Citizens' assemblies for referendums and constitutional reforms: Is there an 'Irish model' for deliberative democracy? *Frontiers in Political Science* 2. https://www.frontiersin.org/article/10.3389/fpos.2020.591983

Elstub, S. (2018). Deliberative and participatory democracy. In A. Bächtiger, J. S. Dryzek, J. Mansbridge, & Warren, M. (eds), *The Oxford Handbook of Deliberative Democracy*, 187 – 202. Oxford: Oxford University Press.

el-Wakil, A. (2017). The deliberative potential of facultative referendums: procedure and substance in direct democracy, *Democratic Theory* 4 (1), 59 – 78.

el-Wakil, A., & Cheneval, F. (2018). Designing popular vote processes to enhance democratic systems. *Swiss Political Science Review* 24 (3), 348 – 358.

Fishkin, J. S. (2009). *When the People Speak. Deliberative Democracy and Public Consultation.* Oxford: Oxford University Press.

Gastil, J., Johnson, G. F., Han, S.-H., & Rountree, J. (2017). *Assessment of the 2016 Oregon Citizens' Initiative Review on Measure 97.* http://sites.psu.edu/citizensinitiativereview.

Geisler, A., & Stojanović, N. (2020). *Citizens' Panel in Sion (Valais, Switzerland, November 2019): Scientific Report.* University of Geneva.

Linder, W., & Mueller, S. (2021). *Swiss Democracy: Possible Solutions to Conflict in Multicultural Societies.* 4th ed. Cham: Palgrave Macmillan.

Neidhart, L. (1970). *Plebiszit und pluralitäre Demokratie: Eine Analyse der Funktion des schweizerischen Gesetzesreferendums.* Bern: Francke.

Parkinson, J. (2020). The roles of referendums in deliberative systems. *Representation* 56 (4), 485–500.

Setälä, M. (2011). The role of deliberative mini-publics in representative democracy: lessons from the experience of referendums. *Representation* 47 (2), 201–213.

Setälä, M., Christensen, H. S., Leino, M., Strandberg, K., Bäck, M., & Jäske, M. (2020). Deliberative mini-publics facilitating voter knowledge and judgement: experience from a Finnish local referendum. *Representation.* First View. DOI: 10.1080/00344893.2020.1826565.

Stojanović, N. (2021). *Multilingual Democracy: Switzerland and Beyond.* London and New York: ECPR Press/Rowman & Littlefield.

Vatter, A. (2000). Consensus and direct democracy: conceptual and empirical linkages. *European Journal of Political Research* 38 (2), 171–192.

Warren, M. E., & Gastil, J. (2015). Can deliberative minipublics address the cognitive challenges of democratic citizenship? *Journal of Politics* 77 (2), 562–574.

Irena Fiket

15 Citizens' assemblies at supranational level: Addressing the EU and global democratic deficit

Abstract: The problems related to the democratic deficit, lack of democratic legitimacy, and widening gap between citizens and decision-makers seem even more striking in the case of decision-making at supranational level. One response to this crisis of democracy at the supranational level has been the creation of citizens' assemblies (CAs) promoted and implemented by the various actors: European Union, NGOs, international organizations, and social movements. Still, although all those actors advocated for the use of CAs at supranational level there are significant differences regarding the capacity of those actors as well as the CAs they promote to address the democratic deficit. Starting from this assumption, in the following pages I will analytically differentiate between CAs implemented by the European Union (EU), a system provided by the political authority and those CAs implemented by supranational actors that lack formally legitimate political authority.

Keywords: global democratic deficit, EU democratic deficit, supranational citizens' assemblies, supranational deliberation, supranational deliberative mini-publics, European citizens' panels

15.1 Introduction

> We recommend that the European Union holds Citizen's Assemblies. We strongly recommend that they are developed through a legally binding and compulsory law or regulation. The citizens' assemblies should be held every 12–18 months. Participation of the citizens should not be mandatory but incentivised, while organised on the basis of limited mandates.
>
> (Report from the European Citizens' Panel 2, Session 3–17, Conference on the Future of Europe, 2021)

As stated in the introduction of this *Handbook*, there is a widespread crisis of democracy, which has been the matter of intense political and academic debate for over 20 years. The problems related to the democratic deficit, lack of democratic legitimacy, and widening gap between citizens and decision-makers seem even more striking in the case of decision-making at supranational level or, to put it in a slightly different perspective, in the case of political decisions that produce effects beyond the local or national borders.

Irena Fiket: University of Belgrade, Serbia.

∂ Open Access. © 2023 the author(s), published by De Gruyter. (cc) BY-NC-ND This work is licensed under the Creative Commons Attribution-NonCommercial-NoDerivatives 4.0 International License. https://doi.org/10.1515/9783110758269-017

One response to this crisis of democracy at the supranational level has been the creation of citizens' assemblies (CAs), participatory institutions which seek to bring together an inclusive group of ordinary people to deliberate formally on a political issue and to exert an influence on public decision-making (see the Introduction to this *Handbook* for a definition of CAs). The use of CAs at supranational level was proposed and promoted by various actors: European Union (EU), NGOs, international organizations, and social movements.

Still, although all those actors carried out CAs and advocated for their use at supranational level, there are significant differences regarding the capacity of those actors as well as the CAs they promote to address the democratic deficit. Starting from this assumption, in the following pages I will analytically differentiate between CAs implemented by the European Union (EU), a system provided by the political authority and those CAs implemented by supranational actors that lack formally legitimate political authority.

The relevance of the idea that CAs could serve as institutions that could help in addressing the democratic deficit could be inferred just by looking at the long list of CAs implemented at the supranational level so far. On the one hand, the EU continuously, since 2005, promoted various types of CAs. The first EU initiatives that took the form of CAs were two Citizens Conferences organized within the 6th Framework Programs (FP) financed by the European Commission. One focused on "the city of tomorrow"[1] while the other one, the "Meeting of Minds: European Citizens' Deliberation on Brain Science",[2] dealt with the impact of new developments in neuroscience.

Those experiments, not formalized institutional processes, created the precedent for other similar projects promoted under the 7th FP, the Plan D for Democracy, Dialogue and Debate (2005) and Debate Europe programme (2008).[3] Under Plan D the First European Citizens Consultation was organized in 2006–2007. It involved 1,789 lay citizens from 27 EU countries. In addition, with the EU institutions' support, two wide European Deliberative Polls involving the random samples of more than 300 European citizens were organized in 2007 and 2009 respectively. The most recent example of the EU institutions' initiative to "reinvigorate democracy" is The Conference on the Future of Europe (CoFoE),[4] promoted by the Presidents of the European Parliament, European Commission, and Council and launched in 2021 in Strasbourg. It comprises four thematic CAs each gathering 200 randomly-selected Europeans reflecting the EU's diversity.

On the other hand, the list of the CAs implemented "globally" seems to be shorter and more diverse. Unfortunately, it is not possible to trace all CAs implemented at the "global" level since, unlike in the case of the EU, there was no unique political entity

---

1 See http://www.raise-eu.org/.

2 Meeting of minds – European citizens' deliberation on brain sciences: final report of the external evaluation (2006), DOI:10.18419/opus-5483.

3 http://eur-lex.europa.eu/LexUriServ/LexUriServ.do?uri=COM:2008:0158:FIN:en:PDF.

4 https://futureu.europa.eu/pages/about.

that promoted them but a wide variety of actors such as NGOs, international organizations, and social movements and those processes are neither systematically documented nor archived in some publicly available databases[5] which means that also a process
of institutional learning from those experiences is impeded. As it is often the case also
in the CAs implemented at the local and national level, we don't have a trace of the
process of discussion or formulation of the policies that took in consideration the recommendations that the CAs produced, so the eventual political influence that the outputs of those processes could have produced is also put in question. Besides, the CAs at
the "global" level were most often part of a broader initiative that had different specific
goals for each phase of the process and were not directly integrated in the formal processes of decision-making. For instance, this is the case of the 13th Association for
Women in Development (AWID) International Forum that was held in Brazil in 2016
that brought together 1,700 activists and women from marginalized groups from
over 140 countries. The CAs that were organized, as one of the elements of the
forum, had a flexible format regarding characteristics of participants, topics, possibility
to choose specific CAs to participate in, and so on. This was also the case in the United
Nations Youth Climate Summit that gathered youth activists and ordinary young people
from all over the world to discuss the world's climate change emergency. The summit
used different forms of CAs such as participatory budgeting, town hall meetings, and
deliberative workshops, but also some formats that are not similar to CAs. One of
the most mentioned examples of the CAs at the supranational level is the World
Wide Views, the large-scale initiative of citizens' deliberation on the climate issues promoted by the Danish Board of Technology Foundation, an independent counselling institution connected to the Danish Ministry of Science, Innovation and Higher Education. So far, three WWVs were held: on Global Warming in 2009, on Biodiversity in
2012, and on Climate and Energy in 2015.

A quick glance at the proclaimed reasons for the promotion of CAs at supranational level confirms that the common political goal of those CAs, both at the EU and global
level, was to offer solutions to the problem of democratic deficit in supranational policymaking. The idea that CAs could tackle the problem of democratic deficit is based on
the assumption of deliberative democracy according to which the political decisions
could be legitimate only if they are reached through a process of inclusive deliberative
discussion that allow arguments of "all" those affected by some political issue, to be
heard (Manin 1987; Bohman 1996).

In order to understand the relevance that CAs could have in terms of reducing the
democratic deficit at supranational level of decision-making, but also the challenges regarding their implementation and benefits they can bring to the actors and political
processes, I argue that we need to distinguish analytically between CAs promoted at

---

5 For example, the OECD report published in 2020 mapped 289 cases of CAs, and identified only three
per cent of those as being supranational. However, we know with certainty for at least nine cases of CAs
organized only at EU level.

EU level and those at global level. In fact, in the following pages we will see that two distinct paths of development of the CAs could be traced; one applies to the introduction of CAs within the European Union (EU), a system provided by the political authority and political constituency in the making (Fiket, Olsen and Trenz 2014), while the other is related to their introduction within the global system of governance that lacks formally legitimate political authority, political constituency, and that is often described as non democratic (Zweifel 2006). The key implications of different features of the EU and global system of policymaking on CAs will be taken into account in the next two sections, where major political and scientific arguments for the introduction of CAs at supranational level will be outlined. Following the systemic approach to deliberation (Parkinson and Mansbridge 2012) I consider that the legitimacy of political decisions is generated through the interdependence and exchange between a variety of institutional and non-institutional (deliberative) actors that are part of that system. Therefore, in this contribution I will rely on political and scientific discussion about the possibility of the CAs to represent one part of the solution to democratic deficit at the supranational level. I will discuss two specific proposals of institutions that are conceived as solutions for the democratic deficit at the supranational level: Popularly Elected Global Assembly (Falk and Strauss 2001) and Deliberative Global Citizens' Assembly (Dryzek, Bächtiger and Milewicz 2011). Before all, I will try to show that, in order to understand the possibilities of CAs to address the democratic deficit at the global level, it is necessary to distinguish between EU and global policymaking systems.

15.2 Political arguments for the institutionalization of citizens' assemblies at the supranational level

The proliferation of the idea that the European Union must find the way to involve citizens in political life can be traced back to the debate on its democratic deficit that started in the early 1990s, when the Danish referendum rejected the Maastricht Treaty, although intense experimentation with the CAs actually stems from the "period of reflection" that followed the 2005 rejection of the EU Constitutional Treaty (Friedrich 2011). On the whole, these facts were taken as clear symptoms of an increasingly tense relationship between the EU and its citizens: the era of "permissive consensus" seemed definitely over and the conviction was that the EU was suffering a legitimacy crisis due to a deficit in its democratic credentials (García-Guitián 2022). This resulted in a process of democratic engineering that consisted of three phases inspired by three different principles related to representative, participatory, and deliberative conceptions of democracy. Each phase also had different targets: elected representatives in the European Parliament (EP), representatives from civil society organizations, lay citizens, and the general public. In the third phase of participatory engineering, the EU opened a space to direct citizens' participation (Abels 2009; Hüller 2010.; Di Mauro and Fiket 2017). Political arguments for the involvement of lay citizens in EU political life were basically the same as for civil society's involvement, and both aimed to create a shared public arena of communication and participation in Europe and were suggested as "solutions" for the democratic deficit of the EU. However, the type of initiatives promoted in the third phase, as well as the language employed in political documents, indicated a clear shift towards the deliberative model of democracy and the involvement of ordinary citizens (and not only organized interests) into the political life of the EU through various forms of CAs.

The Plan D and its follow-ups were a direct European Commission (EC) reaction to the Heads of State and Government call for a "period of reflection", which was meant "to enable a broad debate to take place in each of our countries, involving citizens, civil society, social partners, national parliaments and political parties".[6] The Plan D delineated ambitious objectives identifying goals such as "set[ting] out a long-term plan to reinvigorate European democracy and help[ing] the emergence of a European public sphere, where citizens (...) actively participate in the decision-making process and gain ownership of the European project".[7]

The EU institutions have remained on this path since then and the most recent EU initiative, The Conference on the Future of Europe (2021), while aiming to "giv(ing)e citizens a greater role in shaping EU policies"[8] also improved a method of integrating recommendations from the CAs (European Citizens' Panels) in political decisions. At the final Conference Plenary, in fact, all actors that participate in decision-making will gather in discussion: the citizens that participated in CAs, EP, the Council, and the European Commission, as well as representatives from all national Parliaments.

On the other hand, although a wide variety of actors promoted CAs at the global level, they all aimed to solve problems with democratic deficit of global governance in some specific thematic areas. To give one example: the main proclaimed goal of the WWV project was to respond to the need for global solutions to global problems such as environmental cross-border challenges. As stated in the Policy Report[9] from the first WWVs: "As markets, technologies and environmental issues become increasingly global in scale, so does policymaking. In this new reality, the distance between citizens and policymakers increases, thereby diminishing the citizens' sense of ownership in decision-making. This creates a need for new initiatives to bridge the widening democratic gap."

The reasons for the promotion of CAs at global level were always tied to democratic deficit in decision-making regarding specific issues. The need to democratize the overall system of global governance or to promote global citizenship was not the main focus of those initiatives. Besides, the initiatives to promote CAs at global level

---

6 http://www.coreuropa.eu/migrated_data/com2005_0494en01.pdf.
7 http://www.coreuropa.eu/migrated_data/communication_planD_en.pdf.
8 https://ec.europa.eu/commission/presscorner/detail/en/ip_21_1065.
9 http://globalwarming.wwviews.org/files/AUDIO/WWViews%20Policy%20Report%20FINAL%20-%20Web%20version.pdf.

never made an explicit reference to the movements for an alternative democratic globalization that were on the rise in 1999, 2000, and 2001. Yet, it seems that the political pressures to democratize the international system of governance came exactly from those movements that were reclaiming the right of global citizenry to participate in global decision-making.[10] Those movements in fact pose the questions of both global polity and democratic accountability of international organizations such as the United Nations (UN), World Trade Organization (WTO), International Monetary Fund (IMF), and World Bank (WB) regarding their possibility to influence policies that have direct influence on citizens' lives.

Like in the case of the EU reforms that were implemented in order to make the EU system of governance more democratic, the first phase of reforms in the global system followed the logic of representative democracy and aimed at making international organizations more representative and accountable (Barnett and Finnemore 2004; Weiss and Wilkinson 2018). For example, in 2010 the Campaign for the UN Parliamentary Assembly was launched and supported by a broad range of individuals and institutions from more than 150 countries. The UN Parliamentary Assembly was imagined as an independent watchdog in the UN system and consultative body that would develop into a world parliament over time (UNPA Campaign 2010).

However, there is a shared consensus in the international relations literature that despite calls for more democratic governance at global level and tentative reforms of single organizations, the global system has not been significantly democratized (Zweifel 2006; Belém Lopes and Casarões 2019).

In such an undemocratic system, the sporadic and unsystematic promotion of CAs, that aim to respond to specific challenges that global problems pose, has serious limitations regarding their possibility to address democratic deficit in global policymaking. In the political promotion of CAs by the EU, their potential to build common European identity and European polity (Di Mauro and Fiket 2017) as well as the interrelation of CAs and EU institutions, were, and remained, considered highly relevant for addressing democratic deficit. Instead, the political promotion of global CAs is focused mainly on solving problems in particular policy areas without serious reflection on neither the relationship between institutions and organizations with CAs nor their potential to build common identity and polity.

---

10 Those movements organized a series of protests: those at the gathering of the World Trade Organization in Seattle in 1999, at the gatherings of the International Monetary Fund and the World Bank in Washington and in Prague in 2000, at the gathering of G8 countries in Genoa in 2001, and at the meetings of the World Economic Forum.

15.3 Scientific arguments for the institutionalization of citizens' assemblies at the supranational level

In the political effort to promote CAs, the EU institutions, NGOs, international organizations, and social movements were supported by theorists of democracy who developed a critique of representative democracy, stressing its inner limits and inability to fulfil democratic functions at the supranational level. According to this view, traditional instruments of representative democracy and international governance should be combined with tools of participatory and deliberative models of democracy, based on a broad involvement of citizens in decision-making (Bohman 1999, 2004; Crespy 2013; Smith and Brassett 2008; Fishkin, Luskin and Siu 2014). However, despite a relatively strong consensus about the democratic deficit at supranational level and shared understanding that the nature of the supranational issues requires supranational policy, the literature on deliberative democracy that approached problems of supranational democratic deficit did not advance straightforwardly towards the proposal of CAs as solutions to the problems of global democracy.

Like in the case of political discussion regarding the institutional reforms of the EU or international organizations, the solutions to democratic deficit were initially inspired by the principles of representative democracy. This view suggests that existing elected representative bodies, such as EP, should be empowered or that supranational representative bodies ought to be formed in order to deal with the democratic deficit at supranational level(s) (Stie 2021). Furthermore, the theoretical approaches arguing that the principles of deliberative democracy should be integrated at the supranational level often remained at the level of theoretical discussions and no clear path towards the promotion of institutions of CAs could be traced from that literature (Eriksen and Fossum 2000; Eriksen 2006; Cochran 2002; Dryzek 2006; Smith and Brassett 2008).

Very rarely academic discussion evolving around the principles of representative versus participatory and deliberative democracy focused on specific proposals of institutions that should be implemented at a supranational level of decision-making in order to deal with the democratic deficit.

Richard Falk and Andrew Strauss in their article 'Toward Global Parliament' (2001) approached the question of the democratic deficit in global governance from the perspective of international relations. They proposed the solution in a form of Popularly Elected Global Assembly (PEGA), underlying the need for an international system of decision-making to have elected national representatives to decide for global citizenry within the global assembly.

PEGA basically follows the model of the EU Parliament: it is composed of political representatives of all countries of the world, elected by citizens in elections held at the national level. The authors did not develop in detail the PEGA model but were more focused on arguments that support the necessity of its institutionalization. They were reflecting on political claims of left-wing, anti-globalism movements (movements for democratic globalization) that were insisting on the lack of democratic legitimacy of international organizations to shape citizens' daily lives. Recognizing that globalization is dispersing political authority throughout the international order, they focused on designing the model of global institution that would have legitimate political authority within the framework of electoral democracy.

Dryzek, Bächtiger and Milewicz (2011) accepted the basic justifications for a global democratic institution advanced by Falk and Strauss (2001). Starting from the critique of their PEGA model, they moved beyond electoral democracy logic and elaborated a deliberative model of a global democratic institution – Deliberative Global Citizens' Assembly (DGCA).[11]

The DGCA is structured as a deliberative mini-public or, as we define it in this *Handbook*, citizens' assembly, a citizens' forum in which a sample of citizens, (randomly) selected from the population affected by some public issue, deliberates and makes a decision on that specific issue (Goodin and Dryzek 2006; Ryan and Smith 2014; see the Introduction to this *Handbook*).

The first critique of the PEGA advanced by Dryzek, Bächtiger and Milewicz (2011) is that certain states would be reluctant to concede some part of their own sovereignty and an elected global body such as PEGA could represent a direct challenge to their national institutions. The US and China are taken as examples of the states that already showed preferences to maintain a world order in which there are no more global institutions to bind them. Although both countries have been unwilling to cede formal authority to international elected bodies, this could change with the introduction of innovative institutions such as DGCA. Namely, the hypothesis is that the lack of understanding of the very nature of the deliberative institution such as DGCA, composed of ordinary citizens that through deliberation formulate recommendations, policy proposals, or make decisions, would not look like a threat to the US Congress. The fact that no elections would need to be organized may solve the reluctance of the Chinese and other authoritarian governments that are not organizing competitive democratic elections as legitimate ways to select the representatives. Besides, both China and the US already showed willingness to accept CAs organized at the local level (Dryzek, Bächtiger and Milewicz 2011). Yet, the question of political influence of the DGCA and its eventual contribution to the reduction of democratic deficit remains open if global political actors remain unwilling to cede their formal authority, as underlined by the Dryzek,

---

11 It should be mentioned here that, like in the case of the EU, inclusion of civil society in the global system of governance was also proposed as a response to the problems of democratic deficit. However, no specific model of institution or supranational body of global civil society was formulated so far and those proposals remained at the level of theoretical conceptualizations of a global civil society and its democratic function in the global system (Bartelson 2006). At the same time, the Millennium NGO forum, based on inclusion on various civil society organizations, was implemented by the UN but its function was to provide inputs of NGOs for the UN Millennium Summit and not to address democratic deficit.

Bächtiger and Milewicz (2011). The DGCA could therefore be implemented more as symbolic and not as really empowered institutions that would be able to tackle the democratic deficit of the global decision-making process.

Second, the elections for PEGA would suffer from the same problems as the elections for EP. The democratic nature of elections to the EP is put into question given the lack of European focus of the electoral contest (Follesdal and Hix 2006). Framed by national parties, the EP electoral contest is producing electoral choices based exclusively on the performance of national governments or political programmes framed in terms of national issues (Eijk and Franklin 1996). As Hix noted, "it is not enough to have representative institutions and free and fair elections if these elections are uncontested or do not change political outcomes" (Hix 2008: 76). Additionally, the turnout of the EP elections is very low (Marquart, Goldberg and de Vreese 2020). The ideators of DGCA underline that the empirical research on CAs indicates that there are reasons to believe that the DGCA would suffer less from the above-mentioned problems: citizens who were invited to take part in the CAs showed a high degree of commitment to participate, learn about the issue, discuss with others, and adopt different perspectives before making an opinion or proposals. In that regard, Dryzek, Bächtiger and Milewicz (2011) argue that global citizens could perceive their participation as consequential, especially because they usually do not have a possibility to directly partake in political processes. However, there is also a counter argument based on the research on CAs and indicating that the lack of political will to consider the outputs of deliberation when formulating decisions could also demotivate citizens to deliberate (Jacquet 2017).

An additional argument that the ideators advance in favour of DGCA is related to the procedures of elections for the Assembly. In the case of PEGA the specificities of electoral systems and at the same time the size of the country must be taken into account when designing the model for elections, and the optimal solution might not be easy to find; in contrast, the DGCA would rely on solid sampling procedures.

Besides, the fact that the citizens who participate are not linked to specific national constituencies would also allow the discussion to evolve around common (global) goods problems instead of around constituency interest according to the ideators. Previous research already showed that citizens are able to act in the name of the common good, even at supranational level (Gerber et al. 2014; Fiket, Olsen and Trenz 2014; Di Mauro and Fiket 2017). This seems to be one of two major advantages of DGCA, the other being a long-term perspective that the supranational assembly must take when discussing a global issue. The relevance of these two criteria becomes clear if we think about the climate change issue as a global issue that a hypothetical assembly must discuss (see Knops and Vrydagh's chapter in this *Handbook*). Namely, the relatively short duration of the mandate that elected representatives have is not compatible with the long-term perspective that is needed for climate change policies. Political parties and political representatives, insofar as they aim to be reelected, will likely hesitate to propose unpopular measures that will be costly in the short term. In distinction, ordinary citizens once elected for the DGCA will not suffer from a pressure of reelections and therefore will be more willing to adopt measures, often very relevant for climate change, that will bring benefits only after a period that is longer than political mandates.

The ideators of DGCA, however, do not place DGCA at some specific point within the process of decision-making, instead they argue that its role could be defined ad hoc and contextualized in reference to the specific issue and specific global context. But exactly this undefined position in relation to power holders within the undemocratic global system we showed, could represent the weakness of global CAs specially regarding their main goal, that is, to tackle global democratic deficit.

On the empirical side, our understanding of the challenges and benefits of the supranational CAs is mainly based on those CAs implemented at the EU level. We know that: deliberation is feasible in a transnational and pluri-lingual setting (Olsen and Trenz 2014); the EU unfinished polity can be recognized and taken as a reference point by citizens included in deliberation and finally – deliberation could transform the public sphere and help build citizens' feelings of belonging to the same community (Fiket, Olsen and Trenz 2014; Di Mauro and Fiket 2017). Still, we should be careful when assuming that those benefits of deliberation could be realized through implementation of the global CAs.

15.4 Concluding discussion: Supranational citizens' assemblies as possible remedies for democratic deficit

In the last fifteen years there has been a political interest to adopt the CAs as a solution for democratic deficit at the supranational level. This political interest goes hand in hand with a broader theoretical movement for the introduction of deliberative democracy into global policymaking. However, in the previous pages we have seen that there are relevant differences between the supranational level in the case of the EU, on one hand, and the global political context, on the other, and that those differences must be taken into consideration when discussing the role that CAs could have in addressing the democratic deficit.

First of all, there is a political effort at EU level to democratize the whole system of policymaking, and the introduction of the CAs within this system could be seen as a part of this attempt. On the other hand, in a global setting that has characteristics different from the local, national but also the EU settings, the process of democratization actually never started, although there were some initiatives that aimed to promote it. CAs at global level could indeed be imagined as drivers of development of global deliberative systems and overall democratization of global governance (Dryzek, Bächtiger and Milewicz 2011) but the systemic approach to deliberation (Parkinson and Mansbridge 2012) warns us that the legitimacy of political processes must be seen as determined by the relationship of reciprocity and a mutual dependence between political and social actors that are part of the system.

Even if, as it is the case of already implemented global CAs or as the one proposed by the creators of DGCA, the CAs remain only advisory, they must still be empowered enough to create a real challenge to existing sources of power in global governance in order to address democratic deficit at the global level. Without democratic transformation of the institutional design of a global system that would allow the transparency and accountability of global decision-making procedures and processes, the CAs can be, at best, used to improve the democratic legitimacy of specific political decisions like, for example, those related to climate change. Nonetheless, the possibility of the recommendations produced by the CAs, implemented as ad hoc bodies, to exercise any political influence is hard to imagine in an undemocratic system of global governance. We can also envision CAs planting "the seeds for communicative transformation in global politics" (Dryzek, Bächtiger and Milewicz 2011: 40), but expanding deliberative democratic processes beyond the single CA would be a major challenge in an undemocratic system. The example of the autocratic regime of China and its deliberative experimentation promoted at the local level teaches us that we should be careful when assuming that single deliberative initiatives could initiate the processes of democratization of the entire system in the near future. It is more likely that the deliberative assemblies could provide the stability for the authoritarian regime (He and Warren 2017; see also He's chapter in this *Handbook*). At the same time, even if we formally provide the global CAs with more political power than advisory one, it would make the need to democratize the global system of governance more urgent. It is hard to imagine that the power holders of the global system that are reluctant to the democratization of the global decision-making would gave up on their power to decide, even on specific issues, and give it to the ordinary citizens included in the CAs.

Another difference between the EU and global context that must be thought through when reflecting on the possibilities of the CAs to address the democratic deficit is the characteristics of the constituency and the polity. The potential of CAs to generate democratic legitimacy rests on propensity of the citizens included in the CA to recognize themselves as members of the polity and furthermore to identify as a constituency that could generate legitimate political authority (Fiket, Olsen and Trenz 2014). While in the case of the EU there are certainly some challenges that the polity and the constituency features create, the recognition of political authority and the identification of the constituency in global context are hard to imagine. Even if we, in deliberative fashion, consider polity and constituency as possible outcomes of the process of deliberation (Cooke 2000; Eriksen 2006), it also seems that some preconditions must be fulfilled for outcomes to be successful. In the case where CAs led to the confirmation of the hypotheses of the polity- and constituency-generating power of deliberation, the participants of the CAs were at the same time empowered as potential voters in the EP elections (Fiket, Olsen and Trenz 2014). This, once again leads us to consider the necessity to democratize the overall system of global decision-making, the actors and bodies that participate in the process, and their interactions. The introductions of CAs as remedies to democratic deficit at supranational level must be discussed with reference to the political context. This is not to say that the CAs should not be promoted as discussion forums aiming at socialization of the global "polity" with deliberative logic, but only that we need to be clear when discussing their possible reach, while hoping that they could still trigger the emergence of a global deliberative system and overall democratization of global politics.

References

Abels, G. (2009). Citizens' deliberation and EU democratic deficit: Is there a model for participatory democracy? *Tubinger Arbaitspapiere zur Integrationsforschung* 1/2009, 1–38.

Barnett, M., & Finnemore M. (2004). *Rules for the World: International Organizations in Global Politics.* Ithaca, London: Cornell University Press.

Bartelson, J. (2006). Making sense of global civil society. *European Journal of International Relations* 12 (3), 371–395.

Belém Lopes, D., & Casarões, G. (2019). Can international organisations be democratic? A reassessment. *Contexto Internacional* 41 (3), 481–500.

Brennan, G. & Lomasky, L. (1993). *Democracy and Decision: The Pure Theory of Electoral Preference.* Cambridge: Cambridge University Press.

Bohman, J. (1996). *Public Deliberation.* Cambridge, MA: MIT Press.

Bohman, J. (1999). International regimes and democratic governance: Political equality and influence in global institutions. *International Affairs* 75 (3), 499–513.

Bohman, J. (2004). Constitution making and democratic innovation: The European Union and transnational governance. *European Journal of Political Theory* 3 (3), 315–337.

Crespy, A. (2013). Deliberative democracy and the legitimacy of the European Union: A reappraisal of conflict. *Political Studies* 62 (1), 81–98.

Cochran, M. (2002). A democratic critique of cosmopolitan democracy: Pragmatism from the bottom-up. *European Journal of International Relations* 8 (4), 517–548.

Cooke, M. (2000). Five arguments for deliberative democracy. *Political Studies* 48 (5), 947–969.

Di Mauro, D., & Fiket, I. (2017). Debating Europe, transforming identities: Assessing the impact of deliberative poll treatment on identity. *Italian Political Science Review* 47 (3), 267–289.

Dryzek, J. S. (2006). *Deliberative Global Politics: Discourse and Democracy in a Divided World.* Cambridge: Polity Press.

Dryzek, J. S., Bächtiger, A., & Milewicz, K. (2011). Toward a deliberative global citizens' assembly. *Global Policy* 2, 33–42.

Eijk Van der, C. and Franklin, M. (1996). *Choosing Europe?: The European Electorate and National Politics in the Face of Union.* Ann Arbor, MI: University of Michigan Press.

Eriksen, E. O. (2006). The EU – a cosmopolitan polity? *Journal of European Public Policy* 13 (2), 252–269.

Eriksen, E. O. and Fossum, J. E. (eds). (2000). *Democracy in the European Union: Integration Through Deliberation?* 1st ed. London: Routledge.

Falk, R., & Strauss, A. (2001). Toward global parliament. *Foreign Affairs* 80 (1), 212–220. doi: https://doi.org/10.2307/20050054

Fiket I., Olsen, E. D. H., & Trenz, H. (2014). Confronting European diversity: Deliberation in a transnational and pluri-lingual setting. *Javnost – The Public* 21 (2), 57–73.

Fishkin, J. S., Luskin, R. C., & Siu, A. (2014). Europolis and the European public sphere: Empirical explorations of a counterfactual ideal. *European Union Politics* 15(3), 328–351.

Follesdal, A. and Hix, S. (2006). Why there is a democratic deficit in the EU: A response to Majone and Moravcsik. *Journal of Common Market Studies* 44, 533–562.

Friedrich, D. (2011). *Democratic Participation and Civil Society in the European Union.* Manchester: Manchester University Press

García-Guitián, E. (2022). Citizens' 'permissive consensus' in European integration scholarship: Theoretical reflections on EU politicisation and the democratic deficit discourse. In T. Haapala & Á. Oleart (eds), *Tracing the Politicisation of the EU*, 45 – 66. Cham: Palgrave Macmillan.

Gerber, M., Bächtiger, A., Fiket, I., Steenbergen, M., & Steiner, J. (2014). Deliberative and non-deliberative persuasion: Mechanisms of opinion formation in EuroPolis. *European Union Politics* 15 (3), 410 – 429.

Goodin, R., & Dryzek, J. S. (2006). Deliberative impacts: The macro-political uptake of minipublics. *Politics & Society* 34 (2), p219 – 244.

He, B., & Warren, M. E. (2017). Authoritarian deliberation in China. *Daedalus* 146 (3), 155 – 166.

Hix, S. (2008). *What's Wrong with the European Union and How to Fix it.* Cambridge: Polity Press.

Hüller, T. (2010). Playground or democratisation? New participatory procedures at the European Commission. *Swiss Political Science Review* 16 (1), 77 – 107.

Jacquet, V. (2017). Explaining non-participation in deliberative mini-publics. *European Journal of Political Research* 56 (3), 640 – 659.

Manin, B. (1987). On legitimacy and political deliberation. *Political Theory* 15, 338 – 368.

Marquart, F., Goldberg, A. C., & de Vreese, C. H. (2020). 'This time I'm (not) voting': A comprehensive overview of campaign factors influencing turnout at European Parliament elections. *European Union Politics* 21 (4), 680 – 705.

Olsen, E. D. H. and Trenz, H. (2014). From citizens' deliberation to popular will formation? Generating democratic legitimacy in transnational deliberative polling. *Political Studies* 62 (1), 117 – 133.

Parkinson, J., & Mansbridge, J. J. (eds). (2012). *Deliberative Systems: Deliberative Democracy at the Large Scale. Theories of Institutional Design.* Cambridge: Cambridge University Press.

Ryan, M., & Smith, G. (2014). Defining mini-publics. Iin: K. Grönlund, A. Bächtiger, & M. Setälä (eds), *Deliberative Mini-Publics: Involving Citizens in the Democratic Process*, 9 – 26. Colchester: ECPR Press.

Smith, W., & Brassett, J. (2008). Deliberation and global governance: Liberal, cosmopolitan, and critical perspectives. *Ethics & International Affairs* 22, 69 – 92.

Stie, A. E. (2021). Crises and the EU's response: Increasing the democratic deficit? In M. Riddervold, J. Trondal, & A. Newsome (eds), *The Palgrave Handbook of EU Crises. Palgrave Studies in European Union Politics*, 725 – 738. Houndmills: Palgrave Macmillan.

UNPA Campaign. (2010). *Campaign for the Establishment of a United Nations Parliamentary Assembly.* Available at: http://www.unpacampaign.org/.

Weiss, T. G., & Wilkinson, R. (eds). (2018). *International Organization and Global Governance.* 2nd edn. London: Routledge.

Zweifel, T. (2006). *International Organizations and Democracy: Accountability, Politics, and Power.* Boulder: Lynne Rienner Publishers.

Louise Knops and Julien Vrydagh

16 Between hopes and systemic unsustainability: An analysis of citizens assemblies' potential on climate change

Abstract: Citizens' assemblies (CAs) dealing with climate change have been mushrooming throughout Western democracies. In this chapter, we take stock of recent empirical experiences of CAs to further inspire the theoretical discussions on their potential to respond to the climate crisis. We adopt a problem-based approach to identify four sets of problems which are linked to climate change and the "governance of unsustainability" that characterizes current representative democracies: namely the issues related to territoriality, temporality, conflictuality, and denialism. We discuss for each one of them whether and where CAs can make possible contributions. We then engage in a two-way empirical and theoretical discussion which summarizes key lessons before presenting a set of concluding remarks and paths for further research. Overall, we argue that despite strong hopes placed in the climate and democratic potential of CAs, strong obstacles remain to turn CAs into a real instrument of societal transformation.

Keywords: climate change, climate assemblies, sustainability, climate governance, citizen participation, deliberation, governance of unsustainability, deliberative democracy, climate crisis, deliberative democracy

16.1 Introduction

Citizens' assemblies (CAs) dealing with the question of climate change have mushroomed in recent years throughout Western democracies. They have taken the form of institutional experiments in France, Germany, Ireland, Belgium, and throughout the United Kingdom and have been invoked as key democratic demand by contemporary climate movements (e. g., Extinction Rebellion), and broader civil society networks (e. g., KNOCA, the Knowledge Network on Climate Assemblies).

The dynamism surrounding Climate Citizens' Assemblies (CCA) can be attributed to the increasing salience of climate change as a political issue and the accelerating pace of climate change overall (IPCC report, 2021). As a result, CCA has become an important research topic within the broader scholarly field of deliberative democracy. Here, scholars portray CCAs – and other deliberative democratic designs – as a concrete institutional path to overcome the chronic failures and shortcomings of representative

Louise Knops: Université catholique de Louvain and Vrije Universiteit Brussel, Belgium; **Julien Vrydagh:** University of Stuttgart, Germany.

✆ Open Access. © 2023 the author(s), published by De Gruyter. (cc) BY-NC-ND This work is licensed under the Creative Commons Attribution-NonCommercial-NoDerivatives 4.0 International License. https://doi.org/10.1515/9783110758269-018

democracy on climate and environmental issues (Niemeyer 2013); the "impotence" of representative democracy (Courant 2020), democratic myopia (MacKenzie 2021; MacKenzie and Caluwaerts 2021) and systemic unsustainability (Blühdorn 2013; Felicetti 2021). Yet, this literature has not yet taken stock of the important empirical evolutions and CCA experiments of recent years.

In this chapter, we discuss the concrete potential of CCAs to respond to the climate crisis, both in terms of scope and ambition of policy solutions, and in terms of enhancing the democratic legitimacy of these solutions. We root our discussion in ongoing theoretical debates and the preliminary empirical evidence drawn from the recent CCAs experiences in France, the UK, Scotland, and Ireland in the years 2017–2021.[1] To conduct our discussion, we adopt a problem-based approach (see Lacelle-Webster and Warren, in this *Handbook*) and take inspiration from Saward's (2021) democratic design and Fung's (2007, 2012) pragmatic approach. Instead of reflecting on all the contributions, potentialities and limits of CCAs, we articulate the discussion based on the problem of "climate change", which we unpack here along four political dimensions: *territoriality, temporality, conflicuality, and denialism.* These dimensions were derived from our literature review and our own understanding of climate change and CCAs, drawing on scholarly traditions located both within and outside the field of deliberative democracy. For each one of these dimensions, we discuss whether and where CAs can make a possible contribution (sections 16.3–16.6), and where they fall short. We then engage in a discussion which summarizes our key findings and opens paths for further research (section 16.7).

16.2 Climate change and the governance of (un)sustainability: What role for climate citizens' assemblies?

The climate crisis is a symptom of the Anthropocene, our geological epoch wherein "human influences become decisive in affecting the parameters of the earth system accompanied by the potential to generate instability and even catastrophic shifts in the character of the whole system" (Dryzek and Pickering 2018: 2). Far from being just another "crisis" that needs to be solved, climate change is part of a fundamental ecological and socio-political mutation (Charbonnier 2020; Chakrabarty 2014; 2018) which requires thinking about the place of humans in relation to nonhumans, and thinking of the relation between our economic development and the earth (Dryzek and Pickering 2018: 5) to ensure that humanity can operate within planetary boundaries (Jackson 2009; Rockström et al. 2009).

---

1 See the website of KNOCA https://knoca.eu/previous-climate-assemblies/.

This radical ecological transformation poses a direct threat to democracy, in its current institutional shape. Indeed, as argued by William Ophuls (1992, in Willis 2017: 216), modern democratic societies are only made possible by a reliance on abundant natural resources that are imagined as limitless (see also Charbonnier 2020). Consequently, the scarcity and environmental instability linked to climate change inevitably threatens the viability of liberal democracy itself, by undermining the very conditions upon which it is based. This tension can be thought as a fundamental incompatibility, or a "disconnect" (Niemeyer 2013) between representative democracy and the imperatives linked to climate change. This has been widely documented in the literature on deliberative democracy and democratic innovations which precisely seeks to overcome the limits of representative democracy; a system that is described in this literature as path-dependent for locking-in politics in a short-term bias and for organizing *the governance of unsustainability* (Blühdorn 2013; see also Felicetti 2020; Willis et al. 2022).

A myriad of factors have been attributed to the governance of unsustainability in contemporary democratic systems; from political-economic factors and the grounding of liberal democracy in capitalist and neoliberal ideologies, to the role of vested interests that undermines climate policy (Dunlap and McCright 2015), and institutional path dependency (Mahoney 2000). In this chapter, we explore four dimensions which characterize both climate change and the governance of unsustainability in contemporary representative democracies: *territoriality, temporality, conflictuality, and denialism.* These are also key dimensions around which CCAs may provide some tentative answers, both in terms of institutional designs to overcome some of the shortcomings of representative systems, and in terms of their potential to introduce transformative climate policies. To be sure, we do not aim to provide an exhaustive overview of the many potentialities of CCAs, but rather offer a nuanced discussion on some of the salient issues that revolve around democracy and climate change.

16.3 Territoriality: overcoming the territorial trap?

A recurring theme in the literature on climate change and democratic systems relates to the territorial level of governance that should be mobilized in response to climate change; both to generate ambitious, transformative policies, and more democratic legitimacy around these policies. It is also here that some of the causes for the governance of unsustainability can be found. Climate change is often thought as a *global* issue transcending the national state boundaries, which requires a coordinated *international* political response (Biermann et al. 2012). Nevertheless, as testified for example by the recent disappointing results of the COP26, *states* chronically fail to put their *national* interests aside, and adopt a truly global, international perspective. While climate change requires a concerted global solution, *national states* still remain the decisive institution. Yet, national and subnational levels of authority cannot cope, on their own, with the planetary consequences of climate change. This is referred to as "the territorial trap" (Agnew 1999, in Gupta 2007) in which our political systems are caught and explains the popularity of the adjective "*Glocal*" – a contraction between "Global" and "Local" to describe the multi-level territorial implications of climate change (Swyngedouw 2004). Accordingly, the supranational level is continuously invoked in debates on the governance of climate change, yet it seems ill suited to create the mass political movement needed to generate, support, and legitimize complex and context-relevant climate solutions (Gupta 2007: 132).

In addition, the general trend towards decentralization across most Western democracies also creates a series of challenges when it comes to the climate crisis. The decentralization and dislocation of the state is said to further weaken its capacity to take action. It is dislocated in the sense that it is "divided into an array of different departments and agencies with competing interests (*and which*) act in silos, with little concern for the activities of others or for the external costs of their decisions" (Smith 2021: 18). As a result, states can "muddle through" immediate crisis but often fail to adopt long-term policies which require coordination (Lindblom 1979; Smith 2021), thereby contributing to Blühdorn's (2013) governance of unsustainability. At the same time, it has also been widely documented that local, grassroots policies and politics are key to both mitigate climate change and adapt to it (Schlosberg and Collins 2014)

To be sure, the territorial dimensions do not only concern matters of governance; they also have to do with geographical, biophysical, and historical parameters which have materialized in a dislocation between causes and consequences of climate change across multiple territories. This has created situations of environmental and international injustice – in particular between North and South – which undermines the creation of a "global polity" on climate change, but also within countries, between urban and rural areas, wealthy and poor. This dislocation has also resulted in strong disparities in the experience of climate change-related events, and therefore in the necessary sense of urgency and survival that may underpin more ambitious climate policy (Okereke and Coventry 2016). Overall, and cutting across these dimensions, climate change is perceived as disrupting our relation to territoriality itself by raising the deeply political question of *"how to inhabit the Earth in new ways"* (Latour 2018). In many accounts, climate change is framed as an invitation to redefine "what it means to be a human, a *territory*, a politics, a civilization" (Latour 2018, see also Dryzek and Pickering 2018).

All these territorial considerations are crucial when examining the concrete potential of CCAs. In what follows, we briefly analyse the extent to which CCAs have stimulated a global governance of climate change, and we propose a tentative model of glocal CCA design. At the global level, it is chimerical to imagine that a CCA, or any other single institution for that matter, could create the necessary political impetus to move beyond state-centric preferences or push Northern and Southern countries to solve the sensitive question of environmental justice. They are also unlikely to fully compensate for the lack of democratic control that a delegation of power to a supranational level involves (see Dahl 1994: 33). CCAs can nevertheless make interesting contributions for more democratic control and deliberative reflexivity at the global level (Dryzek and

Pickering 2018), as illustrated by the recent experience of the "Global Assembly" (7 October 2021–18 December 2021). This Global Assembly engaged 100 randomly selected citizens from very different territorial regions which reflect the multi-level and diverse territorial corollaries of climate change. Yet, here, it remains to be seen what concrete evidence and lessons will be drawn from this Global Assembly; whether the broader world population perceive these 100 participants as legitimate; whether a variety of territorial considerations and implications will be included in the final recommendations and whether this bears any influence at all on the global governance of climate change. Moreover, the Global Assembly injects a single element of citizen deliberation at the global level but does not design it in the multi-level way that a more "*glocal*" perspective would require. An interesting experiment in this regard has been the organization of another global CCA: the World Wide Views on Global Warming (WWViews). Drawing on 38 distinct national consultation processes (including several CAs), and gathering in total around 4,000 people, the results of this global CCA were integrated into one single report to the destination of the negotiators of the COP15 (Vrydagh et al. 2020). While there is no evidence of the WWViews' influence on the COP15 (Worthington, Rask and Minna 2013, see part V), the WWViews shows how national CCA can be designed to feed global policymaking, and partially embody a more glocal approach.

When looking at national CCAs, the evidence on their contribution to a glocal perspective and climate change governance, is mixed. On the one hand, national CCAs are not implemented with the goal to improve glocal governance, but rather to help in the elaboration of climate policies at the national level only (as testified in the recent examples in France, Scotland, or Ireland). On the other hand, this does not mean that the global dimension is always absent from the CCA reports. Some do contain proposals with an international dimension: the French CCA for instance recommends the instauration of an international label to flag polluting industries, or the creation of a European eco-contribution. However, overall, national CCAs tend not to explicitly and formally integrate connections to other levels of authorities (be they supranational or subnational). Finally, at the subnational level, local and regional authorities often convene CCAs in order to draw their local climate plans which are commonly imposed by higher levels of authority (OECD 2020).

These examples show how subnational CCAs can help adjust climate plans elaborated at the national or global level to local realities. In this light, democratic designers should consider developing CCAs following a "glocal approach", combining a series of CCAs at different levels of authority that are connected. One could imagine, for example, setting a CCA at the global level so as to involve ordinary citizens (from across the world) in international climate conferences, while also organizing multiple CCAs within a country to ensure the realization of the global climate objectives. Subnational CCAs (at the regional and local levels), in turn, could help adjust the national climate plans to better respond to the local realities. These bottom-up CCAs could take inspiration from the CA at the supranational level (see Irena Fiket's chapter in this *Handbook*) or the Brazilian National Public Policy Conferences (Pogrebinschi and Ryan 2018).

Nevertheless, as much as a glocal approach applied to CCAs could help to solve some of the weaknesses of current representative and deliberative democratic models, this approach won't suffice, on its own, to respond to some of the more fundamental territorial implications of climate change. As we have discussed, these don't only cover questions of governance, but also a redefinition of our relation to territoriality and to the Earth. This will imply policies that reinvent our ways of inhabiting the Earth within ecological boundaries, at all territorial levels, through institutions that may fall outside the scope of currently available democratic designs.

16.4 Temporality: Intergenerational (in-)justice and conflicting temporalities

Climate change brings together different and conflicting temporalities; it "saturates our sense of the now" (Chakrabarty 2009: 197) and questions the historical trajectory that society has followed for the past two centuries (Charbonnier 2020). Climate change raises questions of intergenerational justice (Kenis 2021) and the necessary representation of future generations, both human and nonhuman (Thompson 2010; MacKenzie 2021). Intergenerational justice is explicit both in the fact that climate change will affect younger generations disproportionately, compared to their historical contribution to the climate, and in the demographic evolution of the overall population; as the population is ageing, older generations gain more political influence (Verret-Hamelin and Vandamme 2022). And older generations tend to have shorter-term interests (MacKenzie 2016), which may come at the expense of longer-term policy plans and the interests of young and future generations (Verret-Hamelin and Vandamme 2021).

We can distinguish three temporalities of climate change policymaking. First, policymakers must manage the consequences of climate change in the short-term (e.g., emergency response to climate disasters). Second, they must adopt the necessary urgent mitigation measures to limit the damage (e.g., short-term emission reduction targets, recovery after natural disasters). Finally, policymakers must coordinate and support the more overarching effort of long-term adaptation (change of individual and collective behaviour, insulation, rewilding, restoration, change of societal culture). Whereas CCAs do not seem to be an appropriate tool to manage the short-term temporality of natural disasters (and, to our knowledge, have not been implemented for such purposes), they could in theory overcome the short-term bias – or "democratic myopia" – of representative democracy by injecting long-term thinking into policymaking. Given that democratic myopia is the direct result of electoralism and the fact that "long-term thinking" is not a vote-winning strategy (Mahoney 2000; Smith 2021), institutions that are removed from electoral pressures may be more prone to adopt policies underpinned by a longer-term vision. In this context, deliberative democrats have called for "surrogate representation" – i.e., "representation by a representative with whom one has not electoral relationship" (Mansbridge 2003: 522) to overcome democratic myopia. Here, CCAs are advanced as one possible institutional way to ensure "surrogate representation" because they can increase the representation of the younger and future generations thanks to the "stratified random sampling". As Verret-Hamelin and Van Damme (2022: 5–7) explain, this selection procedure achieves a betterrepresentation of the youth (below 45) and the elderly (above 65) than what elections achieve in parliaments. Moreover, given that CCAs' participants are not subject to electoral pressure, they can be expected to favour long-term perspectives, and adopt more difficult – unpopular – decisions. Research has indeed found that the deliberative credentials of CCAs can ensure a "surrogate" representation of future generations and bring positive outcomes to climate change policies overall. CCAs give the time to participants to inform themselves about the issue at stake and consider the long-term consequences of (the lack of) extant climate policies (Kulha et al. 2021; Smith 2021: 98). In addition, the diversity of its participants (including of age) allows different perspectives to be heard (MacKenzie 2018). Deliberation also involves weighing arguments by their merits, which could eliminate short-term interest and stimulate a more collectivist and sustainable approach to policy proposals (Kulha et al. 2021: 36). Fishkin (2011) for instance reports how participants of American deliberative polls were willing to pay more for their energy bills to support renewable energy. Yet Kuhla et al.'s study also shows that participants found it hard to imagine future generations' perspective, and that deliberation did not necessarily increase the participants' willingness to make sacrifices for the future generations and, when it did, its effects were modest (2021: 45–46).

Looking at the recent experiences of CCAs in general, it remains to be seen whether future-oriented policy proposals will actually materialize. While CCAs could inject some reflexivity in a highly path-dependent system (Dryzek and Pickering 2018), their chances of successfully bringing a change, and longer-term perspectives, is fairly unlikely in some institutional contexts (e.g., public institutions) and very unlikely in others (e.g., economic enterprises). This is partly due to the fact that CCAs have never received binding decision-making power (see the chapters respectively by Lafont and by Minsart and Jacquet, in this *Handbook*), which means that elected officials – who remain constrained by electoralism and path dependency – stay the locus of power. For instance, French President Macron, in the run-up to the "Convention Citoyenne pour le Climat" (the French CCA experiment) promised to take up the French climate convention's recommendations without "filters" or amendments. Yet, he then invoked three "jokers", i.e., three recommendations that he could reject unilaterally. Ultimately, the majority of the recommendations were either toned down or disregarded by the legislative institutions.[2] This illustrates a significant limit of CCAs which are added in an ad hoc fashion to existing democratic institutions: while they artificially create a setting where long-term thinking and inclusive deliberation could flourish the-

---

2 See https://www.lemonde.fr/planete/article/2021/02/10/climat-les-propositions-de-la-convention-citoyen ne-ont-elles-ete-reprises-par-le-gouvernement_6069467_3244.html

oretically-speaking, their recommendations are essentially emptied out when they are re-injected back into the same deficient political system they intended to correct. More research is needed here to design ways to effectively couple the decisions and recommendations of CCAs in a way that overcomes the short-term and unsustainable biases of representative democracy (see Bächtiger and Parkinson 2019; Hendriks 2016 as well as the chapters by respectively Lafont and Geissel in this *Handbook*).

16.5 Conflictuality: Between depoliticization and affective polarization

Conflictuality refers here to the degree of political frictions, oppositions, disagreements, and sometimes "polarization" that revolve around climate change. These conflicts can emerge within the two other political dimensions, such as with intergenerational or frictions between different territorial levels of governance. Beyond these, climate change is caught in multiple tensions: it is expected to exacerbate existing conflicts and create new ones, yet climate change debates have also been marked by decades of "depoliticization", and the lack of explicit conflictuality around the issue. Erik Swyngedouw points out the current paradoxical situation "whereby the environment is politically mobilized, yet this political concern with the environment, as presently articulated, suspends the proper political dimension" (Swyngedouw 2001: 255). This has been illustrated by the dominance of a techno-managerial framing of climate change which summarizes the situation in numerical objectives, and technological problems, without addressing the political implications of CO_2 concentration levels and temperature rises, their unequal effects across society, and the unequal responsibilities across groups and countries in causing climate change itself. Overall, climate change is most often represented as such "a global crisis" that humanity ought to solve (Swyngedouw 2011) which ends up glossing over the fundamental conflicts and inequalities that revolve around climate change and which can't be addressed through technological policy solutions only.

Yet, at the same time, conflicts have recently started to (re-)emerge, as embodied by the inter-generational struggle of the young climate activists (of the global movement Fridays for Future in particular), and new forms of eco-social struggle embodied by the Yellow Vests movement in France (Martin and Islar 2021). Looking ahead, as new climate and environmental agendas and agreements are adopted (e.g., the EU's Green Deal, the Paris Agreement, and the Glasgow Climate Pact), the policies resulting from these agendas will increasingly and unequally affect people's lives, which will give rise to new forms of resistance and conflict. The key question is whether and how CCAs can help in creating the necessary context of political conflictuality around climate change for conflicting and divergent opinions and voices to be heard, without feeding antagonisms and polarization across society.

Important conflicts are expected to emerge in relation to substantive issues, e.g., access to key resources and their use in a sustainable, fair manner. Policies will have to strike the difficult compromise between striving for economic and societal changes in response to climate change, while "leaving no one behind" (as the European Commission's slogan goes, in relation to the Green Deal agenda); ensuring survival for all, rather than the survival of the fittest. Other substantial conflicts relate to the difficult compromise between an awareness for the structural dimensions of the climate crisis and remaining attachments to individual well-being and quality of life. Blühdorn (2013, 2020) speaks here of the fundamental incompatibility between the structural transformations required by climate change and the (still) strong dominance of individualistic values in Western society. Here, CCAs can make a series of interesting contributions. Studies have shown for example that CAs can shift the preferences of their participants thanks to deliberation (Andersen and Hansen 2007; Fishkin 2011) by balancing the biases of individual reasoning (Mercier and Landemore 2012; Setälä and Smith 2018). Other studies also reveal that CAs can stimulate the development of a shared identity (Hartz-Karp et al. 2010) and stimulate their engagement in local communities (Knobloch and Gastil 2015); here again, balancing the remaining Western biases towards individualistic values, freedoms and consumption. Research has also shown that CA can stimulate participants' empathy "towards people whose lives are very different from their own" (Suiter et al. 2020: 264), which may help to bring conflicting views and voices to the fore, without creating affective polarization.

In addition, important conflicts also relate to the inequality of representation, and the under-representation of certain social groups, e.g., future generations, nonhuman others, and socio-economically disadvantaged groups. Here, the recent experiences of CCAs and the literature on deliberative democracy tell us that they make a valuable contribution in tackling these conflictual dimensions; both in allowing conflicts to express themselves in a "deliberative" way (i.e., without leading to antagonism and affective polarization (Calvert and Warren 2014: 208–209; Fishkin and Luskin 2005)), but also in offering a new channel of representation for underrepresented groups. In particular, CAs can be used to include a variety of underrepresented voices and mediate conflict on polarizing themes such as economic and redistributive issues, for example by "democratizing" debates and creating a level-playing field on climate change-related topics. Hammond for example argues that CAs create a setting in which participants can engage in a "domination-free" deliberation, where hidden power of ideological distortion can be uncovered and challenged (Dryzek 2002; Hammond 2020: 221). As Curato et al. (2019: 61) argue, "minipublics have the capacity to redistribute political power by equalizing opportunities to speak and be heard, addressing asymmetries of knowledge, and curbing inequalities in political authorities". Overall, the potential of CCAs to tackle these types of conflicts nevertheless depends on the capacity of scaling up their deliberative effects on the broader population (Niemeyer 2014). If these benefits of CCAs indeed remain restricted to the CA participants, this will leave the broader citizenry, and therefore also, the broader political system untouched. More empirical evidence is still needed to demonstrate whether and how CCAs can generate collective conceptions of climate change (and other issues) which would challenge individualistic biases and rea-soning that truly challenges existing policies and decisions. In particular, as long as CCAs are designed and implemented within a growth-oriented paradigm, they are like-ly to perform a symbolic politics that contribute to the governance of unsustainability (Blühdorn 2007, 2013; Hammond 2020), rather than offering a real contentious space that may challenge the status quo. As was recently illustrated in the Irish CCA, the citi-zens' recommendations remained vague on economic issues, and did not include sys-temic proposals such as limiting economic growth, consumption, or questioning the capitalist economic model overall (Courant 2020: 320).

16.6 Denialism: The paradox of knowing, but not wanting to know

The "truth" about climate change is at the heart of ongoing political debates; be it from the perspective of persistent forms of climate denial, or the exhortations to "follow the sciences" that is being heard across society (most notably by contemporary climate movements). At the same time, scientific expertise and experts play a crucial role in the current institutional set-up of CCAs (Roberts et al. 2020). This offers a starting point to explore where and how CCAs may contribute to overcoming persistent forms of climate denial, and what the implications of the prominent role of experts in their institutional design are.

On the one hand, political institutions depend on climate expertise to adopt sound climate-policy measures, and climate change debates are saturated with references to "sciences" (e.g., in the discourses of climate activists, but also decision-makers, media, and other stakeholders). On the other hand, the hegemonic scientific framing of cli-mate change – e.g., as a matter of CO_2 emissions and temperature thresholds – offers only a narrow view of climate change (Hulme 2009). What is more, it seems that even in contexts where scientific expertise is widely shared, recognized, and inputted into the democratic system in the form of reports and recommendations, political institu-tions tend to ignore or downplay the implications of these scientific recommendations. This is what Kari Marie Norgaard calls the "institutionalization of denial", to denote our societies' systemic incapacity to translate existing scientific knowledge in the ap-propriate political and social action (Norgaard 2011: 11). Based on ethnographic re-search carried out in Norwegian communities, she argues that the lack of proper po-litical action by existing institutions does not come down, per se, to a lack of objective, accurate, and accessible climate expertise and information, but is rather linked to deep psychosocial mechanisms that we mobilize when confronted with inconvenient truths. As she explains, in the case of climate change, this boils down to a collective ability to lead "disjoined lives"; between awareness of the climate-science and its implications, and unchanged daily lives.

This perspective is crucial when examining the potential of CCAs, the implications of their reliance on existing climate-science and experts, and their ability to foster truly transformative policies which overcome institutionalized forms of denial. First, experts fulfil an important role in CCAs because they provide the knowledge and information that is necessary for citizens to engage in sound deliberation (Curato et al. 2021; see also Geissel's chapter in this *Handbook*) This particularly applies to the participation of lay citizens in CCAs, because climate change is notoriously characterized by a high level of complexity and technicity (Smith 2021: 99 – 100). However, while research has shown the positive epistemic effects of expert hearing on deliberation and opinion change (Goodin and Niemeyer 2003; Thompson et al. 2021), their influence on CCAs' participants is also subject to questions and criticisms, because, if poorly designed, expert hearings can end up disempowering citizens and lead to the manipulation of CCAs and their results (Böker and Elstub 2015; Courant 2020: 325 – 327; Drury et al. 2021: 41). Here, scholars have advocated a series of measures to overcome the most adverse impacts of expert participation, such as preparing participants to engage with experts or allowing participants and experts to cooperate throughout the CA process (Drury et al. 2021; Roberts et al. 2020). When the involvement of experts is well and carefully designed, it could help to curb the denialism described above. It first offers experts a new stage where they can present their research and help to democratize and disseminate it across society (Dryzek and Pickering 2018: 130 – 136; Verret-Hamelin and Vandamme 2022).

CCAs could also complement the narrow expert-based view of climate change with the "local knowledge" of its participants, "an expertise found in day-to-day understandings of issues, developed over time, particular to the local culture and context" (Drury et al. 2021: 32; see also Fischer 2000). Moreover, provided the selection of CCAs' experts includes climato-sceptical views, participants can assess their expertise, honesty, and epistemic responsibility (Anderson 2011) and help bush myths and fake news (Niemeyer 2014). On the inclusion of climato-sceptical citizens in a CCA, a recent study on the French Climate Convention suggests that its participants and the broader population have similar opinions on climate change (Fabre et al. 2020). Yet, more research is needed not only to elucidate whether the few climato-sceptical participants change their opinions, but also whether other CCAs succeed in including these political views. Indeed, for CCAs to help overcome climate denialism, it is important that climate deniers also participate, in the hope that deliberation shed light on the limits and inaccuracies of climate-sceptical arguments, and confront them with counter-arguments.

In general, despite the apparent benefits of including climate-experts in CCAs, scholars also point out the ambiguous role of expertise in this context. For example, the strong reliance on scientific expertise in CCAs tends to create confusion, among participating citizens and society, about the type of output that is expected from CCAs: should they formulate broad policy principles and values to be translated by policymakers (Christiano 2012) or should they come up with detailed and informed ready-to-use climate policies? Here the empirical evidence on recent CCA experiences points in different directions. In the case of the CCA in the UK, some committee chairs complained about the detail of the report and its recommendations (Elstub et al. 2021: 83), while in the case of the Irish CCA, Dimitri Courant (2020: 320) criticizes the superficial content of the recommendations. In addition, whilst the provision of credible scientific information is a key component of sound democratic deliberation, Norgaard's findings also show that "information", expertise, and knowledge on their own are not sufficient to produce policies that significantly depart from existing trajectories and unchanged daily lives. Future research should here tackle the specific question of how CCAs can tackle denialism from an emotional and psychosocial perspective (Adams 2021; Brosch 2021) to trigger other emotions in relation to climate change and lay the foundation for transformative climate policies.

16.7 Conclusions: Not a silver-bullet solution

In our chapter, we have attempted to contribute to the dynamic field of CCAs, by providing a nuanced discussion on their democratic and political potential. From our review of the literature and the recent empirical experiences of CCAs, we identified four key dimensions that are relevant to understand climate change as political problem and CCAs' democratic potential: *territoriality, temporality, conflictuality, and denialism.* Overall, our discussion shows that despite strong hopes placed in the potential of CCAs, both in terms of democratic legitimacy and their ability to foster transformative climate policies, strong obstacles remain on each of these dimensions to turn CCAs into a real starting point of societal and political transformation.

On the one hand, CCAs give lay citizens a word on the vital question of climate change and how societies should respond to it; allowing here disadvantaged citizens or underrepresented groups to be better included in policymaking at all levels of authority. Our discussion also shows that CCAs have the potential to encourage individuals to overcome their own individual interests and develop a more collective consciousness. Furthermore, CCAs can artificially suspend some of the structural political obstacles that are tied to climate change politics in existing representative systems, such as the deficient representation of future generations and the youth and a short-term political agenda linked to electoral pressures. On the other hand, it remains unclear to which extent these contributions can be scaled up to the broader public sphere and political system, and truly overcome democratic myopia. In many regards, the use of CCAs appears to be injecting a needed deliberative input into a deeply defective political system, without being tooled with the binding powers to fulfil its promised potential. This is particularly explicit in the context of climate change where CCAs may end up further locking-in practices of unsustainability, by providing the illusion of long-termism, rather than opening-up real spaces for institutional and political reform. It is also clear that some of the political obstacles we lay out in the chapter are out of CCAs' range, scope, and ambition. After all, CCAs' alleged ambition, both in the literature and recent empirical examples, has never been to solve all contemporary issues linked to climate change – whether institutionally, ecologically, or socio-politically speaking. Consequently, it is also clear that CCAs on their own won't be enough to overcome the state-interests or the techno-capitalist bias that currently prevent the adoption of binding environmental policies at the global level; nor will they be able to seriously tackle questions of environmental injustice. Likewise, CCAs seem incapable of injecting some environmental reflexivity into institutional contexts that currently escape democratic control altogether, in particular among large economic actors.

Lastly, it is also unclear how far CCAs can go to reach the heart and root of some of the fundamental questions raised by climate change; from developing new ways to inhabit the earth, to overcoming our own denial vis-à-vis the scale of the transformation that is needed. Dimensions which will require a cultural and value shift across the broader population, well-beyond enlightened experts and a selection of CCA participants. Overall, whilst CCAs can make important contributions to tackle climate change and increase the democratic legitimacy of climate policies, they should neither be conceived as a short cut, nor a silver-bullet solution. Coping with climate change in a democratic way should also involve the longer road of democratic struggle, contestation, and societal conflict – beyond the specific and well-crafted moments of deliberation.

References

Adams, M. (2021). Critical psychologies and climate change. *Current Opinion in Psychology* 42, 13–18.

Agnew J. 1999. Mapping political power beyond state boundaries: territory, identity, and movement in world politics. Millennium 28:499 – 521.

Andersen, V. N., & Hansen, K. M. (2007). How deliberation makes better citizens: The Danish Deliberative Poll on the euro. *European Journal of Political Research* 46 (4), 531–556.

Anderson, E. (2011). Democracy, public policy, and lay assessments of scientific testimony. *Episteme* 8 (2), 144–164.

Bächtiger, A., & Parkinson, J. (2019). *Mapping and Measuring Deliberation: Towards a New Deliberative Quality.* Oxford: Oxford University Press.

Biermann, F., Abbott, K., Andresen, S., Bäckstrand, K., Bernstein, S., Betsill, M. M., Bulkeley, H., Cashore, B., Clapp, J., & Folke, C. (2012). Navigating the Anthropocene: Improving earth system governance. *Science* 335 (6074), 1306–1307.

Blühdorn, I. (2007). Sustaining the unsustainable: Symbolic politics and the politics of simulation. *Environmental Politics* 16 (2), 251–275.

Blühdorn, I. (2013). The governance of unsustainability: Ecology and democracy after the post-democratic turn. *Environmental Politics* 22 (1), 16–36.

Blühdorn, I. (2020). The legitimation crisis of democracy: emancipatory politics, the environmental state and the glass ceiling to socio-ecological transformation. *Environmental Politics* 29 (1), 38–57.

Böker, M., & Elstub, S. (2015). The possibility of critical mini-publics: Realpolitik and normative cycles in democratic theory. *Representation* 51 (1), 125–144.

Brosch, T. (2021). Affect and emotions as drivers of climate change perception and action: A review. *Current Opinion in Behavioral Sciences* 42, 15–21.

Calvert, A., & Warren, M. E. (2014). Deliberative democracy and framing effects: Why frames are a problem and how deliberative mini-publics might overcome them. In K. Grönlund, A. Bächtiger & M. Setälä (eds), *Deliberative Mini-Publics: Involving Citizens in the Democratic Process*, 203–224. Colchester: ECPR.

Chakrabarty, D. (2014). Climate and capital: On conjoined histories, *Critical Inquiry* 41 (1), 1–23.

Chakrabarty, D. (2018). Planetary crises and the difficulty of being modern. *Millennium: Journal of International Studies* 46 (3), 259–282.

Charbonnier, P. (2020). *Abondance et liberté: Une histoire environnementale des idées politiques.* Paris: La Découverte.

Christiano, T. (2012). Rational deliberation among experts and citizens. In J. Parkinson & J. Mansbridge (eds), *Deliberative Systems: Deliberative Democracy at the Large Scale*, 27–51. Cambridge: Cambridge University Press.

Courant, D. (2020). Des mini-publics délibératifs pour sauver le climat? Analyses empiriques de l'Assemblée citoyenne irlandaise et de la Convention citoyenne française. *Archives de philosophie du droit* 62 (1), 485–507.

Curato, N., Farrell, D., Geißel, B., Grönlund, K., Mockler, P., Pilet, J.-B., Renwick, A., Rose, J., Setälä, M., & Suiter, J. (2021). *Deliberative Mini-Publics: Core Design Features.* Bristol: Policy Press.

Curato, N., Hammond, M., & Min, J. B. (2019). *Power in Deliberative Democracy.* Cham: Palgrave Macmillan.

Dahl, R. A. (1994). A democratic dilemma: System effectiveness versus citizen participation. *Political Science Quarterly* 109 (1), 23–34.

Drury, S. A., Elstub, S., Escobar, O., & Roberts, J. (2021). Deliberative quality and expertise: Uses of evidence in citizens' juries on wind farms. *Journal of Public Deliberation* 17 (2).

Dryzek, J. S. (2002). *Deliberative Democracy and Beyond: Liberals, Critics, Contestations.* Oxford: Oxford University Press

Dryzek, J. S., & Pickering, J. (2018). *The Politics of the Anthropocene.* Oxford: Oxford University Press.

Dunlap, R. E., & McCright, A. M. (2015). Challenging climate change. In R. E. Dunlap & R. J. Brulle (eds), *Climate Change and Society: Sociological Perspectives*, 300–332. Oxford: Oxford University Press.

Elstub, S., Farrell, D. M., Carrick, J., & Mockler, P. (2021). *Evaluation of Climate Assembly UK.* Newcastle: Newcastle University.

Fabre, A., Apouey, B., Douenne, T., Giraudet, L.-G., Laslier, J.-F., & Macé, A. (2020). *Convention Citoyenne pour le Climat: Les citoyens de la Convention comparés à des échantillons représentatifs de la population française. Note de travail.*

Felicetti, A. (2021). Systemic Unsustainability as a Threat to Democracy. *Environmental Values* 30 (4), 431–451.

Fischer, F. (2000). *Citizens, Experts, and the Environment.* Durham, NC: Duke University Press.

Fishkin, J. S. (2011). *When the People Speak: Deliberative Democracy and Public Consultation.* Oxford: Oxford University Press.

Fishkin, J. S., & Luskin, R. C. (2005). Experimenting with a democratic ideal: Deliberative polling and public opinion. *Acta Politica* 40 (3), 284–298.

Fung, A. (2007). Minipublics: Deliberative designs and their consequences. In S. W. Rosenberg (ed.), *Deliberation, Participation and Democracy*, 159–183. Basingstoke: Palgrave Macmillan.

Fung, A. (2012). Continuous institutional innovation and the pragmatic conception of democracy. *Polity* 44 (4), 609–624.

Goodin, R. E., & Niemeyer, S. J. (2003). When does deliberation begin? Internal reflection versus public discussion in deliberative democracy. *Political Studies* 51 (4), 627–649.

Gupta, J. (2007) The multi-level governance challenge of climate change. *Environmental Sciences* 4 (3), 131–137.

Hammond, M. (2020). Democratic deliberation for sustainability transformations: Between constructiveness and disruption. *Sustainability: Science, Practice and Policy* 16 (1), 220–230.

Hartz-Karp, J., Anderson, P., Gasti, J., & Felicetti, A. (2010). The Australian Citizens' Parliament: Forging shared identity through public deliberation. *Journal of Public Affairs* 10 (4), 353–371.

Hendriks, C. M. (2016). Coupling citizens and elites in deliberative systems: The role of institutional design: the role of institutional design. *European Journal of Political Research* 55 (1), 43–60.

Hulme, M. (2009). *Why We Disagree About Climate Change.* Cambridge: Cambridge University Press.

IPCC, 2021: *Climate Change 2021: The Physical Science Basis. Contribution of Working Group I to the Sixth Assessment Report of the Intergovernmental Panel on Climate Change.* Cambridge: Cambridge University Press. doi: 10.1017/9781009157896.

Jackson, T. (2009). *Prosperity Without Growth: Economics for a Finite Planet.* London: Routledge.

Kenis, A. (2021). Clashing tactics, clashing generations: The politics of the School Strikes for Climate in Belgium. *Politics and Governance* 9 (2), 135–145.

Knobloch, K. R., & Gastil, J. (2015). Civic (re)socialisation: The educative effects of deliberative participation. *Politics* 35 (2), 183–200.

Kulha, K., Leino, M., Setälä, M., Jäske, M., & Himmelroos, S. (2021). For the sake of the future: Can democratic deliberation help thinking and caring about future generations? *Sustainability* 13 (10), 5487.

Latour, B. (2018). *Down to Earth: Politics in the New Climatic Regime.* Cambridge: Polity.

Lindblom, C. E. (1979). Still muddling, not yet through. *Public Administration Review* 39, 517–526.

MacKenzie, M. K. (2016). Institutional design and sources of short-termism. In A. Gosseries & I. González-Ricoy (eds.), *Institutions for Future Generations*, 24–46. Oxford: Oxford University Press.

MacKenzie, M. K. (2018). Deliberation and long-term decisions. In A. Bächtiger, J. S. Dryzek, J.Mansbridge, and M. E. Warren (eds.) *The Oxford Handbook of Deliberative Democracy*, 251–272. Oxford: Oxford University Press.

MacKenzie, M. K. (2021). *Future Publics: Democracy, Deliberation, and Future-regarding Collective Action.* Oxford: Oxford University Press.

MacKenzie, M. K., & Caluwaerts, D. (2021). Paying for the future: Deliberation and support for climate action policies. *Journal of Environmental Policy & Planning* 23 (3), 317–331.

Mahoney, J. (2000). Path dependence in historical sociology. *Theory and Society* 29 (4), 507–548.

Mansbridge, J. (2003). Rethinking representation. *American Political Science Review* 97 (4), 515–528.

Martin, M., & Islar, M. (2021). The 'end of the world' vs. The 'end of the month': Understanding social resistance to sustainability transition agendas, a lesson from the Yellow Vests in France. *Sustainability Science* 16 (2), 601–614.

Mercier, H., & Landemore, H. (2012). Reasoning is for arguing: Understanding the successes and failures of deliberation. *Political Psychology* 33 (2), 243–258.

Niemeyer, S. (2013). Democracy and climate change: What can deliberative democracy contribute? *Australian Journal of Politics & History* 59 (3), 429–448.

Niemeyer, S. (2014). Scaling up deliberation to mass publics: Harnessing mini-publics in a deliberative system. In K. Grönlund, A. Bächtiger & M. Setälä (eds), *Deliberative Mini-Publics: Involving Citizens in the Democratic Process*, 177–202. Colchester: ECPR.

Norgaard, K. M. (2011). *Living in Denial: Climate Change, Emotions, and Everyday Life.* Cambridge, MA: MIT Press.

OECD. (2020). *Innovative Citizen Participation and New Democratic Institutions: Catching the Deliberative Wave.* Paris: OECD Publishing.

Okereke, C., & Coventry, P. (2016). Climate justice and the international regime: Before, during, and after Paris. *Wiley Interdisciplinary Reviews: Climate Change* 7 (6), 834–851.

Ophuls, W. (1992). *Ecology and the Politics of Scarcity Revisited: The Unraveling of the American Dream.* New York: W.H. Freeman.

Pogrebinschi, T., & Ryan, M. (2018). Moving beyond input legitimacy: When do democratic innovations affect policy making? *European Journal of Political Research* 57 (1), 135–152.

Roberts, J. J., Lightbody, R., Low, R., & Elstub, S. (2020). Experts and evidence in deliberation: Scrutinising the role of witnesses and evidence in mini-publics, a case study. *Policy Sciences* 53, 3–32.

Rockström, J., Steffen, W., Noone, K., Persson, Å., Chapin III, F. S., Lambin, E., Lenton, T. M., Scheffer, M., Folke, C., & Schellnhuber, H. J. (2009). Planetary boundaries: Exploring the safe operating space for humanity. *Ecology and Society* 14 (2).

Saward, M. (2021). *Democratic Design.* Oxford: Oxford University Press.

Schlosberg, D., & Collins, L. B. (2014). From environmental to climate justice: Climate change and the discourse of environmental justice. *Wiley Interdisciplinary Reviews: Climate Change* 5 (3), 359 – 374.

Setälä, M., & Smith, G. (2018). Mini-publics and deliberative democracy. In A. Bächtiger, J. Dryzek, J. Mansbridge, & M. E. Warren (eds), *The Oxford Handbook of Deliberative Democracy*, 300 – 314. Oxford: Oxford University Press.

Smith, G. (2021). *Can Democracy Safeguard the Future?* Cambridge: Polity Press.

Suiter, J., Muradova, L., Gastil, J., & Farrell, D. M. (2020). Scaling up deliberation: Testing the potential of mini-publics to enhance the deliberative capacity of citizens. *Swiss Political Science Review* 26 (3), 253 – 272.

Swyngedouw, E. (2004). Globalisation or 'glocalisation'? Networks, territories and rescaling. *Cambridge Review of International Affairs* 17 (1), 25 – 48.

Swyngedouw, E. (2011). Depoliticized environments: The end of nature, climate change and the post-political condition. *Royal Institute of Philosophy Supplements* 69, 253 – 274.

Thompson, D. F. (2010). Representing future generations: Political presentism and democratic trusteeship. *Critical Review of International and Political Philosophy* 13 (1), 17 – 37.

Thompson, A. G., Escobar, O., Roberts, J. J., Elstub, S., & Pamphilis, N. M. (2021). The importance of context and the effect of information and deliberation on opinion change regarding environmental issues in citizens' juries. *Sustainability* 13 (17), 9852.

Verret-Hamelin, A., & Vandamme, P.-É. (2022). The green case for a randomly selected chamber. *Contemporary Political Theory* 21 (1), 24 – 45.

Vrydagh, J., Devillers, S., Talukder, D., Jacquet, V., & Bottin, J. (2020). Les mini-publics en Belgique (2001 – 2018): Expériences de panels citoyens délibératifs. *Courrier Hebdomadaire Du CRISP* 32, 5 – 72.

Willis, R. (2017). Taming the climate? Corpus analysis of politicians' speech on climate change. *Environmental Politics* 26 (2), 212 – 231.

Willis, R., Curato, N., & Smith, G. (2022). Deliberative democracy and the climate crisis. *Wiley Interdisciplinary Reviews: Climate Change* 13 (2), e759.

Worthington, R., Rask, M., & Minna, L. (2013). *Citizen Participation in Global Environmental Governance*. London: Routledge.

Armando Chaguaceda and Raudiel Peña Barrios

17 Authoritarian participationism and local citizens' assemblies in Latin America: A cross look at three national cases

Abstract: This chapter analyses the legal framework, institutions, and processes of citizens' assemblies (CA) in three Latin American authoritarian contexts. These are the cases of the Popular Councils in Cuba (PC), the Councils and Cabinets of Citizen Power in Nicaragua (CCCP), and the Communal Councils in Venezuela (CC). Under the logic of "authoritarian participationism" these CAs engage citizens, grouped by the State from the place of residence, with functions of mobilization, consultation, and (very limited) impact on local politics and administration, operating as spaces for legitimizing government interests and have not favored the participation of citizens based on autonomy and plurality.

Keywords: local assemblies, authoritarian regimes, participatory authoritarianism, Cuba, Nicaragua, Venezuela

17.1 Introduction

This chapter analyses the legal framework, institutions, and processes of citizens' assemblies (CAs) in three Latin American authoritarian contexts. These are the cases of the Popular Councils in Cuba (PC), the Councils and Cabinets of Citizen Power in Nicaragua (CCCP), and the Communal Councils in Venezuela (CC); all of them fit into the definition of citizens' assemblies since they meet the primary criterion of being participatory instances convened by the authorities to bring together a group of diverse lay citizens in the deliberation of public issues. Under the logic of "authoritarian participationism" (Welp 2022), these CAs engage citizens, grouped by the State from the place of residence, with functions of mobilization, consultation, and (very limited) impact on local politics and administration.

Several structures that enable local participation are formally created but stripped of the autonomy necessary for civic empowerment in all three cases. The subjects of this participation operate as executors, receivers, and/or correctors, at the local level, of political and administrative agendas that do not question the general autocratic design of the political system. A category that we could call "semi-citizens" is halfway to the total dispossession of rights/agency (subjects) and the formal recognition and

Armando Chaguaceda: El Colegio de Veracruz, Mexico; **Raudiel Peña Barrios:** El Colegio de México (COLMEX), Mexico.

♿ Open Access. © 2023 the author(s), published by De Gruyter. (cc) BY-NC-ND This work is licensed under the Creative Commons Attribution-NonCommercial-NoDerivatives 4.0 International License. https://doi.org/10.1515/9783110758269-019

genuine empowerment of those inherent in the citizenship of contemporary liberal democracies.

This chapter has been structured in four sections. The first introduces theoretical remarks, and the second is devoted to analysing the legal-constitutional framework that regulates the organization and operation of each of these councils. The third section refers to their development as an organization and political participation mechanisms, assessing whether they have facilitated the latter from a democratic perspective or operated as spaces for legitimizing and deliberation inside authoritarianism. Finally, conclusions posit that in practice, the Popular Councils, the Citizen Power Councils, and Community Councils operate as spaces for legitimizing government interests and have not favoured the political participation of citizens based on plurality. It also includes references to empirical studies on various local experiences in the three national cases.

17.2 Authoritarianism and citizen assemblies: Introducing a debate

Understood as a contemporary political concept, authoritarianism emerged in the 20th century to name repressive and arbitrary political forms of political power (Lesgart 2020) anchored in different geopolitical contexts. However, its scope and precision have been the subject of recent criticism (Przeworski 2019) that focuses on how authority and power are exercised in the 21st century, a discussion whose theoretical and empirical courses remain open. Far from ignoring it, authoritarian systems often promote some forms of political participation. This section explores how the notion of deliberation in citizens assemblies relates to authoritarian practices.

In that sense, the authoritarian association with phenomena coming from the democratic tradition – such as the notion of deliberation – has proliferated in recent years. It is specially linked to cases in which a modernizing autocratic or despotic regime (such as those existing in China, Singapore, nations of the Persian Gulf, and Southeast Asia) endorses and implements controlled processes of public participation, – including deliberative ones, in institutional and community environments.[1] Experiences are almost always limited to the provision of inputs for government decisions and limited and/or subordinate modes of accountability of political and administrative processes.

Simultaneously, a perennial debate in political science (Carole Pateman, Benjamin Barber) is how to ensure and expand political participation. In the theoretical literature, empirical evidence, and constitutional texts, it is possible to find various mechanisms of direct democracy (Altman 2014: 163) and participatory spaces (Zaremberg 2012), with which it is intended to favour the insertion of citizens in the public sphere.

---

[1] There are several texts that address the subject, some of which I would refer to are: (Dukalskis 2017; Keane 2020; He and Warren 2011; Toepfl 2020; Stockmann, Luo and Shen 2020).

Although these mechanisms' legal regulation and practical implementation are verified in democratic contexts, it is also possible to verify their existence in countries with autocratic political regimes. The central objective of this chapter is precisely to expose how CAs are regulated in three Latin American autocracies (Cuba, Nicaragua, and Venezuela) and to analyze the political practice around these areas of political participation.

Autocracies adopt various forms of concealing the true nature of their power (Przeworski 2019; Gerschewski 2013; Guriev and Treisman 2022). Some examples recognized by political science are the military dictatorship, the one-party regime, sultanism, and/or hybrid modalities. Within this universe, hybrid regimes are those where formal elements of democracy are maintained – elections with a minimum of competition, a legal opposition, rights to demonstrate, independent media – but within an order that gives the ruling party – often in the form of a dominant party and a charismatic leader – the most significant control of institutional resources, material, communicational, that allow him to tip the balance in his favour to the detriment of the opposition. They have been called electoral or competitive authoritarianism (Levitsky and Way 2010). In contrast, one-party regimes are characterized by the existence of a single political party, so electoral competition is excluded. Although there are legally several political parties, those regimes in which a single party holds power are also considered as such (Linz 2000).

Although these are authoritarian regimes, there are organizations for deliberative political participation in local spaces in the three countries in question. However, the CP, CPC, and CC have not established themselves as citizen organizations promoting political participation and currently operate as spaces for ratification and support for the Cuban, Nicaraguan, and Venezuelan governments. From our perspective, we conceive the social actor as those social entities with agency capacity and, therefore, can know and justify problematic situations and organize adequate responses (Long 2007: 442). In addition, they share certain similarities, interests, or values, which allow them to follow specific courses of social action (Long 2007: 120). Such characteristics are not appreciated in the citizens' assemblies of Cuba, Nicaragua, and Venezuela, basically because they do not have agency capacity and do not allow the political participation of citizens opposed to the governments of those countries.

The case studies analysed in this chapter precisely cover both typologies of autocracies. Cuba constitutes a one-party system, while Nicaragua and Venezuela are hybrid regimes, all belonging to the camp of the illiberal left, of revolutionary referents within the Latin American political tradition. The CAs are part of what is known as participatory authoritarianism. These are contexts in which there is a concentration of power in the hands of the leader and/or the party. However, some degree of political support or simulacrum of it is required. Thus, participatory authoritarianism seeks some form of legitimation, inward or outward (Welp 2022).

According to Lafont in her chapter in this *Handbook*, CAs are a generic term for all participatory institutions which bring together an inclusive group of lay citizens who deliberate together on a public issue so as to influence public decisions. However, it will be helpful to contrast to what extent this model of CAs drawn, autonomous, and deliberative, corresponds to the particular versions of the countries analysed here. Our chapter also investigates how local CAs in authoritarian regimes come close or meet the criteria of CAs in democratic regimes.

Some of the characteristics of the CAs are verified in the Cuban, Nicaraguan, and Venezuelan contexts, and others are not. Indeed, these are bodies sponsored by the political authority; they do not rely on (stratified) random selection. These CAs are constituted on a territorial criterion and integrated by popular representatives. In addition, although they are spaces for deliberation and, therefore, where the exchange of information is favoured, they are not constituted based on pluralism. This affects the expert and balanced nature of the information they receive and the availability of solid reasons and arguments on the issues being discussed. Lastly, note that since they are CAs in authoritarian contexts, they do not operate based on transparency, so the information they exchange is not always public.

Citizen participation can be studied by analysing the institutional, social, and cultural dimensions of specific cases, including participatory structures, dynamics, and cultures. The structures refer to the organizational spaces (assemblies, coordinations, etc.), rules (formal or informal), and resources (material and/or symbolic) that give body to the various modalities of participation. The dynamics are the set of sequenced actions through which the participatory agenda is deployed. Finally, cultures are the sets of ideas, values, and beliefs about the participation that actors possess. Both contribute to the empowerment of citizens and those that strengthen state control. Starting from these notions/dimensions, an approximate state of the matter, for the case studies, is shown in Table 17.1.

Table 17.1: Dimensions of citizen participation in three models

Model/Country Analytical Dimension	Popular Power (Cuba)	Citizen Power (Nicaragua)	Communal Power (Venezuela)
Participatory context	Closed Autocracy	Hybrid authoritarianism	Hybrid authoritarianism
Participatory structures	Neighbourhood Assemblies Local government Local structures (committees) of the Communist Party	Neighbourhood Assemblies Local government Local structures (committees) of the FSLN and satellite parties	Neighbourhood Assemblies Local government Local structures (committees) of the PSUV, satellite and opposition parties (limited)
Participatory dynamics	Consultation, Mobilization, Indoctrination Propaganda	Consultation, Mobilization, Co-optation, Propaganda	Consultation, Mobilization, Co-optation, Competition

Table 17.1: Dimensions of citizen participation in three models *(Continued)*

Model/Country	Popular Power (Cuba)	Citizen Power (Nicaragua)	Communal Power (Venezuela)
Analytical Dimension			
Participatory cultures*	Subject, Parochial	Subject, Parochial	Subject, Parochial Participant

Note: *Following Almond and Verba (1963)

17.3 Legal-constitutional regulation of citizens' assemblies in Cuba, Nicaragua, and Venezuela

The legal-constitutional regulation of CAs in these three countries presents differences and similarities, on which we will focus. However, to make these reflections shorter, we will concentrate on those fundamental aspects of its regulation.

Of the three countries analysed, the first one in which CAs were created was Cuba. Between 1988 and 1992, the process of expansion of the CP began throughout the country, which was preceded by an experiment carried out in Havana and other areas of the country, as well as recommendations made by the III Congress of the Communist Party of Cuba (Noguera 2006: 501–502; Chaguaceda, Daubelcour and González 2012: 368). The functions and structure of the CPs were recognized in Article 104 of the Constitution. According to this, they were constituted in cities, towns, neighbourhoods, and rural areas; they were vested with the highest authority for the performance of their duties; they represented the demarcation where they acted and, at the same time, were representatives of the organs of the municipal, provincial and national People's Power. They worked actively for efficiency in developing production and service activities and the satisfaction of the population's assistance, economic, educational, cultural, and social needs, promoting the greater participation of this and local initiatives to solve their problems.

In addition, they coordinated the actions of the existing entities in their area of action, promoted cooperation between them, and exercised control and supervision of their activities. The CPs were constituted from the delegates elected in the constituencies, who chose among themselves who preside over them. The representatives of the mass organizations and the most critical institutions in the demarcation belonged to these. A law would regulate the organization and powers of CPs. This was not adopted until 2000 – Law No. 91, Law on People's Councils, published in the *Official Gazette* on

25 July 2000 – and more precisely defined the prerogatives of the CPs, their directors, and the relations of these CAs with the Municipal Assemblies of People's Power.[2]

This law would be repealed by Law No. 132/2019 on the Organization and Functioning of the Municipal Assemblies of People's Power and People's Councils, adopted after the constitutional reform of 2019. It is important to note that the new constitution did not introduce substantial qualitative changes. Article 186.1 of Law No.132/2019 defines the CPs as a local body of the People's Power of a representative nature, vested with the highest authority for its functions and without constituting an intermediate instance for the political-administrative division. It is organized in cities, towns, neighbourhoods, and rural areas; it is made up of the delegates elected in the constituencies of their demarcation, who must choose from among them who presides over it, as established in article 198 of the constitution. Its powers, which are regulated in article 194 of Law No. 132/2019, are related to the control of the performance of state companies and other administrative entities that develop activities within their demarcation, encouraging the participation of citizens and the promoting of community work, among other aspects. A crucial element is that the National Assembly of People's Power, the Council of State, the President of the Republic, the Municipal Assembly of People's Power, and its President are the only competent authorities to give indications and instructions to the CPs (Article 97, Law No. 132/2019).[3]

The antecedents of the CCCP in Nicaragua are located in 2005. After winning more than half of the country's mayoralties in the municipal elections held in that year, the Sandinista National Liberation Front (FSLN) made public the document "Sandinista Municipal Management Model", which described the main characteristics of what was already called the "direct democracy" model. This model of municipal management aimed to present an alternative approach to government management, different from that of the right-wing governments that preceded it. It also aimed to give the population decision-making powers, responsibility for management, and determination over the use of investments.

Finally, the model presented the FSLN as a force that had come to the local government to hand over power to the people. The main actions of this strategy were to operate a radical change in the community organization of municipalities by electing delegates by territories and sectors to move from consultations to decision-making, to overcome the figure of the mayor as the only reference of authority, and that of the councils as the maximum instance of participation due to their limited consultative role in municipal budgets. Note that in the document to which it has alluded, it was stressed that the implementation of this municipal management model was the responsibility of the FSLN through its territorial structure (party structures) and the Sandinis-

---

2 https://www.parlamentocubano.gob.cu/index.php/documento/ley-de-los-consejos-populares/#:~:text=POR%20CUANTO%3A%20La%20Constituci%C3%B3n%20de,y%20de%20toda%20la%20sociedad (consulted 12 March 2022).

3 https://www.gacetaoficial.gob.cu/sites/default/files/goc-2020-ex5_0.pdf (consulted 12 March 2022).

ta municipal governments. Hence, this model has emerged with a partisan dimension (Prado 2008: 16–17).

The Nicaraguan CCCP is not regulated by law but by Executive Decree No. 112–2007, approved on 29 November of that year by President Daniel Ortega. This decree recognizes that its existence is based on the national constitution and several international legal instruments such as the Universal Declaration of Human Rights and the American Convention on Human Rights. The objective of the CCCP is for the Nicaraguan people to exercise participatory and direct democracy in the different social sectors of the country, to organize and participate in the integral development of the nation actively and directly, and to support the plans and policies of the President of the Republic aimed at developing these objectives. Service in these councils and cabinets shall be voluntary and without pay (article 1). They are organized at the level of communities, counties, neighbourhoods, districts, municipalities, departments, autonomous regions, and at the national level (article 2).[4]

In the Venezuelan case, the CCs gradually acquired relevance after the transition (from 2007) from the Bolivarian model of participatory and representative democracy, to a Cuban-style socialist model. Under this, the Organic Law of the Communal Councils was adopted, which, following article 2 of this normative provision, in the constitutional framework of participatory and protagonist democracy, are instances of participation, articulation, and integration between citizens and the various community organizations, social and popular movements, which allow the organized people to exercise community government and the direct management of the public policies and projects aimed at responding to the needs, potentialities, and aspirations of the communities, in the construction of the new model of a socialist society of equality, equity, and social justice.[5]

Article 3 of the Organic Law of the Communal Councils establishes that the organization, functioning, and action of the communal councils are governed by the principles and values of participation, co-responsibility, democracy, national identity, free debate of ideas, speed, coordination, cooperation, solidarity, transparency, accountability, honesty, common good, humanism, territoriality, collectivism, effectiveness, efficiency, ethics, social responsibility, social control, freedom, equity, justice, voluntary work, social and gender equality, in order to establish the socio-political basis of socialism that consolidates a new political, social, cultural, and economic model. The highest instance of deliberation and decision for the exercise of community power is the Assembly of Citizens.

In addition, it prosecutes popular participation and leadership, and its decisions are binding on the CC within the framework Organic Law of the Communal Councils (article 20). Together with this assembly body, the Community Coordination Collective,

---

4 http://legislacion.asamblea.gob.ni/Normaweb.nsf/164aa15ba012e567062568a2005b564b/2eb73e0d3ee8e de6062573ca007b44ea?OpenDocument&Highlight=2,112-2007 (consulted 12 March 2022).
5 http://www.mppp.gob.ve/wp-content/uploads/2018/05/Gaceta_39335.pdf (consulted 12 March 2022).

the Executive Unit, the Community Administrative and Financial Unit, and the Social Comptroller Unit (article 19), the CCs were the best-structured CAs in the three case studies analysed. These bodies perform various functions, which focus on the coordination, execution, and promotion of plans and measures to strengthen citizen participation within the framework of the communes (articles 23, 25, 29, and 31).

17.4 Political practice and citizens' assemblies: More democracy or more authoritarianism?

An issue that transcends the strictly normative framework of law is the true impact of citizens' assemblies in Cuba, Nicaragua, and Venezuela on political citizen participation and incidence. To respond to this question, it is necessary to assess the impact of local spaces in these three countries on political activities. The body of empirical studies (as referenced) developed by the authors of this chapter and other researchers on these experiences support our view on this point.

In Cuba, a Soviet-type political regime – today in a post-totalitarian phase – that enshrines single parties, state ideology, state control of the economy, education, and the mass media, as well as the widespread actions of powerful political police as elements of social control (Chaguaceda and Viera 2021). The party, the limited expression of a part of the nation, takes precedence over a state that, formally, represents the entire citizenry. Within that scheme, the CPs bring people together at the level of streets and neighbourhood blocks, serving as channels of local participation in Cuba. However, their effectiveness is limited, and they have fewer resources, so their expansion during the 1990s did not produce the expected results since they were inserted in a vertical and centralized order. The weakness of the popular economy, local and national associations, and the absence of legislation and policies for (and from) municipalities have diminished the role of CPs as participation spaces. The CPs only allow limited discussions in their blocks, under the authorities' call, and on parochial matters, such as the State or local services with no aggregation of demands relating to the composition, ownership, and exercise of the organs of local power. On the other hand, political opponents, human rights associations, and independent journalists are penalized so that even the critical left cannot take full advantage of the relative democracy of these local structures. In short, the CPs and other local actors have not served to expand even limited reformist conceptions – in favour of more participatory socialism – and have been unable to generate change within the traditional political culture (Guach 2022; Olvera and Chaguaceda 2010: 10; Chaguaceda 2011: 22).

In Nicaragua, the late construction of modern statehood and the authoritarian framework (Somocista and Sandinista) in which it was implemented led to the fact that until the early 1990s in Nicaragua, there were no democratic participation policies, duly regulated and institutionalized (such as the Municipal Development Councils). These have seen their presence almost disappear due to the prominence of the Cabinets and Councils of Citizen Power, linked to the ability to redistribute resources from the state apparatus and loyalty to the FSLN (Chaguaceda 2015). There is evidence of a progressive reduction in the performance of subnational governments and political submission to the national one within the highly hierarchical model of relations of the Nicaraguan State (Prado 2017). The creation and expansion of CCCP have generated tension in organized civil society by superimposing these new structures with the system of citizen participation established by Nicaraguan Citizen Participation Law (Law No. 475).[6] The CCCPs combine logics of community organization and parastatal and para-party organization for the benefit of the ruling FSLN. With its structures closely linked to the executive power, the political power of the FSLN secretaries fulfils the partisan mandate of controlling the decisions of the CCCPs, ignoring the content of municipal and participatory legislation (Chaguaceda 2015). One of the CCCP model's characteristics is that decisions are reserved for the top of the decision-making pyramid, that is, for the National Cabinet of Citizen Power. The other levels (departmental, municipal, and grassroots) only can propose. Thus, the ability to propose and regroup proposals increases as you go up the scheme. Conversely, the ability to decide decreases as operational functions decrease and increase (Prado 2008: 21–22).

In Venezuela, although the development of participation policies (López 2011) is a relatively recent phenomenon, the period of the Chavista government evidenced an acute dispute over citizen insertion in participatory processes and confrontation with the authoritarian and nationalizing pretensions of the government (León and Chaguaceda 2012). The expansion of a model of participation (Communal Power) that seeks to subsume the institutions at the local level and has essential resources for it has not crystallized with the coherence of the Nicaraguan model for a set of factors ranging from the complexity of the Venezuelan social and territorial structure, the dynamics imprinted by the frequent institutional changes and various political conflicts, as well as by the citizen resistance – of adversaries and sympathizers of Chavismo – to those elements of communal power that they perceive as harmful, both for their meagre performance in the area of public policies and for the exclusionary and polarizing bias they have shown when used from the ruling party (López 2011). In Venezuela, there are tensions between the autonomy of a social movement prior to Chávez – and which primarily was its most potent promoter in 1998 – and the "new" practices of clientelist co-optation by the Bolivarian State. The legal deficiencies in citizen participation and social control erode the capacity of actors such as the Communal Councils to exercise their functions of instrumentation and comptroller concerning public management. Meanwhile, there is a clear intention to integrate these councils into state institutions or turn them into "community bureaucracy" in an environment where the rapid transfer of responsibilities for managing different public services reveals voluntarism and lack of planning. The opposition has sought to use the CCs to activate participation and connect with their bases in the communities, but the ruling party has

---

6 http://www.oas.org/juridico/spanish/mesicic3_nic_ley475.pdf (consulted 22 March 2022).

created or taken over most of the Councils, since the State approves the creation of new CCs and the allocation of resources for their operation and public works.

Indeed, the differences in the framework (regime) leave a mark on the differences of these spaces as frameworks for the development of citizen participation. In a closed autocracy like the Cuban one, the Popular Councils – through their assemblies of neighbours – channel the orientations of the Government and the Communist Party. They generate participatory dynamics fundamentally oriented to consultation, mobilization, and indoctrination in correspondence with participatory cultures that place little value on autonomy and initiative. For their part, the hybrid regimes (electoral authoritarianism) of Nicaragua and Venezuela have allowed the Councils of Citizen Power and Communal Councils to be structures of participation where the ruling party converges, in a structurally asymmetrical way, with very weakened and besieged opposition forces. So, its participatory neighbourhood structures combine Consultation, Mobilization, Co-optation, and Competition; referring to citizens with diverse political cultures.

17.5 Conclusions: The future of citizens' assemblies in authoritarian contexts

Participation policies through which citizens intend to influence the development of government policies and agendas, especially at the local level, are a crucial element of democracy. Following the above, creating citizens' assemblies in Cuba, Nicaragua, and Venezuela to favour deliberative political participation at the local level is remarkable. However, in all three cases, this expansion of participation models occurs in a partisan and nationalized way, together with forms of restriction of autonomous social organization.

In practice, these spaces have become mechanisms for the reproduction of authoritarian practices, hindering the participation of those not identifying with the government. Despite this, it is worth asking what to do to democratize these spaces. From the position of authors close to the governments of the authoritarian regimes studied, it is necessary to transform the CAs into deliberative and decision-making spaces by implementing qualitative changes that make them transcend beyond control and guardianship. This argument ignores the authoritarian nature of the political regimes in Cuba, Nicaragua, and Venezuela and their refusal to implement structural political reforms that empower citizens. (Pérez and Díaz 2015: 388). However, they should avoid forms of participation induced, partial or limited to local scale, unable to influence the frameworks and processes of formation and exercise of state power (Cavini 2011).

Contrary to that hope, the empowerment of CAs clashes with high levels of political centralization in the three countries studied. In all three cases, the idea of local councils as experiences of democratic innovation (Zaremberg, Guarneros-Merza and Gurza 2017) is now subject to question. Given that the Cuban People's Councils, the Nicaraguan Citizen Power Councils, and the Venezuelan Communal Councils, in an environment of political autocratization, the partisanship of public management and devaluation of electoral integrity, lose potential as circuits of representation based on the "people" idea, oriented to an agonist activation of democracy, to become spaces of harmonization and Schmittian suppression of politics.

As Yanina Welp (2018) recalls, the experiences of participation at the local level should always be "a mechanism for empowering citizens and not an instrument at the service of groups or associated with partisan interests: in short, you need will, politics, but also good institutions". In this sense, avoiding a conceptual stretching of the participatory/deliberative that perverts –epistemically and civically – both concepts, the experience of the cases studied here reveals that political authoritarianism, as an institutional framework and form of exercise of power, weakens civic assembly as a process of popular empowerment.

References

Almond, G., & Verba, S. (1963). *The Civic Culture.* Princeton, NJ: Princeton University Press.

Altman, D. (2014). Direct democracy in Latin America. In M. Qvortrup (ed.), *Referendums around the World. The Continues Growth of Direct Democracy*, 162–185. New York: Palgrave Macmillan.

Cavini, L. (2011). *Conselhos e democracia. Em busca da participaçao e da socializaçao.* Sao Paolo: Expressao Popular.

Chaguaceda, A. (2011). The promise besieged: Participation and autonomy in Cuba. *NACLA Report on the Americas* 44 (4), 20–25.

Chaguaceda, A. (2015). El FSLN y la participación ciudadana a nivel local en Nicaragua (2007–2013): ¿un nuevo escenario para la hegemonía política? In F. Carrión & P. Ponce (eds), *El giro a la izquierda: los gobiernos locales de América*, 101–127. Quito: FES-ILDIS.

Chaguaceda, A., & Viera, E. (2021). El destino de Sísifo. Régimen político y nueva Constitución en Cuba. *Polis* 58, 58–77

Chaguaceda, A. Daubelcour, D., & González, L. (2012). Community participation in Cuba: experiences from a popular council. *International Journal of Cuban Studies* 4 (3/4), 366–384.

Dukalskis, A. (2017). *The Authoritarian Public Sphere Legitimation and Autocratic Power in North Korea, Burma, and China.* London: Routledge.

Gerschewski, J. (2013). The three pillars of stability: Legitimation, repression, and co-optation in autocratic regimes. *Democratization* 20 (1), 13–38.

Guach, H. C. (2022). En el nombre del pueblo: consolidación autocrática subnacional en Cuba. *Revista de Estudios Sociales* 79, 22–40.

Guriev, S., & Treisman, D. (2022). *Spin Dictators: The Changing Face of Tyranny in the 21st Century.* Princeton, NJ: Princeton University Press.

He, B., & Warren, M. (2011). Authoritarian deliberation: The deliberative turn in Chinese political development. *Perspectives on Politics* 9 (2), 269–289.

Keane, J. (2020). *The New Despotism.* Cambridge, MA: Harvard University Press.

Léon, M. E,. & Chaguaceda, A. (2012). Los Consejos Comunales en Venezuela: entre el gobierno de los hombres y la administración de las cosas. In G. Zaremberg (ed.), *Redes y jerarquías: Representación, participación y gobernanza local en América Latina*, 213–235. México, D.F.: FLACSO México.

Lesgart, C. (2020). Autoritarismo. Historia y problemas de un concepto contemporáneo fundamental. *Perfiles Latinoamericanos* 28/55. FLACSO-México.

Levitsky, S., & Way, L. (2010). *Competitive Authoritarianism: Hybrid Regimes after the Cold War.* New York: Cambridge University Press.

Linz, J. J. (2000). *Totalitarian and Authoritarian Regimes.* Rienner: Boulder.

Long, N. (2007). *Sociología del desarrollo: una perspectiva centrada en el actor.* México: Centro de Investigaciones y Estudios Superiores en Antropología Social, El Colegio de San Luis.

López Maya, M. (2011). *Democracia participativa en Venezuela (1999–2010): orígenes, leyes, percepciones y desafíos.* Caracas: Fundación Centro Gumilla/Universidad Católica Andrés Bello.

Noguera, A. (2006). La participación popular en Cuba. Análisis jurídico y propuestas dentro del contexto cubano. *Foro Internacional* 185, XLVI (3): 493–512.

Olvera, A., & Chaguaceda, A. (2010). Is there participatory democracy in the ALBA countries? *Envío* 342, Managua.

Pérez, L., & Díaz, O. (2015). *¿Qué municipios queremos? Respuestas para Cuba en clave de descentralización y desarrollo local.* La Habana: Editorial Universidad.

Prado, S. (2008). *Modelos de participación ciudadana y presupuestos municipales. Entre los CDM y los CPC.* Managua: Centro de Estudios y Análisis Político (CEAP).

Prado, S. (2017). Lo que esconde el modelo municipal que viene. *Envío* 429, December.

Przeworski, A. (2019). A conceptual history of political regimes: Democracy, dictatorship, and authoritarianism. In J. Wiatr (ed.), *New Authoritarianism: Challenges to Democracy in the 21st Century,* 17–36. Opladen/Berlin/Toronto: Verlag Barbara Budrich.

Stockmann, D., Luo, T., & Shen, M. (2020). Designing authoritarian deliberation: How social media platforms influence political talk in China. *Democratization,* 27 (2), 243–264.

Toepfl, F. (2020). Comparing authoritarian publics: The benefits and risks of three types of publics for autocrats. *Communication Theory* 30 (2), May, 105–125.

Welp, Y. (2018). *Todo lo que necesitas saber sobre las democracias del siglo XXI.* Buenos Aires/Barcelona/Ciudad de México: Paidós.

Welp, Y. (2022). El 'participacionismo' autoritario, otra vez al ruedo https://agendapublica.elpais.com/noticia/17760/participacionismo-autoritario-otra-vez-al-ruedo (consulted 12 March 2022).

Zaremberg, G. (2012). *Redes y jerarquías, volumen I: Participación, representación y gobernanza local en América Latina.* FLACSO, Ciudad de México.

Zaremberg, G., Guarneros-Meza, V., & Gurza, A. (2017). Introduction: Beyond elections: Representation circuits and political intermediation. In G. Zaremberg, V. Guarneros-Meza & A. Gurza (eds.), *Intermediation and Representation in Latin America. Actors and Roles beyond Elections,* 1–30. London: Palgrave Macmillan.

Laws

Ley de Organización y Funcionamiento de las Asambleas Municipales del Poder Popular y de los Consejos Populares, Ley Nº 132 del 20 de diciembre del 2019. *Gaceta Oficial Extraordinaria Nº 5, de 16 de enero de 2020.*

Ley de los Consejos Comunales de la República Bolivariana de Venezuela. *Gaceta Oficial Nº 39.335, de 28 de diciembre de 2009.*

Decreto Ejecutivo Nº. 112–2007 del Presidente de la República de Nicaragua. *Gaceta Diario Oficial Nº. 230 del 29 de noviembre del 2007.*

Part 3: **Assessment**

Didier Caluwaerts and Min Reuchamps

18 Evaluating citizens' assemblies: Criteria, methods and tools

Abstract: Citizens' assemblies (CAs) have been heralded as a potential antidote to the alleged crisis of democratic legitimacy and effectiveness. However, CAs are used in a variety of designs, on a variety of topics, and in a variety of political and institutional contexts. As the experience with CAs deepens and competing designs proliferate, demands for concrete evaluation standards and tools have risen. This chapter aims to offer a comprehensive account of central evaluation criteria for CAs, both in the input, throughput, and output phases, and it gives an overview of potential methods for evaluating CAs. Moreover, the chapter also outlines a new operational evaluation tool, the CA Evaluation Survey (CAES), which taps into the different dimensions.

Keywords: citizens' assemblies, deliberative democracy, legitimacy, evaluation, institutional designs, methods, input, throughput, output, CA Evaluation Survey (CAES)

18.1 Introduction

Citizens' assemblies (CAs) have witnessed a significant rise in the last decade as a potential antidote to the alleged crisis of democratic legitimacy and effectiveness. Despite its common denominator, however, CAs are used in a variety of designs, on a variety of topics, and in a variety of political and institutional contexts. As the experience with CAs deepens and competing designs proliferate, demands for concrete evaluation standards and tools have risen. After all, the more power is given to CAs, the more we expect them to live up to certain quality standards.

In the wake of the *Catching the Deliberative Wave* report (2020), the OECD has proposed *Evaluation Guidelines for Representative Deliberative Processes* (2021). The framework relies on a twofold evaluation: process evaluation and outcome evaluation. The former taps on two dimensions: process design integrity ("Evaluating the design process that set up the deliberation") and deliberative experience ("Evaluating how a deliberative process unfolds 'in the room' and 'outside the room'"). The latter looks at the pathways to policy impact ("Evaluating influential conclusions and/or actions of a deliberative process") and CAs transformative effects on the wider public ("the secondary and long-term effects on efficacy and public attitudes").

This chapter builds on the OECD's criteria and on previous frameworks for evaluating CAs. Its aim is to offer a comprehensive account of central evaluation criteria for CAs, in the input, throughput, and output phases (Caluwaerts and Reuchamps

Didier Caluwaerts: Vrije Universiteit Brussel, Belgium; **Min Reuchamps:** Université catholique de Louvain, Belgium.

∂ Open Access. © 2023 the author(s), published by De Gruyter. (cc) BY-NC-ND This work is licensed under the Creative Commons Attribution-NonCommercial-NoDerivatives 4.0 International License. https://doi.org/10.1515/9783110758269-020

2015; 2016), and it gives an overview of potential methods for evaluating CAs. Moreover, the chapter also outlines a new operational evaluation tool, the *Citizens' Assembly Evaluation Survey* (CAES),[1] which taps into the different dimensions. In the following sections, we will systematically deal with the input, throughput, and output dimensions of CAs, and offer some core questions evaluators should ask when assessing the quality of CAs. A full version of the CAES can be found in the appendix.

18.2 Input

The first dimension to assess a CA relates to input. Three main criteria can be distinguished. The first one taps into the representativeness of the CA, that is to what extent the composition of the CA reflects the diversity of the society in which the CA takes place. The openness of the agenda comes as a second criterion: it is the question of what is to be discussed by the CA and who decides it. The third criterion is epistemic completion, that is to what extent the participants have access to information and the quality of this information.

18.2.1 Representativeness

CAs aim to gather a public that is ideationally and discursively representative of the wider societal diversity. It is often argued that a key dimension of deliberative democracy is the nature of the *representativeness* it allows. This echoes the principle of "all-affected interests" (Dahl 1970: 49–63), which means that everyone affected by the issue at stake should be included in the deliberation (Young 2000). It entails a twofold question: who are the participants, and how are they recruited?

Several answers can be given to the question of who the participants are and thus how a CA accommodates representativeness. Two main ways of conceiving representativeness are usually put forward. On the one hand, it could call for socio-demographic representativeness, that is trying to reach a descriptive representation of the society (Griffin et al. 2015). On the other hand, it could also call for discursive or epistemic representativeness that would insist on a diversity of opinions and discourses rather than on a diversity of people themselves (Landemore 2013). In assessing the representativeness of a CA, it could be a mixture of both.

In order to assess representativeness, participant surveys are the most often used tools with a focus on socio-demographics in order to compare the sample of participants to the population at large (for the socio-demographic representativeness) and/

---

1 Even though the CAES has been developed for the evaluation of citizens' assemblies and other mini-publics, most of its criteria can be applied to other (more aggregative) types of participatory governance as well.

or on issue-based items (for the discursive representativeness) (Caluwaerts and Reuchamps 2015). Discourse analysis can also be mobilized to assess the discursive diversity among participants during the deliberation. This technique allows to dig further but it is more time and energy consuming. It also requires either a direct observation of the deliberations and/or recording them for a post-hoc analysis. Additionally, the evaluators can focus on citizen perceptions of the diversity of the group or on the question whether they feel like they were in contact with diverse viewpoint. Possible CAES items include:

– "The opinions of the other participants on [the issue under discussion] did not fundamentally differ from my own."
– "As a consequence of my participation in the CA, I have come to understand different viewpoints on [the issue under discussion]."

The technique used to delimit the *who* should also be under close scrutiny, as its consequences for representativeness can vary a lot depending on whether random selection, targeted selection, or self-selection is in operation (Caluwaerts and Ugarriza 2012; Fung 2006). CAs seeks representativeness. It is therefore key to assess not only whether it is achieved but also how it is achieved. The recruitment can indeed be – partly – biased, in particular among traditionally vulnerable groups.

In order to assess the recruitment, an analysis of the script of the selection procedure and recruitment efforts can be performed. In the script, the recruitment procedure should be detailed so that any observer can understand the choices that have been made and possibly their consequences. Some follow-up individual interviews with participants and non-participants could also shed light on this criterion. Non-participants (who are citizens who have been invited but have either declined the inviation or have accepted it but are not part of the final sample) need to be included in the assessment as they provide a view on the recruitment process less biased by their own participation (Devillers et al. 2020).

18.2.2 Openness of the agenda

Another key criterion of the input dimension is *agenda-setting*, that is, the *what* question. Fung has distinguished between "hot" and "cold" issues: the former might be of greater social and political interest but more productive of tension; the latter may provoke less tension but have less social resonance, within both the CA and society at large (Fung 2007). Above all, how the agenda is decided on is of crucial importance to understanding the dynamics of any CA. Several ways of agenda-setting, each fostering different consequences, can be found in practice. The process could have an open agenda: the entire population or all stakeholders are able/invited to set or vote on the agenda in an open-ended process. At the other end of the spectrum, the agenda could be closed, decided on by formal institutions and with little room for introducing new issues. In-between options are also available. For instance, the agenda could be fixed but participants could also be allowed to introduce adjacent issues, and question whether pre-chosen issues should be on the agenda at all. As we will see later on, the choice for an open or closed agenda comes with inevitable trade-offs. The more open and inclusive the agenda-setting process, the harder it will prove to be to generate political up-take.

In order to assess the openness of the agenda, we suggest two tools. On the one hand, a document analysis can be performed in order to apprehend the scope of the mandate given to the CA. This is an external assessment of this criterion. On the other hand, an internal assessment of this criterion is needed, that is how participants perceive the openness of the agenda. In this perspective, the CAES contains some items related to the agenda and ask the participants to position themselves on this question. These include:

- "I feel like I had a genuine say in which issues could be discussed."
- "Even though the CA dealt with [the issue under discussion], I felt we could discuss adjacent issues."

18.2.3 Epistemic completeness

A last dimension of the input dimension is the level of information of the people who deliberate, which can be referred to as "epistemic completeness" (Mucciaroni and Quirk 2006). More specifically, it is not so much what participants know but how they can learn about the issues at stake. Ideally, participants have access to all relevant information and are – made – competent, with access to experts on the question, policymakers and/or resource people. In practice, however, efforts to inform citizens may be limited to information booklets, with little room for extra learning and questioning (Fishkin & Luskin 2005). We can also see here the interactions – and possibly the trade-offs – between the different criteria of the input dimension. For instance, if the aim is to build a CA involving a large and diverse crowd of people, the question of information is even more important, to ensure sufficient epistemic completeness. Above all, while there are interactions within the input dimension, there are also interactions *between* input, throughput, and output dimensions, to which we will turn in the remainder of this chapter.

In order to assess the epistemic completeness, we also suggest an external approach and an internal approach. A media analysis can be used to assess the epistemic completeness from an external point of view. Media reports offer a comprehensive assessment of the information given to participants but also the potential biases. Next to this external approach, participants themselves should be consulted about what they think of the quality of the information they have received. The CAES contains some items related to epistemic completeness as well as the role and influence from the experts met throughout the CA. These include, among others:

- "The information materials/the experts presented balanced views on the [the issue under discussion]."

– "The information materials/the experts helped me to better understand the challenges involved in [the issue under discussion]."

18.3 Throughput

A second important step concerns evaluating the process of deliberation and decision-making itself. This so-called throughput phase is concerned with the distribution of power within the group and the external power exerted over the participants. More specifically, we focus on three complementary criteria for evaluating the process. These are the quality of participation, the quality of decision-making, and the contextual independence of the process.

18.3.1 Quality of participation

As we highlighted above, high quality CAs are diverse and inclusive. They include a group that is by-and-large representative of the wider population or of those affected by the deliberation. However, an assembly with a descriptively representative participant pool is not necessarily substantively representative of the wider maxi-public. It can only be so when the voices that are present are also allowed to be voiced, and this is where participatory quality and equality comes in. A CA can only truly be called deliberative when it is designed in such a way as to bring out everyone's arguments experience and perspectives, and to foster openness towards the arguments of others. In this respect, the quality of participation criterion captures whether the discussion reflects the characteristics of the ideal speech situation (Bekkers and Edwards 2007), even though deliberative democrats have repeatedly argued for a wider definition of the type of discourse that should be considered deliberative. Bächtiger et al. (2010) argue for instance that deliberation should be open to personal experiences, humour, storytelling and rhetoric (see also Dryzek 2000).

Crucial in this respect is participatory equality. Even though broad inclusion is normatively ideal, it could also bring with it some practical problems. After all, some might not be able to live up to the high cognitive and intellectual demands of good deliberation, and others who master the vernacular of good argumentation might use this to dominate the deliberations and impose their own views, simply because they are formulated in a more eloquent manner (Lupia and Norton 2017).

Discursive inequalities can thus undermine the quality and legitimacy of CAs, and one of the most important tasks for deliberative designers consists of massaging out these inequalities. Several simple group-dynamic techniques can help realize the goal of participatory equality. These include, among others, varying group sizes (from large plenary groups to small one-on-one deliberations because large groups have exclusionary tendencies), varying moderator roles (from neutral guarantors of the deliberative rules to more active devil's advocates), and allowing sufficient time for deliberation (more time creates more opportunities to speak) (Caluwaerts and Reuchamps 2015). Other characteristics of CAs (e. g., multilingualism or the level of polarization on the issue under discussion) can also increase inequalities.

Assessing the quality of participation can happen in several ways. First of all, most – if not all – CAs are based on a detailed script outlining the time slots, the goals, and the group dynamic aspects. A script analysis can give the evaluator some first clues as to the group dynamic qualities of the deliberations. However, a genuine evaluation of the participatory quality and equality will inevitably require non-participant observation. After all, formal scripts and formally delineated moderator roles do not tell us much about how deliberation materializes in practice. Equality on paper more often than not results in inequality in practice. Finally, the CAES might be a particularly useful tool for mapping participants' perceptions of the deliberative qualities of the discussions. If participants felt like they were silenced or ridiculed, the CAES survey will inevitably pick up on dysfunctional group dynamics and poor participatory quality. This can be measured using some of the following items:

-   "During the discussion, I had ample opportunity to express my views."
-   "The moderators did not manage to eliminate all inequalities between the participants."
-   "We were offered sufficient time to discuss [the issue under discussion]."

18.3.2 Quality of decision-making

CAs are based on the principle that deliberation can lead to epistemically better and democratically more legitimate decisions than voting. It is therefore important that decisions in a deliberative setting come about through a process of argumentation. Decisions made through CAs must reflect the reasoned opinion and openness to persuasion of all those involved and not the power relations in the group (Caluwaerts and Reuchamps 2016).

However, the aim of reaching some kind of uncoercive consensus, which is central to deliberative theory (Dryzek 2000; Steiner 2012; Steiner et al. 2004), is at odds with the realities of political decision-making. When dealing with salient political issues and when much is at stake, conflicts within a mini-public will inevitably continue to linger. The theoretical ideal of the naturally occurring consensus hits some practical obstacles when deciding on actual policies. If this is the case, the organizers will have to resort to other techniques, and – despite the conflicting logics of aggregation and deliberation – a balance should be struck between talking and voting in the real world of deliberative CAs (Saward 2000: 67–68).

Most deliberative designs therefore rely on some aggregative mechanisms to come to some kind of final decision, so that the power of the majority does play a role. This should not necessarily undermine the quality of decision-making as long as the phase of deliberation outweighs the voting phases, and as long as there is an opportunity for the minority to make its opinions and arguments heard in the final recommendations.

The quality of decision-making thus depends on the sheer number of times aggregation crosses the deliberative process and the binding power of these aggregative decisions. For instance, regularly interrupting the deliberative process for a straw poll to see whether and how opinions have shifted, gives the initial majority group more influence on the process than a final vote at the end of the event. Starting off the CA with a vote might lock people into their initial positions since they want to avoid losing face by switching sides. In contrast, allowing those participants on the losing end of a vote to present their dissenting opinion in the final recommendations, increases the quality of decision-making. Similarly, the type of rule might impact the quality of decision-making as well. After all, super-majority rules have previously been found to lead to more high-quality deliberation than simple majorities, and might therefore increase the legitimacy of the decision (Caluwaerts and Deschouwer 2014).

The assessment of the quality of decision-making in essence boils down to an assessment of the relative weight of deliberation and aggregation in CAs. Evaluators should determine how often, with which rules, at which times, and with what effect the assembly relies on voting procedures. This can – similarly to the quality of participation – be done based on script analysis. The design scripts should give a clear overview of organizers' reliance on voting. Additionally, evaluators should look at the final report with the recommendations and policy proposals. This can offer some indication of whether the dissenting opinions within the participant group are included. Finally, the CAES could be useful in assessing participants' perceptions of ownership during the process and in the final outputs, with items such as:

–   "I feel like the final recommendations reflect all of the participants' ideas."
–   "My own ideas about [the issue under discussion] are sufficiently reflected in the final recommendations."

18.3.3 Contextual independence

Finally, evaluators should not only assess the internal power dynamics within the assembly; external coercion is undesirable as well for the legitimacy of CAs (Caluwaerts and Reuchamps 2015). Deliberation is more legitimate if no outside pressure is exerted on the participants, but at the same time, CAs and their participants are under severe public scrutiny. They often deal with controversial issues lacking any type of political consensus, and their participants are a relatively small subset of a wider population that is not necessarily well-acquainted with deliberative modes of political decision-making. This embeddedness in a wider political ecosystem could create tensions and outside pressures (Caluwaerts and Reuchamps 2016). A legitimate deliberative process should therefore be able to handle these outside influences and should avoid the participants from being forced in a particular course of action. Deliberants should thus be substantively independent from these outside pressures exerted by political parties, public opinion makers, pressure groups or the media.

Evaluating the independence of the CA from external pressures is no mean feat because pressure can be exerted in many different ways. One possible source of data would consist of a (social) media analysis. Media reporting and social media posts in the run up or during the CA are oftentimes revealing because they indicate which actors (politicians, civil society groups...) want the recommendations of the participants to go in which direction. Additionally, the participants might have experienced pressure outside of the public and visible channels. A thorough evaluation would therefore also require an assessment of citizens perceptions via the CAES:

- "I feel that I was pressured into agreeing with recommendations I do not fully endorse."
- "I did not present my own views on [the issue under discussion] because I thought it was expected by politicians or the media."

18.4 Output

With the output dimension, we come to the key fact that a CA does not work in isolation but takes place in a broader public sphere and political system. It is therefore crucial to assess how a CA fits into this larger spectrum. That is how the society at large takes up the issues raised by the CA. In assessing this dimension. Three criteria can be distinguished. First, we suggest assessing public endorsement for the CA and its recommendations. Second, the political uptake needs also to be looked at. Third, the assessment of the political uptake should also be complemented by an assessment of the policy implementation or lack thereof.

18.4.1 Public endorsement

As Dryzek insightfully wrote over twenty years ago: "decisions still have to be justified to those who did not participate" (Dryzek 2001: 654). Indeed, how the public perceives the CA and its recommendations is an important facet of any assessment of a given CA (see the chapter by Rountree and Curato in this *Handbook*). In fact, a CA is a mini-public of the larger so-called maxi-public, or put it simply the public. Even if one does not go as far as Fishkin's argument of "what the public *would* think, if it had a more adequate chance to think about the questions at issue" (Fishkin 1992: 26, emphasis in the original), some form of public endorsement is expected for a CA. Research on CAs on electoral reform in Canada and in the Netherlands has shown that large portions of the society were not aware of the deliberative democracy processes in motion (Fournier et al. 2011).

In order to assess public endorsement, the oft-used tool is a general population survey asking a representative sample whether they have heard about the CA, what they think of it, and how much they support its recommendations. To deepen the understanding of the public endorsement or the lack thereof, respondents' opinions vis-à-vis the CA could be analysed in light of their socio-demographics and political and democratic attitudes as well as policy preferences on the questions at issue. While this direct measurement of public endorsement is needed, an indirect approach can be helpful. A script analysis can highlight the efforts of the organizers and the means they have set to maximize public endorsement, and the following CAES items can measure the participants' perceptions:

- "I shared the recommendations of the CA via mail or social media."
- "I am convinced that a large part of the citizens can endorse the recommendations of the CA."

18.4.2 Political uptake

Next to public endorsement, political uptake is also key to assess (see also the chapter by Minsart and Jacquet in this *Handbook*). By political uptake, we mean the discussion of the CA and its results in conventional political arenas: parliament, government, political parties (Jacquet et al. 2016). Here a distinction needs to be made between political actors at large and, if relevant, those who are the initiators of the CA. For the former, it is useful to assess their awareness and views of the CA, as it was done for the public. For the latter, one could gauge the evolution of their support through time, but it is also particularly relevant to understand their reasons to set a CA in motion and how they envision the follow-up. In fact, some forms of feedback can be foreseen; report on the decisions and progress made to participants and the general public, or only on demand by participants.

In order to assess political uptake, a survey among political actors can be run. When relevant, it can take the same form as the general population survey. It can be complemented by discourse analysis broadly understood. Political actors produce several forms of discourse: in parliament, in the media, in manifestos, to give three main examples. Elite interviews offer another approach to assess political uptake as it always digs into rationales, values, and visions of the CA by the political actors. Finally, the perceptions of the participants might be polled via the following CAES items:

- "It was clear from the start what was going to happen with the recommendations of the CA."
- "I am convinced that politicians will take into account the CAs' recommendations."

18.4.3 Policy implementation

Policy implementation can be seen as the final step of a CA, but not all CAs reach this stage, as the chapter by Minsart and Jacquet argues in this *Handbook*. Most CAs yield recommendations but in most cases there is no automatic implementation. It can be related to the fact that it was not politically foreseen by its initiators or because these recommendations cannot be translated as they are into policies. This criterion focuses on the potential policy implementation brought about by the CA. Such assessment needs to take into account two difficulties: scope and time (Caluwaerts and Reuchamps 2015). On the one hand, it is seldom the case that recommendations are translated into one single policy and rather the implementation is achieved via several policies. On the other hand, implementation takes time, and therefore the assessment needs to take this variable into account.

In order to assess policy implementation, the first suggestion is to perform a policy documentation analysis, seeking to trace the fate of each recommendation. Because the policy implementation processes are multifaceted and include several actors at different stages, Vrydagh and Caluwaerts (2020) propose the Sequential Impact Matrix that distinguishes between the type of influence (continuous, enriching, shifting, innovating, and inhibiting) and the extent of influence (no uptake, partial uptake, full uptake). A systematic and comprehensive approach is needed to fully grasp the policy implementation criterion in assessing any CA, and the citizens perceptions thereof can be measured with the following items:

– "I am convinced that we will find my ideas in tomorrow's policies."
– "I am convinced that we will find the CAs' recommendations in tomorrow's policies."

18.5 Discussion

The criteria outlined above give a comprehensive and theoretically grounded assessment of the overall qualities of a CA. However, the lingering question among most evaluators of deliberative processes is whether all criteria should be met or not in order for CAs to be legitimate. For instance, would we prefer a CA with high levels of representativeness and impact and low levels of deliberation, over a highly deliberative process among likeminded individuals and with low impact? These are normative trade-offs that every evaluator will inevitably encounter.

Several practical considerations are therefore in order. First of all, when conflicting results occur, we do not advocate treating every criterion with the same weight. Normatively, we consider the quality of representation (input), the quality of participation (throughput), and the political uptake (output) to be the primary evaluation criteria. Gross disregard of one of these criteria should be considered a fundamental flaw in the deliberative design of CAs. Secondly, evaluators should refrain from applying these criteria in a binary fashion (either a criterion is respected or disregarded). The evaluation of CAs requires a more fine-grained approach that determines whether some criteria are met to some degree, and that also takes into account contextual factors, such as the overall financial support or the saliency of the topic. Finally, some reflections on positionality are in order. Evaluators should be reflexive of their own role and position within the organization of the CA, of their own socio-demographic and ideational characteristics, and the impact of these characteristics on their observations. They should also avoid one-sided assessments by ideally combining a multitude of data and perspectives. High quality evaluation ideally builds on the triple foundations of non-participant observation, document analysis, and the application of the CAES.

A final consideration is that criteria are also (practically and politically) inter-linked. Design choices implemented to meet one criterion, might affect the evaluation of other criteria as well (Caluwaerts and Reuchamps 2016). For instance, the output dimension works in close interaction with the composition of the CA and of agenda-setting on the input side. Choices made to increase representativeness or the openness of the agenda have an impact on the likely political uptake. All in all, the expert evaluators of CAs should bear in mind that trade-offs are inherent in democracy and democratic innovations, and that any evaluation should be explicit about which instruments are used and how they are calibrated.

References

Bächtiger, A., Niemeyer, S., Neblo, M., Steenbergen, M. R., & Steiner, J. (2010). Disentangling diversity in deliberative democracy: Competing theories, their blind spots and complementarities. *Journal of Political Philosophy* 18 (1), 32–63.

Bekkers, V., & Edwards, A. (2007). Legitimacy and democracy: A conceptual framework for assessing governance practices. In V. Bekkers, G. Dijkstra, A. Edwards, & M. Fenger (eds), *Governance and the Democratic Deficit. Assessing the Legitimacy of Governance Practices*, 35–60. Aldershot: Ashgate.

Caluwaerts, D., & Deschouwer, K. (2014). Building bridges across political divides: Experiments on deliberative democracy in deeply divided Belgium. *European Political Science Review* 6 (3), 427–450.

Caluwaerts, D., & Ugarriza, J. E. (2012). Favorable conditions to epistemic validity in deliberative experiments: A methodological assessment. *Journal of Public Deliberation* 8 (1).

Caluwaerts, D., & Reuchamps, M. (2015). Strengthening democracy through bottom-up deliberation: An assessment of the internal legitimacy of the G1000 project. *Acta Politica* 50 (2), 151–170.

Caluwaerts, D., & Reuchamps, M. (2016). Generating democratic legitimacy through deliberative innovations: The role of embeddedness and disruptiveness. *Representation* 52 (1), 13–27.

Dahl, R. A. (1970). *After the Revolution? Authority in a Good Society.* New Haven: Yale University Press.

Devillers, S., Vrydagh, J., Caluwaerts, D., & Reuchamps, M. (2020). Invited but not selected: The perceptions of a mini-public by randomly invited – but not selected – citizens. *ConstDelib Working Paper Series* (4), 1–21. Retrieved from https://constdelib.com/wp-content/uploads/2020/02/WP4–2020-v.2-CA17135.pdf

Dryzek, J. S. (2000). *Deliberative Democracy and Beyond. Liberals, Critics, Contestations.* Oxford: Oxford University Press.

Dryzek, J. S. (2001). Legitimacy and economy in deliberative democracy. *Political Theory* 29 (5), 651–669.

Fishkin, J. S. (1992). The idea of a deliberative opinion poll. *Public Perspective* 3 (2), 26–27.

Fishkin, J. S., & Luskin, R. C. (2005). Experimenting with a democratic ideal: Deliberative polling and public opinion. *Acta Politica* 40, 284–298.

Fournier, P., van der Kolk, H., Carty, R. K., Blais, A., & Rose, J. (2011). *When Citizens Decide: Lessons from Citizens' Assemblies on Electoral Reform.* Oxford: Oxford University Press.

Fung, A. (2006). Varieties of participation in complex governance. *Public Administration Review* 66 (S1), 66–75.

Fung, A. (2007). Minipublics: Deliberative designs and their consequences. In S. W. Rosenberg (ed.), *Deliberation, Participation and Democracy: Can the People Govern?*, 159–183. Basingstoke and New York: Palgrave Macmillan.

Griffin, J., Abdel-Monem, T., Tomkins, A., Richardson, A., & Jorgensen, S. (2015). Understanding participant representativeness in deliberative events: A case study comparing probability and non-probability recruitment strategies. *Journal of Public Deliberation* 11(1). doi: https://doi.org/10.16997/jdd.221

Jacquet, V., Moskovic, J., Caluwaerts, D., & Reuchamps, M. (2016). The macro political uptake of the G1000 in Belgium. In M. Reuchamps & J. Suiter (eds), *Constitutional Deliberative Democracy in Europe*, 53–73. Colchester: ECPR Press.

Landemore, H. (2013). *Democratic Reason: Politics, Collective Intelligence, and the Rule of the Many.* Princeton, NJ: Princeton University Press.

Lupia, A., & Norton, A. (2017). Inequality is always in the room: Language & power in deliberative democracy. *Daedalus* 146 (3), 64–76.

Mucciaroni, G., & Quirk, P. J. (2006). *Deliberative Choices: Debating Public Policy in Congress.* Chicago: The University of Chicago Press.

Saward, M. (2000). Less than meets the eye: Democratic legitimacy and deliberative theory. In M. Saward (ed.), *Democratic Innovation: Deliberation, Representation and Association*, 66–77. London: ECPR Studies in European Political Science.

Steiner, J. (2012). *The Foundations of Deliberative Democracy: Empirical Research and Normative Implications.* Cambridge: Cambridge University Press.

Steiner, J., Bächtiger, A., Spörndli, M., & Steenbergen, M. R. (2004). *Deliberative Politics in Action. Analysing Parliamentary Discourse.* Cambridge: Cambridge University Press.

Vrydagh, J., & Caluwaerts, D. (2020). How do mini-publics affect public policy? Disentangling the influences of a mini-public on public policy using the Sequential Impact Matrix Framework. *Representation* 1–20. doi:10.1080/00344893.2020.1862901

Young, I. M. (2000). *Inclusion and Democracy.* Oxford: Oxford University Press.

Appendix: An evaluative tool for CAs: The Citizens' Assembly Evaluation Survey (CAES)

Dimension	Criterion	CAES items (Likert scale answering categories)
Input	Representativeness	– The participants in the CA were broadly representative of the wider population. – A broad range of perspectives on [the issue under discussion] was present in the participant group. – The opinions of the other participants on [the issue under discussion] did not fundamentally differ from my own. – As a consequence of my participation in the CA, I have come to understand different viewpoints on [the issue under discussion].
	Openness of the agenda	– I feel like I had a genuine say in which issues could be discussed. – Even though the CA dealt with [the issue under discussion], I felt we could discuss adjacent issues. – The organizers did not allow us to broaden the discussion to other relevant issues. – The moderators did not allow us to broaden the discussion to other relevant issues.
	Epistemic completeness	– The information materials presented balanced views on the issue under discussion. – The experts offered balanced views on the issue under discussion. – The information materials presented diverse arguments for and against [the issue under discussion]. – The experts presented diverse arguments for and against [the issue under discussion]. – The experts during the CA were well chosen. – Did you look up information yourself on [the issue under discussion] before or during your participation in the CA? – As a consequence of my participation in the CA, my knowledge on [the issue under discussion] has improved. – As a consequence of my participation in the CA, I have come to understand other perspectives on [the issue under discussion]. – The experts helped me to better understand the challenges involved in [the issue under discussion]. – The experts used clear and understandable language. – I learned a lot about [the issue under discussion] from my participation in the CA. – I had sufficient information about [the issue under discussion] to engage in a meaningful discussion with the other participants.
Throughput	Quality of participation	– During the discussion, I had ample opportunity to express my views. – No one dominated the discussion and everyone had an opportunity to speak.

Continued

Dimension	Criterion	CAES items (Likert scale answering categories)
		– During the discussion, many people just stated positions without justifying them. (inversely coded)
		– I feel that I was needlessly interrupted during the discussion. (inversely coded)
		– No matter how hard I tried, the other participants seemed unwilling to listen to what I had to say. (inversely coded)
		– Most participants seemed to care only about their own well-being. (inversely coded)
		– I think most of the participants in the discussion tried hard to make a compelling case for their viewpoints.
		– We did not have sufficient time to discuss all issues.
		– I was able to present my opinion on [the issue under discussion] in a nuanced manner within the timeframe of the CA.
		– The moderators did not manage to eliminate all inequalities between the participants.
		– Some topics that I thought were important were not covered during the discussions.
		– We were offered sufficient time to discuss [the issue under discussion].
		– We were offered sufficient time to interview the experts.
		– We were offered sufficient time to write down the final recommendations.
		– It was clear from the start what was expected of me.
		– It was clear from the start what will happen with the recommendations we formulated.
	Quality of decision-making	– I feel like the final recommendations reflect all of the participants' ideas.
		– Even though there was a vote in the end, I do feel that our group discussions are reflected in the final recommendations.
		– My own ideas about [the issue under discussion] are sufficiently reflected in the final recommendations.
	Contextual independence	– I feel that I was pressured into agreeing with recommendations I do not fully endorse.
		– I did not present my own views on [the issue under discussion] because I thought it was expected by politicians.
		– I did not present my own views on [the issue under discussion] because I thought it was expected by the media.
Output	Public endorsement	– I discussed [the issue under discussion] with others outside of the CA (e.g. friends, family, colleagues).
		– I shared the recommendations of the CA via mail or social media.
		– I am convinced that a large part of the citizens can endorse the recommendations of the CA.
		– I am convinced that a large part of the politicians can endorse the recommendations of the CA.
		– I am convinced that a large part of the policy makers can endorse the recommendations of the CA.

Continued

Dimension	Criterion	CAES items (Likert scale answering categories)
	Political uptake	– It was clear from the start what was going to happen with the recommendations of the CA. – I am convinced that politicians will take into account the CA's recommendations.
	Policy implementation	– I am convinced that we will find my ideas in tomorrow's policies. – I am convinced that we will find the CA's recommendations in tomorrow's policies.

Marina Lindell

19 Internal dynamics at work

Abstract: Although CAs vary in design – for example they have a different purpose, composition length, and impact – they are similar in their endeavour to reach high quality deliberation. A plethora of research suggests that the internal quality of the CA (or any citizen deliberation) is crucial for the legitimacy of decision-making but also for how participants are included and affected. For a long time, research looked at knowledge and opinion change as the primary outcome of a deliberative process while largely overlooking the quality of deliberation and its impact on these effects. High-quality deliberation does not imply change per se, but rather evidence that the group processes helped individuals to gain new knowledge and confront different perspectives. This chapter focuses on internal dynamics and their role for these transformations. Features that enhance equality are considered particularly important. Hence, focus is on inclusion, diversity and deliberative disagreement, experts and evidence, reflection and perspective-taking.

Keywords: inclusion, diversity, experts, reflection, perspective-taking, design

19.1 Introduction

Deliberative democracy is both a theoretical endeavour and an empirical project. Theorists have focused on normative ideals, the role of deliberation for informed opinions and collective judgements, and the role of democratic deliberation in the democratic system while empirical researchers largely have focused on analysing deliberative principles, outcomes of deliberation, and the implementation and the quality of deliberative processes (Willis, Curato and Smith 2022). The first citizens' assembly (CA) in 2004 in British Columbia was a milestone for empirical research. For the first time, randomly selected citizens were given the mandate to assess and redesign the province's electoral system. Even though electoral reform did not follow, the CA was seen as an archetype for reforming democracy and developing democratic processes. The last two decades we have seen an increased experimentation with deliberative mini-publics, i.e. deliberative polling, citizens' juries, participatory budgeting, and CAs, in all parts of the world and in various contexts. In the last five years, a plethora of Climate Assemblies has been implemented in many countries (e.g. in France, Spain, United Kingdom, Ireland, Denmark, Scotland, Finland, and Luxembourg). Deliberative mini-publics are increasingly used as long-term institutional remedies to the crisis of democracy, and there is a wealth of studies stating that deliberative forums like these can promote empathy and understanding of other's viewpoints, transform atti-

Marina Lindell: Åbo Akademi University, Finland.

๖ Open Access. © 2023 the author(s), published by De Gruyter. [CC BY-NC-ND] This work is licensed under the Creative Commons Attribution-NonCommercial-NoDerivatives 4.0 International License. https://doi.org/10.1515/9783110758269-021

tudes, increase cognitive complexity, and lead to better alignment between values and preferences (Curato, Vrydagh and Bächtiger 2020; Fishkin 2018; Grönlund, Setälä and Herne 2010; Smith 2021). Improved reasoning, listening, and increased respect for other's opinions are often identified as crucial elements underlying these transformations (Bächtiger and Parkinson 2019).

In 2021, a knowledge network on Climate Assemblies, KNOCA, was established. Its purpose is to share best practices on the design and implementation of CAs. The design of the CA is indeed important. If done well, CAs can be a tool to bring informed views of the public into policymaking, help break political deadlock on policy issues, understand the priorities of citizens, increase the legitimacy of social action, reduce the impact of lobbyists and special interests, and to increase citizen participation (see https:// knoca.eu/). For a long time, research looked at knowledge and opinion change as the primary outcome of a deliberative process while largely overlooking the quality of deliberation and its impact on these effects. As critics started to raise the argument that opinion change *per se* should not be seen as a central outcome of deliberation, research focus shifted towards examining the internal dynamics behind these transformations. In this chapter, I first reflect on the transformations and the effects from deliberative processes, such as CAs, on the participants. I then review the literature on the role of internal dynamics, focusing on features important to enhance equality. Hence, I focus on inclusion, diversity and deliberative disagreement, experts and evidence, and reflection and perspective-taking and their role for these transformations. I end by outlining possible future developments of the research field, specifically in relation to internal dynamics.

19.2 Impact of deliberative processes

19.2.1 From opinion change to clarification of opinion

Empirical studies of citizen deliberation suggest that participants often change opinions. Learning usually serves as a strong stimulus for opinion change, since citizens are not adequately informed about a wide array of social and political issues they have not had to seriously address before. Studies also suggest that those with lower levels of knowledge change their opinions more (Fishkin 2018; Suiter, Farrell and O'Malley 2016). Deliberative theories of democracy largely emphasize the same ideal, namely that decision-making should be preceded by a process in which citizens engage in rational argumentation that shapes and possibly changes their opinions. Decision-making based on deliberation is expected to yield more rational and considered opinions than decisions based solely on individual preferences (Andersen and Hansen 2007; Dryzek 2000; Fishkin 2018; Grönlund, Setälä and Herne 2010; Smith and Wales 2000; Suiter, Farrell and O'Malley 2016).

Moderation is normally seen as the desirable outcome of a deliberative process: by listening to others, participants with extreme opinions realize that there is merit in other positions and arguments. Polarization, by contrast, is frequently considered as a suspicious outcome. According to Sunstein (2002), polarization reflects a dynamic psychological process, whereby groups move to the extreme on the basis of biased information processing and biases in the argument pool. However, studies (see Esterling, Fung and Lee 2021; Grönlund, Setälä and Herne 2015; Lindell et al. 2017) suggest that deliberative dynamics can mitigate polarization tendencies by introducing deliberative norms, trained moderators, and balanced information. Although polarization can make it hard to find common ground and make joint decisions, recent lines of theorizing argue that polarization may have deliberative dimensions: it may simply reflect preference clarification in that participants better understand what they really want (Knight and Johnson 2011). In their influential book on democracy, Knight and Johnson (2011, 145) consider clarification and "structured disagreement" more important than opinion change *per se*; and clarification may well encompass polarization, moderation, or stability of opinions. In accordance with Sunstein (2002), however, deliberative democrats would insist that if polarization (or, moderation) occurs, it should do so in normatively defensible ways and not be the product of undesirable group dynamics or on other non-deliberative pathways.

Habermas (2018) acknowledges that although it is a sign of deliberative failure if there is never a change of minds over a long-running debate, it is not necessary that people change minds in every single venue. It is important to consider outcomes beyond opinion change, i.e. deep learning might not always lead to opinion change but sometimes to opinion stability and clarification. Thus, the concept of opinion change also includes the possibility of opinion stability and clarification. High-quality deliberation does not imply change *per se*, but rather evidence that the group processes helped individuals and groups to gain new knowledge and confront different perspectives (Karpowitz and Mendelberg 2018: 541). There seem to be a broad agreement in deliberative theory that normatively desirable opinion changes should at least reflect a high epistemic quality (and respective capacities of participants), the absence of group pressures, or some ethical aspects (such as empathy and understanding) (Lindell et al. 2017). Opinion change can never in itself be a qualitative criterion of deliberation.

19.2.2 From individual-level effects to societal impact

Many studies demonstrate that participants show a different relation to their community after deliberation. This is visible as an increase in political tolerance, social trust, internal efficacy, practical civic skills, willingness to act politically, and higher civic engagement (Andersen and Hansen 2007; Brown 2006; Carpini, Cook and Jacobs 2004; Hall, Wilson and Newman 2011; Smith 2009; Smith and Wales 2000). However, there is also evidence that deliberation does not have any effect on civic skills, and it might even lead to a decrease in some skills, for example Grönlund et al. (2010: 108) identified a small decrease in internal efficacy suggesting that confrontation with new information and arguments might lead to an increased feeling about the complexity of politics. Deliberation seems to stimulate discursive engagement of participants, for example participation in debates, advising family members, giving talks in the workplace (van der Does and Jacquet 2021). There are also indications of a long-lasting impact on participants' interest in politics, political engagement, and policy attitudes (Fishkin 2018; Luskin, Fishkin and Jowell 2002; Smith 2021; Smith and Wales 2000). Recently research has increasingly focused on relations between CAs and mass democracy including engagement with citizens outside the forum (see Goldberg in this *Handbook*), the role of media (see Maia in this *Handbook*), the importance of a two-way communication and spill-over effects to non-participants (see Curato and Roundtree in this *Handbook*; Curato, Vrydagh and Bächtiger 2020; van der Does and Jacquet 2021).

19.2.3 From isolated initiatives to deliberative systems

Whereas literature on deliberative and participatory processes published in early 2000s tended to focus on isolated initiatives, this latter period has seen a shift towards thinking in terms of democratic systems and the need for embedding deliberative governance into said systems more permanently (Brown 2018). The focus has also slowly shifted from individual effects to meso- and macro-level effects where deliberative mini-publics' relationships with the media and with the public are under scrutiny. Legitimacy is largely evaluated in relation to the societal and wider impact of the mini-publics and transparency with the process itself. Research focus has been on developing institutional designs to increase legitimacy, policy uptake, and the role of deliberative mini-publics (e. g., CAs) in democratic decision-making (see Minsart and Jacquet in this *Handbook*). According to Bächtiger and Parkinson (2019: 155) micro institutions such as mini-publics can exert important deliberative roles in a democratic system when their recommendations affect other sites and they "export" deliberative norms to other sites and places. We need a variety of practices that add deliberative and democratic qualities to the system.

19.3 Internal dynamics and their impact

Knight and Johnson (1997) understand equality in deliberative democracy as the equal opportunity to political influence. Political equality is usually discussed in terms of distribution of power and resources. According to Curato et al. (2019: 61–73) it is essential that deliberation do not reinforce existing power imbalances but redistributes power and voice by empowering marginalized groups. Offering them a seat at the table to reason together is not enough, they also need to have a voice at the table. For this, the role of facilitators is crucial since they can create an environment for less confident speakers to express themselves and thereby give them an opportunity to gain political influence. Well-designed mini-publics can equalize opportunities to speak and be heard as well as correct asymmetries in information and knowledge.

Although there are many internal design features, i.e. dynamics, that are important to take into account, I focus on features that relate to political equality and re-distribution of power: Inclusion, Experts and evidence, Diversity and deliberative disagreement, and Reflection and perspective-taking. Although these features are highly intertwined, I will discuss them separately to better enhance their impact on deliberative transformations and processes.

19.3.1 Inclusion

The selection method largely determines who participates. Legitimacy depends on who participates, how they have been selected, and how representative the group is of the wider society. Sortition, or random selection, was introduced as a method for inclusion in order to promote political equality (Owen and Smith 2018). Sortition gives everyone a theoretically equal chance of being selected and it embodies the idea that all citizens are equally capable of political judgement and equally responsible for the public good (Smith 2021: 100). An open invitation is highly unlikely to gather anything resembling a representative group of citizens. The participants self-selecting through an open invitation are more likely to be older, and are more engaged in the issue. Minorities, the young, and the less advantaged tend to participate less (Fishkin 2018: 15–16). Socioeconomic inequalities also tend to allow wealthier, more educated individuals to participate more easily than poor and less well-educated ones. Sortition might reduce this participation bias (Fung 2005: 407–408).

In large CAs, sortition might ensure that the participants are representative of the population. In smaller assemblies, stratified random sampling might be needed to make sure that all groups, i.e. small ethnic groups, minorities are included. The use of stratification can help to reduce the risk that certain groups are over- or under-represented, but for this to happen it requires the identification of relevant strata. Notably, for example, while there was stratification for gender, geography, and age in the British Columbia CA, it failed to stratify for ethnicity. Representatives from BC's indigenous population were subsequently appointed to correct an initial imbalance arising from random selection (James 2008). With a small number of participants, as in a citizens' jury, the random sample is not statistically representative of the population but rather demographically diverse (Smith 2009; Thompson et al. 2021).

Often, demographic representation is stressed, since it is important that all groups in society are represented in the assembly. A rationale behind this is that people from different demographic backgrounds are most likely to have different views and interests and excluding parts of the population will undermine the process. Other times, attitudinal representation might be equally or more important (Harris 2019: 49; Fishkin 2018: 73). Especially if the deliberating issue is salient, highly polarized, and the decision will influence policymaking, it might be crucial for the sake of legitimacy that the discussion is balanced and that the deliberating group is a representative microcosm of the public opinion. Dryzek and Niemeyer (2008) raise the importance of discursive representation. To have countervailing discourses well represented at the outset can be a way to prevent groupthink and the silencing of uncomfortable or minority voices. "The key consideration here is that all the vantage points for criticizing policy get represented – *not* that these vantage points get represented in proportion to the number of people who subscribe to them" (Dryzek and Niemeyer 2008: 482). As already stated, inclusion is related to political equality. In this sense, it is not only about having a chair at the table but also about having a voice and being listened to. Young (2000) refers to external and internal exclusion and suggests that certain measures, such as facilitators, deliberative norms, decision-rules, and group composition need to be taken into account to make sure internal exclusion does not take place. Although everyone does not need to speak equally, it is crucial that everyone is given the same opportunity to speak and to be listened to. A study from Finland (see Lindell et al. 2017) where citizens deliberated on immigration clearly suggests that the presence of an immigrant in the discussion group have an impact on the participants' opinions. The low physical presence of immigrants in the discussion group was identified as one important factor behind the polarization of opinions in an anti-immigrant direction. This finding is in line with long-standing claims that the physical presence of less privileged or marginalized groups is not only a democratic predicament but matters for outcomes as well (see also Phillips 1995). Also in accordance with social identity theory, members of a group might enhance their similarities, i.e. strengthening in-group identity, and thus seek to find negative aspects of out-groups. This suggests that physical presence is an important factor to reduce such tendencies (Hogg 1993) and to enhance inclusion.

Since members of a CA are not elected, they cannot be held accountable to those affected by their decisions (for a discussion on this see Vandamme in this *Handbook*). This makes representative claims difficult. According to Brown (2018: 176–178) representative claims rest on their descriptive representativeness of diverse social perspectives. Thus, he raises concerns that members from disadvantaged groups speak less and are taken less seriously (see also Gerber et al. 2018). There are also studies indicating that there are gender inequalities, for example that a male deliberator's arguments are taken more into account (Beauvais 2021; Curato, Vrydagh and Bächtiger 2020). This resonates with Sanders (1997) concerns that power relations within a deliberative minipublic tend to reproduce those in society. Deliberative democrats' response has been to identify design aspects and internal dynamics that can help reduce these biases. Even if a CA mirrors the nation in all variables typically deemed important, the public needs to accept its outcomes because they trust the members in order to be legitimate (Gutmann and Thompson 2018). For this, it is highly important that the members of the CA engage with the larger public as well and do their best to achieve a two-way communication (e.g., the British Columbia CA and Australia's Citizens' Parliament met with groups outside the forum to get their perspective).

19.3.2 Experts and evidence

Another key design feature of CAs is that participants gather evidence and receive balanced information on the issue at hand. The main rationale behind such practices is that giving citizens an opportunity to acquire evidence and additional information, citizens can make informed and well-considered judgements on policy issues, deepening their understanding of the topic and its complexities (Fishkin 2018; Leino et al. 2021; Lightbody and Roberts 2019). It also gives participants the possibility to learn and gain knowledge, which is important for levelling differences in initial knowledge and deliberative capacities.

Evidence can be presented in different forms and by different actors. Usually various experts in the field present reports, facts, and research. Experts do not only refer to academic specialists but also to knowledge experts, stakeholders, and experts by lived experience that present their views and arguments. In some CAs, participants are given the chance to call in new experts and to ask for more evidence (Lightbody and Roberts 2019; Thompson et al. 2021). Expert views might have a strong impact on how individuals perceive the issue, what kinds of beliefs they have and, consequently, on their attitudes and views. Even if organizers usually invite experts with various expertise and point of views, citizens may use expert information highly selectively to confirm their pre-existing views. Experts need to be chosen wisely to ensure a plurality of expert views and to make sure all views are valued (Leino et al. 2021). The credibility of the expert, the format, and evidence quality might also have an impact on individuals' opinions (Lightbody and Roberts 2019: 226). According to Thompson et al. (2021) the major role of experts is to stimulate learning and reflection and to make the participants considering various arguments and values.

Leino et al. (2021) suggest that expert hearings should be preceded and followed by deliberation in small groups. This might foster critical reflection on expert information among participants and help avoid blind deference or selective use of expert information. Experts are questioned individually or as a panel and they can provide the participants with written information in advance (Lightbody and Roberts 2019: 232). Lightbody and Roberts (2019) raise concerns that Q&A sessions can undermine the quality of evidence and the argument while encouraging emotional expressions and a debate climate where the best arguer is right. It might be a good idea to also "learn" citizens to scrutinize information and to help them develop critical thinking and support them in weighing evidence (Lightbody and Roberts 2019: 235–236).

CAs usually feature expert hearings, the idea being that expert hearings help participants to reach more considered opinions. Therefore, it is perhaps surprising that there is relatively little research concerning the role of experts in citizen deliberation. As other individuals, experts will differ in terms of views, communication skills and style, charisma, experience, and the ability to get their message through which might also have an impact on the participants. Leino et al. (2021) are one of the few that has analysed how expert hearings in a deliberative mini-public affect participants' knowledge and attitudes (to pandemic policies). They conclude that a deliberative process where people need to justify their views to a diverse group of people is arguably an efficient method of correcting individual biases and for processing expert information (see also Mercier and Landemore 2012).

Thompson et al. (2021) study three citizens' juries in Scotland and conclude that the information phase with brief presentations from experts followed by a session for scrutiny with small group discussions and interrogation of the experts in plenum, had the largest influence on the jurors' opinions (compared to the reflection and deliberation phases). As it seems, the prospect of having to deliberate the issues later, including justifying one's opinions, provides a strong incentive for jurors to listen, consider, and weigh the evidence and values presented to them (see also Goodin and Niemeyer 2003 for a similar discussion). Due to time constraint, experts could not address all questions in the plenary. As a result, the experts provided written answers to the unaddressed questions, and this compilation was circulated to the jurors a week before Day 2. The late change of two experts in one of the citizens' juries did not have any impact on the opinions and Thompson et al. (2021) suggest that it is the complexity of arguments and putting attention to the issue and learning about it that have the largest impact on opinions, not the expert *per se.*

There is a tendency that people (especially with strong opinions) tend to be uncritical of information and arguments that support their initial view while being hypercritical of information and arguments that contradict it (Karpowitz and Mendelberg 2018: 539; Lord, Lee and Lepper 1979; Mercier and Landemore 2012). Sometimes people are also misinformed and (even worse) highly confident about their false beliefs. Thus, it is important to design deliberative processes that make people evaluate arguments consciously, and that increase their knowledge and understanding of others' viewpoints (Karpowitz and Mendelberg 2018). In likeminded groups, there might be a risk of biased assimilation of information. People also tend to rely on the judgements and information of trusted others, making informational cascades a serious problem (Sunstein 2002). Hence, it is important to design the learning and information phase so that the information is balanced, learning takes place, and participants get a chance together to scrutinize the evidence presented to them.

19.3.3 Diversity and deliberative disagreement

Making sure that the deliberating group(s) has a diversity of epistemic resources as well as a diversity of perspectives, is crucial and closely linked to the issues of inclusion and representation. Gutmann and Thompson (2018: 909) enhances the need for deliberative disagreement and suggest that more research is needed on the role of disagreement. In their view, mutual respect is a form of agreeing to disagree, and here lies the importance of deliberative disagreement. Mutual respect might develop over time when citizens realize that there are merits in others' perspectives and viewpoints and that "winner takes it all" solutions are subordinate to solutions where compromises are included and where minority views are given weight as well. According to them:

"Citizens may differ on the right resolution but also about the reasons on the basis of which the conflict should be solved."

Caluwaerts (2012) has analysed a deliberation across language divides in Belgium. He concludes that the discussion was more deliberative, i.e. more similar to Habermas's ideal speech situation in the groups that included participants from both language groups. In these groups, participants listened more thoroughly to the arguments presented and made more effort in presenting their own arguments, than in the group with likeminded people where they assumed that everyone would think like them. When exposed to disagreements and new arguments the participants get a larger argument repertoire and an increased ability to list reasons for various opinions (Karpowitz and Mendelberg 2018: 541).

In heterogeneous groups, participants with lower status, for example lower education, minorities, might have difficulties making their voices heard and to get support for their arguments. There might be merits in creating "safe places" where participants can explore their views together with like-minded people. Indeed, studies indicate that among those with lower resources deliberation in likeminded groups generated a higher sense of equality than discussion in mixed opinion groups (Himmelroos, Rapeli and Grönlund 2016). Mansbridge (1994: 63–64) mentions two disadvantages with deliberating in likeminded enclaves. First, in a discussion with likeminded people, participants are not encouraged to listen to different opinions. Hence, they do not learn to formulate their opinions so that outsiders can take them into account. Second, discussions in enclaves are protected from constructive criticism, which might lead to polarization. She concludes that deliberation with likeminded people needs to be linked to a larger context where the benefits of both likeminded deliberation and deliberative disagreement can be exploited. There is empirical research, for example a study by Grönlund et al. (2015), suggesting that deliberative norms can alleviate the negative consequences (such as opinion polarization and amplification of cognitive errors) in likeminded enclaves. Change of opinion is also due to inconsistent arguments, misconceptions, and unreasonable demands being filtered out in the deliberative discussion. In a deliberation, self-interest does not receive support and in order to get support for their own opinions, they must be more focused on the needs of others and on the common good. Participants are given the opportunity to weigh different interests against each other and this creates a better understanding of different arguments, which means that even if the participants disagree, they have better understanding of what they disagree about (Fishkin 2018; Gutmann and Thompson 2018).

Deliberative democrats strongly agree that a demand for consensus might be counterproductive. An expectation of reaching consensus can create an obstacle to a critical dialogue and individual perspectives may dominate the agenda and define consensus. It might also prevent minority inclusion and force minority opinions to form after the group. Showing disagreement can be preferable in many situations. Thus, finding common ground where everyone benefits might be more feasible than reaching consensus (Gutmann and Thompson 2018; Harris 2019). The cost of consensus might also be a loss of precision and a tendency to make vague formulations that can be interpreted in a number of different ways. It can also result in a tendency to avoid debating more con-tentious issues and work against deeper deliberation (Olaffson 2016: 255–256). On the other hand, the requirement of consensus might also imply that more information is shared, knowledge increases to a greater degree and the deliberation is more thorough (Grönlund, Setälä and Herne 2010).

19.3.4 Reflection and perspective-taking

Dryzek (2000) suggests that deliberation needs both internal reflection and interaction with others. Without interaction with others, arguments are not tested in real political interaction. Deliberation requires citizens, not just hypothetically, to exchange views and rationally argue for their views (Goodin and Niemeyer 2003, Mercier and Lande-more 2012). Goodin and Niemeyer (2003) emphasize the internal reflective process they call "deliberation within" as an important part of the deliberative process. The internal process of deliberation always precedes participation in a discussion. After all, this is how we decide what our views and preferences in the coming discussion are. Hermans (2020) introduces the term "inner democracy" to describe the process of dialogical play between thought and counter-thought in developing our inner positions. He also high-lights the need for interactions with ourselves and with others. The deliberative ideals say that we should have an open mind and be willing to change our opinions, but if no one is prepared to take a stand for or against something, deliberation would have no-where to begin. Self-reflection is thus included when we react to the arguments that others present. The initial process of focusing on a topic, presenting information about it, and inviting citizens to think deeply about it probably provides strong stimu-lus for self-reflective deliberation (Goodin and Niemeyer 2003). Recent research implies that reflection decreases partisan-motivated reasoning and affective polarisation (Mur-adova 2021).

Muradova (2021) has examined the Irish CA and suggests that the process of per-spective-taking, defined as actively imagining others' experiences, perspectives, and feelings, can enhance more reflective judgements. She finds evidence that the diversity of viewpoints and the interplay between rational argumentation and personal stories induce the process of perspective-taking in deliberation. To fully understand and try to see things from others' perspectives we need information on the others' worldviews, perspectives, lives, and values. The process of perspective-taking also needs to be acti-vated and storytelling is one way of doing that by displaying values that are typically not talked about (Muradova 2021). Perspective-taking might be challenging for people, and it is likely that taking the perspective of someone similar to oneself is easier than with someone very different. Even though Muradova finds no evidence for biased per-spective-taking, she suggests that this is something worth paying attention to.

Deliberation is an argument-driven endeavour and some individuals are better than others at articulating their arguments in rational, reasonable terms (Young 2000). Even if researchers have opened up for alternative forms of communication,

e. g., storytelling and greetings, rational argument is still in the heart of deliberative democracy (Dryzek 2000: 67–71). Besides justifying their arguments, deliberative theory
also requires that deliberators consider the arguments of others with respect. Disrespect involves degrading others and their arguments as well as hints of irony and sar-
casm (Bächtiger et al. 2010: 41–42).

Talk-centric deliberative democratic theory has largely tended to focus on voice
and argumentation while overlooking the importance of listening. The quality of listening is expected to have a direct impact on the quality of deliberation. Feeling heard and
being heard are different things and deliberative theorists have increasingly acknowl-
edged the centrality of listening (Scudder 2020). There are good reasons to assume that
listening is a presumption for considering others' arguments and perspectives, and for
understanding others' viewpoints. Hence, listening also affects participants' opinions.

In an experimental study, Baccaro et al. (2016) identified a gap between opinion
change and good procedural deliberative quality. Asking participants to declare their
position at the outset and to justify it, discouraged opinion change but simultaneously
also reduced the impact of the pre-deliberative opinions of the other group members
and encouraged better epistemic deliberative quality. Conversely, asking participants
not to take a stance facilitated opinion change but reduced knowledge gains, lowered
epistemic deliberative quality, and led to strong social influences on individual opinions. This suggests that there may be a trade-off between opinion change and high-
quality deliberation. It also raises the question whether opinion change always is a desirable outcome.

The most comprehensive and most known empirical instrument to analyse the
quality of deliberative discourse is the Discourse Quality Index (DQI) developed by
Steiner et al. (2004). Although this chapter will not discuss the measurement of deliberative quality, the DQI deserves to be mentioned since it has transformed the empirical research by putting focus on normative ideals such as participation (inclusion), justification, respect, and reciprocity. Respect implies valuing others and having a positive
attitude towards their arguments and claims. Respect is more than being polite. It is
about being able to engage even with individuals that one disagrees with. It does not
necessarily imply changing opinion but a willingness to agree also with people who
do not share one's opinions (Bächtiger and Parkinson 2019).

19.4 Conclusion

Although CAs vary in design – for example they have different purpose, composition
length, and impact – they are similar in their endeavour to reach high quality deliberation. A plethora of research suggests that the internal quality of the CA (or any citizen
deliberation) is crucial for the legitimacy of decision-making but also for how participants are included and affected. Inclusion relates to both equality and redistribution of
power. Who is being selected and whether everyone has an equal chance to influence

the discussion have a large impact on the outcome. Learning, seen as an active act, is essential for deliberative processes and is often the driving force behind opinion change. Disagreement is needed to fully understand others' viewpoints, but it might also help oneself to better understand one's own opinions and values. Reflection and perspective-taking as well as reason-giving and listening are core principles of the deliberative discussion and closely linked to deliberative normative ideals.

As more CAs are implemented at a fast pace, we will learn to understand the impact of internal dynamics even better. A large part of the research so far relies on experimental studies and therefore examining real world civic forums will be an important addition to the research on citizen deliberation. How will deliberation and internal dynamics function in the real world of politics? Also, more research is needed on how to re-distribute power and how to address inequalities in both participation and influence. Research by Alice Siu (2017) and Edana Beauvais (2021) has showed that power relations and inequalities are problems that need to be taken more seriously. There are also many assumptions about the potentially low quality of deliberation in likeminded groups. Many of these theoretical assumptions would need further elaboration, i.e. how different viewpoints are taken into account in likeminded small-group deliberations. If CAs are to be widely used as democratic remedies for reducing the gap between decision-makers and citizens, it is crucial that they are inclusive, offer a diversity of epistemic resources, acknowledge diversity and disagreements, and rely on high quality deliberation.

References

Andersen, V., & Hansen, K. (2007). How deliberation makes better citizens: The Danish Deliberative Poll on the euro, *European Journal of Political Research* 46, 531–556.

Baccaro, L., Bächtiger, A., & Deville, M. (2016). Small differences that matter: The impact of discussion modalities on deliberative outcomes. *British Journal of Political Science* 46 (3), 551–566.

Bächtiger, A., & Parkinson, J. (2019). *Mapping and Measuring Deliberation. Towards a New Deliberative Quality.* Oxford: Oxford University Press.

Bächtiger, A., Niemeyer, S., Neblo, M., Steenbergen, M. R., & Steiner, J. (2010). Disentangling diversity in deliberative democracy: Competing theories, their blind spots and complementarities. *The Journal of Political Philosophy* 18, 32–63.

Beauvais, E. (2021). Discursive inequity and the internal exclusion of women speakers. *Political Research Quarterly* 74 (1), 103–116.

Brown, M. B. (2006). Survey article: Citizen panels and the concept of representation, *Journal of Political Philosophy* 14 (2), 203–225.

Brown, M. B. (2018). Deliberation and representation. In A. Bächtiger, J. S. Dryzek, J. Mansbridge, & M. Warren (eds), *The Oxford Handbook of Deliberative Democracy*, 171–186. Oxford: Oxford University Press.

Caluwaerts, D. (2012). *Confrontation and Communication. Deliberative Democracy in Divided Belgium.* Brussels: P.I.E. Peter Lang.

Carpini, M. X. D., Cook, F. L., & Jacobs, L. R. (2004). Public deliberation, discursive participation, and citizen engagement: A review of the empirical literature, *Annual Review of Political Science* 7, 315–344.

Curato, N., Hammond, M., & Min, J. B. (2019). *Power in Deliberative Democracy: Norms, Forums, Systems.* Cham: Palgrave Macmillan.

Curato, N., Vrydagh, J., & Bächtiger, A. (2020). Democracy without shortcuts: Introduction to the Special Issue, *Journal of Deliberative Democracy* 16 (2), 1–9.

Dryzek, J. S. (2000). *Deliberative Democracy and Beyond: Liberals, Critics, Contestations.* Oxford: Oxford University Press.

Dryzek, J. S., & Niemeyer, S. (2008). Discursive representation. *American Political Science Review* 102 (4), 481–493.

Esterling, K. M., Fung, A., & Lee, T. (2021). When deliberation produces persuasion rather than polarization: Measuring and modelling small group dynamics in a field experiment *British Journal of Political Science* 51 (2), 666–684.

Fishkin, J. S. (2018). *Democracy When the People Are Thinking.* Oxford: Oxford University Press.

Fung, A. (2005). Deliberation before the revolution: Toward an ethics of deliberative democracy in an unjust world. *Political Theory* 33 (3), 397–419.

Gerber, M., Bächtiger, A., Shikano, S., Reber, S., & Rohr, S. (2018). Deliberative abilities and influence in a transnational deliberative poll (Europolis). *British Journal of Political Science* 48 (4), 1093–1118.

Goodin, R. E., & Niemeyer, S. (2003). When does deliberation begin? Internal reflection versus public discussion in deliberative democracy. *Political Studies* 51, 627–649.

Grönlund, K., Setälä, M., & Herne, K. (2010). Deliberation and civic virtue: Lessons from a citizen deliberation experiment. *European Political Science Review* 2, 95–117.

Grönlund, K., Setälä, M., & Herne, K. (2015). Does enclave deliberation polarize opinions? *Political Behavior* 37, 995–1020.

Gutmann, A., & Thompson, D. (2018). Reflections deliberative democracy: When theory meets practice. In A. Bächtiger, J. S. Dryzek, J. Mansbridge, & M. Warren (eds), *The Oxford Handbook of Deliberative Democracy,* 900–912. Oxford: Oxford University Press.

Habermas, J. (2018). Interview with Jürgen Habermas. In A. Bächtiger, J. S. Dryzek, J. Mansbridge, & M. Warren (eds), *The Oxford Handbook of Deliberative Democracy,* 871–881. Oxford: Oxford University Press.

Hall, T., Wilson, P., & Newman, J. (2011). Evaluating the short- and long-term effects of a modified deliberative poll on Idahoans' attitudes and civic engagement related to energy options. *Journal of Public Deliberation* 7 (1).

Harris, C. (2019). Mini-publics: design choices and legitimacy. In S. Elstub & O. Escobar (eds), *Handbook of Democratic Innovation and Governance,* 45–59. Cheltenham: Edward Elgar Publishing.

Hermans, H. 2020. *Inner Democracy: Empowering the Mind Against a Polarizing Society.* Oxford: Oxford University Press.

Himmelroos, S., Rapeli, L., & Grönlund, K. (2017). Talking with like-minded people—Equality and efficacy in enclave deliberation. *The Social Science Journal* 54 (2), 148–158.

Hogg, M. A. (1993). Group cohesiveness: A critical review and some new directions. *European Review of Social Psychology* 4, 85–111.

James, M. R. (2008). Descriptive representation in the British Columbia CA. In M. Warren & H. Pearse (eds.), *Designing Deliberative Democracy. The British Columbia CA,* 106–126. Cambridge: Cambridge University Press.

Karpowitz, C. F., & Mendelberg, T. (2018). The political psychology of deliberation. In A. Bächtiger, J. S. Dryzek, J. Mansbridge, & M. Warren (eds), *The Oxford Handbook of Deliberative Democracy,* 535–555. Oxford: Oxford University Press.

Knight, J., & Johnson, J. (1997). What sort of equality does deliberative democracy require? In J. Bohman & W. Rehg (eds), *Deliberative Democracy,* 279–320. Cambridge: The MIT Press.

Knight, J., & Johnson, J. (2011). *The Priority of Democracy: Political Consequences of Pragmatism.* Princeton, NJ: Princeton University Press.

Leino, M., Kulha, K., Setälä, M., & Ylisalo, J. (2021). Expert hearings in mini-publics: How does the field of expertise influence deliberation and its outcomes? Paper presented at NOPSA conference 2021.

Lightbody, R., & Roberts, J. J. (2019). Experts: The politics of evidence and expertise in democratic innovation. In S. Elstub & O. Escobar (eds), *Handbook of Democratic Innovation and Governance*, 225–240. Cheltenham: Edward Elgar Publishing.

Lindell, M., Bächtiger, A., Grönlund, K., Herne, K., Setälä, M., & Wyss, D. (2017). What drives the polarisation and moderation of opinions? Evidence from a Finnish citizen deliberation experiment on immigration. *European Journal of Political Research* 56, 23–45.

Lord, C. G., Lee, R., & Lepper, M. R. (1979). Biased assimilation and attitude polarization: The effects of prior theories on subsequently considered evidence. *Journal of Personality and Social Psychology* 37 (11), 2098–2109.

Luskin, R. C., Fishkin, J. S., & Jowell, R. (2002). Considered opinions: Deliberative polling in Britain. *British Journal of Political Science* 32, 455–487.

Mansbridge, J. (1994). Using power/fighting power. *Constellations* 1 (1), 53–73.

Mercier, H., & Landemore, H. (2012). Reasoning is for arguing: Understanding the successes and failures of deliberation, *Political Psychology* 33, 243–258.

Muradova, L. 2021. Seeing the other side? Perspective-taking and reflective political judgements in interpersonal deliberation. *Political Studies* 69 (3), 644–664.

Olafsson, J. (2016). The constituent assembly: A study in failure. In V. Ingimundarson, P. Urfalino, P., & I. Erlingsdóttir (eds), *Iceland's Financial Crisis*, 252–272. Abingdon: Routledge.

Owen, D., & Smith, G. (2018). Sortition, rotation, and mandate: Conditions for political equality and deliberative reasoning. *Politics & Society* 46 (3), 419–434.

Phillips, A. (1995). *The Politics of Presence*. Oxford: Clarendon Press.

Sanders, L. M. (1997). Against deliberation. *Political Theory* 25 (3), 347–376.

Scudder, M. (2020). *Beyond Empathy and Inclusion: The Challenge of Listening in Democratic Deliberation*. Oxford: Oxford University Press.

Siu, A. (2017). Deliberation & the challenge of inequality. *Daedalus* 146 (3), 119–128.

Smith, G. (2009). *Democratic Innovations: Designing Institutions for Citizen Participation*. Cambridge: Cambridge University Press.

Smith, G. (2021). *Can Democracy Safeguard the Future?* Cambridge: Polity Press.

Smith, G., & Wales, C. (2000). Citizens' juries and deliberative democracy. *Political Studies* 48, 51–63.

Steiner, J., Bächtiger, A., Spörndli, M., & Steenbergen, M. R. (2005). *Deliberative Politics in Action. Analysing Parliamentary Discourse*. Cambridge: Cambridge University Press.

Suiter, J., Farrell, D. M., & O'Malley, E. (2016). When do deliberative citizens change their opinions? Evidence from the Irish CA. *International Political Science Review* 37 (2), 198–212.

Sunstein, C. R. (2002). The law of group polarization. *The Journal of Political Philosophy* 10, 175–195.

Thompson, A. G., Escobar, O., Roberts, J. J., Elstub, S., & Pamphilis, N. M. (2021). The importance of context and the effect of information and deliberation on opinion change regarding environmental issues in citizens' juries. *Sustainability* 13 (17), 9852.

van der Does, R., & Jacquet, V. (2021). Small-scale deliberation and mass democracy: A systematic review of the spillover effects of deliberative minipublics. *Political Studies*.

Willis, R., Curato, N., & Smith, G. (2022). Deliberative democracy and the climate crisis, *Wiley Interdisciplinary Reviews: Climate Change*, e759.

Young, I. M. (2000). *Inclusion and Democracy*. Oxford: Oxford University Press.

Saskia Goldberg

20 Citizens' assemblies and their effects on the population

Abstract: A so-called "deliberative wave" is currently hitting the globe, with citizens' assemblies (CAs) being convened all over the world. While much research has been done both on internal qualities of CAs and macro political uptake, little is known about their effects on the wider public, namely (1) how CAs affect non-participating citizens and (2) how non-participants perceive CAs. This chapter seeks to disentangle, systemize, and summarize effects on the wider public and applies an integrative, yet "realistic" approach to classify effects on non-participants by distinguishing between (a) theoretical claims in conjuncture with CAs, (b) observed effects on the wider public, (c) citizens' expectations, and (d) perceived legitimacy. It argues that CAs do not automatically have positive effects on the population, but can also have no or even negative effects. Further, it argues that such effects hinge both on the awareness and contextualization of CAs.

Keywords: deliberation, legitimacy, public opinion, citizens' perceptions, expectations, awareness, framework

20.1 Introduction

Citizens' assemblies (CAs) have become a promising impetus in the debate about the so-called crisis of democracy (e.g., OECD 2020). And indeed, there is much to like about the idea of bringing together a (quasi-)representative subset of the wider population to have inclusive, informed, and consequential discussions about important policy issues (see Curato et al. 2021: 3). If properly designed, CAs can achieve high quality deliberation with a variety of positive effects on *participants*, including opinion changes and knowledge gains (e.g., Fishkin 2018), and the development of positive political attitudes and faith in democracy (e.g., Boulianne 2019). Moreover, some proponents even claim that CAs can make decision-making processes more inclusive and responsive (see Curato, Vrydagh and Bächtiger 2020: 3). By the same token, CAs increasingly are facing powerful and sound criticisms. Normatively, critics echo a common feature: CAs are illegitimate because they bypass deliberations by the public at large, are not participatory enough, fail to connect with the wider public, and are not authorized to inject po-

Saskia Goldberg: KU Leuven, Belgium. Acknowledgements: This chapter partly draws on the PhD thesis 'Where the grass is always greener: Non-participants' contingent legitimacy perceptions of deliberative citizens' forums' (Goldberg 2022). This project has received funding from the German Research Foundation (project number 432370948) and the European Research Council under the European Union's Horizon 2020 research and innovation programme (grant agreement No 759736).

♻ Open Access. © 2023 the author(s), published by De Gruyter. (cc) BY-NC-ND This work is licensed under the Creative Commons Attribution-NonCommercial-NoDerivatives 4.0 International License. https://doi.org/10.1515/9783110758269-022

litical decisions (e. g., Lafont 2019). Empirically, research often tends to neglect or ignore possible negative effects on the population alike.

Yet, CAs remain a tiny snapshot of the wider public and research has long been focusing either on their internal or systemic qualities with questions about macro political uptake and scaling (e. g., Hendriks 2016; Setälä 2017). However, we still lack knowledge about the effects on the wider public, namely how CAs affect *non-participating citizens* and how the latter perceive the former. While empirical works on "spillover effects" (van der Does and Jacquet 2021) are still scarce, most recently there have been some attempts to address citizens' perceptions, showing that the overall support for CAs is somewhat high (though not overwhelming) among citizens (e. g., Bedock and Pilet 2020, 2021; Goldberg and Bächtiger 2022; Jacquet, Niessen and Reuchamps 2022; Pilet et al. 2022).

This chapter seeks to disentangle, systemize, and summarize effects on the wider public focusing on *non-participating citizens*. It applies an integrative yet "realistic" approach and argues that CAs do not automatically have positive effects on the population, but can have no or even negative effects as well. Further, it argues that such effects hinge on both the awareness and contextualization of CAs. The chapter begins by sketching an integrative framework for assessing effects on the wider public. Based on a review of literature it then summarizes findings for a) theoretical claims in conjuncture with CAs, b) observed effects on the wider public, c) expectations of citizens, and d) perceived effects and legitimacy, before pointing to research gaps and (contextual) challenges.

20.2 An integrative framework for assessing effects on the wider public

Many years ago, James Fishkin put forth a promising argument: CAs are particularly appealing because they start from a reflection of the population, which then experiences the "deliberative filter" and arrives at the best possible decision (see Fishkin 2009: 25). And indeed, a number of studies have shown that CAs can have such transformative effects on *participating citizens* (see the chapter by Lindell in this *Handbook*). But what about *non-participants?* Some advocates stress that CAs are able to affect non-participating citizens as well (e. g., Goodin and Dryzek 2006; Gastil et al. 2018). In this respect, CAs might stimulate public discussions not only because non-participants gain knowledge about a policy issue, but also because they increase visibility among the citizenry. Still, however, CAs are criticized for being detached from the public at large. To this end, outcomes of CAs are nothing but democratic shortcuts that require non-participants to blindly defer to decision of deliberating strangers (Lafont 2019).

Yet, research often fails to differentiate between desirable goals of CAs and actual observable effects. Whereas some works are concerned with goals CAs should ideally achieve (sometimes even equate them with desirable goals of deliberative democracy in general), others take empirical approaches and study effects of CAs on the wider public, making it difficult to draw general conclusions. Moreover, researchers often take a top-down approach and neglect assessments of the citizens themselves. This chapter takes a conceptual point of departure and advocates an integrative approach (Table 20.1) that differentiates between desirable goals of CAs (*expectations*) and actual impacts on the wider public (*effects*) while simultaneously accounting for different perspectives: goals and effects from the perspective of deliberative democracy (*objective/ top-down*) and goals and effects from the eyes of the wider public (*subjective/bottom-up*).

Table 20.1: Integrative framework to assess effects on the population

		Object dimension	
		Expectations	Effects
Perspective	**Objective/top-down** (academic disciplines)	A) Theoretical claims in conjuncture with CAs	B) Observed effects of CAs on the wider public
	Subjective/bottom-up (citizens perceptions)	C) Citizens' expectations about CAs	D) Citizens' perceptions of effects, perceived legitimacy

20.2.1 Theoretical claims of citizens' assemblies

Over the past two decades, a body of literature has identified a number of desirable effects associated with CAs. The debate, however, has continued to change. To this end, Curato et al. (2020) have recently suggested to speak of "generations" of CAs. While *first generation* scholars are concerned with the internal working and quality of CAs, *second generation* scholars have started to address their consequentiality and roles in democratic deepening. Finally, *third generation* scholars have only recently begun to scrutinize the widely held idea that CAs quasi automatically strengthen democracy. Instead, they are interested in (more) appropriate, alternative, or contingent uses of CAs in democratic systems. The main argument this section addresses is that CAs might not be equally useful for all purposes. In practice, CAs sometimes even pursue goals quite different from those envisaged by deliberative democracy theory. Desirable goals can broadly be divided into three categories: *internal goals* (deliberative quality and effects on participants), *external goals* (effects on non-participants, public authorities, and the public sphere), and *democratic goals* (realization of democratic goods such as inclusion). The focus of this chapter is on the second category (external goals), with particular attention to effects on *non-participants*. However, it is important to mention that CAs are organized context-specifically and their desirable effects may differ depending (inter alia) on their purposes (see below).

The literature on desired goals of CAs on the population addresses various effects such as informing the public, influencing public opinion, mobilization, and legitimating policies. First, CAs could *inform the public* (both public officials and non-partici-pants) about the "considered opinions" of participants. Such information may feed into broader discussions among citizens but also among politicians, parties, members of the parliament, and policymakers at various government levels. In that regard, La-font (2019) has most recently suggested alternative roles for a participatory re-orienta-tion of CAs, namely when they anticipate important policy issues which have been ig-nored in the population (anticipatory use), contest the majority opinion (contestatory use), or to alert the citizenry when public authorities ignore public opinions (vigilant use). Moreover, CAs could *influence the public opinion* by signalling what a considered opinion would look like. Similar to partisan cues, CAs then can serve as informational shortcuts for (uninformed) citizens (e.g., Ingham and Levin 2018; Bächtiger and Gold-berg 2020) and thus a remedy to complexity. Particularly in complex governance sys-tems, citizens (even the most politically active ones) need to make "choices for passiv-ity" (MacKenzie and Warren 2012: 98). To this end, MacKenzie and Warren (2012) argue that CAs can serve as "trusted information proxies" that help citizens to make decisions particularly in situations where they lack resources, competencies, and interest to en-gage with political issues. In that regard, CAs are seen as useful tools to prepare and compress information in best possible deliberative circumstances and make it availa-ble to citizens (see also Suiter et al. 2020: 257). In turn, citizens may feel normatively committed to democracy which means that they might be supportive toward CAs and accept their decisions or recommendations for they know how the deliberative process was working including that arguments have been heard and exchanged and also that they could have been participants themselves (see Fishkin 2018: 146–147). Third, DCFs could *mobilize citizens* to talk about their experiences, which then might spill-over to everyday conversations (e.g., Lazer et al. 2015; Mansbridge 1999). Finally, albeit symbolically, the idea for CAs is to *help legitimate policy decisions* (see Goodin and Dryzek 2006: 232). With regard to political decision-making, however, CAs typically lack necessary links of authorization and accountability to the wider public (see also Bächtiger and Parkinson 2019: 35).

20.2.2 Observed effects on the wider public

Empirical research has long been focusing on the internal working of CAs and their effects on participants. In a recent review, van der Does and Jacquet (2021) find that the relevant literature for "spillover effects" on non-participants is still scarce, with only a few studies addressing effects on the wider public. First, research shows that CAs can have both *informing effects on non-participants*, including knowledge gains on policy issues and engagement with new arguments (e.g., Gastil et al. 2018; Már and Gastil 2020; Setälä et al. 2020), and even affect (and change) opinions of non-par-ticipating citizens (e.g., Boulianne 2018; Gastil et al. 2018; Ingham and Levin 2018). Sec-ond, for *influence on the public opinion*, evidence on the Citizens' Initiative Reviews (CIRs) shows that citizens who engaged with the citizens' statements were more likely to vote in accordance with the statements and sometimes even change their voting intentions (e.g., Gastil et al. 2018; Gastil and Richards 2013). Overall, however, results remain mixed, revealing that citizens only sometimes (e.g., depending on the issue at stake) vote or decide in line with the recommendations of CAs (e.g., Fournier et al. 2011), putting an "empirical question mark" on shortcut approaches such as trust-based uses of CAs (for a discussion on outcome favourability see below). Moreover, there seems to be at least anecdotal evidence on the *mobilization of citizens*, showing that CAs can both evoke interpersonal discussions outside the forum (e.g., Gastil, Richards and Knobloch 2014; Lazer et al. 2015) and "stimulate" public participation by increasing the willingness of citizens to participate in future CAs (e.g., Denters and Klok 2010; Gastil et al. 2018). Finally, a very few studies provide evidence for "emanating effects" (Knobloch, Barthel and Gastil 2020), showing that CAs can also influence non-participants *political attitudes* including their sense of internal and external efficacy, political trust (e.g., Boulianne 2018), and empathy (Suiter et al. 2020).

20.2.3 Citizens' expectations on citizens' assemblies

To date, research on citizens perceptions of CAs is overly limited. Only a very few studies (mostly qualitative) exist on citizens' expectations about CAs, which, however, focus on participants only. An exemption is Goldberg (2022) who finds that while a substantial proportion of the German citizens (more than 40 %) have never heard about CAs, only about a third of those who are familiar with CAs stated to have some expectations. However, scant research exists on what citizens concretely expect from CAs. Existing studies usually use in-depth interviews to compare *participants' attitudes* before and after the CAs (e.g., Curato and Niemeyer 2013), or apply retrospective designs in which *participants* are asked for their impressions after having participated in a CA, which allows to reflect on their experiences before and after the processes (e.g., Jacquet 2019; Goldberg 2018). Overall, these studies indicate transformative effects of participants' expectations and show that expectations prior to the CAs differ from expectations citizens have after the deliberations. While participants tend to have "instrumental" or "external" goals that refer to the impact and consequentiality of CAs at the beginning (e.g., good decisions and influence), "expressive" or "internal" aspects of CAs become more important afterwards (e.g., social aspects such as friendships). Note, however, these effects refer to single case studies only. Future research needs to look critically and comparatively at other cases and may even come up with standardized measuring tools that allows to examine expectations of various groups of non-participants.

Some recent attempts try to understand citizens' contingent perceptions and expectations, shedding light on what citizens like or dislike about CAs. For instance, Pow et al. (2020) show that citizens value CAs for they are composed of ordinary citizens. This effect seems to be particularly strong when they think that politicians are not like them. Moreover, Goldberg and Bächtiger (2022) find that citizens want CAs to be advisory only, but tightly coupled to legacy institutions while at the same time providing extra provisions in terms of representation and inclusion. Van Dijk and Lefevere (2022) show that citizens want non-binding recommendations to be honoured by elected representatives (see also Germann, Marien and Muradova 2022). Finally, research indicates that expectations about CAs vary among various "types" or "subgroups" of citizens. For instance, Mar and Gastil (2021) find that particularly politically disadvantaged groups (people of colour compared to Whites, poor compared to rich) tend to trust CAs. Similarly, Jacquet (2019) demonstrates that less engaged citizens develop new expectations during their participation. This suggests not only that expectations hinge on the general interest in political participation, but also that awareness about CAs might induce the overall assessment of CAs. To this end, Goldberg (2022) found that citizens who stated to have at least some experiences (either directly through their own participation or indirectly through, for example, media or reports) are more positive towards CAs in general. Moreover, anecdotal evidence shows that participants may even become more sceptical about the actual impact of CAs (Goldberg 2018). Thus, experiences might contribute to more realistic expectations particularly when it comes to their actual influence on political decision-making. Similarly, albeit for referendums, Werner and Marien (2022) demonstrate that citizens tend to have more realistic expectations on what referenda can (not) contribute to democracy in direct democratic contexts. They show that experienced citizens are more critical about the potential of referendums to address responsiveness issues.

20.2.4 Citizens' perceptions of citizens' assemblies and perceived legitimacy

Let us finally tip our hats to a simple though important question, namely how non-participants perceive CAs. A perception-based approach is interested in the extent to which CAs are perceived as legitimate means of policymaking and assumes that CAs would enjoy very limited respect without sufficient support from the wider public (e.g., Bedock 2017). To date, scarce evidence exists on perceived legitimacy and related research is still in its infancy. Some studies have started to assess perceived legitimacy, but focus on participatory innovations in general (Jäske 2019) or different generic forms of democratic decision-making (e.g., Christensen 2020; Werner and Marien 2022). Furthermore, there have been highly promising attempts to contextualize CAs further by considering the variety of CAs and its different designs (e.g., Bedock and Pilet 2020; Goldberg and Bächtiger 2022; Jacobs and Kaufmann 2019; Jacquet, Niessen and Reuchamps 2022; Pow 2021).

The overall story is told quickly: Citizens' general support for CAs seems to be moderately high (e.g., Bedock and Pilet 2021; Jacquet, Niessen and Reuchamps 2022), but support seems to have an instrumental dimension, namely citizens tend to prefer any alternatives to the status quo of political decision-making. However, a wealth of research shows that citizens tend to have difficulties forming coherent preferences (e.g.,

Bengtsson 2012; Goldberg, Wyss and Bächtiger 2020). Yet, drawing on a contingency argument, recent debates about appropriate uses put further nuance to the idea that CAs quasi automatically strengthen democracy (Bächtiger and Goldberg 2020; Curato, Vrydagh and Bächtiger 2020). Empirical evidence suggests that perceived legitimacy not only on design questions of CAs (e.g., Christensen 2020; Goldberg and Bächtiger 2022, van Dijk and Lefevere 2022), but is also contingent on heterogeneity within the citizenry and citizens' awareness about CAs (e.g., knowledge, visibility, experiences). Finally, research on outcome favourability reveals that substantive considerations play a crucial role for citizens' legitimacy perceptions (e.g., Esaiasson, Gilljam and Persson 2012), which is also found in conjunction with support of CAs (e.g., Goldberg and Bächtiger 2022).

20.3 Contextualization of effects

All findings described above refer either to *single (mostly "successful") cases* (e.g., the CIR in Oregon (and similar "experiments" in Finland and Switzerland), the Irish CAs, the British Columbia CA (BCCA), and the G1000 in Belgium), or *survey experiments* on "fictional" CAs (e.g., Boulianne 2018; Christensen 2020; Goldberg and Bächtiger 2022; van Dijk and Lefevere 2022). To this end, van der Does and Jacquet (2021) note that most evidence is based on very few cases and studies. Still, systematic research on citizens expectations and actual effects is missing. Yet, CAs differ considerably in their design and the political context (Paulis et al. 2021) and therefore the contextualization of expectations and effects is of great importance. A major problem in studying CAs comes with a lack of data and knowledge about the actual population of CAs. Mostly, studies refer to successful cases and ignore failed ones, which ultimately makes it difficult to generalize. Finally, Spada and Ryan (2017) remind us this is also reflected in publication biases in high-impact journals.

The POLITICIZE database has started to systematically cover CAs in Europe between 2000 and 2020 and identified criteria for systemizing them (Paulis et al. 2021). This includes, for example, the *design* (e.g., recruitment strategies, number of participants, and group composition), the *issue* (e.g., environment, planning, immigration, and constitutional electoral changes), and the *linkage to political decision-making* (e.g., recommendations to public officials or referendums). Moreover, a recent OECD report points to a great variety of CAs, putting a particular eye on their various *purposes*. The report differentiates between informed citizen recommendations on issues, citizen opinion on issues, informed citizen evaluation of ballot measures, and permanent CAs such as the Ostbelgien Model (OECD 2020: 35).

Yet still some serious challenges exist beyond the availability of cases. The first is *awareness*. In order to properly assess legitimacy, citizens need to get familiarized with CAs to understand their significance (Lafont 2017: 94). In that regard, citizens need knowledge about CAs, including their role in political decision-making. Conversely, when citizens understand both the purpose and functioning of CAs, their legitimacy perceptions might increase (see also Fung 2003). Awareness therefore has much in common with visibility (Rummens 2016), transparency, and communication to assure quality of access to the wider public (see Pow, van Dijk and Marien 2020). However, except for some "successful" cases, most citizens are not familiar with the concept of CAs (see also Devillers et al. 2021), nor do they know about their (critical) democratic implications. Empirical evidence shows that respondents often choose the middle category when answering survey questions, indicating that citizens tend to have difficulties assessing CAs or even possess non-attitudes. However, a few studies tend to confirm a positive relationship between familiarity and the assessment of CAs, showing that awareness indeed is a key driver of impact on the wider public. Boulianne (2018), for example, demonstrates that being informed about CAs can help increase feelings of external efficacy among citizens. Similarly, Goldberg (2022) shows that support for CAs is higher among citizens who either have some experiences with CAs or have carefully engaged with various information on CAs. In addition, Gastil et al. (2016) suggest that citizens need more information about CAs to make informed and robust trust judgements.

Moreover, recent studies have put forth the idea of *heterogeneity*, i.e. differences across subgroups of citizens. To this end, different strata of citizens may have very different views of CAs, depending for example on their experiences with CAs and views about how political decisions should be made. For instance, research shows that particularly politically disaffected citizens or citizens with low political trust call for greater empowerment of CAs or at least seem to have less of a problem with more radical forms of representative democracy (Bedock and Pilet 2020; Goldberg and Bächtiger 2022; Germann, Marien and Muradova 2022).

Finally, this chapter has argued that effects may have an *ambivalent character:* CAs might have positive but also negative effects on the wider public or even no effects at all. Many studies choose not to employ controlled research designs, but seem to implicitly assume that CAs ultimately have positive effects without distinguishing them from other potential determinants at both the institutional level (e.g., the comparison across various CAs and other alternatives) and the individual level (e.g., varying citizen attitudes). Yet, a problem of empirical research is that studies almost exclusively report positive effects and tend to neglect or ignore negative effects. Oftentimes, however, recommendations from CAs are not honoured (Font et al. 2018; Germann, Marien and Muradova 2022), or costly effort are made for running CAs for rather little return. One exception is the BCCA, where a referendum ultimately failed to mobilize enough citizens to cast their vote. To this end, Curato and Böker (2016) remind us to consider negative or even counterproductive effects as well. Their study of various CAs show that they can also undermine public deliberation (even in cases of high internal quality), for example because of poor media coverage. Moreover, anecdotal evidence from case studies in German municipalities shows that conflicts may even become entrenched or magnified rather than resolved (Vetter, Geyer and Eith 2014). Overall, the thin data base suggests that many CAs might not have any effects on the general public, or at least not the highly promising goals associated with CAs. Crucially, however, individual CAs cannot achieve all desirable goals simultaneously (see also Bächtiger and Parkinson 2019).

But what then are avenues for further research? First, research on non-partici- pants' perceptions and effects on the population needs to become *systematic.* More spe- cifically, there is a need to focus on non-participating citizens in addition to partici- pants in CAs. To date, a very few isolated studies exist that "simulate" CAs (or present hypothetical scenarios of CAs) in controlled survey experiments. With few ex- emptions, there is no evidence on the assessments of non-participating citizens for CAs that actually took place. Research also has to systematically include cases in non-West- ern countries as well as less successful or even failed cases. Second, with regard to le- gitimacy perceptions, a doable route to take are *survey experiments* that allow for in- cluding information packages to raise awareness among citizens. Moreover, survey experiments and factorial analyses allow us to study perceived legitimacy contingently, for example, by varying different characteristics and contexts of CAs. Finally, *qualita- tive case studies* could help understand the mechanisms of why (and how) CAs affect the general public. Such methods could, for example, provide insights into why non- participants trust CAs even though they have not participated themselves.

20.4 Conclusion

This chapter provided an overview of empirical findings of effects on the wider public. Along two dimensions – what is the object we are interested in and which perspective do we take – it sketched a fourfold framework for assessing effects on non-participants and outlined the state of research on a) theoretical claims of CAs, b) observed effects of CAs on the wider public, c) expectations of citizens, and d) perceived legitimacy. Four conclusions can be drawn. First, deliberative democracy theory places high expecta- tions on CAs, but these expectations are not consistently met in empirical studies. Dif- ferently put, CAs simply cannot achieve all desirable goals at once. Second, CAs seem to have effects on the population, but evidence mostly refers to unsystematic single-(best)- case studies that need to be contextualized further. Third, citizens' perceptions (partly) differ from the desirable effects formulated in theory. Fourth, research on citizens' per- ceptions shows that citizens seem to be (moderately) supportive of CAs. Yet, research needs further (systematic) studies, especially in light of the fact that citizens are not a homogeneous group with many of them not even being familiar with CAs. In sum, supportive contexts (namely appropriate designing, support within a polity, and aware- ness) increase the likelihood that CAs have positive effects on (at least parts of) the population. However, although we already have a good feeling of how CAs *might affect* the population, systematic research is still in its infancy and positive results should not be fully overestimated, given that many studies tend to focus on successful cases only.

References

Bächtiger, A., & Goldberg, S. (2020). Towards a more robust, but limited and contingent defence of the political uses of deliberative minipublics. *Journal of Deliberative Democracy* 16 (2), 33–42.

Bächtiger, A., & Parkinson, J. (2019). *Mapping and Measuring Deliberation: Towards a New Deliberative Quality.* Oxford: Oxford University Press.

Bedock, C. (2017). *Reforming Democracy: Institutional Engineering in Western Europe* (Vol. 1). Oxford: Oxford University Press.

Bedock, C., & Pilet, J.-B. (2020). Enraged, engaged, or both? A study of the determinants of support for consultative vs. binding mini-publics. *Representation*, 1–21.

Bedock, C., & Pilet, J.-B. (2021). Who supports citizens selected by lot to be the main policymakers? A study of French citizens. *Government and Opposition* 56 (3), 485–504.

Bengtsson, Å. (2012). Citizens' perceptions of political processes. A critical evaluation of preference consistency and survey items. *Revista Internacional De Sociología* 70, 45–64.

Boulianne, S. (2018). Mini-publics and public ppinion: Two survey-based experiments. *Political Studies* 66 (1), 119–136.

Boulianne, S. (2019). Building faith in democracy: Deliberative events, political trust and efficacy. *Political Studies* 67 (1), 4–30.

Christensen, H. S. (2020). How citizens evaluate participatory processes: a conjoint analysis. *European Political Science Review* 12 (2), 239–253.

Curato, N., & Böker, M. (2016). Linking mini-publics to the deliberative system: a research agenda. *Policy Sciences* 49 (2), 173–190.

Curato, N., & Niemeyer, S. (2013). Reaching out to overcome political apathy: Building participatory capacity through deliberative engagement. *Politics & Policy* 41 (3), 355–383.

Curato, N., Farrell, D. M., Geissel, B., Grönlund, K., Mockler, P., Pilet, J.-B., ... Suiter, J. (2021). *Deliberative Mini-publics: Core Design Features.* Bristol: Bristol University Press.

Curato, N., Vrydagh, J., & Bächtiger, A. (2020). Democracy without shortcuts: Introduction to the Special Issue. *Journal of Deliberative Democracy* 16 (2), 1–9.

Denters, B., & Klok, P.-J. (2010). Rebuilding Roombeek: Patterns of citizen participation in urban governance. *Urban Affairs Review* 45 (5), 583–607.

Devillers, S., Vrydagh, J., Caluwaerts, D. & Reuchamps, M. (2021). Looking in from the outside: How do invited but not selected citizens perceive the legitimacy of a minipublic? *Journal of Deliberative Democracy* 17 (1), 149–159.

Esaiasson, P., Gilljam, M., & Persson, M. (2012). Which decision-making arrangements generate the strongest legitimacy beliefs? Evidence from a randomised field experiment. *European Journal of Political Research* 51(6), 785–808.

Fishkin, J. S. (2009). *When the People Speak: Deliberative Democracy and Public Consultation.* Oxford: Oxford University Press.

Fishkin, J. S. (2018). *Democracy When the People Are Thinking: Revitalizing Our Politics Through Public Deliberation* (Vol. 1). Oxford: Oxford University Press: Oxford University Press.

Font, J., Smith, G., Galais, C., & Alarcon, P. (2018). Cherry-picking participation: Explaining the fate of proposals from participatory processes. *European Journal of Political Research* 57, 615–636.

Fournier, P., van der Kolk, H., Carty, R. K., Blais, A., & Rose, J. (2011). *When Citizens Decide.* Oxford: Oxford University Press.

Fung, A. (2003). Survey article: Recipes for public spheres: Eight institutional design choices and Their Consequences. *Journal of Political Philosophy* 11 (3), 338–367.

Gastil, J., & Richards, R. (2013). Making direct democracy deliberative through random assemblies. *Politics & Society* 41 (2), 253–281.

Gastil, J., Knobloch, K. R., Reedy, J., Henkels, M., & Cramer, K. (2018). Assessing the electoral impact of the 2010 Oregon Citizens' Initiative Review. *American Politics Research* 46 (3), 534–563.

Gastil, J., Richards, R., & Knobloch, K. R. (2014). Vicarious deliberation: How the Oregon Citizens' Initiative Review influenced deliberation in mass elections. *International Journal of Communication* 8, 62–89.

Gastil, J., Rosenzweig, E., Knobloch, K. R., & Brinker, D. (2016). Does the public want mini-publics? Voter responses to the Citizens' Initiative Review. *Communication and the Public* 1 (2), 174–192.

Germann, M., Marien, S., & Muradova, L. (2022). Scaling Up? Unpacking the Effect of Deliberative Mini-Publics on Legitimacy Perceptions. Political Studies, 0(0), 1–24.

Goldberg, S. (2018). *A Bottom-Up Perspective on Deliberative Participation Processes: What Citizens Want and How Expectations Affect Perceived Legitimacy.* Paper presented at the 2018 ECPR General Conference, Hamburg, 22–25 August.

Goldberg, S. (2022). Where the grass is always greener: Non-participants' contingent legitimacy perceptions of deliberative citizens' forums. PhD thesis, University of Stuttgart (defended 02.02.2022).

Goldberg, S., & Bächtiger, A. (2022). Catching the 'deliberative wave'? How (disaffected) citizens assess deliberative citizen forums. *British Journal of Political Science*, 1–9.

Goldberg, S., Wyss, D., & Bächtiger, A. (2020). Deliberating or thinking (twice) about democratic preferences: What German citizens want from democracy. *Political Studies* 68 (2), 311–331.

Goodin, R. E., & Dryzek, J. S. (2006). Deliberative impacts: The macro-political uptake of mini-publics. *Politics & Society* 34 (2), 219–244.

Hendriks, C. M. (2016). Coupling citizens and elites in deliberative systems: The role of institutional design. *European Journal of Political Research* 55 (1), 43–60.

Ingham, S., & Levin, I. (2018). Can deliberative minipublics influence public opinion? Theory and experimental evidence. *Political Research Quarterly* 71 (3), 654–667.

Jacobs, D., & Kaufmann, W. (2019). The right kind of participation? The effect of a deliberative mini-public on the perceived legitimacy of public decision-making. *Public Management Review* 23 (1), 91–111.

Jacquet, V. (2017). Explaining non-participation in deliberative mini-publics. *European Journal of Political Research* 56 (3), 640–659.

Jacquet, V. (2019). The role and the future of deliberative mini-publics: A citizen perspective. *Political Studies* 67 (3), 639–657.

Jacquet, V., Niessen, C., & Reuchamps, M. (2022). Sortition, its advocates and its critics: An empirical analysis of citizens' and MPs' support for random selection as a democratic reform proposal. *International Political Science Review* 43 (2), 295–316.

Jäske, M. (2019). Participatory innovations and maxi-publics: The influence of participation possibilities on perceived legitimacy at the local level in Finland. *European Journal of Political Research* 58 (2), 603–630.

Knobloch, K. R., Barthel, M. L., & Gastil, J. (2020). Emanating effects: The impact of the Oregon Citizens' Initiative Review on voters' political efficacy. *Political Studies* 68 (2), 426–445.

Lafont, C. (2017). Can democracy be deliberative & participatory? The democratic case for political uses of mini-publics. *Daedalus* 146 (3), 85–105.

Lafont, C. (2019). *Democracy Without Shortcut: A Participatory Conception of Deliberative Democracy.* Oxford: Oxford University Press.

Lazer, D. M., Sokhey, A. E., Neblo, M. A., Esterling, K. M., & Kennedy, R. P. (2015). Expanding the conversation: Multiplier effects from a deliberative field experiment. *Political Communication* 32 (4), 552–573.

MacKenzie, M. K., & Warren, M. E. (2012). Two trust-based uses of minipublics in democratic systems. In J. Parkinson, J. Mansbridge, J. Parkinson, & J. Mansbridge (eds), *Deliberative Systems*, 95–124. Cambridge: Cambridge University Press.

Mansbridge, J. (1999). Everyday talk in the deliberative system. In S. Macedo (ed.), *Practical and Professional Ethics Series. Deliberative Politics: Essays on Democracy and Disagreement*, 211–242. New York: Oxford University Press.

Már, K., & Gastil, J. (2020). Tracing the boundaries of motivated reasoning: How deliberative minipublics can improve voter knowledge. *Political Psychology.* Advance online publication.

Már, K., & Gastil, J. (2021). Do voters trust deliberative minipublics? Examining the origins and impact of legitimacy perceptions for the citizens' initiative review. *Political Behavior* 1–20.

OECD (2020). *Innovative Citizen Participation and New Democratic Institutions Catching the Deliberative Wave.* Paris: OECD Publishing.

Paulis, E., Pilet, J.-B., Panel, S., Vittori, D., & Close, C. (2021). The POLITICIZE dataset: an inventory of deliberative mini-publics (DMPs) in Europe. *European Political Science* 20, 521–542. Advance online publication.

Pilet, J.-B., Bol, D., Vittori, D. & Paulis, E. (2022). Public support for deliberative citizens' assemblies selected through sortition: Evidence from 15 countries. *European Journal of Political Research.*

Pow, J. (2021). Mini-publics and the wider public: The perceived legitimacy of randomly selecting citizen representatives. *Representation*, 1–20.

Pow, J., van Dijk, L., & Marien, S. (2020). It's not just the taking part that counts: 'Like Me' perceptions connect the wider public to minipublics. *Journal of Deliberative Democracy* 16 (2), 43–55.

Rummens, S. (2016). Legitimacy without visibility? On the role of mini-publics in the democratic system. In M. Reuchamps (ed.), *ECPR – Studies in European Political Science. Constitutional Deliberative Democracy in Europe*, 129–146. Colchester: ECPR Press.

Setälä, M. (2017). Connecting deliberative mini-publics to representative decision making. *European Journal of Political Research* 56 (4), 846–863.

Setälä, M., Christensen, H. S., Leino, M., Strandberg, K., Bäck, M., & Jäske, M. (2020). Deliberative mini-publics facilitating voter knowledge and judgement: Experience from a Finnish local referendum. *Representation*, 1–19.

Spada, P., & Ryan, M. (2017). The failure to examine failures in democratic innovation. *Political Science & Politics* 50 (3), 772–778.

Suiter, J., Muradova, L., Gastil, J., & Farrell, D. M. (2020). Scaling up deliberation: Testing the potential of mini-publics to enhance the deliberative capacity of citizens. *Swiss Political Science Review* 26 (3), 253–272.

Van der Does, R., & Jacquet, V. (2021). Small-scale deliberation and mass democracy: A systematic review of the spillover effects of deliberative minipublics. *Political Studies* 1–20.

Van Dijk L. & Lefevere, J. (2022) Can the Use of Minipublics Backfire? Examining How Policy Adoption Shapes the Effect of Minipublics on Political Support among the General Public. European Journal of Political Research, 1–21.

Vetter, A., Geyer, S., & Eith, U. (2015). Die wahrgenommenen Wirkungen von Bürgerbeteiligung. In Baden-Württemberg Stiftung (ed.), *Demokratie-Monitoring Baden-Württemberg 2013/2014*, 223–342. Wiesbaden: Springer Fachmedien Wiesbaden.

Werner, H., & Marien, S. (2022). Process vs. outcome? How to evaluate the effects of participatory processes on legitimacy perceptions. *British Journal of Political Science* 52 (1), 429–436.

Elisa Minsart and Vincent Jacquet

21 The impact of citizens' assemblies on policymaking: Approaches and methods

Abstract: The chapter aims to contribute to the debate on citizens' assemblies' impacts on the policymaking process. It reviews the different ways to envision this impact by distinguishing three ways to conceptualize and measure it: (1) congruence between the recommendation and public decisions, (2) consideration in the policymaking process, and (3) structural changes. The chapter concludes by discussing the remaining points of attention for future research on the matter. It highlights the need for a multidimensional approach of the notion of impact, for a more complex vision of public action when questioning the impact, and for more comparative analyses to understand the explanatory factors of such impacts.

Keywords: citizens' assemblies, impacts, influence, policy-making, political uptake, public action

21.1 Introduction

"What will come out of this convention, I pledge, will be submitted without filters either to the vote of Parliament, or to a referendum, or to direct regulatory applications" (Macron 2019: 9, our translation). These words of President Emmanuel Macron, pronounced during the inaugural session of the Citizens' Climate Convention in France, had not gone unnoticed. And yet, a few months later, the optimism of the beginning seemed far behind. At the closing session of the Convention, participants gave a score of 3.3 out of 10 to the government's consideration of their recommendations (Barroux and Garric 2021). "From the convention to the citizen's disappointment" (Rosy 2021, our translation), "Citizens' Convention for the climate: a concrete betrayal" (Pascal-Moussellard 2021, our translation), the disappointment of the citizens drawn by lot to participate in the experiment seems great. Voices are raised: the citizens' assembly is denounced as being a form of tokenism.

While citizens' assemblies (CA) have become particularly common in recent years, the question of their broader impact on the policymaking process seems unclear. The establishment of these assemblies has long been justified by their intrinsic qualities, namely their capacity to create a space for free exchanges of opinion between "ordinary" citizens selected by lot (Setälä 2014). Their educative effects on participants have also been a source of justification, being seen as mechanisms that would improve citizenship (citizens having better issue knowledge, better civic skills, etc.) (Michels 2011). Their ability to have a broader impact on the decision-making process is also a central

Elisa Minsart: Université de Namur, Belgium; **Vincent Jacquet:** Université de Namur, Belgium.

∂ Open Access. © 2023 the author(s), published by De Gruyter. (cc) BY-NC-ND This work is licensed under the Creative Commons Attribution-NonCommercial-NoDerivatives 4.0 International License. https://doi.org/10.1515/9783110758269-023

objective for the advocates of such mechanisms (Fishkin 2018). However, the experimental nature of many assemblies has kept the focus on their internal design for a long time, leaving aside the question of their wider external effects (Elstub, Ercan and Mendonça 2016).

The place to be given to those mechanisms in the institutional political system also remains open to debate. Some see them as a way "to support our existing system of representative democracy" (Curato et al. 2021: 9) and are then expected to provide input to policymaking by influencing decision-makers directly or indirectly by stimulating deliberation in the wider public debate (before a referendum). Others, on the contrary, conceive CA more as a first step towards more radical democratic reforms. In this line, some argue for a transformation of some existing assemblies composed of elected representatives into CAs (Van Reybrouck 2014; Verret-Hamelin and Vandamme 2022). Landemore (2020) also envisages a completely new political system in which CAs would occupy a central role. Those assemblies would be institutionalized at every level of power and connected to each other to form a network of assemblies shaping what she calls open democracy (Landemore 2020). Although CAs are thus the source of great enthusiasm, the conceptions underlying their promotion can vary considerably (Courant 2021). In this respect, opinions also diverge on the weight to be given to these mechanisms and their recommendations: while some advocate for the recommendations to become binding decisions (Fishkin 2011), others consider them more as mechanisms that can only be consultative given their lack of accountability and an explicit form of authorization by the public, and their risk to bypass the goal of mass participation (Chambers 2009 ; Lafont 2015 ; Landa and Pevnick 2021). In any case, at present, CAs remain purely consultative (Paulis et al. 2021), even in the most institutionalized cases such as the permanent citizen dialogue of the German-speaking community of Belgium (Macq and Jacquet 2021; Niessen and Reuchamps 2022). The question therefore arises as to the weight given to the recommendations and, more broadly, to the CA in the policymaking process, without which the assembly "would be little more than a form of democratic experimentation without practical use" (Caluwaerts and Reuchamps 2016: 15).

Moreover, the issue of CA impact does not only interest democratic theorists. The impression of a lack of impact of those assemblies is one of the main arguments put forward by citizens drawn by lot who refuse to participate (Jacquet 2017: 14). Equally, their establishment and multiplication create expectations among participants, as shown by the public reactions following the Citizens' Climate Convention in France. The risk is then, by multiplying CAs with little impact on the policymaking process, to only reinforce an already existing crisis of confidence of citizens towards the political system (Blondiaux 2007).

The aim of this chapter is therefore to contribute to the reflection on CAs' impacts on the policymaking process. To do so, it starts with questioning the general lack of insight on the subject before presenting a recent conceptualization which could help to structure the debate on the issue. It finally ends with a discussion of the remaining points of attention for future research on the matter.

21.2 A general lack of insight into the impact of citizens' assemblies

Despite a great deal of attention to their subject matter, CAs have so far been mostly studied in terms of their internal design and dynamics. Established to realize the Habermasian ideal of a debate between free and equal citizens where the "force of the better argument" would prevail, the question has arisen as to how to ensure a good deliberative quality within these assemblies composed of "ordinary" citizens (Dryzek et al. 2019). It is also the capacity of these assemblies to transform the participants selected by lot that has been discussed at length, with research having succeeded in showing a transformation of preferences (Fishkin and Luskin 2005), an improvement in civic capacities (Grönlund, Setälä and Herne 2010) as well as a deepening of knowledge (Caluwaerts and Reuchamps 2014). In recent years, researchers have tried to move from studying CAs as isolated experiments to consider their interactions with the larger political system (Mansbridge et al. 2012), which means moving from a focus on the *internal* design of these assemblies to one on their broader *external* effects (Jacquet and van der Does 2021a; Setälä and Smith 2018).

The question of the impacts of CAs on the policymaking process has been raised by several researchers, often under different terms (Vrydagh and Caluwaerts 2020): political responsiveness, output, fate of proposals, influence, or political uptake. All of them question the fate of the recommendations, but also, and more broadly, of the CAs' impact on the decision-making process. However, the notion remains ambiguous. There is no common definition of what is meant by "impact on the policymaking process". Is there "impact'" when recommendations are translated into public policy? Is there "impact" when the CA succeeds in changing the broader mindset of policymakers on the issue of citizen participation? Does "impact" still mean that the CA has succeeded in influencing the public debate by stimulating it, by indirectly inducing a richer deliberation and exchange of arguments on the issue at stake? The polysemy of the notion and the difficulty in defining its limits seem to be major obstacles to establishing a common analytical framework. The majority of research on the question of the impact of CAs on the decision-making process has indeed very often focused on single case studies. Different types of impacts were highlighted, but the low number of cases systematically studied makes it difficult to get an overview of the potential impacts that an assembly could have on the policymaking process. More comparative studies, such as those conducted by Caluwaerts and Reuchamps (2016) or Dryzek and Tucker (2008), are still needed.

Besides the definition of impact, it is also the methodological challenge of measuring impact that is raised (Vrydagh 2022). It is often difficult to trace the links of influence between various elements, and the question arises even more when it is a matter of entering the black box of policymaking process. Seeing a recommendation formulated by a CA translated in public policy does not mean *de facto* that without the assembly it would not have been implemented. In the policymaking process, the CA and its recommendations are only input policymaking besides many other groups and factors that can influence policymaking (Vrydagh and Caluwaerts 2020: 2). It is therefore more widely the generalized difficulty in tracing and measuring impact in a process as complex and multi-stakeholder as the policymaking one that prevents the emergence of an overall view on the issue.

Moreover, a majority of studies on the matter seem to have focused on the impacts for specific local issues as explained by Pogrebinschi and Ryan (2018) seeking to shift the focus on impacts to a macro level. Yet, democratic innovations have often been criticized for their "scalability" problem. As Bua observes, the "impact that they can, both practically (Dahl 1989) and legitimately (Parkinson 2006), claim to have on policy-making decreases as scale increases", with the risk of concluding that mechanisms such as CAs could only be introduced for "local issues of little strategic importance" (Bua 2017: 160). While this criticism has been relativized by studies showing the importance of an appropriate institutional design in the "transferability" of these innovations (Pogrebinschi 2013; Smith 2009), the question of scale remains an important issue and there is currently a lack of a systemic approach of CAs' impacts on a larger scale (Pogrebinschi and Ryan 2018).

21.3 A conceptualization

Jacquet and van der Does (2021b) have conceptualized the different ways to think about CAs' impacts on policymaking. A systematic literature review of all research published on the matter before 2019 was conducted. The 131 different studies retained have then been classified and enabled them to identify the three main ways in which the impact on the policymaking process is generally envisioned. This section considers each of these ways of looking at the impact on policymaking in turn (summarized in Table 21.1) and highlights some illustrative studies.

Table 21.1: Conceptualization: three ways to think about CAs' impacts on policymaking (Sources: Jacquet and van der Does 2021b).

Conceptualization of consequences	Underlying research question	Number of publications
Congruence with decisions	Are mini-publics' recommendations translated into policies?	105
Consideration in the policy-making process	Do actors consider the minipublic in the public sphere and in empowered institutions?	128
Structural changes	Does the minipublic change policy practices (in a particular domain)?	16

One of the most obvious impacts on the decision-making process is probably the one on the content of public policies, namely *congruence with decisions*. This impact largely echoes much of the rhetoric of the assembly organizers, presenting the CA to participants as mechanisms whose recommendations aim to be translated into public policy. The "congruency approach" can be defined as "a desk-based research method which assesses impact based on the textual correspondence between a citizen-created idea and public policy documents" (Vrydagh 2022: 66). Although a couple of authors have studied this type of impact, a criticism has recently been made of the general lack of consideration of the pre-existing policy preferences of decision-makers (Vrydagh 2022; Vrydagh and Caluwaerts 2020). The risk is therefore to conclude that a CA has impacted the policymaking process because a recommendation has been translated into a public policy, even though the policymakers were already in favour of this recommendation before the setting up of the CA. The problem of *cherry-picking* (Font et al. 2018) – namely the selection by policymakers of recommendations aligned with their initial preferences – is well known, but seems rarely translated into practice in the methodology used to measure this precise type of impact on the content of public policies (Vrydagh and Caluwaerts 2020).

Taking these criticisms seriously, Vrydagh and Caluwaerts (2020) have developed a model called "The Sequential Impact Matrix (SIM)". Built on the necessity to take into account pre-existing policy preferences of policymakers, this matrix offers a framework which distinguishes between different types of influence that the CA can have on the initial preferences of decision-makers: continuous, enriching, innovating, shifting, or inhibiting influence. This matrix has then been applied to the case of the citizens' panel "Make Your Brussels Mobility" initiated by the Brussels Parliament in Belgium. The policy preferences were formalized as follows: for the initial policy preferences, by analysing the coalition agreement and the electoral programmes of all parties; for the preferences of the CA, on the basis of the recommendations made; and finally, the final preferences were documented by analysing the Brussels Mobility Plan that was adopted by the Brussels government. From this matrix, they showed that while at first sight this assembly seems to have had an important impact on subsequent decisions, with two thirds of the recommendations translated into the mobility plan, in reality, a large number of the recommendations followed were aligned with the initial preferences of the policymakers: almost 50 % of the recommendations had a continuous (limited) influence, while on the other hand only 4.9 % and 2.4 % respectively had an innovative or shifting influence.

A second way of thinking about the impact on the policymaking process is no longer to focus on the *content* of public policies as such but on the broader decision-making *process*, which includes a plurality of actors: elected politicians, civil servants, interest groups, political parties, or even citizens (Popoola 2016). Jacquet and van der Does (2021b) refer to this second aspect as *consideration*, meaning that the CA and/or its recommendations are "considered" at some point in the policymaking, whether in state institutions or in the broader public area. "Considered" has here to be understood as references to the CA in the discourses of the different actors. This way of envisioning "impact" makes particular sense when taking a "systemic approach" to deliberation, considering that CAs' impacts should rather be more indirect (than directly shaping public policy) and promote deliberation in the wider political system (Curato and Böker 2016).

In contrast to congruence with decisions, assessing the consideration of the CA or its recommendations can be done in a very broad way, especially because it includes a large number of spheres and actors in society: documentary analysis of parliamentary debates, analysis of media coverage (press, social networks, etc.), or interviews with policymakers or civil society representatives. The possibilities are numerous when it comes to measuring the extent to which the CA or its recommendations have been discussed, debated in all spheres that are closely or remotely related to the policymaking process.

This kind of impact is well represented in the works of McGovern and Thorne (2021) who have analysed the impact of the Irish Citizens Assembly – of which two weekends were dedicated to the issue of climate change – on climate reporting in the media. They have realized a content analysis of four newspapers before, during, and after the assembly, among which three had a dedicated environmental correspondent following the work of the latter. Concretely, they analysed the impact the assembly had had on climate reporting in the media by focusing on different aspects: (1) the frequency of climate reporting, (2) the framing of climate change issues (positive/negative/neutral), (3) the reliance on evidence (from none to very high), and (4) the themes related to climate change put forward (agriculture, energy, etc.). Findings show that even if the level of climate reporting has varied differently from one newspaper to another, making it difficult to draw conclusions regarding the influence of the CA on the frequency of climate reporting, this reporting had "become more neutral in tone and more divergent in its relationship to evidence after the Irish Citizen's Assembly" (McGovern and Thorne 2021: 228). When it comes to the topic put forward, some themes that were particularly highlighted at the assembly, such as agriculture and energy, were reflected in the media, even if this was not the case for all, such as transportation. This case illustrates therefore the possible influence CAs can have on the policymaking process *beyond* direct influence on public policies, by bringing, for example, a change in the media's framing of the issue at stake. It also highlights the possibility of thinking about impact beyond explicit references to CAs, something that has been very rare in research on impact to date.

The last type of impact is a longer-term one on *structure*, understood as an enduring set of practices and rules that characterize a particular policy domain (Jacquet and van der Does 2021b: 477). "Structural change" then means a more or less significant change in decision-making practices and/or formal rules. This type of impact is certainly the one that has been the least studied, particularly because it requires thinking about impact beyond the fate of the recommendations as such and thus broadening the focus, also with a longer-term approach. As with impact consideration, the methodology used to measure structural change is potentially very broad including surveys, interviews with civil servants or political leaders, and ethnographic observation.

The work carried out by Gourgues, Mazeaud and Nonjon (2021) who have worked on the bureaucratization of participatory democracy in France perfectly illustrates the latter type of impact. The starting point of their study is the observation of a lack of empirical research on what the administration and civil servants actually do when it comes to procedures related to citizen participation, including CAs (Gourgues, Mazeaud and Nonjon 2021). The idea was then to grasp what it means in practical terms for civil servants to implement participatory procedures. This was done by synthesizing a whole series of materials studied between 2000 and 2019 in France, through the combination of several methods: the observation of spaces of socialization and professionalization of public agents working in the field of participation (training, fieldwork, etc.), the realization of qualitative and biographical interviews with these agents, surveys as well as a documentary analysis of job offers intended for public agents and other case studies carried out elsewhere. They argue that while the participatory imperative (i.e. the fact that citizen participation has become, in a context of crisis of the representative system, a form of "norm" or "imperative" that cannot be ignored) has indeed become commonplace in the administrative sphere, it has been "integrated, absorbed, […] diluted" (Gourgues, Mazeaud and Nonjon 2021: 13). There has been a form of bureaucratization of participatory democracy instead of a democratization of bureaucracy, which is particularly materialized by a procedural surplus that has led to "an event-based approach to participation – to the detriment of any political project" (Gourgues, Mazeaud and Nonjon 2021: 13).

21.4 Remaining challenges for future research

This threefold conceptualization of the CA impact raises several challenges and avenues for future research. First of all, it shows that the notion of impact is a multidimensional phenomenon. Limiting oneself to studying the impact by asking whether the recommendations made have become public policy means therefore taking the risk of missing some other impacts on policymaking. Since the policymaking process is highly complex, the impact can be more indirect, for example by influencing the public debate upstream of the policymaking. The impact can also, in an even more indirect way, be revealed years later, by the progressive integration of citizen participation in the very practice of public action. The case of the citizen-led mini-public G1000 in Belgium is, in this respect, particularly emblematic. It did not have any short-term impact on public policy, but has led to important long-term consequences, particularly by impacting politicians' and citizens' conceptions of citizen deliberation (Caluwaerts and Reuchamps 2018). This CA has also been an important source of inspiration for a whole series of subsequent deliberative events in Belgium and beyond. While CAs multiply because they are expected to bring about a democratic renewal (Van Reybrouck 2014), the broader structural impact of CAs seems to be largely overlooked here, underexplored. There is thus a risk – by considering only the short-term impacts (congruence and consideration) – of missing the broader debate about the capacity of these CAs to transform the current governance system towards more citizen participation and deliberation.

This conceptualization and some recent research have also shown the importance of a complex vision of the policymaking process when it comes to questioning the impact of a CA on the latter. The research carried out by Vrydagh and Caluwaerts (2020) highlighted the importance of integrating the initial preferences and positions of policymakers into the reflection process in order to avoid prematurely concluding that there are links of influence when the implementation of a recommendation in public policy can be explained elsewhere than by the holding of the CA in question. When, on the contrary, a recommendation does not seem to lead to a policy change, this does not mean that the assembly was not listened to, heard, or did not influence the decisions in some way: perhaps the recommendation was discussed, but was found to be in conflict with other alternative proposals, or was deemed not feasible or even desirable. Perhaps it did not become public policy as such, but it did help to reorient existing policies. Since the policymaking process is particularly complex and fragmented, the study of the impact of a CA can only be done through a more complex vision of the future of the recommendations, on the one hand, and of the assembly on the other.

Beyond the question of "whether" a CA has had some impacts on the policymaking process, there is also a lack of understanding of the explanatory factors of such potential impacts. This issue is not entirely ignored in the literature. Several factors have already been put forward as likely determinants of the impacts of CA. These include design (Smith 2009), the institutional anchorage and the degree of rupture of the CA with existing power relations (Caluwaerts and Reuchamps 2016), the content of the recommendations and their degree of congruence with existing policies (Font et al. 2018; Michels and Binnema 2018), the link of the assembly with civil society (Pogrebinschi and Ryan 2018) as well as the participatory tradition in which the CA is part of (Nabatchi and Leighninger 2015). However, more comparative studies on the matter are still needed, as the one carried out by Font and al. (2018) explaining the fate of 571 recommendations from participatory processes in three Spanish regions, or Pogrebinschi and Ryan (2018) on the basis of 31 cases of National Public Policy Conferences organized in Brazil. Using a Qualitative Comparative Analysis (QCA) approach, the latter, for example, have explored how different institutional designs – such as the policy area at stake, the degree of influence of the civil society, etc. – have influenced the policy outputs and outcomes, namely the impacts of the CA on the agenda-setting stage for the former and on the decision-making stage for the latter. Their study showed, the positive influence of a massive participation in the process, of a small number of bodies involved, as well as participatory procedures whose central topic concerns redistributive policies. Beyond the necessity of more comparative studies, it is also more detailed process-tracing (Beach and Pedersen 2019) of single case that are needed, to understand the causal mechanisms at stake when a CA has (or not) some impacts on policymaking.

21.5 Conclusion

The purpose of this chapter was to summarize the points of attention that persist in the analysis of the impact of CAs on the decision-making process. The proliferation of CAs in recent years has not been met with unanimous approval. While some see them as a real means of democratizing public action by actively involving citizens in the decision-making process (Landemore 2020), others fear that they are nothing more than a form of manipulation by political elites (Pateman 2012). At present, the question remains open, as the broader impacts of these assemblies on the decision-making process are still relatively unknown. Despite a growing interest in the subject, the question of the impacts of these mechanisms deserves to be asked more than ever, impacts without which they cannot claim to represent a form of democratic renewal. A more complex vision of public action, a broader – and longer term – vision of "potential impacts", comparative analyses of the factors that can explain the impact or lack of impact, … Some avenues have been opened up for future research on the subject.

References

Barroux, R., & Garric, A. (2021). La convention citoyenne pour le climat se sépare sur une note sévère au gouvernement. *Le Monde*, 1 March.

Beach, D., & Pedersen, R. B. (2019). *Process-Tracing Methods: Foundations and Guidelines*. Ann Arbor, MI: University of Michigan Press.

Blondiaux, L. (2007). La démocratie participative, sous conditions et malgré tout: Un plaidoyer paradoxal en faveur de l'innovation démocratique. *Mouvements* 50 (2), 118–129.

Bua, A. (2017). Scale and policy impact in participatory-deliberative democracy: Lessons from a multi-level process. *Public Administration* 95 (1), 160–177.

Caluwaerts, D., & Reuchamps, M. (2014). Does inter-group deliberation foster inter-group appreciation? Evidence from two experiments in Belgium. *Politics* 34 (2), 101–115.

Caluwaerts, D., & Reuchamps, M. (2016). Generating democratic legitimacy through deliberative innovations: The role of embeddedness and disruptiveness. *Representation* 52 (1), 13–27.

Caluwaerts, D., & Reuchamps, M. (2018). *The Legitimacy of Citizen-Led Deliberative Democracy: The G1000 in Belgium*. London: Routledge.

Chambers, S. (2009). Rhetoric and the public sphere: Has deliberative democracy abandoned mass democracy? *Political Theory* 37 (3), 323–350.

Courant, D. (2021). Les démocraties du tirage au sort: Légitimités et modèles institutionnels en conflit. *Raisons politiques* 82 (2), 13–31.

Curato, N., & Böker, M. (2016). Linking mini-publics to the deliberative system: A research agenda. *Policy Sciences* 49 (2), 173–190.

Curato, N., Farrell, D. M., Geissel, B., Grönlund, K., Mockler, P., Pilet, J.-B., Renwick, A., Rose, J., Setälä, M., & Suiter, J. (2021). *Deliberative Mini-Publics: Core Design Features*. Bristol: Bristol University Press.

Dryzek, J. S., Bächtiger, A., Chambers, S., Cohen, J., & Landemore, H. (2019). The crisis of democracy and the science of deliberation. *Science* 363 (6432), 1144–1146.

Dryzek, J. S., & Tucker, A. (2008). Deliberative innovation to different effect: Consensus conferences in Denmark, France, and the United States. *Public Administration* 68 (5), 864–876.

Elstub, S., Ercan, S., & Mendonça, R. F. (2016). Editorial introduction: The fourth generation of deliberative democracy. *Critical Policy Studies* 10 (2), 139–151.

Fishkin, J. (2011). *When the People Speak: Deliberative Democracy and Public Consultation.* Oxford: Oxford University Press.

Fishkin, J. (2018). *Democracy When the People Are Thinking: Revitalizing Our Politics Through Public Deliberation.* Oxford: Oxford University Press.

Fishkin, J. S., & Luskin, R. C. (2005). Experimenting with a democratic ideal: Deliberative polling and public opinion. *Acta politica* 40 (3), 284–298.

Font, J., Smith, G., Galais, C., & Alarcon, P. (2018). Cherry-picking participation: Explaining the fate of proposals from participatory processes. *European Journal of Political Research* 57 (3), 615–636.

Gourgues, G., Mazeaud, A., & Nonjon, M. (2021). From the participatory turn of administrations to the bureaucratisation of participatory democracy: Study based on the French case. *International Review of Administrative Sciences.* 88 (4), 1141–1158.

Grönlund, K., Setälä, M., & Herne, K. (2010). Deliberation and civic virtue: Lessons from a citizen deliberation experiment. *European Political Science Review* 2 (1), 95–117.

Jacquet, V. (2017). Explaining non-participation in deliberative mini-publics. *European Journal of Political Research* 56 (3), 640–659.

Jacquet, V., & van der Does, R. (2021a). The consequences of deliberative minipublics: Systematic overview, conceptual gaps, and new directions. *Representation* 57 (1), 131–141.

Jacquet, V., & van der Does, R. (2021b). Deliberation and policy-making: Three ways to think about minipublics' consequences. *Administration & Society* 53 (3), 468–487.

Lafont, C. (2015). Deliberation, participation, and democratic legitimacy: Should deliberative mini-publics shape public policy? *Journal of Political Philosophy* 23 (1), 40–63.

Landa, D., & Pevnick, R. (2021). Is random selection a cure for the ills of electoral representation? *Journal of Political Philosophy* 29 (1), 46–72.

Landemore, H. (2020). *Open Democracy.* Princeton, NJ: Princeton University Press.

Macq, H., & Jacquet, V. (2021). Institutionalising participatory and deliberative procedures: The origins of the first permanent citizens' assembly. *European Journal of Political Research.* 62 (1), 156–173.

Macron, E. (2019). *Conférence de presse à l'issue du Grand Débat national—Propos liminaire.* https://www.elysee.fr/front/pdf/elysee-module-3079-fr.pdf

Mansbridge, J., Bohman, J., Chambers, S., Christiano, T., Fung, A., Parkinson, J., Thompson, D. F., & Warren, M. E. (2012). A systemic approach to deliberative democracy. In J. Parkinson & J. Mansbridge (eds), *Deliberative Systems*, 1–26. Cambridge: Cambridge University Press.

McGovern, R., & Thorne, P. (2021). Citizens assemble: A study on the impact of climate reporting in the Irish media 'before', 'during' and 'after' the *Citizens' Assembly* on 'how the state can make Ireland a leader in tackling climate change'. *Irish Political Studies* 36 (2), 214–234.

Michels, A. (2011). Innovations in democratic governance: How does citizen participation contribute to a better democracy? *International Review of Administrative Sciences* 77 (2), 275–293.

Michels, A., & Binnema, H. (2018). Deepening and connecting democratic processes. The opportunities and pitfalls of mini-publics in renewing democracy. *Social Sciences* 7 (11), 236.

Nabatchi, T., & Leighninger, M. (2015). *Public Participation for 21st Century Democracy.* Hoboken, NJ: John Wiley & Sons.

Niessen, C., & Reuchamps, M. (2022). Institutionalising citizen deliberation in parliament: The permanent citizens' dialogue in the German-speaking community of Belgium. *Parliamentary Affairs* 75 (1), 135–153.

Pascal-Moussellard, O. (2021). *Convention citoyenne pour le climat : Une trahison en béton.* 2 October. https://www.telerama.fr/debats-reportages/convention-citoyenne-pour-le-climat-une-trahison-en-be-ton-6818844.php

Pateman, C. (2012). Participatory democracy revisited. *Perspectives on Politics* 10 (1), 7–19.

Paulis, E., Pilet, J.-B., Panel, S., Vittori, D., & Close, C. (2021). The POLITICIZE dataset: An inventory of deliberative mini-publics (DMPs) in Europe. *European Political Science* 20 (3), 521–542.

Pogrebinschi, T. (2013). The squared circle of participatory democracy: Scaling up deliberation to the national level. *Critical Policy Studies* 7 (3), 219–241.

Pogrebinschi, T., & Ryan, M. (2018). Moving beyond input legitimacy: When do democratic innovations affect policy making? *European Journal of Political Research* 57 (1), 135–152.

Popoola, O. O. (2016). Actors in decision making and policy process. *Global Journal of Interdisciplinary Social Sciences* 5 (1), 47–51.

Rosy, M. (2021). *De la convention à la déception citoyenne.* 4 June. https://www.lesechos.fr/idees-debats/cercle/opinion-de-la-convention-a-la-deception-citoyenne-1304378

Setälä, M. (2011). The role of deliberative mini-publics in representative democracy: Lessons from the experience of referendums. *Representation* 47 (2), 201–213.

Setälä, M. (2014). *Deliberative Mini-Publics: Involving Citizens in the Democratic Process.* Colchester: ECPR Press.

Setälä, M., & Smith, G. (2018). Mini-publics and deliberative democracy. In *The Oxford Handbook of Deliberative Democracy*, 300–314. Oxford: Oxford University Press.

Smith, G. (2009). *Democratic Innovations: Designing Institutions for Citizen Participation.* Cambridge: Cambridge University Press.

Van Reybrouck, D. (2014). *Contre les élections.* Paris: Editions Actes Sud.

Verret-Hamelin, A., & Vandamme, P.-E. (2022). The green case for a randomly selected chamber. *Contemporary Political Theory* 21 (1), 24–45.

Vrydagh, J. (2022). Measuring the impact of consultative citizen participation: Reviewing the congruency approaches for assessing the uptake of citizen ideas. *Policy Sciences* 55 (1), 65–88.

Vrydagh, J., & Caluwaerts, D. (2020). How do mini-publics affect public policy? Disentangling the influences of a mini-public on public policy using the Sequential Impact Matrix Framework. *Representation* 1–20.

Baogang He

22 Citizens' assemblies in authoritarian regimes: China, Cuba, and Libya

Abstract: China, Cuba, and Libya each face a challenging question of whether each would establish and improve citizens' assemblies (CAs) through the introduction of deliberative and partially empowered institutions and practices. This gives rise to questions of why and how partial empowerment and deliberative mechanisms arise and exist within the confines of an authoritarian regime. This chapter compares the similarities, differences, and variations of CAs in the three authoritarian states, with a particular focus on whether the assemblies are partially empowered or not. It offers three possible explanations of the phenomenon of partial empowerment through investigating the three conditions – leadership, ideology, and market development – that enable or constrain empowerment and deliberation. The conditions that enabled or constrained the incidences of partial empowerment surveyed here hold significance for political emancipation under authoritarian regimes in the 21st century.

Keywords: CAs, authoritarian deliberation, partial empowerment, leadership, ideology, market development, China, Cuba, Libya

22.1 Introduction

China, Cuba, and Libya each face a challenging question of whether each would establish and improve citizens' assemblies (CAs) through the introduction of deliberative and partially empowered institutions and practices. This gives rise to questions of why and how partial empowerment and deliberative mechanisms arise and exist within the confines of an authoritarian regime. The conditions that enabled or constrained the incidences of partial empowerment surveyed here hold significance for political emancipation under authoritarian regimes in the 21st century. Rather than dismissing these developments from an advanced democratic perspective, political theorists have an obligation to study the conditions that enable some progress although within the limit of authoritarianism.

Authoritarian regimes use partial empowerment devices to address the common dilemma they face. Without public participation, authoritarian regimes lack legitimacy and support. But fully empowered CAs would lead to large-scale public demonstrations, democratization, and potentially even revolution. China has managed this dilemma of political participation through partial empowerment. It has transformed CAs from a political learning tool to one that has been partially empowered to solve practical problems. Such a transformation has helped the Chinese Communist Party (CCP) stabilize

Baogang He: Deakin University, Australia.

∂ Open Access. © 2023 the author(s), published by De Gruyter. (cc) BY-NC-ND This work is licensed under the Creative Commons Attribution-NonCommercial-NoDerivatives 4.0 International License. https://doi.org/10.1515/9783110758269-024

the system and avoid regime change, but more importantly, it offered citizens the opportunity to express their voice and have an influence on decision-making. Whereas China developed an advanced form of partial empowerment, Cuba is still undergoing the transformation process, and the personalized authoritarianism under Gaddafi failed to achieve such a transformation at all.

This chapter compares the similarities, differences, and variations of CAs in the three authoritarian states, with a particular focus on whether the assemblies are partially empowered or not. It offers three possible explanations of the phenomenon of partial empowerment through investigating the three conditions – leadership, ideology, and market development – that enable or constrain empowerment and deliberation.

22.2 Comparative framework

China, Cuba, and Libya are each socialist countries, at least constitutionally, and fall into the category of authoritarian regime. There are many differences between them in terms of size, geography, history, culture, and race. A key political difference is that the authoritarianism of China and Cuba is more party-centric than Libya's was under Gaddafi, whose form of authoritarianism was more akin to a personality cult. Gaddafi created an ideology of direct democracy, exercising decentralized and de-institutionalized rule in which all political parties were illegal.

All three countries have much in common with the practice of CAs. Their names or terms vary, for example, the Basic People's Councils (or Committees, Conference, and Congress) in Libya, Popular Councils in Cuba, and local People's Congress in China. They are the lowest level of governments that directly connect to people. Below them, there are various self-governing or social organizations or institutions like neighbourhood associations in Cuba, or villagers' meetings (or assemblies), village councils, and village deliberative forums in China. Despite differences in form, design, and process, however, they each meet a loose and minimal definition of CAs: a place where citizens can (theoretically or practically, formally or informally) influence legislative power, exercise popular control, express their voice, and have an impact on decision-making.

These assemblies capture a large portion of the citizenry and have multiple functions. They are a critical part of socialist or authoritarian political systems, designed to gain legitimacy, discipline citizens, and ensure regime survival and resilience. All three countries CAs also share the same problems (though to different extents), including the dilemmas of symbolism, manipulative tendencies, the powerlessness of citizens, the domination of state power, the constraints of rigid control on civil societies, territorially fragmented and thematically parochial public consultation, and vast political inequality (He and Warren 2011; Chaguaceda, Daubelcour and González 2012).

Each considered using consultative or deliberative devices to defuse the regime change pressure and improve governance and accountability without threatening the position of those in power. Each prioritizes consultative forms of participation at the cost of electoral democracy. However, there were significant differences in how they went about it. Chinese CAs have some partially empowered and deliberative elements or mechanisms. Cuba remains in an early stage of the development and improvement of public consultation. Libya represents the case of failure, the consequences of which led to the February 2011 revolt during the Arab Spring. It is these critical differences that makes a comparative study interesting and appealing.

How do we explain the presence of partial empowerment of CAs in China, its absence in Libya, and a situation in between in Cuba? What are the necessary conditions for authoritarianism to develop empowered and deliberative CAs? Among many others like the American democracy promotion and/or regime change policy, or power struggles, this paper selects and examines three key factors:
- whether political leaders have the capacity and skill to navigate the dilemma of political participation within an authoritarian context;
- whether an authoritarian state has a personalized ideology that disfavours deliberation, or whether it introduces Western theory of deliberative democracy that promotes deliberation;
- whether there exists a strong market economy that leads to partial empowerment practices.

I acknowledge that there are some methodological issues like data access and measure of deliberativeness that arise here (He and Warren 2011). National comparisons can encounter difficulties with relation to distinctive national elements such as size, culture, and history. Moreover, China is so diverse that some local governments still maintain older practices that are closer to those of Cuba and Libya under Gaddafi. And some local governments in Cuba may also develop similar practices to those in China. Nevertheless, comparison is possible and valuable, as will be demonstrated below. This analysis should therefore be understood not as an explicit predictive tool, but more as an illustrative, explanatory device.

22.3 Have citizens' assemblies been partially empowered and deliberative?

23.3.1 China: Partial empowerment

Since the early 2000s, local *urban* communities have developed several new participatory and deliberative institutions and mechanisms. In the Shangcheng district of Hangzhou, a residential meeting is held once a month. Citizen evaluation, first introduced in Shangdong and Shengyang, and then in Shanghai and Hangzhou, is designed to give the ordinary people an opportunity to rate and evaluate the performance of local cadres. Practices and procedures vary; Ya'An city, for example, required at least 40 % of participants being ordinary citizens in 2003 (He 2006). Chinese villages have also developed village representative meetings wherein major decisions on village affairs are discussed, debated, and deliberated by village representatives. In a 2005 survey, 10% of respondents reported that decisions on schools and roads in their villages over the previous three years were decided by an all-villagers' assembly. 20.7% said these decisions had been made by village representative meetings, and 25% by villager leaders. If we combine the first and second responses, roughly 30.7% of respondents confirmed that villagers were able to make decisions through village deliberation. In a 2016 survey, 36% of villagers confirmed that major decisions were determined by all villagers' meetings (or assemblies) or villagers' representative meetings. At the same time, the percentage of villagers who believed major decisions were completely made by the village party secretary or village chief dropped from 25% to 14.3% (He et al., 2021).

Regularized participatory and deliberative institutions and meetings empower citizens with a set of rights and procedures, such as the right of public consultation, the right to equal concern in public, and the right to initiate a meeting and make motions. In 2004 in Wenling, for example, a law was put in place to regularize deliberative institutions. Citizens can use this law to demand that a local official hold a deliberative meeting. National law stipulates that all major public policies that affect the life of all citizens must go through a consultative and deliberative process before being implemented. Citizens are entitled to the right to ask the government to respond to the result of deliberation.

In Zhejiang Province, Zeguo Township has, over the past decade, combined deliberative polling and participatory budgeting to decide its annual budget, developing a kind of deliberative participatory budgeting (He 2019). The application of deliberative polling at Zeguo meets the criteria of public deliberation in terms of representative sampling through random selection, significant changes in opinions, and the creation of public spirit (Fishkin et al. 2010).

As shown above, Chinese citizens at both the individual and community level do achieve a certain degree of empowerment through deliberation, but we should not understand these achievements as fulfilled normative inspiration. Empowerment of this kind, including opportunities for voluntary enrolment, access to relevant information, and freedom of speech during deliberations, does not necessarily afford citizens the significant achievement of their goals (Qin and He 2022).

22.3.2 Cuba: The potential of empowerment and deliberation

In the early 1990s, Popular Councils consisting of municipal representatives as well as citizens and leaders of social organizations in the local area, tried to deal with the daily issues that the Municipal Assemblies had struggled to resolve. However, these Councils did not allow forums for debate concerning decisions; citizens complained about problems rather than engaged in discussions over potential solutions (Libya and China shared the same problem!). Information was often inadequate, and the process was characterized by an overly rigid agenda and the rejection of dissent (Bengelsdorf 1994: 163–165; Rodríguez 2009: 104–113).

In the 1990s the Workshops for the Integral Transformation of the Neighbourhood (TTIB) were launched and expanded into 20 Havana neighbourhoods. They were essentially local, informal, and territorial. They promoted neighbourhood participation and trained women's leaders in developing community projects and participation. They were closely linked to Popular Councils, whose leaders tended to interfere with the TTIB's work (Evenson 2009, and Chaguaceda, Daubelcour and González 2012).

In more recent times new steps have been taken in Cuba to encourage greater public discussion of important issues. In 2007, over three million people participated in more than 215,500 meetings in which they discussed problems relating to numerous aspects of life in Cuba. Social debate was broadening with the publicizing of scholarly debate. There was a greater diversity of opinion in the media, which was backed by President Raúl Castro's call for greater open exchange of opinions. The government implemented several projects, like workshops for community leaders and citizens to foster a culture of participation, enable stronger communication and collective decision-making, and develop skills that would help to undermine hierarchical relations (Evenson 2009).

In 2018, more than seven million Cubans (64% of the population) participated in twelve weeks' public discussion in neighbourhoods and towns across the country on a constitutional proposal process that generated 10,000 proposals. Yet, the process was under state control and citizens lacked influence on the final constitution (Welp 2021: 281). Seven obstacles to empowerment and deliberation were identified: fear of risk, the siege syndrome, monopoly on information, unintelligible ambiguities, extreme puritanism, comprehensive planning, and the language of tasks (cited in Treto 2009:13). Despite these obstacles, neighbourhood assemblies constitute a potential for promoting community participation – if bureaucratic and central practices of the central state level and Party mechanism interference are to be modified (Chaguaceda, Daubelcour and González 2012: 380).

22.3.3 Libya: The absence of deliberative citizens' assemblies

During the 1970s approximately 2,000 Basic People's Councils (or Committees, Conference, or Congress) were established in Libya (Martinez 2007: 21). Citizens were theoretically supposed to exercise political authority, but they often expressed criticism and grievances in a highly scripted form. These organizations functioned to mobilize and educate the population and serve as listening devices through which Gaddafi was able to discover popular sentiments and then himself publicly express popular criticisms of the political system (Vandewalle 2006: 145–146).

There was widespread passivity on the part of the public, however, due to an unfamiliarity with the system, unwillingness to take part in discussions, or a negative attitude towards the Committees. Obeidi surveyed Libyan university students in 2001 and found that only 6% said they regularly attended meetings of their Basic People's Congress. 43% attended occasionally, and 50% never attended. 32% of the survey respondents indicated they felt they could influence decisions taken by a People's Congress while 66% said they could not. When asked if they could change a decision taken by a People's Congress, 74% responded no and 23% responded yes (Obeidi 2001: 142, 156, 160).

22.4 Why is partial empowerment present or absent in different authoritarian regimes?

22.4.1 The role of leadership

China

When China entered the World Trade Organization in 2001, immense investment flowed into China, affecting its utilities sectors. The National Development and Reform Commission (NDRC) developed guidelines about the procedure of public hearings in 2002 and 2008. The 2008 guideline specifies that participation must involve different interest groups to ensure diversity and representativeness, with consumers (i.e., citizens) comprising at least 40% of all participants. Authorities must distribute information relevant to the issue to participants at least 15 days before the event to provide sufficient time for contemplation. Authorities must make public the methods of participant selection at least 30 days before the event to ensure the opportunity for voluntary registration, post selection results, and participant name lists online for reference. Authorities must announce pricing decisions online with detailed feedback for each participant's questions. These procedures marked a critical difference from Mao's mass line participation as they embody partial empowerment mechanism. Some local leaders even gave their power to make CAs truly consequential in that the result of CAs would be honoured to be adopted by the local governments.

In 2012, the term socialist deliberative (or consultative) democracy was for the first time adopted by the 18th Party Congress. In 2015 the CCP issued a guideline that outlined how to develop deliberative democracy in China. Chinese scholars have likewise studied and promoted Western theories of deliberative democracy.

Nevertheless, Chinese political participation is 公民有序政治参与 (gongmin youxue zhengzhi canyu) – literally, citizen's orderly political participation, and aims to address the dilemma of political participation. The CCP's priority is to improve governance without threatening the domination of CCP rule. In this context, participatory and deliberative forums were promoted as they were much more attractive than taking steps to allow the deepening of civil society organizations.

The CCP has developed and improved its art of ruling and governing method. On the one hand, Chinese leaders encourage citizens to decide on and have input into local matters. This phantom democracy lets people feel that they do impact the decision process. It is the 21st-century form of voluntary servitude in which citizens seem to give their implicit consent and feel comfortable with it. It creates the edifice of free and equal discussion but glosses over issues of manipulation and domination.

On the other hand, the CCP controls the scope and extent of deliberation, and does not allow public deliberation to undermine or weaken political power. Thus, it is a controlled form of political participation. It promotes local deliberative democracy to discipline local officials and tame the exercise of power by local governments at the periphery, but it maintains authoritarian power at the centre. Often it blames local officials for corruption, for problems, for slow development, or poor social service. This is a smart technique to exercise political control. The authoritarian empowerment strategy channels citizens' awakened demand for political power into institutionalized devices and transforms it into orderly political engagement. It acts as a filter that encourages some types of participation and precludes those that the CCP deems too risky. This is consistent with China's long-existing agenda of seeking a substitute for electoral democracy to respond to its growing governance burdens.

Cuba

During the early 2000s, the Bush Administration hoped that the seemingly imminent death of the ill and aging Fidel Castro would release grassroots pressure among Cubans for democratic change. It prepared for a political transition in helping Cubans to conduct free and fair elections. USAID, for example, has funded the Cuba Transition Project since 2002.

Cuba completed a stable, peaceful, and successful succession transition from Fidel Castro to his brother Raúl Castro before the former died, however, thwarting the US plans. Raúl Castro took power in 2006 and consolidated his power in 2008. On 26 July 2007, he launched the national consultation process calling for dialogue, debate, and deliberation and inviting every citizen to discuss the issue of socialism. He said that "We are not going to refuse to listen to anyone's honest opinion, which is so useful and necessary". In December 2007, he emphasized again the need for all party or government leaders to stimulate the broadest debate and consultation among citizens (Treto 2009: 4).

While Raúl Castro launched political initiatives, he also allowed private farmers to lease idle state-owned land in 2008. In April 2011, Raúl promoted the development of private initiative and encouraged foreign investment. A significant move was to introduce a limitation on presidential terms, including his own. In 2018, Miguel Díaz-Canel, a non-Castro family member, took over as President of the Council of State, who implemented a more ambitious economic reform agenda and introduced a large-scale public consultation through popular participation in 2018 as mentioned earlier.

One wonders whether and when Cuba is following the Chinese path to slowly develop partially empowered and deliberative CAs. Without these new citizens' initiatives,

Cuba will not be able to handle the new social conflicts that arise from economic reforms. Doing nothing would run the risk of intensifying public dissatisfaction and fomenting social unrest.

Libya

There was potential for the development of deliberative democracy in Libya in the 2000s. Muammar Gaddafi had met with Western democratic theorists like Robert Putnam, Benjamin Barber, and Anthony Giddens. He asked Joseph Nye how Libya could increase its soft power on the world stage. His discussion with Giddens and Barber was televised in the UK (Human Rights Watch 2006: 4).

Saif al-Islam, Gaddafi's son, had a plan of establishing a Centre for Democracy and Civil Society in Tripoli under the guidance of David Held, using the £1.5 million donated by Saif's Qaddafi International Charity and Development Foundation. The Foundation received 470 complaints and led the way in publicly criticizing the human rights record of the regime within Libya, including calling for greater civil society freedoms. This was largely allowed due to the protection it was afforded given its close connections with the Gaddafi family (Human Rights Watch 2006: 74). Ronald St John (2008: 104), however, doubted the old regime would entertain the slightest thought of significant change to the direct democracy system.

Gaddafi failed to manage the dilemma of political participation. His supposed opening and liberalization of Libya raised democratic expectation to a level he was not prepared to allow. In April and May 2005, Human Rights Watch conducted its first visit to Libya and released its 2006 report. The report noted that Gaddafi and his elite circle seemed to be unwilling to implement genuine reform, especially in the area of free expression and association (Human Rights Watch 2006: 1). Between 2005 and 2008, Human Rights Watch made three more visits to Libya. Their 2008 report stated that Libya had made modest improvements in recent years but pointed out a long list of ongoing problems and serious incidents in which human rights were violated (Human Rights Watch 2008: 1).

If Gaddafi had implemented a large-scale consultative or deliberative democracy experiment like China did, perhaps he would have addressed some practical issues, controlled the level of social conflict, and reduced the scale of popular resistance. This might have helped him to maintain the regime. The failure of the popular committees and councils to respond to the needs of the public, however, and the lack of cohesion that resulted from the extreme decentralization of the committee system, made it more brittle and therefore prone to a violent uprising. As Alison Pargeter (2006:225–6) pointed out in 2006: whilst these endless committees might serve to mop up some of the public sector workforce and to strengthen Qadhafi's hand, they ultimately stand in the way of meaningful reform. This view seems to be supported by Putnam's observations regarding his meeting with Gaddafi. According to Putnam, Gaddafi dismissed his suggestion that civil society could strengthen democratic stability and instead claimed that this would only create social division along tribal lines, which he saw his existing direct relationship with individuals as insuring against.

22.4.2 Ideology

Each of the socialist and authoritarian states appealed to the notion of people or popular sovereignty, and required input from the people, at least rhetorically. However, the personalized ideology downplays the importance of collective leadership and the necessity of communal wisdom, thus making popular sovereignty symbolical. Personalized ideology favours one-way communication from an individual leader to the masses, thus undermining the two-way communication required for public deliberation. It privileges the authority and wisdom of one individual leader, and thus fails to meet the normative condition that public deliberation needs, namely collective reasoning. It prefers coercive governance to deliberative governance. In summary, the abolishing of a cult of personality is the necessary condition for partial empowerment because it removes a key obstacle to meeting the normative requirements of deliberation and empowerment. Below I examine how three cases meets or refuse to meet this normative condition differently.

China

During Mao's time, the mass line emphasized the need for public consultation to give value to the voice of the people in the political process. However, Mao's personalized ideology and his personality cult overrode the consultative process. All public discussions and revolutionary committees were supposed to study his great work (the Little Red Book). In such an ideational condition, there was no genuine deliberation, neither was there partial empowerment.

It was Deng Xiaoping's pragmatism that paved the way for partial empowered process. Former President Jiang Zemin made a theoretical contribution in developing the idea of three representatives, that is, that the CCP should represent all advanced productive forces, and that it should therefore recruit businesspeople to join the Party. This opened the door for the logic of market economics to impact upon empowered deliberation, which will be discussed next. For his part, President Hu Jintao introduced the new idea of scientific development to improve the decision-making process, including consultative and deliberative input. Western deliberative democracy theories were likewise introduced into China and prevailed in domestic academic discourse. Between 2003 and 2017, there were 1,229 academic articles discussing deliberative democracy and citing Western theories of deliberative democracy according to data from the CSSCI. The works of J. Bohman, Habermas, John Dryek, Amy Gutman, and J. Valadez were frequently cited, with citation rankings of 2, 5, 6, 9, and 10 respectively.

Currently, President Xi Jinping has returned to the politics of personalized ideology. Xi Jinping Thought was added into the PRC Constitution in 2018, and numerous study centres on Xi Jinping Thought have been established in recent years. This spread of the personalized ideology is likely to undermine public deliberation. The promotion of correct thinking associated with the official line precludes critical thinking by establishing an appropriate political line of thought that has negative consequences if not followed. This is anathema to the democratic idea of public deliberation, which is rooted in openness, debate, and critique. Ideological control mechanisms clash with the fundamental concept of deliberative democracy.

Cuba

Fidel Castro attempted to develop Fidelismo, an ideology centred around himself (Szulc 2003). However, unlike Mao and Gaddafi, Fidel Castro failed to build a strongly personalized ideology. Cuba's ideology is largely nationalist, radical, and anti-imperialist. It suffered the series crisis after the collapse of the Soviet Union. Raúl Castro, coming from military background, was unable to recover and rebuild a strong ideology.

Around 2007–2008 a national social science conference was proposed to meet Raúl Castro's call for national dialogue. Cuban Academy of Sciences sent a delegation to Australia to visit John Dryzek, the leading deliberative democracy theorist, and consult this author about China's deliberative polling experiment in the 2000s. Carlos Alzugaray Treto, a Cuban diplomat and educator, advocates for the creation of a new form of governance and the broadening of democracy through developing deliberative democracy in Cuba (Treto 2009). His advocacy looks very much like the promotion of deliberative democracy by Li Qunru, the vice President of Central Party School in China.

Libya

Like Mao, Gaddafi wrote his own famous Green Book which was widely distributed. The Green Book outlined a conception of direct democracy. It argued that humans have evolved from absolute kings to elected presidents – who only represent about half the people – to direct democracy for all citizens and stated that his goal was to move Libya towards this third phase (Nye 2007). Gaddafi argued that representative democracy results in a dictatorship of the majority over the minority under the cover of false democracy. Political parties are simply ways to organize those with common interests into a collective force to exercise domination over the rest of the people, so his argument went. The party system is the dictatorship of the modern age and constituted a modern equivalent of the tribal or sectarian system. According to the Green Book, the people were divided into Basic Popular Councils. All public institutions were to be run by People's Committees which would be accountable to the Basic Popular Councils that dictated government policy and supervised its execution.

While the Green Book attempted to address some real problems with representative democracy, the solutions it proposed were seriously flawed. It is never clearly explained how the General People's Congress differs from a parliament in practice, or how the various Secretariats are chosen (presumably not by voting, since that has already been labelled a dictatorship of the majority). It seems to propose a kind of compulsory participation at the grassroots level as the solution to the problems of representative democracy. Citizens were supposed to learn about, rather than engage in real deliberation to address political problems. Under this personalized ideology, there was no hope of developing any kind of empowered or deliberative CAs.

Saif al-Islam, the second son of Gaddafi, who was awarded a PhD degree in 2008 from the London School of Economics, wrote his thesis entitled *The role of civil society in the democratization of global governance institutions: from "soft power" to collective decision-making.* He criticized Libyan democracy for its lack of free press (Barber 2007). He also had plans to introduce deliberative democracy practices, however, he did not have a chance to do so. Even if he had introduced partially empowered CAs, it would have been a case of far too little, far too late.

22.4.3 Market economy

China

In China, private businesses account for 90 % of all companies, generate over 60 % of GDP, and contribute half of the country's total tax revenue. The market economy drives partial empowerment in China via the following mechanisms. First, market development increased social conflict, which in turn lead to the widespread development of public consultations in China in order to ease and manage these conflicts. With a set of rights enjoyed by workers, peasants, and residents, firms and companies, villages, townships, and street-level governments are forced to develop a set of voice mechanisms or public deliberations to address conflictual issues that arise.

Second, market economics and the private sector economically empowers citizens to control their financial life and fate to a much higher degree than was previously the case before reform. In this context, citizens do not have infinite time to debate semantics or abstract concepts in public forums or assemblies; they want to come up with real and tangible solutions to the problems they face. Under such pressure, local governments must ensure that public consultations are meaningful; otherwise, ordinary citizens would not bother to turn up. Smart local governments make public hearings meaningful in that they occasionally follow citizens' suggestions and recommendation.

Third, a modern market economy brings together a diversity of plural interests and groups, thus leading to various criticisms of and resistances to controversial projects like the building of a chemical plant or rubbish dump near residences. To manage these criticisms and resistance, cleaver local governments have started to develop citizens' forums and have even let citizens make decisions on thorny issues.

In summary, the above economic logic has led to a change in the function of CAs and public forums. The political communication between cadres and the citizenry has transformed away from political education toward a model that seeks conflict resolution for economic development purposes. The Chinese approach therefore takes the lead in terms of authoritarian innovation apropos the function of public consultation, followed by Cuba, and with Gaddafi's Libya lagging.

Cuba

Fidel Castro began economic reform in the 1980s but at the same time closed small farmers' markets. While he claimed that peasants were getting too rich too quickly by selling piglets and chickens, the real worry was that he would not be able to maintain effective political control. If peasants gained more economic power and autonomy, they would not bother to attend empty public discussions as their counterparts did in China. In 2006, Fidel Castro handed over power to his brother Raúl who tolerated and encouraged private enterprise. However, it was not until 2021 that President Miguel Díaz-Canel legally allowed private enterprises with up to 100 employees.

The absence of a strong private economy has impacted the function of CAs in Cuba. As long as most citizens rely on the state for their income, they are compelled by the state to attend political studies meetings, and CAs remain a political study tool. The forums for public deliberation do not function as they should because the public participants treat them as an opportunity to complain and to vent their frustration with authorities rather than to discuss how to solve problems. The lack of economic resources at the local level encouraged the public perception that popular grassroots participation in local government had little ability to solve problems. Local delegates felt that they must focus their resources on the agenda prioritized by the central authorities even when that agenda did not address the concerns of their constituents (Rodríguez 2009: 109–110).

Now, economic empowerment has begun, and with the advent of limited economic reform, businesses have more opportunity to engage and participate within Popular Councils and contribute to the dynamics of social debate (Evenson 2009: 100). Whether a more market-based economy will lead to empowerment and deliberative CAs in Cuba remains to be seen, however.

Libya

Gaddafi's Green Book advocated for the abolishing of private retail trade, rent, and wages, criticizing them as forms of exploitation. He likewise forbade ownership of more than one private dwelling, and state-owned people's supermarkets replaced private trade operations in the early 1980s. Gaddafi undertook cautious economic liberalization of Libya in the 1990s, but it was not sufficient to instigate any changes in the political system by the 2000s. Indeed, it mainly served to enhance the wealth of Gaddafi and his family, thereby acting as a mechanism by which the regime has consolidated itself rather than an economic process conducive to the reinforcement of democracy (Martinez 2007: 151).

The 2011 revolution in Libya was triggered by rising food prices, high unemployment, and elites defecting due to frustration with closed, corrupt, and unresponsive political systems. Since 1990, the proportion of the total population of Libyan's aged 15 – 29 had increased by 50 %, and university enrolments had increased tenfold, making it very difficult to create enough jobs to satisfy demand (Goldstone 2011). A lack of basic goods and services exacerbated widespread corruption. The capricious cruelty of the regime broke down trust in the government and trust within society. Gaddafi's efforts to divide and rule by weakening institutions such as the press, bureaucracy, and military led to a lack of social and governmental cohesion (Anderson 2011).

22.5 Conclusion

This chapter has examined the driving forces and conditions for the presence or absence of partially empowered and deliberative CAs in China, Cuba, and Libya. The discussion on incentives and conditions is relevant to the development of CAs in the Western democratic countries. For example, as I argue elsewhere (He 2019), if some townships in the authoritarian state of China can implement such deliberative participatory budgeting, many other local towns or cities in democratizing and well-established democratic countries should also be able to carry out similar experiments. If so, the case of China offers some useful lessons in terms of technical designs and novel solutions to the issues arising from such innovative practices.

China's story demonstrates the formation of a kinder, gentler, and smarter authoritarianism although its future is uncertain, and its normative force is in doubt. It can be called the ideal type of deliberative authoritarianism (He and Warren 2011). It departs from much of the literature on competitive authoritarianism (Levitsky and Way 2002, Diamond 2002), or consultative Leninism (Tsang 2009). This new authoritarian ruling is based on public reasoning, persuasion, and utilizing a diversity of consultative and deliberative devices. It aims to control society and manage and cultivate people through community engagement and political participation. Public deliberation serves a similar function to a fire alarm. It is a critical mechanism of crisis management that is driven by authoritarian leaders to manage democratic pressure.

From the perspective of normal citizens living under authoritarian rule, partial empowerment is better than its total absence. Perhaps, some Western commentators need to revise their simplistic view that authoritarian CAs are completely meaningless, symbolic, and manipulative. A nuanced and balanced analysis reveals important new developments in deliberation and partial empowerment within authoritarian regimes.

Deliberative authoritarianism is an advanced form of authoritarianism. It is the result of a long historical evolution of authoritarianism. Military authoritarianism first developed in Africa and Asia in the early postcolonial decades (1950–1970), followed by bureaucratic authoritarianism in Latin American in the 1980s, and electoral authoritarianism in Asia and elsewhere in the 1990s (Geddes 1999). Deliberative authoritarianism began to develop in the 2000s in China, Vietnam, and Cuba. Unlike military authoritarianism's reliance on naked force, deliberative authoritarianism leans on public opinion to develop its social policies, and public deliberation to deal with local conflicts. Distinct from bureaucratic authoritarianism's dependence on a small circle of professional experts and governmental agencies to run government, deliberative authoritarianism broadens the scope of the polity by involving and mobilizing the citizenry in community building and development. Unlike electoral authoritarianism's deployment of manipulative electoral devices to win elections, deliberative authoritarianism uses instruments like public hearings, deliberative polling, and participatory budgeting to win the trust of citizens. Each of these mechanisms increases the relative legitimacy of the regime.

Deliberative authoritarianism is superior to either personalized, militarized, or bureaucraticized forms of authoritarianism precisely because it allows space for partial empowerment processes and problem-solving mechanisms. Among many other factors, it has partially contributed to authoritarian resilience (Nathan 2003) in China and Cuba. The absence of empowered deliberation, contrarily, was a factor in the collapse of Gaddafi's personalized authoritarian regime in Libya. Nevertheless, it is debatable whether it is better than electoral authoritarianism. Electoral authoritarianism, as the case of Singapore shows, is better than deliberative authoritarianism in terms of representation, empowerment, political competition, and taking people's voice seriously. Moreover, the recent retreat in deliberative and partially empowered practices under Xi Jinping demonstrates the fundamental limits and the difficulties of maintaining the democratic direction of CAs.

References

Anderson, L. (2011). Demystifying the Arab Spring: Parsing the differences between Tunisia, Egypt, and Libya. *Foreign Affairs* 90 (3), 2–7.

Barber, B. (2007). Yes, Saif a Gaddafi. But there is still a real reformer insider. *Guardian*, 13 April. http://www.guardian.co.uk/commentisfree/2011/apr/13/saif-gaddafi-real-reformer-inside.

Bengelsdorf, C. (1994). *The Problem of Democracy in Cuba: Between Vision and Reality*, Oxford: Oxford University Press.

Chaguaceda, A., Daubelcour, D., & González, L. (2012). Community participation in Cuba: Experiences from a Popular Council. *International Journal of Cuban Studies* 4 (3/4), 366–384.

Diamond, L. (2002). Elections without democracy: Thinking about hybrid regimes. *Journal of Democracy* 13 (2), 21–35

Evenson, D. (2009). Opening paths to renewed popular participation. *Latin American Perspectives* 36 (2), 95–103.

Fishkin, J., He, B., Ruskin, B., & Siu, A. (2010). Deliberative democracy in an unlikely place: Deliberative polling in China. *British Journal of Political Science* 40 (2), 435–448.

Geddes, B. (1999). What do we know about democratization after twenty years? *Annual Review of Political Science* 2, 115–144.

Goldstone, J. A. (2011). Understanding the revolutions of 2011: Weakness and resilience in Middle Eastern autocracies. *Foreign Affairs* 90 (3), 8–16.

He, B. (2006). Intra-party democracy: A revisionist perspective from below. In K. E. Broedsgaard & Y. Zheng (eds), *The Chinese Communist Party in Reform*, 192–209. London and New York: Routledge.

He, B. (2019). Deliberative participatory budgeting: A case study of Zeguo Town, China. *Public Administration and Development* 39 (3), 144–153.

He, B., & Warren, M. (2011). Authoritarian deliberation: The deliberative turn in Chinese political development. *Perspectives on Politics* 9 (2), 269–289.

He, B., Huang, Z., & Wu, J. (2021). Village deliberative democracy and village governance in China. In B. He, M. Breen & J. Fishkin (eds), *Deliberative Democracy in Asia*, 19–37. London: Routledge.

Human Rights Watch. (2006). *Words to deed: The urgent need for human rights reform*, Report Vol. 18, No. 1, available online at https://www.hrw.org/reports/2006/libya0106/ (accessed 6 May 2011).

Human Rights Watch. (2008). *Libya: Rights at risk*, available online at http://www.hrw.org/en/reports/2008/09/02/libya-rights-risk (accessed 6 May 2011).

Levitsky, S., & Way, L. A. (2002). The rise of competitive authoritarianism. *Journal of Democracy* 13 (2), 51–65.

Martinez, L. (2007). *The Libyan Paradox* (translated by John King), London: C. Hurst and Co.

Nathan, A. (2003). Authoritarian resilience. *Journal of Democracy* 14, 6–17.

Nye, J. (2007). Tripoli Diarist, *The New Republic*, December 10, http://www.tnr.com/article/tripoli-diarist.

Obeidi, A. (2001). *Political Culture in Libya*. Richmond, Surrey, UK: Curzon.

Pargeter, A. (2006). Libya: Reforming the impossible? *Review of African Political Economy* 33 (108), 219–235.

Putnam, R. D. (2011). With Libya's megalomaniac 'philosopher-king'. *The Wall Street Journal*, 26 February. Available at http://online.wsj.com/article/SB10001424052748703408604576164363053350664.html.

Qin, X., & He, B. (2022). The politics of authoritarian empowerment: Participatory pricing in China. *International Political Science Review* 43 (5), 613–628.

Rodríguez, E. N. (2009). Participation and decision making in local spaces in Cuba: Notes for a debate on the challenges facing popular power after 30 years. *Latin American Perspectives* 36 (2), 104–113.

St John, R. B. (2008). Redefining the Libyan Revolution: The changing ideology of Muammar al-Qaddafi. *The Journal of North African Studies* 13 (1), 91–106.

Szulc, T. (2003). Fidelismo: The unfulfilled ideology. In I. L. Horowitz and J. Suchlicki (eds), *Cuban Communism 1959–2003*, 173–184. London: Routledge.

Treto, C. A. (2009). Continuity and change in Cuba at 50: The revolution at a crossroads. *Latin American Perspectives* 36 (3), 8–26.

Tsang, S. (2009). Consultative Leninism: China's new political framework. *Journal of Contemporary China* 18 (62), 865–880.

Vandewalle, D. (2006). *A History of Modern Libya*. Cambridge: Cambridge University Press.

Welp, Y. (2021). Deliberation in the constitutional reform process: Cuba in comparative context. In B. Hoffmann (ed.), *Social Policies and Institutional Reform in Post-COVID Cuba*, 281–299. Berlin: Verlag Barbara Budrich.

Part 4: **Different perceptions of citizens' assemblies**

David Talukder and Jean-Benoit Pilet

23 Citizens' support for citizens' assemblies

Abstract: In this chapter, David Talukder and Jean-Benoit Pilet analyse support for a greater use of citizens' assemblies among citizens. They combine new analyses of recent comparative survey data with published studies on support in various countries in order to examine how much citizens would like to give a greater role to citizens' assemblies and what are the main characteristics that split citizens in their support for CAs. Their contributions are threefold. First, they show that while CAs might enjoy wide support as additions to representative institutions, they are not seen by the majority of citizens as an institution that could replace assemblies composed of elected politicians. Second, they show that the greatest support for CAs is found among citizens who are politically dissatisfied, who are politically engaged and who trust the political skills of other citizens. Finally, they show that support for CA is context-contingent and is especially dependent on how CAs are institutionalized (composition, prerogatives, …) and on the topics they will be in charge of.

Keywords: democratic innovations, citizens' assemblies, deliberation, democracy; citizens' perception, sortition

23.1 Introduction

During the last decades, citizens' assemblies (CAs) have become widespread, especially in Europe, and to a certain extent in North America and Oceania. In Europe, since 2000, the POLITICIZE dataset lists at least 127 *Deliberative Mini-Public* (DMPs, a generic appellation for citizens' assemblies). CA as an object is often analysed and discussed by scholars, yet little is known regarding support for those types of reforms. Literature on this later topic has however grown significantly over the last decade (Landwehr and Faas 2016; Caluwaerts et al. 2018; Bedock and Pilet 2020, 2021; Gherghina and Geissel 2020; Colm and Elkink 2021). Insights could also be found in the broader literature on citizens' support for different models of democracy, and that covers deliberative democracy as one of the models (Font, Wojcieszak and Navarro 2015; Bengtsson and Christensen 2016; Fernandez-Martinez and Font 2018; Gherghina and Geissel 2019; Goldberg, Wyss, and Bächtiger 2020).

In this chapter, we propose to build upon this consolidating literature and to provide a comprehensive view regarding what we know about citizens' support for CAs. First, relying on empirical data, we describe how widespread citizens' support for instruments of deliberative democracy is. The data show that many citizens tend to be in

David Talukder: Université libre de Bruxelles, Belgium; **Jean-Benoit Pilet:** Université libre de Bruxelles, Belgium.

∂ Open Access. © 2023 the author(s), published by De Gruyter. [cc BY-NC-ND] This work is licensed under the Creative Commons Attribution-NonCommercial-NoDerivatives 4.0 International License. https://doi.org/10.1515/9783110758269-025

favour of those instruments. Nonetheless, a majority of the citizens are against CAs to replace elected politicians. Bearing those elements in mind, we then discuss more specifically what are the factors that could explain citizens' support (or not) for CAs. Indeed, although rather recent, several theories and empirical studies might provide explanatory elements regarding why citizens are in favour or against CAs. More specifically, scholars underline four approaches to better understand citizens' support for CAs: political engagement, political frustration, social trust, and ideology. Finally, going further than those approaches, we discuss the role of general and contingent support for CAs. As recent studies suggest, while analysing political reforms, one should take into account the fact that there might be differences between general support for CAs and support for CAs regarding specific policy issue.

23.2 Do citizens support the organizations of citizens' assemblies?

The first question one might be tempted to ask when it comes to discussing CAs as a new instrument to associate citizens to policymaking could be to know if citizens are willing to have such a reform. More specifically: "Are citizens in favour of the organizations of CAs?" and "How widespread the support for CAs?". In this section, we propose to have a brief look at support for CAs among citizens in general. In order to do so, we rely on data from the EPIS web-based survey coordinated by Damien Bol and André Blais (see Blais et al. 2021), in which 15,406 citizens from 15 European countries[1] were surveyed between 13 March and 2 April 2020. The countries are quite different and cover different types of political systems which allow to draw a general picture of citizens' support toward CAs as a replacement for elected politicians and to identify cross-country variations.

However, one of the common criticisms when it comes to studying citizens' support for CAs is related to the fact that citizens do not necessarily know in detail what CAs are. Indeed, despite the popularity of deliberative democracy in academia and among practitioners it is likely that many citizens have never heard of/never been confronted with an actual CA. In order to take that into account, we relied on a very specific question asked in the EPIS web-based survey which is the following:

> We live in countries in which citizens vote for politicians who then make decisions on various topics. People sometimes talk about the possibility of letting a group of citizens decide instead of politicians. These citizens will be selected by lot within the population and would then gather and deliberate for several days in order to make policy decisions, like politicians do in parliament.

---

1 Austria (976), Belgium (1,845), Denmark (997), Finland (977), France (977), Germany (934), Greece (787), Ireland (989), Italy (990), the Netherlands (973), Norway (992), Portugal (1,003), Spain (991), Sweden (1,001), and the United Kingdom (974). Representative samples of each countries' population were recruited by a polling company (DyNata) based on age, gender, education, and region quotas.

Overall, do you think it is a good idea to let a group of randomly-selected citizens make decisions instead of politicians on a scale going from 0 (very bad idea) to 10 (very good idea)?

The question is rather specific as it allows to measure citizens' perception of deliberative tools after being briefly described to them. The vignette mentions two crucial components of CAs: they are composed of citizens selected by lot, and those citizens gather to deliberate. It does not stress, however, that in most CAs, deliberation starts with an information phase with auditions of experts and various actors affected by the policy issue at stake. Moreover, the formulation of the question asks citizens' perception of letting a group of *randomly-selected* citizens to make decisions *instead of politicians.* As a consequence, the question captures support for the replacement of politicians by citizens as well as support for randomly selected citizens, while in most real-life cases, CAs are formulating policy recommendations and do not take decisions. Nevertheless, data from this survey is the first one to provide a view on support for CAs across a wide range of countries. The graph below shows the distribution of citizens in each country. More specifically citizens are divided into three groups, those who hold a negative view of CAs to replace politicians (answer between 0 and 4), those who are neutral (answer of five) and those who hold a positive view (answer ranging between 6 and 10).

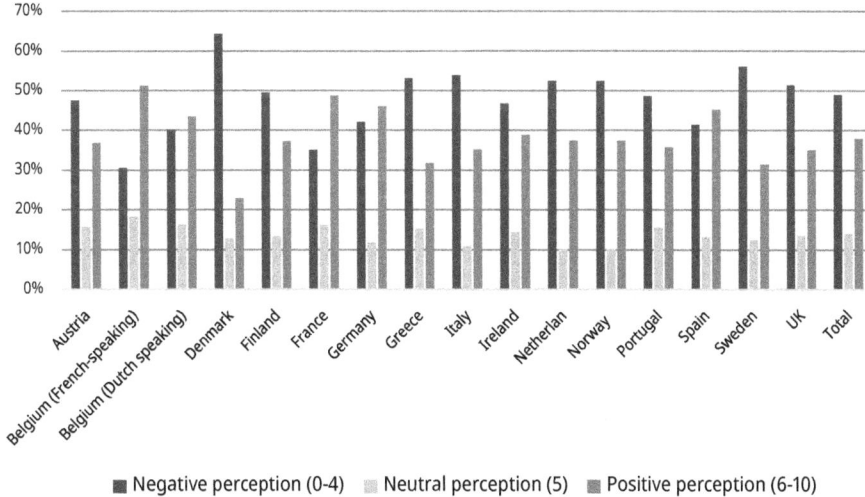

Figure 23.1: Support for the replacement of elected politicians by citizens' assembly

The graph (Figure 23.1) shows that citizens tend to be rather opposed to the replacement of elected politicians by randomly selected CAs. In almost each country, the largest group of respondents are those who think that it is a *very bad idea* to replace elected politicians by randomly selected citizens or those who are neither against nor in favour. The mean of the answer is higher than 5 for only one country (France with a mean of 5.2) and for French-speaking Belgium (with a mean of 5.3).

The descriptive statistics suggest that citizens tend to be rather opposed to the idea of replacing the elected politicians by a body of randomly selected citizens. Those results echo the study of Vandamme and colleagues (2018) in which similar results are found regarding the Belgian case; or Goldberg and Bächtiger's (2022) recent study in Germany. Nonetheless, other studies (Bedock and Pilet 2020; Gherghina and Geissel 2019, 2020; Pilet, Talukder, et al. 2020) regarding the support for *consultative* deliberative mini-publics, show that citizens might be more in favour of initiatives, such as CAs, to complement (rather than replace) the work of elected politicians. Those preliminary elements lead us to investigate the matter further by examining theoretically the different reasons that could explain citizens' support for CAs.

23.3 What factors appear to drive citizens' support for citizens' assemblies?

The question of attributing a greater role for citizens in the policymaking process has been investigated by several scholars and among those studies, some scholars have tried to understand citizens' support for instruments of deliberative democracy (Font, Wojcieszak and Navarro 2015; Bedock and Pilet 2020, 2021; Gherghina and Geissel 2020). More specifically, in this section we focus on the following question: "Why would citizens be in favour of instruments of deliberative democracy instead of the classic representative system?" The existing literature regarding citizens' support for CAs highlights four key factors that are discussed in the following paragraphs: citizens' dissatisfaction, citizens' engagement, social trust, and ideology.

The main approach to explain citizens' support for CAs as well as other forms of democratic innovation (like referendums or participatory budgeting) is related to citizens' dissatisfaction with the political system. The rationale behind this approach is rather simple. Citizens who are dissatisfied with the way politics works in their country would be willing to have reforms of the political systems that enhance the role of citizens in the policymaking process. This argument, first used to explain support for a greater use of referendums (Bowler, Donovan and Karp 2007; Schuck and de Vreese 2015), has been studied regarding support for deliberative democracy and has been referred to the "enraged citizens" hypothesis (Bedock and Pilet 2020).

When it comes to the relationship between political dissatisfaction and support for CAs, studies generally use generic measures of political dissatisfaction such as the classic indicator of "satisfaction with democracy". However other studies suggest that rather than relying on generic support toward the political system, one might go back to Easton's (1965) classical distinction between specific support for actors of the system and diffuse support for the principles of the political system in itself. In this regard, Gherghina and Geissel (2019) found that dissatisfaction with specific institutions such as the government and the parliament are affecting support for citizens as decision-makers in Germany. Nonetheless, they also found an effect regarding dissatisfaction with the political system in general. Alternatively, other scholars rather distinguish between different objects of political support such as the political regime, political institutions, and political actors (see Norris 2011). Bedock and Pilet (2021a) found, for instance, that support for mini-publics among French citizens was strong when support was low for political actors, but was even stronger when support was lower for institutions and the regime.

If the "enraged citizens" hypothesis is often mentioned when one studies support for reforms of the representative system, another line of explanation regarding support for CAs is the so-called "engaged citizens" hypothesis (Schuck and de Vreese 2015). Further than dissatisfaction with politics, this approach argues that citizens' perception of their own characteristics might explain their support for CAs. More specifically, the rationale behind this approach is referring to the fact that citizens who are interested in politics and who feel competent might be more in favour of reforms, such as CAs, that give a direct say to citizens in the policymaking process (Colm and Elkink 2021). In other words, citizens who feel competent in terms of political skills might be more in favour of reforms that could enhance their possibility to have an impact on policymaking processes. These elements connect to traditional explanations of political participation: citizens with more resources and more (perceived) ability to participate support more opportunities to have a say in politics (Almond and Verba 1963; Brady, Verba and Scholzman 1995; Dalton 2004). Several studies have confirmed that it was also playing a role in shaping opinions towards deliberative democracy (Jacobs, Cook and Carpini 2009; Bedock and Pilet 2020; Gherghina and Geissel 2020).

A third group of explanations examined, though to a lesser extent, in the literature relates to factors associated with political under-representation (Gherghina, Mokre and Miscoiu 2021; Talukder and Pilet 2021). The question posed is whether citizens belonging to groups that are politically disadvantaged and less represented in elected institutions such as women, younger citizens, lower educated citizens, or citizens with more precarious jobs would hold different views towards CAs. Two contradictory expectations might be formulated in that respect. On the one hand, citizens from those groups are often underrepresented in parliament. By contrast, CAs are composed to be representative of society in its diversity. Specific attention is therefore paid to the inclusion of citizens from those groups. It might consequently be expected that citizens from groups underrepresented in representative institutions would be more in favour of CAs (Traber et al. 2022). On the other hand, as explained above, political science has widely demonstrated that citizens from those groups tend to participate less in politics (Almond and Verba 1963; Brady Verba and Scholzman 1995). They could therefore be less in favour of CAs as they require greater and wider citizens' participation. The few studies published on the attitudes of citizens from traditionally underrepresented groups provide mixed findings (Talukder and Pilet 2021). Some of these characteristics, and especially being a woman, are indeed associated with greater support for CAs and deliberative instruments. Yet, other characteristics such as lower education or precarious job conditions do not produce the same effects. Those findings seem to validate the idea that underrepresentation in representative institutions could trigger support for CAs as more inclusive alternatives, but this link does not cancel out the negative impact of resources on support for greater citizens' participation.

Another, less common approach has been developed to explain citizens' support for CAs: the role of social trust or the evaluation of the competences of fellow citizens. The logic behind this approach is directly related to the use of sortition and deliberation. Indeed, in the case of an election and a referendum almost all citizens are entitled to participate. By contrast, in CAs, only a handful of unelected citizens are invited to take part (commonly via sortition mechanisms). In most cases, it means that most of the citizens would not directly participate in CAs and would have to delegate their sovereignty completely to other citizens (MacKenzie and Warren 2012). Trusting the political competence of the fellow-citizens therefore becomes more important. Consequently, one might expect citizens who trust their fellow citizens to be more in favour of CAs than those who believe that their fellow citizens are not competent enough to take part in the decision-making process. The role of social trust regarding support for CAs has been emphasized in several studies. It had been earlier underlined in Spain by Adrian del Río and his colleagues (2016) and had been central in the qualitative work of García-Espín and Ganuza (2017) on "participatory sceptics", which demonstrated that a good share of citizens might be opposed towards deliberative democracy because they doubt that most citizens would have the competence to take part. More recently studies on French (Bedock and Pilet 2021a) and Belgian (Talukder and Pilet 2021) citizens showed that trust in fellow-citizens is one, if not the main, explanatory factor regarding support for CAs.

Finally, a last approach to explain citizens' support for CAs might be related to ideology. In particular, a few studies have tried to connect support for CAs with citizens' positions along the left/right cleavage. There is not much research on the positions on other cleavages. The dominant finding is that left-wing citizens are more in favour of reforms that are supportive of a greater citizens' involvement (Bedock and Pilet 2021a; Bengtsson and Mattila 2009; del Río, Navarro and Font 2016; Donovan and Karp 2006; Webb 2013). Right-wing citizens, on the other hand, tend to be more in favour of reforms that involve citizens less and to develop *stealth democratic* attitudes (Hibbing and Theiss-Morse 2002; Webb 2013). Those differences between left-wing and right-wing citizens are empirical regularities. They have not been widely theorized, but might be associated with research showing that left-wing actors tend to have a more inclusive vision of politics, willing to involve all social groups into politics. This has especially been examined regarding political parties in relation to electoral institutions (Bol 2016; Bowler, Donovan and Karp 2006). Several studies (Jacquet, Niessen and Reuchamps 2020; Junius et al. 2020; Rangoni et al. 2021) found that left-wing MPs were more supportive of CAs than right-wing MPs. The same line of reasoning could be expanded to citizens and how they evaluate instruments increasing citizens' participation (see the chapter by Niessen in this *Handbook*). More left-wing citizens would be supportive of CAs based on the idea that they would guarantee the fair inclusion of citizens with various backgrounds to ensure that participants would reflect the diversity of society. Left-wing citizens also tend to be in favour of a redistribution of power within society towards a more egalitarian structure. They support, in particular, the empowerment of citizens from more disadvantaged groups. Empowerment is precisely one of the goals of deliberative democracy (Curato, Hammond and Min 2019; Fishkin 2011; Fung 2006).

23.4 Is it only a matter of process? General vs. contingent support for citizens' assemblies

All the studies that we have discussed above are built on the assumption that citizens would show some kind of generic support (or opposition) to deliberative mini-publics. Yet, over recent years, new research has been published showing that citizens' attitudes towards such form of democratic innovation could also be contingent on how the citizens' assembly is going to be implemented or would perform. First, it has appeared that the institutional characteristics of the CA could influence how citizens evaluate its use. More specifically, research identifies at least two types of institutional characteristics that could have an effect of support for CAs: the composition of CAs and its (non-)binding nature.

The composition of the CAs is an important factor regarding support for this type of democratic innovation. Indeed, as suggested above, CAs by definition imply that a representative subset of the wider population is drawn by lot to deliberate on specific topics (Curato et al. 2021). In other words, it means that each citizen does not have the opportunity to participate. Moreover, the representative relationship in a CA is different from one with elected representatives. In the case of CAs, participants are drawn by lot and are not bonded by a representative relationship in the sense that they are not directly accountable to their fellow citizens (see the chapter by Vandamme in this *Handbook*). Therefore, one might expect that citizens might not be in favour of CAs unless they have good reason to be in favour of CAs such as evaluating negatively political elites. Several empirical studies tend to corroborate this argument. In Northern Ireland, Pow, Van Dijk and Marien (2020) find that the perception of CAs participants as "like them" tend to increase citizens' support for CAs. In Norway, Arnesen and Peters (2018) found something similar through a survey experiment in which they showed that citizens were more inclined to accept a political outcome when the decision-makers were descriptively representative.

The other institutional element that might impact citizens support for CAs can be related to the prerogatives given to the assembly. If the outputs of a CA are binding rather than consultative, then support for CAs might differ. Indeed, several studies (see Pilet, Bedock and Vandamme 2021) emphasize the fact that several groups of citizens are not against complementing the current representative system with democratic innovations but are not necessarily in favour of bypassing elected representatives. In a survey experiment conducted in the United States, Rojon and colleagues (Rojon, Rijken and Klandermans 2019: 219) found that public support for deliberative assemblies was slightly lower for binding models than for advisory ones. Examining support for CAs at the local level in Belgium, Bedock and Pilet (2020: 8) found the same pattern. Almost half of their respondents were in favour of advisory mini-publics, while about 31% wanted citizens selected by lot to form the local council, with all related policy prerogatives. These findings are actually in line with the recommendations in favour of advisory mini-publics made by Curato and colleagues (2021: 113).

Second, recent studies have also shown that some citizens evaluate CAs taking into account their policy outputs. They demonstrate that citizens are not policy blind. They primarily care about the policies that will be implemented, and less about the procedures and institutional arrangements to reach a decision (Arnesen 2017; Esaiasson et al. 2019). Pilet, Bol and colleagues (2020) found, for example, that across 15 Western European countries, support for CAs was higher when citizens knew that their policy preferences were shared by a majority of fellow citizens, and would therefore be likely to be well represented in a CA. By contrast, citizens knowing that they held minority position tended to be less supportive of gathering citizens in CAs when those citizens were likely to hold different policy preferences. Those findings concur with the findings of Beiser-McGrath and colleagues (2022: 548) who studied citizens' process preferences in Germany, Switzerland, and the UK, and concluded that such preferences should be perceived as stable and generic. They are susceptible to change when citizens examine the policy outputs associated to a process like a CA.

These last findings show that citizens' support for deliberative mini-publics as captured in surveys might not translate into the same evaluation when an actual mini-public would be installed. There might be differences between how citizens answer survey questions about the concept of mini-publics, and how they would evaluate an actual mini-public being held in their country, region, or municipality (see the chapter by Goldberg in this *Handbook*). In the latter case, their judgement will also be influenced by the information they would receive on citizens who composed the CA as well as on the content of the policy recommendations formulated. The spill-over effect of CAs on the wider public is often dependent on many factors (see van der Does and Jacquet 2021). For example, several studies underline that non-participants are often ill-informed about mini-publics and that there is a need for greater publicity around mini-publics that are held if we want them to have an influence on the citizenry at large (Boulianne 2018; Michels 2011). As Bächtiger and Goldberg (2020, p. 35) wrote: "In order to be trustworthy (in their views towards mini-publics), citizens must have acquired some knowledge of how mini-publics work internally and why they trump other venues in terms of trustworthy input." In the same logic, Germann and colleagues (2021) have shown that mini-publics could increase legitimacy perceptions, but it also depends on what elected authorities do with recommendations that have emerged from CAs. If elected authorities decide to ignore those recommendations, the boost in perceive legitimacy fades away.

23.5 Conclusion

Citizens' assemblies as an instrument of deliberative democracy have been studied for decades by scholars. Yet, most of the studies were focused on the instrument in itself and little was known regarding citizens' support for CAs. Recently, several researchers tackled this question and the aim of this chapter was to gather and underline the factors that could explain citizens' support for CAs.

First, based on a comparative survey, we have shown that a majority of the citizens were not in favour of replacing elected politicians by CAs. However, a significant part of the citizens tends to be "not opposed/in favour of" such a reform. Citizens tend to be even more in favour of consultative CAs which complement the current decision-making process.

Second, we identified the factors that could drive citizens' support for CAs based on recent empirical studies. According to the literature on the topic, four elements can be underlined when it comes to citizens' support for CAs. The first element is citizens' dissatisfaction with political actors and the political system (which refers to the "enraged" hypothesis). The second element refers to the "engaged" hypothesis and focuses on citizens' personal characteristics such as their resources, their background, and their (perceived ability) to participate. The third element refers to social trust and, more specifically, to citizens' trust in their fellow citizens to be competent enough to participate. Finally, the fourth element refers to citizens' ideology as several empirical studies found that left-wing citizens were more in favour of participatory reforms than right-wing citizens who are more inclined to develop stealth democratic attitudes.

Finally, further than the factors that drive support for CAs in general, we discussed in detail the contextual elements that can impact citizens' support for CAs. Indeed, several studies have shown that the context can matter a lot when it comes to citizens' support for CAs. More specifically, institutional elements as well as the potential performance of CAs are underlined by scholars. The former refers to how CAs might be implemented such as their composition or their prerogatives (consultative/binding). The latter refers to the potential policy outputs of CAs and their congruence with citizens' preferences.

Research has developed significantly across recent years on the topic. Yet, it should still be consolidated. Indeed, our examination shows that research is still very much needed regarding how to explain citizens' support for CAs. We can identify at least two directions for future research. First, most of the literature relies on case studies, looking at citizens' attitudes towards CAs in one country, or examining their impact on political legitimacy in one specific context. They implicitly assume that findings in one country will be exportable to other contexts. It is not self-evident, and several studies show contradictory findings in different countries. Comparative research is therefore more than needed. Second, few studies are examining citizens' attitudes towards deliberative CAs in the context of real mini-publics taking place (see Gastil et al. 2018). Most studies would be experimental (see Boulianne 2018). But research shows that citizens are attentive to the details of the mini-public and to its output when evaluating it. Therefore, we would need more research following citizens in real situations of CAs running.

References

Almond, G., & Verba, S. (1963). *The Civic Culture.* Princeton, NJ: Princeton University Press.

Arnesen, S. (2017). Legitimacy from decision-making influence and outcome favourability: Results from general population survey experiments. *Political Studies* 65 (1_suppl), 146–161.

Arnesen, S., & Peters, Y. (2018). The legitimacy of representation: How descriptive, formal, and responsiveness representation affect the acceptability of political decisions. *Comparative Political Studies* 51 (7), 868–899.

Bächtiger, A., & Goldberg, S. (2020). Towards a more robust, but limited and contingent defence of the political uses of deliberative minipublics. *Journal of Deliberative Democracy* 16 (2).

Bedock, C., & Pilet, J.-B. (2020). Enraged, engaged, or both? A study of the determinants of support for consultative vs. binding mini-publics. *Representation*, 1–21. https://doi.org/10.1080/00344893.2020.1778511

Bedock, C., & Pilet, J.-B. (2021). Who supports citizens selected by lot to be the main policymakers? A study of French citizens. *Government and Opposition* 56 (3), 485–504.

Beiser-McGrath, L. F., Huber, R. A., Bernauer, T., & Koubi, V. (2022). Parliament, people or technocrats? Explaining mass public preferences on delegation of policymaking authority. *Comparative Political Studies*, 55 (4), 527–554.

Bengtsson, Å., & Mattila, M. (2009). Direct democracy and its critics: Support for direct democracy and 'stealth' democracy in Finland. *West European Politics* 32 (5), 1031–1048.

Bengtsson, Å., & Christensen, H. (2016). Ideals and actions: Do citizens' patterns of political participation correspond to their conceptions of democracy? *Government and Opposition* 51 (2), 234–260.

Blais, A., Bol, D., Bowler, S., Farrell, D. M., Fredén, A., Foucault, M., Heisbourg, E., Lachat, R., Lago, I., & Loewen, P. J. (2021). What kind of electoral outcome do people think is good for democracy? *Political Studies*, 00323217211055560.

Bol, D. (2016). Electoral reform, values and party self-interest. *Party Politics* 22 (1), 93–104.

Boulianne, S. (2018). Mini-publics and public opinion: Two survey-based experiments. *Political Studies* 66 (1), 119–136.

Bowler, S., Donovan, T., & Karp, J. A. (2006). Why politicians like electoral institutions: Self-interest, values, or ideology? *The Journal of Politics* 68 (2), 434–446.

Bowler, S., Donovan, T., & Karp, J. A. (2007). Enraged or engaged? Preferences for direct citizen participation in affluent democracies. *Political Research Quarterly* 60 (3), 351–362.

Brady, H. E., Verba, S., & Scholzman, K. L. (1995). Beyond SES: A resource model of political participation. *American Political Science Review* 89 (2), 271–294.

Caluwaerts, D., Biard, B., Jacquet, V., & Reuchamps, M. (2018). What is a good democracy? Citizens' support for new modes of governing. In K. Deschouwer (ed.), *Mind the Gap. Political Participation and Representation in Belgium*, 75–90. Colchester: ECPR Press.

Ceka, B., & Magalhaes, P. C. (2020). Do the rich and the poor have different conceptions of democracy? Socioeconomic status, inequality, and the political status quo. *Comparative Politics* 52 (3), 383–412.

Colm, D. W., & Elkink, J. A. (2021) The dissatisfied and the engaged: citizen support for citizens' assemblies and their willingness to participate, *Irish Political Studies* 36 (4), 647–666.

Curato, N., Farrell, D., Geissel, B., Grönlund, K., Mockler, P., Pilet, J.-B., Renwick, A., Rose, J., Setälä, M., & Suiter, J. (2021). *Deliberative Mini-Publics: Core Design Features.* Bristol: Bristol University Press.

Curato, N., Hammond, M., & Min, J. B. (2019). *Power in Deliberative Democracy.* Cham: Palgrave Macmillan.

Dalton, R. J. (2004). *Democratic Challenges, Democratic Choices: The Erosion of Political Suppori In Advanced Industrial Democracies.* Oxford: Oxford University Press.

del Río, A., Navarro, C. J., & Font, J. (2016). Citizens, politicians and experts in political decision-making: The importance of perceptions of the qualities of political actors. *Revista Española de Investigaciones Sociológicas (REIS)* 154 (1), 83–120.

Donovan, T., & Karp, J. A. (2006). Popular support for direct democracy. *Party Politics* 12 (5), 671–688.

Easton, D. (1965). *A Systems Analysis of Political Life.* New York: John Wiley.

Esaiasson, P., Persson, M., Gilljam, M., & Lindholm, T. (2019). Reconsidering the role of procedures for decision acceptance. *British Journal of Political Science* 49 (1), 291–314.

Fernández-Martínez, J. L., & Font Fábregas, J. (2018). The devil is in the detail: What do citizens mean when they support stealth or participatory democracy? *Politics* 38 (4), 458–479.

Fishkin, J. S. (2011). *When the People Speak: Deliberative Democracy and Public Consultation.* Oxford: Oxford University Press.

Font, J., Wojcieszak, M., & Navarro, C. J. (2015). Participation, representation and expertise: Citizen preferences for political decision-making processes. *Political Studies* 63 (S1), 153–172.

Fung, A. (2006). Varieties of participation in complex governance. *Public Administration Review* 66, 66–75.

García-Espín, P., & Ganuza, E. (2017). Participatory skepticism: Ambivalence and conflict in popular discourses of participatory democracy. *Qualitative Sociology* 40 (4), 425–446.

Gastil, J., Knobloch, K. R., Reedy, J., Henkels, M., & Cramer, K. (2018). Assessing the Electoral Impact of the 2010 Oregon Citizens' Initiative Review. *American Politics Research* 46 (3), 534–563.

Germann, M., Marien, S., & Muradova, L. (2021). Scaling Up? Unpacking the Effect of Deliberative Mini-Publics on Legitimacy Perceptions. https://dx.doi.org/10.2139/ssrn.3954035

Gherghina, S., & Geissel, B. (2019). An alternative to representation: Explaining preferences for citizens as political decision-makers. *Political Studies Review* 17 (3), 224–238.

Gherghina, S., & Geissel, B. (2020). Support for direct and deliberative models of democracy in the UK: understanding the difference. *Political Research Exchange* 2 (1), 1809474.

Gherghina, S., Mokre, M., & Miscoiu, S. (2021). Introduction: Democratic deliberation and under-represented groups. *Political Studies Review* 19 (2), 159–163.

Goldberg, S., & Bächtiger, A. (2022). Catching the 'deliberative wave'? How (disaffected) citizens assess deliberative citizen forums. *British Journal of Political Science* 1–9. doi:10.1017/S0007123422000059

Goldberg, S., Wyss, D., & Bächtiger, A. (2020). Deliberating or thinking (twice) about democratic preferences: What German citizens want from democracy. *Political Studies* 68 (2), 311–331.

Hibbing, J. R., & Theiss-Morse, E. (2002). *Stealth Democracy: Americans' Beliefs About How Government Should Work.* Cambridge: Cambridge University Press.

Jacquet, V., Niessen, C., & Reuchamps, M. (2020). Sortition, its advocates and its critics: An empirical analysis of citizens' and MPs' support for random selection as a democratic reform proposal. *International Political Science Review* 43 (2), 295–316.

Jacobs, L. R., Cook, F. L., & Carpini, M. X. D. (2009). *Talking Together: Public Deliberation and Political Participation in America.* Chicago: University of Chicago Press.

Landwehr, C., & Faas, T. (2016). Who wants democratic innovations, and why? Working Papers 1705. Mainz: Universität Mainz.

Junius, N., Matthieu, J., Caluwaerts, D., & Erzeel, S. (2020). Is it interests, ideas or institutions? Explaining elected representatives' positions toward democratic innovations in 15 European countries. *Frontiers in Political Science* 2, 584439.

MacKenzie, M. K., & Warren, M. E. (2012). Two trust-based uses of minipublics in democratic systems. In J. Parkinson & J. Mansbridge (eds.), *Deliberative Systems: Deliberative Democracy at the Large Scale*, 95–124. Cambridge: Cambridge University Press

Michels, A. (2011). Innovations in democratic governance: How does citizen participation contribute to a better democracy? *International Review of Administrative Sciences* 77 (2), 275–293.

Norris, P. (2011). *Democratic Deficit: Critical Citizens Revisited.* Cambridge: Cambridge University Press.

Pilet, J.-B., Bedock, C., & Vandamme, P.-E. (2021). *Improving, Bypassing or Overcoming Representation?* Lausanne: Frontiers Media SA.

Pilet, J.-B., Bol, D., Paulis, E., Vittori, D., & Panel, S. (2020). *Public Support for Citizens' Assemblies Selected through Sortition: Survey and Experimental Evidence from 15 Countries.*

Pilet, J.-B., Talukder, D., Sanhueza, M. J., & Rangoni, S. (2020). Do citizens perceive elected politicians, experts and citizens as alternative or complementary policy-makers? A study of Belgian citizens. *Frontiers in Political Science* 2, 10. https://doi.org/10.3389/fpos.2020.567297

Pow, J., van Dijk, L., & Marien, S. (2020). It's not just the taking part that counts: 'Like Me' perceptions connect the wider public to minipublics. *Journal of Deliberative Democracy* 16 (2), 43–55.

Rangoni, S., Bedock, C., & Talukder, D. (2021). More competent thus more legitimate? MPs' discourses on deliberative mini-publics. *Acta Politica.* https://doi.org/10.1057/s41269–021–00209–4

Rojon, S., Rijken, A. J., & Klandermans, B. (2019). A survey experiment on citizens' preferences for 'vote-centric' vs.'talk–centric'democratic innovations with advisory vs. binding outcomes. *Politics and Governance* 7 (2), 213–226.

Schuck, A. R. T., & de Vreese, C. H. (2015). Public support for referendums in Europe: A cross-national comparison in 21 countries. *Electoral Studies* 38, 149–158.

Talukder, D., & Pilet, J.-B. (2021). Public support for deliberative democracy. A specific look at the attitudes of citizens from disadvantaged groups. *Innovation: The European Journal of Social Science Research* 34 (5), 656–676.

Traber, D., Hänni, M., Giger, N., & Breunig, C. (2022). Social status, political priorities and unequal representation. *European Journal of Political Research* 61 (2), 351–373.

van der Does, R., & Jacquet, V. (2021). Small-scale deliberation and mass democracy: A systematic review of the spillover effects of deliberative minipublics. *Political Studies*, 00323217211007278.

Vandamme, P.-É., Jacquet, V., Niessen, C., Pitseys, J., & Reuchamps, M. (2018). Intercameral relations in a bicameral elected and sortition legislature. *Politics & Society* 46 (3), 381–400.

Webb, P. (2013). Who is willing to participate? Dissatisfied democrats, stealth democrats and populists in the United Kingdom: Who is willing to participate? *European Journal of Political Research* 52 (6), 747–772.

Christoph Niessen

24 How do elected officials perceive deliberative citizens' assemblies?

Abstract: Despite their increasing use, citizens' assemblies are far from being unanimously supported by elected officials. While citizens' assemblies offer the opportunity to increase the quality and acceptance of decision-making, they may also require to give away power and engage with alternative legitimacies. In light of this ambiguity, the objective of this chapter is to explore how elected officials perceive CAs, i.e. when they support and when they oppose them? The question is addressed from two angles. First, the theoretical bases of why elected officials may (dis)like CAs are considered. Secondly, the results of existing empirical research on the matter are reviewed. These findings are then discussed vis-à-vis their theoretical relevance and the main lessons for the prospects of CAs as a democratic reform proposal are derived.

Keywords: deliberative democracy, democratic innovation, elite attitudes, deliberative wave, citizen deliberation

24.1 Introduction

To regain popular trust after decades of its decline, or to receive diversified and reasoned public feedback on problems of governance that are increasingly complex, there are more and more elected officials around the world associating citizens with decision-making through deliberative citizens' assemblies (CAs) (Česnulaitytė 2020: 69).[1] CAs are gatherings of ordinary citizens that meet to deliberate on a political issue and, after expert hearing and collective discussions, formulate recommendations on how it should be addressed (Ryan and Smith 2014). CAs vary in size and form but should be large enough to realize a certain descriptive representation of society – usually achieved through random selection – and small enough to allow for high quality deliberations (Goodin and Dryzek 2006). While they are usually used for a specific policy problem on an ad hoc basis, some countries have started to use them repeatedly or even institutionalized their use (Farrell, Suiter and Harris 2019; Niessen and Reuchamps 2022).

Christoph Niessen: Leiden University, Netherlands.

1 Between 1986 and 2019, the OECD counted 282 representative deliberative processes in its member countries. On average, there was 1 every year between 1986 and 1990, 2 between 1991 and 1995, 7 between 1996 and 2000, 5 between 2001 and 2005, 6 between 2006 and 2010, 16 between 2011 and 2015, and 25 between 2016 and 2019.

Open Access. © 2023 the author(s), published by De Gruyter. (cc) BY-NC-ND This work is licensed under the Creative Commons Attribution-NonCommercial-NoDerivatives 4.0 International License. https://doi.org/10.1515/9783110758269-026

Despite this increasing trend, CAs are far from being unanimously supported by decision-makers. One reason for this is that decision-makers need to give away a part of their power when initiating a CA. They may indeed like some of the recommendations of CAs but not others – be it for ideological or strategic reasons. Yet, decision-makers need at least to engage with CAs' recommendations, i.e. explain which of them are implemented (or not) and why, and may sometimes even feel obliged to implement them, depending on the expectations raised by citizens (Jacquet 2019). Another reason is that CAs rely on a fundamentally different rationale of composition (descriptive rather than electoral) and decision-making (deliberative rather than adversarial) that can compete with elected officials' own legitimacy (Mansbridge 1983; Vandamme 2018). Notwithstanding these challenges, CAs offer decision-makers the opportunity to increase both the legitimacy and quality of political decisions because they have been inspired by the reasoned exchange of a diverse and independent group of citizens (Bohman 2006; Parkinson 2006).

In light of this ambiguity, one may wonder *how elected officials perceive CAs*, i.e. when they support and when they oppose them?[2] This question is not only of theoretical interest but also touches upon the relevance of CAs as a proposal for democratic reform. Put differently, since elected officials are those who eventually decide on the reform of existing political institutions, their attitude towards CAs and its determinants provide us with further insights into the likelihood and direction of democratic reform processes.

To answer this question, I explore in this chapter the theoretical bases of why elected officials may (dis)like CAs (Section 1) and review the results of existing empirical research on the matter (Section 2). After discussing the findings vis-à-vis their theoretical relevance, I conclude with their main lessons for the prospect of CAs as a democratic reform proposal (Section 3).

24.2 A conceptual framework for understanding elite attitudes towards deliberative citizens' assemblies

As illustrated above, there are good reasons for elected officials to both support and oppose CAs. But how best to understand their preferences? In this section, I develop a conceptual framework with which to categorize elected officials' attitudes towards CAs and review the factors that could influence their position.

At first, one should note that beyond the basic premises of support and opposition, there is a broad continuum of positions that elected officials can adopt vis-à-vis CAs. On

---

2 Which is not to be confused with the question of when elected officials implement mini-publics' recommendations (e.g. Jacquet and Van der Does 2021).

this continuum, *four ideal-typical positions* seem particularly distinctive to me, as summarized in the header of Table 24.1. First, there is the simple negative view. Elected officials who take this position do not want CAs to influence decision-making and prefer decisions to be taken by elected politicians only, with or without consulting stakeholders, and not by lay citizens in any case (Umbers 2021). Secondly, there is the positive view that sees CAs as a complement to traditional representative institutions – but on a consultative level alone. Elected officials supporting this position may support occasional CAs on an *ad hoc* basis, or even go as far as to systematize if not institutionalize CAs. But the main premise is that CAs and elected officials co-exist and complement each other, and that elected officials are those who take the final decision (Rummens 2016). Thirdly, there are those who have an equally positive and complementary view of CAs, but who want to go further and entrust CAs with co-decision-making power – be it through a form of bicameralism (Gastil and Wright 2019) or a mixed setting with both elected and sortitioned members (Suiter, Farrell and Clodagh 2016). Fourthly, there exists the positive view that wants CAs to disrupt and replace traditional representative institutions. Elected officials backing this position aim to replace themselves and build a new political system based on sortition and deliberation – at least for some political functions (Bouricius 2018).

The factors that influence the position of elected officials on this continuum are diverse and have been approached in different ways in the past (Thompson 2019). Drawing on Hall's (1997) seminal framework – prominent in political economy and policy sciences but also used by existing empirical research on elite preferences towards electoral institutions (Bowler, Donovan and Karp 2006) and democratic innovations (Junius et al. 2020) – it seems useful to me to group and understand potential explanatory factors around the three main concepts of *interests*, *ideas* and *institutions*. Each of these "three is" corresponds to a grand theory – rational-choice, interpretivism, and institutionalism – providing different perspectives on why elected officials might support or oppose CAs to different extents. While presented as distinct in the remainder of this section, the factors of these theoretical strands should be seen as complementary and interacting when influencing the position of elected officials. Table 24.1 gives a summary.

A first set of potential factors accounting for elected officials' position towards CAs relates to officials' strategic interest. In terms of political power, the possibility of using a CA to make better policy decisions and increase popular acceptance because they have been inspired by a diverse group of independent citizens can constitute a strong incentive for reform and lead officials to a complementary view of CAs – consultative or co-decisive (Boix 1999). The same can be said about the potential for officials to increase their popularity and votes. However, as said, this comes at the price of accepting some external influence into the decision-making, which may temper officials' enthusiasm and lead them to negative views. The latter might be especially true if they (expect to) disagree with the outcome of a CA, i.e. with the recommendations formulated by citizens (Esaiasson et al. 2019). If, on the contrary, they (expect to) agree with them, giving away power comes at a lower cost and can be expected to lead to positive views.

Table 24.1. Potential factors influencing elected officials' perception of CAs

View	Negative	Positive	
		Complementary	Disruptive
Decision-making power	None	Consultative/ Co-decisive	Solely decisive

Factors:				
Interests	Power	Losing power	Gaining popularity/votes Better decisions/ acceptance	
	Outcome	Disagreeing	Agreeing	
Ideas	Representative legitimacy	Electoral representation Electoral accountability	Both legitimacies	Descriptive representation Justification and rotation
	Capacity	Through selection, professionalizat. and adversarial exchange	Both forms of capacity	Through epistemic diversity, independence and deliberation
	Complementarity	Non-complementary	Complementary	Non-complementary
	Ideology	Conservative	Progressive	
Institutions	Socialization	Long political career	Short/no political career	
	Experience with elected institutions	Positive	Problematic	Negative
	Experience with citizen deliberation	Negative	Positive	

The expectation of (always) agreeing with citizens' recommendations seems to me like the only interest-based factor that could explain why an elected official would adopt a disruptive view of CAs. When accounting solely for its power, an official would indeed never want to give it away altogether.

Another set of factors potentially explaining the extent to which elected officials support or oppose CAs relates to their political ideas. We can distinguish four ideational factors in particular. First, there is the officials' view of representative legitimacy. While that of elected officials relies on electoral representation and accountability, that of CAs relies on descriptive representation, justification to the macro-public, and rotation (Parkinson 2006). Secondly, there is the officials' view of political capacity. That of elected officials comes with the idea of selecting the best, who then professionalize and compete in adversarial majority vs. opposition dynamics, while that of CAs relies on epistemic diversity, independence, and deliberation (Thompson 2008). Depending on how elected officials envision representative legitimacy and political capacity, support-ing only one of the two or both, they may be more or less in favour of CAs. Thirdly, and related to the former, there is the extent to which elected officials see the respective virtues and the functioning of electoral institutions and CAs as complementary or not – regardless of whether they support them (Vandamme et al. 2018). If they do not see them as complementary, they may be more inclined to a negative or a disrup-tive view of CAs – depending on which legitimacies and capacities they see as superior. Fourthly, there is the elected officials' political ideology. While conservative positions can be expected to be associated with negative views of CAs, progressive ones should lead to positive views – complementary or disruptive (Sintomer, Röcke and Herzberg 2016). Beyond individual officials' ideology, it has furthermore been argued that the general political culture in a country could influence officials' openness towards inte-grating (deliberative) citizen participation into decision-making (Dryzek 2012: 170–175).

A third and final set of potential factors accounting for elected officials' position towards CAs are of an institutional nature. The amount of time elected officials have spent working in electoral institutions and the amount of time they still want to may influence them (Weber 1919) – leading to a negative or at most complementary view. Conversely, political newcomers or those who do not want to make a career living from electoral institutions might be more open for reforming them – be it to comple-ment or disrupt them. The exact line between the two, i.e. when career lengths lead to a consultative or a co-decisive view is difficult to draw theoretically. Moreover, officials' actual experience with both elected institutions and citizen deliberation might equally influence their opinions. Those who are disenchanted with the functioning of electoral institutions should be more inclined towards reforming them – a little, if officials see that only a few problems could be solved by complementing existing institutions with CAs; a lot, if they see them as inherently flawed (Niessen et al. 2018). Similarly, a pos-itive past experience with CAs can be expected to open elected officials to their use, while a negative past experience should do the opposite.

24.3 How elected officials perceive deliberative citizens' assemblies: Review of existing research

Now, beyond the theoretical soundness of all these factors, which of them have actually been proven to influence elected officials' positions towards CAs? The objective of this section is to answer this question by reviewing existing empirical research. While the literature on elite preferences towards all kinds of democratic innovations as well as towards the reform of electoral institutions in general is quite broad (e.g. Bowler, Do-novan and Karp 2002, 2006; Hendriks and Lees-Marshment 2019), I limit my review to studies that focus on the attitude of elected officials (legislative or executive) towards CAs.[3]

24.3.1 Quantitative studies

To my knowledge, there are as of today four studies surveying elected officials' opinions on CAs and analysing them quantitively. In their survey of Finnish national members of parliament (MPs), ministers, and party officials in 2018 (n=124), Koskimaa and Rapeli (2020) found that these were quite sceptical of deliberative citizen forums. On a 5-point trust scale (none-little-some-a lot-full), 57.6% had at least some trust in them advising decision-makers on "which problems should be given priority". But only 37.6% had some trust in them advising decision-makers on "how they should make decisions about particular political issues", and trusted them even less to "oblige elected officials to vote in a certain way on specific political issues" (9.8%). The authors did not inquire if certain types of officials were more positive than others, but found much higher approval scores among citizens, which leads us to expect a relationship with the political function.

Similar opinions were found among regional and national Belgian MPs in 2017 (n=124) by Jacquet et al. (2022). While 48.2% of them were rather or fully in favour of the use of "a participatory citizen panel [composed] by random selection" (10.7% remained neutral), only 7.3% rather or fully supported the "institution of a legislative chamber that is composed of randomly selected citizens" (6.6% remained neutral). The "institution of a mixed legislative chamber that is composed of both elected and randomly selected citizens" collected 26.9% of rather or full approval rates (6.4% remained neutral). Like their Finnish colleagues, the authors found much higher approval rates among citizens, pointing *a priori* to a relationship with politicians' profession. However, approval rates did not differ when related to the length of MPs' political careers or their degree of disaffection with electoral institutions. In turn, they did find MPs from leftist parties to be more in favour of sortitioned citizen panels and a mixed chamber.

Besides these two single-country studies, a cross-national survey was conducted from 2009 to 2012 among MPs in 15 European countries by the *PartiRep* consortium (Deschouwer and Depauw 2014). It asked how desirable it was for them to "increase the number of deliberative events, where groups of ordinary citizens debate and decide on particular issues". In her analysis of national MPs from 14 of these countries (n=836–927), Close (2020) found an overall approval rate of 68.6%, which can be deemed high – certainly if one considers that the question comprised the conferral

---

3 Within this limit, I have tried to be as exhaustive as possible and include all studies I could find. However, considering the abundance and steady increase of work on CAs – also beyond the English, French, and German literature I am able to read – I cannot guarantee full exhaustivity.

of some decision-making power. In particular, she found MPs from opposition parties, leftist parties, and identifying as a woman to be more in favour of such deliberative events than others. This was also the case for those who saw citizens as politically competent and with "clear preferences".

The same dataset was analysed by Junius et al. (2020) for both national and regional MPs from all 15 countries (n=1770–2064). In addition to their colleague's findings, they showed that higher approval rates also existed both among MPs who thought that "politicians are out of touch with people's concerns" and among what they call "delegates" (i.e. MPs who thought they "should vote according to the opinion of his/ her voters", as opposed to "according to his/her own opinion'). In turn, they did not find significant differences across electoral systems (proportional vs. non-proportional) and political levels (regional vs. national) or based on MPs' "electoral vulnerability" (their perceived re-election chances), age and seniority.

24.3.2 Qualitative studies

In my review of qualitative research looking into elected officials' perceptions of CAs, I came across ten studies. While five of them looked for typical discourses on CAs among officials and their determinants, five tried to retrace the factors leading officials to implement CAs.

In their interviews with 41 chairs and staff of the United Kingdom House of Commons select committees between 2018 and 2019, Beswick and Elstub (2019) found deliberative mini-publics were appreciated for their capacity to test ideas on citizens, to legitimize the committee and increase its power vis-à-vis the government and to give citizens a better understanding of the functioning of parliament. However, their interviewees also saw deliberative mini-publics as potential competitors and a threat to parliament's own legitimacy; considering electoral representation to be of superior democratic legitimacy, which did not require the contribution of other forms of legitimacy.

Similar statements were collected by Hendriks (2016) between 2012 and 2015 in her interviews with six members of the Public Accounts Committee of the New South Wales Parliament in Australia, as well as by Bottin and Schiffino (2022) in their interviews with nine municipal councillors and advisors on a local deliberative mini-public in Belgium. In particular, Hendriks (2016) showed that a deliberative mini-public can attract more attention and appreciation from MPs when they are "coupled", i.e. when the latter are integrated into the mini-public process. This points to the importance of actual experience with CAs for the opinions of officials. Bottin and Schiffino (2022), in turn, found more positive statements about CAs among female, young, and leftist officials.

Two existing qualitative studies have tried to typologize elite opinions on CAs. In their analysis of interviews with 91 regional and national MPs in Belgium in 2018, Rangoni et al. (2021) identified three ideal-typical discourses on CAs: an elitist discourse, reserving decision-making to elected officials only; a consultative discourse, supporting the complementary and consultative use of CAs; and a power-sharing discourse, which envisions CAs with co-decision-making power. They showed that these discourses are related to MPs' vision of representation and of ordinary citizens' political capacity. In 2016, I found similar views among 28 politicians, associations, and companies on a local mini-public in Belgium (Niessen 2019). As a fourth additional typical position, I identified an expert position requiring public consultation to rely on experts and stakeholders but not on lay citizens. Furthermore, I showed that supportive discourses on CAs came from leftist politicians and those agreeing with the outcome – both of which may potentially be correlated when considering the progressive stances often taken by deliberative mini-publics.

A further strand of qualitative research has shown how the experiments of constitutional or electoral system reform through deliberative mini-publics came about in British Columbia, the Netherlands, Ontario (Fournier et al. 2011), Iceland (Landemore 2015) and Ireland (Farrell et al. 2021). They share the common background of having originated in a climate of political crisis – be it the aftermath of the 2008–2009 bank crisis for the Icelandic and Irish experiences, or the visible lack of fairness and proportionality in existing electoral systems in British Columbia, the Netherlands, and Ontario. Against this backdrop, electoral commitments (in British Columbia, Ontario, and Ireland), the particular motivation of individual politicians (in British Columbia and the Netherlands), as well as the inspiration of one case for others (British Columbia for the Netherlands and Ontario) were found by the respective authors to be triggering factors. The bad experience with a referendum (in the Netherlands) or the fear of its polarizing potential (in Ireland) were also signalled as having contributed to the choice of deliberative approaches. To prevent the processes from immediate politicization, which could have made them fail, the preparation by an all-party committee (in Ontario), by external independent designers (in British Columbia), or an external independent chair (in Ireland) and multi-party compromises (in Iceland) were pointed out as key.

The slightly different experience in East-Belgium, of a CA that has for the first time been associated permanently as an advisory body to a legislative assembly, has attracted equal scholarly attention (Macq and Jacquet 2023; Niessen and Reuchamps 2022). It was also shown to have originated in a climate where elected officials perceived a certain democratic fatigue, leading them to a first test of citizen deliberation, which was successful. Particular to these officials was that the majority of them were not full-time politicians. The possibility to be the first to go further and institute something permanent, presenting themselves as a kind of model, was seen as an additional incentive. Just as with the preceding experiences of electoral and constitutional reform, the avoidance of politicization was key during preparation: through an all-party steering in parliament rather than government, through the neutral facilitation by a group of experienced deliberation academics and activists, and through the joint agreement between parties not to campaign on the project in the upcoming elections.

24.4 A deliberative wave, but a shallow one as yet?

From this review of the literature, it follows that despite the steady increase of deliberative citizens' assemblies (CAs) around the world, they are still received with a certain caution by many elected officials. Approval rates for consultative uses vary, from 30% to 70% depending on the country, with uses envisioning (co-)decision-making power scoring much lower. These rates are reflected in the main political discourses collected as of today, seeing CAs very often as a tool for consultation and information, and often preserving a strong vision of traditional electoral representative democracy.

When going back to our conceptual framework, expecting elected officials' attitudes to vary depending on their interests, ideas, and institutions, we see that the relevance of each of the "three Is" is confirmed by the existing literature. Although not always easy to prove, evidence of interests and power considerations among officials was found in their discourses, portraying CAs amongst others as a means to collect public support. Vote-seeking strategies and majority vs. opposition dynamics were identified by both case studies and quantitative research. Although only partly explored by one qualitative study as of today, officials' opinions on CAs' outcome also seems to influence their opinions.

Elected officials' ideas – be it considerations about representative legitimacy or citizens' political capacity – were omnipresent in their discourses. While it remains difficult to disentangle whether those ideas influence their opinions or whether their opinions (determined by something else – interests, for example) influence their ideas, both seem intimately related. Some of these considerations also touch upon the question of complementarity. Elected officials' political ideology is found in different quantitative and qualitative studies to influence their attitude towards CAs, with greater openness coming on average from leftist politicians. Case studies show, however, that politicians from all types of parties can support CAs if the cross-party context is consensual, even if their degree of enthusiasm varies.

Surprisingly, the investigation of institutional factors did not find supporting evidence of elected officials' attitudes being related to the length of their political career. This means either that other factors, be it rational or ideological ones, outweigh it, or that institutional socialization is very quick and leads politicians swiftly to defend electoral institutions over CAs. Not the length but the way elected officials experienced electoral institutions, however, was shown to matter in most quantitative[4] and case studies – with negative experiences leading to higher support for CAs. The same can be said of their actual experience with CAs, which was shown by qualitative research to be a positive factor.

---

4 In Jacquet et al.'s (2022) study where electoral disenchantment did not appear to make a difference, the number of observations was much lower than in the one by Junius et al. (2020) where it did make a difference.

Despite these very interesting insights, many avenues remain to be explored. Three seem particularly promising to me. First, although explored qualitatively, there is at this stage little quantitative research on the impact that elites' knowledge and experience of CAs has on their opinions. This is understandable, given the recent nature of the phenomenon. But as a potentially strong factor, it should be taken up by future research. Secondly, since the relevance of both interests and ideas for elected officials' opinions on CAs has been proven, it would be interesting to investigate when and what happens when their interests and ideas conflict. Although CAs seem to be more supported by progressive officials, and although they also often come to rather progressive conclusions, it is possible that they come to conclusions that are not shared by all officials who supported the institution. It would be very interesting to explore when this happens and what kind of political dynamics follow. Thirdly, it would be interesting to trace elected officials over the longer term and see if and when some of them become more supportive of or, on the contrary, more opposed to CAs.

Finally, we are left with the question of what these results tell us about the prospects of CAs as a democratic reform proposal? As it stands, the "deliberative wave" we are seeing in the increasing number of CAs around the world (Česnulaitytė 2020) seems steady but rather shallow if we judge it by the actual transformation it brings to elected officials' conceptions of democracy. Many of them see CAs as a device for public consultation but largely stick to traditional conceptions of electoral representative democracy. A more radical reform of decision-making that reconsiders democratic legitimacies and redistributes decision-making power, as envisioned by political theorists and aimed for by activists (Mansbridge et al. 2012; Van Reybrouck 2016), has not yet reached or convinced large numbers of elected officials. Based on the determinants of their opinions found relevant in the present review of existing research, the support for more radical deliberative reforms can be expected to come especially from left and female officials. It can be expected to obtain greater political support in moments of political crisis and when initiated and steered in a non-politicized way. When considering officials' low support rates for more compelling uses of deliberation, certainly when compared to citizens, it may be more likely that radical reform proposals, if they succeed, will emerge bottom-up rather than top-down.

Despite this rather sceptical appraisal of the prospects of CAs as a profound democratic reform proposal, as of today, the "deliberative wave", even if it is shallow as yet, might still have a significant deliberative impact on the broader political system. Through their increasing use, even if it remains consultative, CAs prompt elected officials and the broader public to think not only about the legitimacy of citizen deliberation and the place it should take in the political system, but also about the legitimacy of existing institutions. This already has the potential to contribute now to a deliberative (re)consideration of how political decisions should be taken.

References

Beswick, D., & Elstub, S. (2019). Between diversity, representation and 'best evidence': Rethinking select committee evidence-gathering practices. *Parliamentary Affairs* 72 (4), 945–964.

Bohman, J. (2006). Deliberative democracy and the epistemic benefits of diversity. *A Journal of Social Epistemology* 3 (2), 175–191.

Boix, C. (1999). Setting the rules of the game: the choice of electoral systems in advanced democracies. *American Political Science Review* 93 (3), 609–624.

Bottin, J., & Schiffino, N. (2022). Les élus et la participation citoyenne. *Emulations – Revue de sciences sociales*, doi: 10.14428/emulations.varia.039.

Bouricius, T. (2018). Why hybrid bicameralism is not right for sortition. *Politics & Society* 46 (3), 435–451.

Bowler, S., Donovan, T. & Karp, J. (2002). When might institutions change? Elite support for direct democracy in three nations. *Political Research Quarterly* 55 (4), 731–754.

Bowler, S., Donovan, T. & Karp, J. (2006). Why politicians like electoral institutions: Self-interest, values, or ideology? *Journal of Politics* 68 (2), 434–446.

Česnulaitytė, I. (2020). Key trends. In OECD (ed.) *Innovative Citizen Participation and New Democratic Institutions: Catching the Deliberative Wave.* Paris: OECD Publishing.

Close, C. (2020). Rapport au système représentatif et soutien à la démocratie directe et délibérative. Analyse comparée des attitudes des élus nationaux en Europe. *Participations* 1, 193–222.

Deschouwer, K., & Depauw, S. (eds). (2014). *Representing the People: A Survey among Members of Statewide and Substate Parliaments.* Oxford: Oxford University Press.

Dryzek, J. S. (2012). *Foundations and Frontiers of Deliberative Governance.* Oxford: Oxford University Press.

Esaiasson, P., Persson, M., Gilljam, M., & Lindholm, T. (2019). Reconsidering the role of procedures for decision acceptance. *British Journal of Political Science* 49 (1), 291–314.

Farrell, D. M., Suiter, J., & Harris, C. (2019). 'Systematizing' constitutional deliberation: The 2016–18 Citizens' Assembly in Ireland. *Irish Political Studies* 34 (1), 113–123.

Farrell, D. M., Suiter, J., Harris, C., & Cunningham, K. 2021. Ireland's deliberative mini-publics. In D. M. Farrell & N. Hardiman (eds), *The Oxford Handbook of Irish Politics*, 627–645. Oxford: Oxford University Press.

Fournier, P., van der Kolk, H., Carty, R. K., Blais, A., & Rose, J. (2011). *When Citizens Decide: Lessons from Citizen Assemblies on Electoral Reform.* Oxford, Oxford University Press.

Gastil, J., & Wright, E. O. (eds) (2019). *Legislature by Lot. An Alternative Design for Deliberative Governance.* London and New York: Verso.

Goodin, R. E., & Dryzek, J. S. (2006). Deliberative impacts: The macro-political uptake of mini-publics. *Politics & Society* 34 (2), 219–244.

Hall, P. A. (1997). The role of interests, institutions, and ideas in the comparative political economy of the industrialized nations. In M. I. Lichbach & A. S. Zuckerman (eds), *Comparative Politics: Rationality, Culture, and Structure*, 174–207. Cambridge: Cambridge University Press.

Hendriks, C. M. (2016). Coupling citizens and elites in deliberative systems: The role of institutional design. *European Journal of Political Research* 55 (1), 43–60.

Hendriks, C. M., & Lees-Marshment, J. (2019). Political leaders and public engagement: The hidden world of informal elite–citizen interaction. *Political Studies* 67 (3), 597–617.

Jacquet, V. (2019). The role and the future of deliberative mini-publics: A citizen perspective. *Political Studies* 67 (3), 639–657.

Jacquet, V., & Van der Does, R. (2021). Deliberation and policy-making: Three ways to think about minipublics' consequences. *Administration & Society* 53 (3), 468–487.

Jacquet, V., Niessen, C. & Reuchamps, M. (2022). Sortition, its advocates and its critics: An empirical analysis of citizens' and MPs' support for random selection as a democratic reform proposal. *International Political Science Review* 43 (2), 295–316.

Junius, N., Matthieu, J., Caluwaerts, D. & Erzeel, S. (2020). Is it interests, ideas or institutions? Explaining elected representatives' positions toward democratic innovations in 15 European Countries. *Frontiers in Political Science* 2 (9), 1–14.

Koskimaa, V., & Rapeli, L. (2020). Fit to govern? Comparing citizen and policymaker perceptions of deliberative democratic innovations. *Policy & Politics* 48 (4), 637–652.

Landemore, H. (2015). Inclusive constitution-making: The Icelandic experiment. *Journal of Political Philosophy* 23 (2), 166–191.

Macq, H. & Jacquet, V. 2023. Institutionalising participatory and deliberative procedures: The origins of the first permanent citizens' assembly. *European Journal of Political Research*, 62(1), 156–173.

Mansbridge, J. (1983). *Beyond Adversary Democracy*. Chicago: University of Chicago Press.

Mansbridge, J., Bohman, J., Chambers, S., Christiano, T., Fung, A., Parkinson, J., Thompson, D. F., & Warren, M. E. (2012). A systemic approach to deliberative democracy. In J. Parkinson & J. Mansbridge (eds), *Deliberative Systems: Deliberative Democracy at the Large Scale*, 1–26. Cambridge: Cambridge University Press.

Niessen, C. (2019). When citizen deliberation enters real politics: How politicians and stakeholders envision the place of a deliberative mini-public in political decision-making. *Policy Sciences* 52 (3), 481–503.

Niessen, C. & Reuchamps, M. (2022). Institutionalising citizen deliberation in parliament: The permanent citizens' dialogue in the German-speaking Community of Belgium. *Parliamentary Affairs* 75 (1), 135–153.

Niessen, C., Schiffino, N., Jacquet, V. & Deschamps, L. (2018). Critical candidates: Elite attitudes toward the functioning of representative democracy. In A. Vandeleene, L. De Winter, & P. Baudewyns (eds), *Candidates, Parties and Voters in the Belgian Partitocracy*, 341–364. Basingstoke: Palgrave Macmillan.

Parkinson, J. (2006). *Deliberating in the Real World: Problems of Legitimacy in Deliberative Democracy*. Oxford and New York: Oxford University Press.

Rangoni, S., Bedock, C., & Talukder, D. (2021). More competent thus more legitimate? MPs' discourses on deliberative mini-publics. *Acta Politica*, online first.

Rummens, S. (2016). Legitimacy without visibility? On the role of mini-publics in the democratic system. In M. Reuchamps & J. Suiter (eds), *Constitutional Deliberative Democracy in Europe*, 129–146. Colchester: ECPR Press.

Ryan, M., & Smith, G. (2014). Defining mini-publics. In K. Grönlund, A. Bächtiger, & M. Setälä, M. (eds), *Deliberative Mini-Publics. Involving Citizens in the Democratic Process*, 9–26. Colchester: ECPR Press.

Sintomer, Y., Röcke, A. R. & Herzberg, C. (2016). *Participatory Budgeting in Europe: Democracy and Public Governance*. London, Routledge.

Suiter, J., Farrell, D. M. & Clodagh, H. (2016). The Irish Constitutional Convention: A case of 'high legitimacy'? In M. Reuchamps & J. Suiter (eds.) *Constitutional Deliberative Democracy in Europe*, 33–54. Colchester: ECPR Press.

Thompson, D. (2008). Who should govern who governs? The role of citizens in reforming the electoral system. In M. E. Warren & H. Pearse (eds), *Designing Deliberative Democracy: The British Columbia Citizens' Assembly*, 20–49. Cambridge and New York: Cambridge University Press.

Thompson, N. (2019). The role of elected representatives in democratic innovations. In S. Elstub & O. Escobar (eds), *Handbook of Democratic Innovation and Governance*, 255–268. Cheltenham & Northampton, MA: Edward Elgar Publishing.

Umbers, L. M. (2021). Against lottocracy. *European Journal of Political Theory* 20 (2), 312–334.

Van Reybrouck, D. (2016). *Against Elections. The Case for Democracy*. London: The Bodley Head.

Vandamme, P.-É. (2018). Le tirage au sort est-il compatible avec l'élection? *Revue française de science politique* 68 (5), 873–894.

Vandamme, P.-E., Jacquet, V., Niessen, C., Pitseys, J. & Reuchamps, M. (2018). Intercameral relations in a bicameral elected and sortition legislature. *Politics & Society* 46 (3), 381–400.

Weber, M. (1919). *Politics as a Vocation*. Philadelphia: Fortress.

Jehan Bottin and Alice Mazeaud

25 The deliberative public servants: The roles of public servants in citizens' assemblies

Abstract: For several decades, numerous citizens' assemblies involving citizens in public decision-making have been multiplying at all levels of power. This development of a more participatory, deliberative or collaborative democracy implies the transformation of public administrations and public servants. Various studies show that civil servants are key actors in the organization of participatory processes, in their institutionalization and in their follow-up. However, they remain under-analyzed. In this chapter, we define and analyze more specifically the profile and role of public servants specialized in participation, those we call deliberative public servants. Then, we review the results of research on the relationship between civil servants' perception of participation and the processes they implement. We conclude by identifying research perspectives for the analysis of public officials and CAs.

Keywords: citizens' assemblies, deliberative democracy, public servants, participatory democracy, public participation professionals, public administration, facilitators

25.1 Introduction

For several decades, numerous citizens' assemblies (CAs) involving citizens in public decisions have been multiplying at all levels of power (Smith 2009; Font, della Porta and Sintomer 2014). This irruption of citizens into decision-making processes, encouraged by the critique of the bureaucratic model based on the agents' expertise (Dryzek 1994; Schneider and Ingram 1997; Bherer 2011), is a challenge for public administrations, which are invited to change (Moynihan 2003; Nabatchi 2010). Administrations are pushed to consider citizens, formerly mere beneficiaries of public services, as partners in the construction and implementation of public policies (Kathi and Cooper 2005). For many authors, this change in administrative culture conditions the consideration of participatory products in public action, which today remains limited and context-dependent (Bherer, Dufour and Montambeault 2016; Michels and De Graaf 2017). In the absence of significant changes in administrative practices, participation implemented by a bureaucratic administration may lead to disappointing or even traumatic outcomes for both citizens and public officials as it may create hope of political change that will not be met (King, Feltey and Susel 1998). In other words, and this has long been stressed, the transformation of the administration and the development of a more participatory, deliberative, or collaborative democracy are necessarily linked. The promotion of new and more participatory forms of democracy necessarily leads

Jehan Bottin: Université catholique de Louvain, Belgium; **Alice Mazeaud:** Université de La Rochelle, France.

∂ Open Access. © 2023 the author(s), published by De Gruyter. [CC] [BY-NC-ND] This work is licensed under the Creative Commons Attribution-NonCommercial-NoDerivatives 4.0 International License. https://doi.org/10.1515/9783110758269-027

to a change in the role of public servants, and to the emergence of new public servants' profiles (Blijleven, Hulst and Hendriks 2019). However, it must be noted that while the relationship between administration and participation has long interested specialists in administrative science, it is only belatedly that specialists in participatory democracy have taken an interest in it. Even so, public servants are still under-analyzed in studies on participatory processes, and are almost invisible in studies on CAs, even though they play a key role in their organization.

In the literature on participation, it is in the frame of the work on the professionalization of participation (Bherer, Gauthier and Simard 2017a; Christensen 2018; Mazeaud and Nonjon 2018; Martínez-Palacios 2021) that the first surveys were conducted on the administrative institutionalization of citizen participation and on the public agents specializing in this field were conducted. Indeed, after having noted that the institutionalization of citizen participation had led to the emergence of the figure of the participation professional – defined as "an individual working in the public or the private sector who is paid to design, implement, and/or facilitate participatory forums" (Bherer, Gauthier and Simard 2017a) – a growing number of researchers have focused on studying their profile and their role, first focusing on professionals working outside of administrations, such as consultants and associative actors, and then on public agents. As a sign of a scientific and professional field that has not yet stabilized, these participation professionals go by different names in the literature: "facilitators", "deliberative practitioners" or "public engagement professionals" (Moore 2012; Forester 1999; Escobar 2013; Lee 2015). The terms used to designate them reveal the variety of the processes concerned and the place, central or peripheral, allocated to these professionals in these processes. These terms have been constructed mainly from the observation of participation professionals, but they also make it possible to describe the role and practices of public servants who organize CAs or other deliberative processes, which we refer to in this chapter as "deliberative public servants". In a nutshell, the "deliberative public servants" carry out all the tasks carried out by the participation professionals, but as civil servants hired by an administration. This lack of conceptual distinction between public officials and external consultants in the scientific literature and this diversity of terms used to describe their roles reminds us that participation is still in the process of being institutionalized.

On the basis of these observations, our chapter proceeds in three stages. First, we will review the results of research on the relationship between public servants' perception of participation and the processes they implement. Secondly, we will define and analyze more specifically the profile and role of public agents specialized in participation, those we call deliberative public servants. Finally, as a conclusion, we will identify research perspectives for the analysis of public servants and CAs.

25.2 The perception of citizen participation by public agents and its effects on the systems

For a long time, the literature, particularly in administrative sciences, has emphasized the importance of studying the administration in the development of a more participatory, deliberative, or collaborative public action (King, Feltey and Susel 1998; Yang 2005; Eckerd and Heidelberg 2020; Kübler et al. 2020; Migchelbrink and Van de Walle 2022a, 2022b). Indeed, it is widely accepted "that public administrators' trust in citizens is a relevant and valid construct and a predictor of proactive citizen involvement efforts" (Yang 2005: 1). Also, many quantitative studies have aimed to measure and explain the administrations' attitudes towards participation in various national contexts (Pierre, Røiseland and Gustavsen 2017; Oh, Shin and Park 2022). A recent literature review, based on evidence from 99 peer-reviewed journal articles, allowed the authors to highlight four categories of determinants of agents' attitudes towards participation: personal characteristics, process characteristics, organizational structures and culture and lastly contextual features (Migchelbrink and Van de Walle 2022a). The agents' perceptions of participation are very important because they guide the design of the processes. Given the importance of this role, it is surprising that there is so little data on these agents among the many studies on participation. Surveys show that from the public agents' point of view, the value of citizen participation is less democratic than instrumental, which influences the type of processes public agents carry out carry out (Eckerd and Heidelberg 2020; Värttö 2021). In their study of an American environmental administration, Eckerd and Heidelberg (2020) have shown that the processes implemented are more or less democratic depending on the meaning and value that the agents give to public participation. Their study shows that agents can adopt four types of attitudes towards the public during a participatory process: public as a partner, public as a student, public as an informational source, public as a hurdle. We can also mention the work of Migchelbrink and Van de Walle (2022b) who developed a typology of attitudes and role perceptions of public managers in participatory budgeting. According to this study, agents can adopt a managerial attitude, a city-centred attitude, a technocratic attitude, or a sceptical attitude. They also show how these role perceptions affect their behaviours and decisions in participatory budgeting practices. These results should be linked to recent quantitative studies which, in their analysis of the variables involved in the implementation of mini-publics in Switzerland, have highlighted the important role of the administration and the weight of instrumental issues. This leads them to conclude that the development of these mechanisms reflects a search for governability rather than a search for democratization of decision-making processes (Kübler et al. 2020).

Table 25.1: Agent's attitudes and roles towards participation

Agent's attitudes towards partici-pation	Public managers' attitudes and role perceptions in participatory budgeting	Agent's types of attitudes towards the public during a participatory process
– Personal characteristics – Process characteristics – Organizational structures and culture – Contextual features	– Managerial attitude – City-centred attitude – Technocratic attitude – Sceptical attitude	– Public as a partner – Public as a student – Public as an informational source – Public as a hurdle
Migchelbrink and Van de Walle 2022a	Migchelbrink and Van de Walle 2022b	Eckerd and Heidelberg 2020

25.3 Who are the deliberative public servants?

The research we have just cited highlights the interest of studying the relationship between public agents and citizen participation, but does not address the characteristics of these actors and the concrete role they play. Although deliberative public servants are rarely the focus of systematic investigation, different research shed light on their presence and role in different national contexts: in Brazil (Sa Vilas Boas 2020), in the UK (Cooper and Smith 2012; Chilvers 2013; Escobar 2013 2017), in Finland (Puustinen *et al.*2017), in the United States (Lee 2015), in France (Gourgues 2012; Mazeaud 2012; Mazeaud and Nonjon 2018), in Germany (Cooper and Smith 2012), in Quebec (Bherer, Gauthier and Simard 2017a; McMullin 2020), in Italy (Lewanski and Ravazzi 2017), in Spain (Martínez-Palacios 2021) and in Australia (Christensen 2020). It emerges that the integration of participatory expertise within administrations has taken place according to a double dynamic of diffusion and specialization (Gourgues, Mazeaud and Nonjon 2021) which leads us to distinguish two types of agents: agents whose mission is to design and organize participatory mechanisms, and those who are in charge of a sectoral policy and who are impacted by the implementation of a deliberative process. In the first group the agents are assigned primarily to tasks related to the organization of deliberative processes or to the promotion of these processes within their administration. The second group, which is much more numerous, consists of the agents whose work is affected by the organization of participatory and deliberative processes within their administration, without having organized it themselves. For these agents, participatory products are a new source of information to be integrated (or not) into their daily activities. These agents are impossible to typify as their profiles are so varied. They occupy all administrative functions and are present at all levels of power. However, they are more present in the land use and urban planning sectors. Generally speaking, these agents are required to carry out their tasks by combining the insights of their technical expertise with the lay knowledge of citizen-users. This irruption of lay knowledge in the work of these agents disrupts their work habits and generates new tensions that they have to manage with regard to citizens, with regard to agents of other services (and notably deliberative public servants), and with regard to citizens. In this chapter, we mainly focus on the first category of agents, the participation specialists, whom we call "deliberative public servants".

The existence of deliberative public servants has mainly been identified in local authorities (Mazeaud and Nonjon 2018; Christensen 2020). On the other hand, it is impossible to identify a typical profile of deliberative public servant. While women seem to be more numerous than men in this profession (Mazeaud and Nonjon 2018; Christensen 2020), their personal characteristics are varied (social origin, experience, skills, etc.). It should be noted, however, that several surveys highlight that many of them come from the sectors of community organizing, teaching, popular education, or development (Craig, Mayo and Popple 2011; Mazeaud and Nonjon 2018; Escobar 2019). But it should also be noted that the agents studied in these surveys manage a wide variety of participatory mechanisms: participatory budgeting, local participatory assemblies, project-based consultations, etc.

The lack of a typical profile can be related to the low level of institutionalization of participation within administrations. Administering participation is similar to an "unclear job" (Jeannot 2011); this leads agents to invent their job during the course of their daily activities (Mazeaud 2012; Gourgues 2012). This work mentions that a significant majority of agents share certain common values and conceive their profession as a militant commitment to the dissemination of participatory and deliberative practices within their administration, public institutions, and in society in general. They are overall promoters of democracy, and more specifically, they are often responsible for leading a real "culture change project" (Escobar 2017) within their administration in favor of citizen participation. If this activist commitment can be seen as a cause of their commitment to participation, it can also be understood as the product of the weak institutionalization of participation in administrations (Mazeaud 2012). This absence of a typical profile can also be explained by the weight of national contexts and political-administrative and cultural structures that strongly affect the modalities of the implementation of participation in the administrations. Indeed, on this issue, the rare comparative analyses (Mazeaud and Nonjon 2017; Martinez-Palacios and Mazeaud 2019) are consistent with the elements pointed out in the previously cited literature review (Migchelbrink and Van de Walle 2022a).

Table 25.2: Who are the deliberative public servants?

- Varied characteristics (social origin, experience, skills, etc.) but most of them are women
- Previous experience outside the administration in the sectors of community organizing, teaching, popular education or development
- Manage a wide variety of participatory mechanisms
- Common values and conceive their profession as a militant commitment to the dissemination of participatory and deliberative practices within their administration, public institutions and in society in general.

25.4 What are the deliberative public servants' roles in citizens' assemblies?

Several pieces of work have produced typologies of the roles of deliberative public servants (Bherer, Gauthier and Simard 2017b; Blijleven, Hulst and Hendriks 2019; Sa Vilas Boas 2020). It emerges that these roles depend strongly on the agents' profile, the characteristics of the participatory processes they are in charge of, but also the political-administrative characteristics of the administrations in which they carry out their activities: department dedicated to participation with a strong autonomy, transversal department, technical department, general secretariat in direct link with the elected officials. Indeed, public participation agents are at the heart of a system in tension between citizens, elected officials, consultants, and other public agents. Although employed by public authorities, they must appear as neutral mediators between citizens and public authorities (Escobar 2017). They must also articulate the logic of the participatory process and the bureaucratic functioning. Thus, for example, Agger and Sørensen (2018) identify four roles that managers of collaborative innovation have to play: Pilot, Whip, Culture-maker, Communicator. These roles oscillating between pilot of a process and promoter of a participation culture in their administrations appear more or less clearly in the case studies (Bherer, Gauthier and Simard 2017b; Mazeaud and Nonjon 2018). Escobar (2013) emphasizes that the role of promoter of a culture of participation within the administration leads the other services to develop a love-hate relationship with them: they will sometimes be seen as useful resources to involve citizens in their projects, sometimes as threats to their autonomy and workload.

The tasks of the deliberative public servants are more or less visible according to the stages of the participatory process, and scholars agree that attention must be paid not only to the visible face (frontstage) such as the animation but also to all the less visible moments (backstage) of the deliberative processes (Forester 1999; Escobar 2019). Concerning the less visible tasks, Forester (1999: 8) talks about the "messy, conflicted, dirty-hands experience of practitioners". Before the participatory event, agents play a role in the design of the process. It is in this design activity that the agents' perceptions of participation and their role exert a strong influence. However, agents are not totally free to define the design of the devices; it is most often the product of the relationships they have with elected officials (Røiseland and Vabo 2020) and consultants (Mazeaud and Nonjon 2020). These agents also play a role in the animation of the process. During the process, the activities that these agents carry out can be analyzed as "micropolitical work" of the agents, that is, "the work that facilitators carry out to develop processes that meet participatory standards of inclusion, interaction and impact" (Escobar 2019: 5).

In particular, their work often consists of preventing elected officials from taking up too much space at the expense of citizens during participatory processes (Escobar 2017). They are regularly called upon to facilitate processes, this is defined as "the craft of enabling conversations that are inclusive, meaningful and productive" (Escobar 2011:

178). Although studies have sought to investigate the influence of facilitators on the quality of deliberations and their outputs (e.g., Carcasson and Sprain 2016; Spada and Vreeland 2020), few have undertaken to understand whether the facilitators' status as a public agent changes the quality of facilitation.

Finally, the deliberative public servants play a role after the participatory processes in monitoring the outcomes of participation. In many cases, and in the absence of any rules, monitoring is initiated and carried out by the agents on their own initiative. This research is particularly important since many studies have shown that the clash with the administrative culture can be a hindrance to administrations taking into account the products of participation; these products may be misunderstood by agents or considered incompatible with the organizational culture of their administration (King, Feltey and Susel 1998; Cooper and Smith 2012; Bherer, Dufour and Montambeault 2016). As a result, their role is often to negotiate with other public officials to ensure that public engagement will have an impact on public policy (Blijleven and van Hulst 2021). This direct link that deliberative public servants have with the administration and elected officials is a considerable advantage over private consultants (Escobar 2017). In some situations, the choice of public authorities to outsource the organization of the participatory process is made in order to allow them to avoid political and administrative responsibilities (Wan 2018). Conversely, as participation is institutionalized within their administration, these agents, whose militant commitment is well known, manage to "convert" agents from other departments to participation as the processes are organized (Escobar 2017).

On the one hand, the analysis of the missions carried out by these agents allows us to understand that they play a real political role (Escobar 2019): the agents manage, in their daily practices, the power relationships and the competition between actors that often takes place through anecdotical actions (Morley 2006). From then on, these agents are the real entrepreneurs of the transformation of administrations through participation. On the other hand, studies have shown that the concrete tasks carried out by these agents (monitoring the public, reporting, logistical organization, monitoring, and evaluation) were quite similar to those carried out by other public agents, and as such reveal the process of bureaucratization of participation (Gourgues, Mazeaud and Nonjon 2021).

Table 25.3: What is the deliberative public servants' role in CAs?

Agents' roles in CAs depend on:
– the profile of the agents
– the characteristics of the deliberative process they oversee
– the political-administrative characteristics of the administrations

Their role oscillates between pilot of a process and promoter of a participation culture in their administrations	Before the CA: role in the design and the organization. Their influence is the product of their relationships with elected officials and	As participation is institutionalized within their administration, these agents manage to "convert" agents from other departments to

Table 25.3 *(Continued)*

(Escobar 2013; Bherer, Gauthier and Simard 2017b; Mazeaud and Nonjon 2018).	consultants (Røiseland and Vabo 2020; Mazeaud and Nonjon 2020).	participation as the processes are organized (Escobar 2017).
Agger and Sørensen, (2018) identify four roles that managers of collaborative innovation have to play:	During the CA: "micropolitical work", including facilitation (Escobar 2011 2019).	They play a real political role (Escobar 2019) as they manage, in their daily practices, the power relationships and the competition between actors that often takes place through anecdotical actions (Morley 2006).
Pilot Whip Culture-maker Communicator	After the CA, role in monitoring the outcomes of participation. In the absence of any rules, monitoring is initiated and carried out by the agents on their own initiative. As a result, their role is often to negotiate with other public officials to ensure that public engagement will have an impact on public policy (Blijleven and van Hulst 2021).	They are entrepreneurs of the transformation of administrations through participation. Some tasks carried out by these agents reveal the process of bureaucratization of participation (Gourgues, Mazeaud, Nonjon 2021).

25.5 Conclusions and perspectives for the study of the role of deliberative public servants in citizens' assemblies

Despite the development of a recent literature on the professionals of citizen participation, few researchers have undertaken to study the role of public agents responsible for organizing democratic innovations. Yet the work we have listed in this chapter shows to what extent these under-studied actors are key players in participatory processes. These results show the importance of taking these actors into account in the study of CAs. Indeed, the organization of CAs without the involvement of the administration and a paradigm shift in the way public servants view citizen participation are essential for the long-term institutionalization of CAs. Moreover, the agents' detailed knowledge of the administration is a considerable advantage over private consultants regarding the consideration of the outcomes of participation by public authorities to ensure that CAs have an impact. There is much to be gained from systematically studying the profile and activities of public agents of participation, as well as public agents' perceptions of CAs. In the numerous case studies of CAs, research should take as much care in studying the administrative conditions of their deployment as in studying the deliberative dynamics.

Two perspectives seem to be particularly fruitful in shedding light on the logic of the implementation of CAs and its effects. Firstly, beyond the analysis of the role of public participation agents in the design of mechanisms, and more broadly in the success of mini-publics, it seems necessary to consider the perverse effects of the professionalization and institutionalization of citizen participation. Several investigations have pointed out that the dynamics of institutionalization – the love-hate relationships between actors (Escobar 2013), the struggles of jurisdictions (Mazeaud and Nonjon 2018) – could explain some of their effects. We can mention here the fact that the more they are known and appreciated within their administration, the more the deliberative public servants can be drawn into multiple organization of participatory devices whose quality can only decrease due to a lack of resources (Escobar 2013). We can also mention that the need to be recognized in their administration and the impossibility of controlling their jurisdiction partly explains the tendency to focus attention on the participatory event rather than on the participatory outcome intended to guide a change in public policy (Gourgues, Mazeaud and Nonjon 2021), and thus to feed the phenomenon of proceduralization of participation, (Ganuza and Baiocchi 2012; Lee 2015), which may explain why processes with limited effects continue to multiply.

Secondly, and most importantly, it is essential to question the perception that non-specialist agents have of CAs. Indeed, these agents have often not been involved in the design and implementation of the mechanisms. However, it is these agents in charge of sectoral policies who must concretely integrate CAs outcomes into public policies. Moreover, as we have seen, public participation agents invest a great deal of energy in monitoring participatory outcomes and ensuring that participation has an impact. However, research on local participatory processes has shown that these processes can be difficult for front-line agents (Tawa Lama-Rewal 2019) and technicians because these processes push them to transform their identities and professional practices in order to integrate citizens' opinions (Blondiaux and Michel 2007; Mazeaud 2009). Indeed, these agents are required to make decisions not only on the basis of their technical expertise as they did before but also by integrating the lay knowledge of citizen-users. These are all avenues to be explored in order to understand the logic and effects of CA at both local and national levels.

References

Agger, A., & Sørensen, E. (2018). Managing collaborative innovation in public bureaucracies. *Planning Theory* 17 (1), 53–73.

Bherer, L. (2011), Les relations ambiguës entre participation et politiques publiques. *Participations* 1, 105–133.

Bherer, L., Dufour, P., and Montambeault, F. (2016). The participatory democracy turn: An introduction. *Journal of Civil Society* 12 (3), 225–230.

Bherer, L., Gauthier, M., & Simard, L. (2017a). *The Professionalization of Public Participation*. London: Routledge.

Bherer, L., Gauthier, M., & Simard, L. (2017b). Who's the client? The sponsor, citizens, or the participatory process? Tensions in the Quebec (Canada) public participation field. in L. Bherer, M. Gauthier, & L. Simard, *The Professionalization of Public Participation*, 87–114. London: Routledge.

Blijleven, W., & van Hulst, M. (2021). How do frontline civil servants engage the public? Practices, embedded agency, and bricolage. *The American Review of Public Administration* 51 (4), 278–292.

Blijleven, W., Hulst, M. van, & Hendriks, F. (2019). Public servants in innovative democratic governance. In S. Elstub & O. Escobar (eds), *Handbook of Democratic Innovation and Governance*, 209–224. Cheltenham: Edward Elgar Publishing.

Blondiaux, L., & Michel, L. (2007). L'expertise en débat: jeux d'acteurs et conflits de savoirs autour d'un débat public local dans le Lot. In F. Cantelli, S. Jacob, G. Genard, and V. de Visscher (eds) *Les constructions de l'action publique*, 181–201. Paris: L'Harmattan.

Carcasson, M., & Sprain, L. (2016). Beyond problem solving: Reconceptualizing the work of public deliberation as deliberative inquiry. *Communication Theory* 26 (1), 41–63.

Chilvers, J. (2013), Reflexive engagement? Actors, learning, and reflexivity in public dialogue on science and technology. *Science Communication* 35 (3), 283–310.

Christensen, H. (2018). Community engagement and professionalization: Emerging tensions. *Research in Ethical Issues in Organizations* 20, 117–133.

Christensen, H. E. (2020). Participatory and deliberative practitioners in Australia: How work context creates different types of practitioners. *Journal of Deliberative Democracy*, 15 (3).

Cooper, E., & Smith, G. (2012). Organizing deliberation: The perspectives of professional participation practitioners in Britain and Germany. *Journal of Public Deliberation* 8 (1).

Craig, G., Mayo, M., & Popple, K. (eds). (2011). *The Community Development Reader: History, Themes and Issues*. Bristol: Bristol University Press.

Dryzek, J. S. (1994). *Discursive Democracy: Politics, Policy, and Political Science*. Cambridge: Cambridge University Press.

Eckerd, A., & Heidelberg, R. L. (2020). Administering public participation. *The American Review of Public Administration* 50 (2), 133–147.

Escobar, O. (2011). *Public Dialogue and Deliberation: A Communication Perspective for Public Engagement Practitioners*. Edinburgh: UK Beacons for Public Engagement.

Escobar, O. (2013). Public engagers and the political craft of participatory policy making. *Public Administration Review* 73 (1), 36–37.

Escobar, O. (2017). Making it official: Participation professionals and the challenge of institutionalizing deliberative democracy. In L. Bherer, M. Gauthier, & L. Simard (eds), *The Professionalization of Public Participation*, 141–164. London and New York: Routledge.

Escobar, O. (2019). Facilitators: The micropolitics of public participation and deliberation. In S. Elstub & O. Escobar (eds), *Handbook of Democratic Innovation and Governance*, 178–195. Cheltenham: Edward Elgar Publishing Ltd.

Font, J., della Porta, D., & Sintomer, Y. (2014). *Participatory Democracy in Southern Europe: Causes, Characteristics and Consequences*. London: Rowman & Littlefield (Book, Whole).

Forester, J. F. (1999). *The Deliberative Practitioner: Encouraging Participatory Planning Processes*. Cambridge, MA: The MIT Press.

Ganuza, E., & Baiocchi, G. (2012). The power of ambiguity: How participatory budgeting travels the globe. *Journal of Public Deliberation* 8 (2).

Gourgues, G. (2012). Les fonctionnaires participatifs : les routines d'une innovation institutionnelle sans fin(s). *Socio-logos. Revue de l'association française de sociologie* [Preprint], (7).

Gourgues, G., Mazeaud, A. and Nonjon, M. (2021). From the participatory turn of administrations to the bureaucratisation of participatory democracy: study based on the French case. *International Review of Administrative Sciences* [Preprint].

Jeannot, G. (2011). *Les métiers flous – Travail et Action publique*. 2nd edition. Toulouse: Octares Editions.

Kathi, P. C., & Cooper, T. L. (2005). Democratizing the administrative state: Connecting neighborhood councils and city agencies. *Public Administration Review*, 65(5), 559 – 567.

King, C. S., Feltey, K. M., & Susel, B. O. (1998). The question of participation: Toward authentic public participation in public administration. *Public Administration Review* 58 (4), 317 – 326.

Kübler, D., Rochat, P. E., Woo, S. Y., & van der Heiden, N. (2020). Renforcer la gouvernabilité plutôt qu'approfondir la démocratie: les raisons qui amènent les gouvernements locaux à introduire la gouvernance participative. *Revue Internationale des Sciences Administratives* 86 (3), 427 – 444.

Lee, C. W. (2015). *Do-It-Yourself Democracy: The Rise of the Public Engagement Industry.* Oxford and New York: Oxford University Press.

Lewanski, R., & Ravazzi, S. (2017). Innovating public participation: The role of PPPs and institutions in Italy. In L. Bherer, M. Gauthier, & L. Simard, *The Professionalization of Public Participation*, 17 – 39. London: Routledge.

Martínez-Palacios, J. (2021). *El giro participativo neoliberal: institucionalización y profesionalización de laparticipación ciudadana en España (1978 – 2017).* Bilbao: Universidad del País Vasco.

Martínez-Palacios, J., & Mazeaud, A. (2019) La institucionalización de la participación ciudadana: un diálogo entre España y Francia. In P. P. Yáñez, R. Rébola, & M. S. Elías (eds), *Procesos y Metodologías Participativas*, 149 – 167. CLACSO (Reflexiones y experiencias para la transformación social).

Mazeaud, A. (2009) La modernisation participative vue d'en bas : entre militantisme et malaise identitaire. *Pyramides. Revue du Centre d'études et de recherches en administration publique* 18, 267 – 290.

Mazeaud, A. (2012). Administrer la participation: l'invention d'un métier entre valorisation du militantisme et professionnalisation de la démocratie locale. *Quaderni. Communication, technologies, pouvoir* 3 (79), 45 – 58.

Mazeaud, A., & Nonjon, M. (2017) Les enseignements d'une comparaison manquée. Les professionnels de la participation en France et au Québec. *Politix*, 120(4), 61 – 86.

Mazeaud, A., & Nonjon, M. (2018) *Le marché de la démocratie participative.* Vulaines-sur-Seine: Editions du Croquant.

Mazeaud, A., & Nonjon, M. (2020). The participatory turn in local policies: A product of the market. *Governance* 33 (2), 407 – 424.

McMullin, C. (2020). the role of public servants in supporting local community projects: Citizen-led co-production in Quebec. In Sullivan, S., Dickinson, H., & Henderson, H. (eds), *The Palgrave Handbook of the Public Servant*, 921 – 936. Cham: Palgrave Macmillan.

Michels, A., & De Graaf, L. (2017). Examining citizen participation: local participatory policymaking and democracy revisited. *Local Government Studies*, 43(6), 875 – 881.

Migchelbrink, K., & Van de Walle, S. (2022a). A systematic review of the literature on determinants of public managers' attitudes toward public participation. *Local Government Studies* 48 (1), 1 – 22.

Migchelbrink, K., & Van de Walle, S. (2022b). Serving multiple masters? Public managers' role perceptions in participatory budgeting. *Administration & Society* 54 (3), 339 – 365.

Moore, A. (2012). Following from the front: theorizing deliberative facilitation. *Critical Policy Studies* 6 (2), 146 – 162.

Morley, L. (2006) Hidden transcripts: The micropolitics of gender in Commonwealth universities. *Women's Studies International Forum* 29 (6), 543 – 551.

Moynihan, D. P. (2003). Normative and instrumental perspectives on public participation: Citizen summits in Washington, D.C. *The American Review of Public Administration* 33 (2), 164 – 188.

Nabatchi, T. (2010). Addressing the citizenship and democratic deficits: The potential of deliberative democracy for public administration. *The American Review of Public Administration* 40 (4), 376 – 399.

Oh, Y., Shin, H., & Park, J. (2022), Exploring managerial attitudes toward various participation mechanisms in response to citizen satisfaction signals on public service quality. *Administration & Society* 54 (5), 878 – 902.

Pierre, J., Røiseland, A., & Gustavsen, A. (2017). Comparing local politicians' and bureaucrats' assessments of democratic participation: the cases of Norway and Sweden. *International Review of Administrative Sciences* 83 (4), 658–675.

Puustinen, S., Mäntysalo, R., Hytönen, J., & Jarenko, K. (2017). The "deliberative bureaucrat": Deliberative democracy and institutional trust in the jurisdiction of the Finnish planner. *Planning Theory & Practice* 18 (1), 71–88.

Røiseland, A., & Vabo, S. I. (2020). Administrators as drivers of democratic innovations. *The Innovation Journal – Public Sector Innovation Journal* 25 (1), 1–20.

Sa Vilas Boas, M.-H. (2020) Implementing public participation in Brazil. Sociology of secondary actors. *Caderno CRH*, 33, 1–17.

Schneider, A. L., & Ingram, H. (1997). *Policy Design for Democracy*. Lawrence: University Press of Kansas.

Smith, G. (2009). *Democratic Innovations: Designing Institutions for Citizen Participation*. Cambridge: Cambridge University Press.

Spada, P., & Vreeland, J. R. (2020). Who moderates the moderators? The effect of non-neutral moderators in deliberative decision making. *Journal of Deliberative Democracy*, 9 (2).

Tawa Lama-Rewal, S. (2019). La résistible émergence d'une gouvernance participative à Delhi. *Revue Gouvernance / Governance Review* 16 (2), 21–40.

Värttö, M. (2021). The value of public engagement: Do citizens' preferences really matter? *Scandinavian Journal of Public Administration* 25 (2), 23–41.

Wan, P. Y. (2018) Outsourcing participatory democracy: Critical reflections on the participatory budgeting experiences in Taiwan. *Journal of Deliberative Democracy*, 14 (1).

Yang, K. (2005). Public administrators' trust in citizens: A missing link in citizen involvement efforts. *Public Administration Review* 65 (3), 273–285.

Kristof Jacobs

26 Populists and citizens' assemblies: Caught between strategy and principles?

Abstract: This chapter examines the relationship between populism and CAs. It does so from the perspective of populist parties and that of populist citizens. For both types of actors I first develop a theoretical framework juxtaposing rational choice inspired factors to more principled ones. Afterwards, the framework is applied using novel data. Regarding populist parties, the framework is applied to the case of the French 2019 Climate CA; regarding populist citizens it is applied to three cases of participatory budgeting in the Netherlands. These studies highlight that there is a discrepancy between populist parties and populist citizens. Populist parties are only supportive when CAs deliver the outcomes they themselves want. Regarding populist citizens, the message is more optimistic. When they participate, they seem content and grade the event similar to non-populist citizens. Furthermore, they do not seem more motivated by a desire "to get what they want".

Keywords: populism, deliberation, political parties, populist citizens, democratic innovations

26.1 Introduction

Populism is on the rise and the feeling that politicians do not listen to the people is widespread (see Rooduijn et al. 2019). One response to this trend is to give citizens more options to make their voice heard. Indeed, many scholars studying deliberative democracy believe that deliberation, such as in citizens' assemblies (CAs), can counter-act populism (Dryzek et al. 2019: 1145). But is this the case? It is often claimed that populist parties (Taggart 2000; Mudde 2004) and citizens, at least in theory, support referendums (Jacobs, Akkerman and Zaslove 2018). Yet, less is known about populists' affinity with deliberative tools such as CAs.

Indeed, more in general one can wonder: what explains actors' relationship with democratic innovations? This question has been puzzling scholars for quite some time. Initially applied in the field of electoral system change, most researchers assumed that political *parties* would simply support those *innovations* (to the electoral system) that would benefit them. After all, not doing so would equate to "turkeys voting for Christmas" (Katz 2005). However, when shifting the focus (1) from parties to parties *and citizens* and (2) from electoral system changes to *democratic innovations*, more principled or normative motivations become plausible.

Kristof Jacobs: Radboud Universiteit Nijmegen, The Netherlands.
 Funding: Part of this research was financed via Dutch National Science Fund (NWO) as part of the NWO-VIDI project no. 195.085.

𝗮 Open Access. © 2023 the author(s), published by De Gruyter. [CC] [BY-NC-ND] This work is licensed under the Creative Commons Attribution-NonCommercial-NoDerivatives 4.0 International License. https://doi.org/10.1515/9783110758269-028

In this chapter I outline both approaches and apply them to populist political parties and populist citizens. I zoom in on populist parties' outcome- and act-contingent motivations and compare them to more principled, ideational motivations. Regarding populist citizens, I zoom in on outcome-contingent motivations on the one hand and ideational fit on the other. Afterwards, I present two case studies to illustrate how those approaches shed more light on populists' relationship with CAs. Specifically, I analyse how *La France Insoumise* and *Rassemblement National* spoke about the French CA on the climate (2019–2020). Regarding populist citizens, I analyse populist participants of three Dutch participatory budgeting cases (Duiven, Maastricht, and Amsterdam Oost 2019–2021). All three were cases seeking to bring together an inclusive group of ordinary people to deliberate formally on political issues in order to influence public policies.

26.2 Theoretical framework: Populism and citizens' assemblies

To be able to theorize the relationship between populism and CAs, I will first define both concepts, starting with populism. While it may seem that populism is a contested concept, increasingly scholars agree about the key components of the populist set of ideas.[1] Specifically, populists consider "society to be ultimately separated into two homogeneous and antagonistic groups, 'the pure people' versus the 'corrupt elite,' and which argues that politics should be an expression of the volonté générale (general will) of the people" (Mudde 2004: 543).

Mudde's definition of populism focuses on three key aspects of populism that are relevant when studying CAs. First, defined as such populism is *people-centred*. For populists "the people" are considered as one homogenous whole and are "good" and "pure". Populists "see wisdom as residing in the common people. From common people comes common sense and this is better than bookish knowledge" (Taggart 2000: 94–95). Second, the people are juxtaposed with the elite. It is the "evil elite" who threaten the people-centred notion of democracy. Third, populists believe that politics should be centred on the general will. Hence, intermediary organizations or non-electoral institutions should be taken out of the equation as much as possible (see Rosanvallon 2008) and power should reside with the people. Populist parties are defined as parties that

---

1 Related, there is also broad agreement in the academic community about what populism is *not*. It is not the same as *demagogy* (providing simple solutions to complex problems) or *electoral opportunism* (changing one's policy positions depending on what is popular) (Mudde 2004). Nevertheless, there is still is debate about the ontology of populism when applied to political parties. Some scholars consider populism to be a strategy, others a communicative style and still others consider it a thin-centered ideology. Regarding populism among citizens such debates do not occur, for the simple reason that citizens are not in the business of getting elected, it makes little sense to consider populism a strategy or communication style of citizens.

adhere to the aforementioned populist set of ideas. Populist citizens are defined as citizens who adhere to this set of ideas.

Clearly, there is an affinity between this set of ideas and democratic innovations such as referendums, especially if they are binding and citizen-initiated (see Jacobs, Akkerman and Zaslove 2018). Regarding CAs the affinity is perhaps less straightforward as such instruments tend to centre on a pluralist, non-homogenous view of "the people". More on this below.

Regarding CAs, many labels have been used to describe related or even similar types of democratic innovations. Citizen juries, mini-publics, CAs, or constitutional conventions are just a few of these. For the purpose of this study, I will use the same definition that is used throughout this *Handbook*, namely I consider a CA a participatory institution which seeks to bring together an inclusive group of ordinary people to deliberate formally on a political issue, so as to exert an influence on public decision-making.

As mentioned in the introduction, in general, there are two approaches to studying the relationship between actors and democratic innovations, an instrumental, rational choice inspired one and a more principled approach. Below I discuss and apply each of them first to political parties and then to citizens.

26.3 Populist parties and citizens' assemblies

26.3.1 Theoretical assessment of the relationship

The literature on how parties position themselves on a given democratic reform – i.e. a reform implementing democratic innovations – stresses two strategic motivations: outcome-contingent and act-contingent motivations (Reed and Thies 2001). *Outcome-contingent* motivations deal with whether or not parties will benefit from the reform. Importantly, such motivations are subjective: they are about perceptions, not the actual results of the reform after it is implemented. *Act-contingent* motivations deal with the perceived electoral benefits or costs attached to the act of supporting a reform or innovations. In essence, act-contingent motivations are about whether it "looks good" to support the innovation.

Next to these two instrumental motivations, scholars have highlighted that there can be *principled* motivations to support an innovation. Specifically, scholars have highlighted the role of motivations centred around a desire to improve democracy (Katz 2005: 74). Often this concerns enhancing the representativeness of the system, but typically such motivations are grounded in the specific ideology and ensuing model of democracy a party adheres to. Regarding populist parties, scholars have for instance assessed to what degree referendums "fit" with the populist ideology (Jacobs, Akkerman and Zaslove 2018; Gherghina and Silagadze 2020).

Strategic motivations: outcome-contingent motivations

While in theory CAs can be institutionalized (e.g., Ostbelgien), in practice, most CAs are ad hoc events about a certain topic. In such cases, the question is hence: is the (expected) policy outcome of the CA in line with what the party advocates? If outcome-contingent motivations prevail, one would expect populist parties to favour CAs on topics where they anticipate the outcome to be in line with their political programme. For instance, one can expect a populist radical left party to support a CA on reforming the labour market if that party expects the outcome of the CA to be a strengthening of the position of ordinary workers.

Strategic motivations: act-contingent motivations

Populist parties have act-contingent motivations to support a CA when the mere act of supporting it is advantageous to them. But when is that the case? Jacobs (2011) outlined several factors that matter when judging act-contingent motivations. For CAs three in particular are relevant, namely (1) support for the instrument and its outcomes, (2) the degree of media support for the CA, and (3) the degree of public disenchantment at the time (e.g., Jacobs 2011: 104). When available, public opinion data form the most direct measure of act-contingent motivations: if an instrument and its outcomes are popular among the population, parties have act-contingent motivations to be in favour of it. But often such data is not available to parties. Then two other proxies are typically used by parties, whereby media narratives are the most crucial of the two. Indeed, public disenchantment is often mainly visible in the media. On top of that, the media can judge the CA to be an adequate response to the "crisis" or not. This frame in return determines whether or not it is worthwhile for a party to support the CA. If act-contingent motivations prevail, one would expect populist parties to follow public polling data. If no such data is available, they are expected to follow the judgement of the media. If the media are silent on the CA, one would expect the degree of public disenchantment to be decisive. For instance, one can expect a populist party to support a on the climate if polls show a majority of citizens support this, when the media support that CA's introduction or when this is absent, when there is widespread public disenchantment about this issue.

Principled motivations: ideological "fit"

As mentioned earlier, the populist set of ideas consists of three dimensions: anti-elitism, people-centrism, and a desire for popular sovereignty. Earlier research has established that there is a great fit between populism and referendums. But to what extent does this fit also exists with CAs? (1) CAs are not anti-elitist by definition, though they can be. The Belgian G1000 and Icelandic 2011 CAs were fairly anti-political in their set-up

(Van Reybrouck 2016), but the Canadian and Dutch CAs on electoral reform were not (Fournier et al. 2011). Whether or not a CA is anti-elitist thus depends on its context and content. (2) Regarding people-centrism, similar ambiguity exists. CAs are based on the foundation that citizens have the capacities to deliberate and therefore share populists' optimism about the virtue of the people. However, CAs have a pluralist notion of the people. Diversity, exchanging ideas, emotions and views, and changing one's opinion are a central part of it. This is somewhat different from the populist interpretation of what the notion of "the people" is. Indeed, populists view "the people" as a homogenous whole. As Taggart (2000: 92) puts it:

> [t]he people are portrayed as a unity. They are seen as a single entity devoid of fundamental divisions and unified and solidaristic. 'The people' are, in populist thinking already fully formed and self-aware.

For populists, deliberation is a superfluous exercise, as "the people" are already self-aware. This does not necessarily mean they are against it, it is just considered a pointless exercise. Worse, a CA risks being seen by populists as a place where "special interests" try to corrupt the will of the people. (3) Regarding the third dimension, the picture is clearer and more positive. Indeed, that CAs at least to some degree increase popular sovereignty is by definition the case, as they are about citizen involvement in the decision-making process. Indeed, CAs strive "to exert an influence on public decision-making" (viz. supra). To sum up the potential relationship between populists and CAs: it's complicated. If principled motivations prevail, we would expect populists to favour CAs if they clearly empower the people, are anti-elitist in their set-up, and limit the influence of what populists would call "special interests" (such as civil society organizations and "biased" experts).

Which of the three motivations is likely to prevail? In analysing populists' relationship to referendums, Gherghina and Silagadze (2020) found that populists were first and foremost strategic in their support and use of referendums. While they are less likely than non-populists to call referendums, they are more likely to win them, suggesting that outcome-contingent motivations are the most important drivers of support for referendums. Given that the fit between populists and referendums is more straightforward and clearer than the one with CAs and that despite this, principled motivations did not seem to matter, one can expect populists to support CAs primarily when they benefit them strategically.

26.3.2 Empirical exploration of the relationship: the French citizens' assembly on the climate (2019–2020)

In this section I explore the empirical relationship between populist parties and CAs in the case of the French CA on the climate.

Some brief methodological notes. I selected this case because (1) it is an extreme, but typical case and (2) it has a clear link with populism (in the form of being the direct consequence of the "Yellow Vest" protests). Regarding the first, the case is extreme in that it was high profile and national level, while it is nevertheless typical in that CAs on the climate have become fairly common in the past five years. This combination allows me to examine traces of the three types of motivations. After all, when parties are silent on a topic we lack data to properly analyse their position on a given matter. Moreover, the findings on the French climate assembly are likely to travel to future CAs on a similar topic. Regarding the second, this link with populism once again makes it more likely that populist parties speak explicitly about it. Regarding data sources, I use secondary analyses of the case and combine these with an analysis of parliamentary minutes and the parties' public communication about the Citizens' Assembly. I am primarily interested in the populist parties, specifically *La France Insoumise* and *Rassemblement National* (see Rooduijn et al. 2019). While I will mention some other parties' positions to sketch the context of the overall debate at the time, I will not systematically compare all the parties as it would go beyond the scope of this chapter.[2]

The French CA on the climate consisted of 150 citizens using sortition and stratified sampling. It took place during nine months from October 2019 till June 2020. The assembly proposed 149 measures and was supposed to have a tangible impact on policy. Indeed, President Macron said that he would not filter the proposals and either submit them to the parliament directly or put them directly to a referendum (Caulcutt 2021). However, he abandoned his referendum promises and faced criticism regarding the minimal implementation of the proposals (Giraudet et al. 2021). The two populist parties under study mainly made themselves heard after the assembly made its recommendations. Interestingly, they took opposite positions in the debate, despite their shared populist worldview. *La France Insoumise* considered the assembly an integral part of democracy, whereas the *Rassemblement National* wanted to de facto overrule the work of the assembly via a "counter-referendum". This already indicates that principled motivations are not the main driving force of how they related themselves to the CA. In what follows I assess the three types of motivations in more detail.

Outcome-contingent motivations.

Just like most of its European sister parties, the *Rassemblement National* can be considered climate sceptic or at best "ambivalent" when it comes to climate change policies. The party for instance denounces international climate treaties as a breach of sovereignty (e.g., Jeffries 2017). Nevertheless, after the CA on the climate it tried to brand itself as a party embracing a more nationalist ecological ideology (Rassemblement National 2021). In practice, however, this still meant that the proposals of the CA were

---

2 Given its tiny size, I do not analyse the position of *Debout La France*.

considered beyond the pale. It explicitly mentioned the speed reduction pledge as a bad idea (Pajot 2020), but also stressed that other proposals were "crazy" and disconnected from economic reality and had no social or ecological pertinence (Le Pen 2020). The party pushed to have the CA have as little impact as possible (Pajot 2020). *La France Insoumise* on the other hand is a party that favours taking climate action. It welcomed the proposals made by the CA, especially those that were in line with its manifesto. The party by and large supported the outcomes of the CA, though clearly indicated where these proposals did not align with its own election manifesto. Where this was the case, the manifesto took precedence (La France Insoumise 2020a). In short, the reaction of the two parties is entirely in line with outcome-contingent motivations.

Act-contingent motivations

The act-contingent motivations concerning the CA are similar for both parties. Because of its large scale, there was a fair amount of polling data available. According to that data, some 70% of the population had heard of the work of the CA at the time of presenting its propositions, and 60% of the French found its work legitimate (ELABE 2020: 3–4). Moreover, the content of the most prominent of these propositions was widely supported, with the exception of reducing the speed limits on highways (Odoxa 2020: 10). In short, if act-contingent motivations had prevailed they should have supported the proposals and the CA. Clearly, this is not the case for the *Rassemblement National*. However, it should be noted that Le Pen did aim to give citizens a say about this topic by proposing a "counter-referendum" on 15 questions (Rassemblement National 2021), a non-consequential pledge to make as she was in opposition and did not have the votes to make the referendum possible. Regarding *La France Insoumise*, the party by and large supported the outcomes of the CA, though clearly indicated where these propositions did not align with its own election manifesto. Where this was the case, the manifesto took precedence (La France Insoumise 2020a). Other than that, the party stressed that the CA case showed that the government insulted democracy by ignoring the assembly's proposals (La France Insoumise 2020b). The latter does align with act-contingent motivations, but even in this speech the party cherry-picked these outcomes that aligned with the electoral manifesto of the party.

Principled motivations

Where mainstream parties stressed the illegitimacy of the CA, the two populist parties were less keen on doing so. *La France Insoumise* considered the CA to be an integral and important part of democracy, though once again it needs to be stressed that the party cherry-picked those proposals of the assembly that aligned with the party (La France Insoumise 2020b). While *Rassemblement National*'s Marine Le Pen mainly criticized the results of the assembly, her colleague Ludovic Pajot stressed that the assembly consisted of 150 "persons" drawn by lot (not "citizens"). Moreover, Le Pen did not propose to hold a new assembly but rather wanted a referendum, suggesting that she preferred that tool over a CA.

Table 26.1: Summary of the different types of motivations

	Outcome-contingent	Act-contingent	Principled
La France Insoumise	++	(+)	(+)
Rassemblement National	++	–	–

In short: populist parties only seem to support CAs when they deliver the outcomes they themselves want. This is a sobering message for those hoping that CAs as a tool of more popular involvement in the decision-making process placate populist parties.

26.4 Populist citizens and citizens' assembly

Whereas the rational choice approach to studying political parties' positions towards democratic reform is well-developed, until recently this was not the case for citizens' positions. The last few years have nevertheless seen a burgeoning literature adopting a rational choice approach (see Werner 2020). Most earlier studies used the framework of "engaged" versus "enraged" citizens. The notion of engaged citizens was inspired by modernization scholars (see Dalton 2004; Bowler, Donovan and Karp 2007). In this view, societies were experiencing a cultural value change driven by "forces of social modernization" such as improved socio-economic conditions during one's formative years and increased levels of education (Dalton 2004: 95). This value change specifically entailed the rise of postmaterialist values and the accompanying preferences for a different model of democracy, one where citizens had more say. In response, other scholars stressed that certain groups in society were "enraged" and desired a different type of democracy, one that included elements of expert and direct democracy and combined these in a so-called "stealth democracy" (Hibbing and Theiss-Morse 2002). Fundamentally, both approaches stressed principled motivations where the fit between the model of democracy a citizen adheres to and a given instrument determines whether she supports it or not.

As said, strategic motivations have received less attention. Specifically, Werner's landmark study about support for referendums tried to address this "neglected" dimension of support for democratic reforms (2020: 315). She starts from the insight that election losers are more likely to support referendums directly after that election. Under such circumstances, referendums still give these voters a chance to reach at least some of their desired policy outcomes. Werner extends this idea and expects that those citizens who oppose the status quo on a certain topic, will be more likely to support a referendum on it. Additionally, she expects that majority perceptions play an important role. Citizens who believe they are in the majority on a certain topic are expected support a referendum on that topic. Below I apply both approach to populist citizens' position vis-à-vis CAs.

Strategic motivations: outcome-contingent motivations

Regarding citizens, the rational choice approach merely focuses on outcome-contingent motivations. Indeed, citizens do not need to win elections, so supporting a democratic reform for electoral gains is irrelevant here. So which outcomes matter? CAs come in many shapes and forms and may be designed to have a big or fairly small impact on actual policymaking. However, all of them produce a proposal, or list of proposals. This is a useful benchmark to assess outcome-contingent motivations. Indeed, if outcome-contingent motivations prevail, one would expect a populist citizen to favour CAs on topics where the outcome is in line with their own preferences. Populism may moderate this relationship, in that populists typically have the idea that they are the "silent majority" (see Taggart 2000). If they don't get what they want, they may be even more frustrated with the CA as this may signify to them that "special interests" captured the process.

Principled motivations: "fit"

In the introduction of this section we noted that principled motivations typically stress the fit between the model of democracy a citizen adheres to and the instrument in question. While typically a distinction is made between postmaterialist, engaged citizens and enraged, stealth democrats, populism is distinct from these two (see Webb 2013). Contrary to postmaterialism it has a homogenous view of the citizenry and believes the elites are corrupt and contrary to stealth democracy it desires more popular sovereignty and an active role of citizens.[3] In the section on populist parties we already highlighted the complex fit between populism and CAs. Populist citizens are expected to support these types of CAs that limit the role of elites and special interests and clearly empower the people.

Which of the two motivations is likely to prevail? In analysing populist citizens' acceptance of a referendum loss, Werner and Jacobs (2022) found that populists were more willing to accept a loss than non-populists. This leads them to conclude that populist citizens' referendum support may actually be principled rather than instrumen-

---

3 Indeed, Kaltwasser and Van Hauwaert find that in Europe, citizens with a higher degree of populist attitudes also tend to have a high degree of political interest and want a "democratization of democracy (2020:15).

tal. However, it remains to be seen to what extent this is also the case for CAs: the fit between populism and CAs is less straightforward than the one with referendums.

26.4.1 Empirical exploration of the relationship: Populist citizens in three cases of participatory budgeting

There is some empirical evidence that populist citizens support tools of deliberative democracy such as CAs (e.g., Zaslove et al. 2021). However, we do not know what happens if populist citizens actually participate. This matters as outcome-contingent motivations can only be examined in a context where there are outcomes. Below I will analyse populist citizens who participated in participatory budgeting. This instrument combines deliberation of an inclusive group of citizens with actual impact on policy. I analyse three cases in the Netherlands: Duiven (2019), Maastricht (2021), and Amsterdam Oost (2020). One municipality was small, one bigger, and one was a big city; additionally there was geographical spread over the country. All three cases used a largely similar template inspired by the one used in the city of Antwerp. This template consisted of three sessions on separate days ('rounds'): small-scale deliberation about which topics should be prioritized; small-scale deliberation and bargaining about allocating the budget to these topics, and a third voting round. I zoom in on the first round of the events as this round involved the most extensive deliberations and resembled deliberations in classic CAs the most. The three cases are representative of other participatory budgeting events in the Netherlands, which typically are binding and have allocated budgets. In that sense they are a most likely case for the impact of populists' principled motivations: there is genuine citizen empowerment and the role of elites is limited. It is also a good testing ground for outcome-contingent motivations as the process yields tangible outcomes and can have a meaningful impact: the stakes are real.[4] We first surveyed the participants when they entered. In the pre-questionnaire we included a standard battery measuring populist attitudes (Akkerman, Mudde and Zaslove 2014). At the end of the event we surveyed them again and asked a series of questions about the event. The response rates ranged from 68.9% (post survey Amsterdam Oost) to 96.6% (post survey Maastricht). In total 285 respondents filled in at least one survey.

How did populist citizens experience the session? As Table 26.2 shows, the differences between populist participants and non-populist ones are negligible. If anything, the populist participants seemed to be happier with the quality of the discussions and were slightly more likely to change their mind after the discussions. This suggests that

---

4 Though the respective budgets to allocate were modest, they were large enough to make a tangible and visible impact: – Duiven: 25,000 €, – Maastricht: 300,000 €, – Amsterdam Oost: 400,000 € (200,000 € per neighbourhood).

populists and non-populists were equally satisfied with the deliberations.[5] So clearly once a populist citizen participates, she is not that different from non-populist ones in her judgement of the experience.

Table 26.2: Scores on quality of discussions

	Non-populist citizens	Populist citizens[1]
I had ample opportunity to express my opinion during the discussions.	4.14	4.24
The opinions of the other participants did not differ so much from my own opinions.	3.60	3.80
In general, everyone showed respect for the others in the discussion.	4.51	4.67
I have changed my mind as a result of the discussion.	2.36	2.60

[1] The cut-off point was 3.67 on a scale from 1 to 5. A stricter cut-off (4 instead of 3.67) yielded similar results.

Note: T-tests show that none of the differences are statistically significant. Note though that the numbers refer to population data: we did not sample among the citizens present, but rather surveyed all of them. Statistical significance in such a context mainly tells us something about the consistency of the answers. Hence, the non-significant findings highlight that there is more difference within the group of (non-)populist citizens than between them.

Next, we tested the role of populist attitudes and outcome-contingent motivations. The dependent variable is how a respondent graded the event on a scale from 0 to 10. My main independent variables are populist attitudes and a variable measuring satisfaction with the outcome. The latter was measured by the question: "to what extent do you agree with the choices the group made during the event?" The scale ranged from not at all satisfied (1) to fully satisfied (5). I also include standard controls (gender, age, and education). Outcome satisfaction is by far the most important determinant of the grade a participant gave the event. Populist attitudes play no role, independently, nor in strengthening or weakening the effect of outcome satisfaction (see insignificant moderator effect). In short, populists seem to behave the same as non-populists. One important note is that outcome satisfaction in general was very high: the average satisfaction was no less than 4.22 on a scale from 1 to 5. Hence, dissatisfied participants were the exception rather than the rule. Most participants, be they populist or not, were very satisfied with the outcome.

---

5 This is also corroborated by a T-test examining differences in the overall evaluation of the event (in the form of a grade on a scale from zero to ten. Here non-populists on average scored 6.9 whereas populists scored a 7.33; a non-significant difference.

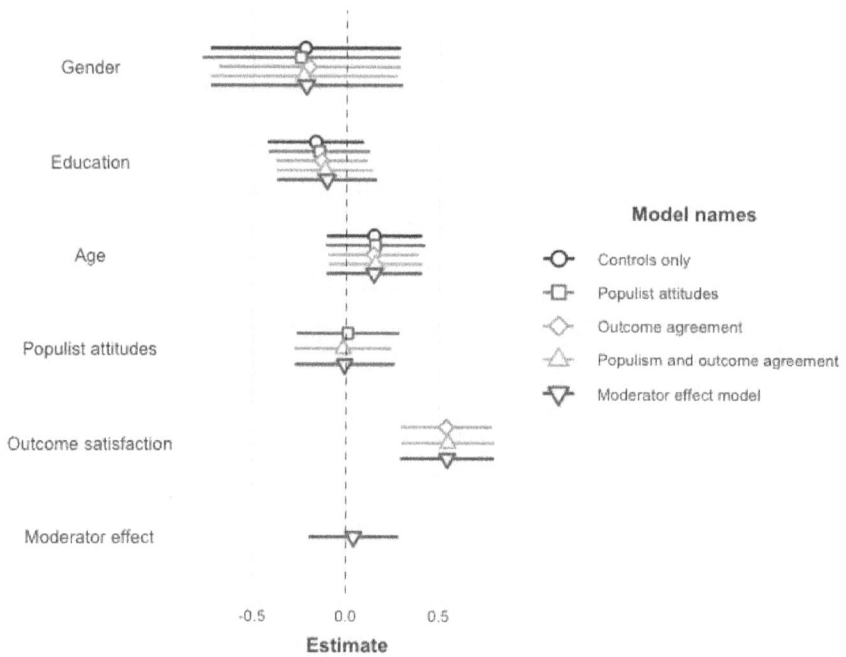

Figure 26.1: Coefficient plot of effect of populist attitudes and outcome satisfaction on event grade
Note: Variables are mean-centered and scaled by 1 standard deviation. N = 122, 119, 118, 116 and 116.

26.5 Conclusion

How do populists view CAs? It appears that when it comes to populist parties, this largely depends on the outcomes of that CA. If they like these outcomes, they will support the CA, if not, they will denounce it. This is a sobering message for reformers hoping to win over populist parties by implementing CAs. Adding a referendum after the CA may help, but populists may well campaign against the position of the CA in such a referendum, e.g. claiming that the process was hijacked by special interests or the elites.

For populist citizens, the message is more optimistic. When they participate, they seem content and grade the event similar to non-populist citizens. Furthermore, they do not seem more motivated by a desire to get what they want: there is no difference between populists and non-populists and both groups gave the events a fairly high grade. Those that were dissatisfied with the outcome did significantly grade the event lower. Again, outcome-contingent motivations play a substantial role, but the process seems to have been good at creating satisfaction with the outcome: only very few participants were dissatisfied. That "magic" of deliberation seems to work for both populists and non-populists.

Some caveats though. *First*, it could be that these positive feelings erode over time, especially when political elites slow or halt the implementation of the outcomes of the process. Especially populists may be vulnerable to this as they tend to be more sceptical of political elites. *Second*, it remains to be seen how populist non-participants feel about CAs. It is not unlikely that they are more driven by outcome-contingent motivations and that they doubt the legitimacy of the process when confronted with outcomes they do not like. *Third*, CAs are one-shot events, but multiple such assemblies can occur consecutively (see Ireland). For both populist parties and populist citizens, the first of such events may be the defining one: it sets the stage for following events, creating goodwill or scepticism.

All in all, much remains to be investigated – this is still a nascent field of research. However, the present study does suggest that CAs are no panacea. Dryzek et al.'s claim that deliberation "counteracts populism" (2019: 1145) seems only partially true.

References

Akkerman, A., Mudde, C., & Zaslove, A. (2014). How populist are the people? Measuring populist attitudes in voters. *Comparative Political Studies* 47 (9), 1324–1353.

Bowler, S., Donovan, T., & Karp, J. A. (2007). Enraged or engaged? Preferences for direct citizen participation in affluent democracies. *Political Research Quarterly* 60 (3), 351–362.

Caulcutt, C. (2021). It's crunch time for Macron's climate bet. https://www.politico.eu/article/emmanuel-macron-climates-fair-weather-friend/, last accessed 2/1/2022.

Dalton, R. J. (2004). *Democratic Challenges, Democratic Choices.* Oxford: Oxford University Press.

Dryzek, J. S., Bächtiger, A., Chambers, S., Cohen, J., Druckman, J. N., Felicetti, A., Fishkin, J., Farrell, D., Fung, A., Gutman, A., Landemore, H., Mansbridge, J., Marien, S., Neblo, M., Niemeyer, S., Setala, M., Slothuus, R., Suiter, J., Thompson, D., & Warren, M. E. (2019). The crisis of democracy and the science of deliberation. *Science* 363 (6432), 1144–1146.

ELABE, (2020). *Convention Citoyenne pour le climat, qu'en pensent les Français?* https://elabe.fr/conv-cit-climat/, last accessed 16/2/2022.

Fournier, P., Van Der Kolk, H., Carty, R., Blais, A., & Rose, J. (2011). *When Citizens Decide: Lessons from Citizen Assemblies on Electoral Reform.* Oxford: Oxford University Press.

Gherghina, S., & Silagadze, N. (2020). Populists and referendums in Europe: Dispelling the myth. *The Political Quarterly* 91 (4), 795–805.

Giraudet, L.-G., Apouey, B., Arab, H., Baeckelandt, S., Begout, P., Berghmans, N., Blanc, N., Boulin, J.-Y., Buge, E., Courant, D., Dahan, A., & Adrien F. (2021). *Deliberating on Climate Action: Insights from the French Citizens' Convention for Climate.* Working Papers hal-03119539, HAL.

Hibbing, J. & Theiss-Morse, E. (2002). *Stealth Democracy: Americans' Beliefs about How Government Should Work.* Cambridge: Cambridge University Press.

Jacobs, K. (2011). *The Power or the People? Direct Democratic and Electoral Reforms in Austria, Belgium and the Netherlands* (Doctoral dissertation).

Jacobs, K., Akkerman, A., & Zaslove, A. (2018). The voice of populist people? Referendum preferences, practices and populist attitudes. *Acta Politica* 53 (4), 517–541.

Jeffries, E. (2017). Nationalist advance. *Nature Climate Change* 7 (7), 469–471.

Katz, R. (2005). Why are there so many (or so few) electoral reforms. In M. Gallagher & P. Mitchell (eds), *The Politics of Electoral Systems*, 55–77. Oxford: Oxford University Press.

La France Insoumise, (2020a). *Convention Citoyenne pour le Climat: 90% des propositions sont compatibles avec l'Avenir en Commun.*
https://lafranceinsoumise.fr/2020/06/26/convention-citoyenne-climat-propositions-compatibles-avenir--en-commun/, last accessed 16/2/2022.

La France Insoumise, (2020b). *Enterrement de la Convention citoyenne pour le climat: éloge funèbre.*
https://lafranceinsoumise.fr/2020/10/13/enterrement-de-la-convention-citoyenne-pour-le-climat-eloge--funebre/, last accessed 16/2/2022.

Le Pen, M. [@MLP_officiel] (2020, 21 June). La #ConventionCitoyenne, censée repondre à la crise des #GiletsJaunes, accouche de propositions toutes plus loufoques les unes que les autres, sans conscience des réalités économiques et sans aucune pertinence sociale et écologique. Tout ça pour ça... MLP. [tweet]. Twitter. https://twitter.com/mlp_officiel/status/1274742621169225729.

Mudde, C. (2004). The populist zeitgeist. *Government and Opposition* 39 (4), 541–563.

Odoxa, (2020). *La Convention Citoyenne pour le Climat.*
http://www.odoxa.fr/sondage/mesures-de-convention-citoyenne-seduisent-francais-a-lexception-notable-110-km-h/, last accessed 16/2/2022.

Pajot, L. (2020, 14 July). Question N° 31062. https://questions.assemblee-nationale.fr/q15/15–31062QE.htm, last accessed 16/2/2022.

Rassemblement National, (2021). *15 questions sur l'écologie qui doivent être tranchées par les Français par la voie référendaire.* https://reporterre.net/IMG/pdf/le_contre-projet_du_rn_pour_l_ecolologie.pdf, last accessed 16/2/2022.

Reed, S., & Thies, M. (2001). The causes of electoral reform in Japan. In M. Shugart & M. Wattenberg (eds), *Mixed-Member Electoral Systems: The Best of Both Worlds*, 380–403. Oxford: Oxford University Press.

Rooduijn, M., Van Kessel, S., Froio, C., Pirro, A., De Lange, S., Halikiopoulou, D., Lewis, P., Mudde, C., & Taggart, P. (2019). *The PopuList: An Overview of Populist, Far Right, Far Left and Eurosceptic Parties in Europe.* www.popu-list.org, last accessed 16/2/2022.

Rosanvallon, P. (2008). *Counter-Democracy: Politics in an Age of Distrust.* Cambridge: Cambridge University Press.

Rovira Kaltwasser, C., & Van Hauwaert, S. (2020). The populist citizen: Empirical evidence from Europe and Latin America. *European Political Science Review* 12 (1), 1–18.

Taggart, P. (2000). *Populism.* London: Open University Press.

Van Reybrouck, D. (2016). *Against Elections: The Case for Democracy.* London: The Bodley Head.

Webb, P. (2013). Who is willing to participate? Dissatisfied democrats, stealth democrats and populists in the United Kingdom. *European Journal of Political Research* 52 (6), 747–772.

Werner, H. (2020). If I'll win it, I want it: The role of instrumental considerations in explaining public support for referendums. *European Journal of Political Research* 59 (2), 312–330.

Werner, H., & Jacobs, K. (2022). Are populists sore losers? Explaining populist citizens' preferences for and reactions to referendums. *British Journal of Political Science* 52 (3), 1409–1417.

Zaslove, A., Geurkink, B., Jacobs, K., & Akkerman, A. (2021). Power to the people? Populism, democracy, and political participation: A citizen's perspective. *West European Politics* 44 (4), 727–751.

Appendix: Table with effects for Figure 26.1

Table 26.3: Effect of populist attitudes and outcome satisfaction on grade of the event

	Model 1	Model 2	Model 3	Model 4	Model 5
Intercept	7.37 (0.87)***	7.25 (1.11)***	3.92 (1.20)**	3.87(1.37	4.88 (3.23)
Populist attitudes (1 – 5)		0.01 (0.18)		−0.02 (0.17)	−0.34 (0.95)
Outcome satisf. (1 – 5)			0.80 (0.18)***	0.81 (0.19)***	0.54 (0.79)
Pop. attitudes x outcome satisf.					0.08 (0.23)
Female	−0.22 (0.25)	−0.25 (0.27)	−0.20 (0.25)	−0.23 (0.25)	−0.22 (0.26)
Education (1 – 6)	−0.15 (0.12)	−0.13 (0.13)	−0.13 (0.11)	−0.11 (0.12)	−0.10 (0.13)
Age	−0.01 (0.01)	0.01 (0.01)	0.01 (0.01)	0.01 (0.01)	0.01 (0.01)
N	122	119	118	116	116
R^2	0.00	0.00	0.14	0.13	0.13

Note: where appropriate, scale between brackets. * 0.05>p, ** 0.01>p, * 0.001>p

Rousiley C. M. Maia

27 Citizens' assemblies and communication studies

Abstract: This chapter discusses the growing analytical interest of citizens' assemblies (CAs) research in the neighbouring field of political communication in recent years. This involves (i) rethinking internal advances in CA theoretical and empirical research after the systemic turn, including the effort to use the media to expand mini-public initiatives to a wider body of citizens, and (ii) common concerns about the digitization of communication, circulation of dysfunctional information, and threats posed by illiberal and authoritarian uprisings in electoral democracies. This chapter argues that including media and digital landscape studies in the AC research agenda is useful in enabling scholars to address connections between institutions and wider publics, as well as the interplay of deliberative and non-deliberative practices. To advance an integrative research agenda, the author points out some lines of investigation and practical actions to shape the future directions of participatory deliberative processes and improve CAs' programmatic response to disruptions in the public sphere today.

Keywords: citizens' assemblies, mini-publics, media, public sphere, digital communication, political communication, deliberative system, systemic approach, non-deliberative behaviours, communication studies

27.1 Introduction

Relevant developments have taken place in the last two decades that allow us to rethink the interfaces between citizens' assemblies (CAs) and communication studies. Rather than investigating whether discussions in a particular citizens' forum or experiment meet deliberation standards or not, researchers have become increasingly interested in articulating micro, forum-based analyses, with macro deliberation issues and contextual factors. Throughout this intellectual movement, media studies arguably acquired a new relevance for the understanding of deliberative politics and the functioning of CAs. In this chapter, I argue that the growing analytical interest in citizen forum studies towards the neighbouring field of communication studies comes from two complementary sources: i) internal advances in theoretical and empirical research towards a systemic approach, including interdisciplinary collaboration in distinct fields, and ii)

Rousiley C. M. Maia: Federal University of Minas Gerais, Brazil. I am grateful to members of the Research Group on Media and Public Sphere, EME/ UFMG for their critical comments, and specially to Daniella Francione, Gabriella Hauber and Maria Eduarda Carvalho, for their assistance in formatting this chapter. The following funding agencies have supported this research: CNPq 308609/2015 – 8; CNPq 306492/2018 – 0; Capes/ INCT MCTI N° 25/2015.

∂ Open Access. © 2023 the author(s), published by De Gruyter. [CC BY-NC-ND] This work is licensed under the Creative Commons Attribution-NonCommercial-NoDerivatives 4.0 International License. https://doi.org/10.1515/9783110758269-029

a growing concern with the digitization of communication, the need to repair ruptures in the public sphere (Habermas 1991, 1996) and counteract illiberal or authoritarian uprisings in electoral democracies.

My basic argument is that CAs' holistic approach cannot ignore the interfaces between discussions in deliberately designed forums and the more mundane discussions outside those forums. I argue that a better understanding of the interconnectedness of parts in the political system and complex interactive processes between a set of political institutions and a set of actors is crucial to any attempt to successfully build CAs. Including media studies and platform digitization on the research agenda is helpful for allowing us to think across institutions and wider publics, as well as the interplay of deliberative and non-deliberative practices. An integrative research agenda, including mini-public initiatives and media studies, seems badly needed to shape future directions when democracy is seen under threat.

This chapter is structured as follows. The first section indicates the divide between CAs and media studies. The dynamic that unites CAs and media research in recent years is mapped in the second and third sections. In the fourth section, I point out some lines of investigation on how studies on political communication can help deliberative politics and suggest possible actions in the mass media and in the field of digital communication. In conclusion, I argue that it is worth seeking to deepen the dialogue between these disciplines to open a new perspective on participatory deliberative processes and improve the programmatic response to disruptions in the public sphere today.

27.2 The split between citizens' assemblies and media studies

For a long time, scholarly work on CAs and media studies seemed to be nested in separate fields of inquiry. Typically, CA initiatives are carefully designed to engage citizens in qualified discussions, offering opportunities for learning, expressing thoughtful reflections, and understanding the opinions of others in conditions that are as close to ideal deliberation as possible, as well as making more consequential recommendations for decision-making (Dryzek and Hendriks 2012; Fishkin 2018; Strandberg and Grönlund 2014). Relevant lines of research offered practical steps to mitigate asymmetries among participants and power imbalances in discussions and decision-making processes (Dryzek and Hendriks 2012; Karpowitz, Mendelberg and Shaker 2012) or to open spaces for deeply divided groups to engage in constructive discussions and seek collaborative conflict resolution (Caluwaerts and Reuchamps 2014; Maia et al. 2017; Steiner et al. 2017; Ugarriza and Caluwaerts 2014). In contrast, discussion in settings outside of deliberately designed forums is often characterized by poor information, participants' inattention, inequality, and power-based relationships. In this sense, the CA focus on mini-publics and media research on broader publics seemed essentially dichotomous.

In this first phase of the CA research, media studies played a relatively peripheral role. Generally speaking, scholars and practitioners were, above all, interested in publicity issues. This means attracting media attention or making CA messages more compelling (or understandable) to larger audiences. The visibility offered by the mainstream media is certainly important; and publicity matters to mobilize public opinion to support certain decisions on issues of common interest (Escobar and Elstub 2017; Karpowitz and Raphael 2014; Pomatto 2019; Rinke et al. 2013). However, research on media coverage of CAs often result in disappointment. Journalists usually produce limited coverage of citizens' meetings, do not provide sufficient and qualified information, and use certain frames that reduce the relevance of the issues under discussion (Pomatto 2019; Rinke et al. 2013). Even the local media provide scant informational material about CA (Escobar and Elstub 2017; Karpowitz and Raphael 2014; Warren and Pearse 2008). The literature indicates that citizen participatory initiatives in general have limited ability to influence news production routines and news values (della Porta 2013; Caemmerts, Mattoni and McCurdy 2013). The government's political agenda dominates the news, voices from official sources and knowledgeable elites are prevalent, while civic causes and civic association speakers are largely ignored (Häussler 2018; Maia 2012a; Wessler 2018). In this context, activists also report that when they gain media attention, the media's logic, referring to simplification of what is happening and what is at stake, and tendency to personification, frequently change the character of their actions (Caemmerts, Mattoni and McCurdy 2013; Esser and Strömbäck 2014). Assuming that theoretical problems and empirical research have an internal logic and development, also anchored in broader sociocultural contexts, I argue that CA literature and media studies have been more closely linked in recent years.

27.3 Bringing together citizens' assemblies and media studies: A systemic approach

As the CA theory developed, it incorporated a series of inquiries from deliberative thinkers themselves, as well as critiques from scholars working in adjacent fields. In this section, I argue that the CA literature has been reconstructed "from the inside out" so that wider publics gain increasing influence on theoretical and analytical framework, so to speak. When scholars adopt a holistic perspective, everyday discussions and media-based communication, both mediated and through social media, acquire new analytical relevance. In this sense, a holistic approach helps researchers to go beyond previous concerns about deliberation within forums, putting new issues on the research agenda (Bächtiger and Parkinson 2019; Dryzek et al. 2019; Hendriks, Ercan and Boswell 2020; Maia 2018; Maia, Hauber and Choucair 2023; Mansbridge et al. 2012).

The criticism that isolated discussions (and policymaking recommendations) represent a problem to democratic legitimacy in CAs is recurrent among deliberative scholars themselves (Chambers 2009, 2017; Lafont 2015; Neblo 2015). Simone Chambers (2009) has long argued that while mini-publics are often seen as antidotes to various evils in democratic societies (citizen apathy, low level of political trust, and a lack of sense of political effectiveness), broader citizenship, however, cannot be overlooked. Focusing exclusively on mini-publics risks bypassing the political judgement of a broader body of citizens; and political decision-making on pressing issues and long-term reforms requires the support of a larger public (Böker 2017; Boswell, Niemeyer and Hendriks 2013; Lafont 2015). In addition to the issues of authorization and accountability, CA participants go through an experience that their opinions cannot be considered representative of the general public. They are given the opportunity to learn, eventually watch expert debates, and engage in deliberation on fairly egalitarian terms that broader publics cannot replicate (Boswell, Niemeyer and Hendriks 2013; Lafont 2015).

Shifting from diagnosis to tentative remedies, theorists and practitioners have become increasingly interested in finding ways to "scaling up" deliberation or "spread the effects" of mini-publics beyond deliberative forums (Gastil and Knobloch 2020; Niemeyer 2014; Niemeyer and Jennstäl 2018; Setälä et al. 2020; Warren and Gastil 2015). Thompson (2008) suggested that this gap can be bridged if the broader public is prepared to accept the conclusions of an assembly because they trust the members. Along these lines, Niemeyer (2014) highlighted that mini-public participants can provide "distilled information" to help a larger body of people to make good judgements about complex issues, with reduced cognitive effort. In his words, mini-publics can be used as "a ladder for increasing the deliberative nature of the overall system" (Niemeyer and Jennstäl 2018: 339). Warren and Gastil (2015) also argued that forum members could operate as "enabling trust agents" among broader publics (see also Gastil and Knobloch 2020). According to Curato and Böker (2016), members of CAs could be induced to play a "discursive role", to counteract manipulative discourses or non-deliberative strategies.

Media-based communication acquires new analytical relevance in a context in which scholars have become increasingly concerned with finding ways to interact with broader publics; and exerting influence on a larger group of people (Dryzek et al. 2019; Fishkin 2018; Gastil, Richards and Knobloch 2014; Lazer et al. 2015). After all, to spread (or expand) supposed gains from deliberation – acquisition of knowledge, reasoned reflection, greater motivation to listen to those who think otherwise, trust, greater political effectiveness – require interaction with other socially distant people (who have not participated in a specific deliberative initiative). This approach captures well the complexity of pragmatic communicative interactions, in dynamic practices of making and receiving claims, rather than merely "transmitting" messages.

However, the concern with deliberation beyond the protected environment of CAs brings back problems of public opinion and preference formation conceived as broader processes (Curato, Hammond and Min 2019; Fishkin 2009, 2018; Maia 2018; Warren and Gastil 2015). The literature on communication and media studies helps shed light on a number of issues in this field, and prospects for responding to these challenges require more collaboration across disciplines.

27.4 Media and the micro-macro linkage

Developments in theoretical and empirical research towards a systemic approach paved the way for more interdisciplinary collaboration among deliberative and political communication scholars. In this section, I argue that the second movement that increased the relevance of everyday discussions and media-based communication is related to technological developments in the digital media landscape. Thinking about deliberation at the mass level poses enormous challenges on the research agenda, as it reintroduces some variants of citizens' cognitive and information deficits and a lack of interest in understanding others' opinions. Although digital media offer multiple communication opportunities, problems of circulating disinformation, harmful micro-targeting, hate speech, algorithmic manipulation, polarization, and mass surveillance become central worries in the research agenda of both participatory, deliberative, scholars and media and political communication scholars alike (Bennett and Pfetsch 2018; Dahlgren 2018; Miller and Vaccari 2020; Pfetsch 2018; van Aelst et al. 2017). The growing concern with such threats urges scholars to find ways to repair ruptures in the public sphere and counteract illiberal or authoritarian uprisings in electoral democracies.

I argued in the first section of this chapter that CA initiatives are particularly valued in the literature of deliberative democracy because these forums can be carefully constructed as "more perfect public spheres" (Fung 2003: 338). In contrast, everyday discussions and media-based communication are typically seen as unstructured and plagued by various democratic deficiencies, deliberately speaking, fragmentation and communication between like-minded people (Benkler, Faris and Roberts 2018; Sunstein 2017); absence of mechanisms to curb intolerance and informational disorders (Chadwick 2019; Vaccari and Chadwick 2020); inattention of most participants, unequal participation conditions; and prevalence of voices or interests of the most powerful actors, at the expense of the underprivileged and actors with fewer resources (Bimber and Zúñiga 2020; Maia 2014 Bennett and Pfetsch 2018; Dahlgren 2018; Pfetsch 2018; van Aelst et al. 2017).

Deliberative scholars continue to develop refined versions of citizen forums, searching for institutional resources and procedures to improve the quality of discussions, but with increasing sensitivity to the complexity of processes interrelated with external publics (Boulianne 2017; Setälä et al. 2020; Suiter et al. 2020; Vrydagh, Devillers and Reuchamps 2020). When the analysis of parliaments and mini-publics is expanded to external political contexts, deliberativeness is less likely to be found. In this context, maintaining rigid boundaries between discursive practices in formal and informal settings can therefore be a fruitless effort. I fully agree that communicative exchange outside the properly designed forums hardly looks like deliberation (Bächtiger and Parkinson 2019; Chambers 2017; Maia 2017). Yet, it is common to conceive the digital landscape in an abstract way and combine this generic approach straightforwardly with users' inattention, spread of lies, hate speech, etc. Perhaps, pessimism about the threats posed by the social media is moving very fast and far towards generalizations about citizens' incompetence and partisan motivations (Chambers 2020; Miller and Vaccari 2020). In this highly differentiated terrain, the nature and purpose of online settings, affordances for communication, moderation, among other factors, are important for shaping the interactions at play (Chadwick 2017, 2019; Ekström and Shehata 2018; Maia, Hauber and Choucair 2023; Strandberg and Grönlund 2014). The distinctions on people's affective identification to groups, partisan alignments under different conditions and specific situations, should also be critically surveyed (Boulianne 2017; Gastil et al. 2018; Lindell et al. 2017).

A caveat is needed before we proceed further. First, I start with the general premise that deliberation is not a purely natural behaviour likely to be found in any circumstances. Proper conditions for democratic interactions should be kept in perspective when seeking to craft discursive engagement in informal settings (Bächtiger and Parkinson 2019; Chambers 2017, 2020; Habermas 2017; Mansbridge et al. 2012; Maia 2017). Deliberation is a particular mode of communication and interaction (Cohen 1997; Habermas 1996), and scholars in this research field should definitely not abandon normative commitments when observing and analysing communicative exchanges. By holding normative conceptions, one can make fundamental distinctions in practical ways, for instance, between reciprocal interactions in contrast to hierarchical ones; equalitarian cooperative effort of persuasion in contrast to power-based interactions; respectful behaviours and reasoned disagreement in contrast to disruptive or intolerant ones, and so on (Maia et al. 2017; Steiner et al. 2017). Thus, normative criteria remain important as ever to deal with situations that violate democratic deliberative principles and corresponding expected behaviours.

Having said that, it is important to know more about how deliberative and non-deliberative practices may intertwine. Demands and recommendations generated by CA initiatives are likely to compete with the views and discourses of other actors in different settings, as politicians, media professionals, celebrities, religious leaders, etc. continually provide inputs to communicate with ordinary citizens and obtain direct feedback (Benkler, Faris and Roberts 2018; Bimber and Zúñiga 2020; Neuman 2016; Swart, Peters and Broersma 2018). More theoretical and empirical research is needed to understand the processes of preference formation, opinion building, and coordination of political action, through continuous communicative loops in digital media (Chambers 2020; Maia 2012b; Mansbridge and Macedo 2019). Systematic comparison between specific discussion taking place in different locations (Esau, Fleuß and Nienhaus 2020; Maia and Rezende 2016; Maia et al. 2020) helps evincing where, when, and to what extent actual processes approximate to deliberative standards and expectations; and in different moments of communicative interactions. Informal settings and everyday discussions should be investigated with equal serious attention and meticulous measurement as those discussions occurring in legislatures and deliberatively designed forums.

One of the main contributions of a large body of empirical research on CAs has been to demonstrate how to design deliberative forums in practical ways – providing qualified information, moderation strategies, and procedures to motivate thoughtful reflections and respectful reciprocal interactions (Caluwaerts and Reuchamps 2014; Fishkin 2009 2018; Karpowitz, Mendelberg and Shaker 2012; Ugarriza and Caluwaerts 2014). The crucial question, then, seems to be: beyond the protected environment of the mini-public, is it possible to build incentives for respectful listening and discursive exchange, including strategies to compensate for suboptimal conditions? In addition to current efforts, a common research agenda across different scientific and professional fields driven by ideals of democratic inclusion and plurality seems better equipped to find answers and build promising interventions to face contemporary challenges to deliberative politics.

27.5 What can be done?

The reflections developed in the previous sections lead us to the bleak scenario from which we started: the decline of citizens' trust in democratic institutions; increased incivility among elected leaders and polarization among political groups. Systems thinking does not provide any specific remedy, but it facilitates the exploration of complex issues of various levels of discursive engagement and types of communication. Against the general criticisms that CAs need to be reconnected with broader publics, media and communication studies can (and should) play a central and strategic role today. In this scenario, I would like to propose three lines of inquiry for actions: (i) within the mass media, (ii) digital communication, and (iii) incentives for CA members' own agency and communication with non-participants.

27.5.1 Within conventional media organisations

Literature on civic associations, NGOs and social movements has long indicated that building a systematic knowledge of the overall media ecology – including a set of opportunities and constraints of media practices, assumptions and attitudes towards different media formats and technologies – is important to effectively interact with media professionals (della Porta 2013; Maia 2014; Mattoni 2013; McCurdy 2013). Civic associations, while being highly specific about the topic they choose to promote (e.g., public health, children's issues, LGBTQ issues, domestic violence, people with disabilities, climate change), offer examples of a range of initiatives to achieve consequential change in mainstream media approaches to citizen demands. These initiatives comprise: (a) capacity building for media professionals: offering workshops and training for media professionals helps familiarize them with relevant aspects of the subject matter and bringing them into close contact with experts; the elaboration a set of principles to guide the reports and become regular and reliable sources among other important stakeholders, contribute to change frame-building and issue-relevance (Caemmerts, Mattoni and McCurdy 2013; Karpowitz and Raphael 2014; Waisbord 2009); b) systematic media monitoring: maintaining regular forms of surveillance on the volume and quality of media content helps to reflexively constrain biased news coverage, media stereo-types, and marginalization. Press observatories and media watchdogs also develop (or sponsor) research on media content in order to disseminate and share study data with media organizations to identify media achievements, deficiencies, and improvement actions (Maia 2014; Porto 2012; Waisbord 2009; Wardle and Derakhshan 2017; Wessler 2018); and (c) media criticism: dissemination of ratings of media programmes with the highest level of complaints; giving awards to recognize quality reporting and creat-ing discussion forums for media content that adversely affects members of disadvan-taged groups, causes harm, or violates public interests helps to improve the context of regular reporting.

These initiatives suggest that the shortcomings of mass media reporting should not be treated as fatal but as demonstrative of the need to do more than simply send letters to editors, issue press releases, or give interviews to journalists. CA organizers could motivate media professionals, who work on conventional media organizations, to be-came collaborators. Once included in the chain of experts involved in CA planning, im-plementation, and outcome analysis, media professionals could take place in discussion panels, media monitoring strategies, and enhance public communication at different levels. Obtaining mass media attention and supporting citizens' demands (to promote changes in a desired direction) requires engaging with media professionals on a more regular basis, and planning actions for the different components of the information ecosystem.

27.5.2 Multiplatform digital communication.

Mini-publics are embedded in larger contexts and CA organizers and professionals are now forced to operate in the interconnected digital environment. Previous studies have shown that deliberately designed forums can exert considerable influence over a large number of people (Gastil and Knobloch 2020; Lazer et al. 2015; Boulianne 2017; Suiter et al. 2020). Perhaps, the central challenge now might be to communicate with wider au-diences, through a democratic form of communication that generates intelligible pat-terns of some sort in an adverse terrain, such as authoritarian discourses or illiberal values, for example.

Thus, the CA communication across platforms and discursive agency needs more elaboration. It is important to explore the link between online and offline behaviours, and design local, contextualized, interventions. For instance, CA organizers and media professionals could produce activist videos to circulate at different scales, in order to find their way back to the messaging and social media applications now incorporated into the daily work of reflection, contestation, and mobilization (Ekström and Shehata 2018; Maia 2018; Valenzuela et al. 2019).

27.5.3 Citizens' assembly participants' own communication

In addition to implementing a set of initiatives related to conventional media and developing their own cross-platform communication, CA organizers could engage participants themselves to craft media practices to advance desired goals. This would require support and directives for forum participants through a more programmatic response to dysfunctional information. Efforts to "scaling up" deliberation or "spreading the effects" of mini-publics beyond deliberative forums remain little more than speculative at this point (Gastil and Knobloch 2020; Niemeyer 2014; Niemeyer and Jennstäl 2018; Warren and Gastil 2015). However, mini-public participants as "trust-enabling agents" are called upon to play a broader and more constructive role to counteract the spread of disinformation and strengthen democratic values, goals, and motivations.

Several studies (Chadwick 2017, 2019; Ekström and Shehata 2018; Miller and Vaccari 2020) have advanced our understanding of direct, bidirectional, and multidirectional communication with ordinary citizens on digital platforms. Still, much remains to be done to integrate this knowledge with practical democratic innovations. At least partially, current research on social media supports the view that enthusiastic politically active users could operate well as amplifiers of corrections and deliberative-capacity building agents, in the "brighter" side of information diffusion. For instance, research that detects the impacts and dissemination of dysfunctional information and harmful activities to which citizens must respond can be articulated with critical thinking and digital media literacy. Surveys have indicated that higher media awareness and citizens' concern with reputable sources have positive effects on curbing spread of dysfunctional information (Newman 2019; Guess, Nagler and Tucker 2019). Moreover, research on repetition of misinformation, social correction, and political engagement suggests that pernicious effects are diminished when coherent correction is delivered immediately, when it is consistent with the message recipient's worldview, and when users engage in ways to legitimately gain the trust of their communication partners (Valenzuela et. al. 2019; Walter and Tukachinsky 2020; Rossini et al. 2021).

In this line, planning ethical and regulatory interventions, as well as combating the harmful effects of social media, could become frequent themes for collective discussion in CAs. Concerns about public ignorance, spread of lies, and illiberal commitments demand finding ways for fellow citizens to become more informed about how to acquire accurate information, develop motivation to listen to those who think otherwise, and articulate mutually accepted solutions to conflicts of views and interests. Existing fact-checking organizations, for monitoring and data measurement at the individual, community, platform, and social level, can be associated with mini-public initiatives to build common frameworks to mitigate toxic communication and strengthen democratic interventions (Guess et al. 2019; Newman 2019; Wardle and Derakhshan 2017). Often, elected representatives are not the central promoters or supporters of deliberative democracy initiatives. But one thing is clear: engaging CA participants is crucial to building resilience across wider publics and broadening support for deliberative practices more consistently along systemic lines.

27.6 Conclusion: Rethinking a common research agenda for citizens' assemblies and communication studies

I began this chapter by arguing that research on mini-publics and research on media communication were nested in different fields, as scholars' interests seemed divorced. Continued engagement with system thinking and the growth of digital communication have created an awareness of common concerns. The link between CA and media studies does not, of course, eliminate specific interests and objectives. However, the dialogue between these disciplines helps to structure innovative research projects, providing conceptual tools to facilitate empirical analysis inside and outside the forums, and to move from one level of analysis to another.

Models of media and political communication serve deliberative studies poorly unless the normative dimension is maintained. Throughout this chapter, I have argued that examining political discussions, whether in formal, semi-formal, or informal arenas, requires careful identification of the specificities of each context, with equal analytical rigour. Rather than ignoring the boundaries between environments, tracking communicative practices across a set of institutions and a set of actors seems a promising research agenda for better understanding the complexities that emerge in everyday life communication and rethinking the active role of citizens in deliberative politics. With a rich philosophical foundation and a remarkable body of empirical research, CA has always implied that conditions can be rebuilt and resources or incentives be provided for emancipatory personal development and democratic social inclusion – even as the social world may be increasingly becoming more averse to deliberation.

References

Bächtiger, A., & Parkinson, J. (2019). *Mapping and Measuring Deliberation: Towards a New Deliberative Quality.* Oxford: Oxford University Press.

Benkler, Y., Faris, R., & Roberts, H. (2018). *Network Propaganda: Manipulation, Disinformation, and Radicalization in American Politics.* New York, NY: Oxford University Press.

Bennett, W. L., & Pfetsch, B. (2018). Rethinking political communication in a time of disrupted public spheres. *Journal of Communication* 68 (2), 243–253.

Bimber, B., & Gil de Zúñiga, H. (2020). The unedited public sphere. *New Media & Society* 22 (4), 700–715.

Böker, M. (2017). Justification, critique and deliberative legitimacy: The limits of mini-publics. *Contemporary Political Theory* 16 (1) 19–40.

Boswell, J., Niemeyer, S., & Hendriks, C. M. (2013). Julia Gillard's citizens' assembly proposal for Australia: A deliberative democratic analysis. *Australian Journal of Political Science* 48 (2), 164–178.

Boulianne, S. (2017). Mini-publics and public opinion: Two survey-based experiments. *Political Studies* 66 (1), 119–136.

Caluwaerts, D., & Reuchamps, M. (2014). Does inter-group deliberation foster inter-group appreciation? Evidence from two experiments in Belgium. *Politics* 34 (2), 101–115.

Cammaerts, B., Mattoni, A., & McCurdy, P. (2013). *Mediation and Protest Movements.* Bristol: Intellect Books.

Chadwick, A. (2017). *The Hybrid Media System: Politics and Power.* Oxford: Oxford University Press.

Chadwick, A. (2019). *The New Crisis of Public Communication: Challenges and Opportunities for Future Research on Digital Media and Politics.* Loughborough: Loughborough University.

Chambers, S. (2009). Rhetoric and the public sphere: Has deliberative democracy abandoned mass democracy? *Political Theory* 37 (3), 323–350.

Chambers, S. (2017). Balancing epistemic quality and equal participation in a system approach to deliberative democracy. *Social Epistemology* 31 (3), 266–276.

Chambers, S. (2020). Truth, deliberative democracy, and the virtues of accuracy: Is fake news destroying the public sphere? *Political Studies* 69 (1), 147–163.

Cohen, J. (1997). Procedure and substance in deliberative democracy. In J. Bohman & W. Rehg (eds), *Deliberative Democracy: Essays on Reason and Politics*, 407–437. Cambridge, MA: The MIT Press.

Curato, N., & Böker, M. (2016). Linking mini-publics to the deliberative system: A research agenda. *Policy Sciences* 49 (2), 173–190.

Curato, N., Hammond, M., & Min, J. B. (2019). *Power in Deliberative Democracy.* Cham: Palgrave Macmillan.

Dahlgren, P. (2018). Media, knowledge and trust: The deepening epistemic crisis of democracy. *Javnost – The Public* 25 (1–2), 20–27.

Della Porta, D. (2013). Bridging research on democracy, social movements and communication. In B. Caemmerts, A. Mattoni, & P. Mccurdy (eds), *Mediation and Protest Movements*, 21–38. Bristol, UK: Intellect.

Dryzek, J., & Hendriks, C. (2012). Fostering deliberation in the forum and beyond. In F. Fischer & H. Gottweis (eds), *The Argumentative Turn Revisited: Public Policy as Communicative Practice*, 31–57. Durham, NC: Duke University Press.

Dryzek, J. S., Bächtiger, A., Chambers, S., Cohen, J., et al. (2019). The crisis of democracy and the science of deliberation. *Science* 363 (6432), 1144–1146.

Ekström, M., & Shehata, A. (2018). Social media, porous boundaries, and the development of online political engagement among young citizens. *New Media & Society* 20 (2), 740–759.

Esau, K., Fleuß, D., & Nienhaus, S. M. (2020). Different arenas, different deliberative quality? Using a systemic framework to evaluate online deliberation on immigration policy in Germany. *Policy & Internet* 13 (1), 86–112.

Escobar, O., & Elstub, S. (2017). Forms of mini-publics: An introduction to deliberative innovations in democratic practice. *New Democracy. Research and Development Note 4.* newDemocracy Foundation.

Esser, F., & Strömbäck, J. (2014). *Mediatization of Politics: Understanding the Transformation of Western Democracies.* London: Palgrave Macmillan.

Fishkin, J. S. (2009). *When the People Speak: Deliberative Democracy and Public Consultation.* Oxford: Oxford University Press.

Fishkin, J. S. (2018). *Democracy When the People are Thinking: Revitalizing Our Politics Through Public Deliberation.* Oxford: Oxford University Press.

Fung, A. (2003). Survey article: Recipes for public spheres: Eight institutional design choices and their consequences. *Journal of Political Philosophy* 11 (3), 338–367.

Gastil, J. & Knobloch, K. (2020). *Hope for Democracy: How Citizens Can Bring Reason Back into Politics.* Oxford: Oxford University Press.

Gastil, J., Knobloch, K. R., Reedy, J., Henkels, M., & Cramer, K. (2018). Assessing the electoral impact of the 2010 Oregon Citizens' Initiative Review. *American Politics Research* 46 (3), 534–563.

Guess, A., Nagler, J., & Tucker J. (2019) Less than you think: Prevalence and predictors of fake news dissemination on Facebook. *Science Advances* 5 (1), 4586.

Habermas, J. (1991). *The Structural Transformation of the Public Sphere: An Inquiry into a Category of Bourgeois Society*, trans. T. Burguer. Cambridge, MA: MIT Press. [orig. German ed 1962].

Habermas, J. (1996). *Between Facts and Norms*, trans. W. Rehg. Cambridge, MA: MIT Press. [orig. German edn 1992].

Habermas, J. (2017). *Postmetaphysical Thinking II: Essays and Replies*, trans. C. Cronin, Kindle edn. Malden, MA: Polity Press. [orig. German edn 2012].

Habermas, J. (2022). Reflections and Hypotheses on a Further Transformation of the Political Public Sphere. *Theory, Culture & Society*, 39 (4), 145–171.

Häussler, T. (2018). *The Media and the Public Sphere: A Deliberative Model of Democracy*. New York, NY: Routledge.

Hendriks, C. M., Ercan, S. A., & Boswell, J. (2020). *Mending Democracy: Democratic Repair in Disconnected Times*. Oxford: Oxford University Press.

Karpowitz, C., & Raphael, C. (2014). *Deliberation, Democracy, and Civic Forums: Improving Equality and Publicity*. Cambridge: Cambridge University Press.

Karpowitz, C. F., Mendelberg, T., & Shaker, L. (2012). Gender inequality in deliberative participation. *American Political Science Review* 106 (3), 533–547.

Lafont, C. (2015). Deliberation, participation, and democratic legitimacy: Should deliberative mini-publics shape public policy? *Journal of Political Philosophy* 23 (1), 40–63.

Lazer, D. M., Sokhey, A. E., Neblo, M. A., Esterling, K. M., & Kennedy, R. (2015). Expanding the conversation: Multiplier effects from a deliberative field experiment. *Political Communication* 32 (4), 552–573.

Lindell, M., Bächtiger, A., Grönlund, K., Herne, K., Setälä, M., & Wyss, D. (2017). What drives the polarization and moderation of opinions? Evidence from a Finnish citizen deliberation experiment on immigration. *European Journal of Political Research* 56 (1), 23–45.

Maia, R. C. (2012a), *Deliberation, the Media and Political Talk*. New York, NY: Hampton Press.

Maia, R. C. (2012b). Non-electoral political representation: expanding discursive domains. *Representation* 48 (4), 429–443.

Maia, R. C. (2014). *Recognition and the Media*. Houndmills, Basingstoke: Palgrave Macmillan.

Maia, R. C. (2017). Politicization, new media and everyday deliberation. In P. Fawcett, M. Flinders, C. Hay, & M. Wood (eds), *Anti-Politics, Depoliticization, and Governance*, 68–87. Oxford: Oxford University Press.

Maia, R. C. (2018). Deliberative media. In A. Bächtiger, J. S. Dryzek, J. Mansbridge, & M. E. Warren (eds), *The Oxford Handbook of Deliberative Democracy*, 348–364. Oxford: Oxford University Press.

Maia, R. C., & Rezende, T. A. (2016). Respect and disrespect in deliberation across the networked media environment: Examining multiple paths of political talk. *Journal of Computer-Mediated Communication* 21 (2), 121–139.

Maia, R. C., Cal, D., Bargas, J., & Crepalde, N. J. (2020). Which types of reason-giving and storytelling are good for deliberation? Assessing the discussion dynamics in legislative and citizen forums. *European Political Science Review* 12 (2), 113–132.

Maia, R. C., Cal, D., Bargas, J. K., Oliveira, V. V., Rossini, P. G., & Sampaio, R. C. (2017). Authority and deliberative moments: Assessing equality and inequality in deeply divided groups. *Journal of Public Deliberation* 13 (2).

Maia, R. C., Hauber, G., & Choucair, T. (2023). *The deliberative system and interconnected media in times of uncertainty*. London: Palgrave Macmillan.

Mansbridge, J., & Macedo, S. (2019). Populism and democratic theory. *Annual Review of Law and Social Science* 15 (1), 59–77.

Mansbridge, J., Bohman, J., Chambers, S., Christiano, T., Fung, A., Parkinson, J., Thompson, D. F., & Warren, M. E. (2012). A systemic approach to deliberative democracy. In J. Parkinson & J. Mansbridge (eds), *Deliberative Systems*, 1–26. Cambridge: Cambridge University Press.

Mattoni, A. (2013). Repertoires of communication in social movement processes. In B. Cammaerts, A. Mattoni, & P. McCurdy (eds), *Mediation and Protest Movements*, 39–56. Chicago, IL: Intellect Ltd.

McCurdy, P. (2013). Mediation, practice and lay theories of news media. In B. Cammaerts, A. Mattoni, & P. McCurdy (eds), *Mediation and Protest Movements*, 57–74. Chicago, IL: Intellect Ltd.

Miller, M. L., & Vaccari, C. (2020). Digital threats to democracy: Comparative lessons and possible remedies. *The International Journal of Press/Politics* 25 (3), 333–356.

Neblo, M. A. (2015). *Deliberative Democracy between Theory and Practice.* Cambridge: Cambridge University Press.

Neuman, W. R. (2016). *The Digital Difference: Media Technology and the Theory of Communication Effects.* Cambridge, MA: Harvard University Press.

Newman, N. (2019). Executive summary and key findings. *Reuters Institute Digital News Report 2019.* https://www.digitalnewsreport.org/survey/2019/overview-key-findings-2019/

Niemeyer, S. (2014). Scaling up deliberation to mass publics: Harnessing mini-publics in a deliberative system. In K. Grönlund, A. Bächtiger, & M. Setälä (eds), *Deliberative Mini-Publics: Involving Citizens in the Democratic Process*, 177–202. Colchester, UK: ECPR Press.

Niemeyer, S., & Jennstäl J. (2018). Scaling up deliberative effects: Applying lessons of mini-publics. In A. Bächtiger, J. S. Dryzek, J. Mansbridge, & M. E. Warren (eds), *The Oxford Handbook of Deliberative Democracy*, 329–347. Oxford: Oxford University Press.

Pfetsch, B. (2018). Dissonant and disconnected public spheres as challenge for political communication research. *Javnost – The Public* 25 (1–2), 59–65.

Pomatto, G. (2019). Journalists: The role of the media in democratic innovation. In S. Elstub & O. Escobar (eds), *Handbook of Democratic Innovation and Governance*, 269–280. Cheltenham: Edward Elgar Publishing.

Porto, M. (2012). *Media Power and Democratization in Brazil: TV Globo and the Dilemmas of Political Accountability* (Vol. 8). New York: Routledge.

Rinke, E. M., Knobloch, K. R., Gastil, J., & Carson, L. (2013). Mediated meta-deliberation: Making sense of the Australian Citizens' Parliament. In L. Carson, J. Gastil, J. Hartz-Karp, & R. Lubensky (eds), *The Australian Citizens' Parliament and the Future of Deliberative Democracy*, 260–273. University Park, PA: Pennsylvania State University Press.

Rossini, P., Stromer-Galley, J., Baptista, E. A., & Veiga de Oliveira, V. (2021). Dysfunctional information sharing on WhatsApp and Facebook: The role of political talk, cross-cutting exposure and social corrections. *New Media & Society* 23 (8), 2430–2451.

Setälä, M., Christensen, H. S., Leino, M., Strandberg, K., Bäck, M., & Jäske, M. (2020). Deliberative mini-publics facilitating voter knowledge and judgement: Experience from a Finnish local referendum. *Representation*, 1–19. https://doi.org/10.1080/00344893.2020.1826565

Steiner, J., Jaramillo, M. C., Maia, R. C., & Mamelli, S. (2017). *Deliberation across Deep Divisions: Transformative Moments.* Cambridge: Cambridge University Press.

Strandberg, K., & Grönlund, K. (2014). Online deliberation: Theory and practice in virtual mini-publics. In K. Grönlund, A. Bächtiger, & M. Setälä (eds), *Deliberative Mini-Publics: Involving Citizens in the Democratic Process*, 93–113. Colchester, UK: ECPR Press.

Suiter, J., Muradova, L., Gastil, J., & Farrell, D. M. (2020). Scaling up deliberation: Testing the potential of mini-publics to enhance the deliberative capacity of citizens. *Swiss Political Science Review* 26 (3), 253–272.

Sunstein, C. R. (2017). *#republic – Divided Democracy in the Age of Social Media.* Princeton, NJ: Princeton University Press

Swart, J., Peters, C., & Broersma, M. (2018). Shedding light on the dark social: The connective role of news and journalism in social media communities. *New Media & Society* 20 (11), 4329–4345.

Thompson, D. F. (2008). Deliberative democratic theory and empirical political science. *Annual Review of Political Science* 11 (1), 497–520.

Ugarriza, J. E., & Caluwaerts, D. (2014). *Democratic Deliberation in Deeply Divided Societies: From Conflict to Common Ground.* Basingstoke: Palgrave Macmillan.

Vaccari, C., & Chadwick, A. (2020). Deepfakes and disinformation: Exploring the impact of synthetic political video on deception, uncertainty, and trust in news. *Social Media + Society*, 6 (1).

Valenzuela, S., Halpern, D., Katz, J. E., & Miranda, J. P. (2019). The paradox of participation versus misinformation: Social media, political engagement, and the spread of misinformation. *Digital Journalism* 7 (6), 802 – 823.

Van Aelst, P., Strömbäck, J., Aalberg, T., Esser, F., de Vreese, C., Matthes, J., Hopmann, D., Salgado, S., Hubé, N., Stępińska, A., Papathanassopoulos, S., Berganza, R., Legnante, G., Reinemann, C., Sheafer, T., & Stanyeret, J. (2017). Political communication in a high-choice media environment: A challenge for democracy? *Annals of the International Communication Association* 41 (1), 3 – 27.

Vrydagh, J., Devillers, S., & Reuchamps, M. (2020). The integration of deliberative mini-publics in collaborative governance through the perspectives of citizens and stakeholders: The case of the education reform in French-speaking Belgium. *Representation*, 1 – 22. https://doi.org/10.1080/00344893.2020.1853599

Waisbord, S. (2009). Bridging the divide between the press and civic society: Civic media advocacy as "media movement" in Latin America. *Nordicon Review* 30, 105 – 116.

Walter, N., & Tukachinsky, R. (2020). A meta-analytic examination of the continued influence of misinformation in the face of correction: How powerful is it, why does it happen, and how to stop it? *Communication Research* 47 (2), 155 – 177.

Wardle, C., & Derakhshan, H. (2017). Information disorder: Toward an interdisciplinary framework for research and policy making. *Council of Europe*, 27. http://tverezo.info/wp-content/uploads/2017/11/PREMS-162317-GBR-2018-Report-desinformation-A4--BAT.pdf

Warren, M. E., & Gastil, J. (2015). Can deliberative minipublics address the cognitive challenges of democratic citizenship? *The Journal of Politics* 77 (2), 562 – 574.

Warren, M. E., & Pearse, H. (eds) (2008). *Designing Deliberative Democracy: The British Columbia Citizens' Assembly*. Cambridge: Cambridge University Press.

Wessler, H. (2018). *Habermas and the Media*. Cambridge, Medford, MA: Polity Press.

Andrea Felicetti

28 Social movements and citizens' assemblies

Abstract: Social movements and citizens' assemblies are drawing closer to each other. Besides engaging in internal practices of participatory and deliberative politics, some social movements are now increasingly advocating for and taking a role in the implementation of citizens' assemblies, arguably the main instrument through which deliberative democracy has been pursued. This phenomenon raises theoretical and empirical issues which we need to better understand to exploit its democratic potential. This chapter reviews some of the ongoing interactions between social movements and citizens' assemblies. It points out to some key developments in research on the topic and envisages the strengths and weaknesses of this relationship. Movements and CAs can develop a mutually beneficial relationship that benefits democracy. Nevertheless, citizens' assemblies and activism tend to be informed by different logics. If they are not carefully dealt with, they might put these forms of democratic life at odds with each other.

Keywords: democracy, deliberation, participation, social movements, activism, citizens' assemblies, representation

28.1 Introduction

This chapter explores the way social movements and citizens' assemblies (CAs) are drawing closer to each other in one of the most interesting developments in the contemporary democratic landscape. To be sure, social movements have long engaged in forms of "assembleary" democracy giving prominence to group discussions and decision making (Mansbridge 1983; Polletta 2012). Sometimes, they have also been agents of democratic innovation, for instance, by asking for referendums and citizen initiatives as della Porta and colleagues (2017) have documented in the case of Catalonia, Greece, Iceland, Italy, and Scotland in recent times. Today an increasing number of social movements, intended as instances of collective action aimed at conflict against opponents, characterized by dense inter-organizational networks and by actors sharing lasting identities and forms of solidarity (Diani 1992), are now advocating for and taking a role in the implementation of CAs, arguably the main instrument through which deliberative democracy has been pursued. This phenomenon raises theoretical and empirical issues which we need to better understand to exploit its democratic potential.

In the next section, I offer an overview of ongoing interactions between CAs and social movements. Then, I review some of the key developments in research on the topic and offer some thoughts on the strengths and weaknesses of this relationship.

Andrea Felicetti: Scuola Normale Superiore, Italy.

∂ Open Access. © 2023 the author(s), published by De Gruyter. (cc) BY-NC-ND This work is licensed under the Creative Commons Attribution-NonCommercial-NoDerivatives 4.0 International License. https://doi.org/10.1515/9783110758269-030

Movements and CAs can develop mutually beneficial relationships, and indeed this strengthens the possibility of promoting political change. However, if not carefully dealt with, the different logics informing public deliberation and activism might easily put these forms of democratic life at odds with each other. I conclude with an invitation to pay greater systematic attention to this topic given its growing significance and great democratic potential.

28.2 Citizens' assemblies and social movements today

In the last few years, a host of ground-breaking processes have given CAs a new scope and relevance (OECD 2020). One of such processes, the 2019 Great National Debate of France provides insights into the interaction between public deliberation and activists, as this assembly was created in reaction to a social movement, the Yellow Vests. Briefly, this movement, born in 2018 as a protest against an environmental tax on fuel, engaged in relentless contestation of the perceived injustice of political and economic systems in France, and generated mobilization on a scale unseen in the country since the World War II. Interestingly, among its political claims, the Yellow Vests movement featured a demand for direct democracy and the introduction of popular initiatives. After months of stalling and concessions, President Macron, organized a Great National Debate, which was a national-level deliberative and participatory process with the stated objective of learning about the grievances raised with the intention of envisaging future developments. That is one of the largest, initiatives involving CAs including 19 through France (overseas regions included). However, this unprecedented development met with the staunch resistance of activists who denounced it as an attempt to use deliberation against mobilization. In retaliation, many Yellow Vests activists engaged in what they called a True National Debate. This consisted of a series of initiatives that were aligned with the movement's direct democratic and grassroots ethos. The movement's attitude toward the Great National Debate undermined the legitimacy of this experience, reviving long-standing concerns about the use of innovations to exclude critical voices (Ehs and Mokre 2020).

Another well-known case is the French Citizens' Convention on Climate (Eymard 2020), which was conceived in response to the popular mobilizations of the Yellow Vests movement and climate change activists. This assembly has enjoyed the support of movements, and, in effect, it has led to an ambitious recommendation plan. The adoption of these recommendations and their implementation, however, proved to be a challenging aspect since parliament accepted only part of the proposals advanced by citizens, very much to the discontent of environmental activists (see Paulis 2020; Giraudet et al. 2021). Such dynamics suggest that understandably the relationship between public deliberation, including CAs, and social movements, is not set in stone but made of dynamic phenomena that are bound to evolve over time.

Going beyond these illustrations from France, many national-level CAs are being established systematically across Europe. As well as the ongoing Citizens' Assembly model adopted in Ireland in 2016 to deal with matters of constitutional relevance (Farrell, Suiter, and Harris 2019), numerous other national deliberations have been instituted to deal with climate change. CAs on climate change have already been convened in many countries, for example, Denmark, France, Germany, Ireland, and the UK, and they are being planned for many more, including, the Netherlands, Sweden, and Spain. Frequently, in such cases, mobilizations have played an important role, often driving the action. Examples of these are Extinction Rebellion, one of whose three core goals is the creation of climate assemblies, and Fridays for Future, whose activists demand more meaningful involvement of citizens in politics. There are other such movements including #RiseForChange and networks of groups whose claims include the institutionalization of deliberative and participatory democracy (Mellier and Wilson 2020). In point of fact, we do not know if constructive interactions between innovators and activists will occur. These experiments are fundamental means to revitalize democracy (Dryzek et al. 2019) but, of course, there might be flaws that could undermine their democratic potential and jeopardize that of future initiatives.

The body of cases from which we can learn is growing steadily in size and variety, and a lot of these are from the lower levels of government, which are the traditional loci of democratic innovations (Geissel 2012). While for the sake of this chapter I will focus on Europe, interesting cases are by no means limited to that area.[1] Chile, for instance, hosted one of the most remarkable processes of political change driven by activism. It featured democratic innovations, in some of the foremost institutions of the country up to the constitutional level and had a role for citizens' assemblies too (see Pogrebinschi and Ross 2019). Coming to Europe, in Belgium, there has been an unprecedented effort to establish permanent bodies of randomly selected citizens in regional governments, pioneered by the Permanent Citizens' Dialogue of the German-speaking Community of Belgium, the so-called Ostbelgien Model (see Niessen and Reuchamps 2022). In addition, in an unconventional attempt to modernize the traditional channels of representative democracy, the Agora Party managed to elect a representative to the Brussels Regional Parliament to speak for a network of self-developed bodies of randomly selected citizens whose overarching aim was to promote participatory democracy (see Junius et al. 2021). Across Europe, there is also a wealth of hybrid democratic innovations, which feature a mix of deliberative and participatory elements, online and face-to-face interaction, and top-down and bottom-up processes at all levels of government (Geissel 2019). Further, there are CAs such as the one in Gdansk in Poland. The decisions of this particular assembly are ratified by the mayor, provided they are approved by the majority of deliberators (Gerwin 2018). Activists' demands often contribute to these developments. This is the case, for example, with regard to the establish-

---

1 Websites such as https://participedia.net/ and https://www.latinno.net/ offer an extensive list of cases of democratic participation including those led by social movements and citizens' assemblies.

ment of dozens of local climate assemblies across Europe and the recent wave of local assemblies from Budapest in Hungary to Oxford in the UK that have been created to deliberate on local measures for combating ecological destruction.

Besides pressuring for deliberation, movements contribute to initiate CAs. For instance, they might urge political leaders to use these devices to address a certain problem. Movements can also be enclaves where deliberative and participatory democracy ideas, sympathetic to CAs, are hosted, producing leaders that will eventually enter political institutions and enable change, as we see in Southern and Eastern Europe with local municipalities, most notably, in Spain, Slovenia, Croatia, and Serbia. Also, the movements' role is important to pressure decision-makers to take up the deliberations of citizens (della Porta and Felicetti 2022). Finally, movements cannot only contribute to input and implementation of CAs. They can also contribute to citizens' deliberation by speaking before them as experts, advocates, and testimonials (see Talpin 2015).

Current developments offer a promising prospect for strengthening democracy, but it is important to understand that they also offer substantial grounds for misunderstandings and opposition (see Gastil and Knobloch 2019). That risks happening when deliberation is introduced as a top-down project, with unclear credentials as to expected impacts, disconnected from the wider democratic system, in the context of communities that did not ask for public deliberation in the first place (Felicetti and della Porta 2019). For example, in Italy, the construction of a high-speed railway line connecting the city of Turin to Lyon across the French border resulted in hotly contested attempts to mimic public deliberation on the topic (Esposito et al. forthcoming). Parkinson (2006) noted similar worrying dynamics of exclusion in the context of his research on deliberative democracy in relation to health reform in the UK. Not all democratic innovations are beneficial for democracy, and it is important that scholars consider such cases (Spada and Ryan 2017).

28.3 Public deliberation and social movements research

As Cristina Lafont has recently argued, scholars need to better understand how the current phase of democratic innovations affects democratic life. This is particularly true for CAs that are making inroads into mainstream political arenas and debates (Lafont 2019). A conspicuous body of research helps us in this regard. For instance, scholars have studied the design of innovations in general and CAs in particular (Dean, Boswell, and Smith 2020; Saward 2021), and their relationship with decision-makers (Hendriks and Lees-Marshment 2019), administration (Boswell 2016), the wider public (Bedock and Pilet 2020; Jacquet 2019), and even with the burgeoning democratic public engagement industry (Lee 2014).

Both academic debate and public commentary report on CAs being initiated in response to the mobilization of social movements (Mellier and Wilson 2020). However, activists have played a key role in processes of democratic renewal even before movements such as the Yellow Vests, Extinction Rebellion, and Fridays for Future started to engage prominently with democratic innovation processes. For example, the innovative Icelandic attempt at crowdsourced constitutional reform, which included citizen deliberation, was a reaction to anti-austerity protests (Landemore 2015), and the G1000 in Belgium, an original civil society-based deliberative and participatory process, was established in response to protests against the ineffectiveness of the political system (Caluwaerts and Reuchamps 2014). Even if they did not lead to policy changes, and in the Belgian case there was no direct institutional innovation either, in effect, these attempts brought deliberative democracy into the political debate in these two countries and beyond (Jacquet et al. 2021).

As is known in the field of democratic innovations, democracies have continuously devised innovations at different levels of government to deal with an ever-expanding set of political problems (Saward 2003). From a deliberative democracy standpoint, CAs have long been the main forum of choice to promote meaningful forms of engagement. These are specifically designed venues to engage randomly selected citizens loosely representative of a community of reference who take part in facilitated interactions to exchange views about a certain problem under examination and then make recommendations to policymakers and/or the wider public (Grönlund, Bachtiger and Setälä 2014). Pioneering efforts in this direction have come from deliberative experiments in Europe such as the consensus conferences in Denmark and the German planning cells in the 1980s, and these were paralleled by similar experiments in the USA such as citizens' juries. In the following decades, mini-publics have differed widely, taking the form, for example, of deliberative polls (Fishkin 2018) or CAs (such as the pioneering assemblies on electoral reform in Canada). There has also been a plethora of local deliberative bodies that have started to achieve political relevance and that feature interaction with activists (Elstub and McLaverty 2014). Generally, activists' engagement with these consensus-oriented and randomly selected bodies has been more modest than their involvement with participatory organizations (Polletta 2015). By comparison, the greater role of movements in the current wave of CAs might create more radical forms of democratic participation (Sintomer 2018).

The field of social movement studies, in which the relationship between popular mobilizations and democracy has long been studied (Tilly and Wood 2020; Giugni, McAdam, and Tilly 1998), is also a vital source of scholarship. Departing from a view of mobilizations as threats to democracy, which have been fuelled by the pathological behaviour of some citizens, activism has long been recognized as a constitutive element of any democratic society (Markoff 2015). Historically, movements have contributed to the democratization of Western democracies, as a wealth of scholarship on women's, workers', and student movements testifies (Meyer and Tarrow 1998). Long before CAs attracted attention from the government, movements have been key actors in all waves of the democratization of European states, and they continue mobilizing for democracy also elsewhere (Della Porta and Mattoni 2014). More generally, movements have often considered their political struggles to be a fight for democracy, as exemplified by the wave of anti-austerity movements in Southern Europe and beyond (Gerbaudo 2017).

Extant scholarship details how movements have engaged extensively in participatory and, successively, deliberative forms of internal democracy (Polletta 2014). Activists' ideas and practices have inspired developments in participatory and deliberative theories of democracy (Floridia 2017). These, in turn, have contributed to informing the practices of new activists (Mansbridge 2003). Today, activists are also engaging in innovative democratic practices that spread widely across publics and bring about institutional change in some cases (Felicetti 2021). Particularly after the Great Crisis, movements tend to address their grievances at the systemic level, targeting representative institutions and claiming the need for them to work more inclusively and effectively (Giugni and Grasso 2018). Besides invoking more direct democracy and reclaiming spaces for agonistic democracy close to or apart from the state (Mouffe 2014), movements' claims have also often resonated with participatory and deliberative forms of democracy (Della Porta 2013). Research on social movements has highlighted the contribution of activists to maintaining and deepening democracy (Fominaya and Feenstra 2019), and researchers have shed light on how social movements help initiate important conversations that address deficiencies and various governance problems in democracies (Elstub and Escobar 2019; Della Porta and Doerr 2018).

28.4 Assessing interactions between social movements and citizens' assemblies

An increasing number of CAs in particular and deliberative forums more generally seem to be initiated in the wake of movements' mobilization (Mellier and Wilson 2020). A growing literature highlights how disruption, interruption, and contestation on the one hand, and co-creation, inclusive governance, and collaboration on the other, can all offer valuable forms of interaction between actors in a democracy (Doerr 2018; Curato 2019). Nonetheless, why and how the interaction between CAs and movements develops has not received due attention yet. In particular, there is no clear theory as to what interactions might be considered desirable for democratic systems.

In democratic theory, this effort is today conducted usually within the context of debates around the notion of democratic systems (Warren 2017; Mansbridge et al. 2012). Starting in the field of deliberation, the systemic approach to democracy is evolving fast, and is being refined through the incorporation of concerns from other approaches to democracy. Nevertheless, the ability of the systemic approach to capture and assess the complexities of the interactions between movements and activists should not be taken for granted (Drake 2021). One promising way of assessing the interaction is the democratic ecologies concept proposed by Pickering (2019), which goes beyond functionalist approaches and makes more room for complexity.

Further, the relationship between movements and CAs tends to be understood with reference to two distinct views on activists' politics and democratic innovation. Specifically, on the one hand, innovations and movements are seen as potential partners for democracy (Della Porta 2013; Fung and Wright 2003); on the other hand, however, they are deemed as likely opponents (Mouffe 1996; Pateman 2012). Potential for cooperation is rooted in different factors. Innovators and activists tend to share a commitment to democracy. They might benefit from engaging with each other. For instance, gaining the support of movements could be an asset for innovations trying to involve the public, as it happened during the Icelandic attempt at constitutional reform. On the other hand, movements could benefit from public deliberation on problems representative systems fail to address, as, for example, Extinction Rebellion's proposal for CAs on climate change illustrates. Also, institutional recognition can sometimes be a valuable resource for movements. This, for instance, occurs when movements are publicly recognized as political actors invested with knowledge and political clout on a problem. Activists could also provide a valuable perspective and advocacy in democratic forums, and participating in such assemblies might prove to be a learning experience for activists. Finally, movements might have an additional chance to affect politics because of their involvement with innovations, whereas innovators might benefit from obtaining the support of movements in the implementation of the outcomes of a process. As the French Citizens' Assembly on climate change now illustrates, political commitment at the highest level and high quality deliberation of citizens is no warranty still that radical, systemic political change can overcome the entrenched dynamics of representative politics. Similar to what happens with the participatory wave most famously embodied by the early Participatory Budgeting in Brazil, social movements' support remain an essential element to hard won, democratic change. Overall, the prospect of radical democracy and democratic renewal can hardly be established if the value of CAs and social movements as carriers of more participatory and deliberative visions of democracy is not affirmed (Cini and Felicetti 2018).

Substantial advantages, however, correspond to a plethora of potential hindrances, especially when innovations are proposed as shortcuts to democracy (Lafont 2019). Epistemologically, involvement in often short processes of public deliberation will hardly lead citizens to grasp the radical positions that activists have developed through long-standing socialization and engagement in groups (Fung 2009). In terms of power, CAs might be used to give the impression of involvement with the public without ceding any power (Johnson 2015), as an instrument of cooptation, or to exclude radical critiques of policy ideas from discussion (Lee and Romano 2013). There can be tensions between the more radical aims of movements and institutional innovators' wish to appease the needs of the neoliberal state (Young 2001; Lee 2014). Deliberative engagement implies challenges, for example, movements having to adapt to the terms of engagement set by organizers, thereby putting aside their adversarial repertoire of action to pursue more consensual methods instead. Strategically, involvement with innovations limits the ability of movements to question the organizers, who could be political adversaries, and enhances the risk of their being sidelined in the contest to submit ideas. Activists would then be faced with a dilemma as to whether and how to proceed (Polletta 2016).

Finally, it is necessary to take into account the fact that social movements have varying levels of concern about democracy itself. Even movements explicitly promoting democratization might behave differently and even sceptically toward participatory or deliberative bodies (Felicetti, Niemeyer, and Curato 2015). Although, in general, movements rooted in far-right and religious groups (Castelli Gattinara and Pirro 2019) are not openly adverse to liberal democratic norms and institutions, with the exception of extremist groups, their openness to processes of democratization has been questioned and deemed opportunistic. Not all innovators see activists' role in CAs favourably. Funders and facilitators responsible for democratic processes may need to be responsive to institutional, professional, and industry logics that may be at odds with activists' way of thinking (Lee 2014). The former might, for example, envisage a substantially different process by which the social movement's concerns could be recognized or expect the movement to play a role it did not expect. As recently argued by Felicetti (2021), close observations of the real-life practices through which actors engage remains fundamental to understand how in different contexts they consider the opportunity to build ties with each other and how the timing of this interaction enables or hinders their collaboration.

28.5 Conclusions

The current rise in CAs and its increasing proximity with social movements is one of the most interesting and potentially positive developments for contemporary democracies. As this phenomenon evolves it becomes increasingly important to understand it in its complexities. Research from the fields of deliberative democracy and social movement studies has taken us beyond a stage where CAs or social movements could just be dismissed as minor, ancillary elements in democratic life. Theoretical refinements and empirical studies show that neither overly optimistic nor exceedingly critical views help us gain a realistic assessment of what happens when these two democratic phenomena meet. Nevertheless, the study of the relationship between activism and deliberation is far from mature. The current trend towards greater interaction between movements and CAs' commands and would certainly benefit from greater research efforts on this topic.

References

Bedock, C., and Pilet, J.-B. (2020). Enraged, engaged, or both? A study of the determinants of support for consultative vs. binding mini-publics. *Representation*, 1–21.

Boswell, J. (2016). Deliberating downstream: Countering democratic distortions in the policy process. *Perspectives on Politics* 14 (3), 724–737.

Caluwaerts, D., & Reuchamps, M. (2014). The G1000: Facts, figures and some lessons from an experience of deliberative democracy in Belgium. In Caluwaerts, D., Reuchamps, M., Jacobs, K., Van Parijs, P., & Van Reybrouck, D. (eds), *The malaise of electoral democracy and what to do about it*, 10 – 33. Brussels: Re Bel.

Castelli Gattinara, P., & Pirro, A. L. P. (2019). The far right as social movement. *European Societies* 21 (4), 447 – 462.

Cini, L., & Felicetti, A (2018). Participatory deliberative democracy: toward a new standard for assessing democracy? Some insights into the Italian case, *Contemporary Italian Politics* 10 (2), 151 – 169.

Curato, N. (2019). *Democracy in a Time of Misery: From Spectacular Tragedies to Deliberative Action*. Oxford: Oxford University Press.

Dean, R., Boswell, J., & Smith, G. (2020). Designing democratic innovations as deliberative systems: The ambitious case of NHS citizen. *Political Studies* 68 (3): 689 – 709.

Della Porta, D. (2013). *Can Democracy Be Saved: Participation, Deliberation and Social Movements*. Cambridge: Polity Press.

Della Porta, D., & Doerr, N. (2018). Deliberation in protests and social movements. In A. Bächtiger, J. Dryzek, J. Mansbridge, & M. Warren (eds), *The Oxford Handbook of Deliberative Democracy*, 392 – 406.

Della Porta, D., & Felicetti, A. (2022). Innovating democracy against democratic stress in Europe: Social movements and democratic experiments, *Representation* 58 (1), 67 – 84.

Della Porta, D., & Mattoni, A. (eds). (2014). *Spreading Protest. Social Movements in Times of Crisis*. Colchester: ECPR Press.

Della Porta, D., O'Connor, F., Portos García, M., & Subirats Ribas, A. (2017). *Social Movements and Referendums From Below: Direct Democracy in the Neoliberal Crisis*. Bristol: Policy Press.

Diani, M. (1992). The concept of social movement. *The Sociological Review* 40 (1), 1 – 25.

Doerr, N. (2018). *Political Translation: How Social Movement Democracies Survive*. Cambridge Studies in Contentious Politics. Cambridge: Cambridge University Press.

Drake, A. (2021). *Activism, Inclusion, and the Challenges of Deliberative Democracy*. Vancouver: University of British Columbia Press.

Dryzek, J. S., Bächtiger, A., Chambers, S., Cohen, J., Druckman, J. N., Felicetti, A. Fishkin, J. S. Farrell, D. M., Fung, A., Gutmann, A., Landemore, H., Mansbridge, J., Marien, S., Neblo, M. A., Niemeyer, S., Setälä, M., Slothuus, R., Suiter, J., Thompson, D., & Warren, M. E. (2019). The crisis of democracy and the science of deliberation. *Science* 363 (6432), 1144 – 1146.

Ehs, T., and Mokre, M. (2020). Deliberation against participation? Yellow Vests and Grand Débat: A perspective from deliberative theory. *Political Studies Review* 19 (2), 186 – 192.

Elstub, S., & Escobar, O. (2019). *Handbook of Democratic Innovation and Governance*. Cheltenham: Edward Elgar Publishing.

Elstub, S., & McLaverty, P. (2014). *Deliberative Democracy: Issues and Cases*. Oxford: Oxford University Press.

Esposito, G., Felicetti A., and Terlizzi A (forthcoming). "The limits of participatory governance in megaprojects: the Lyon-Turin high-speed railway between structure, agency, and democratic participation." *Policy and Society*

Eymard, L. (2020). From the French Citizens' Convention on Climate to the Conference on Future of Europe: A participatory science and democracy perspective. *European Law Journal* 26 (1 – 2), 136 – 140.

Farrell, D. M., Suiter, J., & Harris, C. (2019). 'Systematizing' constitutional deliberation: The 2016 – 18 Citizens' Assembly in Ireland. *Irish Political Studies* 34 (1), 113 – 123.

Felicetti, A. (2021). Learning from democratic practices: New perspectives in institutional design. *The Journal of Politics* 83 (4), 1589 – 1601.

Felicetti, A., Niemeyer, S., & Curato, N. (2015). Improving deliberative participation: Connecting mini-publics to deliberative systems. *European Political Science Review* 8 (3), 427 – 448.

Felicetti, A., & Della Porta, D. (2019). Joining forces: The sortition. In J. Gastil & E. O. Wright (eds), *Legislature by Lot: Transformative Designs for Deliberative Governance*, 145 – 165. London: Verso

Fishkin, J. S. (2018). *Democracy When the People Are Thinking: Revitalizing Our Politics through Public Deliberation.* Oxford: Oxford University Press.

Floridia, A. (2017). *From Participation to Deliberation. A Critical Genealogy of Deliberative Democracy.* Colchester: ECPR Press.

Fominaya, C. F., & Feenstra, R. A. (2019). Introduction: Contemporary European social movements: Democracy, crisis and contestation. In C. F. Fominaya & R. A. Feenstra (eds), *Routledge Handbook of Contemporary European Social Movements*, 1–14. London and New York: Routledge.

Fung, A., & Wright, E. O. (2003). *Deepening Democracy: Institutional Innovations in Empowered Participatory Governance.* Vol. 4. London: Verso Books.

Fung, A. (2009). *Empowered Participation: Reinventing Urban Democracy.* Princeton: Princeton University Press.

Gastil, J., & Knobloch, K. (2019). *Hope for Democracy: How Citizens Can Bring Reason Back into Politics.* Oxford: Oxford University Press.

Geissel, B. (2012). Impacts of democratic innovations in Europe: Findings and desiderata. In B. Geissel & K. Newton (eds), *Evaluating Democratic Innovations*, 173–193. London and New York: Routledge.

Geissel, B. (2019). Democratic innovations in Europe. In S. Elstub & O. Escobar, *Handbook of Democratic Innovation and Governance*, 404–428. Cheltenham: Edward Elgar Publishing.

Gerbaudo, P. (2017). The indignant citizen: Anti-austerity movements in Southern Europe and the anti-oligarchic reclaiming of citizenship. *Social Movement Studies* 16 (1), 36–50.

Gerwin, M. (2018). *Citizens' Assemblies: Guide to democracy that works.* Kraków: Otwarty Plan.

Giraudet, L. G., Apouey, B., Arab, H., Baeckelandt, S., Begout, P., Berghmans, N., ... & Tournus, S. (2021). *Deliberating on Climate Action: Insights from the French Citizens' Convention for Climate* (No. hal-03119539).

Giugni, M. G., McAdam, D., & Tilly, C. (1998). *From Contention to Democracy.* Lanham, MD: Rowman & Littlefield Publishers.

Giugni, M., & Grasso, M. (eds). (2018). *Citizens and the Crisis: Experiences, Perceptions, and Responses to the Great Recession in Europe.* Palgrave Studies in European Political Sociology. Cham: Palgrave Macmillan.

Grönlund, K., Bachtiger, A., & Setälä, M. (eds). (2014). *Deliberative Mini-Publics:Involving Citizens in the Democratic Process.* Colchester: ECPR Press.

Hendriks, C. M., & Lees-Marshment, J. (2019). Political leaders and public engagement: The hidden world of informal elite–citizen interaction. *Political Studies* 67 (3): 597–617.

Jacquet, V. (2019). The role and the future of deliberative mini-publics: A citizen perspective. *Political Studies* 67 (3), 639–657.

Jacquet, V., Talukder, D., Devillers, S., Bottin, J., & Vrydagh, J. (2021). Deliberative minipublics has made it to mainstream politics: A dispatch From Belgium. *Journal of Deliberative Democracy.*

Johnson, G. F. (2015). *Democratic Illusion: Deliberative Democracy in Canadian Public Policy.* Toronto: University of Toronto Press.

Junius, N., Caluwaerts, D., Matthieu, J., & Erzeel, S. (2021). Hacking the representative system through deliberation? The organization of the Agora party in Brussels. *Acta Politica*, 1–19.

Lafont, C. (2019). *Democracy without Shortcuts: A Participatory Conception of Deliberative Democracy.* Oxford: Oxford University Press.

Landemore, H. (2015). Inclusive constitution-making: The Icelandic experiment. *Journal of Political Philosophy* 23 (2), 166–191.

Lee, C. W. (2014). *Do-It-Yourself Democracy: The Rise of the Public Engagement Industry.* Oxford: Oxford University Press.

Lee, C. W., & Romano, Z. (20130. Democracy's new discipline: Public deliberation as organizational strategy. *Organization Studies* 34 (5–6), 733–753.

Mansbridge, J. J. (1983). *Beyond Adversary Democracy.* Chicago: University of Chicago Press

Mansbridge, J. (2003). Practice-thought-practice. *Deepening Democracy: Institutional Innovations in Empowered Participatory Governance* 4, 175.

Mansbridge, J. J., Bohman, J., Chambers, S., Christiano, T., Fung, A., Parkinson, J. R., Thompson, D. F., & Warren, M. E. (2012). A systemic approach to deliberative democracy. In J. Parkinson & J. Mansbridge (eds), *Deliberative Systems: Deliberative Democracy at the Large Scale*, 1–26. Cambridge: Cambridge University Press.

Markoff, J. (2015). *Waves of Democracy: Social Movements and Political Change.* London and New York: Routledge.

Mellier, C., & Wilson, R. (2020). Getting climate citizens' assemblies right. *Carnegie Europe.* https://carnegieeurope.eu/2020/11/05/getting-climate-citizens-assemblies-right-pub-83133.

Meyer, D. S., & Tarrow, S. (1998). *A Movement Society: Contentious Politics for a New Century.* Lanham, MD: Rowman & Littlefield.

Mouffe, C. (1996). Democracy, power, and the 'political'. In S. Benhabib (ed.), *Democracy and Difference: Contesting the Boundaries of the Political*, 245–256. Princeton, NJ: Princeton University Press.

Mouffe, C. (2014). Democratic politics and conflict: An agonistic approach. In M. Lakitsch (ed.), *Political Power Reconsidered: State Power and Civic Activism between Legitimacy and Violence*, 17–29. Vienna: Lit Verlag.

Niessen, C., & Reuchamps, M. (2022). Institutionalising citizen deliberation in parliament: The permanent citizens' dialogue in the German-speaking community of Belgium. *Parliamentary Affairs* 75 (1), 135–153.

OECD. (2020). *Innovative Citizen Participation and New Democratic Institutions: Catching the Deliberative Wave.* Paris: OECD Publishing.

Parkinson, J. (2006). *Deliberating in the Real World: Problems of Legitimacy in Deliberative Democracy.* Oxford and New York: Oxford University Press.

Pateman, C. (2012). Participatory democracy revisited. *Perspectives on Politics* 10 (1), 7–19.

Paulis, E. (2020). Jury duty for global warming: Citizen groups help solve the puzzle of climate action (Interview). *Science Magazine.*

Pickering, J. (2019). Deliberative ecologies: Complexity and social–ecological dynamics in international environmental negotiations" *Global Environmental Politics* 19 (2), 61–80.

Pogrebinschi, T., & Ross, M. (2019). Democratic innovations in Latin America. In S. Elstub & O. Escobar (eds), *Handbook of Democratic Innovation and Governance*, 389–403. Cheltenham: Edward Elgar Publishing.

Polletta, F. (2012). *Freedom Is an Endless Meeting.* Chicago: University of Chicago Press.

Polletta, F. (2014). Participatory democracy's moment. *Journal of International Affairs* 68 (1), 79–92.

Polletta, F. (2015). Public deliberation and political contention. In C. W. Lee, M. McQuarrie & E. T. Walke (eds), *Democratizing Inequalities: Dilemmas of the New Public Participation*, 222–244. New York: New York University Press.

Polletta, F. (2016). Social movements in an age of participation. *Mobilization: An International Quarterly* 21 (4), 485–497.

Saward, M. (2003). *Democratic Innovation: Deliberation, Representation and Association.* London and New York: Routledge.

Saward, M. (2021). *Democratic Design.* Oxford: Oxford University Press.

Sintomer, Y. (2018). From deliberative to radical democracy? Sortition and politics in the twenty-first century. *Politics & Society* 46 (3), 337–357.

Spada, P., & Ryan, M. (2017). The failure to examine failures in democratic innovations. *PS: Political Science & Politics* 50 (3): 772–778.

Talpin, J. (2015). Democratic innovations. In D. della Porta & M. Diani, *The Oxford Handbook of Social Movements*, 781–792. Oxford: Oxford University Press.

Tilly, C., & Wood, L. J. (2020). *Social Movements, 1768–2008.* London and New York: Routledge.

Warren, M. E. (2017). A problem-based approach to democratic theory. *American Political Science Review* 111 (1), 39 – 53.

Young, I. M. (2003). Activist challenges to deliberative democracy. In J. S. Fishkin & P. Laslett, *Debating Deliberative Democracy*, 102 – 120. Oxford: Blackwell Publishing.

Part 5: **Conclusion**

Yanina Welp

29 Citizens' assemblies: Beyond utopian and dystopian approaches

Abstract: The concluding chapter identifies outcomes and main trends emerging from the collections of contributions included in the *Handbook*. The goal is to help relocate the conversation about citizens' assemblies on a pragmatic and well documented ground, leaving aside both over-optimistic (utopian expectancies looking for a "magic solution") and over-pessimistic portrayals (that foresee any action addressed to produce change as worsening the problems intended to resolve, failure or at too high of costs). Following Albert Hirschman (1991), it is assumed that there are dangers in both action and inaction, so CAs need to focus on canvassing and assessing and guarding against risks as much as possible. To develop this strategy, the text is structured along the following lines: the global spread of CAs beyond ethnocentric views; the discussion on their authorization, accountability, and legitimacy; their outcomes and evaluation; their scalability and best design; their public support and potential to provide answers to global challenges (climate change, global democracy); and their connection to regime type (authoritarian or democratic).

Keywords: citizen's assemblies, ethnocentrism, authorization, accountability, legitimacy, evaluation, institutional designs, public support, global challenges, regime type

29.1 Introduction

The collection of chapters presented in this first *Handbook of Citizens' Assemblies* (CAs) offers a comprehensive and broad overview of the ongoing political and theoretical debate around CAs as well as its multifaceted empirical assessment. This final chapter does not pretend to end such a rich discussion with closed conclusions but rather to identify both outcomes and main trends emerging from the contributions. The goal is to help relocate the conversation about CAs on a pragmatic and well documented ground, leaving aside both over-optimistic (utopian expectancies looking for a "magic solution") and over-pessimistic portrayals (that foresee any action addressed to produce *changes* as worsening the problems intended to resolve, failure or at too high of costs).[1] Following Albert Hirschman (1991) we assume here that there are dangers in both action and inaction, so CAs must focus on canvassing and assessing and guarding against risks as much as possible. The chapters presented in this *Handbook*

Yanina Welp: Albert Hirschman Centre on Democracy, Graduate Institute in Geneva, Switzerland.

1 Inspired by *The Rhetoric of the Reaction* (Hirschman 1991), where the author identifies the perversity thesis, futility thesis and jeopardy thesis as conservative narratives of reaction.

∂ Open Access. © 2023 the author(s), published by De Gruyter. [cc] BY-NC-ND This work is licensed under the Creative Commons Attribution-NonCommercial-NoDerivatives 4.0 International License. https://doi.org/10.1515/9783110758269-031

share in common multiple reflections, developments, and evaluations to seriously identify their potentialities and limits to reinforce democracy. The text is structured along the following lines: the global spread of CAs beyond ethnocentric views; the discussion on their authorization, accountability, and legitimacy; their outcomes and evaluation; their scalability and best design; their public support and potential to provide answers to global challenges (climate change, global democracy); and their connection to regime type (authoritarian or democratic).

29.2 A Western focus on a global phenomenon

The *Introduction* by Julien Vrydagh (Chapter 1) sets the floor by defining our approach to CAs in a broad sense, which allows for moving beyond the narrow understanding of democratic innovations and deliberative democracy as belonging to Western democracies. Vrydagh recognizes both that CAs have historical roots and a global incidence, while the current CA revival is linked to Western democracies' developments of mini-publics and more specifically CAs. The main assumptions behind the promotion of these participatory institutions have been related to achieving conditions for consequential democratic deliberation (CAs are expected to draw a unique picture of what the whole citizenry would think about a public issue if it had the time to deliberate on the matter), to produce inclusion (understood as a result of descriptive representation of ordinary citizens, by selecting them by lot) and to have influence (effects on policymaking). But these assumptions are being challenged internally: by criticism on the theoretical approaches to CAs and their empirical evaluations, as well as externally, by works from critical perspectives and from several disciplines. The introduction acknowledges potential answers, sometimes complementary and sometimes contradictory, to the numerous questions that emerge alongside the proliferation of CAs.

29.3 Citizens' assemblies under the lens of authorization and accountability

A main objection posited to CAs are their lack of authorization and accountability, considered hallmarks of democratic representation. It is a fact that randomly selected representatives are not authorized or accountable in the same ways as elected representatives. However, Michael K. MacKenzie (Chapter 2) argues that this is flawed logic given that "CAs will be useful and valuable only if they *add* something to our democratic systems, as opposed to merely reproducing more of what we already have". MacKenzie suggests to change the focus from individuals to the institutions and calls for understanding the role played by CAs within the ecologies of other democratic institutions which are authorized and accountable to the publics they serve. In doing so, CAs are well suited to provide descriptive, discursive, surrogate, and gyroscopic representation, all forms that do not require direct links to accountability. For instance, a randomly selected second chamber – a sort of permanent CA with a continually rotating membership – would not be directly accountable, in electoral terms, to the people it serves, but it would have its decisions scrutinized and sanctioned or rejected by an elected chamber. The example makes evident that the specific design and features of the CA (permanent or not, with mandatory or advisory capacities, among others) are relevant for the discussion. It is also important to remember that there are many other bodies playing central roles which are not directly accountable neither, like judges and jurors in many systems (in others they are also elected).

Agreeing with MacKenzie on considering accountability a less salient problem of CAs when they are embedded in a broader democratic system (e.g. ecologies of democratic institutions), Pierre-Etienne Vandamme (Chapter 3) invites consideration of different forms of understanding accountability. Following Jane Mansbridge's (2014) work, the author stresses that there are at least two different forms of accountability: sanction-based and trust-based, and the former could operate independently of electoral sanction. Vandamme offers some arguments in the literature about limiting individual accountability to avoid individual citizen representatives being exposed to public pressure and lobbying (for example, with the use of secret ballot). The right to recall the CA is also listed as an option to introduce institutional accountability. A remarkable point to take into account is the reconfiguration of the classical trade-off between accountability and independence when talking about CAs. This is because it is often the independence of CAs from electoral promises and public pressure that is invoked to justify their epistemic added value. "Yet, if they cannot deviate from public opinion without sanction, these epistemic benefits (including the possibility to leave room for the interests of foreigners and future generations) might be jeopardized", affirms Vandamme.

29.4 Controversial legitimacy and capacity to strengthen democracy

There is an ongoing discussion about the different types of decision-making authority CAs should have, with merely consultative on one extreme and binding on the other. For Cristina Lafont (Chapter 4) the central question is not simply about how much power their participants ought to exercise, but rather, and above all, the specific capacity in which they are supposed to exercise that power. If the goal is to enhance the democratic legitimacy of political decision-making, a positive outcome will be achieved when CAs have a positive impact and improve the quality of the deliberative process of opinion and will-formation in which the citizenry participates. Lafont's central concern in this chapter is that "If the aim of institutionalizing CAs is to empower a few participants to do the thinking, deliberating and deciding for the rest of the citizenry, then it is hard to see how these innovative institutions can have a positive democratic impact".

On a more favourable view than Lafont, Antonin Lacelle-Webster and Mark Warren (Chapter 8) explore the role of CAs in democratic systems and the ways in which they can strengthen democracy. Their first focus is on the normative problems a political system needs to solve in order to count as "democratic". And the answer provided is that a democratic system must (a) empower inclusion of those affected by collective decisions; (b) form preferences and interests into collective agendas and wills; and then (c) convert these into collective decisions, such that people rule over themselves. They look at potential sites in which CAs can strengthen democracy by supplementing other institutions and practices (elections, ballot measures, legislatures, executive agencies, public spheres, political parties, and constitutional processes) and conclude advocating for CAs in places where they can strengthen the deliberative and representative dimension of democratic polities.

A broader approach to the legitimacy challenge is offered by Stephen Elstub and Zohreh Khoban (Chapter 9), who discuss the six most prominent critiques to CAs: (1) that members of the public do not have the capacity to engage in meaningful deliberation and decision-making; (2) that CAs do not contest power relationships in society; (3) that CAs are excessively manipulated spaces, with participants having little control over the design; (4) that CAs are easily co-opted by public authorities and have little policymaking impact; (5) that CAs only include small numbers of participants, and therefore exclude most of the public from deliberation and decision-making; and (6) that because CAs are representative, they do not do enough to promote the voice and interests of minorities and marginalized groups who are most adversely affected by the policy issues. Elstub and Khoban develop a proposal within the deliberative system approach to connect CAs with other democratic institutions embedded in the political system. The main point is then to provide concrete and established links between CAs and other parts of the political system, including civil society, parliaments, government, and the media, to enhance their impact on policy debate and opinion formation in the informal and formal public spheres.

29.5 But do citizens' assemblies work for improving democracy and good governance?

Moving from theoretical approaches to literature reviews and empirical assessments, several chapters in the *Handbook* discuss the impact of CAs. Focusing on the uses of CAs to solve the crisis of democracy, Rasmus Ø. Nielsen and Eva Sørensen (Chapter 10) argue in favour of a systemic turn able to achieve more dialogue between the practitioners working to develop, refine, and institutionalize mini-public innovations and the academics who critically scrutinize their contributions to democracy. Their argument is illustrated with the assessment of four different formats of mini-publics (the Citizens' Jury and the Planning Cell; Open Space Technology, Future Search, and World Café; the Consensus Conference and the Deliberative Poll; and the Citizens' Assembly pioneered in British Columbia). Their basic idea is "to shift or expand the scope of how mini-public formats are evaluated: from the direct and measurable effects of individual experiments to the broader functional effects that putting different mini-public formats in the toolbox of decision-makers and institutions has on the democratic system".

To answer the question about the working of CAs to improve democracy, there is a need to evaluate outcomes. Thus, how can we measure the effects of CAs? Didier Caluwaerts and Min Reuchamps (Chapter 18) build a framework for evaluating CAs inspired in the OECD *Evaluation Guidelines for Representative Deliberative Processes* (2021) that focuses on the evaluation of both process design integrity and deliberative experience. Caluwaerts and Reuchamps develop a set of criteria based on input (representativeness of the CA composition, the openness of the agenda and the epistemic completion, or in other words, the quality of information accessed), throughput (quality of participation, the quality of decision-making, and the contextual independence of the process), and output (public endorsement for the CA and its recommendations, the political uptake, and an assessment of the policy implementation). But not all criteria have the same value. The authors argue that the quality of representation (input), the quality of participation (throughput), and the political uptake (output) are primary evaluation criteria while binary assessments should be avoided.

Elisa Minsart and Vincent Jacquet's (Chapter 21) starting point is that multiplying CAs with little impact on the policymaking process would only reinforce an already existing crisis of confidence from citizens towards the political system. There is a need to know the impact of CAs on policymaking that at the same time requires a definition of impact and an accurate method to measuring it. Minsart and Jacquet identify three types of impacts: congruence with decisions, defined as "a desk-based research method which assesses impact based on the textual correspondence between a citizen-created idea and public policy documents"; consideration of CA recommendations, what is understood as references to the CAs in the discourses of different actors; and impact on structure, as enduring practices in decision making. While the previous methodology is based on discourse analysis, impact on structure can be assessed using different approaches such as surveys, interviews with civil servants or political leaders and ethnographic observation.

29.6 The scope and scalability of citizens' assemblies' recommendations

One of the most common criticisms of CAs is that they serve as symbolic or "simulative" participation or even as distracting participation. Recommendations could be well grounded but would be ignored or misused for political cherry-picking – politicians may choose recommendations they like and neglect those they dislike. Manipulation and co-optation are also typical criticisms. Brigitte Geissel (Chapter 5) focuses on the options that could ensure recommendations made by CAs are taken into account. Basing her proposal on the participatory system approach that advocates the systematic and systemic connection of collective will-formation with decision-making, Geissel envisages five models of CAs: (1) with different tasks, (2) Multi-level (3) Multi-issue Referendum (4) Randomly selected parliament and (5) Deliberation Day, all of which connect CAs to either decision-making by representatives or by citizens.

Drawing on the recent developments in the theory of deliberative democracy and their own empirical work on various other democratic practices, John Boswell, Carolyn Hendriks, and Selen A. Ercan (Chapter 7) suggest expanding the repertoire of democratic reform in contemporary democracy. Their central proposal moves the current focus on democratic reform from designing to "mending". This addresses a key criticism by opening the room to include citizens, administrators, and decision-makers in a debate that was until now controlled by "democratic designers" because "the pursuit of democratic repair needs to move away from a 'social laboratory' mode and towards an approach associated with 'reflexive governance'".

Participatory system approaches and a more flexible and inclusive understanding of CAs for democracy are complemented in the *Handbook* by a chapter devoted to proposing the interaction between different forms of referendums and CAs. In the past, deliberative and direct democracy were seen as opposites, one focusing on the quality of deliberation and opinion change and the other on empowering decisions. Nenad Stojanović (Chapter 14) offers a combination of both. He differentiates the actor who is entitled to initiate a process (institutional actors, reform advocates, or citizens at large) and the outcome of a popular vote (binding or consultative) and elaborates a conceptual roadmap regarding the linkage between CAs and mechanisms of direct democracy to present an overview of the various points within the process leading to a popular vote, in which deliberative mini-publics could be meaningfully employed. One of the limits of the proposal comes from the scant use of instruments of direct democracy. However, there are promising experiences such as the Irish model and the Citizens Initiated Referendums (CIR) or Oregon model, as well as the Swiss practice.

29.7 Who should organize citizens' assemblies and who should participate?

There is an idealized conception of ordinary citizens, whose deliberation would be epistemically superior as well as an idealized view connecting bottom-up initiatives with a more democratic approach than top-down initiatives. Sonia Bussu and Dannica Fleuß (Chapter 11) identify the two models generally in discussion when designing a CA based on who initiates the CA: bottom-up or top-down approaches. The authors make it evident that the distinction is too narrow on one hand (there are more dimensions to be taken into account) and the assumptions on their limitations and potentialities incomplete (the connection of top-down CAs with political elites and less disruptive goals and the connection of bottom-up CAs with disruptive aims to challenge established

power relations). To classify a CA, not only the initiator (public agencies or state institutions *vs* social movements, civil society, grassroots initiatives) matters, but also the
level of openness in the process and the normative values and conceptions of democracy and the core aims. After reviewing concepts and evidence, Bussu and Fleuß argue
that "bottom-up approaches are not necessarily better than top-down initiatives at
bringing in disempowered interests and ensuring more inclusive processes, top-
down CAs do not seem to have such a good record in terms of impact just because
they work closely with state institutions". Thus, they favour flexible combinations of
both approaches.

Standard or more common CAs are composed by so-called "ordinary citizens".
Nonetheless, there are also many forms of hybridization that open room to discuss
pros and cons. Clodagh Harris, David M. Farrell, and Jane Suiter (Chapter 12) analyse
the topic feeding their argument in the currently best-known example of a mixed-member mini-public, the Ireland's Convention on the Constitution (2012–2014). If a central
concern refers to the ways in which the politician members can frame and influence
the process at the input stage, it is applicable to "pure" assemblies as well as to mixed-
member forums for deliberation (MMDFs). But in the case of MMDFs, there are additional issues related to parity of esteem between the citizen members and the elected
officials, as well as parity between the politician members themselves (governing and
opposition parties, etc.). Harris, Farrell, and Suiter list as benefits of mixed forms that
(1) the inclusion of elected representatives directly in the deliberations can ensure visibility for the recommendations, (2) it may increase politicians' and the political establishment's trust and confidence in deliberative processes, (3) including politicians may
lend greater epistemic value to the process as they allow for learning by bringing different perspectives and lived experiences to bear on the given topic, and (4) mixed
forms have the potential to increase trust in politics, politicians, political institutions,
and the wider policymaking and legislative process. However, these benefits can be undermined by power asymmetries and elite domination.

29.8 The mini-public's opinion and the general public's opinion

Another central argument against CAs is their supposed lack of connection with the
general debate – the "shortcut to democracy" to use Cristina Lafont's term (Chapter 4) –,
a more general concern on public opinion and opinion change within the CAs and on
the broader public. John Rountree and Nicole Curato (Chapter 6) consider how CAs
form a link with the wider citizenry by contributing to public deliberation; inviting
public deliberation; and triggering a meta-deliberation on the value of these assemblies
in public life. In making this link, three different routes are considered: (1) members of
the public may watch the deliberations unfold live or through recordings of the proceedings; (2) citizens can learn about the deliberations through the media; or (3) citi-

zens may review the final report from the assembly. These different routes may present challenges: for instance, opening public consultations could show cases where an assembly's recommendations do not align with public input. Rountree and Curato acknowledge this and argue that it does not necessarily signal a problem because deliberation is a transformative process, and assembly members after going through deliberation would not be expected to mirror public opinion.

Still, little is known about the effects of CAs on the wider public. Saskia Goldberg (Chapter 20) focuses on how CAs affect non-participating citizens and how non-participants perceive CAs. In doing so, she differentiates between theoretical claims, observed effects, citizen's expectations, and perceived legitimacy. A central claim of Goldberg's chapter is that deliberative democracy theory places high expectations on CAs, but these expectations are not consistently met in empirical studies. There are some positive empirical findings but evidence mostly refers to unsystematic single-(best)-case studies that need to be contextualized further. Finally, citizens' perceptions and support for CAs are moderately positive regarding their implementation. However, as stressed in many other chapters, context matters.

Beyond the previous discussion on the connection between public opinion and the work and recommendations of CAs, there is a discussion about the knowledge aims of CAs. Marina Lindell (Chapter 19) underlines that too much emphasis has been placed on opinion change as the primary outcome of a deliberative process while largely overlooking the quality of deliberation and its impact on these effects. Her work focuses on inclusion, diversity, and deliberative disagreement, experts and evidence, and reflection and perspective-taking and their role for these transformations. As some highly relevant findings, Lindell argues that clarification and "structured disagreement" could be more important than opinion change *per se*; and clarification may well encompass polarization, moderation, or stability of opinions. Making sure that a deliberating group has a diversity of epistemic resources as well as a diversity of perspectives, is crucial. Finally, Lindell agrees that the demand for consensus from many deliberative democrats may be counterproductive. "An expectation of reaching consensus can create an obstacle to a critical dialogue and individual perspectives may dominate the agenda and define consensus. It might also prevent minority inclusion and force minority opinions to form after the group."

CAs have been studied relatively in isolation. Many chapters here support the need to move to a systemic turn but there is also a growing request to develop a contextual approach. Rousiley C. M. Maia (Chapter 27) argues that the holistic approach to CAs cannot ignore the interfaces between discussions in deliberately designed forums and the more mundane discussions outside those forums. Maia focuses on the connection between CAs and communication studies. Including media studies and platform digitization on the research agenda is helpful to think across institutions and the wider public, as well as the interplay of deliberative and non-deliberative practices. Maia argues that "Rather than ignoring the boundaries between environments, tracking communicative practices across a set of institutions and a set of actors seems a promising research agenda for better understanding the complexities that emerge in everyday life communication and rethinking the active role of citizens in deliberative politics."

29.9 Children, climate change and global democracy

Some challenges democracies currently face are connected to the political definition of the future in times of growing and increasingly controversial globalization. We have decided to include chapters on children participation, climate change, and supranational democracy and CAs to explore the extent to which CAs could produce solutions or are charged with unfounded expectations.

On the basis of their age and lack of capacity, children are excluded from electoral politics as well as from CAs. Against this argument, Kei Nishiyama (Chapter 13) argues for the inclusion of children providing three arguments: inclusion of children is epistemically beneficial for adult citizens to gain a deeper understanding of perspectives and interests of future generations. Inclusion of children is also beneficial for children themselves as it enables them to act as agents of democracy who communicate with various political agents (e. g., lay citizens, experts, elected officials) and influence the policymaking process, which is usually difficult to achieve in other popular simulative practices such as mock elections or mock parliaments. Finally, some forms of inclusion of children in CAs are synergistic in many ways with existing political engagement practices for children (e. g., children's parliament, social movements). Nishiyama shows the different forms in which children can be included, such as imaginary and symbolic inclusion; a*dult–child collaboration* and *adult-centric practice; and children participation, direct and consultative.* On this topic, childrens' contribution to CAs could be powerful and straightforward.

One of the most prominent topics tackled by CAs relates to global warming and climate change. CAs with this focus have been launched in France, Germany, Ireland, Belgium, and the United Kingdom, among others, and are invoked and demanded by social movements such as Extinction Rebellion as well as broader civil society networks like KNOCA, the Knowledge Network on Climate Assemblies. Louise Knops and Julien Vrydagh (Chapter 16) discuss the potential of Citizens' Climate Assemblies (CCAs) to respond to the climate crisis, both in terms of scope and ambition of policy solutions, and in terms of enhancing the democratic legitimacy of these policies. They organize the discussion around four key dimensions: territoriality (a global issue whose management is based on the nation state), temporality (policymakers face short-term consequences of their decisions and need to combine solutions for different challenges at the same time), conflict (that refers to frictions and disagreements around climate change), and denialism (the fight for the "truth" that opposes science to conspiracy at the extremes). Knops and Vrydagh show the extent to which some challenges faced are beyond the scope of CCAs:

it is clear that CCAs on their own won't be enough to overcome the state-interests or the techno-capitalist bias that currently prevent the adoption of binding environmental policies at the global level; nor will they be able to seriously tackle questions of environmental injustice. Likewise, CCAs seem incapable of injecting some environmental reflexivity into institutional contexts that currently escape democratic control all-together, in particular among large economic actors.

The authors believe that CCAs can make important contributions to tackle climate change and increase the democratic legitimacy of climate policies, but caution CCAs as providing a silver-bullet solution.

As with climate change, there is an expectancy on CAs to promote global democratic governance. In this regard, there are several experiments at the European Union level launched by NGOs, international organizations and social movements to trigger CAs at the supranational level. Irena Fiket (Chapter 15) offers an overview of these developments based on the systemic approach to deliberation. Fiket shows that in the last fifteen years, there has been a political interest to adopt CAs to resolve the democratic deficit at the supranational level. It goes hand in hand with a broader theoretical movement for the introduction of deliberative democracy into global policymaking. However, she finds relevant differences between the supranational level in the case of the EU, on one hand, and the global political context, on the other. The first and more relevant difference is that there is a political effort at the EU to democratize the entire system of policymaking in which CAs are just a small part, while the process of democratization actually never started at the global level. With this in mind, the author does not reject the promotion of CAs as remedies to the democratic deficit at the supranational level, but calls attention to the need to discuss CAs with reference to the political context. This consideration is fundamental to avoiding the spread of symbolic experiments with high ambitions and yet less capacity to have effects.

29.10 Who supports citizens' assemblies?

Why would citizens be in favour of instruments of deliberative democracy instead of the classic representative system? Relying on empirical data, David Talukder and Jean-Benoit Pilet (Chapter 23) describe citizens' support for instruments of deliberative democracy. The authors show that many citizens tend to be in favour of such instruments, but a majority is against CAs to replace elected politicians (data come from EPIS web-based survey, in which 15,406 citizens from 15 European countries were interviewed between 13 March and 2 April 2020). They attempt to understand which factors explain or correlate with citizens' support for CAs and explore the role of political engagement, political frustration, social trust, and ideology. Evidence in general offers results conditioned by context. The study shows a difference between left-wing and right-wing citizens that has been under-theorized, and could be related to a more inclusive vision of politics by left-wing actors. Finally, the overview shows that some citizens evaluate CAs by taking into account their policy outputs, indicating that "citizens are not policy blind. They primarily care about the policies that will be implemented, and less about the procedures and institutional arrangements to reach a decision."

CAs are far from being unanimously supported by decision-makers and there are intuitive explanations: decision-makers need to give away a part of their power when initiating a CA and then need to deal in some ways with the recommendations produced, whether implementing them or explaining why they should not be implemented. But CAs also provide decision-makers with the opportunity to increase both the legitimacy and quality of political decisions. Christoph Niessen (Chapter 24) analyses how elected officials perceive CAs, examining when they are supported and when they are opposed. Niessen builds a conceptual framework expecting elected officials' attitudes to vary depending on their interests, ideas, and institutions:

> Surprisingly, the investigation of institutional factors did not find supporting evidence of elected officials' attitudes being related to the length of their political career. This means either that other factors, be it rational or ideological ones, outweigh it, or that institutional socialization is very quick and leads politicians swiftly to defend electoral institutions over CAs.

It is self-evident that changes in the way in which policymaking is framed would affect public servants. The promotion of participatory forms of democracy would necessarily lead to changes in the role of public servants, and to the emergence of new public servants profiles, such as the figure of an individual working in the public or the private sector who works to design, implement, and/or facilitate participatory forums. Jehan Bottin and Alice Mazeaud (Chapter 25) review available data and find that "from the point of view of public agents, the value of citizen participation is less democratic than instrumental, which influences the type of processes they carry out". The study distinguishes two types of agents: those whose mission is to design and organize participatory mechanisms, and those who are in charge of a sectoral policy and who are impacted by the implementation of a deliberative process. The second group is not only much more numerous but is also affected by the organization of participatory and deliberative processes without having organized it themselves.

Finally, despite that many global and local social movements are supportive of CAs, the interaction between CAs and the development of social movements is yet to receive due attention. In the words of Andrea Felicetti (Chapter 28),

> Theoretical refinements and empirical studies show that neither overly optimistic nor exceedingly critical views help us gain a realistic assessment of what happens when these two democratic phenomena meet. Nevertheless, the study of the relationship between activism and deliberation is far from mature. The current trend towards greater interaction between movements and citizens' assemblies commands and would certainly benefit from greater research efforts on this topic.

Thus, far from showing a clear path and trend, again, there is a call for developing more research and looking more carefully at specific political processes.

29.11 "Participatory authoritarianism" and populist support to citizens' assemblies

CAs are associated with democratic settings. However, careful concern is required when examining how CAs can fit and serve political purposes in authoritarian regimes. Baobang He (Chapter 22) analyses the different uses of deliberative citizens' assemblies in China, Cuba, and Libya. In China, the authoritarian ruling is based on public reasoning, persuasion, and utilizing a diversity of consultative and deliberative devices.

> It aims to control society and manage and cultivate people through community engagement and political participation. Public deliberation serves a similar function to a fire alarm. It is a critical mechanism of crisis management that is driven by authoritarian leaders to manage democratic pressure.

What He identifies as deliberative authoritarianism would show that some forms of empowerment, even if controlled, contribute to authoritarian resilience. While this is more evident in China and to some extent in Cuba, it is not present in Libya and would explain to some extent the collapse of Gaddafi's personalized regime.

Focusing on three Latin American experiences – the Popular Councils in Cuba (PC), the Councils and Cabinets of Citizen Power in Nicaragua (CCCP), and the Communal Councils in Venezuela (CC) – Armando Chaguaceda and Raudiel Peña Barrios (Chapter 17) show how these councils which fit within our definition of CAs, work to mobilize and consult the population with very limited impact on local politics and administration. This is because several structures that enable local participation are formally created but stripped of the autonomy necessary for civic empowerment. Moreover, the subjects of participation operate as executors, receivers, and/or correctors, at the local level, of political and administrative agendas coming from above. Chaguaceda and Peña Barrios propose the category of "semi-citizens", which is halfway to the total dispossession of rights/agency (subjects) and formal recognition and empowerment. As a final conclusion, the authors stress that

> in an environment of political autocratization, the partisanship of public management and devaluation of electoral integrity, lose potential as circuits of representation based on the "people" idea, oriented to an agonist activation of democracy, to become spaces of harmonization and Schmittian suppression of politics.

And what about the connection between CAs and populism? Do populist parties and populist citizens support CAs? Kristof Jacobs (Chapter 26) identifies two strategic motivations for populists: Outcome-contingent motivations, which deal with whether or not parties will benefit from the reform; and Act-contingent motivations, which deal with the perceived electoral benefits or costs attached to the act of supporting a reform or innovations. The findings are mixed. Populist parties only seem to support CAs when they deliver the outcomes they want. This is a message for those hoping that CAs as a tool of more popular involvement in the decision-making process placate to populist parties. More optimism brings the analysis of populist citizens. When they participate, they seem content and grade the event similar to non-populist citizens. Even more, they do not seem more motivated by a desire to get what they want: there is no difference between populists and non-populists and both groups gave the events a fairly high grade. Once again, "outcome-contingent motivations play a substantial role, but the process seems to have been good at creating satisfaction with the outcome: only very few participants were dissatisfied".

29.12 What then, for or against citizens' assemblies?

Citizens' assemblies have generated enormous expectations, idealized in their ability to lead to the best decisions based on a supposed (and highly questionable) epistemic superiority. Lately, more concerns have emerged on their lack of accountability and the limits of their legitimacy. CAs have been activated with incipient frequency, undoubtedly due to their lower political cost (compared to, for example, the calling of binding referendums, which have a direct effect in challenging authorities' power and decisions). The representativeness of CAs is understood as based on descriptive representation or on representing "ordinary people", but their lack of accountability or lack of authorization are some of the supposed weakest aspects. This review allows us to maintain that it is the isolation in which most CAs tend to be designed that presents the main challenge to their success. The lack of accountability will not be a problem if CAs are included in participatory ecologies and even combined with referendums. But their lack of incidence and embeddedness and laboratory design will undermine their capacity to reinforce democracy.

Despite support by some social movements, the available evidence shows that there is not majoritarian support to replace a representative system with CAs. Utopian approaches to CAs do not contribute to understanding their potential from a realistic approach. Even more, it would be wrong to assume that CAs are by default democratic. As the prominent example of China shows, CAs can be implemented in authoritarian contexts with relative success (some degree of incidence in the definition of public affairs perceived as non-conflictive by the regime). This evidence does not play against CAs but it does play against simplified approaches to controversial processes. Current developments show that there has also been an idealization of bottom-up mechanisms and the benefits of activating assemblies made up "purely" by ordinary citizens (ignoring or undermining the role of public servants and practitioners and the potential benefits of hybrid models that include politicians). The different chapters included in this *Handbook* relocate the debate on more pragmatic and complex bases, which did not reveal binary and definitive classifications, but rather invite us to consider the contexts and dynamics of the democratic process outside design laboratories.

References

Hirschman, A. O. (1991). *The Rhetoric of Reaction. Perversity, Futility, Jeopardy.* Cambridge, MA: Harvard University Press.

Mansbridge, J. (2014). A contingency theory of accountability. In M. Bovens, R. Goodin, & T. Schillemans (eds), *The Oxford Handbook of Public Accountability*, 55 – 68. Oxford: Oxford University Press.

Index

ᵃ Open Access. © 2023 the author(s), published by De Gruyter. (cc) BY-NC-ND This work is licensed under the Creative Commons Attribution-NonCommercial-NoDerivatives 4.0 International License. https://doi.org/10.1515/9783110758269-032

www.ingramcontent.com/pod-product-compliance
Lightning Source LLC
Chambersburg PA
CBHW080642270326
41928CB00017B/3160